To Brad

Enjoy, and
give comments
for next edition.
Your friend
Ward

>Internet Marketing & e-Commerce

WARD A. HANSON
STANFORD UNIVERSITY

•

KIRTHI KALYANAM
SANTA CLARA UNIVERSITY

THOMSON
SOUTH-WESTERN

Australia · Brazil · Canada · Mexico · Singapore · Spain · United Kingdom · United States

THOMSON
™
SOUTH-WESTERN

Internet Marketing & e-Commerce
Ward A. Hanson and Kirthi Kalyanam

VP/Editorial Director:
Jack W. Calhoun

Publisher:
Neil Marquardt

Developmental Editor:
John Abner

Marketing Manager:
Nicole C. Moore

Marketing Communications Manager:
Sarah Greber

Content Project Manager:
Amy Hackett

Manager, Editorial Media:
John Barans

Technology Project Manager:
Pam Wallace

Senior Manufacturing Coordinator:
Diane Gibbons

Production House:
GEX Publishing Services, Inc.

Printer:
Transcontinental Interglobe
Beauceville, QC

Art Director:
Stacy Jenkins Shirley

Internal Designer:
Diane and Nick Gliebe

Cover Designer:
Diane and Nick Gliebe

Cover Images:
© Getty Images

Photography Manager:
Deanna Ettinger

Photo Researcher:
Terri Miller

Library of Congress Control Number:
2006908239

For more information about our
products, contact us at:

Thomson Learning Academic Resource
Center

1-800-423-0563

Thomson Higher Education
5191 Natorp Boulevard
Mason, OH 45040
USA

brief contents

Part 1	Foundations	1
Chapter 1	Introduction	2
Chapter 2	A Digital World	36
Chapter 3	Networks	68
Chapter 4	Individuals Online	104

Part 2	Essential Skills	141
Chapter 5	Web Business Models	142
Chapter 6	Online Branding	176
Chapter 7	Usability, Credibility, and Persuasion	212
Chapter 8	Traffic Building	248
Chapter 9	Personalization	286
Chapter 10	Creating Commitment	324
Chapter 11	Innovation and the Net	356
Chapter 12	Pricing in an Online World	390

Part 3	e-Commerce	427
Chapter 13	Internet Retailing	428
Chapter 14	Consumer Channels	468
Chapter 15	B2B e-Commerce	500
Chapter 16	Online Research	534
Chapter 17	Organizing for Online Marketing	566
	Glossary	593
	References	605
	Index	623

contents

Part 1	Foundations	1
Chapter 1	**Introduction**	**2**
	Creating a Commercial Internet	5
	The Noncommercial Net: 1969–1994	*6*
	The Internet Explosion	*8*
	The Internet as a Global Resource	*14*
	Technology and Marketing	21
	Technology Impacts	*21*
	General Purpose Technologies and Marketing	*25*
	Our Approach	30
	Book Material	*30*
	Endnotes	33
Chapter 2	**A Digital World**	**36**
	Being Digital	38
	Digital Technology	*38*
	Digital Benefits for Marketing	*39*
	Moore's Law and Digital Power	39
	A Trillion Times Cheaper	*39*
	Using Moore's Law	*42*
	Will Moore's Law Continue?	*48*
	Digital Environments	49
	The Folly of Business-as-Usual	*49*
	Digital Environment Components	*50*
	Digital Convergence	57
	Converging Industries and Technology	*57*
	How Digitizing Works	*59*
	Digitizing Marketing Processes	*62*
	Endnotes	65
Chapter 3	**Networks**	**68**
	The Network Evolves	71
	Maturing and Expanding	*71*
	Content and Communication	*73*
	Blogs	*79*
	Technology Standards	*81*
	Network Science	85
	The Geometry of Social Networks	*85*
	Marketing with Networks	94
	Creating Value with Networks	*94*
	Endnotes	101

Chapter 4   **Individuals Online**   **104**

Patterns of Internet Usage   107
   The Necessary Internet   *107*
   The Behavioral Internet   *118*
Individualization as a GPT   130
   The Individualization GPT   *130*
Endnotes   138

Part 2   **Essential Skills**   **141**

Chapter 5   **Web Business Models**   **142**

Valuing Contacts   146
   Marketing Actions and Responses   *147*
   The Value of a Customer Contact   *149*
   Customer Lifetime Value   *157*
Web Benefits to Firms   159
   Improved Processes   *160*
   Revenue Benefits   *165*
Endnotes   173

Chapter 6   **Online Branding**   **176**

Brands and Online Brand Building   179
   The Branding Business   *179*
   Connecting Branding Strategy to Online Presence   *183*
Online Brand Presence and Enhancement   185
   Establish Proper Brand Identity   *185*
   Enhance Brand Meaning   *193*
   Reinforce Right Brand Responses   *195*
   Forge Brand Relationships   *202*
Endnotes   208

Chapter 7   **Usability, Credibility, and Persuasion**   **212**

The Web Site Visit   217
   Visit Dynamics   *217*
Creating Useful Information   224
   Usability   *224*
   Customer Support   *233*
Credibility and Persuasion   238
   Web Site Credibility   *238*
   Persuasive Designs   *241*
Endnotes   246

Chapter 8   **Traffic Building**   **248**

The Difficult Battle for Web Traffic   250
   Value and Scarcity   *250*
A Web Traffic Plan   254
   Traffic-Building Sources   *254*
   Traffic Volume and Quality   *258*
   Traffic-Building Goals   *262*

Search Engine Marketing 266
   Site Optimization 266
   Keyword Advertising 269
Traffic by Association 279
   Banner Ads 279
   Co-Branding and Placement 282
Endnotes 283

Chapter 9   **Personalization** **286**
Personalization Benefits 289
   Why Personalization? 289
   The "Democracy of Goods" 291
   Turning Experience Goods into Search Goods 291
   Personalization and the Total Product 292
   The Personalization Balance 296
Personalization Approaches 298
   Overview 298
   Mass Customization 302
   Choice Assistance 307
   Personalized Messaging 316
Endnotes 322

Chapter 10   **Creating Commitment** **324**
Online Community 327
   Community and Loyalty 327
   Community Content 331
   Learning from Online Communities 341
Retention Marketing 345
   Customer Base Analysis 345
   Dialogue Marketing 349
Endnotes 353

Chapter 11   **Innovation and the Net** **356**
The Need for Speed 360
   Internet Time 360
   Business Implications of Internet Time 361
Standards Marketing 364
   The Importance of Standards 364
   The Two Types of Standards 365
   Standards Strategy 370
New Product Development Online 373
   Improving Traditional New Product Development 373
   Modular New Product Development 379
   Early Feedback 383
   Rapid Release 386
Endnotes 387

Chapter 12	**Pricing in an Online World**	**390**
	Pricing and the Net	393
	The Power of Pricing	*393*
	The Standard Pricing Answer	*394*
	Price Sensitivity and Online Information	*396*
	Advanced Pricing Online	408
	Time-Based Pricing	*409*
	Personalized Pricing	*419*
	Bundle Pricing	*420*
	Endnotes	424

Part 3	**e-Commerce**	**427**
Chapter 13	**Internet Retailing**	**428**
	Online Retailing Develops	431
	Internet-Enabled Retailing	436
	iPACE and the Online Shopping Process	*437*
	Implementing iPACE	*448*
	Multi-Channel Retailing	460
	Multi-Channel Shopping Behavior	*460*
	Multi-Channel Challenges	*461*
	Endnotes	464

Chapter 14	**Consumer Channels**	**468**
	Consumer Channels and the Internet	471
	Overview	*471*
	Channel Design	*471*
	Existing Customers	475
	Presales Information	*475*
	Selling Through Online Intermediaries	*476*
	Direct Sales	*480*
	Expanding Markets	490
	New Domestic and International Locations	*491*
	Selling the Long Tail	*492*
	Versioning	*493*
	Online Closeouts	494
	Endnotes	497

Chapter 15	**B2B e-Commerce**	**500**
	B2B e-Commerce Evolves	503
	Customers and Channels	508
	New Sales and Buying Centers	*509*
	Facilitating Repeat Purchase	*512*
	eProcurement	514
	Indirect Materials	*514*
	Services	*517*
	Direct Materials and Dynamic Bidding	*519*
	Marketplaces	*522*

Supply Chain Coordination   526
  Demand Visibility and Vendor Managed Inventory   526
  The New Product Introduction Process   527
  Global Data Synchronization   529
Endnotes   531

Chapter 16   Online Research   534
Running a Survey   537
  Types of Online Surveys   538
  Survey Quality   541
Finding the Right Audience   545
  Panel versus Log File Measurements   545
  Domains and Tracking   547
  Trends and Duplication   548
  Source and Loss Analysis   550
  Demographic and Behavioral Composition   552
  Reach, Frequency, and CPM Analysis   554
Monitoring Congestion and Delay   556
  Sources of Delays   556
  Monitoring and Managing Delays   561
Endnotes   564

Chapter 17   Organizing for Online Marketing   566
Organizing for Online Tasks   569
  Aligning Structure and Strategy   569
  Avoiding Legal Pitfalls   577
Looking Forward   587
  The Long View   587
  If the Net Marketing GPTs Continue to Develop...   590
Endnotes   591

Glossary   593

References   605

Index   623

preface

It has been a little more than a decade since the Internet deregulated and opened for commerce. There has been much experimentation. Throughout the wild ride of the 1990s or the financial doldrums of the early 2000s, the Internet continued to grow in reach and importance. This broader base of users, applications, and capabilities now fuel what some are calling "Web 2.0." Companies have had time to alter some of their business processes. Rational, hardheaded managers justify their online investments and services with far fewer speculative projections. Real results, real customers, and substantial profits are available.

These developments make it much easier to discuss online marketing and ecommerce with a feeling of realistic optimism. The goal for this book is to provide a foundation for understanding how and why the Internet is changing business in general, and marketing in particular. Beyond this foundation, specific chapters develop the skills, strategies, and tactics that experience and research demonstrate to be important.

Submitting the final chapter of a book is one of the most pleasant events any author experiences. How this happened mirrors many of the recent Internet changes. While all expect the Internet to work in the offices of Silicon Valley, as it has for decades, a commercial and public Internet now covers much of the planet. The medieval city walls of Avignon, a place steeped in fourteenth-century history and religious controversy, were suddenly no barrier as a multi-megabyte file wirelessly made its way onto the Internet. Within seconds it appeared in North America, at no cost. We now barely notice such a feat; it has become a commonplace part of our daily life. Within a minute, we move on to the next thing—checking the sports scores perhaps or making a new travel reservation. Yet this transmission, and the devices making it possible, would surely have seemed an act of a deity, or perhaps a demon, to the citizens of Avignon past.

The Internet is lowering walls both metaphorical and real, including the walls of distance, time, experience, and social connection. Five measures—out of many—help provide perspective: 1 billion, 113 million, 1,384,605, 129.20, and 2.7%. These metrics illustrate the scale and growth in Internet users, communication, content, innovation, and revenue seen online.

One billion refers to the approximate number of Internet users worldwide. It took the human species until the beginning of the nineteenth century to reach a billion in population. Reaching 2 billion took about 130 more years. Now, the world holds a little more than 6 billion people. Of these, the latest estimate has 1/6 of them online. Only two countries, China and India, have populations larger than the number of Internet users. As we will see, these 1 billion users control far more than their per capita share of wealth and income. The Internet user base is one of the largest economic entities in the world, connected by near-instantaneous communication.

One hundred thirteen million refers to the number of online users with a Skype account. Skype is a leading example of companies using the Internet for direct voice and video communication. It charges no monthly fee. Skype users can freely place calls, send messages, even conduct video conferences between themselves anywhere in the world. With drastically reduced rates compared to normal telecom providers, Skype users can call traditional landline and cellular phones. The cost of direct communication continues to fall dramatically, at the same time expanding capabilities, reach, and mobility. While email remains the primary direct online interaction method, the richness and flexibility of services such as voice-over-IP is growing rapidly. Organizations have many more options to cost effectively reach potential customers and partners.

Content continues its startling growth and becomes ever more collaborative. Our third number, 1,384,605 current Wikipedia articles in English, demonstrates the ability of an organization to serve as a focal point for thousands of collaborators to create valuable and diverse content. Wikipedia, and open source systems as a whole, encourage contributions without monetary reward (contributions are unpaid and without royalties) or even widespread recognition (Wikipedia articles are unsigned). Harnessing distant collaborators, and understanding when it may or may not work, is a new skill for many managers.

Lowered transaction costs lead to surprises. The fourth number, 129.20, is the exchange rate between U.S.$ and 1000 pieces of "Aegwynn US-Alliance" *World of Warcraft* "gold." That is, it is the exchange rate available on one of the trading sites between actual money and the virtual currency used in one of the most popular multi-person online games. Gamers worldwide, some operating as for-profit companies in China and elsewhere, invest their time accumulating virtual world currency for the purpose of exchange. In a page right out of an international trade text on comparative advantage, impatient gamers trade dollars for "gold" to raise their status and accumulate online possessions. While the idea of rooms full of workers slaying dragons for money may seem perverse and wasteful, it illustrates the power of innovation in the marketplace.

The final number of 2.7% is cautionary and shows that the Internet is growing inside a well-developed marketplace capable of fighting back. Which is bigger: total U.S. Internet retail sales or the U.S. retail sales of Wal-Mart? The answer, somewhat surprisingly, is still Wal-Mart by a factor of two (based on first quarter results of 2006; $24.5 billion in retail sales online; $52.5 billion in U.S. Wal-Mart sales). While the U.S. Census Bureau has tracked a four-fold increase in share during the last five years, at 2.7% online sales remain a small fraction of total retail activity. The economy is a big place and inertia matters greatly in both markets and consumer habits.

Indirect impacts of a technology often exceed direct results. A much larger share of sales are influenced online than are transacted fully online—through information about products, from detailed price comparisons and reviews, and web sites of multi-channel retailers willing to sell through any method convenient to the customer. The Internet does not exist in a vacuum, and the battle for customer dollars is a highly competitive environment.

Readers of my previous book, *Principles of Internet Marketing*, will recognize some material and certainly many of the topics contained here. At the same time, five years of dramatic change and evolution of the Internet led to enough changes and additions that calling this work simply a new edition did not seem appropriate. The Internet of 2006 is a more developed, more rational, and more comprehensive business and marketing environment than in 2000. Changes in depth, topics covered, new research, and understanding must reflect these developments.

One of the most notable changes contained here is a major expansion in the treatment of ecommerce, with Kirthi Kalyanam taking the lead for the material in Chapters 13 to 16. Exchanging insights and having a colleague share some of the tasks of a 600 page text makes the book both more balanced and more complete. Kirthi brings a deep knowledge of retailing and marketing through his experience, his research, and his years of involvement in the Retail Management Institute at Santa Clara University as well as Shop.org. The original discussion of the ecommerce framework in my *Principles* book fit into one chapter. We now cover a much wider range of ecommerce topics—with separate chapters devoted to online consumer retailing, manufacturer direct sales, business-to-business sales, and online market research. The perspective is the same as the leading practitioners of this new multi-channel approach: provide the customer with the proper information, the proper offerings, and the proper channel to deliver these products and services. The goal is not to sell online but to sell with online. Kirthi also contributed to the greatly expanded treatment of branding in Chapter 6.

ACKNOWLEDGMENTS

It is hard to believe that 10 years have gone by since I created the first class in Internet Marketing at the Stanford Graduate School during the winter quarter of 1996. Since then I have taught it many times, along with specialized seminar classes, executive education classes, and more recently courses on Internet economics and online discussions of public policy. My earlier book cited many of the academics, industry practitioners, and former students that have enriched my understanding of the Internet, its potential, and its limitations. I thank you all again and ask your indulgence in not repeating the long list. I also thank the team at Thomson South-Western, especially Neil Marquardt, Amy Hackett, John Abner, and Nicole Moore, for handling a challenging book with many images, permissions, and other production hoops.

I would be remiss in not acknowledging some of my more recent colleagues for explicit thanks in understanding emerging topics. My knowledge of the telecom industry, wireless Internet, and many of the controlling regulations surrounding the Internet is much deeper thanks to co-teaching with Gregory Rosston of Stanford. Brad Inman of *HomeGain* and *TurnHere* continues to be a source of insight about Internet entrepreneurship. Placing the digital—network—individualization framework in the context of general purpose technologies has benefited from discussions with Tim Bresnahan, Manuel Trajtenberg, and Ove Granstrand. Class visits and discussions with Hal Varian of U.C.-Berkeley, Micah Baldwin, Ellen Siminoff of *Efficient Frontier*, and Jonathan Rosenberg of *Google*, helped in discussing the especially important topic of search marketing. Kirthi is grateful to his colleague Dale Achabal for his support over the years and to Scott Silverman and Ray Greenly of Shop.org for their help in providing access to Shop.org research. He also thanks Howard Lester and Pat Connelly of Williams Sonoma, Gene Domecus of Macys.com, Bill Cleary, founder of CKS Partners, Pat Guerra of Lions Peak, and Bill Bass, formerly of Sears/Lands' End for their valuable insights.

The Stanford Institute for Economic Policy Research (SIEPR) generously supported this book with both time and resources, and I strongly thank SIEPR director John Shoven, my SIEPR colleagues, and SIEPR's contributors. SIEPR is an exciting place, mixing superb academic support with stimulating colleagues. A number of intriguing policy questions confront the continued growth and success of the Internet, such as Net neutrality, broadband investments and capabilities, the proper rules governing personal privacy and personal data, intellectual property regulation, and various governments' proclivity to monitor and censor Internet use.

A gratifying supply of comments and insights came from readers of my previous book, both in English and in multiple translations. Knowledge of the Korean Internet market benefited greatly from the gracious hosting of a visit by the Hanaro Company, the China market through visits sponsored by SIEPR and Tsinghua University, and the European market by extended visits to Sacro Cuore University of Piacenza. I strongly hope this current book reflects this international input.

As always, our biggest thanks go to our families. We both wish to honor the memories of our parents: Neelakantan and Nirmala Kalyanam and James and Dorothy Hanson. Any book steals time from family life, yet they provided constant support and encouragement. Kirthi would like to thank his wife Pavitra Maragani for her generous support. Many of my ideas first get their airing, and improvements, through discussions with my wife, Camille Townsend. Helpful reality checks, and enthusiasm, came from my daughters, Cressida and Eve, for whom the Internet is second nature.

Ward Hanson
Stanford, California
September, 2006

INSTRUCTIONAL SUPPORT MATERIALS

Instructor's Manual

The Instructor's Manual provides chapter by chapter resources designed to assist instructors with all the tasks of their course including class preparation, in-class execution, and student evaluation. To assist with pre-class planning, the Manual contains an overview of each chapter, with objectives, and a detailed outline. For use in the classroom, the Manual provides for each chapter thought-provoking, real-world teaching recommendations and exercises to engage students. A selection of test items including multiple choice, true/false, and essay questions are also provided for each chapter to assist with student evaluation. The Instructor's Manual is available to adopters as a download from the *Internet Marketing and e-Commerce* web site: www.thomsonedu.com/marketing/hanson/.

PowerPoint Presentation

More than 300 slides integrating select visual elements from the pages of *Internet Marketing and e-Commerce* are available to assist instructors in bringing this dynamic course to life. The PowerPoint Presentation is available to adopters as a download from the *Internet Marketing and e-Commerce* web site: www.thomsonedu.com/marketing/hanson/.

about the authors

Ward Hanson, Stanford University

Dr. Ward Hanson is a member of the Stanford Institute for Economic Policy Research, where he is a Fellow and Policy Forum Director. Previous faculty positions include the Stanford Graduate School of Business, Purdue University Krannert School of Management, and the University of Chicago Graduate School of Business. He is an adviser, expert witness, and consultant to leading firms in Silicon Valley and beyond. He has a Masters and Ph.D. in Economics from Stanford University and a B.A. from the University of Wisconsin-Madison.

Dr. Hanson analyzes the economics and marketing of new technology. His current areas of Internet research include governmental policy choices and their impact on the Internet, the rise of individualization as a general purpose technology, and quantitative models of online business. Other research interests include product line pricing, competitive strategy, and the diffusion of innovative energy alternatives.

Professor Hanson created the first Stanford Graduate School of Business Internet marketing class in 1996 (one of the first in the world and repeated many times), pioneered an online version of the class in 2000, teaches a course on the economics of the Internet, and is developing a class in the use of online tools for policy analysis and persuasion. His previous book, *Principles of Internet Marketing*, has been adopted worldwide and translated into multiple languages, including Chinese, Italian, Japanese, Russian, and Spanish. Offline, he enjoys golf, cycling, political debates, and family.

Kirthi Kalyanam, Santa Clara University

Dr. Kalyanam is the J.C. Penney Research Professor and Director of Internet Retailing in the Retail Management Institute at the Leavey School of Business at Santa Clara University. A recognized leader in the field of Internet Marketing and Retailing, he co-produces Internet Retailing Boot Camps with Shop.org and has served as an advisor to the State of Retailing Online (SORO) research study.

Dr. Kalyanam's current research interests focus on Internet Marketing, Retailing, and Multi-Channel marketing. He teaches on these topics in undergraduate, graduate, and executive programs and has won awards for his teaching and research. He also advises early stage start-ups and serves as an expert witness.

Professor Kalyanam has a Ph.D. from the Krannert School of Management at Purdue University. He was also most recently the Senior Vice President and Chief Marketing Officer of SpinCircuit Inc. He is an avid mountain and road biker and enjoys swimming, surfing, time with his family, and travel.

part 1: Foundations

Chapter 1: Introduction

Chapter 2: A Digital World

Chapter 3: Networks

Chapter 4: Individuals Online

Introduction

> **"** The goal is to move from the **"**
> current situation of complexity
> and frustration to one where
> technology serves human needs
> invisibly, unobtrusively: the
> human-centered, customer-
> centered way.
>
> Donald Norman
> *The Invisible Computer*[1]

> **"** In any given era there typically **"**
> exist a handful of technologies
> that play a far-reaching role in
> widely fostering technical
> change and thereby bringing
> about sustained and pervasive
> productivity gains.
>
> E. Helpman and M. Trajtenberg
> *General Purpose Technologies
> and Economic Growth*[2]

Organizing the World's Information

Millions begin their daily Internet experience at the Google home page. Uncluttered and focused, few online sites reflect the goal of simplicity hiding power better than Google. With the "I'm Feeling Lucky" button, Google takes the user to the single web page it believes best matches the search term out of the billions of pages in the Google index. Only slightly less ambitious, the Google search button prioritizes the matches, attempting to display the best matches on the first page of results.

The Google story reflects many of the trends and developments of the Internet and how it is changing peoples' lives. From humble beginnings in the cubicles of two Stanford graduate students, Google was ranked the world's top brand in 2004[3], the same year of its highly successful initial public offering. It is a part of popular culture, with "googling" as a verb for checking information online. Millions use it as their automatic choice to find people, web sites, telephone numbers, or movie reviews.

Contained within Figure 1.1 are hints of the breadth of information available online. Gone are the days when a search engine highlighted only web pages. The Images tab on the page lets a user search over a billion images. A traveler wishing to find a picture of the Hoover Dam outside of Las Vegas or the Imperial Hotel in Tokyo can quickly find hundreds of alternative photos. The Groups tab covers discussions for thousands of topics.

this chapter

The commercial Internet is transforming global business. This first chapter highlights some of the main steps in the evolution of the commercial Internet during its first decade and some of the creative applications. Technology and marketing interact, and the Internet builds upon three major technological foundations. The chapter closes with a look ahead at the main topics of the book.

Topics covered in this chapter include:

> Googling

> Creating a Commercial Internet

> Technology and Marketing
  - Technology impacts
  - General purpose technologies

> Our Approach

Figure 1.1

Google's Home Page

Source: Courtesy of Google Inc.

News feeds, capturing material too recent for normal search indexing, appear under the News tab and change by the hour. Froogle is a gateway to shopping, where search technology compares listings on web pages and catalogs. Local search narrows results by geography, turning search technology into an interactive Yellow Pages. Desktop search uses Google technology to create an index of the user's hard drives, letting the user automatically combine results from emails and personal files with web results. A click further leads to many additional tools and search over video, library holdings, and more.

Google began as an innovative way to improve online search. As the Web grew from thousands of pages to millions, it became increasingly difficult to sort through the many matches resulting from a search. Early search engines tried rules of thumb. If a search term appeared repeatedly in the title or some other prominent location on a page the page would appear higher on the search list. These simple rules were not sufficient as the Web grew to hundreds of millions of pages and web site marketers manipulated their content to improve their search list ranking. Better approaches were needed.

Google's PageRank algorithm prioritizes searches by treating links pointing at a web page as a form of popularity voting. Pages and sites with many votes are treated as more important than sites with fewer. Popularity is contagious, as sites linked to popular sites receive higher weights as well.[4] The founders of Google developed a mathematical system that could be applied to the entire Web, assigning to each page importance weights in a manner that gave much better search performance while remaining fast and easy to use. The Google system uses the entire web to rank web sites and web pages. The Internet partially organizes itself.

The commercial potential of Google developed gradually and somewhat surprisingly. At first, Google had traffic but no revenue. The breakthrough for Google was the AdWords system, which lets advertisers put simple text-based ads on the same page as search engine results.

When users click on an ad, taking them to the advertiser's web site, Google receives a fee. The relevance and focus of the ad proves to be highly effective, as it is triggered by the searchers own words. AdWords are easy to create and let the advertiser carefully track the profitability of their keyword advertising. Fees are set by auction, generating much more revenue than a flat fee.

The core of Google's activities and revenue remains in search, which receives 70% of funding. Google expands beyond search with a rule they call "70-20-10".[5] Adjacent products, such as Froogle and Groups, receive 20% of the research and development funding. The remaining 10% is used for experimental activities, which may never be commercialized, but allow Google to explore new opportunities and test new ideas.

Another core strategy of Google is to hire the "best and the brightest" among engineers and programmers. Partly seriously, partly for fun, Google posted the billboard shown in Figure 1.2 in the San Francisco and Boston area. Once someone finds the answer and types it into their browser, they arrive at a site run by Google. There another problem is posted, finally leading to the Google Labs employment page.[6] Individuals quickly deduced that the fastest way to solve the problem was with a Google search for a page with the answer, somewhat defeating the billboard's initial purpose but demonstrating the power of search.

Although committed to a simple interface on its core search page, and resisting a common tendency to clutter the most valuable initial contact with advertisements and

Figure 1.2

Google's Recruiting Technique – A Billboard Domain Puzzle

Source: Courtesy of Google Inc. Photographer: Matt Walsh (www.mattwalsh.com).

commercial offerings, Google designers are not averse to having a little fun. Whether it is artist Van Gogh's birthday, Google's anniversary, international water day, mathematician Mandelbrot's birthday, or Valentines Day (as in Figure 1.3), the home page occasionally has a little surprise. These swaps of the Google logo reinforce the friendly, socially conscious and helpful brand image that Google nurtures.

The tendency of online companies to build on their initial success through expansion leads to increasing overlap and competition between services. Google expanded into ecommerce when it added its Froogle capability, while Yahoo! bolstered its advertising capabilities by purchasing the Overture keyword search service. No company can rest easy, as new competitors emerge and market boundaries change. Though occasionally confusing, online users benefit greatly as this dynamic competition proceeds. Like the Internet itself, each month brings new features and challenges. Google demonstrates the power of a startup to rise to global stardom in only a few years.

Figure 1.3

Google Having a Little Fun or Supporting a Cause

Source: Courtesy of Google Inc.

CREATING A COMMERCIAL INTERNET

Few technologies have the scope and scale of impact as the Internet. Two of its pioneers became *Time* magazine "Persons of the Year" in the 1990s,[7] hundreds of thousands of press articles covered its emergence, new print and online magazines focused online, and U.S. presidential hopefuls fought over credit for stimulating Internet development. Hundreds of millions of users became Net citizens in all corners of the globe. Bursts of investment activity swamped previous records, and sent the stock market shooting up and reeling down. Net impacts include improvements in economic productivity, changes in the location of work, educational resources surpassing the grandest encyclopedia, and new cheap online communication channels. There have also been failed companies, governmental censorship, email boxes cluttered with objectionable content, lost jobs, and failed industries due to obsolescence.

Though all aspects of business have been affected by the commercial Internet, few areas have had as big a leadership role as marketing. This was natural, and reflects the pattern seen in other great communication technologies such as radio and television. Reaching both current and potential customers is a fundamental role of marketing. Marketing embraced many of the new techniques of email, web advertising, web site support, and online commerce. At the same time, savvy web entrepreneurs such as Internet powerhouses AOL and Yahoo! were able to tap into the widely available investment money and demand multi-million-dollar marketing partnerships from these new entrants.

The roller coaster ride of boom and bust of the past decade should not obscure the fundamental truth: Nearly a billion Internet users worldwide have integrated the Internet into their lives. This popularity and user base means that any marketer must understand the challenges and opportunities provided by the Internet. Global information on all products and services is at least partially available for any Net surfer. No marketing education is complete without the skills needed to compete online. At the same time, these skills must include an appreciation for the weaknesses of the Internet and the blending of traditional and innovative marketing approaches.

An Internet marketer faces the continual and difficult challenge of mixing established best practices while creatively exploiting the newest opportunities and techniques. The only thing constant about the Internet is its continual evolution, whereby costs fluctuate, markets change, and new technologies appear. An appreciation of the history of the commercial Internet is helpful in understanding how best to handle such a dynamic environment. This section quickly reviews how the Internet has grown from a small experimental technology to a worldwide critical resource.

The Noncommercial Net: 1969–1994

For the first 25 years of its existence, commercial use of the Internet was improper. From 1969 to the early 1990s, the Internet was restricted to military, academic, and a few corporate research users. Most of the 1 billion Internet users would be surprised to learn that 1994, the beginning of the explosion in public interest, actually marked the 25th anniversary of the Internet.

Theoretical work on the Internet started in the early 1960s. The first implementation of the Net occurred in 1969, hooking the University of California at Los Angeles to the Stanford Research Institute (see Figure 1.4). Over the next five years many of the procedures still in use today were developed. These included email and the @ symbol in addresses (1971), remote accessing of computers through telnet (1972), multiple-person chat sessions (1973), and the downloading of files through ftp (1973).[8] A select few had decades of online experience by the time the Net was opened for business.

This early Internet served two purposes. The first was as a robust emergency military communication network. The second was as an experimental communications system within the academic community. The goal was to stimulate sharing between researchers, many with government research grants.

The long-distance backbone of the Internet was maintained by the U.S. National Science Foundation (NSF). The NSF had an acceptable-use policy that explicitly prohibited all but the most indirect commerce online.[9] It was considered acceptable for private researchers to send files and email messages to academic members in their own research areas. Technical support was a bit of a gray area, allowed in most cases. Commercial information and transactions were expressly prohibited.

Figure 1.4

Earliest Internet Hardware

Source: Courtesy of the Computer History Museum.

Despite these restrictions, the Internet grew rapidly as many universities and labs found it an effective way to keep in touch. In fact, its growing value caused many to feel that bans against commercial use were hurting the economy. Researchers, seeing the benefits of sharing academic information, started arguing that the rest of society would also benefit.

The key driver of this growth was email. Users found email a surprisingly efficient method of communication, eliminating telephone tag and allowing users to communicate at any time. Researchers found that up to 70% of telephone calls fail to reach the intended party. At the time, answering machines and voice mail were scarce. Email took advantage of asynchrony, separating a message's sending and receiving time. Email could be instantaneous, or it could be spread over days and weeks. The research community quickly adapted email as a preferred method of communicating with colleagues. Email's indifference to time zones worked well in the widely dispersed academic community and helped foster a sense of community, allowing many colleagues to keep in touch between face-to-face meetings. This remains true to the present day.

The early Internet was painfully slow and expensive by twenty-first-century standards. Computers costing tens of thousands of dollars were required. Modems to hook to the network were very slow. Congestion was common. Software was limited and difficult to use, with arcane commands required to access the network and find specific information.

The Internet's deregulatory "big bang" happened in the early 1990s. Political and technical leaders realized that it was time to share the productivity and potential of the Internet to a much wider audience. At the time, the subsidy provided by the NSF was running at about $15 million a year. The U.S. government announced that it was eliminating the acceptable-use policy as well as the subsidy. In 1994, the new Internet backbone that allowed commercial operations became operational.[10] The Internet could now be used for commercial activities, including marketing.

One more fundamental breakthrough was needed: the World Wide Web, an innovation from Europe which quickly spread throughout the Net.[11] The Web combines ease of use, much simpler navigation between pages and sites, and multimedia. Suddenly it was possible to mix pictures, sound, and even video with the simple text of the earlier innovations. Just as importantly, the Internet became much more intuitive for users. Gone were many of the obscure and complicated commands. Now there was a simple way to navigate by clicking on links and typing in web addresses.

Companies found that they could use the Web to communicate effectively. This new web, combined with power of the earlier email technology, created an entirely new and effective mechanism for relating to customers. Marketers in companies across the planet seized this new tool.

Companies and organizations suddenly found themselves able to create marketing material that had global reach for very low cost. Small firms could compete on a much more even footing with the largest companies in the world. Customers found they could quickly find product and company information at the click of a mouse. Even more exciting, companies and customers could engage in a dialogue and learn from each other. This new tool, a commercially available and easy to use Internet, created a revolution.

The Internet Explosion

> *Fascination and Functionality*

Fundamental new technologies have the power to inspire. Users are able to project beyond the immediate limitations and imagine what might exist in a year, in a decade, in a generation. This vision can be so compelling that it makes them buy the product just to participate in the vision, even if it is nowhere near able to perform those feats in its present shape.

The early days of radio provide insight. Radio was the original WWW, worldwide wireless. When the RCA Corporation took the logo shown in Figure 1.5 in 1920, it saw itself in the business of wireless telegraphy and wireless telephony. It had the U.S. rights to send telegrams and messages to ships and other hard-to-reach locations. As part of a settlement following World War I, the Marconi Company of England had been forced to give up its monopoly of the world wireless market and turn the American rights over to the newly formed RCA. Wireless was viewed as a security matter, with little impact on commercial activity.

In 1922, radio suddenly transformed from a low-cost niche business into a consumer and business phenomenon. It was "top of the charts" and seemed to point the way to the future. The number of broadcasting stations mushroomed from five at the end of 1921 to more than 575 a year later. Starting radio stations was the height of entrepreneurship. Listening to radio became a runaway consumer fad.[12] "Combing the ether" was the hit of the day.

This reaction surprised RCA. When the company was created, it based its entire business plan on the traditional ways that radio had been used by the military and by shipping companies, which involved point-to-point communication. Within three years, the revenues from broadcasting were more than 100 times larger than these original sources. Like the Internet 75 years later, the transition from limited military and experimental uses to commercial adoption meant an enormous increase in use and revenue.

Radio created more than a product or an industry. Although it now seems merely an appliance, radio had a huge impact on the society of the 1920s. It changed the way the average person thought about distance and time. Simultaneity no longer required proximity. Global events could be experienced as they happened. Performances in distant cities could be heard in the neighbor's living room. Fast-breaking world stories, or simply news about impending weather, were available with a flip of a switch and the turn of the dial.

Figure 1.5

RCA Logo: 1920

Source: David Sarnoff Collection, Inc.

Radio changed business, especially marketing. Radio accelerated the economy's transformation to a mass market. It greatly facilitated the creation of national brands. A firm could launch national marketing campaigns simultaneously, backed by a nationally created image. New-product store introductions could be synchronized with advertising campaigns building consumer interest. Product positioning became more flexible. Businesses of all kinds learned to use this new powerful method of reaching customers.

Radio changed the everyday life of millions of listeners, altering aspects of their lives from church attendance to newspaper reading.[13] A scheduled mass culture emerged. As early as 1923, the Happiness Boys had become famous as "your Friday-night date, from seven thirty to eight."[14] Timeslots, lead-ins, and prime time became familiar concepts.

In making the transition from hobby to industry, radio as an industry struggled with the basic requirement of generating a self-sustaining revenue base. Providing value to customers created opportunities, but it was necessary to make a profit to sustain a business. Radio had to solve the business model problem. There were major competing visions. Some argued bitterly against advertising support and commercialization. In many European countries, this stance led to government support of radio. The U.S. administration was opposed to government control and pushed for a purely private solution.

For a time, a private solution did not look promising. By the end of 1924, 581 broadcast stations were operating. Many of these stations found it impossible to be profitable, and by the middle of 1926, stations were failing at a rate of almost 15 percent per month. At the same time, consumers continued to rush to purchase new radios. Ultimately the emergence of national networks combining local and national advertising made radio profitable.

Montgomery Ward first sold a radio in its 1922 catalogue (Figure 1.6). It was extremely popular. A close inspection shows that a number of basic radio features are lacking. The automobile battery on the floor was necessary because the radio could not be plugged into a wall outlet. Headphones were used because the radios could not run speakers effectively with their limited power. Photos from the time show groups of people sitting around a table, each wearing headphones.

The external antenna had to be strung for considerable distances, often to a nearby building. An antenna became a serious hazard during thunderstorms. Finally, tuning was limited. Most areas only allowed broadcasts on one frequency. Local stations had elaborate time-sharing arrangements to avoid interfering with other signals.

The early days of the Web shared many of these characteristics. In 1995, when the Internet commercial explosion took off, Web sites lacked many of the features now taken for granted. Sites were static—with little dynamic content personalized to individual use. Only a few pioneering sites had database retrieval capabilities.

Figure 1.6

Montgomery Ward's First Radio

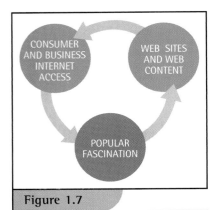

Figure 1.7

The Virtuous Cycle for Net Growth

Frames, tables, and styles were not available. Security mechanisms and encryption were rare and cumbersome. Streaming media, both sound and video, were nonexistent.

The early Internet had limited content. In early 1995, it would have been possible to store the entire Internet in fewer than 50 compact discs of data, less than a typical college student's music collection. Even so, it was a struggle to find the correct material and the techniques of web directories and search engines were just emerging.

> The Virtuous Cycle of the Early Web

Although the early commercial Internet lacked many features we now consider basic, it did have the power to fascinate. Users, providers, and investors could imagine many opportunities and future capabilities. Entrepreneurs realized that a gold rush was on, with many brands and services to be created. Interested amateurs, often graduate students, created directory services such as Yahoo! and the search engine WebCrawler. The popularity of these sites exploded, and quickly became full-time activities and businesses.

The commercial Internet spawned a virtuous cycle, shown in Figure 1.7. A virtuous cycle is a business system with positive feedback. Each element feeds off one and onto the other, leading to rapid development and, often, a large amount of speculation. Consumers and firms feel the need to participate and contribute to the development, even if a clear business plan is missing. The desire not to miss the "next great thing" causes many to join in. If this cycle is strong enough, it can actually be a self-fulfilling expectation. Belief in the new industry helps it succeed.

The virtuous cycle speeds technology adoption far ahead of the pace it would have without these positive feedback loops. Figures 1.8 and 1.9 are two examples of many possible versions of the rapid diffusion occurring during the initial boom years. Consumers came to expect all businesses to be experimenting with web sites and web pages—even Larry with his lunch truck. This was possible due to the rapid development of web access and simple web services. Figure 1.9 shows how widely the distribution of Internet service providers had penetrated by 1998. Even sparsely settled counties in the United States were served, often by individuals starting up their own small business to serve their neighbors.[15] The boom in Net access was extremely diversified.

There is a long research tradition in marketing, economics, and sociology studying the spread of new products. The adoption of a technology depends on the pool of possible adopters and how quickly they can be turned into buyers. Key motivators of trial are the expected benefits of the new technology and social influences such as word of mouth.

The important feature of a virtuous cycle is that several different diffusion processes are linked and reinforce each

Figure 1.8

Experiments with Online Information

Source: © The 5th Wave, www.the5thwave.com.

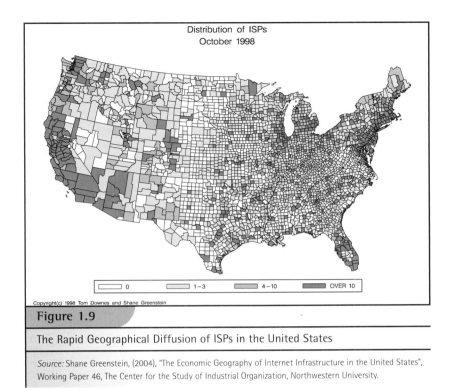

Distribution of ISPs
October 1998

| | 0 | | 1–3 | | 4–10 | | OVER 10 |

Copyright(c) 1998 Tom Downes and Shane Greenstein

Figure 1.9

The Rapid Geographical Diffusion of ISPs in the United States

Source: Shane Greenstein, (2004), "The Economic Geography of Internet Infrastructure in the United States", Working Paper 46, The Center for the Study of Industrial Organization, Northwestern University.

other. The diffusion of web sites depends on both web-site diffusion and user-base diffusion. User diffusion is positively affected by the growth in web sites.

> *Financial Booms and Busts*

Web users were not the only ones captivated, fascinated, and contributing to this virtuous cycle. Venture capitalists, stock market investors, and marketing executives all poured money into online ventures. Venture capital financing, money available for startups and risky new approaches, grew especially rapidly during the late 1990s. Venture investments in all areas of the economy, but heavily tilted toward the Internet, rose to six times higher in 2000 than just two years earlier. This was an unsustainable boom, with too much money chasing too many similar opportunities.[16] Inevitably, there were bad investments and disappointed investors. The same experience occurred in radio and in other major technology innovations. While investors end up losing money, a speculative boom kick starts an industry faster than it might have otherwise. Unfortunately, the bust that follows causes major disruptions as well.

Rapidly growing venture capital investment reflects enthusiasm for starting new companies. Going public and a public company's stock price measures how the wider investment community views a company's future. Figure 1.10 shows the history of Yahoo! stock, one of the most successful of Internet companies. From its public debut in 1997, Yahoo! grew dramatically in value until it reached its peak in early 2000. The fall in value from this peak was steep and painful; at one point Yahoo! was worth less than 10% of its 2000 peak.

Many companies launched during the peak of the investment boom were not as fortunate as Yahoo!, did not survive, failed to recover, and closed their doors. Others merged with another

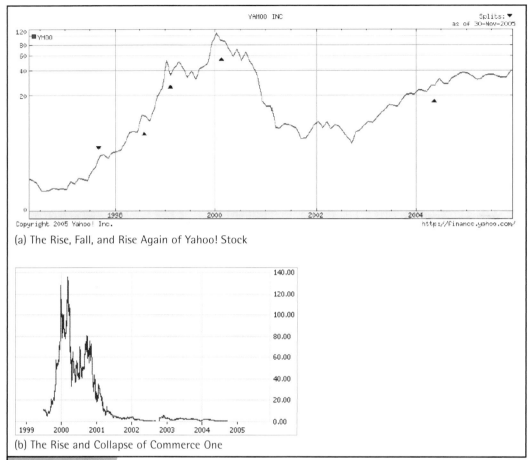

(a) The Rise, Fall, and Rise Again of Yahoo! Stock

(b) The Rise and Collapse of Commerce One

Figure 1.10

The Roller Coaster Ride of Stock Valuations During the Boom

Source: 1.10a http://finance.yahoo.com. Reproduced with permission of Yahoo! Inc. © 2005 by Yahoo! Inc. YAHOO! and the YAHOO! logo are trademarks of Yahoo! Inc.; 1.10b © Quotemedia.com.

company at a fraction of their peak value. An example of the roller coaster ride is Commerce One, a high profile company aiming to be the "EBay of business to business commerce."[17] During the boom it seemed to be succeeding, with revenues rising into the hundreds of millions and a stock market value in the billions. However, it failed to become profitable and its stock market value plunged, layoffs ensued, and eventually it ran out of cash.

The same force that propelled the rapid growth in the revenues of companies such as Yahoo! and AOL during the boom spelled the doom of many Internet startups—a highly aggressive battle for new customers that caused companies to spend more acquiring customers than these customers would ever contribute to the company.[18] Eventually these extremely high marketing expenditures needed to be scaled back, and much more rational and cost-effective marketing plans emerged. Companies with the discipline and ability to make this transition began to thrive.

Figure 1.11 shows the steep rise in online advertising that occurred from 1998–2000. While much of this occurred at the largest sites, the demand for traffic at almost any cost percolated throughout the online advertising system. In 1996, the first year of data collection by the IAB (Internet Advertising Bureau), online advertising spending was only $30 million per quarter. In 1997 spending tripled, doubled in 1998, and tripled again in 1999. At the same time, online companies were spending lavishly on traditional media. Magazines were created covering the Net, driven by the high levels of spending. Radio and television ads for new online sites became commonplace. Companies such as Monster.com and Pets.com ran Super Bowl ads, the most expensive of all media advertising, to advance their brands. Again the peak was the January 2000 game, where 17 dot-coms spent at least $2.2 million for a 30-second television spot.

By 2002, venture capital funding, stock prices, and customer acquisition spending had declined to more typical and sustainable levels. Historians will long debate the exact causes and consequences of this burst of investment in venture capital and technology stocks. One consequence for some observers is to conclude that the Internet was a passing fad, and the decline in the boom meant a fall in Internet adoption and real impact on the economy. The truth is very different.

Booms and busts can obscure underlying trends, and the financial swings of company fortunes can hide the movements in underlying real variables. Even during the shakeout phase of dot-coms, the fundamentals of real growth continued for the Net. Financial trends have stabilized and resumed their growth. As seen in Figure 1.11, online spending now exceeds even the peak of the boom times, but with a very different composition. Gone are almost all of the unaccountable and occasionally irrational portal sponsorship deals. Replacing them are much more accountable and flexible search engine key word and click-through arrangements. Companies can now bid on very small increments of traffic, judge their profitability carefully, and engage in highly accountable customer acquisition. While growth remains an important goal, both marketers and investors place a premium on profitability and reward companies for good management and proper practices.

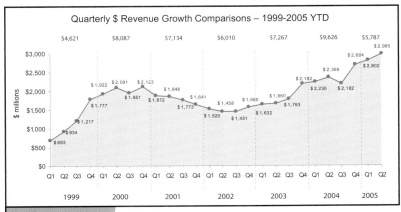

Figure 1.11

Quarterly Online Advertising U.S. Revenues

Source: IAB Internet Advertising Revenue Report: An Industry Survey, Conducted by PricewaterhouseCoopers and Sponsored by the Interactive Advertising Bureau (IAB), 2005 Second Quarter and First Six-Months Results, September 2005, p. 5. Copyright PriceWaterhouseCoopers LLP.

| The Internet as a Global Resource

Despite the roller coaster behavior of the stock market, the actual pattern of usage and impacts of the Internet has shown a much steadier pattern of growth and expansion. The user base continues to grow rapidly, especially outside of the early adopter countries. Computers and servers hooked to the Net provide ready access, with an increased emphasis on broadband and wireless access. The Internet is diversifying further with the ability of more devices to connect. Applications relying at least partially on Net connectivity continue to be incorporated into a wide range of products.

At the heart of Internet growth is a better appreciation of the potential and sources of productivity increases it provides. Rather than rely on speculation and hype, companies are now insisting on demonstrable results. During the beginning of the boom a Nobel Prize–winning economist could rightly say that "computers appear everywhere but in the productivity statistics."[19] That has changed, and researchers are documenting both the magnitude and the type of improvements caused by the Net.

> Internet Users

Approximately 15% of the world's 6.3 billion population is online. This remarkable achievement creates a valuable global resource with substantial additional room for growth. It creates an infrastructure capable of sharing content and communications nearly instantly around the planet. Far from declining in importance, it is boosting productivity and supporting entire new industries around the world.

The dominance of U.S. users is disappearing. Americans are less than 20% of the world's Internet user base. This is a dramatic fall in the U.S. share of Net users over the past five years, relative to other advanced and emerging economies. The share of Internet users in developing countries has more than doubled since 1998.[20]

Table 1.1 demonstrates that the Internet is becoming much more diverse in its geographic, cultural, and economic user base. Especially notable growth is happening in countries such as China, India, and South Korea. China already

Table 1.1

Top 15 Countries for Internet Access, 2004			
	Country	Population	Internet Users	% online
		6,302,309,691	934 Million	14.8%
Rank				
1	United States	290,342,554	185.5	63.9%
2	China	1,286,975,468	99.8	7.8%
3	Japan	127,214,499	78.1	61.4%
4	Germany	82,398,326	41.9	50.8%
5	India*	1,065,070,607	37.0	3.5%
6	United Kingdom	60,094,648	33.1	55.1%
7	Korea, South	48,289,037	31.7	65.6%
8	France	60,180,529	25.5	42.4%
9	Italy	57,998,353	25.5	44.0%
10	Brazil	182,032,604	22.3	7.68%
11	Russia	144,526,278	21.2	14.7%
12	Canada	32,207,113	20.5	63.7%
13	Mexico*	104,959,594	13.9	13.2%
14	Australia	19,731,984	13.0	66.0%
15	Indonesia*	238,452,952	12.9	5.4%
	Share of total	60.3%	70.1%	

* New to list in 2004.

Source: CIA Factbook

has the second largest base of Net users, despite a low per capita income and a small percentage of market penetration. In 2004, China passed Japan as the number two online country and may soon challenge the United States for the largest user base. Between 2002 and 2004, India jumped from not being on the top-15 list to fifth place. Also in 2004, the first predominately Islamic country (Indonesia) joined the list. In richer countries, saturation of the market seems to be occurring as market penetration exceeds 60% of the total population. Missing from the top 15 is any African country, and a number of other populous but poor countries. The top 15 countries have approximately 70% of the world's online users, with a population base of roughly 60% of the world total.

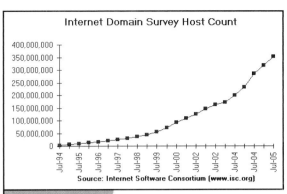

Figure 1.12

Continuing Growth in Net Hosts

Source: Internet Software Consortium (www.isc.org).

> Connection Devices

A traditional metric for Internet access devices has been the number of Internet hosts, which are computers with a permanent Internet addresses. The chief strength of this measure is its longevity. Available since the earliest days of the Internet, the graph in Figure 1.10 clearly shows the rapid host growth that dominated the 1990s. By the end of 2002, the host count seemed to indicate a maturing and slowing of the growth of access devices. However, this seems to have been just a pause, with renewed strong growth appearing in 2004 and 2005.

Internet hosts are becoming a less useful measure of Net access devices. Web-enabled cell phones, wireless handheld devices, home wireless networks connecting multiple devices, and other shared resources are spreading rapidly, suggesting that Figure 1.12 substantially understates the total number of access devices. Indeed, the International Telecommunications Union (ITU) detected an intriguing transition in 2003. Throughout the 1980s and 1990s, computer usage far outweighed Internet usage.[21] Recently, the online user base continues to grow rapidly while computer growth slows (see Table 1.2). A combination of phone-based access, wireless personal digital assistants,

Table 1.2

Worldwide Networks of Landlines, Cellular Phones, Personal Computers, and Internet Users		1996	1997	1998	1999	2000	2001	2002	2003e
Main telephone lines	(millions)	738	792	846	905	983	1,053	1,129	1,210
Mobile cellular subscribers	(millions)	145	215	318	490	740	955	1,155	1,329
International telephone traffic minutes	(billions)	71	79	89	100	118	127	135	140
Personal computers	(millions)	275	325	375	435	500	555	615	650
Internet users	(millions)	74	117	183	277	399	502	580	665

Source: Reproduced with the kind permisson of the ITU (International Telecommunications Union).

shared access through Net cafes and schools in less developed countries, and the standard inclusion of the Internet in personal computers means that the online user base is surpassing the number of personal computers.

The quality of access is also changing, moving to much faster broadband connections. More than 15% of the world's Internet users had access to broadband by 2005. Broadband connectivity is much like Net access was several years ago, uneven and biased toward richer countries. However, broadband also reflects governmental and telecommunication company policy decisions. Countries such as South Korea and Singapore have made strategic investments and have aggressively pushed broadband. In Japan, broadband served as an entry strategy by competitors, shaking up the Internet access market. For example, Yahoo! has become very successful providing Japanese Internet access by offering very low prices and very fast connection speeds. The United States is something of a laggard in the broadband market. Broadband is typically "always on," lowering a substantial convenience barrier and simplifying access for many applications. Broadband greatly improves the quality of services such as video-on-demand, file downloading, swapping of photos, shared computing, and voice-over-IP. Broadband encourages the use of applications that rely on data only available online.

A different form of diversity and maturity is occurring with connection devices as they become information appliances. An information appliance is a move away from general purpose computing toward a dedicated device which becomes simpler by focusing on limited functions. Two of the most popular current information appliances are the Apple iPod and the Tivo personal video recorder. Both are "computers," containing processing power, hard disk storage, and connectivity. Both use the Internet in a powerful and seamless method. The Tivo is an information appliance for video recording, the iPod for audio downloading and listening.

Tivo connects to the Net using either dial-up or broadband, and downloads information for its electronic programming guide. This allows a viewer to program and view television content as they wish. Viewing information can also be shared with Tivo headquarters, leading to interactive audience measurement. The iPod works through its cradle connected to a computer, synchronizing its media content and allowing a listener to obtain music online for consumption at any time. Both devices have won rave reviews from their owners, allowing simple and elegant consumption of media (see Figure 1.13). They are an emerging kind of Internet connection device. Combining low cost computing, storage, and connectivity with a simple design based on human usage factors, these devices make the Internet and the computing necessary for their working nearly invisible. They still, however, retain many of the internal capabilities of more general purpose tools.

Following these information appliances are actual familiar household appliances, such as refrigerators, heating systems, lights, and ovens, fitted with Net capabilities. While still mostly expensive prototypes, engineers and designers are searching for opportunities to integrate the Net into familiar appliances without burdening users with complex commands. The goal is both ubiquitous access and smarter home automation.

Businesses typically incorporate high technology into daily operations earlier than consumers. Businesses have the support and maintenance staff necessary to solve problems, train staff, and search for productive solutions. An example is office and commercial building

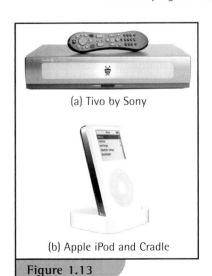

(a) Tivo by Sony

(b) Apple iPod and Cradle

Figure 1.13

Information Appliances

Source: 1.13a © AP/Wide World Photos; 1.13b © Getty Images.

automation. For years, Otis elevator has incorporated networking devices into their elevators and escalators. When a problem occurs, these modules automatically send a message over a network connection letting service personnel know they are needed. Companies such as Xerox and Canon are building these diagnostics and service modules into their large copiers and printers. Whether these should be counted as Net access devices is debatable, but they are taking advantage of the Net to routinely communicate from machine to human or machine to machine.

> *Innovative Marketing Applications*

Within a decade of its inception, marketers for all organizations have come to rely on the Internet for an expanding number of functions. New products debut online, advertisements contain Web URLs providing additional details, politicians steer voters to their web sites during debates, special sales are only available online, and promotional efforts build valuable traffic and consumer information from their online presence. Prosperous companies exist that could only operate online, needing the low cost and rapid communication provided by the Net. Just as users and devices have continued their healthy growth, the number of online marketing applications continues to expand.

No simple metric captures this diversity of applications. However, a quick review of these expanding uses helps set the stage for the detailed discussion throughout the rest of the book. Consider how the world's most popular sporting event merges the Net into its quadrennial activities.

> The World's Game Online

No sporting event generates more viewers and more continued fan interest than the World Cup. Months before the opening ceremonies, countries must qualify for the games. These qualifying rounds arouse intense discussion, and billions of fans around the world trace the fortunes of their country's team or arch rivals. The World Cup provides an illustrative case study of how marketers are using the Net to reach their fan base and are evolving in sophistication.[22]

(a)

(b)

Figure 1.14

The "World's Game" is Heavily Online

Source: 1.14a KIMINORI SAWADA/EPA/Landov; 1.14b Bernd Weissbrod/ EPA/Landov.

Popularity of the Cup Online

World Cup 98 was the first championship with a commercial Net as part of many soccer fans' enjoyment. There was diverse coverage, with over 60 sites springing up devoted to the Cup.

The most popular site, France98.com, amassed impressive viewership for a web site at the time. Between June 12 and July 12 of 1998 it received 1.14 billion hits.[23] Its peak day was June 30, when it received 73 million hits in a day. Its peak hour was on June 29, with 10.3 hits million hits in an hour.[24] This rivaled the performance of almost any other web site up to that time.

The planning and execution of the 2002 World Cup, this time jointly held in South Korea and Japan, revealed both the growing pains and increased importance of the Net in commercial ventures. Rather than a diverse and open policy, the FIFA (Fédération Internationale de Football Association) governing body exerted substantially more control over content. Limits were placed on live online feeds, with concerns that it would cannibalize regular broadcasts. Even with these restrictions, more than 79 million page viewings occurred on the peak day of the matches.

Planning for the 2006 matches in Germany highlights online lessons learned from the successes of 1998 and the relative disappointments of 2002. The importance of early fan interest shows in the daily match coverage, which started almost two years prior to the finals. Information is available in multiple languages, with automatic translations into others. In-depth information, including classic World Cup matches and goals can be watched. Video from classic moments and players from past Cups provides excitement. Planning is made much easier with travel, tickets, and surroundings described in detail.

Static Publishing

The online World Cup shows an expansion in the interactivity and sophistication of Net usage and site design. It also dramatizes continuing battles over commercial interests, business models, choices of strategy, and different execution alternatives.

Many web sites begin as simple publishing sites, providing the same information to all. It can be as simple as one page of contact information, or a multimedia experience with in-depth material retrieved by clicking on links. The common thread is a fixed set of information available to all.

While most static sites are fairly modest, they are not necessarily limited or dull. A site can contain thousands of pages, pictures, sound, and video. The design and graphics can be stunning. What is limited is the dialogue between web site and users. A static site broadcasts. Information flows from the web site to the viewer, with only the clicks of readers and viewers providing any feedback.

Modern web tools make such simple web sites easy and inexpensive to produce. Almost any document can be converted and moved online. Software programs make it possible to manage a stage I web site almost as easily as using a word processor. Because of this, many company's first web site reflects a static publishing approach.[25] With experience and investment they move on to richer and more dynamic content.

Dynamic Selection

A second stage of web sophistication combines the publishing power of a static site with the ability to retrieve information in response to user requests. The responses are dynamically turned into web pages or email. Interactivity and dialogue has started, although it is limited to a series of "ask-respond" interactions.

Some of the most popular and useful features of World Cup sites use these capabilities. Clicking on the qualifying matches of the day retrieves layers of information and additional detail. Additional drill-down material can lead to nearly unlimited content, accessible in unique mixtures depending on the interests of the visitor. Fans can list all players, matches, and schedules of each team. Specialized programs provide recaps of all the contests, with details about scoring, penalties, substitutions, and top moments of the match.

Templates allow the unique aspects of each game to be presented automatically. While each match is different, all share the same underlying structure of players, scores, penalties, referees, timing, weather, location, and highlights. Templates must be flexible enough to handle the full range of possibilities that can occur (such as a 0-0 tie or a lopsided 6-1 win), while allowing the information to flow into the proper content areas.

Ecommerce

Most ecommerce, where goods or services are purchased online, is accomplished with dynamic selection capabilities. Instead of players and scores, the information is often products and prices. Ecommerce is certainly one main area of content for the FIFA site. On the 2006 site is a map showing the various German cities hosting the matches. Clicking on the links for Köln, Berlin, or any of the other 12 cities gives a view of amenities, scheduled groups, and travel facilities. Further links retrieve ticketing for games, hotels, local additional events, and airfare.

The ability to use the Web as an access point to images, sound, and databases is a valuable tool. Dynamic sites can help users find directions, buy tickets, listen to a sports hero, or see a stadium from many angles.

Personalized Information

A personalized site dynamically creates pages catering to a specific individual. It moves beyond an "ask-respond" interaction into a dialogue, and may anticipate user choices and suggest possible alternatives. A personalized site does more than just react to requests typed into forms or selected by clicking on an image. These sites are the most challenging and least used. They require both static and dynamic selection capabilities plus a direct connection to a specific user. A user must reveal at least part of their identities and wants, and the site must be able to respond appropriately.

The 2006 World Cup explicitly emphasizes these full capabilities. Users are encouraged to set up alerts to receive email information about upcoming matches and specific team and player information. Even more directly, FIFA is partnering with Yahoo! to take advantage of Yahoo's personalization system to customize World Cup information. This lets FIFA use a system capable of mass customizing information for millions of users.

Several factors worked against personalization for earlier World Cup sites. Personal web sites are useful for creating a relationship between the web site sponsor and the visitor. Unless efforts begin early, or work through a system such as Yahoo!, the logistics and costs of creating a relationship system are hardly justified. By engaging alliances with partners, FIFA can move increasingly toward dynamic and individualized content.

Personalization tools and applications are developing rapidly. Many companies have followed this same train of thought and are laying the foundation of their online marketing with simpler sites, and adding personalized capabilities as they gain experience, develop compelling applications, or take advantage of new tools.

> Keyword Advertising

One of the biggest changes in the time since the first online Cup is the rise of search engines and keyword advertising. The turnaround in advertising spending seen in Figure 1.9 is heavily influenced by the ability of leading search engines to sell text links tied to search terms. A fan planning their trip to the games would often start with a search such as that shown in Figure 1.15, keying in the terms "World Cup," "tickets," and perhaps the name of the city they are interested in. Figure 1.15 shows the query, with the top results listed first, the purchased links on the right, and the latter results the unpaid-for responses. The sponsored links can lead to actual match tickets, hotel, and airfare booking. Rather than scattered through the 1,620 links found from the 4 billion pages searched by Google, these advertising sites are given top billing.

Figure 1.15

Using Keyword Advertising for the Games

Source: Courtesy of Google Inc.

Several factors contribute to the success of keyword advertising. Relevance is key, as searchers using these search terms are primed for further information tied to the Games. In the words of direct marketing, they are hot leads that have self-identified their interest. Second, keyword advertising is flexible. Rather than set a fixed price for this combination of terms, advertisers at major sites such as Yahoo! and Google can bid in an ongoing auction. The intensity of demand determines the price. In Chapter 8 we consider this process in detail. It has numerous benefits, both in terms of accountability to advertisers and profitability to the search engines.

Keyword advertising highlights the many different businesses that can be interested in these search terms. The sponsored links include stadium ticket vendors, eBay auctions on soccer collectibles, and airline and hotel bookings. Visiting a major sporting event is a trigger event for a wide range of potential purchases. A trigger event is an action or choice that is naturally connected to a variety of follow-on purchases or actions. Connecting advertising to trigger events increases the effectiveness of the advertising, raising its commercial value and its benefit to the audience it targets.

The common mixture of free and commercial material, some of it relevant and some of it not, also stands out. Keyword search returns free results that partially overlap with the advertisers. There are sites not among the advertisers. There are listings that might be considered mistakes, such as the World Cup of Hockey that also took place in Köln. In some cases this information could be useful, as a fan might want to know that Köln is experienced in holding international sporting events. Search terms themselves don't indicate which of the World Cup events the searcher intends.

> Integrated Media Planning

Advertisers prefer to advertise where customers are. Over the course of a day this changes. During workdays, marketers have grown to realize that the Net is the principal source of messages and communication. On the other hand, during drive times or evenings, radio and television lead the marketing venues.

Rather than focus only online, or only on mass media, an increasing number of advertisers are using an integrated media plan to follow their audience. Each of these media can reinforce the others, and hand the audience to the media by highlighting the upcoming events. When World Cup matches are months away, few games will be seen and stories in the mass media are less frequent. This makes the Net an ideal spot for coverage. In geographic regions far from Germany, coverage of the games may be scarce. Providing travel and supporting information online works best.

Marketers are following this pattern in their support of the World Cup. As part of their licensing revenue, FIFA created 15 sponsorship packages. These were taken by a range of consumer goods companies, such as Adidas, Anheuser-Busch, Avaya, Coca-Cola, Continental, Deutsche Telekom, Emirates, Fujifilm, Gillette, Hyundai, MasterCard, McDonald's, Philips, Toshiba, and Yahoo!. As the matches progress, media shifts from purely online promotions to a mixture of online and mass media advertising. These 15 global corporations then mix their ads with a combination of information and branding.

> Blogs, Chat, and Peer-to-Peer Material

One of the fascinating and challenging online changes since the first Internet coverage of the Cup is the growth of direct consumer interaction through tools such as instant messaging, online chat, and Blogs. These peer-to-peer tools start to change the flow and balance of information. The ability of marketers to shape perceptions by presenting a unified mass market branding image is tested by the counter-flow of dissenting opinions, alternative sources of information, and messages.

Blogs are especially active during times of controversy and rapid change. This occurs during the heat of a match or when some controversy erupts surrounding a player or a call. Combining elements of personal messaging, call-in talk radio, and instant editorial pages Blogs are often long on emotion and somewhat short on verified facts. Still, the emotional content and immediacy can be highly influential on like-minded fans and participants.

TECHNOLOGY AND MARKETING

| Technology Impacts

> *A Century of Technology Changes*

At the beginning of the twentieth century, even in the richest countries, the majority of the population lived in small towns or farms. At the end of the century, in Europe, Japan, South Korea, or America,[26] most individuals lived in cities or suburbs. At the beginning of the century, social life was mostly local; at its end, the culture and economy was increasingly global.

Technology drove these changes. Electric engines substituted for steam and waterpower. Businesses learned to substitute a telephone or email for travel, the radio for storytelling, and television for a trip to a distant theater. Railroads, cars, trucks, and planes brought distant markets and people together. Computers substituted for tedious calculating and massive record keeping.

These changes shape the possibilities and conduct of business. Marketing is especially tied to communication and transportation revolutions. Marketing is the area of business that deals most with the external world. As the tools and reach of marketing increase, the job and responsibilities of marketers have evolved with them.[27]

> Mass Production

Keith[28] was one of the first marketers to observe that this technological development initially caused a "depersonalizing" of business. Mass production ruled, and the power of product and service standardization dominated. Over time, technological change has moved steadily back toward the individual. Kotler formalized this evolution as the stages of production, sales, and brand management. Each of these is strongly motivated by technological opportunities, which permit new methods and new opportunities. As the new technology of the Internet develops it reinforces a new marketing emphasis, a focus on the individual consumer. Technology is returning marketing to the emphasis that existed prior to mass production.

Scale dominated the early twentieth century. Business people such as Henry Ford, with innovations like the moving conveyor belt in 1913, invented the factory system. The factory system led to a huge increase in the scale of production and rapidly falling costs. The key to mass production is volume.[29] In such a system, marketing's main job is to get distribution so as to ship to as wide a marketplace as possible (Figure 1.16). Kotler labels this the production concept.

The production concept holds that consumers will favor those products that are widely available and low in cost. Managers of production-oriented organizations concentrate on achieving high production efficiency and wide distribution coverage.[30]

Mass production requires cheap transportation to move products to increasingly distant markets. By the start of the twentieth century, an extensive railroad system existed in most developed countries. This continued to expand, providing connections to rapidly growing cities. Soon trucks and cars augmented rail and ship. Cars and trucks brought products from the rail depots and docks to stores throughout the country. Even homes could be ordered mail order, and delivered to a farm or small town. Much of marketing at this stage is logistics and supply chain management, dealing with suppliers and creating an effective channel to the consumer.[31]

Figure 1.16

In 1926 Sears Roebuck Supplied the Country from Its Catalog

Source: "Sears Brands, LLC" sole property.

> Selling

The "problem" with mass production is its incredible efficiency. Companies soon realized that this efficiency resulted in very low prices for basic demands. Additionally, rising income levels permitted consumers to want something more than just basic, no-frill products. Developing and building category demand, for items such as new electric appliances or national product lines of consumer packaged goods, became the focus of marketing. Along with this market expansion were much more complicated distribution systems.

> The selling concept holds that consumers, if left alone, will ordinarily not buy enough of the organization's products. The organization must therefore undertake an aggressive selling and promotion effort.[32]

The selling phase is the introduction of the national market and national brands. The number of strongly identified brands exploded during the first couple of decades.[33] Companies created product lines out of standardized products, and tied these new brands to fundamental needs and insecurities.

Communications technology was key to the selling phase, and none more so than radio. Never before had it been possible to create instant awareness of new and different products. Radio allowed for the near-instantaneous rollout of brands, which then became household names. On-air or movie celebrities, such as Ginger Rogers in Figure 1.17, endorsed these emerging products and needs.

In the 1940s, the ability to broadcast information to consumers reached a new height with the launch of television. Invented years earlier, its launch was delayed by World War II. Television's power as a visual medium reinforced commercial messages and its branding power.

Figure 1.17

Celebrity Endorsements Help Sell Soap in 1935

Source: Baden, Sandra & Gary, Collection of Celebrity Endorsements in Advertising, 1897–1979, Archives Center, National Museum of American History, Smithsonian Institution.

> Brand Management

At about the same time as the rise of television, many companies were creating a new system of marketing. Companies moved to a system of brand management, which emphasized individual management of the advertising and logistics of the specific brands. A brand manager handled one particular line of product. This focus on a single brand allowed careful planning of new product campaigns, promotional activities, and advertising management. Companies carefully tracked market share and profitability of each brand.

> The brand management concept holds that the key to achieving organizational goals consists in determining the needs and wants to target markets and delivering the desired satisfactions more effectively and efficiently than competitors.[34]

Brand management emerged as the dominant emphasis for the second half of the twentieth century. Brand management reflects the role of the customer, and also that of competition; it states that the object of marketing is the provision of consumer "needs and wants."

Figure 1.18

Imprinting the McDonald's Brand – Right Down to Toy Drive-Ins

Source: Courtesy of M.T.H. Electric Trains

Yet despite its definition in terms of target market, brand management emphasized the product, with success measured in terms of market share and brand image. Brands such as Coca-Cola, Levi's, and McDonald's came to dominate, and even symbolize America throughout the world (Figure 1.18).

Segmentation and brand proliferation expanded dramatically with the mainframe computer's arrival. Starting in the 1960s, and rapidly developing during the next two decades, computerized databases became a vital part of sophisticated marketing. Part of this was simple record keeping. To accurately track sales and promotional activity, it was necessary to assemble and correlate huge amounts of information.

Computerized databases allowed entire new methods of segmentation. Brand managers started to use purchase location, customer demographics, and even psychological profiles to get a better picture of customer segments. However, the total number of segments and the number of products to serve them were still limited.

> Customer Management

The 1980s saw the rapid development of direct marketing, which uses sophisticated printing combined with computerized databases to directly target much smaller groups of consumers. Not only could smaller segments be created, but customized products could be offered. Catalog sales, custom credit card offerings, and magazine promotions exploded in popularity.

Retailers with computerized databases began to realize the power of specific customer focus. An early result of customer management was a realization of the importance of the very best customers. The second main lesson was the power of customer loyalty. Lands' End has found repeat business to be absolutely critical: "If we don't keep the customer for several years, we don't make money" is how the CEO of Lands' End, puts it.[35] Customer retention is needed to offset the costs of recruiting new customers.[36]

The fundamental limitation of mail-based direct marketing is its one-way flow of information. The company collects information about individuals, but individuals don't shape the process. The Internet is changing that, leading to an emphasis on individual customer measures and relationships.

The individual marketing concept holds that the key to effective marketing is to treat the consumer as an individual, and to use interactive dialogue to provide personalized products and services, improve quality, membership in communities, and to provide support (Figure 1.19).

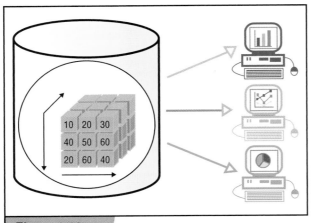

Figure 1.19

Data Mining Identifies Customer Differences with Technology

Source: Masuteru Sekiguchi, Tokyo University of Information Sciences.

The individual marketing concept builds on the trends of the previous century. The product space, which started with one in the era of mass production, grows to an astronomical number of potential products. Unique products become possible. At the same time that the product space is exploding, market segment size shrinks. During the production phase, the goal was to ship the same thing to everyone. As the selling and marketing phase took hold, target markets shrunk. With the individual phase, it reaches the minimum size possible of one. The goal is to treat each customer uniquely and individually.

Competitive skills change under the different regimes. Under mass production, the fundamental skill was production. Any error in production is magnified thousands or millions of times over. Under mass customization, the key is customer information management and flexible production. As customers get unique products based on their choices, quality customer data is critical. Interaction and dialogue assume a much more important position. A firm creates increasingly individualized messages to consumers, and the consumers respond differently.[37]

This focus on individual customers brings a new discipline to marketing efforts. Once the purchase and activity levels of customers are traced and recorded, it becomes meaningful to talk about the lifetime profitability of a specific customer. This is the discounted net present value of the profits that are expected over the entire future dealings with a specific individual. We will consider this in detail in Chapter 5. A firm has a portfolio of customers it is currently serving, and another group it might attract. The value of its customer base becomes the most important measure of how well the company is doing.[38]

Anyone comparing marketing in the economy before the phases of mass production, selling, brand management, and customer management to the present day global market would be struck by the huge change in opportunities and practices stimulated by these new approaches. We seem to be at another such transition point, as the many opportunities of online marketing reveal new changes stimulated by new technology. To understand how marketing is driven by major innovation, it is very useful to consider the key general purpose technologies behind these changes.

General Purpose Technologies and Marketing

> *General Purpose Technologies as Engines of Growth*

The technologies driving marketing changes over the past century were not isolated or special purpose, but rather were fundamental breakthroughs, causing numerous spin-offs and associated inventions. They were general purpose technologies (GPTs), and they have been identified as core engines of growth throughout the economy.[39] The technologies were pervasive, they had much room for improvement, and they spawned many innovations.

> Pervasive Presence

Marketing was one of the many application areas changed by twentieth-century technological GPTs. The optimal scale and scope of corporations changed, requiring new and more scientific forms of management. Change occurred in housing and production patterns, with relocation to the suburbs and more distant but lower cost production areas. The balance of automation, worker productivity, and worker skills needed to adapt to the new methods. Over time a GPT was incorporated into more segments of society, industries, and applications. This pervasiveness has a cumulative positive effect on productivity and growth, as people and organizations acquire the skills and infrastructure necessary to take best advantage of the new approach. Combined across the entire economy, there is a substantial improvement in economic performance.

A multiple-sector impact is at the heart of a general purpose technology. GPTs have a tree-like structure, and they branch out and diffuse into increasingly more application sectors as time goes by. Lessons and cost reductions achieved by early adopters filter out to other applications, which become achievable and cost effective.

> Have Much Room for Improvement

GPTs do not appear fully developed; they improve over time. Increasingly inventors and customers find the new technology the least cost solution and substitute new for old. As this occurs, problems are solved and improvements are made. Industries learn from each other, borrow best practices, and share skilled workers. Investments that incorporate the newer versions of the technologies show higher performance and lower operating costs than partially converted legacy approaches.

Central to these improvements are complementary components to the GPT, often supplied by different inventors and different firms. Computers benefit from an entire array of better software, computer monitors, hard disks, printers, and other aspects of a full computer system. Internet usage benefits from improvements in modems, whether dial-up, Ethernet, or WiFi. All technologies benefit from changes in education systems that train users to understand and work with the new approaches.

There may be a short-term down side to the appearance of general purpose technologies. One of the implications of multiple companies training for and adopting a new technology is a short-term fall in worker effectiveness during a skill and systems transition. There is an especially sharp fall in the training of workers for the old technology, and the new technology has not diffused fast enough to take up the slack. This process of adopting a GPT has been called a "time to sow and a time to reap."[40] Theoretical and historical models suggest a pattern of short-term boom and bust; followed by more sustainable and rapid longer term growth. However, it can take decades for the full benefits to be realized, and slowdowns in short-term performance can trigger a recession.

> Spawn Many Innovations

A general purpose technology makes it easier to invent and produce new products or processes. The new technology relieves bottlenecks, creates new possibilities, and generates new ideas and new ways of seeing old problems. Changes in the cost structure, higher speed and accuracy, or other dramatic alterations brought about by the new technology create new potential for invention.

These three aspects of a general purpose technology provide momentum and importance to the innovation. They change the way business operates in new and exciting ways, and create a path of improvements and productivity changes.

Some researchers consider only the most fundamental and dramatic technologies as GPTs. The title of GPT is reserved only for such path-braking tools as agriculture, writing, and printing. From this point of view, the broad grouping of breakthroughs in computers, communications, and networking is called the information and communications technology GPT. Such a view is too strict, and sets too high a bar. A definition based on the three conditions of pervasiveness, improvement, and innovation spawning leads to more technologies considered GPT. The "GPT perspective" is particularly useful and important for Internet marketers, as three related general purpose technologies provide the driving force behind many of the online marketing changes now underway.

> *The Three GPTs of Internet Marketing*

The Internet enables individuals using a network to access digital information. These individuals may be home consumers or workers as part of their job. The network is the open standard of

TCP/IP,[41] with a wide array of devices and interfaces able to transmit and receive over it. Digital information is also diverse, including text, photos, video, and computer programs.

A general purpose technology drives each of these expanding capabilities. Each of these GPTs goes far beyond marketing in their reach, and their usage in business is only part of their influence. Each forms a basis for the opportunities, problems, and likely direction for future online marketing. They form Internet marketing's foundation, and what makes it different, innovative, and creative relative to existing methods. The best strategy leverages their strengths and understands their impact. In addition, for sustainability, there must be viable business models that reward the firms and organizations for their efforts.

The three general purpose technologies that form the foundation of Net marketing, create momentum and opportunities for innovation, and lead to many additional opportunities are:

1. The digital revolution,
2. Networking, and
3. Individualization.

Two of these GPTs, digital computing and networking, are well established and have provided the fuel for many of the most important changes in the economy over recent decades. The third GPT, individualization, is less developed and builds on the earlier two. Understanding these key technologies, and how they evolve, allows us to understand the interaction between technology and marketing. For online marketers, this is a fundamental skill for medium- and long-term planning, and can help make better short-term tactical decisions.

> GPT 1: The Digital Revolution

The first of the GPTs underlying Net marketing is digital computing and digitization. As is the case for many GPTs, the digital revolution has taken decades to work itself throughout the economy. The digital revolution began as room-sized mechanical computers in 1945. Sixty years later, it pervades all sectors of the economy. As we will see in Chapter 2, the scope of improvement in the underlying computing performance has been staggering. Figure 1.20 compares the first commercial computer in the United States, the Univac 1 released in 1951, against a modern personal computer laptop available for $1000.

The vast differences between these two machines indicate how far the computing GPT has progressed. In comparable dollars, the Univac 1 is almost 7,000 times

a) UNIVAC 1: 1951

Speed: 1,905 operations per second

Memory size: 1,000 12-digit words

Technology Vacuum tubes, Floor space: 943 cubic feet

Cost: $750,000 plus $185,000 for a high speed printer. Adjusted for inflation: $6.7 million

b) IBM Thinkpad

Speed: Millions of operations per second

Technology: Microprocessor

RAM: 500 Million bytes

Hard Disk: 30 billion bytes

Additional features: Color screen, DVD, wireless Internet, . . .

Floor space: 1 sq. foot.

Cost: $1000, plus free printer

Figure 1.20

Early and Modern Computers

Source: 1.20a Courtesy of the Computer History Museum; 1.20b © Getty Images.

as expensive. It has a speed roughly 1,000 times slower, a random access memory almost 500,000 times smaller, and it fills an entire machine room. Operating cost was extremely high, with large power consumption and rapidly failing vacuum tubes. There was no visual display, punch card data entry, or modern programming languages. Everyday current applications such as word processors and spreadsheets did not exist.

The power of digital computing to create entire new products, processes, and economic activities has also been phenomenal. A common laptop is now a multimedia engine, with the ability to play music, movies, display photos, and access streaming video wirelessly. Behind these possibilities are the digitization of multimedia, which converts formerly incompatible media to the same stream of bits and bytes. Movies and music easily slip into a DVD player, a standard feature in today's computer.

Arguably more important than the obvious improvements in computers are the invisible uses of computing and digitization throughout the economy. A phone call begins on a hidden computing device, such as a cell phone, and relies extensively on computers to route and transmit the call. Modern automobiles use computers in all major components, such as engine control, braking, transmission, and pollution control. Almost every home appliance has some degree of digital control and capability.

Digital innovations illustrate how difficult it can be to identify exactly when a technology moves from the realm of promising to a widespread GPT. While there was great potential in the Univac 1, its actual impact on society and the economy was minimal. It took decades before many of the common features of the ThinkPad (such as modern operating systems, word processors, spreadsheets, multimedia) became common in computers. Computers didn't escape the glass room of dedicated computing until the 1970s, and didn't enter homes or individual offices until the 1980s. Organizational changes, supply chain changes, and direct marketing all built on computing techniques and database learning acquired over decades.

While the exact transition point into a GPT can be hard to identify, the value and power of the GPT concept is to focus on the implications of its pervasiveness, its natural opportunities for improvement, and the types of innovation that flow from the ongoing improvements. In Chapter 2 we consider what marketers need to appreciate and benefit from using the digital GPT.

> GPT 2: Networking

What begins as a spin-off from a preceding GPT can acquire sufficient power and generality to become its own GPT. This has happened with networking, the second fundamental GPT at the heart of Internet Marketing. While modern networking began as a complementary innovation that made computers more efficient, by the 1970s computer networking had acquired sufficient independence and influence that it can be viewed as its own source of innovation and improvement.

Although modern networking is tightly connected to computing, telecommunication networks predate the computer by more than a century. Figure 1.21 illustrates one of the earliest telecommunication networks, the extensive French system of "optical telegraphs" of the early 1800s. Messages were relayed by line of sight, and a system for signaling messages with different positions of a rotating tower. First used in the 1790s, the system could transmit military and financial information throughout France.

The electrical telegraph eventually replaced the use of optical signaling, and dramatically expanded its reach and speed. It had a profound impact on financial markets, military affairs, news organizations, commercial operations, and personal communications. For the first time in history it was possible to send a message, nearly instantaneously, around the globe. Telegraph networks reached the far corners of the planet, linked by cables crossing both the Atlantic and

Pacific. The telegraph network dominated long-distance communication from its early use in the 1850s until well into the twentieth century.

The telegraph's influence began to wane as it yielded to the telephone network and its ability to carry both voice and data. The telephone incorporates fundamental technological and social changes. Most obviously, it substitutes voice for telegraph text messages. This requires much more information carrying ability. Over long distances, it requires sophisticated switching and amplification. The telephone connects individuals directly, rather than relying on an intermediary (telegraph operators) to encode and decode messages. This radically changes the social uses of the network, making it much more personal and emotional than just informational.

The telephone network became central to other media. Radio networks in the 1920s grew by using the telephone system to transmit their network programming nationwide, and used international lines to trans-

Figure 1.21

The French Chappe Semaphore Network

Source: http://chappe.ec-lyon.fr/carte.html.

mit radio coverage from around the world. The print news media took advantage of the additional capacity of the telephone network with such new devices as the fax machine, able to send photos and news copy instantly. This pattern reappears with the Internet, as older media adopt and customize the new media capabilities to augment their capabilities and expand their reach.

Chapter 3 introduces the modern aspects of networking and its uses in business and marketing. Many of the themes of both the telegraph and telephone networks reemerge. The power of short text messages is still strong, as seen in email and instant messages. The power of direct communication, which is so important online, echoes the transition from the centralized and impersonal telegraph to the direct and "peer-to-peer" telephone. The value of increased expressiveness, such as the move from text to voice, is seen in the power of the visual when we move to the Web or to streaming media. Just as these earlier network inventions altered the social connections in society, the newer media have impacts on social community and distant individuals.

> GPT 3: Individualization

The first two general purpose technologies, digitization and networking, are economywide and important enough to drive innovation in widely separated sectors of the global economy. Business in general, and marketing in particular, are sectors like many others driven to grow and change by these technical opportunities. Our third GPT is different in an important way; it is more organizational than just technical. That is, it is more of a general purpose technology devoted to the manner in which business and marketing is conducted than a specific set of hardware and software devices. In this way, it is like the earlier organizational GPTs of the factory system and mass production.

The third GPT for Internet marketing is individualization, the ability to create messages, marketing campaigns, and products geared toward individuals rather than the aggregate crowd. This increasing ability of one-to-one marketing is based on the interrelated capabilities of

1. identification
2. the ability to associate and connect identified individuals with descriptive information, and
3. the ability to interact appropriately with identified people or objects.

Individualization allows marketers to infer much more detailed information about their customers, learn about their wants and desires, store information about their choices in the past, and form predictions about their choices in the future.

Individualization is based on both new technical capabilities and new organizing principles. Important technical innovations include cookies to track online browsing, secure web access based on personal information, metadata to describe web content much more precisely, RFID chips embedded in products to identify individual purchases, and other methods of tracking and identifying individual products, individuals, and information. The most important of these will be discussed in Chapters 4 and 9.

The most important marketing organization transition that builds on the individualization GPT is customer management and its emphasis on customer lifetime value. Computing power and transaction databases shift emphasis from brand management to customer management. At the heart of this change is a change in the fundamental measure of marketing success. While brand management emphasizes a battle over market share and brand value, customer management emphasizes measures of individual customer profitability and the "share of wallet" that an individual devotes to a company.

OUR APPROACH

Book Material

The book has three major parts. Part 1 (Chapters 1–4) provides the foundation for understanding Internet marketing and associated business models. Part 2 (Chapters 5–12) develops the essential skills an Internet marketer needs to adequately cover the many responsibilities and opportunities the Net creates. Part 3 (Chapters 13–17) emphasizes online commerce, with the techniques and challenges of using the Internet to sell.

> A Web Framework

Chapters 2 to 4 develop the Net Marketing framework. The core is the DNI (Digital Network Individualization) approach, building on the three general purpose technologies driving Internet marketing. Chapters 2 through 4 expand on each of the critical forces in greater detail.

Chapter 2 provides the digital fundamentals. Three digital forces shape Net Marketing. The fuel driving much of the Net is the rapid decrease in the cost of computing. This spills over into lower costs and increased power for all digital technologies. Not only do digital technologies continually get cheaper, they increasingly share the same design, components, and technological standards. Televisions, computers, cell phones, and music players build on the same platforms. These expanding digital technologies create expanding digital environments.

Chapter 3 introduces the fundamental network issues. The Internet is both a physical and social network. The physical network is evolving and improving. The social network increasingly changes how individuals communicate and learn about the world. The new science of networks allows marketers to build upon these social relationships and understand their importance. Networks encourage new skills, such as speed, credibility, and the ability to gather and refine information. Networks bring together resources from around the world, and reduce the importance of geography.

Chapter 4 focuses on the individual, and the changes that occur when marketing activities move from the mass market to a much more targeted level. Individuals have very different patterns of access and usage, and bring very different skills and experience with them online. The general purpose technology of individualizing creates the capability to interact, to learn, and to communicate in a much more customized and personalized manner.

> *Online Marketing Skills*

Effective online marketing utilizes a variety of skills, some closely related to traditional marketing and some that require new abilities and new training. Part 2 highlights these and provides examples of successful applications of these skills by a wide variety of organizations.

Chapter 5 begins the skills part by looking at profitability and Net business models. Both startups and traditional companies have embraced the Internet and can profit using online marketing. Each must have an online strategy and a set of online goals. These can include indirect benefits to brand, efficiency, and effectiveness. Companies can make money directly online, through sales, commissions, or advertising. One of the most important developments is the concept of closed-loop marketing, where marketing actions can be followed through to actual results. It also encourages new measures of marketing success, relying on customer-specific metrics such as acquisition cost and lifetime value.

Chapter 6 looks at online branding and persuasion, including the ability to work from general brand strategy to appropriate online branding activity. This includes domain name branding, creating a supportive and consistent brand presence, using the Net to extend and enhance the brand, and developing a sense of community around a brand.

Online material needs to be usable, credible, and persuasive. Chapter 7 focuses on how visitors use a site, how they form judgments about the information contained on the site, and common problems limiting credibility and persuasion. These vary by the nature of the visit and site, the type of device used for access, and the timing of access.

Chapter 8 investigates traffic building and the challenge of acquiring visitors. Sophisticated techniques for managing a company's online presence let marketers carefully compare traffic-building alternatives. Banner ads, search engines, publicity links, and affiliate arrangements all create a funnel of visitors with different conversion rates and profitability. A marketer must be able to build traffic efficiently given their strategic goals. Measurement tools allow increasingly scientific approaches to advertising and traffic building, and tie back to specific measures of customer value.

Chapter 9 studies learning and personalization. Companies are using exciting new personalization techniques. These permit highly customized, even individualized, products and services. The chapter looks at when personalization has value, and what concerns it raises. Personalization and customization is impossible without the ability to understand important differences among individuals, and requires a system of learning about customers and building accurate profiles.

Chapter 10 looks at building commitment and loyalty among visitors. Marketers must be able to understand the pattern and drivers of loyalty. Important drivers are community building and switching costs. Marketers need to understand the elements of true community and ways they are appropriate to commercial ventures. Community is closely tied to communication and shared content. Stimulating this creates a sense of belonging, and encourages frequent visits and use of a site. Switching costs can also build commitment, but are resisted by customers fearing lock in. Managing this tradeoff requires skills of demonstrating the benefits of participation and collaboration.

Chapter 11 concentrates on innovation, including ways that the Net is changing the new product development process. One of the most important issues is speed and the acceleration of product cycles. As part of this new product development process, companies are learning how to simultaneously discover new features and release new products. This includes the role of early releases, the sampling of customer opinion, and the gathering of statistics online. Using modularity assists rapid learning and rapid innovation, and takes advantage of the emerging technical standards.

Chapter 12 looks at an area of marketing that is being dramatically affected by the Net: pricing. The Net alters many of the determinants of pricing, such as consumer awareness, the number of rivals, and the level of competitive interaction. It creates a new arsenal of pricing tools, including email deals, online auctions, and real-time pricing. Information goods, which sell well online, provide special opportunities for such techniques as bundling and versioning.

> *Commerce with the Net*

While the Net is useful for many things other than selling, its impact on commerce is central to much of the attention it receives. The effect is widespread, with the impact occurring both offline and online. It affects the evolution of channels of distribution and methods of retailing. While issues of privacy, intellectual property, and globalization are important even without commerce, they come to the fore when companies sell across borders.

Chapter 13 looks at retailing online. While the Internet still is a small fraction of total retail sales, some of the most intriguing innovations in retailing are being developed online. Consumers respond to the power of online retailers to provide detailed information, offer lower prices, create a huge assortment, and make shopping convenient. On the other hand, online retailers have been slow to create the level of ambiance and entertainment present in physical shopping outlets.

Chapter 14 looks at online selling to consumers from a manufacturer or service provider's perspective. This includes the design of distribution channels, and the choice between direct and indirect sales. Many manufacturers want a hybrid channel, attempting to get the benefits of both direct and indirect distribution. While this may work, it runs the risk of channel conflict and confusion. Online channels can also permit a company to reach out to new and off-price markets.

Chapter 15 focuses on business-to-business commerce. Important issues include electronic procurement, supply chain applications, and the power of online tools for fostering collaboration. While less noticeable than consumer sales, business-to-business ecommerce is reaching substantial volume and pioneering techniques of integration and specialization.

Chapter 16 covers market research tools that firms use to measure their online success. Online commerce generates large amounts of consumer data. Using this data requires caution to avoid mistakes and biases. One of the strongest competitive advantages of online commerce is rapid feedback. With proper methodology, this learning can be extremely valuable. Some of this learning comes from information collected internally. Many larger firms also purchase dedicated studies from consumer research firms.

Chapter 17 looks at the organizational and legal challenges an online marketer needs to be aware of when operating a globally connected site. A familiarity with some of the main legal issues, such as privacy and taxation, are required for good business decision making. The book ends with a consideration of the future. Technology forecasting is fraught with risk. Nevertheless, if William Gibson is right, the future is already here in pieces and important trends are already emerging.

ENDNOTES

1. Donald A. Norman. (1999). *The Invisible Computer: Why Good Products Can Fail, the Personal Computer is so Complex, and Information Appliances are the Solution.* MIT Press, Cambridge, p. ix.
2. Elhanan Helpman and Manuel Trajtenberg. (1998). "A Time to Sow and a Time to Reap: Growth Based on General Purpose Technologies." In *General Purpose Technologies and Economic Growth*, Chapter 3.
3. In 2005 it finished second, yielding the title back to another Silicon Valley legend—Apple.
4. Much more about Google PageRank and search engine optimization is in Chapter 8.
5. Matt Hicks. (2005). "Google Reveals its Product Formula." *eWeek*, February 9.
6. For a description of the solution, see http://www.regulators.org/archives/000283.html.
7. Andrew Grove of Intel in 1997 and Jeff Bezos of Amazon.com in 1999.
8. For this timeline see Hobbes' Internet Timeline v. 8.0 at http://www.zakon.org/robert/internet/timeline/ and also K. Hafner and Matthew Long. (1996). *Where Wizards Stay up Late: The Origins of the Internet.* New York: Simon & Schuster.
9. See, for example, Philip Baczewski. (1992). "The Rules of the Internet." *Benchmarks* (13(5), p. 12). It is also available online by searching the author's name and article title.
10. The timeline for this transition ranged from 1991 to 1994. Connections became operational in 1994 and later. For example, see Merit (1994), Status of NSFNET Transition, October 3, available at http://www.merit.edu/mail.archives/nanog/1994-10/msg00000.html.
11. Tim Berners-Lee. (1999). *Weaving the Web: The Original Design and Ultimate Destiny of the World Wide Web by its Inventor* Harper-Collins, New York.
12. Jome (1924) documents how rapidly radio took off—faster even than automobiles had 20 years earlier. Hiram Jome. (1924). *Economics of the Radio Industry.* A.W. Shaw, esp. pp. 69–79.
13. See Paul Lazarsfeld and Frank Stanton (eds). (1941). *Radio Research.* Duell, Sloan, and Pearce, New York.
14. Susan Smulyan. (1994). *Selling Radio: The Commercialization of American Broadcasting, 1920–1934.* Smithsonian Institution Press, Washington, DC.
15. Greenstein (2004) documents the extensive market penetration of very small Internet service providers and their surprising longevity. Shane Greenstein. (2004). "The Economic Geography of Internet Infrastructure in the United States." Working Paper 46, The Center for the Study of Industrial Organization, Northwestern University.
16. Scott Herhold, op.cit. Also see http://www.sjmercury.com/svtech/companies/moneytree/.
17. Stacy Cowly. (2004). "Commerce One Runs out of Cash." *ComputerWorld* September 24.
18. The scale of these early portal deals was very large. An example of the aggressive spending by Internet startups for a presence among AOL and Yahoo! was Homestore.com. Homestore signed a deal with AOL as late as May 2000 committing to pay $20 million per year in cash for five years for exclusive sponsorship and advertising on AOL's real estate pages.[17] Other very expensive AOL portal deals included Tel-Save ($100 million, long-distance telephone service), Barnes & Noble ($40 million, books), Dr. Koop (1999, $89 million over 4 years, health), and 1-800-Flowers ($42 million over four years, flower delivery).
19. Discussed in Federal Reserve Bank of Minneapolis. (2002). "Interview with Robert Solow," *Banking and Policy Issues Magazine* September. Available online.
20. ITU. World Telecommunications Development Report 2002: Executive Summary. The share in 1998 was approximately 12%, and rose to 23% by 2001. By 2003 it exceeds 25%.
21. Available online at the ICT Free Statistics Home Page.
22. Bruno Giussani. (1998). "World Cup Sites Target Ticketless Fans." *New York Times* May 12.

23. A hit is a separately transmitted file. A web page is typically composed of more than one hit. The text on the page counts as one hit, and each picture on the page counts separately as another hit. Thus, a web page with text and five pictures would be six hits.

24. Rory Thompson. (1998). "World Cup Record." *InformationWeek* October 12.

25. However, just as a word processor does not turn everyone into a best-selling author, a good stage I web site requires considerable skill and design to best reach the audience.

26. According to the U.S. Census Bureau, the U.S. rural population in 1900 was 60.4% and the urban population was 39.6%. By year 2000, the rural population was 21% and urban 79%. Similar percentages apply to European countries.

27. For an essay on how the research on marketing is driven by technology, see Steven M. Shugan. (2004). "The Impact of Advancing Technology on Marketing and Academic Research." *Marketing Science* 23(4, Fall), 469–475.

28. Keith, Robert J. (1960). "The Marketing Revolution." *Journal of Marketing* January, 35–38. Reprinted in Thompson. (1981). *The Great Writings in Marketing.*

29. Online Encyclopedia Britannica, Search: mass production.

30. Kotler, 6th Edition, p. 13.

31. An excellent discussion of these stages is also to be found in Richard Tedlow. (1996). *New and Improved: The Story of Mass Marketing in America.* Harvard Business School Press, Cambridge, MA.

32. Kotler, ibid.

33. A discussion of early brands and branding can be seen in Aaker, *Building Strong Brands.*

34. Kotler, ibid.

35. Quoted in Blattberg and Deighton. (1996). "Manage Marketing by the Customer Equity Test." *HBR* July-August, 136–144.

36. See Sunil Gupta and Donald Lehman. (2003). "Customers as Assets." *Journal of Interactive Marketing* 17(1, Winter), 9–24.

37. For example, using multiple channels for their shopping behavior. See Arvind Rangaswamy and Gerrit Van Bruggen. (2005). "Opportunities and challenges in multichannel marketing: An introduction to the special issue." *Journal of Interactive Marketing* 19(2, Spring), 5–11, or V. Kumar and Rajkumar Venkatesan. (2005). "Who are the multichannel shoppers and how do they perform?: Correlates of multichannel shopping behavior." *Journal of Interactive Marketing* 19(2, Spring), 44–62.

38. For an example, see Rajkumar Venkatesan and V. Kumar. (2004). "A Customer Lifetime Value Framework for Customer Selection and Resource Allocation Strategy." *Journal of Marketing* 68, October), 106–125.

39. See Timothy F. Bresnahan and Manuel Trajtenberg. (1995). "General Purpose Technologies: Engines of growth?" *Journal of Econometrics* 65, 83–108.

40. Elhanan Helpman and Manuel Trajtenberg. (1998). A Time to Sow and a Time to Reap: Growth Based on General Purpose Technologies." In *General Purpose Technologies and Economic Growth,* Chapter 3.

41. Transmission Control Protocol/Internet Protocol.

chapter 2:

A Digital World

Figure 2.1

Humans and Digitally Simulated Orcs in Battle
Source: "The Lord of the Rings: The Return of the King" Copyright MMIII, New Line Productions, Inc.™ The Saul Zaentz Company d/b/a Tolkien Enterprises under license to New Line Productions, Inc. All rights reserved. Photo by Pierre Vinet. Photo appears courtesy of New Line Productions, Inc.

Middle Earth Comes to Life

As World War II ended, two very different inventions were nearing release. In England, J.R.R. Tolkien was finalizing the first book of his Lord of the Rings trilogy.[3] At the same time, both in the United States and in England, engineers and scientists were completing the first general purpose computers. Sixty years later, these two creations combined in an overwhelming commercial and critical success. Despite costing AOL-Time Warner more than $270 million to create (shooting all three installments of the trilogy at once), it became extremely profitable in the first month of release of the first film.[4] In only a month, *The Fellowship of the Ring* grossed more than $500 million in global box office revenues.[5] Critical reviews were glowing. Success continued with the rest of the trilogy and their release onto DVD.

Neither the movie, nor its rapid distribution and further commercialization, would have been possible without computers, 60 years of technical progress, and the digital revolution they created. Tolkien's novels have fantastic mythical creatures, many engaged in battles by the thousands. Even a blockbuster's budget could not produce these special effects with costumed actors. The imagery of the Middle-Earth world is a lush hybrid of real actors, New Zealand scenery, and thousands of digital animations and computer creations. Few scenes are completely real, and few are entirely animated. Merging these elements required over 600 computers running continuously for months. This produces individual digitally rendered frames

this chapter

Falling digital costs, improved digital quality, and the convergence of many different industries to the same core digital technology are a foundation of the Internet's rise and a key to future opportunities.

Topics covered in this chapter include:

> Being Digital
> Digital Environments
> Digital Convergence
> A Working Digital Economy
> How Digitizing Works
> Making Marketing Processes Digital

that are archived on a hard disk and available for future use.

Special effects are only a small part of the digital transformation of the movie and television industry. After leaving theatres, Lord of the Rings DVDs were next. DVD movie sales now far surpass analog VHS sales. DVD provides numerous advantages over VHS, such as smaller physical size, higher resolution playback, random access to scenes, and room for additional footage about the movie. Digital televisions, increasingly with purely digital flat panel screens, recreate the theatrical feel in individual homes. The analog VCR is also losing ground to digital video recorders (DVRs) such as Tivo, which bring the digital advantages to broadcast television. These personal video recorders further blur the line between computers, television, and the Internet.

The filmmaker's archive of every screen shot makes it easy for filmmakers to reinforce the movie buzz and satisfy the demands of fans. Visitors to the Lord of the Rings web site can download scenes from the movie as backgrounds for their computers, get screensavers of their favorite characters, select a movie character as an icon for their AOL instant messaging system, send an email card to a friend with a movie scene and link to the web site, and download software to a Palm or Pocket PC personal organizer (Figure 2.2).

Not every aspect of the movie industry is smoothly transitioning to the digital world. Digital distribution and projection is a notable roadblock to the purely digital cinema, where a

movie could move from creation to viewing entirely in digital form. Movie prints are a costly part of movie distribution, and force studios to guess each film's popularity. Digital cinema changes this by electronically shipping the movie, nearly instantaneously, directly to the projection booths of theaters. Despite considerable advantages over the costly and slow creation and distribution of celluloid prints, digital distribution has stumbled.[6]

Barriers to digital cinema are both economic and technological. A sizable fixed cost—over $100,000 per theatre for conversion—slows

Figure 2.2

Customizing Your PDA With Downloaded Images

the transition. A rapid buildup of multiplexes during the 1990s created excess capacity, tough business conditions, and a stock of relatively new but traditional projection systems. A lack of digital standards is also a problem, as competing vendors use different approaches both for distribution and projection systems.

There have been truly phenomenal cost declines in the six decades since the computer's invention. This continues to create new opportunities for digitalization. A key strategic skill is judging which digital applications are about to become viable.

BEING DIGITAL

Digital Technology

The world is increasingly digital. A single search engine retrieves over 115 million web pages with the word digital in it, an increase from 35 million just two years earlier.[7] Newspaper stories yield a list of digital devices: digital cameras, digital kiosks, digital telephones, digital television, even digital noses. These devices lead to a host of digital uses: digital special effects, digital commerce, digital democracy, and a digital beach.[8]

Despite the vast range of digital technologies and uses, the digital concept is very simple. Something is digital when all of its properties and information are stored as a string of zeros and ones. All of the text, pictures, and video seen through a computer, digital television, or over the Internet are just different sequences of zeros and ones passing through the machine.

These zeros and ones are called bits. A bit is a single piece of information, the smallest piece of the digital puzzle. One of the visionaries of digital technology, Nicholas Negroponte of the MIT Media Lab, describes the essence of bits.

> A bit has no color, size, or weight, and it can travel at the speed of light. It is the smallest atomic element in the DNA of information. It is a state of being: on or off, true or false, up or down, in or out, black or white.[9]

Everything on the Internet is digital. All of the technology used on the Net shares the advantages and disadvantages of being digital. Understanding the technical and economic factors behind the digital revolution allows a marketer to anticipate and take better advantage of digital opportunities.

The digital revolution is the most established of the general purpose technologies forming the foundation of online marketing. Although there are hints and beginnings with earlier inventions, the effective beginning is with the introduction of computing in the 1940s. From this beginning, digital technology now permeates our lives.

Digital Benefits for Marketing

Three factors make the translation into bits such a powerful process. The first is Moore's Law, and it has historically been the most important. Moore's Law is a shorthand phrase for a technological force that has been operating over the last 60 years and promises to continue for the foreseeable future. Moore's Law causes bits to become radically cheaper to use, a process that includes the power to store and manipulate bits. If a single reason was chosen to explain why the Internet has become so explosively popular, Moore's Law would have to be it.

The second force making the digital world important to marketing is its ability to create digital environments. Not only are digital technologies becoming cheaper, but programmers and designers are learning how to make entire digital worlds. These digital environments are much more flexible and adaptable than simple computing. Digital environments have important properties that shape messages and marketing communications.

The third force driving the use of bits is convergence. As devices become digital, the separation between products breaks down. Televisions become more like computers, and computers become more like TVs. Telephones acquire computing power, and you can use your laptop computer to place a call.

Products that handle bits in a consistent and powerful manner increasingly surround consumers and firms. Converting to a digital technology makes formerly distinct industries share a common technological base and similar solutions. Products such as record albums, photographs, movies, and computer disks once required unique packaging and display hardware. The same DVD player can now handle all of these functions. Telephone voice calls and Internet data travel as digital packets over the same digital fiber-optic cable.

It is not necessary to understand all of the technologies of the Internet to be an effective Internet marketer. However, knowing the core technology principles is vital to anticipating new approaches as they emerge and matching the marketing approaches to technological capabilities. The digital, networked, individual framework starts with the foundation of it all—the move to a digital economy.

MOORE'S LAW AND DIGITAL POWER

A Trillion Times Cheaper

The falling cost of digital technology is one of the most powerful economic forces in modern society. Digitization has resulted in a huge array of new products, computing by the masses, and a tremendous increase in the flow of information. It is one of the major factors behind the economy's ability to grow without inflation.[10] Many political observers even believe it played a crucial role in the demise of communism and the spread of democracy in eastern Europe.

Moore's Law started as simply an engineering observation by Gordon Moore, one of the co-founders of Intel Corporation. Founded in the 1960s, Intel hoped to take advantage of the emerging semiconductor technology. Semiconductors allowed engineers to put transistors, which used to be individually packaged, and combine them on a single flat piece of silicon (a die). Intel's initial products were computer memory chips. Soon it added microprocessors to its semiconductor line.

Moore noticed that his engineers (and others in the industry) kept learning how to shrink transistors, thus packing more and more onto the same sized chip. The rate of miniaturization was about 30% every 18 months; that is, the separation between the transistors and other circuit elements shrunk about 30% every 18 months. As integrated circuits are created on a flat piece of silicon, the surface area needed for the same number of components is then only 70% * 70% = 49% as much in the new chip as the one it replaced. This observation on engineering skill, which Moore highlighted in a speech, became Moore's Law. Each new generation of chip technology, released at a rate of about every 18 months, packs the same number of elements into half the space. More commonly, twice as many components squeeze into the same surface area to create twice as much computing power.[11] Hundreds of chips, each with tens of millions of components, come from the silicon wafer shown in Figure 2.3.

Research has shown that Moore's Law is a deeper and more powerful phenomenon than even Moore expected. If we measure computing power, rather than chip density, we can compare performance over a much longer timeframe. It is even possible to stretch the comparison back into the 1800s for mechanical calculators and tabulators. Moore's Law is fundamentally about computing, not chip making.

The result of this analysis is very surprising. Rather than starting with the integrated circuit or even semiconductors, economist William Nordhaus and others have documented that exponential cost reduction has been occurring since the earliest days of computers.[12] After decades with essentially no improvements in the cost of computation, whether done by machine or by humans, there was a dramatic change in technical opportunities starting in the mid-1940s.

The impact of this longer time horizon is dramatic. From the beginning of the computer age in 1945 until 2002, there has been an increase in computer speed of approximately 75 billion times. The price per calculation is even more dramatic, with an improvement in computing performance of 600 billion times. A computer in the year 2002 could do 600 billion calculations for the same cost as one calculation in 1941. As each doubling of performance is equal to the cumulative benefit, by 2006 the improvements are well into the trillions of times cheaper than before the computer. Nordhaus also finds that the rate of improvement shows signs of accelerating. That is, the rate of improvement in the 1990s was considerably faster than the rate of improvement in the 1970s and 1980s.

Exponential growth surprises us with its power. Imagine a baby, call her Joan, is born in 1984. Joan's parents buy a personal computer. They choose to spend an extra $1000 on expanded memory chips. By mid-1985, that same amount of memory would only cost $500. By the end of 1987, its price would $250. By late 1990, with Joan starting first grade, the same memory price is $62.50. In just six years, the cost of memory has fallen by over 94%.[13]

The revolutionary power of exponentials emerges when doublings continue beyond the point where it already seems cheap. Consider the cost of memory as Joan graduates from high school in 2002. By now Moore's Law has

Figure 2.3

Gordon Moore and Silicon Wafer

Source: © AP/Wide World Photos.

had a chance to cut costs in half 12 times—and the cost of that $1000 memory has fallen to a little less than 25 cents. A quarter can buy what a thousand dollars did when she was born. In 18 years, there is a fall of 99.97%. Obviously, when Joan heads off to college, she buys vastly more memory for her computer.

Storage technology has also seen dramatic improvement, even faster than semiconductors during the past decade. Hard disks cost over $100 per megabyte in the 1970s. Computer hard disk prices are now less that $.0005 a megabyte and falling very rapidly.[14] As can be seen in Figure 2.4, digital storage became much cheaper than paper or film during the late-1990s. Again, the rate of progress seems to be increasing.

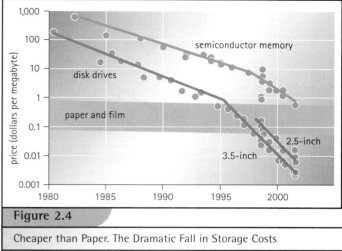

Figure 2.4

Cheaper than Paper. The Dramatic Fall in Storage Costs

Source: Brian Hayes, "Terabyte Territory," *American Scientist* 90 (May–June 2002), 212–216.

If this trend continues for another decade, affordable individual storage capacity is striking. Hayes[15] estimates that by 2012 a personal computer could have a 120-terabyte hard disk as standard equipment, capable of holding 180,000 CD-ROMs. This single disk could hold all the books in the Library of Congress (24 million volumes), plus 100 photos a day for 80 years, plus enough music to listen to 24 hours a day for 80 years, and still have room left over. Of course, the cost of this content might be prohibitive, but the capacity is not. An Apple iPod now can store 60 gigabytes of music, but its potential to store all music ever recorded may be only a decade or so away (Figure 2.5). An iPod Nano, using semiconductor (flash) memory, is much smaller in size but with a smaller disk capacity due to the higher costs shown in Figure 2.4.

An intriguing use of this storage is the extensive pre-loading of the Internet and marketing material onto computers prior to purchase. A user could have huge quantities of the Net readily available, with updates provided in the background when available or as requested. A major use might be in-depth video linked to a company's web presence, avoiding the need for expensive bandwidth usage later on. This use of local storage is a form of "edge storage" currently provided by companies that put content caches nearer to Net users, thus relieving Net congestion and speeding up performance. Local massive storage would help remove the "last mile congestion" created by relatively slow consumer Internet access.[16]

The "big iron" of the computing world, supercomputers costing millions of dollars and capable of performing massive computations rapidly, have grown exponentially more powerful as well. The vertical axis of Figure 2.6 measures computing speed of the top 500 supercomputers over time. At the bottom are megaflops, roughly a million computations per second

Figure 2.5

The iPod Uses this Storage Cost Decline

Source: © Getty Images.

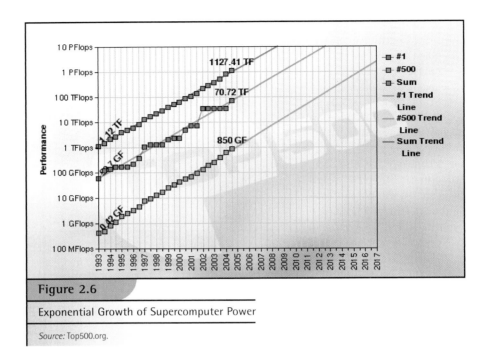

Figure 2.6

Exponential Growth of Supercomputer Power

Source: Top500.org.

using a standard set of benchmark tests. Next comes gigaflops (a billion per second), then teraflops (a trillion per second), and then pentaflops (a quadrillion per second). The bottom line is the slowest of the current top 500. The middle line is the speed of the current world record supercomputer. The top line is the sum of the computing speeds of the top 500 computers in the world.

In 1997 the world record supercomputer speed passed a teraflop; in 2002 the fastest computer passed 10 teraflops, and by 2005 the IBM BlueGene/L set the mark at 280 teraflops per second.[17] These modern supercomputers achieve their high speed by spreading the computation among thousands of linked microprocessor chips.

Computers with teraflop power begin to rival the estimated computing power of mammal brains. Although controversial, estimates of human brain computing power are in the range of a pentaflop. This is not to say that pentaflop computers will suddenly have human-level intelligence through sheer power, as the "software" and wiring of humans is highly complex and almost totally unknown. However, these very large computers are capable of extremely rapid data analysis. Extracting patterns in large customer databases, in real time, is one of many opportunities for the pattern recognition power of these innovative supercomputers. Accessed online as part of a computing grid, companies will increasingly tap into high-power supercomputing whenever needed.

Using Moore's Law

> Input Substitution

The cost of handling bits is falling so fast, and the power to calculate with bits is rising so quickly, it makes sense to substitute bits for atoms whenever possible. This is one of the foundations of Internet marketing. It is, however, not always easy to accomplish and smooth to implement.

How Much Digital Content to Substitute?

A profit-maximizing firm attempts to choose the best combination of production inputs. How should a firm trade off digital *marketing content* against *marketing labor*? The basic economics answer uses the ratio of marginal products (MP) to price for these inputs:

$$\frac{\text{MP(digital content)}}{\text{Price(digital content)}} = \frac{\text{MP (marketing labor)}}{\text{Price(marketing labor)}}$$

An input's marginal product is the additional output that would result from adding one more unit of an input (say a worker) while holding other inputs fixed. Marginal product typically falls as an input is used more intensively without adding more of other inputs.

Moore's Law dramatically drives down the price of generating and using digital content. As labor prices and labor productivity change slowly, the profit-maximizing firm must expand the use of digital content. However, the marginal product of digital content will decline as it is heavily used.

The switch from "bits to atoms" is an example of input substitution. When an input to production gets cheaper, input substitution guides us to substitute that cheaper input for other inputs that have stayed the same or gotten more expensive. Another way of expressing this is in terms of relative prices. It is most economical to use more of the inputs whose relative prices have fallen.

The price of bits has fallen dramatically while the other marketing costs have not. Energy prices rise. Newsprint becomes scarce. Sales calls get more expensive. Time is ever more precious. Digital technology can help offset each of these increasing costs. Input substitution is such a basic economic force it guarantees the importance of online marketing.

Early use of digital material in marketing led to large savings. As early as 1995, Sun Microsystems was saving hundreds of thousands of dollars by using online methods of customer support. Sun substituted the Web and email for costly telephone contacts. Web support yielded almost pure savings. Email still requires staff response, but is usually much more efficient and flexible than the phone. Chapter 7 will consider online support in detail.

Savings were even more dramatic for software distribution. By late 1995, Sun estimated they were saving over $1.5 million a quarter compared to their traditional software distribution methods. By some calculations, they were saving much more than that. Because the web is so much easier and cheaper for customers to use, customers were downloading software fixes and upgrades much more frequently than they had with the old methods. The increased cost of supporting this higher level of usage with the old methods would have been over $12 million per month.[18]

U.S. banks have found online customer service and digital substitution highly cost-effective and are rapidly expanding their use. By late 2002 the substantial majority had already adopted online FAQs (87%), online credit self service (80%), and online deposit self-service (77%).

Campaigns: Using Digital Marketing to Launch a Digital Convergence Product

Each of these trends, Moore's Law, digital convergence, and digital environments was present in the pre-launch campaign for the Handspring Treo Communicator (which has since merged with Palm). The Treo was Handspring's first effort to integrate a personal organizer (with the Palm OS), cell phone, and pager. Digital convergence and Moore's Law are critical for the very existence of this convergence between communication and computing.

Handspring always relied on the Net as an important sales channel. They launched their earliest product, the Handspring organizer, online. With the Treo, they use an online digital environment geared to building buzz, reputation, and early orders. This multimedia environment included a gallery of images, a demo of the product's use, a streaming video from a recent trade show by a top

Handspring executive, text reviews by industry trade writers, and more. U.S. residents willing to supply their email address received an alert as soon as the new models are available. The cell phone built into the Treo requires cellular activation, and a potential buyer can use the web site to investigate cellular system coverage in their area. Merging with Palm has not reduced the use of online promotion of the Treo, which continues with the latest models.

Figure 2.7

Part of the Digital Environment Promoting the Treo 650

Source: Courtesy of Palm, Inc.

Leading banks had adopted online check images (23%), online bank statements (23%), and natural language search (17% using and another 13% piloting the process). Digital features still in the experimental stage with few adoptions were an interactive knowledge base (4%) and virtual representatives (7%).[19]

Creating and using digital marketing content builds on past digital investment. Pharmaceutical companies such as Bristol-Meyers, Eli Lily, and Merck have long provided laptops and PDAs to their sales force. Sales staff use them to demonstrate new drugs and provide training to physicians in the field. They are now going wireless, able to connect from the field and provide real-time quotes, on-demand instruction, and immediately forward doctors' questions back to the home offices.[20] While somewhat controversial, both in effectiveness and implications, hundreds of thousands of physicians are also adopting the basic digital infrastructure of laptops and handhelds for their patient rounds.[21] This creates the digital platform necessary for further breakthroughs in digital substitution, including such costly healthcare issues as drug formulary coverage and patient records.

Lord of the Rings provides an example of cumulative digital substitution. As part of its marketing campaign, New Line Cinema hired a direct marketing consulting firm to help it create and manage word of mouth efforts. Initially the marketing company hired student interns to search online, collect email addresses of Tolkien fans, and monitor discussions taking place in Tolkien online forums. The task was tedious, time consuming, and the interns had low productivity. Facing this, and the imminent return of students to college classes, the company spent $12,000 on a software system that automatically and intelligently sifts through this same online material and converts it to usable direct marketing material. The company estimates a saving in labor costs of 95%, with much faster and more accurate results.[22] Previous knowledge about online chat showed its value. Adding more digital capabilities in the form of the software system lets chat monitoring become a cost-effective ongoing marketing capability.

> Creating New Capabilities

Substituting "bits for atoms" not only saves money, it also creates new capabilities. Digital substitution provides new avenues for information customization, intelligent targeting, and real-time interaction.[23] One example of many is the ability to communicate and target in multiple languages simultaneously.

Reaching out to consumers can be expensive. Worldwide, companies currently spend over $300 billion to communicate their messages to consumers.[24] One of the most challenging tasks facing global companies is getting the proper messages in the right language.

One of the best ways of taking advantage of cheap bits is to have multiple languages available. Shown in Figure 2.8 are two versions of the main page of Banco Itau, one of the major banks of Brazil. As you would expect, the initial home page (Figure 2.8a) is in Portuguese. However, a simple click brings up alternate web sites in either English or Spanish. Further links stay within the selected language. Not only does this allow Banco Itau to serve the multi-lingual society of Brazil, it can easily reach out to international investors and companies interested in the financial health of Brazil.

Figure 2.8 reveals an important lesson about parallel sites—there is no reason for them to be identical. The Portuguese site is oriented much more to the daily transactional needs of its customers. The English site is more investor oriented, and emphasizes issues surrounding the international traveler.[25]

Not all sites or languages justify parallel translations. Automatic translation is a leap beyond parallel language sites. While it still leads to many humorous mistakes, automatic translation is advancing. For example, a search on Google for "Deutsche Telecom" produces a high ranking for the German language homepage for the largest telecom firm in Germany. To the right of the listing is the option "translate this page," which automatically produces an English version of the page. The grammar is not always the best, and some phrases are incorrect, but overall it produces a comprehensible page that a non-German speaker can use effectively. Translation need not be perfect to be useful.

Contrast the performance of Google's translation software running on a 2006 large-scale server against the early and highly disappointing performance of the Apple Newton released in 1993 (and spoofed by Doonesbury in Figure 2.9). Trying to build a free-script language recognizer into a very limited early handheld resulted in terrible performance. Indeed, industry experts feel the over-reaching digital goals of the Newton crippled the digital organizer market for

(a) Portuguese

(b) English

Figure 2.8

The Banco Itau Portuguese and English Site

Source: Courtesy of Banco Itaú.

Figure 2.9

Digital Substitution Doesn't Always Work (At Least Right Away)

years.[26] This is an important lesson for marketers. The exact timing of digital substitution, especially when pioneering very different applications, can be challenging and risky.

Techniques such as automatic translation and automated agents highlight a nearly unlimited source of demand for Moore's Law improvements. In these and other cases, the essential capability is machine intelligence. The fundamental reason the Newton (and often Google translations) produce nonsense is their lack of any sense of context. In a digital system such as the Newton, or in the voice recognition systems built into Windows XP, the software uses statistical routines to match the user's entry against libraries of actual words or phrases. These systems do not understand context, the "what" of what is being said.

A classic example is the phrase "Let's talk about how to recognize speech." As Raymond Kurzweil points out,[27] a current voice recognition system is apt to translate this into "Let's talk about how to wreck a nice beach." Read aloud these sound very similar. Both are grammatically correct, and use words that appear in the dictionary. One is obviously the correct translation if the topic is machine intelligence. Making a system understand context is an ongoing and fundamentally difficult challenge in computer science.

Opportunities created by increased digital power and designer creativity are difficult to predict. The Newton attempted handwriting recognition not because people can write faster than they can type, but to eliminate the need for a bulky and inconvenient keyboard. Designers try to solve problems, with new designs often based on "form following failure."[28] Keeping handhelds small seemed to engineers to require screen or voice recognition. Other alternatives exist. A Silicon Valley startup is offering keyboards based entirely of projected light. A handheld emits a virtual keyboard onto a desk, and the user types as if it is there. Typing is fast and familiar, with digital bits substituting for keyboard atoms (see Figure 2.10).

Figure 2.10

Inventors with their Virtual Keyboard

Digital input substitution and new digital applications are themes that run throughout this book. More uses become feasible every year. Continued steep declines in digital costs create new, unpredictable, and exciting opportunities. Even more marketing information and marketing processes build on the digital GPT.

Will Moore's Law Continue?

Will Moore's Law continue? Ultimately, it must slow down or stop. Skeptics complain that supporters adjust the doubling period to keep the "law" going. Originally, Moore described his Law based on a one-year doubling. As time went on it seemed that 18 months fit the data better. Other skeptics claim that eventually available technologies will not be able to operate with the very small separation between circuit elements that the continuation of Moore's Law requires, and we have finally hit the "bottom" that Richard Feynman was alluding to in 1959 when he pointed out how tiny devices could really become. Even sooner, factories to make the more complicated chips get prohibitively expensive.

Nonsense, claim Moore's Law supporters. The industry has always operated with a known window of technology and an unknown future beyond that. Andy Grove, the former CEO and chairman of Intel, has likened it to driving a car at night. The headlights only shine so far, with darkness beyond. The darkness may hide a wall and a collision. Historically, it has just been more open road. Engineers have always been able to plow ahead with the dizzying pace of change. Intel has stated they see "no theoretical or practical challenges that will prevent Moore's Law being true for another 20 years at least".[29]

The Nordhaus finding emphasizes the decreasing cost of computation as the essential feature of Moore's Law, rather than the density of transistors that Moore considered. From this perspective, there are other ways in which digital cost reduction may continue and even accelerate. For example, research groups are developing methods of combining distributed computers to solve problems previously reserved for the highest end supercomputers. Engineers can combine even relatively obsolete individual computers, turning them into a highly effective parallel computer.

An ambitious extension of this is to create the equivalent of the electrical grid for computing power. A user, such as a marketer wishing to translate a set of pages into high-quality German, might request increased digital power to perform the first phase of the task.[30] A subscription to the "computing grid" would be able to scale this request up to supercomputer status, adding as much contextual knowledge as possible to the translation task. A skilled human translator can then fine-tune the machine's version.

Available evidence suggests Moore's Law reductions are technically achievable for at least a decade. Declines in storage costs are also predictable, with no near term end in sight. Hardware cost decreases and performance increases are a continuing source of opportunity.

Consumer choice, rather than physics or engineering, may present the most serious limit to Moore's Law. Consumer demand for higher performance is at the heart of the "digital spiral"[31] of increasing hardware capabilities. For decades, new features and more complete software solutions consumed the enhanced computer power and additional storage. Finding new applications that need this power is becoming more difficult. While it is always possible to take advantage of more and better computers, market observers worry that consumers may not be willing to spend the money and time to upgrade at the rate they have in the past.[32]

Competition for consumer dollars may further limit consumer demand for more powerful computers. Slower economic times typically reduce demand for consumer durables. Consumers are also spending a considerable amount of money on the transformation to digital television and multimedia entertainment. Several expensive items are included in the move to high definition and digitally oriented television. DVD players have been an extremely successful consumer electronic product, breaking sales records for market penetration. Both hardware sales and movie library purchases take money away from discretionary computer upgrades. Other digital television devices are even more expensive. Digital video recorders promise a set of enhanced digital capabilities, but cost several hundred dollars for hardware and an ongoing service commitment. Flat-panel televisions deliver high-resolution pictures and require much less space, but are expensive. Moore's Law reductions in these items will tempt many consumers to spend their money more on video entertainment than online and computing expenditures. Due to convergence, these new digital technologies will ultimately be highly complementary to the Net. However, in the short term, they may put severe pressure on computer makers to compete for consumer attention and upgrade dollars.

An ongoing challenge for Net marketers is to turn increased digital power into improved products and services. This ultimately determines whether we see continued digital improvements in the marketplace. The next two parts outline two areas where these capabilities are applied: the creation of digital environments and the digital convergence of many disparate industries.

DIGITAL ENVIRONMENTS

The Folly of Business-as-Usual

In 1943, Thomas Watson Sr. of IBM made one of the worst technology predictions ever. He estimated the total world market potential to be "about five computers." A common fallacy underlies this dismal prediction. Technology forecasters often assume that future uses of a machine will be the same as initial uses. Computers in 1943 generated mathematical tables, especially for military gunners. There is a very limited demand for that application.

The current situation is far different. Quarterly worldwide PC sales exceed 30 million. While Moore's Law allows growth due to cost reductions, there is an even more important reason why Watson was completely wrong. Digital technology is both powerful and flexible. Computers, especially networked computers, have gone far beyond simple computation. One of the most powerful visions of digital technology is immersion, the creation of an entire digital world. These digital worlds can be a classroom, a storefront, or a simulated city street. New technology continually pushes the capabilities of richer, more engrossing digital worlds.

Digital technology creates environments. These digital environments may store and display information, develop a story, educate visitors, and create amusing diversions. Understanding the key components of digital environments lets marketers use these emerging digital tools more effectively. The first step involves understanding the key components of digital environments. Marketers can use these components either in immersive digital environments or in hybrid environments that overlay digital environments onto the physical world to create an augmented reality.

| Digital Environment Components

In her studies of digital communication, Janet Murray has identified a useful framework for understanding digital environments.[33] Digital environments are procedural, participatory, spatial, and encyclopedic. Each of these components of digital environments creates opportunities and problems for their proper use. They set the stage for the sophisticated use of this ever-cheaper capability and help marketers harness these tools.

> *Digital Environments are Procedural*

One of the strongest restrictions on digital environments is the simple-mindedness of computers. Computers are logic engines. They follow rules. Nothing happens on a computer that is not pre-programmed. As we move to creating more in-depth and realistic digital worlds, the programming challenges become ever more complex.

> Hardware May Be Cheap, but Software Is Difficult to Get Right and Expensive to Create

The cheap hardware resulting from Moore's Law only sets the stage for digital environments. Software is also critical, and there is not a Moore's Law for software. Computer programming is difficult, requires considerable natural talent and training, and is difficult to manage. Errors are hard to detect and even harder to eliminate. Indeed, one of the classic books about managing software development has the revealing title *The Mythical Man Month*. Man months are mythical due to the legendary difficulty of estimating and completing large projects on time and on budget.

Managers eventually learned that to make a programming project predictable required re-use. Programmers rely on integrated packages to make a digital project much easier to manage.[34] The fundamental evolution of best practice has been to build upon complete solutions whenever possible (see Table 2.1).

The first digital environment procedural lesson for marketers is simple to understand but hard to obey—avoid the "not invented here" syndrome. Custom solutions often fail, rarely arrive on schedule, and normally overrun the budget. Despite this painful history of software development, many managers feel that no commercial package really fits their needs and are tempted to build one from scratch. This is usually wrong. It is typically far better to rely on standard tools, with customization held to the minimum.

The second lesson is more controversial and may not fit in all cases: avoid "best-of-breed" solutions and choose the best of the integrated solution packages. A best-of-breed solution

Table 2.1

Best Practice in Software Development Re-Uses Integrated Standard Tools		
Conventional: 1960s–1970s	**Transitional: 1980s–1990s**	**Current**
Environments/tools: Custom	Environments/tools: Off-the-shelf, separate	Environments/tools: Off-the-shelf, integrated
Size: 100% custom	Size: 30% component-based 70% custom	Size: 70% component-based 30% custom
Process: Ad-hoc	Process: Repeatable	Process: Managed/measured

Source: Walker Royce, (1998), *Software Project Management: A Unified Framework* (Reading, MA: Addison-Wesley), p. 23.

tries to identify the best vendor for each major marketing function, such as sales force automation, email system, and customer database management. Implementation and consistency are often major problems with a best-of-breed solution. On the other hand, any integrated solution will have components lacking state-of-the-art features or performance. Despite this, management ease with integrated solutions normally dominates individual tool limitations.

> Rules Lead to Adaptive Results

Although difficult to create, procedural rules can be very flexible. Murray argues that the essence of a computer is its ability to "embody complex, contingent behaviors". A well-programmed computer can create wonderful illusions of intelligence, spontaneity, and attention to detail.

An example is the sophistication and graphic content of a web site. Leading sites have tools that make a one-size-fits-all strategy unnecessary. If the user has a fast connection, and the net is not congested, full graphics access is possible. If the connection speed is slower, reduced graphics are possible. If the user is accessing with a PDA or cell phone, the system can supply text-only content. Modern streaming media systems sample the current congestion on the Net and adjust automatically. By using adaptive rules, the intelligence and power of digital technology can provide the best possible quality available at this instant. Real conditions, not average conditions, are the basis of the transmission.

> Rules Require Explicit Understanding of Business Decisions

The central procedural challenge facing marketers is the need to make business policies and rules explicit. Much of traditional marketing relies on implicit rules of conduct. Managers instruct sales people to treat the customer well, listen to their concerns, and respond with enthusiasm or empathy. While helpful, these are highly incomplete guides to action. Individuals must also know what it means to be helpful or empathetic. Marketing trainees have a lifetime of stored experience and context they can draw on. Indeed, some of the most effective training is through simple observation. Trainees watch and benefit from the actions and methods of superiors with a minimal amount of explicit instruction.

This human-oriented training does not work for digital components. Computers, and the software they run, must have clear-cut rules governing their actions. This forces a much deeper understanding of the underlying business and joint efforts between marketers and software engineers. The procedural demands of computers require those closest to customers, the marketers, to interact with web site designers and programmers to make sure rules do not override the customers' wishes.

Computer usability expert Donald Norman stresses that digital systems operate very differently from people, and programmers often confuse which is better.[35] He argues that it is always important to understand the difference between a machine-centered and a human-centered view. In particular, it is important to understand that successful marketing must satisfy the human-centered views of customers (Table 2.2).

> *Digital Environments are Participatory*

Computer users become excited when the computer responds to a choice, a command, or a preference they have expressed. Digital environments achieve much of their power when they encourage a sense of participation.[36] Participation leads to both success in finding the proper information, and satisfaction with the online experience.

One of the most important aspects of participation is ease of use. Digital environments can be difficult to use in many ways. A virtue of the Web is its ability to provide a simple and consistent method of accessing millions of different web sites. Murray argues the combination of procedural rules and participation leads to interactivity. Participation provides the

Table 2.2

Whose Procedural Point of View?					
The Machine-Centered View			The Human-Centered View		
People	*Machines*		*People*	*Machines*	
Vague	Precise		Creative	Dumb	
Disorganized	Orderly		Compliant	Rigid	
Distractible	Undistractible		Attentive to change	Insensitive to change	
Emotional	Unemotional		Resourceful	Unimaginative	
Illogical	Logical				

Source: Donald Norman, "Why It's Good That Computers Don't Work Like the Brain," in P. Denning and R. Metcalfe, *Beyond Calculation: The Next Fifty Years* (New York: Copernicus, 1997), 103–126. Reprinted with kind permission of Springer Science and Business Media.

feedback between computer and user. Procedural rules turn this user feedback into insight and make the environment respond to the user.

At the heart of any personalization system is a set of rules for deciding what to show each web visitor. There can be rules that determine what text to display based on previous choices. There can be rules that suggest a tie if an online shopper has chosen a new dress shirt or suit. There can be rules that only show low-fat foods if an online grocery shopper has indicated she is on a diet.

A web site becomes interactive when procedural rules combine with user participation. Almost any popular web site provides examples. The best are those that tap into curiosity, a sense of challenge, or some other natural human motivator. A simple example is the Amazon Gold Chest. Every 24 hours, Amazon puts a new set of sale items into the Chest. Each offer is sequential, on a "use it or lose it" limited-time basis. Once declined, the user cannot go back and buy the product. The motivation is both the love of a deal and impulse buying.

Auction sites were early learners of interaction's motivating power. When an auction begins, basic information about the product is posted, complete with text, pictures, and links to reviews of the product or product category. As the auction progresses, a bidder can view the history of the bids. Sites commonly allow for automatic notification by email if you are outbid, a personalized page showing the auctions you have recently been a member of, and the status of any pending shipments and orders.

What emerges from this combination of procedural rules and individual information is an interactive social environment. Bidders can warn about "crossing this line,"[37] point out negative information about the product, or issue pleas about needing to win this bid. As the bidding continues, a real feeling of presence and competition can emerge.

Not all technological attempts to create interaction work well or receive praise by customers and critics. An early example of technological substitution is the automated teller machine. The cost savings of ATMs over bank tellers are substantial. However, critics have faulted their procedural implementation:

> To enter the space constructed by the ATM system's software you have to submit to a potentially humiliating public examination—worse than being give the once-over by

some snotty and immovable receptionist. You are either embraced by the system (if you have the right credentials) or excluded and marginalized by it right there in the street. You cannot argue with it. You cannot ask it to exercise discretion. You cannot plead with it, cajole it, or bribe it. The field of possible interactions is totally delimited by the formally stated rules.[38]

> *Digital Environments are Spatial*

> Visions of Cyberspace

The ability of digital environments to create a virtual space has captured the imagination of science fiction writers. This has created high hopes, expectations, and anxieties about digital worlds. In a 1984 path-breaking book by William Gibson, *Neuromancer*, digital environments are so addictive and compelling that participants dismiss the real world and their real bodies as "just meat." Users live for their next connection, and go to great lengths to "jack in." Science fiction writers, movies, and television shows have speculated on the power and impact of fully developed digital environments. In *Snow Crash* by Neal Stephenson, the digital environments can leak out into the brains of their users and cause permanent damage. More playful and positive, the holodeck of Star Trek fame has created a vision of a digital environment so real it can mix with actual individuals in a three-dimensional simulation. In the Matrix movies, digital environments are a complete substitute for a grim reality.

For the near future, these types of digital environments remain fiction. The closest approach to digital worlds is the efforts by digital game creators. Advertising for Riven, a best-selling sequel to the blockbuster Myst, was explicitly spatial. Phrases such as "enter a deceptively beautiful world," "you must search, you must explore," and "You must let Riven become your world—before an entire world is lost" explain the game.[39]

These games achieve much of their power by combining rich material with a first-person point of view. The digital content to create these illusions is substantial. Riven includes 4,000 pictures, three hours of animation, and two hours of music stored on five compact disks (see Figure 2.11). Modern top sellers, such as the Grand Theft Auto series, contain much more digital content and include highly controversial visible and hidden material.

So-called "God games," such as Sims, dramatically expand the use of spatial immersion. In a Sims game, the goal is to create a functioning and entertaining virtual world populated by virtual citizens named Sims. Recently, the publisher of Sims signed a marketing arrangement with companies such as McDonalds and Intel to include their products and brands into the Sims worlds. This product licensing expands the product placement strategies of Hollywood movies in the virtual world of digital environment games.

Figure 2.11

Pioneering Digital Worlds and Interactive Digital Storytelling

Source: © Cyan Worlds, Inc.

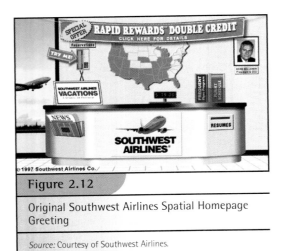

Figure 2.12

Original Southwest Airlines Spatial Homepage Greeting

Source: Courtesy of Southwest Airlines.

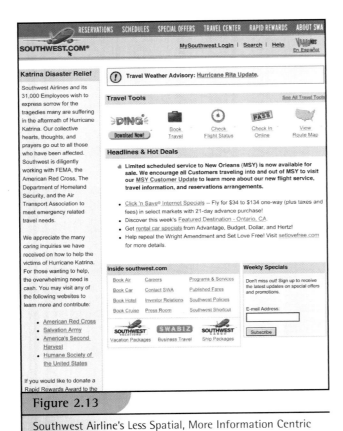

Figure 2.13

Southwest Airline's Less Spatial, More Information Centric Home Page

Source: Courtesy of Southwest Airlines.

> Currently Limited Web Spatial Environments

Current online efforts are much simpler and basic than even these modern games. Partly this is the scale of the exercise. Creating Warcraft is almost like making a major motion picture, with multi-million-dollar costs spread over millions of purchasers worldwide. Most web sites do not have that user base. Those that do must still battle with limitations of distributing digital content. As will be seen in the next chapter, many users of the Internet do not have connection speeds that can handle the level of digital content used by dedicated games.

Nonetheless, there are strong and important spatial elements in modern online systems. The most popular button on web browsers, by far, is the "back button." A common complaint among new users to the web, or to a site, is that they "get lost." Navigation on a web site typically uses spatial sounding phrases, such as forward, top, and bottom.

One of the uses of spatial digital environments is to provide familiarity and comfort to users. Southwest Airlines originally greeted visitors with a homepage that is immediately friendly and familiar (Figure 2.12). It is a desk with representations of familiar functions. Clicking on the newspaper leads to news stories. Phone numbers are available, of course, next to the phone. Click on a picture of the company president, and you get further information. Spatial metaphors can be effective methods of making online content easy to use and friendly.

Metaphor has limitations as well. Jakob Nielsen criticizes the original Southwest page for poor usability. He argues the metaphor is unnecessarily complex, and forces web designers to extend the metaphor beyond what is helpful. In his view, the much less spatial redesign of the Southwest page in Figure 2.13 is more focused and usable.[40]

Spatial digital environments may have their first extensive usage as part of augmented reality. Augmented reality is a hybrid of digital information and the real world. American football fans have grown accustomed to one pioneering use of augmented reality with the virtual first down line now common on television broadcasts (Figure 2.14).

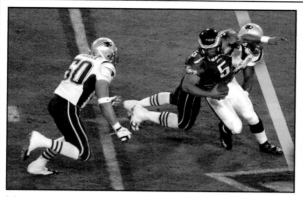 

(a) No, there really isn't a yellow first down line on the field.   (b)

Figure 2.14

Future Augmented Reality Merges Digital Environments with the Real World

Source: 2.14a ELIOT J. SCHECHTER/EPA /Landov; 2.14b Art by Pat Rawlings/SAIC.

The system is quite clever, using a computerized three-dimensional model of the field, rules for detecting what is grass versus what is a player, and multiple computers able to transform the raw video feed to an enhanced feed in real time. The system is smart enough to allow players to "run over" the line as if it were actually painted on the field.[41] The line is so useful that fans may well find its absence odd and annoying when viewing a game live.

Much more ambitious uses of augmented reality are under development. One goal of researchers is to combine real time, networked information with images not of a television broadcast but the actual physical world. Both corporate and university scientists are developing display technologies that users can wear while they go about their daily activities. These systems, using wireless Internet connections and GPS-location finders, can graft digital information onto the real spatial world. Possible applications include maps, advertisements, special offers, and available services in the neighborhood. This interface may be superior to other portable digital devices, such as cell phones and digital organizers.

The crucial challenge for marketers is to combine creativity and discipline. The continual creation of new capabilities spills over into new areas. Companies need to be on the lookout for innovations, and borrow and adapt those most suitable for their setting. Discipline is required as well, as digital capabilities demand precise programming and suitable supporting technologies. Innovations are often more expensive than planned.

> Digital Environments are Encyclopedic

The low cost of digital storage leads to the final feature of digital environments. It is possible to store huge amounts of information easily and cheaply. Digital environments are inherently encyclopedic. Storage is cheap and compact, with little need to delete content. This allows the volume, and value, of the digital environment to grow over time.

A good example of this capability is the Internet Movie Database (IMDB). Even the thickest print version of a movie guide must limit its entries. Not so online. IMDB stores whatever text is available about a movie in a database, always ready to be accessed. For example, in August of 1998 the database contained over 165,000 movies. By August of 2005, this had grown to over 327,000 movies. As Table 2.3 shows, there is much more than just movie titles and reviews. A wide range of business, creative, and social information is included.

Cheap bits allow a marketer to avoid the difficult choice between costly multiple product versions or ignoring smaller markets. Book publishers have discovered that, for many titles, it is possible to put multiple formats of their material, such as Mac and Windows, on the same CD-ROM. This creates savings in a version's shelf space, production costs, and inventory. As seen in Figure 2.4, storage costs show no sign of stopping their rapid decrease. The incentive to make digital environments more encyclopedic is increasing.

Table 2.3

The Internet Movie Database Content			
327,524	movies	34,221	TV series
		71,595	with plot summaries
18,183	with movie links	17,148	with merchandising links
25,783	with trivia	1,840,960	people
218,616	with ratings (44,137,742 votes)	3,953	with crazy credits
16,096	with quotes	17,387	with soundtrack listings
341,202	with genre descriptions	294,382	with production company info
7,193	with special effects company info	204,965	with distribution companies
90,439	with locations	191,740	with sound mix info
241,766	with running times	86,035	with certificate info
31,077	with tag lines	29,717	with literature info
148,603	with technical info	7,515	with laserdisc info
6,613	with alternate version info	34,694	with business info
7,272	with MPAA reasons	431,987	with their country of origin
266,730	with their release dates	5,281	with in-production status
39,610	with a complete and verified cast list	16,738	with completed crew lists
395,074	commentary or reviews	377,298	with color/B&W info
38,186	newsgroup reviews	357,171	with language info
54,420	with URLs for images, sounds, official sites, fan pages etc (49,316 URLs in all)		

Source: Information courtesy of The Internet Movie Database (http://www.imdb.com). Used with permission.

DIGITAL CONVERGENCE

Converging Industries and Technology

Cheap and powerful digital technology has another impact: digital convergence. Digital convergence is the merging of industries, technologies, and content that used to be separate but now overlap (see Figure 2.15). The three most important converging industries are computing, communications, and media content.[42]

Even before the Internet boom, these three industries were a crucial part of the U.S. economy. Computing is the most familiar. This includes computers, software, and computer services. This is the biggest of the converging parts of the economy. In 1996, for the United States alone,

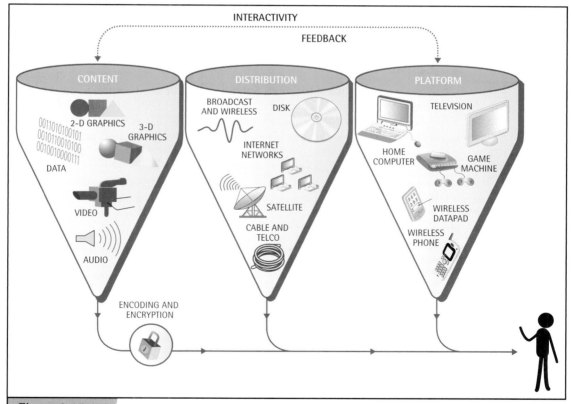

Figure 2.15

Converging Digital Industries and Technology

Source: Special Report: The Future of Digital Entertainment/Creating Convergence; November 2000; by Peter Forman, Robert W. Saint John; 7 page(s) *Scientific American.*

this was a $419 billion industry.[43] Communications follows, at $267 billion. This includes the telephone, cable, satellite, and wireless industries. Tied in size with communications are the content industries, including entertainment, publishing, and information providers.

What is happening in each of these areas is a convergence of technology and technique. The same hardware and software calculates an equation, makes a telephone call, or creates the graphics on a weather broadcast. This same technology then ships and displays the results. A compact disk can be used to store software, data, or a new music release. These joint capabilities, interactive multimedia, form a trillion dollar digital industry.

Not only are the technologies merging, but the leading companies in the separate-but-converging industries are combining as well. None of these mergers was more dramatic than the acquisition of Time-Warner by America Online in January 2000. The merger brought together the leading online company of the time with a powerhouse of music, movies, and cable distribution. Cartoons extrapolated the merger to all consumers' lives (Figure 2.16).

By many measures, the AOL-Time Warner merger was a failure and slowed digital convergence mergers. From its peak in early 2000, the stock fell sharply. Lawsuits, turnover in management, and controversy quickly followed. AOL has had difficulty transitioning to an environment of broadband Net access, and the hoped-for joint marketing opportunities have been disappointing. An indication of the difficulties is when the joint company dropped the AOL brand (and stock symbol) as its name and reverted to Time Warner and TWX.

The full promise of multimedia convergence has not yet happened. A study of the convergence of local area computing and telephony found a wide array of differences in the way these industries sell very similar digital technology. Companies deal with different wholesalers and the sales force talks to different parts of buyers' organizations. Each industry has its own jargon, often with different phrases for the same basic hardware or software. Business practices are converging slower than technology.

Convergence gives Internet marketers great flexibility. As the barriers between industries fall, marketers can rely on the medium that works the best. The special abilities of the Internet augment the traditional power of the mass-market media. The coming digital changes in television and cable systems mean the scope of Net marketing is growing dramatically.

There is an important part of the economy that proves an entire industry can go digital. The financial sector dwarfs in size even the converging triangle of computing—communicating—content. On a normal day it involves not millions, or billions, but trillions of dollars. It is almost purely digital and networked. It is the world's network of large banks and financial institutions.

Many consumer transactions already take place entirely digitally. Many consumers have direct deposit of their paychecks. By 2001, 65.1% of the private workforce used direct deposit of paychecks.[44] Consumers are also actively using direct payments. There are also automated payments of mortgages,

Figure 2.16

Expansive Views at the Time of the AOL and Time Warner Merger

Source: Bob Gorrell, Creators Syndicate, Inc.

utility payments, alimony, and even state lottery tickets. This all takes place through the Automated Clearing House (ACH), which had over 3.9 billion transactions in 2002.

Even larger amounts are transacted between banks. FedWire is a system operated by the Federal Reserve System to settle accounts and transfer money between banks within the United States. The annual volume of money transferred using FedWire in 2002 was $405 trillion. The Clearing House Interbank Payment System, CHIPS, is the electronic banking system that transfers money internationally. It transfers more than $1.2 trillion daily.[45] In all of these systems, there are no actual tangible transactions of money or goods. It is simply the digital exchange of bits. However, they are very valuable bits.

Though there is much to be learned from the financial sector, online commerce and consumer online marketing have elements that make it more challenging than the ACH or CHIPS systems. Security systems are costly and impractical for many small commercial and consumer transactions. Consumers may desire anonymity, and this complicates security measures. Sophistication of bank operatives is much higher than the average web user. The number of participants is radically different. Instead of hundreds of banks transferring trillions of dollars, there will be millions of individuals each spending $50. This is a huge change in the number of participants and in a dramatic lowering of the amount per transaction.

How Digitizing Works

The first step in harnessing the power of Moore's Law, digital environments, and digital convergence is to make something digital. Often these days it is digital from the start. We create books in digital word processors. We create an illustration in a computer graphics program. We create photographs with a digital camera.

Other times we use older methods, or take pre-existing books, illustrations, and pictures and capture them digitally. This capture must somehow transfer the information stored in the physical item into a digital representation. Through innovation, market competition, and standards bodies, literally hundreds of different procedures exist for making the world digital. The important issue is that all of these methods of analog to digital transformation, no matter what they start with, end up with the same result—a string of zeroes and ones.

Text provides a simple example of how digitizing works. Digital formats translate text in a manner similar to old childhood codes, where each symbol is associated with a specific letter. Each letter of the alphabet receives a code. Every time an "A" appears, the symbol for "A" is used. Every time an "a" is encountered, the symbol for lowercase "a" is used. Each character gets a unique code. Unicode 4.0 provides a widely established system capable of handling all of the leading languages.[46]

Digitizing a picture provides a useful illustration of a more complicated digital transformation. Figure 2.17 is a Martian meteorite that may contain the first evidence of life on other planets. Figure 2.18 illustrates one method of digitizing this picture, making it sharable around the world.

Step 1 is to make a grid of picture elements, or pixels. The more pixels, the higher the resolution of the picture. As part of making this grid of pixels, we decide how many colors or shades of gray to use.

Figure 2.17

A Martian Meteorite

Source: NASA Jet Propulsion Laboratory (NASA-JPL) # PIA00289.

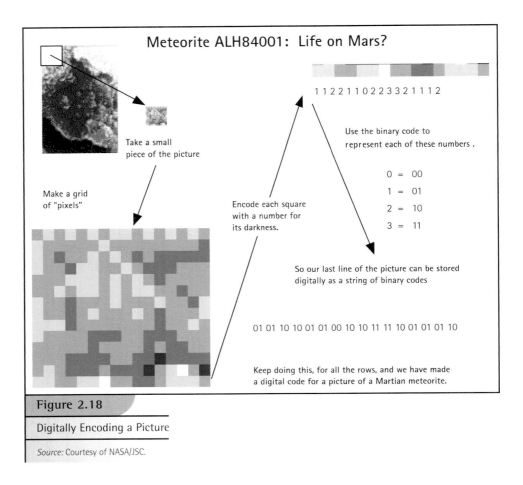

Figure 2.18

Digitally Encoding a Picture

Source: Courtesy of NASA/JSC.

Now assign the closest available color to each of these pixels. This is now a picture represented by a string of numbers.[47]

At several points in the digitizing process, tradeoffs and decisions occur. The number of pixels used in the original scan of the item is a measure of the highest resolution possible. The resolution of the picture will in turn dictate how big of a file results from the digitizing process. It is often advantageous to have multiple images of the same picture. A popular commercial system for storing pictures is the Kodak PhotoCD. The standard Kodak PhotoCD stores five different resolutions for each picture. Depending on a user's need for quality and sharpness, each of these levels is retrievable. The highest quality uses 2048 × 3072 pixels to represent the picture image. The other quality levels are 1024 × 1536 pixels (the same resolution as high definition television), 512 × 768 pixels (the same resolution as U.S. TV), 256 × 384 pixels (the "Thumbnail" version), and 128 × 192 pixels (the "Small Thumbnail" version).[48] For color pictures, these are very different file sizes. The highest resolution needs 18 Mb per image; the lowest resolution requires a file size of 70 K.

Digital designers have become very clever in shrinking file size. Each digital picture, movie, and sound is run through compression routines before being shipped to the network. In the World Wide Web, picture images commonly use either the GIF or the JPEG compression routines. These systems allow users to further tradeoff size of file versus picture quality. This can be very important in speeding up performance, and not forcing users to wait for long periods to download multiple graphic files.

Technology is at a stage where massive two-dimensional digitalization is rapidly taking place. Pictures, maps, icons, historical documents, diagrams, and catalogs are rapidly converting to digital form. Google searches over 1 billion online images. Already a huge number, it is growing rapidly. Archives of Ansel Adams, the Vatican collection, the Louvre in Paris, and hundreds of other museums are available in partial or complete form.

Digitizing three-dimensional objects is technically more challenging, but results in files that can be stored, shipped, and viewed with the same technologies as any other digital content (see Figure 2.19). Efforts are under way to create standards and methods for capturing a feeling of three dimensions. A first step toward three dimensions is to allow a two-dimensional screen to scroll. An example of this technique is the surround picture technology of IPIX. Their approach gives at least an illusion of three dimensions by allowing scrolling in whatever direction the user desires.

The first step of the IPIX approach is to capture the view. A standard camera takes two precisely opposite pictures using a "fish eye" lens. Specialty software then digitizes and processes the image to eliminate the curved distortion that a fish eye lens creates. After running the images through this software and blending the two views, they create an effective composite image. Using a specialty viewer application, or a plug-in to the main browsers, a user can see a

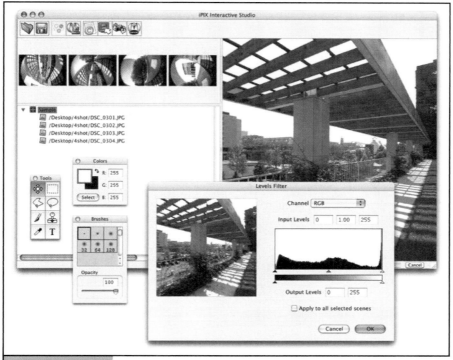

Figure 2.19

3D Views

Source: Courtesy of IPIX Corporation.

complete view of what someone standing in the middle of the view and looking in all directions would see. Toyota has applied this technique to create a virtual showroom. With it, you can "sit" in the driver's seat of any of its cars and look at a complete view of the interior of the car, truck, or land cruiser.

For many cases, the challenge of digitization is cost, both in time and money. An industry that would love to have complete 360 views of an environment is real estate. Rather than escort prospective buyers to 50 new houses, most of which are unacceptable, digital technology allows prescreening of properties. Research by the National and the California Association of Realtors strongly indicates that online viewing of properties is highly effective for brokers, buyers, and sellers.

| Digitizing Marketing Processes

> *Steps in Digitizing Marketing*

The very flexibility of digital technology is daunting. It can be difficult to choose the best place for marketers to take advantage of Moore's Law, digital environments, and the convergence of digital technologies and companies. Firms need to know where to look and how to prioritize their efforts.

The sequence shown in Figure 2.20 is an evolutionary process that many firms follow. It reflects many of the automation steps in other business areas. First it creates the foundation of the digital transition, then it chooses the easiest targets, and finally it redesigns the marketing step to fully use the digital capabilities.

The first step is to capture, store, and maintain the material in digital form. Brochures, product documents, and product development materials should be kept in both electronic and printed form. This makes it easy to create online versions, even years later. This can be valuable as a permanent record of older product lines. Companies should also capture and archive major presentations and corporate training sessions. Multimedia digitization is advancing rapidly. As network access speeds increase there will be increasing demands for video and sound. Saving the material makes it available for future use.

The second step is to substitute digital material wherever practical. Chapter 7 looks at many of the customer support uses that are saving companies millions of dollars. There are many high cost activities, such as publishing complicated manuals, which digital material can completely replace.

The final stage is redesign around digital capabilities. Careful studies of technology adoption show that this step takes considerable time, but also is the source of the greatest payoffs in new efficiency and new capabilities.

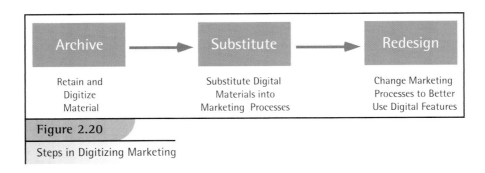

Figure 2.20

Steps in Digitizing Marketing

> *Using the Business Process Point of View*

> Identifying Marketing Processes

One of the most active areas of marketing strategy and consulting is business process improvement. These efforts create a deeper understanding of the steps and people involved in each marketing function. It can be of considerable use in spotting opportunities for digitalization.

The business process point of view breaks down an area of a company, such as marketing, into essential value-creating steps. Shapiro et al. (1992) provide an example. They argue that marketing managers should "staple yourself to an order".[49] By following all the steps involved in taking and fulfilling orders many delays, gaps, and problems with the process can be spotted. The level of detail developed by process analysis assists in substituting digital capabilities. Table 2.4 is an example of one market process categorization.[50]

First-level processes are the basic value creation that marketing performs. Each first level process is a broad category of capabilities. Companies must understand their customers, design

Table 2.4

Marketing Business Processes That Can Be Digitized

Marketing Processes for Identifying, Developing, and Retaining Customers

First-Level Processes

Understand Markets and Customers	Involve Customers in the Design of Products and Services	Market and Sell Products and Services	Involve Customers in the Delivery of Products and Services	Provide Customer Service	Manage Customer Information

Second-Level Processes

| Understand the Market Environment

Understand Customers' Wants and Needs

Segment Customers | Develop New Concepts and Plans for Products and Services

Design, Build, and Evaluate Prototypes

Refine and Customize Products or Services, Then Test Their Effectiveness | Secure Channels of Distribution

Establish Pricing

Develop Advertising and Promotion Activities

Develop and Deploy a Sales Force

Process Orders

Develop Customers | Offer Broad Delivery Options to Become the "Supplier of Choice"

Use Delivery Customization to Attract and Retain Core Customers

Identify Customers' Delivery Needs

Develop Distribution Capability | Establish "Points of Contact" Excellence

Build Cross-Functional "Points of Contact" Cooperation

Train Employees to Improve Customers' Expectations for Projects and Services | Build Customer Profiles

Establish Service Information

Measure Customer Performance and Satisfaction |

Source: Adapted from Hiebeler et al., *Best Practices: Building Your Business with Customer-Focused Solutions.*

new and improved products, bring these products to market, achieve efficient distribution and benefits, provide after sales support, and manage customer data to do a better job in the future.

A business process point of view is most useful when first level processes are broken down further (see Table 2.4). Companies can then compare individual business processes from organizations in very different industries. For example, a catalog company might be the best in its industry in handling packages and shipping. However, it still could learn much from FedEx or UPS in the way they handle large volumes of boxes. By focusing on the process of package handling, companies have a much richer source of ideas than simply their immediate industry competitors.

> Substituting Digital Material in Marketing Processes

The process point of view is well suited for identifying digital substitution opportunities. Marketers can look for new ideas and methods of adding digital content by looking at a much wider range of online examples. A trucking company can learn from airlines how to design complicated schedules. Customer support methods from a computer company can be a valuable lesson for an air conditioner maker. Chains of dry cleaners can mimic dealer locator pages from cellular phone companies.

Each of the main processes benefits from digital substitution. Take the first requirement of a marketing department, to understand markets and customers. At the second level, this is broken down into three steps, each of which provides many opportunities for digital substitution.

There are numerous ways companies are using the digital capabilities of the Net to better understand and track their market environment. The Gallup Organization conducted a poll of how European firms were using the Net. More than 85% of companies had an online connection in the United Kingdom, 86% of companies in Germany, and 85% of French firms cited collecting information about competitors and their market. Rather than compile a stack of yellow newspaper clippings and file folders, online material is sortable, storable, and analyzable using spreadsheets and databases.

Some companies are taking the digital capabilities quite far in understanding customer wants and needs. Levi Strauss has always been committed to extensive market research on a wide range of issues. One of its most valuable qualitative techniques is the focus group, in which consumers come together to talk about general issues or to respond to new product ideas.

Providing this information to marketing staff has long been a challenge. Rather than forcing staff to view multiple hours of sessions or videotape, Levi's has digitized and put this material on its corporate intranet. As part of the digitizing process, editing and categorization occurs. Suddenly anyone in marketing throughout the world can focus on exactly the 20-minute discussion of a particular item of interest with exactly the focus group of interest.

Research is showing that substituting low-cost online market research for costly physical surveys and demonstrations can provide accurate data at a fraction of the cost. This allows lower cost research that saves money and allows more in-depth studies.

> Redesigning Marketing Processes to Use Digital Capabilities

The process point of view can be even more important when moving to the third step, the redesign of marketing processes to take advantage of digital capabilities. For example, one of the main obstacles for the major airlines use of information technology was the traditional need to get a ticket in the hands of travelers. Despite being able to handle the complete transaction without a travel agent in many cases, the need for a physical ticket was a critical bottleneck. The invention and adoption of etickets solved a big part of this problem. By redesigning the ticketing process to allow for purely electronic versions, the full reservation and travel sequence could be made digital. Although some travelers have resisted etickets, this process redesign dramatically increases the ability of the airlines to make reservations directly with the consumer.

Redesign leads to much more widespread process improvements than substitution alone, but it often requires time and training.[51] New skills complement and reinforce the new capabilities. Reorganizations provide a management structure compatible with the new abilities. Digitization requires management skill, both in the selection of digitization efforts and the proper staffing required. Managers must prioritize and build on earlier successes. Existing workers may require training to acquire new skills, and different types of worker backgrounds may be required under the new system. While gains from reorganization can be large, reorganization can be difficult.

ENDNOTES

1. Nordhaus, William. (2002). "The Progress of Computing." Working Paper, *Yale University and National Bureau of Economic Research*, March 4, Version 5.2.2.

2. Title of a classic talk given by Richard Feynman, December 29th, 1959, to the American Physical Society. Text available at: http://www.zyvex.com/nanotech/feynman.html. Much of the vision for shrinking digital circuits to their atomic scale is outlined here.

3. Michael White and Laura Gilman. (2001). *J.R.R. Tolkien*, Alpha Books, New York.

4. Joe Morgenstern. (2001). "A Magical Start for Tolkien Epic on the Screen." *Wall Street Journal* December 28.

5. *Variety* weekly box office, http://www.variety.com, January 24, 2002.

6. For example, a leading system by Boeing uses a satellite network to digitally distribute films.

7. Google search engine, http://www.google.com, September 2004, September 2002.

8. These are all examples of a search on the word "digital" in the *New York Times* online archive, for example K. Cavanaugh. (1996). "A Trip to the Digital Beach: MTV Brings Sound and Chat To Virtual Reality Web Site." *New York Times* August 2.

9. Nicholas Negroponte, *Being Digital*, p. 14.

10. Federal Reserve Board Chairman Alan Greenspan noted, "...our nation has been experiencing a higher growth rate of productivity—output per hour—worked in recent years. The dramatic improvements in computing power and communication and information technology appear to have been a major force behind this beneficial trend." *The Emerging Digital Economy*, (1998), U.S. Department of Commerce, http://www.commerce.gov.

11. For a restatement and forecast by Gordon Moore, see "An Update to Moore's Law" speech given September 30, 1997, transcript available at http://www.intel.com/pressroom/archive/speeches/gem93097.htm.

12. Nordhaus, William. (2002). "The Progress of Computing." Working Paper, *Yale University and National Bureau of Economic Research*, March 4, Version 5.2.2.

13. Moore's Law is a predictor of longer term engineering trends, and market conditions can result in slower or faster short-term changes. During the late 1980s there was actually a temporary shortfall of chips, import restrictions into the United States, and temporary price rises. These quickly disappeared, and did not change the long-term Moore's Law trends.

14. Montgomery Phister. (1979). *Data Processing Technology and Economics*, Second Ed. p. 143 for original costs, September 2004 street price for current hard disks at retail.

15. Brian Hayes. "Terabyte Territory." *American Scientist* (90, May–June 2002), 212–216.

16. While there are many legal issues involved, such as copyright violation and fair use that would need to be worked out, many companies would find this a cost-saving arrangement. Some form of encryption and approval method might allow the information to be stored on the disks while still requiring approval by the ultimate owner of the material. This ideas of "super distribution" was discussed in an early book by Brad Cox. (1996). *Superdistribution*, Addison Wesley, Upper Saddle River, NJ.

17. 27th TOP500 List.

18. Will Snow, Senior Staff Engineer, Sun Microsystems quoted by Jim Sterne. (1996). *Customer Service on the Internet*, John Wiley and Sons, New York.

19. Catherine Graeber. "Online Service: The Next Generation." *Forrester Research*, September 2002.

20. Philip Clark. (2001). "B to B: Bristol-Meyers Prescribes Sales Solution." *Crain Communications* 86, p. 1, September 3.

21. Kenneth De Ville. (2001). "The Ethical and Legal Implications of Handheld Medical Computers." *Journal of Legal Medicine*, 22:447–466.

22. E-Business. (2001). "The Web at Work/ Memetic Systems, Cassius Software." *Wall Street Journal* December 17.

23. For example, merging video and advertising: Arthur A. Raney, Laura M. Arpan, Kartik Pashupati, and Dale A. Brill. (2003). "At The Movies, On the Web: An Investigation of the Effects of Entertaining and Interactive Web Content on Site and Brand Evaluations." *Journal of Interactive Marketing* 17(4, Autumn), 38–53.

24. Forecasts global spending between 2002 and 2004 range between 320 and 360 billion U.S. dollars. The key uncertainty is the state of the worldwide economy. Internet ad spending is forecast at $9.7 billion in 2002 rising to $12.9 billion in 2004. *Zenith Media*. http://www.zenithmedia.com/ pradsp02.doc.

25. Behavioral researchers are finding that the same person consumes information differently depending on the language it is presented in. David Luna and Laura A. Peracchio. (2005). "Advertising to Bilingual Consumers: The Impact of Code-Switching on Persuasion." *Journal of Consumer Research* 31(4, March), 760–765.

26. Although even a failed brand can generate intense feelings. Albert M. Muniz Jr. and Hope Jensen Schau. (2005). "Religiosity in the Abandoned Apple Newton Brand Community." *Journal of Consumer Research* 31(4, March) pp. 737–747.

27. Raymond Kurzweil. (1996). "When Will HAL Understand What We Are Saying: Computer Speech Recognition and Understanding." In *Hal's Legacy: 2001's Computer as Dream and Reality*, edited by David Stork, MIT Press, Cambridge, MA.

28. Henry Petrosky, *The Design of Everyday Things*.

29. Intel. "Focus Moore's Law: Changing the PC Platform for Another 20 Years", http://www.intel.com.

30. See, for example, the many cites contained at http://www.gridcomputing.com.

31. This phrase has been popularized by Intel Corporation.

32. *New York Times*, September 29, 2002.

33. Janet H. Murray. (1997). *Hamlet on the Holodeck: The Future of Narrative in Cyberspace*, Free Press, New York, see especially pp. 71–94.

34. Walker Royce. (1998). *Software Project Management: A Unified Framework*, Addison-Wesley, Upper Saddle River, NJ, p. 23.

35. Donald Norman. (1997). "Why It's Good That Computers Don't Work Like the Brain." In Peter Denning and R. Metcalfe, *Beyond Calculation*, Copernicus, New York, pp. 103–126.

36. See, for example, Ann E. Schlosser. (2003). "Experiencing Products in the Virtual World: The Role of Goal and Imagery in Influencing Attitudes versus Purchase Intentions." *Journal of Consumer Research* 30(2, September), 184–198.

37. An online warning by one bidder about overbidding for an item.

38. William Mitchell. (1995). *City of Bits: Space, Place, and the Infobahn*. MIT Press, Cambridge, MA, p. 112.

39. Broderbund web site for purchasing Myst and Riven.

40. Jakob Nielsen. *Designing Web Usability*. New Riders, LOCATION, 2000, pp. 182–183.

41. A more complete description is available from Shel Brannan. (2003). "How the First-Down Line Works," available at HowStuffWorks.com.

42. Don Tapscott. (1996). *The Digital Economy: Promise and Peril in the Age of Networked Intelligence*, McGraw-Hill, New York. Also see David Yoffie. (1996). "Competing in the Age of Digital Convergence." *California Management Review* 38(4, Summer), pp. 31–53.

43. Numbers and graph are from D. Tapscott, op. cit., pp. 9, 325, 329.

44. *Direct Deposit/Direct Payment General Information*, NACHA—The Electronic Payments Association, June 2003.

45. Statistics from the New York Federal Reserve, www.newyorkfed.org.

46. See the information at www.unicode.org.

47. There is typically one more very important step: compression. After encoding the picture in a binary code, software goes through and looks for ways to make the stream of bits smaller. It does this by looking for repeating patterns. For example, color 1 may repeat at some point for 300 pixels. Rather than have a string of 01 01 01 . . . . for 300 entries, a compression scheme will store the color and how many times it is repeated. When the picture is to be viewed, this compression scheme must be run in reverse.

48. Kodak information from Kodak web site, http://www.kodak.com.

49. Benson Shapiro, V. Kasturi Rangan, and John Sviokla. (1992). "Staple Yourself to an Order." *Harvard Business Review* July–August.

50. Hiebeler, Robert, Thomas Kelly, and Charles Ketteman. (1998). *Best Practices: Building Your Business with Customer-Focused Solutions*. Simon & Schuster, New York, p. 44.

51. Erik Brynjolfsson and Lorin Hitt. (2003). "Computing Productivity: Firm-level Evidence." *Review of Economics and Statistics* 85(4), pp. 793–808.

chapter 3:

Networks

Smart Mobs and the Mobile Net

Internet usage in Japan differs dramatically from
the United States or Europe. Japanese embrace
mobile access to email and online information
more than other areas of the world. The leader of
this mobile Internet is NTT DoCoMo, with their
i-mode and FOMA systems. I-mode is one of the
most popular methods of Internet access in Japan,
with more than 43 million users in 2006. This base
of users can access tens of thousands of sites providing customized web content in the i-mode format. Beyond that, they can use their i-mode
phones to access the general Web. FOMA is the
next generation of mobile access, much faster with
new and innovative features.

Surprisingly, i-mode achieved rapid growth
with a user interface and speed that few computer-
based Net users would tolerate. I-mode's core service provides a data speed of less than 20K per
second, painfully slow compared to broadband
and less than half the rate of normal dial-up
computers. As it uses a phone for access device,
the screen is small and the keyboard tiny. Even so,
the combination of pent-up demand for Internet
use, the ability to access the Net during long
Japanese commutes, the bundling of the Net with
a sleek and modern cell phone, and the "always
on" nature of i-mode led to a runaway hit.

The relative difficulty and cost of Japanese
computer-based Internet also contributed to the
success of i-mode. Character-based computer
keyboards are more difficult to use than those
based on Western alphabets, and require more

this chapter

Connecting millions of people through a network creates a powerful new marketing environment. Three aspects of the Internet as a network are fundamental: it is a social network, it is a content network, and it is a technological network.

Topics covered in this chapter include:

> The Internet in Japan

> Network Growth and Diversification

> A Science of Networks

> Marketing with Networks

computer power. Space is at a premium for Japanese homes and businesses.[3] When i-mode launched, Japanese residential dial-up connection fees were triple of those in the United States or Europe. All of these factors made a wireless solution attractive.

In 2002, NTT introduced FOMA (freedom of mobile access), a third-generation (3G) mobile data service and the first widespread introduction in the world. FOMA phones have high-speed data connections that allow rapid downloads of games, pictures, music, or other large files. It is fast enough to allow video calls and streaming video media. By 2006, the FOMA subscriber base exceeded 23 million and was still growing. An example of this type of high-speed data connection is shown in Figure 3.1.

Escaping the desktop changes how individuals use the Internet. One of the most popular and profitable uses of i-mode is short messaging (SMS). While instant messaging is popular among some regular Internet users, especially teenagers, it is even more common with i-mode. SMS augments and partially substitutes for phone calls or email. Quick little notes communicate with friends and family without interrupting and forcing an immediate reply.

I-mode reveals interesting trends for geographically oriented Net usage. As it is a cell phone, it is easy for DoCoMo to locate any particular i-mode phone. This permits the system to highlight nearby stores, movie theaters, restaurants, or other small businesses. Using a combination of phone and SMS, friends can

Figure 3.1

A Video Call Using Wireless Internet in Japan

Source: © ERNEST GOH/AFP/Getty Images

coordinate their daily lives and locate others who happen to be physically close.

One of the most interesting patterns of i-mode use is clustering, where small groups of users have extensive communication. These "thumb tribes" and "smart mobs," to use Howard Rheingold's description, strongly demonstrate the social aspects of network communication. Individuals show widely different patterns of messaging close friends, more distant friends, or mere acquaintances. While many individuals have a moderate number of contacts, some individuals have an extremely large network of contacts. I-mode also provides the ability to "self-organize," where short messages between like-minded individuals can suddenly lead to crowds that appear planned and structured.[4]

The success story of i-mode contains a common pattern for many network competitions. There is a virtuous cycle of system popularity and available content. As i-mode took off, it became attractive for content providers to supply information. As more content providers emerge, the i-mode system becomes even more attractive. This positive feedback loop magnifies leads and makes it more difficult for competitors to catch up.

Popular content for i-mode has its own distinctive flavor. Top revenue producers include downloadable ring tones, horoscopes, and games. The strong entertainment aspect of i-mode content further reflects the social aspects of this information and communication system.

Another lesson of i-mode is the importance of managing technology standards. System designers chose a version of HTML that was suited to mobile use while still being easy to convert from normal HTML. This use of established standards made it very easy to leverage existing content and quickly roll out i-mode sites. On the other hand, the proprietary aspects of the i-mode phone makes it possible for DoCoMo to fend off clones and rivals and profit from the service.

Japanese Internet use is changing again. A partnership between Softbank and Yahoo! Japan pioneered inexpensive, fast broadband Internet access.[5] This change, also coupled with the online experience gained from previous exposure, has stimulated rapid adoption of broadband in Japan. The ITU rates Japanese broadband more than 300 times more cost effective, in terms of monthly cost per speed delivered, than systems common in the United States. The broadband systems increasingly common in Japanese homes are fast enough to download high-quality video, on demand, in real time.

The developments in Japan, both DoCoMo FOMA and Yahoo! Broadband, show that Internet innovation is truly worldwide. While the first-generation commercial Internet relied heavily on U.S. companies, the emerging second-generation Internet demands a global perspective. This second generation Internet is a much more diverse network, a network with smarter information and with companies around the world introducing new features.

Networking is the second of three core foundations of Internet marketing. The DoCoMo experience highlights the rich mixture of technology and social interaction that marketers face when using networks. The nature of the technology is important, the impact of the network on communication is important, and the shift in value caused by the network is important. The first part of the chapter considers how the network itself has grown, in terms of users, devices, and content. Following that is a discussion of the new science of networks. The chapter ends with an overview of the important skills and sources of value that networks introduce into marketing.

THE NETWORK EVOLVES

Wireless i-mode and FOMA demonstrate important features of networking, both wired and wireless, as a general-purpose technology useful for marketing. Recall from Chapter 1 that four defining features of a GPT are (a) a substantial scope for improvement, (b) eventual wide use, (c) a variety of applications, and (d) many spillover effects. The rapidly growing and evolving Net demonstrates each of these properties.[6]

First, we consider the growth in the width and breadth of the Net. This includes:

> People using network devices to access the Net,
> Content available using the network and communication happening through the network, and
> Technology standards that make the network possible.

After considering the adoption of the Net, we consider some of the many uses of networks in marketing and business.

Maturing and Expanding

It is striking how fast the Internet became an essential part of everyday life for users around the world.[7] In little more than a decade, once the Internet was open for commercial activities, a billion individuals became Net users. Table 1.2 showed this rapid pattern of adoption, plus the even more rapid adoption of mobile phones. Both of these technologies have succeeded despite their relatively expensive and complicated technical capabilities. Desktop Internet access requires a computer, modem, Internet access line, and the software for making contact. Cell phone access requires substantial infrastructure, phone purchase or rental, service charges, and at least some learning by users.

The increasing ability of mobile subscribers to tap into Internet resources provides additional reach and coverage for the Net. Mobility extends Internet connectivity, and provides access where a desktop device is not possible. Any analysis of the role of the Internet must pay attention to the impact of the billion cell phone users as well as computer users.

Rapid growth for a decade must inevitably slow because of market saturation. Many of the advanced economies are finding it challenging to encourage more than 70% of the population to use the Internet, while most of the wealthy countries in the world have Net adoption rates exceeding 50%. As we saw in Table 1.1, the United States, Japan, South Korea, Canada, and Australia all have adoption rates between 60% and 70% of the population. Later in this chapter, we consider the major barriers for expanding the Internet for both wealthy and less developed countries. Figure 3.2 highlights how Asia Pacific and European user bases have surpassed the United States, with Asian access forecast to grow the most.[8]

Market maturation has a number of impacts. More experienced users are more likely to engage in ecommerce, upgrade to broadband, and use more services.[9] On the other hand, more experienced users tend to have more of an online routine, and engage in less exploratory surfing.[10] Internet companies are reacting to this change from a decade of access expansion to an upcoming decade of deepening of the online connections.[11]

Many of the most innovative applications of the Net require broadband for effective performance. Broadband is typically "always on," lowering a substantial convenience barrier and simplifying access for many applications. Broadband greatly improves the quality of services

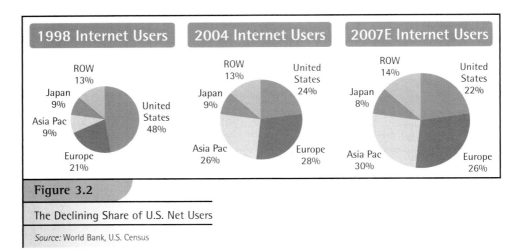

Figure 3.2

The Declining Share of U.S. Net Users

Source: World Bank, U.S. Census

such as video-on-demand, file downloading, swapping of photos, shared computing, and voice-over-IP. Broadband encourages the use of applications that rely on data only available online.

An especially influential form of broadband is WiFi, a rapidly growing protocol for local-area wireless connections.[12] WiFi has a number of intriguing aspects. First, it combines many of the benefits of wireless access without the limitations of slow speed and screen size inherent in phone-based systems. Second, it distributes access throughout the home or office without costly rewiring of existing buildings. Broadband to the home stimulates adoption of WiFi and the purchase of an access point (AP) and network cards (NICs) that create a WiFi network. Third, in many urban or campus settings it creates roaming broadband access available to all. One problem with WiFi is its relatively limited range of coverage from any given access point. WiFi enthusiasts share lists of public access points and map out coverage zones.

Hardware makers are reacting to WiFi's growth, and further stimulating it, by bundling WiFi capability into new laptops and home computers. Chipsets with built-in WiFi lower the cost of adopting wireless, create market momentum for establishing wireless access points, and make wireless an expected part of a new computer's features. This sets the stage for an entirely new set of uses.

Figure 3.3

Home WiFi Networks for Sharing Music, Video Files

Source: Courtesy of Linksys

Consumer electronics firms are releasing WiFi-enabled entertainment systems, capable of wireless distribution of music, video, and gaming capability throughout the home. Home automation companies are building WiFi Internet access into traditional appliances, such as heating, lighting, and kitchen devices, allowing average consumers to create elaborate home automation capabilities. Some simply add a converter box to attach to existing systems, some build the capabilities into new players. Microsoft's Media Center operating system or Apple's wireless formats simplify both manufacturer challenges for home automation and consumers' use of these devices. The WiFi music server shown in Figure 3.3 is just one of the many devices entering the market to make the fully connected multimedia home a reality.

Content and Communication

> *Total New Information*

> Stored Information

Networks link people to information and people to people. Each is an essential aspect of using the network for marketing purposes. This section highlights the information environment existing today. Society faces a rapid, some say overwhelming,[13] increase in available information. This growth creates a difficult struggle to gain attention in a world of information overload.

This connected information comes in many forms. Each year artists release new music, publishers release new books, movie studios release new DVDs, software companies ship software on data CDs, millions of office workers create spreadsheets and word processing documents, medical technicians take X-rays, web site designers release launch new web pages, and proud parents take home movies. Researchers at the University of California have undertaken the ambitious effort of estimating annual new global information production. Table 3.1 presents a summary of their findings. We are awash in a sea of information.

The most striking finding is the dominance of magnetic media, primarily videotape and computer hard disks. More than 92% of the world's new stored information is on magnetic media. Ranking the magnetic storage reflects the importance of full motion video and hard disks: (1) hard disks, (2) videotape (primarily VHS), (3) MiniDV (primarily for digital video camcorders), (4) digital tape, (5) audiotape, and (6) all others (audio md, zip, flash, floppy disk). All the original optical storage, paper storage, and film storage was less than 8% of total original information in 2002. Note that this is original information, which explains how the optical storage category can be so low despite the hundreds of millions of DVDs shipped during the year. For example, this calculation only considers the first copy of *Pirates of the Caribbean* as original content, not the millions of additional copies sold.

Total world information production is so large that the Berkeley researchers need to use information measurement units as large as an exabyte. Consumers are familiar with hard disks measured in gigabytes (10^9 bytes). One thousand gigabytes is a terabyte, 1,000 terabytes is a petabyte, and 1,000 petabytes is an exabyte (10^{18} bytes). The lower limit estimate of original

Table 3.1

Worldwide Production of Original Information if Stored Digitally, 2002 Units are terabytes of information (1000 gigabytes, 10^{12} bytes)				
	Upper est.	Lower est.	% of total	Growth since 1999
Paper	1,634	327	0.029%	36.17%
Film	420,254	76,690	7.492%	−2.65%
Magnetic	5,187,130	3,416,230	92.477%	86.60%
Optical	103	51	0.002%	27.16%
Total	5,609,121	3,493,298		

Source: Table 1.2, Lyman, Peter and Hal R. Varian, "How Much Information," 2003. Retrieved from http://www.sims.berkeley.edu/how-much-info-2003.

information is 3.4 exabytes in 2002, a growth of more than 62% from their estimate for 1999.

Multimedia, primarily video, dominates the production of original information. In Chapter 2, we saw how the digital world is using increased digital power to handle video and sound as well as text and data. This includes digital video, displays capable of moving between alternative forms of content, and storage capacities sufficient to handle video requirements. The results of the Berkeley study show that this trend creates an ability to tap the vast reserve of new stored information.

> New Information Flows

Information storage is only part of the information landscape. Table 3.2 highlights a different view, the flow of new information. The important media are traditional broadcast (radio, television), the Internet (email, Web, messaging, file transfer), and voice communication (wire line, cellular). The total across these four information channels is 17.9 exabytes, or 17,900 terabytes. The surprising features of this table are the very large amount of new information in telephone calls and the relatively minor new information role played by mass media broadcasting.

As researchers have long realized, communication dramatically outpaces content in information flow.[14] Although listeners and viewers spend considerable time each day consuming broadcast media, the overlap in consumption is very high. Telephone calls, on the other hand, are nearly always unique. Each call between two individuals creates a unique dialogue and exchange of information. It is the rare case, such as in taped telemarketing or broadcast investor calls, that multiple recipients receive the same phone content.

Internet content is an intermediate case between the extremes of telephone and television. There is considerable overlap in broadcast email (such as spam), but email between individuals is much more like a phone call. Standard web pages and shared files (such as MP3s) are common across a wide audience, but personalized web pages and searches contain considerable original content.

The volume of voice communication continues to grow, even as mobile begins to substitute for the traditional wireline connections of standard telephony. Table 3.3 illustrates the

Table 3.2

Summary of Electronic Flows of New Information in 2002 (Terabytes)		
Flows of Original Information		
Medium	In 2002	% of Total
Radio	3,488	0.02%
Television	68,955	0.39%
Internet	532,897	2.98%
Telephone	17,300,000	96.62%
Total	17,905,340	

Source: Table 1.9, Lyman, Peter and Hal R. Varian, "How Much Information", 2003. Retrieved from http://www.sims.berkeley.edu/how-much-info-2003 on March 15, 2006.

Table 3.3

Communication Volume in the United Kingdom			
	Wireline calls *All operators*	Wireless calls *All operators*	SMS & MMS *All operators*
2003 Q2	14,657	84,848	5,241
2003 Q3	15,128	82,467	5,277
2003 Q4	15,198	82,520	5,719
2004 Q1	15,035	85,352	6,122
2004 Q2	15,504	77,465	6,154
	(Million minutes)	(Million minutes)	(Million messages)

Source: U.K. Office of Telecommunications

growth and relative shares in the United Kingdom, where the government publishes a detailed breakdown.

As the i-mode example shows, the distinction between telephony and the Internet is blurring. Messaging and email can substitute directly and through the same handset for a phone call. Voice-over-IP is a technology for conducting phone calls using exactly the same technology as for other Internet files. Researchers in the future will have a challenging time segmenting between telephony and the Internet as the Internet evolves.[15]

> *Online Communication*

> Email

Email continues to be the leading driver of online usage. The importance of email stems from several sources. One, it is the leading online communication method between friends, family, and co-workers. Two, it is the major driver of Internet usage frequency. Once online to read their email, web page visits become more popular. Three, email has evolved to include more HTML and Web-like capabilities, making email a more effective communications and marketing device.

From a marketing perspective, perhaps the most important characteristic of email is the potential of a dialogue with current or prospective customers. Brondmo emphasizes that a wide range of consumer activities can trigger this dialogue, and includes a mixture of manual and automated response capabilities using web sites and email.[16]

One of the fundamental aspects of email is its ability to conduct asynchronous dialogue, with messages distributed over time. Each of the steps in Table 3.4 can occur rapidly, but they can take hours or days to complete. This permits a more flexible communication structure, reinforces the efficiency of email, and allows users to respond when convenient. Critical messages and alerts can lead to rapid response. Conversely, later sessions handle email newsletters, distribution lists, and less pressing social messages.

This asynchronous feature is, in the phrase of software engineers, "both a bug and a feature." While efficient, email marketers cannot rely on immediate attention or processing. Lack of or late response to time-sensitive messages may lead to frustration and resentment when received after the offer or opportunity expires. While some workers are increasingly adopting technologies such as Blackberry or cell phone email, most consumers have not. Marketers must build into their messaging a reasonable lag between offer and expiration. As we will see in Chapter 12, this limits some of the valuable opportunities of instant offers.

Time lags can also impair email as a method of shared experience between friends. Rather than use email, many online participants are turning to a more immediate online communication method. One of the leading alternatives to email is instant messaging, which combines the direct communication capabilities of email with the immediacy of synchronous communication.

> Instant Messaging and SMS

Instant messaging is the second leading direct communication method behind email (Table 3.5). By the summer of 2004, more than 43% of U.S. Internet users engaged in instant messaging at least once a month. On a typical day, 12% of Internet users use instant messaging.[17] Usage tilts heavily toward younger demographics, especially those age 18–27. Many in this demographic use instant messaging more than email, logging in to their instant messaging system several times a day. They log on for longer stretches of time, with more than 35% of Gen Y (born between 1981 and 1995) users on for about an hour on a typical day.

Table 3.4

Incorporating Email into a Customer Dialogue			
Dialogue Action	**Action Type**	**Dialogue Response**	**Response Type**
Consumer first visits web site.	(M) Manual	Greeted as first-time visitor; invited to sign up for email newsletter.	(A) Automatic
Consumer signs up for newsletter.	(M)	Personalized sign-up sequence; personalized welcome email.	(A) (A)
Consumer returns to web site.	(M)	Greeted by name; presented with relevant content and/or promotions.	(A) (A)
Marketer sends email notification.	(A/M)	Open email; clicks on link.	(M) (M)
Consumer makes purchase.	(M)	Purchase confirmation email; automatic cross-sell email.	(A) (A)
Marketer email promotion.	(A/M)	Opens email; clicks to purchase.	(M) (M)
Consumer sends customer service email.	(M)	Confirmation email; automated email response; human email response; live chat response.	(A) (A) (M) (M)
Marketer sends customer service email follow-up.	(A/M)	Click-through to web site.	(M)
Marketer sends email newsletter.	(A/M)	Opens email; clicks though for more information.	(M) (M)

Source: Hans Peter Brondmo, (2000), *The Engaged Customer: Email Strategies for Creating Profitable Customer Relationships,* *Harper Business,* pp. 114–115. Reprinted by permission of HarperCollins Publishers.

The most active instant messaging users multi-task. Multi-tasking while messaging tilts toward the youngest demographic that Pew tracks. Instant messaging is social in two ways, allowing direct communication and letting participants share ongoing real-world experiences with their friends. As seen in Japan, messaging that combines mobile capabilities can be a powerful social force. Younger users, some using mobile phones and PDAs, regularly link to their computer-based friends. Marketing implications are obvious and potentially very important.

> *Online Content*

> The Shape of the Web

The most influential online content for most Internet users is the Web, with a collection of more than 8 billion pages, appearing on millions of web sites. These web sites and pages vary dramatically in size and importance. Some sites, such as Yahoo! or MSN, have tens of thousands of pages. Others are a simple landing page with minimal information.

Table 3.5

Trading Off Online Communication Methods		
Email vs. IM Which do you use most frequently?		
	The percent of internet users in each generation who use IM	Percent of IM users who use IM more than email	Percent of IM users who use email more than IM
Gen Y	62%	57%	19%
Gen X	37	16	24
Trailing Boomers	33	18	24
Leading Boomers	29	7	16
Matures	25	<1	7
After Work	29	<1	5

Source: Pew Internet & American Life Project Training Survey, February 2004. Reprinted by permission of Pew Internet Project.

Research is discovering the shape of the Web, regularities that have emerged in its first decade of life. First, the Web has a "bow tie" shape critical to the working of search engines.[18] At the heart of the Web is a core set of highly linked web sites. Starting with any web site in the core, a web searcher can follow links and eventually visit all of the other web sites in the core.

A second feature of the Web is its unequal nature, especially within the core. Google's PageRank uses a weighting measure that views links as a form of importance voting. Highly connected sites are important, and the links that they establish to other sites create additional importance for these target sites. As we will see in Chapter 7, the distribution of links within the core has very wide variability and follows a power distribution.

A third important feature of the Web is origination and termination sites. Origination sites are sites with outward links pointing into the core, but without links on other sites pointing toward them. They can become isolated and difficult to find. Termination sites are the opposite, with pages in the core pointing at them but without outbound links pointing traffic back. While not shown in Figure 3.4, there are also many isolated "islands," web sites and web pages without links in or out.

The bowtie shape of the web is a snapshot of the entire shape of the Web. Web searchers find a different structure when they study smaller portions of the Web.[19] At a medium or even smaller scale of "magnification," such as a snapshot of the organization of part of the core, a different picture emerges. Figure 3.5 shows the web structure at two progressively smaller scales. At medium scale, the most apparent feature is clustering, where communities of interest have a high degree of linkage to each other. Clustering is extremely important for the social analysis of networks, discussed later in this chapter. Drilling down even further on one of these clusters, we get the structure on the right. This indicates the structure at the level of a small set of focused web pages. These are the scales especially relevant both for usability (see Chapter 7) and traffic building (see Chapter 8).

Change is another important feature of the Web. While the identity of core, termination, and origination sites tend to be stable, within these sites many pages change weekly. A sample of web sites tracked weekly over a full year found that on average 8% of the sites' pages change

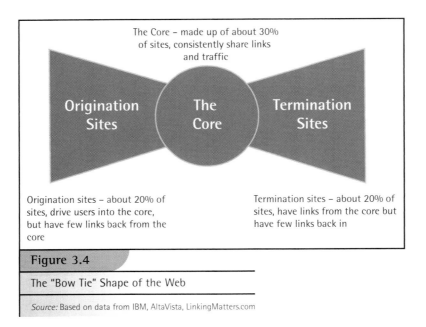

The Core – made up of about 30% of sites, consistently share links and traffic

Origination sites – about 20% of sites, drive users into the core, but have few links back from the core

Termination sites – about 20% of sites, have links from the core but have few links back in

Figure 3.4

The "Bow Tie" Shape of the Web

Source: Based on data from IBM, AltaVista, LinkingMatters.com

every week, with a low of 3% and a peak of 15% (Figure 3.6). This high rate of page creation and deletion resulted in fewer than 50% of the pages from these sites surviving for a year. While the goal of the study was to demonstrate the challenges and difficulties of maintaining accurate search engines and archives, it also demonstrates the high volume of new content contained in the Web at any one time.

The rapid change in pages, and the large size of the Web, raises the cost and complexity of maintaining a search engine. A marketer trying to improve search engine placement and the

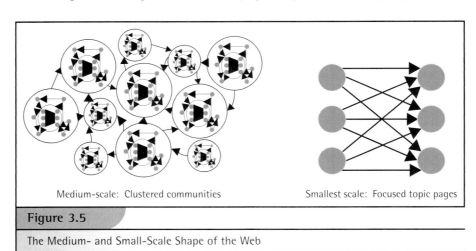

Medium-scale: Clustered communities

Smallest scale: Focused topic pages

Figure 3.5

The Medium- and Small-Scale Shape of the Web

Source: Gary W. Flake, David M. Pennock, and Daniel C. Fain, "The Self-Organized Web: The Yin to the Semantic Web's Yang," IEEE Intelligent Systems, 2003, 2.

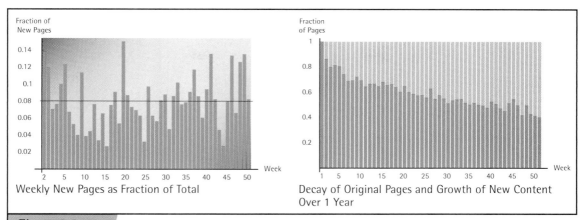

Weekly New Pages as Fraction of Total

Decay of Original Pages and Growth of New Content Over 1 Year

Figure 3.6

The Highly Dynamic Form of the Web Shown by the Creation and Deletion of Pages

Source: Alexandros Ntoulas, Junghoo Cho, and Christopher Olston, (2004), "What's New on the Web? The Evolution of the Web from a Search Engine Perspective," Proceedings of the WWW2004, May 17–22, New York, New York.[20]

quality of their search engine listings (discussed in Chapter 8) needs to assist these engines by linking closely into the core. This requires mixing the novelty of new pages with the benefits of stable content capable of generating links from other sites.

Figure 3.7 illustrates the slowdown in the growth of new public web sites after the rapid growth expansion of the 1990s.[21] However, despite the slowdown in the addition of web sites, the earlier results on page turnover shows that content is neither static nor durable. Anyone attempting to attract attention online is battling a constantly changing landscape of content and links.

Blogs

One of the fastest growing areas of online influence are blogs, web sites comprised of short and frequent postings by one or more authors, either on a focused subject or ranging over many topics. Blogs are an evolution of the much older bulletin boards and USENET discussion boards, with an increased emphasis on individual point of view and frequent commentary.

As measured by incoming links (which is the main metric in the PageRank algorithm of Google), blogs rival the leading media sites in importance and online popularity. Blogs such as Slashdot, Plastic, and Davenetics rival the *Washington Post* or the *Guardian*. During the presidential campaign of 2004, blogs were often the "rapid response" avenue of the candidates or interested supporters. In other areas, such as technology developments, they become the leading source of breaking news.

By the end of 2003, researchers documented more than 4 million active blogs. Marketers are interested in blogs as a source of consumer word-of-mouth. Market researchers are experimenting with techniques of collecting mentions of brands, products, and services to detect trends and problems in the marketplace.

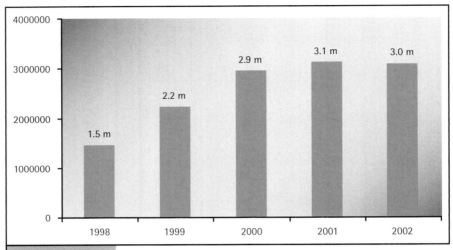

Figure 3.7

Number of Public Web Sites: 1998–2002

Source: Edward T. O'Neill, Brian Lavoi, and Rick Bennett, "Trends in the evolution of the Public Web: 1998–2002."
Copyright © 2003 OCLC Computer Library Center, Inc., appearing in *D-Lib Magazine,* April 2003.

Figure 3.8

Not All Communication is Desirable

Source: Copyright Guardian Newspapers Limited 2005

> RSS and Podcasts

Blogs require a visitor to remain sufficiently interested to repeatedly come back and visit a site. While some readers will actively do this, especially during high-interest times, competition over time, inertia, or some other distraction can lead to long lapses between visits. One rapidly growing alternative is the use of RSS, an acronym for really simple syndication. RSS allows a reader to subscribe to a blog or other content source as an actively monitored channel. Whenever content changes, the system automatically notifies and forwards descriptions of the changes. RSS readers, such as is built in to the FireFox browser, make a quick glance and link to subscribed channels much more likely than simply browsing.

Building on the RSS system, podcasts let a user subscribe to audio content. Subscribed through podcast readers, these podcasts play over desktop computers or MP3 players such as the iPod. These subscribed channels appear as playlists, right next to songs and other media, ready for consumption whenever convenient.

Several features of RSS in general and podcasts in particular, make this an exciting concept. First, the inertia of users goes from a negative with blogs to a positive for subscribed podcasts. Subscribed content automatically appears whenever a MP3 player synchronizes. A sponsored channel, much like dedicated and segmented radio stations, becomes feasible with a very low budget and communication costs. Audio is highly evocative and can be much more persuasive than text, and it allows consumption while involved in other tasks.

Technology Standards

> *A Key to Growth: Scalability Through Standards*

The Internet often resembles a living ecosystem more than any specific product or technology. Each day brings growth, decline, change, and surprising developments. Clever entrepreneurs and designers are constantly at work, with new ways of using old approaches and completely new means of seeing and interacting with the world. Successful innovations catch the attention of more innovators, investors, and customers. Entire communities of customers, suppliers, products, and services spring into existence.[22]

> Open Standards

Growth has been possible because of open technology standards. Open standards exist when the software protocols and operations are made readily available, documented widely, and not controlled by any single organization.[23] Throughout the history of computing, innovations and technological systems relied heavily on proprietary standards, owned and controlled by specific companies.[24] Open standards relax this control by a dominant firm and permit many firms to compete and innovate.

The cross-platform podcast receiver

Figure 3.9

iPodder Podcasting Software

Source: Courtesy of iPodder Lemon Team

Open standards have had many benefits. One benefit is to provide a widely shared set of tools available to Internet users. Another is to encourage specialization. Once standards are set, producers can specialize in pieces of the solution, confident that their products will mesh with other software components. Prior to standardization, consumers tend toward "one-stop" solutions from single providers. In this early phase before standardization, proprietary solutions may be necessary to simultaneously provide the many solution pieces needed.

Open systems are one of the major reasons the Internet has spawned such entrepreneurial activity. As long as it follows the open standard rules, a startup company can focus on doing one thing very well. These many small innovations can add up and lead to much better performance for the system as a whole. Blogs, podcasts, RSS, and even HTML arose initially from small organizations or even individuals pioneering the approach.

> Scalability

Internet standards are crucial for allowing the network to grow rapidly, and to be scalable. Scalability is the capability to grow and add many new destinations, locations, paths, capabilities, and resources to a network without having to reengineer the design of the Net.

The Internet grows by allowing different, extensive systems of networks to develop and then specifying just enough detail to let these independent networks talk to each other and exchange packets. Standards develop that allow very different computers, speeds of connection, and sophistication of systems to coexist gracefully.

Scalability allows the Internet to operate without anyone owning or controlling the entire network. Someone responsible for its performance and capacity owns each portion of the Internet. Larger portions of the Net, controlled by regional Internet service providers (ISPs), negotiate agreements between themselves on transmitting packets to recipients on their networks. Their networks connect at a variety of exchange points, where packets make the transition between these private networks, in order to reach the worldwide audience.

> *A More Intelligent Internet*

> First-Generation Internet

As we saw in Chapter 1, disruptive innovations often experience a phase of rapid growth while still suffering from serious limitations. The same has been true for the Net. The most rapid growth of Internet hosts occurred prior to widespread broadband access, prior to effective online multimedia, prior to effective wireless networks, and without many of the technologies allowing secure Net access. What are now core features of the Internet experience were missing. Despite these gaps, the user base doubled more than seven times during the decade of the 1990s.

Internet technology is changing in important ways. A wide variety of supporting tools, such as web publishing software, have become routine. These better systems and services make it much easier for all to engage in basic Internet publishing without specialized staff and difficult initial investments. The technologies of basic web site design, maintenance, and flow of transactions are being simplified and streamlined.

A more profound change in the nature of the Internet network is also under way. Two core simplifications exist at the heart of the early Internet. This first-generation Internet served basic documents to anonymous users. These two simplifications have great power in promoting widespread usage, low entry costs, and freewheeling participation. They also greatly limit the power of the Internet to perform intelligently and securely.

> Second-Generation Internet

The second-generation Internet combines documents with much more descriptive information about their content with reliably authenticated users. The combination of content with meaning and users with reliable profiles creates many more opportunities and challenges for the intelligent matching of information to individual needs. We first consider the changes in content and then the changes in user identification.

The Semantic Web

HTML, the basic language of the Web, contains minimal information about the meaning of the information on web pages. HTML is a markup language, with a goal of helping to display information such as tables, titles, and text appropriately. The emphasis is appearance. Whether a table contains information about the weather, product prices, or names of friends is immaterial in HTML. HTML focuses on issues such as whether the table has highlighted text, uses Times Roman font, or centers the row.

Figure 3.10 gives an example of basic HTML. This is a page of information regarding the 2004 Toyota Prius. Each of the HTML tags utilize brackets, such as <title> for the title of the page, <table> for the beginning of a table. Note that the Prius picture is actually located on a remote Toyota web site and remotely accessed for the page. Below the code is what the page actually looks like.

A human looking at the simple web page can quickly identify that this is a web page about a car, it is made by Toyota, and what the price is. While a human can quickly comprehend the meaning of the information, automated processing systems are lost. Intelligent automatic processing of information requires much more careful labeling of information and content. Automated systems need keys identifying which text items are weather reports, what specific items are (for example) location, time, and temperature. Adding sufficiently descriptive tags and definitions makes it possible for information to sorted, combined, and "understood" by automated systems. Tim Berners-Lee, the original architect of

Basic HTML Commands for a First-Generation Web Page

```
<html>
<title>Toyota Prius</title>
<body>
<p align="center"><b><font size="4">Toyota Prius </font></b></p>
<table border="0" cellpadding="0" cellspacing="0" width="82%"
height="120">
  <tr>
    <td width="50%" height="19">Car maker: Toyota</td>
    <td width="50%" rowspan="5" height="1">
    <img alt src="http://www.toyota.com/prius/minisite/exterior/
    images/photo_2.jpg"
    align="top" border="0" width="254" height="133"></a></td>
  </tr>
  <tr>
    <td width="50%" height="19">Engine type:  Hybrid</td>
  </tr>
  <tr>
    <td width="50%" height="19">Price: $19,995</td>
  </tr>
  <tr>
    <td width="50%" height="19">Anti-lock brakes: yes</td>
  </tr>
  <tr>
    <td width="50%" height="1">...</td>
  </tr>
</table>
</body>
</html>
```

What It Looks Like

Toyota Prius

Car maker: Toyota

Engine type: Hybrid

Price: $19,995

Anti-lock brakes: yes

Missing Information that an Automated System Needs

> A description of what the page is about,
> Which specific words describe the engine, and
> What the price is.

Figure 3.10

First-Generation HTML is Missing Semantic Information

Source: © JEFF CHRISTENSEN/Reuters /Landov

the World Wide Web and a leader in improving the understanding of content, calls this the Semantic Web.[25]

Ontologies and metadata are central to a semantic web. An ontology is an agreed upon set of definitions, essentially a subject-oriented dictionary, for how information is organized and categorized. For example, a book has an author, a publisher, a title, a year, and a number of other descriptions. A semantic web begins to emerge when online book information includes agreed upon descriptors. These descriptive metadata are special tags that coexist with basic page layout HTML. For example, a book ontology including tags such as <author>, <publisher>, <language_used>, and <year published> allows an automated system to effectively locate all books by a certain author written after a certain year or all the books in a certain subject area published in Chinese.

Even a basic semantic web facilitates automated agents and search assistance. For example, imagine someone interested in buying a secondhand telescope. Currently, the best online route is to visit a main auction site such as eBay. When online content contains appropriate descriptors, a much wider continuous search is possible. Individualized search bots can monitor the Internet for postings of the relevant telescopes for sale, including the ability to identify what appear to be excellent values. Depending on the urgency of the opportunity, the system notifies the user through email, a cell phone call, instant messaging, or some other method. The better the ontology, the less chance of being interrupted for a poor match or missing a desired product.

The Authenticated User

The semantic web becomes even more powerful when combined with an understanding of individual tastes, history, and choices. Chapters 4 and 9 consider the many challenges, applications, and debates surrounding authenticated users. It lies at the heart of personalization, the control of intellectual property, the ability to keep Internet sites and data private, and the ability of marketers to accurately track the impact of messages and campaigns from release to final impact.

At the center of the process of identification are many standards needed to reliably authenticate individuals. This can be as simple as a secure password system, or as complicated as a process of biometric authentication based on fingerprints, eye scans, or voice recognition. Some Internet access devices, such as a cell phone, are by their very nature closely identified with a particular user. Others may require additional standards and add-ons to create identification. Chapter 4 considers these issues in depth.

The legal system exerts pressure on web site operators to utilize authentication standards. For example, in the United States the Child Online Privacy Protection Act (COPPA)[26] makes it illegal to collect personally identifiable information from anyone under 13 years of age. Web sites need to somehow verify that a visitor to their site is older than this before they can comfortably decide to collect names and other contact information. Countries around the world have special rules for online actions allowed or prohibited to their citizens. Simple convenience also encourages identification technologies. Online merchants such as Amazon.com try to make the shopping and checkout customized and convenient for the shopper, as when they store previous shipping and payment information. This convenience requires the ability to easily verify shopper identity. Robust authentication standards enable authentication with fewer questions, user ids, and passwords.

NETWORK SCIENCE

| The Geometry of Social Networks

> *Growth of a New Science*

New measurements often trigger scientific discoveries. Surprising patterns appear that do not fit conventional understanding and stimulate research. Studies reveal a complexity not appreciated before. The Internet itself provides a laboratory for exploring how networks grow and self-organize.

The past ten years of Internet growth and usage created a wealth of new measurements. Detailed web logs, search engine results, email logs, and other digital data revealed surprising patterns and complexity in network growth and usage. There has been an explosion of research by a wide variety of academics, creating a new "network science."[27] Researchers combine insights from marketing, economics, sociology, and even physics to understand the patterns in the structure of the Net and how individuals communicate and share information. In fact, Internet data is so useful it has helped discover patterns subsequently found in other social, biological, and physical networks.

Researchers contributed hundreds of articles on the new network science over the last decade. Five key features of the shape and evolution of networks are especially important for online marketers. These are:

> *Feature 1:* Network connections grow much faster than the number of participants. The growth of a communications network strongly enhances its value.
> *Feature 2:* Real networks typically have high local clustering. Friends tend to have the same group of friends and not know many other participants in the network.
> *Feature 3:* Social networks are small worlds. Connecting any two people on a network is usually possible with a small number of links.
> *Feature 4:* There is a very wide spread in participation by network members. Specifically, there are critical hubs and connectors, network members with far more links than average that dominate the network. Involvement of a network hub member dramatically speeds communication.
> *Feature 5:* Most networks are robust to losing members randomly, but are vulnerable to deliberate targeted attack.

These five features of network science shape online marketing. We consider each in detail.

> *Feature 1: Metcalfe's Law and Network Value*

> The Number of Conversations

A network's value grows quickly as participants join. Named for a networking company founder who popularized it, Metcalfe's Law captures the idea that the number of possible connections between members of a network expands much faster than the count of the members. Metcalfe's Law illustrates the important difference between an individual's value of a network and the value of the network as a whole. It provides a beginning framework for quantifying the strength of ties between network members, a method of thinking about spam, and such aspects of permission-based marketing as opt-in and opt-out. Metcalfe's Law is not an engineering result like Moore's Law. Rather, it results from the basic logic of pair-wise communication. When communication is valuable, a new user creates value for everyone already on the network. Every current member now has one more possible link.

Figure 3.11 shows the number of possible conversations among people in a group. If there are only two persons, only one conversation is possible. With three persons, three conversations can take place. A few more members show the accelerating growth rate. Metcalfe pointed out that the number of links in a fully connected network grows at a rate that is the square of the size of the network.

A simple formula shows how fast this grows. If there are n members of a network, they can connect to (n−1) other members. For undirected links (for example, person 1 linking to person 3 is the same as person 3 linking to person 1) we divide by 2.

Possible conversations in a complete undirected network $= n\times(n-1)\div2$ (3-1)

Even in a small network of 100, this gives $100\times99\div2 = 4950$ possible conversations. Moderate-sized networks create a rich communication setting.

> Metcalfe's Law and Community Value

Metcalfe's Law translates the number of connections in a network into a value for the network. In the original formulation, the translation is very simple. If each member of a conversation values it at a value $v = \$1$, the full value of a conversation is $2 per conversation. This gives us Metcalfe's Law:

Metcalfe's Law with everyone connected, each valuing connections at

$$\$1 = \$2 \times n\times(n-1)\div2 = \$n\times(n-1)$$ (3-2)

For situations that are more complicated it is useful to define network value based on individual values. Each member of the network above has an individual value of the network. This is the benefit that individual gets from joining the network. In the situation above, everyone

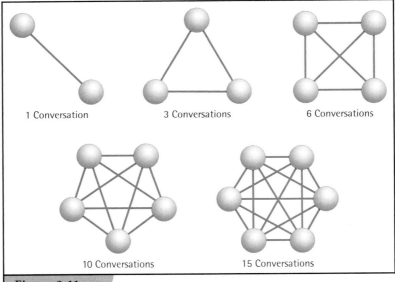

1 Conversation   3 Conversations   6 Conversations

10 Conversations   15 Conversations

Figure 3.11

The Value of a Complete Network Grows Rapidly

benefits the same from a connection. The full value of the network, the community value, is just the summation of each of these individual values.

$$\text{Community network value} = \Sigma \text{ (individual values in network)} \qquad (3\text{-}3)$$

Table 3.6 demonstrates this for a rising number of users. Equation (3-3) is true even when individuals have very different values and links to others.

The community value of a network grows at a much faster rate than individual values. When there are only a few members in the network, the community value is comparable to the individual values. As the network grows, the added links accelerate the growth of community value. Each new user benefits from joining the network and contributes a new value-laden connection to all the existing members of the network.

While the individual value of the network drives most individual's willingness to join a network, the community value is the main driver behind the actions of organizations, governments, and businesses. These organizations can often act collectively and work to capture the full benefits of a large network. This aggregation has been vital for the Internet. The earliest users of the Net were the U.S. military and universities around the world. While there were many reasons for this, these groups could justify the investment because they valued the network based on the total community value and not just on the payoff to the next individual. Community value also explains the strong commitment to network access by many companies. The community value grows rapidly as the total network grows. For a company, this translates into productivity, cost savings, and effective communication. The most fundamental insight of Metcalfe's Law is that networks can generate increasing returns. The bigger the network, the more valuable it becomes. It pays to be ubiquitous.

For example, consider a company with 40 employees in which each gets a value of $10/month for every email and intranet connection between its employees. The monthly community value is

$$(\$10)\times(40^2-40) = (1,600-40) \times \$10 = \$15,600/\text{month}$$

A value this high justifies extensive investments in networking equipment, training, and maintenance.

> Network Value When v Varies by User

If different consumers have very different values in using a network, the equal-value assumption will do a poor job of predicting which people benefit most from the network. If there are large groups of individuals who never communicate with each other, then the equal-value assumption will overvalue the network. In other cases, a user's connection value v may rise steeply once the network reaches a critical size threshold. An estimate based on an equal-value assumption would miss this spike in v and, consequently, understate the network's value.

To get an accurate value of a network with changing communication values, we need to reflect

Table 3.6

Individual and Community Values of a Network

Network Size	Individual A's Value	Community Value
1 (just A in network)	0	0
2 (A, B in network)	v	$2v = 2\times1\times v$
3 (A, B, C in network)	$2v$	$6v = 3\times2\times v$
...	...	...
26 (A, B, C, . . ., Z)	$25v$	$650v = 26\times25\times v$
n (A, B, C, . . ., Z, . . ., n)	$(n-1)v$	$n\times(n-1)v = (n^2-n)v$

how the value of communication differs among individuals. This depends on communication-value pairs, and the network is directed. Each link in Figure 3.11 now has arrows at each end, indicating that a link may not have the same value in each direction.

We denote these link values by v_{ij}, the value v to person i of a network link to person j. High-value communication, say between a supplier and a vendor, will show up as a large positive value for v_{ij}. Low-value communication, say between two acquaintances who rarely exchange emails, have a low but positive value. In some important cases, v_{ij} is negative. This happens when the presence of a communication link between i and j imposes costs on individual i. Spam is the most important example of this.

We can now calculate the personal and community value of a network that work in many situations. As noted earlier, for all different individuals who might be on the network, we define v_{ij} as the value of user i having a link to user j. We define $\delta_{ij} = 1$ if a link actually is present (a link pair) and $\delta_{ij} = 0$ if it is not. A link can be missing either because of a missing physical connection or because of filters. Filters allow users to screen and eliminate communication links selectively. With filtering technology, messages may be able to go from individual i to j, but not from j to i. In that case, we would have $\delta_{ij} = 1$, but $\delta_{ij} = 0$.

With these definitions, we have a more useful formula for both individual and network values. It is helpful to have the shorthand INV_i for the individual network value of individual i.

$$\begin{aligned} \text{Individual Network Value } i \quad &= INV_i = \Sigma_j \, v_{ij} \times \delta_{ij} \\ \text{Community Network Value} \quad &= \Sigma_i \, INV_i = \Sigma_i \Sigma_j \, v_{ij} = \delta_{ij} \end{aligned} \tag{3-4}$$

A consumer may have very different values for different clusters of users. For example, a consumer might have a small group of 50 friends and business interactions where the connection value is $5, a larger group of 500 with a connection value of $0.10, and a much larger group of 5,000 where the expected benefit is only $0.01 per connection. For this consumer, all other links could have zero value. This individual has $INV = (50 \times \$5) + (500 \times \$.10) + (5,000 \times \$.01) = \$250 + \$50 + \$50 = \$350$.

The community value in clustered networks rises considerably slower than Metcalfe's law. If this total network had 25,000 members, each with the same pattern of values as the previous example, then the total community value would be $25,000 \times \$350 = \$8,750,000$.

> Opt-In, Opt-Out, and Spam

Spam clearly demonstrates the negative impact a limited number of network members impose on the community value of the network. System operators and spammers engage in an escalating "arms race" of spamming and filtering techniques. Spam filters must balance two types of errors. False positives are the legitimate messages classified as spam that do not make it to their intended recipients. False negatives are the actual spam messages that clog in boxes with hoaxes about Nigerian fortunes, promises of increased physical performance, cheap mortgages, prescriptions, porn sites, or any number of other products.

Spammers attach a small positive value to any one user, while recipients have a negative value for the unsolicited communication. Many individuals, as well as AOL and other online services, try to break the links between themselves and the spammers with filters. On the Web, many parents and schools want to set link pairs equal to zero for "adult" sites. Being able to set some of the $\delta_{ij} = 0$ restores value for both email and the Web.

This issue occurs for many Net marketers during online user registration. As part of software registration, online publications, or other customer interactions, it is possible for a marketer to collect personalized information. Email addresses are especially useful. Marketers must choose what terms they offer for these names. They can choose

> *No restrictions.* The company accepts no restrictions on its use of information, including unsolicited email and the selling of information to others. Many of the v_{ij} may be negative as email lists get sold and used by spammers.
> *Opt-out.* The customer can choose not to receive any solicitation. However, without making this effort, the information (including email address) may be used or sold. Negative v_{ij} may exist but tend to be limited over time if the opt-out provision is available and honored.
> *Opt-in.* The customer must actively give permission before any use of the personalized information is allowed. Almost all v_{ij} will be positive for messages received, but many of the $\delta_{ij} = 0$ because of failure to opt in.
> *No sharing.* No personalized information is used or made available to any other organization. Many of the $\delta_{ij} = 0$ because of lack of knowledge of audience email addresses.

The most important choice is between no restrictions and the other alternatives. The cost of sending email is so low that unrestricted and unwanted email can quickly become a source of Internet pollution. This harms both consumers and email providers. Consumers respond by aggressively adopting filters, dropping service, and complaining to authorities.

The choice between opt-in and opt-out is complicated by a marketer's plans and by legal issues. Evidence suggests that opt-in leads to fewer customers connected, but they are likely to be more interested and valuable customers.[28] An opt-out plan may be the best choice for a company that will self-regulate and send only a limited number of email offers.

> *Feature 2: Clustering*

> What is Clustering?

One of the oldest recognized patterns in social networks is clustering. Clustering is the tendency for individuals to share close friends, co-workers, and family members. In a clustered network, if A and B and A and C are friends, then it is likely that A and C are also friends. The social networks of friends overlap. This is seen in Figure 3.12, where Ego has links to nearby members of the network. If we look closely at the links of these friends, individuals linked to Ego are much more likely to be linked themselves than are more distant network members.

We measure an individual's clustering coefficient by looking at the number of links between friends compared to the maximum number of possible links. For

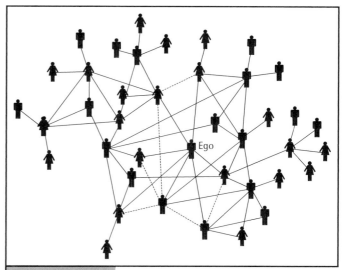

Figure 3.12

Clustering is Standard in Social Networks

Source: Albert-Laszlo Barabasi, *Linked: The New Science of Networks,* (New York: Perseus Publishing, 2002), 43.

example, imagine being able to look at the email address book of Ego. Assume there are 99 addresses in Ego's book. The denominator of Ego's clustering coefficient is just the Metcalfe number for these 100 people (Ego plus her 99 acquaintances). As we saw earlier, this number is $(1/2) \times 100 \times (100-1)$. For the numerator, we find how many actual connections there are. Ego has 100, person 1 may have 30 of these names in their book, person 2 might have 12, person three may have 52, all the way up to person 99. In other words, Ego's clustering coefficient is the actual number of connections between these 100 people divided by the maximum number of these connections.

$$C_{Ego} = \frac{\text{(Actual number of connections among Ego's friends)}}{\text{(Maximum number of connections between Ego's friends)}}$$

Clustering coefficients must lie between zero and one. In a fully connected network, where every one of Ego's friends links to each other, the clustering coefficient is exactly one. On the other hand, if friends are much more randomly determined, then anyone's clustering coefficient will be very close to zero. There are hundreds of millions of people with email accounts. If people acquired email addresses randomly, then shared addresses in any two people's account would be rare. But acquaintances aren't random. Research demonstrates a high degree of sharing of friends and acquaintances, with clustering coefficients in the 10–40% range.[29]

> Clustering, Strong Ties, and Weak Ties

A major impact of clustering is the high overlap in information among friends and acquaintances. Information, word-of-mouth, opinions, and computer viruses tend to flow very rapidly within clusters.

A second implication of high clustering is the tendency of information to "get stuck." When there is high clustering, information travels quickly within a single cluster but has a hard time jumping to another cluster. Clustering makes it difficult for information to flow throughout the entire network. Fads and disease tend to "die on the vine" with clustering.

This leads to one of the most important insights about networks and clustering. Individuals have uneven degrees of strength of friendship and connections. Links with members of "their cluster," such as close friends and colleagues, tend to be deep. These are strong ties, frequent contact, idea sharing, and mutual reliance. However, individuals also have more remote casual connections with individuals in distant social groups. These are weak ties.

In one of the classic studies in social networks, Grannovetter documented the crucial importance of weak ties for the flow of information.[30] Weak ties provide the bridge between clusters that prevent information from being stuck. Eliminating a strong tie tends not to limit information flow, as another friend will pass it along. Eliminating a weak tie can be more serious and can block the flow of communication. One of the powers of the Internet, especially email, has been to expand the range of weak ties. Email distribution lists make it easy to gather information from distant groups and individuals, without imposing the cost and social obligation of phone calls or personal meetings. Instant messaging, on the other hand, strengthens strong ties while not incorporating many weak ties.

Recent research on clustered networks stresses the importance of cluster categories as an alternative to weak ties. Individuals actually have a range of groups they belong to with relatively strong ties. Work colleagues form one type of cluster, family another, and parents of children another. Each of these clusters may be highly connected. However, if we look at the entire network of individuals, these clusters may not overlap much. An individual's membership in these different groups is central to the sharing of information.

Email can reinforce many of these different cluster categories. Parents share email about their children's school or sports activities. Families create email distribution lists. Work sites mix email links, intranets, and other shared resources to speed and deepen the flow of information.

> *Feature 3: It IS a Small World After All*

Within hours of its release, the SoBig.F virus spread around the world, clogging email systems and overloading email servers. At its peak, AOL found the virus in more than half of the 40.5 million emails it processed in one day.[31] While one of the fastest spreading email viruses on record, it was hardly unique.[32] Clearly, the high clustering described above does not stop the spread of the email viruses. One of the major reasons for this is another important property of most realistic complicated networks: they share the small world property.

The small world property exists when it is possible to connect any two members of the network with a relatively small number of links. In a complete network, such as we see in Figure 3.11, the small world property immediately follows from the direct connection between each pair of members. With clusters, it is more surprising. Somehow, clusters connect more closely than the picture in Figure 3.13 would suggest.

Insight into the small world property comes from a game played with movie stars—the *Six Degrees of Kevin Bacon*. The goal is to link Kevin Bacon with some other actor based on a shared presence in a movie cast. Define Kevin Bacon's number as 0. If actors, such as Kevin Costner or Tom Cruise, have appeared in a movie with Bacon they have a Bacon Number of 1. Those who have been in a movie with someone with a Bacon Number of 1 have their own Bacon Number of 2, and so on. With this definition, we find Tim Curry has a Bacon Number of 2 via Tom Cruise or one of 3 through Susan Sarandon. Using the minimum, Curry's Bacon Number is 2. There can be multiple routes to this same shortest path. For example, another route would be Bacon and Laura Linney in *Mystic River*, Linney and Curry in *Congo*. Curry can only shorten his Bacon Number (to 1) by acting directly in a movie with Kevin Bacon.

Researchers at the University of Virginia have taken the argument out of the game by creating a web site that can calculate any actor's Bacon Number. Indeed, the small world property of the social network of movie actors is very clear from their results. Figure 3.14 gives Bacon Numbers for all the half-million actors that appear in the Internet Movie Database, one of the most comprehensive movie industry databases in existence. As of August 2003, no actor in the database has a Bacon Number more than 8. The vast majority of actors have a Bacon Number 5 or less, and the average Bacon Number is 2.941.

The key insight from networks of actors holds true for networks such as email systems. Clustering is consistent with the small

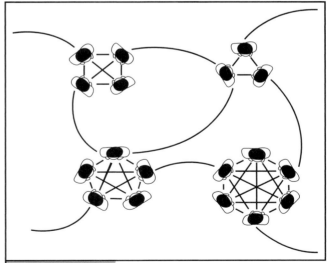

Figure 3.13

Clustered Networks Rely on Weak Ties for Sharing Information

Source: Albert-Laszlo Barabasi, *Linked: The New Science of Networks,* (New York: Perseus Publishing, 2002), 43.

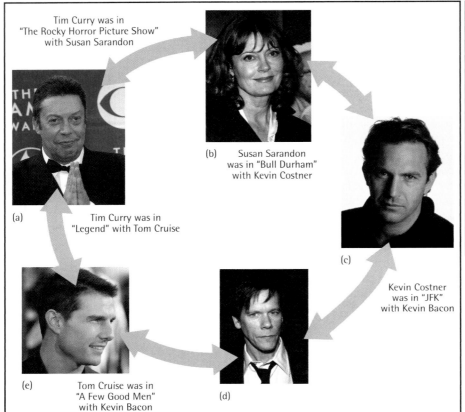

Tim Curry was in
"The Rocky Horror Picture Show"
with Susan Sarandon

(a)

Tim Curry was in
"Legend" with Tom Cruise

(b)   Susan Sarandon
was in "Bull Durham"
with Kevin Costner

(c)

Kevin Costner
was in "JFK"
with Kevin Bacon

(e)   Tom Cruise was in
"A Few Good Men"
with Kevin Bacon

(d)

Bacon Number	# of people
0	1
1	1673
2	130851
3	349031
4	84165
5	6718
6	788
7	107
8	11

Figure 3.14

The Six Degrees of Kevin Bacon and the Small World of Hollywood

Source: 3.14a © Frederick M. Brown/Getty Images; 3.14b © FRANCIS SPECKER/Landov; 3.14c © LAURA CAVANAUGH/UPI /Landov; 3.14d © Byron-SYG PARIS NEWMAN/CORBIS SYGMA; 3.14e © LAURA CAVANAUGH/UPI /Landov; 3.14 (table) From the Oracle of Bacon, based on data from the Internet Movie Database, http://www.cs.virginia.edu/

world property as long as there are enough links to "distant" parts of the network.[33] The weak links of Figure 3.13 are not enough to create a small world if the links are only to neighboring clusters. However, if some of the weak links jump to distant clusters it provides a dramatic fall in the average path length. With enough "bridges," the world is small for all (Figure 3.15).

One of the impressive features of the web site run by the University of Virginia is how quickly it finds its way through the maze of possible paths to create a shortest path between actors. A variety of startups are taking these algorithms and attempting to create similar capabilities using real networks of email addresses and personal acquaintances. LinkedIn is one of those companies.

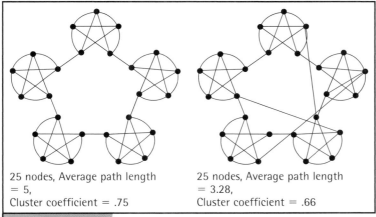

25 nodes, Average path length = 5,
Cluster coefficient = .75

25 nodes, Average path length = 3.28,
Cluster coefficient = .66

Figure 3.15

Distant Links Help Create a "Small World"

Source: Melissa A. Schilling and Corey Phelps, (2003), "Inter-firm Knowledge Networks and Knowledge Creation: The Impact of 'Small-World' Connectivity," Working Paper, New York University, September

Members invite other members to join in their network using an opt-in approach to build trust and permission. The system can then help find resources, such as job possibilities, based on information contained in each member's profile.

In Chapter 10, which discusses community, we will investigate some of the commercial and nonprofit applications of the small world property. These include referral networks and online community building. In these systems, the goal is to find short and trusted paths between individuals.

> Feature 4: The Importance of Hubs and Authorities

The key to ranking high in the actor game is a long career with many movies, thus becoming a hub of the acting network. Bacon is well connected because he has acted alongside 1,673 other actors. It turns out that Kevin Bacon is not, at least yet, the most connected actor in Hollywood. The same game can be played for any other actor, with average path distance calculated to the rest of the half million actors. As of June 2004, the most connected actor is Rod Steiger, with an average distance number of 2.68. Rod Steiger acted with 2,693 others before his death.[34]

The secret for an email virus to travel rapidly is to infect the email in-boxes of a few highly connected emailers, which rapidly transmits the virus throughout the entire network. Marketers have long understood the power of community centers and highly connected thought leaders. Hubs and authorities play a crucial role in communication through networks.

The vast amount of data from web site visits, email logs, and other online activity has shown that the "pattern of connectedness" often follows a very skewed but predictable pattern. While most people have a small- or modest-sized network of connections, some special members have many more links than average. Understanding this pattern can help marketers understand the likely patterns of information flow, word-of-mouth, and other communication that is based on trust and referrals.

The same pattern is true for links on web pages. While most pages have a modest number of outbound links (those on the page pointing to other pages) and inbound links (those on other pages pointing to it), there are some pages and sites far above average. From this, we get the concept of hubs and authorities. A hub is a network member with a large number of outbound links and an authority is a network member with a large number of inbound links.

> *Feature 5: Random Failure versus Deliberate Attack*

Clustering, the small world property, and the importance of hubs and authorities have immediate implications for the ability of a network to perform well even in the face of network members "dropping off" the network. If this failure or defection is random, it is unlikely to cause much of a change because of clustering and the small world property. Information or capabilities of the missing network member are likely to be present in other members of its cluster, which just as easily flows to the rest of the network. A deliberate attack on a network hub or authority can have a much more damaging result. The failure of a hub or authority simultaneously disrupts a large number of links, lowering performance and increasing congestion on alternative pathways.

MARKETING WITH NETWORKS

| Creating Value with Networks

The impact of networks on marketing is a new and rapidly changing field. For the Internet marketer, the findings of network science suggest several critical implications:

> *Ubiquity*—the ever-present power of a communication network accessible by all.
> *Speed*—networks accelerate many aspects of business and life.
> *Expectations*—the importance of network participants' views of successful technologies.
> *Sharing*—the efficiency that comes when a network allows reciprocity.
> *Specialization*—the newly found freedom firms and providers have to specialize in their key capabilities because of the network.
> *Virtual value activities*—the power of a network to deliver useful information.

Each of these implications creates new opportunities and challenges for marketers. Internet-only companies are using them to create new types of services. Traditional companies are using them to enhance their existing products and to create new divisions and capabilities. This section highlights some of the themes important to Internet marketing that arise because of networking. Remaining chapters discuss these themes in much more detail.

> *Ubiquity*

Networks are most valuable when ubiquitous. Any network, such as telephones, faxes, or cellular phones, is more valuable as its user base grows and it becomes a standard method of communication. A ubiquitous network allows customers, suppliers, and vendors to share the same data and technology costs. With ubiquity, both the individual and community values of the network are high.

As the Net reaches the mainstream in a country, marketers can rely on it to reinforce and complement the full range of marketing activities. Instead of a medium to reach only early adopters, it becomes a fully integrated part of marketing strategy and tactics. The same is true of innovations, such as the semantic web, which extend the basic network.

A ubiquitous network forces a shift in perspective and approach. Businesses find it much easier and cheaper to access global information. Using the network as a communication medium, whether through email, messaging, or dedicated private web networks, companies can trace their incoming supplies, their shipments in transit, and often the outgoing sales of their customers. This is changing the design of a number of distribution and supply channels. As network-aware software evolves, much of this production and sales information is automatically available, further improving speed and accuracy.

Ubiquity also drives a wide range of consumer software and devices. Users receive automatic protection from the most recent viruses with automatic updates downloaded with the Net. Music players work in the background and go online to access descriptive data, so songs display the proper artist and track information. New home systems rely on a wide range of standards to communicate effectively in the home. Small, cumulative improvements can have a big effect over time. The mainstream Net fosters "learning by doing" and "learning by using" by everyone. Over time, this results in dramatic improvements in performance and efficiency.[35]

> *Speed*

The small world property of the Net makes information flow more rapidly than ever before. The Web permits in-depth and persuasive information to be accessible whenever desired, email accelerates promotions and dialogue opportunities over regular mail, instant messaging feeds communication among friends and co-workers, and blogs create new authorities that create a powerful word-of-mouth.

One of the main areas for firms to take advantage of this is in their speed of learning. These new communication mechanisms, and an appreciation of their relative strengths and weaknesses, enhance the ability and necessity of tracking the market more closely. New avenues of feedback from consumers, both positive and negative, let a firm find new opportunities and fix errors faster than before. Sales rates can be tracked in near real time, allowing a change in production and distribution capabilities.

In Chapter 10, which discusses new products, we will see numerous examples of how the speed of the network is shortening product cycles, creating the ability to introduce beta versions and more rapid improvements in many offerings. Just as important, the speed of market research allows companies to find and fix difficulties. New communication mechanisms allow companies to increasingly substitute these online information methods for much more expensive traditional market research surveys and focus groups.

A ubiquitous Net makes it easy to take advantage of time zones by moving work as the day progresses. Online accesses can just as easily be arriving from eight time zones away as eight blocks away. The needs for customer support and interaction become more challenging in this new online world. Traditional office hours break down and service becomes "24/7" (twenty-four hours a day, seven days a week). Some companies have adapted to this new rigor by distributing support and development teams strategically around the world. A team in Europe begins the day, handing off to the United States as the European workday ends. The U.S. team can then transfer responsibility to a team in Asia, completing a 24-hour cycle.

Use of worldwide resources normally is unavailable to small business. Small businesses cope either by developing online-automated responses or by extending their day. One of the challenges facing effective customer support is to create 24/7 support without the need for the "three-shift" way of life.

> *Expectations*

> Publicity and Celebrity

Hype played an especially large part in early Net marketing efforts. At the height of the "dot com" boom thousands of articles covered the comings and goings of leading companies and entrepreneurs. Many major Internet firms made celebrities out of their key executives, especially young and visionary leaders.

One reason for the prevalence of hype and celebrity is the power of consumer expectations when networks are involved. As the personal value of a network grows with network size, and the community value grows even faster, companies are eager to create the impression that the network is rapidly growing. This is true for a wide range of Internet products and services.

> The Economic Logic of Hype

Expectations matter when an investment in a network makes sense for a user if the network reaches a critical mass. For simplicity, again assume that the individual value of a connection is given by v_i, so that an individual i values each possible connection the same. Assume that every user of a network must spend C to be connected, which again for simplicity is over the same time horizon as the benefit v.[36]

A user will find it valuable to belong to a network if the value of the network exceeds the cost:

$$v_i \times (n-1) > C$$

This inequality means the individual worth needs to be larger than the hookup cost divided by the number of possible conversations. Obviously, it is easier to satisfy this requirement when n is large.

$$v_i > C \div (n-1)$$

This inequality illustrates why expectations and hype can be valuable to anyone trying to create a network. It also shows how expectations of a large network can be self-fulfilling. The larger n is believed to be the lower the value of v_i that justifies joining the network. As long as everyone believes a network will be large, consumers will join and the network will be large. But if consumers think that the network will be small, only the highest-value users will join, and the network will remain small.[37]

When expectations matter so much, consumers want to pick winners and to feel good about their choices. Celebrity endorsements, media stories, and a general "buzz" around a product all create the impression that many other consumers are also making the same choice.[38] A big challenge for many companies is to make the endorsements convincing and believable.

> *Sharing*

Sharing resources online magnifies their capabilities. One such example is grid computing, in which hundreds, thousands, or occasionally even millions of standalone computers volunteer or sell spare capacity to attack difficult computing problems. SETI@home pioneered in these efforts. SETI has utilized nearly 500,000 "computer years" of idle machines over a span of three years to process radio astronomy signals in search of distant civilizations. As part of a screen saver program, fans of the effort permit SETI to make calculations with their idle machines. Network links exchange data for analysis and the results from each machine.[39]

Additional research teams are utilizing the power of grid computing. Both Folding@Home and Genome@Home connect thousands of computers to simulate the behavior of DNA and the proteins they produce.[40] Without the ability to parcel out these problems to thousands of individual computers automatically, the difficulty of the calculations would overwhelm any available computing resources. See Figure 3.16.

Scientific use of the Net often paves the way for commercial applications. Many of the file swapping and content sharing systems such as Kazaa and Gnutella take advantage of shared storage and

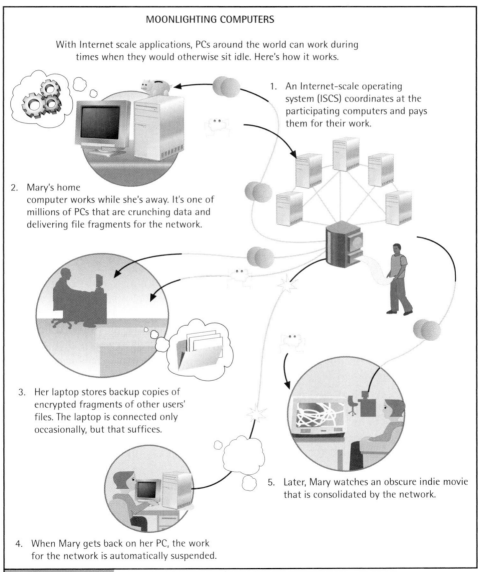

MOONLIGHTING COMPUTERS

With Internet scale applications, PCs around the world can work during times when they would otherwise sit idle. Here's how it works.

1. An Internet-scale operating system (ISCS) coordinates at the participating computers and pays them for their work.

2. Mary's home computer works while she's away. It's one of millions of PCs that are crunching data and delivering file fragments for the network.

3. Her laptop stores backup copies of encrypted fragments of other users' files. The laptop is connected only occasionally, but that suffices.

4. When Mary gets back on her PC, the work for the network is automatically suspended.

5. Later, Mary watches an obscure indie movie that is consolidated by the network.

Figure 3.16

Networks and Specialization

computing. While challenged by the recording industry as illegal, many users tap into a shared library of music, videos, and other digital information.

The ability to share does not imply equal participation. A study of Gnutella revealed very high levels of "free riding," where users tap into the library of online music without simultaneously allowing others to share. Adar and Huberman sampled the Gnutella system and found that more than 70% of Gnutella users share no files and more than 90% of users answer no queries. Free riding was widespread among all types of users.[41]

Entrepreneurs are actively developing grid computing for use by businesses and individuals. The goal is to turn supercomputing into a form of utility, where users can tap the grid when necessary just as they tap a grid for electricity or water. Users facing a problem beyond their home computer, such as on-demand voice recognition, can also use the Net to tap into shared resources. Some of the obstacles for commercializing a computing grid are the establishment of a cost-effective payment system and an "Internet operating system" capable of coordinating the sharing. Early demonstration projects such as SETI or Folding@Home avoid payment systems altogether, relying on the volunteer spirit of Net users. For more mundane and commercial operations, altruism is unlikely. Nonetheless, a fast and widespread network has the potential for tapping millions of powerful computers (growing more powerful every year) to leapfrog the computing capabilities of even the fastest single computer.

Sharing knowledge and experience in the form of reviews and ratings provide another rich source of marketing insights, opportunities, and challenges. We will consider this in detail in later chapters, and the mechanisms that encourage users to provide reviews and ratings, the credibility of these contributions, and the occasional need to intervene to counter negative information.

> *Specialization*

In 1776, Adam Smith wrote in *The Wealth of Nations*, "the division of labor is limited by the size of the market."[42] At the dawn of the Industrial Revolution, as new technologies and new markets were rapidly expanding, Smith's famous example of making pins showed how specialization leads to dramatically increased productivity. Other early examples of the virtues of specialization, such as the manufacture of guns in Birmingham, England, confirmed Smith's principle that jumps in productivity are possible as specialized firms and processes develop.

Education, consulting, banking, and insurance are some of the markets moving from local to national to global by going online. More important for many firms is the power of the Net to open many marketing processes to competition and specialization. This is furthering the trend of outsourcing such activities as customer and technical support. The network creates many more opportunities for specialization.

The Internet makes it much easier to bring together resources from a wide range of alliance partners specializing in providing particular content. Alliances and sharing have many benefits. They are fast and cheap, and they make it much easier for a company to expand offerings. Networks encourage this sharing by being able to deliver real-time information from many sources simultaneously. An ongoing marketing challenge is how to present these alliances. Should brands remain independent, or should they be merged? What is the impact of this decision on each member of the sharing arrangement? Many Web marketers are puzzled over these questions. These branding issues show up throughout our discussion, especially with respect to business models and traffic building.

> *Virtual Value Activities*

Creating value with information is one of the main skills of online marketing. The goal is to use and transform information in a manner that stands out from the ocean of information created each year and satisfies customer needs. Rayport and Sviokla refer to this process as creating virtual value.[43] Virtual value activities (VVAs) are the methods firms use to enhance information.

The virtual value steps are gathering, selecting and organizing, synthesizing, and distributing. Each improves value by raising the relevance and impact of information; allowing the customer to solve problems, make better decisions, or find more entertaining content. Virtual value analysis gives online marketers a tool for spotting information collection, design, and distribution opportunities to make their site a more valuable resource.

We briefly introduce virtual value in this section using the web site of Edmunds.com. Later chapters expand on the details of personalizing VVAs, building revenue models around different virtual value choices, improving usability with VVAs, and the appropriate use of the VVAs during new product design and pricing. An understanding of virtual value activities is one of the most important practical tools for online marketers in designing their communication and content strategies.

> Gathering

The first virtual value step is information gathering, using creativity, resources, and technology to collect a wide array of information as an input. In Chapter 2, we saw how digital cost reduction encourages archiving and building encyclopedic collections of information. The power of the network further encourages this by creating low-cost methods of information gathering from widely dispersed sources.

For Edmunds, which acts as an information intermediary for car and truck buyers and sellers, several sources of important information are obvious. Edmunds brings together new and used vehicle specifications, prices, and reviews. Archiving previous years' content makes it easy for Edmunds to maintain extensive information about cars and trucks ranging back a decade. Edmunds invests in gathering very detailed information about actual inventory and transaction prices of vehicles in markets around the country. They also collect a wide range of data that affect the actual prices paid by car buyers, such as current manufacturer incentives and dealer programs. Alliances with a variety of data providers and partners let them update this information in near continuous time (Figure 3.17).

Gathering information directly from other car owners is a very different source of material. Edmunds encourages this relatively cheap source of content by creating the "Town Hall," where visitors can chat about their experiences, post questions to other car owners, or enter their own evaluation of a make or model. While customer reviews can vary widely in quality and usefulness, they provide a valuable check on the accuracy and relevance of the other sources.

> Selecting and Organizing

Information organization, sometimes termed information architecture, is an emerging discipline. Well-organized information is easy to find, intuitively structured, and helps a visitor discover new material. It must also balance the business goals and objectives of the web site. In Edmunds's case, the balance is tilted toward the user, with multiple approaches to structuring and finding material.

For a marketer, the organizing phase starts with an analysis of customer needs and abilities. In Chapter 4, we look in detail at opportunities, problems, and biases consumers have in using the Web. Ease of use is one of the most important factors. Companies must also worry about language and cultural differences users have in accessing and using online material.

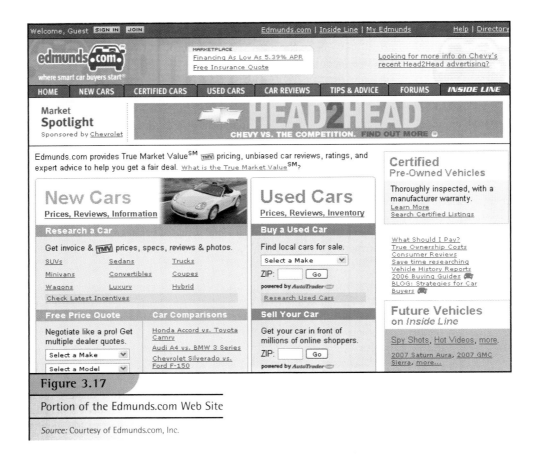

Figure 3.17

Portion of the Edmunds.com Web Site

Source: Courtesy of Edmunds.com, Inc.

Edmunds uses a variety of organizational approaches. At the level of the home page there are distinctions based on the vehicle being research, such as new versus used or the type of vehicle (car, SUV, truck). Material is organized in the navigation bar around product, research, ownership, or discussion. Farther down the home page there is a detailed topical directory allowing quick access using browsing. Highlighting new material lets frequent visitors distinguish what is most relevant for a return visit.

Selection must balance relevance against comprehensiveness. A good search capability allows users quick access to the most relevant material. Selecting high-quality reviewers provides readers with better insights and confidence. Selecting the right balance of news, information, and education makes the site both informative and enjoyable.

> Synthesizing

Proper synthesis of information is closely tied to the market segmentation and personalization strategies of a web site. Sophisticated sites try to build up a profile of usage so the most relevant material is the most obvious. For example, registered users of the Dell support site get better and more helpful responses as the system learns more about the computer systems they own and the sophistication of the user. Sites can implement this by allowing customers to reveal their abilities and needs. They learn from simple ratings that accompany articles from earlier searches. They can combine responses from other users that appear to have similar requirements and abilities.

Synthesis reflects business strategy as well. Low-cost or free information can be provided if it does not threaten more lucrative arrangements. Preferred customers may get more complete and timely reports than the general base of users. E*trade has used this strategy for access to industry analyst reports. Customers with larger balances and trading accounts qualify for a much wider range of studies and reports.

Edmunds uses synthesis as a competitive advantage with its development of an in-depth methodology for its True Market Pricing. This is a branded attempt to capture the actual prevailing prices for new and user cars. An explicit goal is to make True Market Pricing superior to the competitor Kelley Blue Book Value, which is based on more aggregate and national data.

> Distributing

Distributing information relies heavily on network capabilities. Simple web technologies make it easy to provide the service to any web user. Pages are designed to make them fast loading and easy to access. Common data formats allow the collection of data from many different providers in different locations. Most importantly, using the standard web browser format makes the Web an accessible and low-cost publishing system. Other mechanisms, such as downloading information to PDAs or cell phones, lets Edmunds push information out into users' hands when they visit an actual dealer.

The virtual value activities are a very useful framework for understanding many of the nuances of creating value with information. We cover these activities and their use in customer support and online quality improvement in much more detail in Chapter 8.

ENDNOTES

1. *Barry Wellman. (2001).* "Physical Place and CyberPlace: The Rise of Personalized Networking." *International Journal of Urban and Regional Research* 25(2), 227–252.

2. Duncan J. Watts. (2003). *Six Degrees: The Science of a Connected Age.* Norton, New York, p. 299.

3. See John M. Ratliff. (2002). "NTT DoCoMo and Its I-mode Success: Origins and Implications." *California Management Review*, 44 (3, Spring).

4. Howard Rheingold. (2002). *Smart Mobs: The Next Social Revolution*, Perseus, Cambridge, MA, 2002.

5. Reuters. (2003). "Japan leaps to world No. 2 in broadband-survey." July 14.

6. Early discussion of GPTS were motivated, in part, by the example of the Net. See, for example, Bresnahan and Trjtenberg. (1995). "General Purpose Technologies: Engines of growth?" *Journal of Econometrics* 65:83–108; Richard G. Harris. (1998). "The Internet as a GPT: Factor Market Implications." In *General Purpose Technologies and Economic Growth*, edited by Elhanan Helpman, MIT Press, Cambridge, MA.

7. And as part of consuming. See Yoram Wind and Vijay Mahajan. (2002). "Convergence Marketing." *Journal of Interactive Marketing* 16(2, Spring), 64–79.

8. Susan Decker, Chief Financial Officer of Yahoo!, presentation to the Stanford Institute for Economic Policy Research, December 2, 2004.

9. See various reports by Pew Internet & American Life Project at http://www.pewinternet.org/.

10. For example, Eric J. Johnson, Wendy W. Moe, Peter S. Fader, Steven Bellman, and Gerald L. Lohse. (2004). "On the Depth and Dynamics of Online Search Behavior." *Management Science* 50 (3, March), 306.

11. Decker, op.cit.

12. The most common form is 802.11.

13. For an example of this discussion, see John Seely Brown and Paul Duguid. (2000). *The Social Life of Information.* Harvard Business School Press, Boston. A very early discussion is present in Jacques Vallee. (1982). *The Network Revolution: Confessions of a Computer Scientist.* And/Or Press, Berkeley.

14. See Andrew Odlyzko, (2001), "Content is Not King," *First Monday*, February, available online. Also see Alfred D. Chandler Jr. and James W.

Cortada, editors, (2000), *A Nation Transformed by Information: How Information Has Shaped the United States From Colonial Times to the Present*, Oxford Press, Oxford.

15. Mirella Kleijnen, Ko de Ruyter, and Martin Wetzels. (2004). "Consumer Adoption of Wireless Services: Discovering the Rules, While Playing the Game." *Journal of Interactive Marketing* 18 (2, Spring).

16. Hans Peter Brondmo. (2000). *The Engaged Customer: Email Strategies for Creating Profitable Customer Relationships*. Harper Business, New York, NY, 114–115.

17. Pew/Internet. (2004). "How Americans Use Instant Messaging." *Pew Internet & American Life Project* September 1, 2004.

18. For example, A. Broder et al. (2000). "Graph Structure in the Web: Experiments and Models." *Proceedings of the 9th World Wide Web Conference*, Elsevier, New York, NY.

19. For example, Gary W. Flake, David M. Pennock, and Daniel C. Fain. (2003). "The Self-Organized Web: The Yin to the Semantic Web's Yang." *IEEE Intelligent Systems*.

20. Alexandros Ntoulas, Junghoo Cho, and Christopher Olston. (2004). "What's New on the Web? The Evolution of the Web from a Search Engine Perspective." *Proceedings of the WWW2004*, May 17–22, New York.

21. Edward T. O'Neill, Brian Lavoi, and Rick Bennett. (2003). "Trends in the evolution of the Public Web: 1998–2002." *D-Lib Magazine*, April 2003.

22. We will see more of this in Chapter 5. On this idea of business ecosystems, see J. Moore. (1996). *The Death of Competition*. Harper Business, New York, NY, especially pp. 66–68.

23. Many texts document the role of Net standards. A good source is Larry L. Peterson and Bruce S. Davie. (2003). *Computer Networks: A Systems Approach*, 3rd Ed., Morgan Kaufmann, San Francisco. For an industry leaders' perspective, see National Research Council. (2001). *The Internet's Coming of Age*. National Academy Press, Washington, D.C.

24. For example, Paul A. David and Dominique Foray. (2002). "Economic Fundamentals of the Knowledge Society." working paper, Stanford Institute for Economic Policy Research, 01–14, February.

25. Time Berners-Lee, James Hendler, and Ora Lassila. (2001). "The Semantic Web," *Scientific American*, May, 34–43.

26. Text of the law available at http://www.ftc.gov/ogc/coppa1.htm.

27. Albert-Laszlo Barabasi. (2002). *Linked: The New Science of Networks*, Perseus Publishing, Cambridge, MA.

28. For example, opt-in email lists cost substantially more per name than opt-out or unrestricted lists.

29. Duncan J. Watts. (2002). *Small Worlds: The Dynamics of Networks between Order and Randomness*, Princeton University Press, Princeton, p. 40.

30. M. Grannovetter. (1973). "The Strength of Weak Ties." *American Journal of Sociology* 78(6), 161–178.

31. Bill Tucker. "SoBig.F breaks virus speed records." CNN.com, August 22, 2003.

32. For a more complete discussion see Jeffery Boase and Barry Wellman. (2001). "A Plague of Viruses: Biological, Computer, and Marketing." *Current Sociology* 49(6), 39–54.

33. For an application see Melissa A. Schilling and Corey Phelps. (2003). "Inter-firm Knowledge Networks and Knowledge Creation: The Impact of 'Small-World' Connectivity." Working Paper, New York University, September.

34. Rounding out the top ten are Christopher Lee (2.659737), Dennis Hopper (2.678602), Donald Pleasence (2.682544), Donald Sutherland (2.682981), Max von Sydow (2.685544), Anthony Quinn (2.695204), Charlton Heston (2.695928), Harvey Keitel (2.697524), and Martin Sheen (2.700971).

35. See Nate Rosenberg. (1983). *Inside the Black Box*. Cambridge Press, Cambridge, for an extended discussion of learning by doing and learning by using.

36. In other words, if v is measured in months then C is the monthly amount of the sunk cost. Alternatively, v could be a benefit over the same useful life as the connection fee.

37. This has become a very active area of economics and is starting to be widely discussed in marketing. For early papers see Michael Katz and Carl Shapiro. (1986). "Technology Adoption in the Presence of Network Externalities." *Journal of Political Economy* 94:822–841. Joseph Farrell and Garth Saloner. (1985). "Standardization, Compatibility, and Innovation." *Rand Journal of Economics* 16:70–83; Brian Arthur. (1983). "On Competing Technologies and Historical Small Events: The Dynamics of Choice Under Increasing Returns." International Institute for Applied Systems Analysis, Working Paper WP-83-90. Ward Hanson. (1985). Bandwagons and Orphans: Dynamic Pricing of Competing Technological Systems Subject to Decreasing Cost, Ph.D. Dissertation, Stanford University Department of Economics. See Chapter 8 for more discussion.

38. For an early look at it see Nancy Austin. (1998). "Buzz: In Search of the Most Elusive Force in All of Marketing." *Inc.* May, 44–50. A more complete treatment is Emanuel Rosen. (2000). *The Anatomy of Buzz: How to Create Word of Mouth Marketing*. Currency Doubleday, New York.

39. See, for example, David P. Anderson and John Kubiatowicz. (2002). "The Worldwide Computer." *Scientific American* February.

40. Larson et al. (2002). R. Grant, ed. "Folding @ Home and Genome @ Home: Using Distributed Computing to Tackle Previously Intractable Problems in Computational Biology." *Computational Genomics*. Horizon Press.

41. Eytan Adar and Bernardo A. Huberman. (2000). "Free Riding on Gnutella." working paper, Internet Ecologies Area, Xerox Palo Alto Research Center, Palo Alto, CA 94304. This is one reason the record industry legally targeted the leading sources of music, who serve as hubs of the free music system.

42. Adam Smith. (1776). *An Inquiry into the Nature and Causes of the Wealth of Nations*. Strahan and Codell, London.

43. Jeffrey Rayport and John Sviokla. (1995). "Exploiting the Virtual Value Chain." *Harvard Business Review* November/December.

chapter 4:

Individuals Online

❝ I know you. You tell me what **❞**
you want. I make it. I remember
next time.

D. Peppers and M. Rogers[1]

❝ Every culture has developed **❞**
activities designed primarily
to improve the quality of
experience.

M. Csikszentmihalyi[2]

Figure 4.1

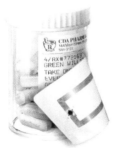

RFIDs on Prescription Bottles
Source: Copyright © 2005 by Computerworld,
Inc. Framingham, MA 01701. All Rights
Reserved.

Creating Identity

In 2004, the General Accounting Office (GAO) of the U.S. Congress was asked to investigate Internet-based prescription drug sales to determine whether these drugs were handled properly and to assess the reliability of online pharmacies.[3] To do this they placed 10 different orders for each of 13 top-selling drugs or drugs requiring special handling or safety procedures.[4] Online pharmacies were located both in the United States and overseas. The GAO was successful in obtaining 11 of the 13 drugs, most without providing a prescription, and completed orders with pharmacies in 12 different countries.

The most problematic orders were from foreign countries other than Canada. Of these 21 completed orders all were missing the FDA-required pharmacy labels and instructions, 13 had improper or damaged shipping status, and 4 were counterfeit drugs. No counterfeits were found among the U.S. or Canadian sources, although counterfeiting of pharmaceuticals is a growing crime problem in all countries. Notably, the GAO did not report the pricing of the drugs and the possible savings from buying online.

For both safety and business reasons, the pharmaceutical industry is very interested in tracking and monitoring their drugs throughout the supply chain. To accomplish this, they are turning to a technology called radio frequency identification (RFIDs, as in Figure 4.1) that lets a company track each individual bottle of pills at every step from manufacturer to consumer. Like package tracking from shippers such as FedEx or UPS, this "electronic pedigree" will show every handling step and verify

this chapter

Whether anonymous or identified, individual inter-actions form the heart of online activity. This chapter begins with a review of online activities by users and countries. Next is the behavioral aspects of the Net, and the manner in which individuals interact with online tools. We then consider the third GPT of online marketing, the individualization of people, products, and information.

Topics covered in this chapter include:

> Following Everything

> The Necessary Internet

> The Behavioral Internet

> Individualization and Marketing

the drug has the proper history. A number of pharmacies, such as Wal-Mart, CVS, and Walgreens have all indicated they intend to adopt an RFID system for product tracking.

An RFID system works by embedding a small electronic circuit into the labeling of a package. RFIDs come in two fundamental types. A passive RFID is an unpowered chip with a unique identifier code for that specific package, which draws its power from the reader signal used to access the information. When it is scanned, the system must match this unique code with a database record and update the database. As it draws power from the reading signal, its range is limited. In contrast, an active RFID chip contains its own battery. This permits a stronger signal and more distant access. It also makes writing of information onto the RFID chip easier. A passive chip is much cheaper to produce, while an active RFID can be read with less investment in readers.

Several factors make RFID more powerful than traditional bar coding. A critical difference is the ability to read the code at a distance. The read rate is much faster, up to 1,000 tags per second. The read/write capability of some RFIDs allows the creation of an electronic manifest, tracking each of the steps of the product with difficult-to-forge information.

These differences permit many new applications, such as the concept of smart shelves. By reading the RFID chips on each package on the shelf, inventory tracking is automatic and accurate. Specific items can be instantly identified, located, and characterized.

The movement to RFID throughout the rest of the economy is well underway. New U.S. passports will include an RFID chip containing personal information and a digital picture, with other countries expected to comply as well. Two of the biggest organizations pushing RFID technology are Wal-Mart and the U.S. military. In 2005, Wal-Mart is requiring all of its top 100 suppliers to put an RFID chip on each product case delivered. All suppliers are expected to comply in 2006. Estimates of the companywide cost savings are quite large, dominated by the savings in labor costs of scanning bar codes.[5] The U.S. military is going further, making all of their suppliers put RFID chips on every piece of equipment or supply.[6] The military is spending tens of millions of dollars putting RFID scanners and database systems throughout their logistics network.

RFIDs are controversial. If an RFID is embedded into a product, rather than just the packaging, it creates an ongoing record throughout the product's life. In particular, it can be used to identify and track its purchaser. For example, an RFID embedded in a jacket would be readable by scanners whenever the owner wore that jacket. Systems could identify and track individuals by matching up their product RFID identifiers against sales records, following them throughout a store and over time.

RFIDs are a notable example of an ongoing trend throughout the economy, especially pronounced online, of the increasing individualization of business. The substitution of an RFID for a bar code creates an individual identity of a specific pallet, or case, or product itself. Things begin to have their own identity and meaning. It is possible to match these items to the identity of the owner, both before and after purchase. As we saw in the last chapter, with the discussion of the semantic web, web pages are undergoing a similar refinement and increase in identification.

A major change occurs when products and information can be individually and intelligently understood and matched against the goals of a specific person. This increases the power to learn from both shopping and purchasing behavior. When an individual's shopping behavior and purchase choices can be tracked, far more refined models of their preferences and desires are possible. Many new forms of advice giving, customer support, and relationship tracking become possible. At the same time, privacy concerns and unequal treatment also become more serious.

Over the longer term, an RFID system may provide a critical and necessary technology for the use of personalized drug development. Researchers are beginning to match individual DNA differences with differences in the effectiveness and side effects of pharmaceuticals.[7] The same drug that is a safe and powerful treatment for one person may harm, and even kill, another due to differences in their genome. Without an ability to screen and track these differences, these drugs cannot be used to treat anyone. With tracking, those that benefit can be helped without the risk of injury to the susceptible. In other cases the difference is less extreme but still important. Some individuals require much lower dosages than others, simply because of differences in their genes.

Personalized medicine requires innovations still to come, many of them involving the sharing of information between patient, doctors, pharmacies, and drug makers. The Internet will be vital in this, requiring secure and accurate methods of connecting personal medical history with customized diagnosis and treatment. Medicine that varies at the individual level will require using RFID capabilities to cost-effectively and accurately match medicine to individual. Investments in tracking for inventory purposes set the stage for the evolution to a more personal form of medicine.

Other changes will be needed as well. While over 40% of American adults use prescription drugs, and many search online for drug information, only 4% of adults have purchased their drugs online.[8] Multiple factors cause this number to be so low. There are hassles involved in providing prescriptions to online pharmacies and trust in online pharmacies is lower than with conventional pharmacies. Perhaps most fundamentally, prescription drug use tilts heavily toward seniors. As we will see in this chapter, this group has proven the most challenging to move online. Those over 65 are far less likely to use the Internet at all, much less likely to purchase any product, and far more fearful about such a high-cost and high-involvement product as their prescription drugs.

Online individualization does not require anything quite as intrusive as RFIDs. However, firms may learn even more about an individual by using cookies, passwords, Internet address, email address, search behavior, credit card numbers, or other information. Currently, the Internet is a hybrid of anonymous and identifiable transactions. Understanding how to refine marketing from the mass market toward individualized approaches is a challenging and fundamental skill for Internet marketers. Understanding how to do this individualization while respecting privacy rights and providing control by the individual is even more of a challenge.

The rise of an individualization general purpose technology provides detailed information about products and people, which changes the nature of interaction between companies and consumers.

PATTERNS OF INTERNET USAGE

| The Necessary Internet

> *Individuals and Individualization*

The first two pillars of Net marketing, digital computing, and networking are well-established general purpose technologies. Ten years ago, only the digital foundation was clear with net-working just emerging. The situation today is similar for the third Net marketing foundation, individualization. This is the GPT creating individual interaction between users, content, and even physical goods.

As an emerging GPT, the winning implementations of the different aspects of individualization are challenging to predict. The situation was similar in 1995, when it was unclear which firms and systems would dominate the technologies of networking or the most important features of online social networks. The early phases of a GPT are exciting but chaotic. Companies introduce different formats into the market, different clusters of innovations occur, and alliances form.

For example, RFIDs may emerge as the foundation for individualized product identification. Conversely, cost reductions may not occur fast enough to move from high-cost individual items and cases of goods to the particular product. Other particular technologies may emerge with lower costs and higher quality.

It is unlikely that the individualization GPT will develop evenly across online applications. High-value interactions will tend to lead lower value situations. Certain industries will invest in the underlying tools faster than others will, sometimes due to external forces and regulations. These lead industries are especially interesting, as they create many of the standards and expectations that spill over into later adopting industries.

What is clear about individualization is that operating at an individual level of person-content-thing is an important step forward for online marketing. It supports more secure interaction, it is essential for low-cost personalized information and product customization, it creates much more accountability and traceability, and it becomes the basis for a wide variety of innovative business practices. These are the important spin-offs characteristic of any powerful general purpose technology.

Individualization changes the nature and the quality of online interactions. It allows the online world to be much more adaptive, secure, and intelligent. Among these benefits are

> Interaction can react to the sophistication and knowledge of the user,
> Interaction can react to the specific immediate needs and access method of the user,
> Interactions can mix and match content addressable to many individuals with unique communication between individuals, and
> Interaction can begin to build intelligence into the system.

Changes can be as simple as automatically connecting to a buddy list, or as complicated as a system offering personalized travel information based on real-time changes in location and flight conditions. Interactions can take full advantage of a high-speed desktop connection or reduce the formatting and images to send to a mobile device.

Operating at an individual level benefits from increased precision about people, content, and things. Chapter 3 illustrated how the semantic web connects descriptions to individual online content. The same information may have multiple descriptions, such as creator, last edited, the meaning of the information, and persons allowed to see it. Chapter 9 investigates personalization systems connecting this identified and described information to a person's immediate needs.

Understanding individual-level interaction is challenging. The next part reviews many of the important trends of how people are using the Internet as part of their everyday lives. Next, the most important biases and behavioral factors shaping online usage reveal how the online world compares to more traditional settings.

The chapter closes with a detailed look at the individualization GPT. Three capabilities are most important. The first is authentication, which is the ability to identify an individual accessing the Net. Next is association, which is the ability to categorize and understand the individual. Third is interaction, which is the ability to communicate appropriately with the individual. This includes choosing the proper communication technology, but it also includes choosing the right messages, timing, and detail.

> *The Dual Budget: Time and Money*

> Time and Money Tradeoffs

Consumers face two fundamental constraints, time and money, that limit their daily activities. Spending time on leisure generates entertainment. Spending time working generates more income. Income spent on goods and services gives consumption value.[9]

It is easy to overemphasize the money side of the constraint. Ecommerce is rapidly growing, and the flow of money is relatively simple to trace. Chapters 5, 12, and 13 focus primarily on the impact of the Net on consumer expenditures. However, the impact of the Net on consumer time is still much larger than its impact on consumer money. Chapter 1 highlighted how the Net still accounts for less than 5% of consumer retail expenditures, while it accounts for a higher fraction of consumer time.

The Internet makes the tradeoff between time and money complicated. Studies show the Net blurs the lines between work and play. Workers organize leisure activities during work hours. Alternatively, checking work email at home is a common activity for many. The Net chops an individual's day into finer and finer blocks of time, mixing work and play.

Some online activities are time-saving, while others are time-using. It is challenging to divide online time into simple time-saving and time-using. Online activities may be enjoyable in their own right. Reading an online magazine, commenting in an online blog, reading about a possible vacation destination are all possible time-using activities. Alternatively, visiting an online store may be a highly effective means of shopping quickly and conveniently. A ten-minute online shopping excursion, with included shipping, may save hours in the store, time spent packing and running the package to the post office.

The objectives of these time-saving and time-using applications are different. The benefit of a time-saving use is to expand the total time left over for other activities. Thus, a quicker shopping trip using an online store frees up time for work or other leisure. The benefit of a time-using application or product is to enhance the quality of the time available. For example, a better sound system raises the quality of the time spent listening to music.

Interesting differences occur in the dynamics of consumer adoption between time-saving and time-using durable goods. Time-saving appliances, such as an electric washing machine, lower the time necessary to complete a household task. Time-using appliances, such as the radio, enhance the quality of time spent in leisure. Bowden and Offer looked at a variety of consumer appliances during the twentieth century in the United States and Britain.[10] There was a striking difference in speed of adoption, with time-using appliances penetrating the market much faster than time-saving appliances. Consumers seem to be much more motivated to raise the average quality of their leisure time than they are to add additional leisure time. Time-using appliances diffuse more rapidly.

The Internet's dual capability as efficiency enhancer and entertainment provider has intriguing implications. As high-speed broadband, powerful search engines, and other online innovations

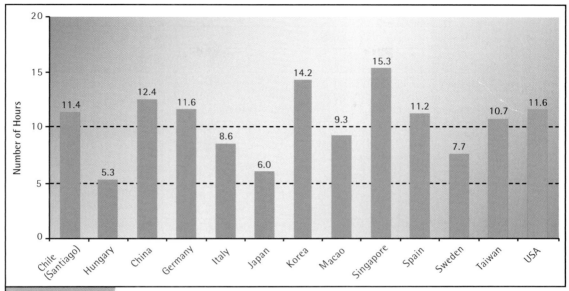

Figure 4.2

Total Hours Using the Internet per Week by Average Net User

Source: The World Internet Report - "Surveying the Digital Future," Center for the Digital Future, USC Annenberg School.

occur, they change the opportunities for both time-saving and time-using. The "always on" nature of broadband makes it a rapid response tool for answering many questions. It also creates the capability for online media entertainment. Search engines help find quick answers to productive questions, while also connecting hobbyists with the latest information for their amusement. The Internet is especially compelling due to its simultaneous ability to free up more time through efficiency and to then consume this greater stock of free time in enjoyable activities.

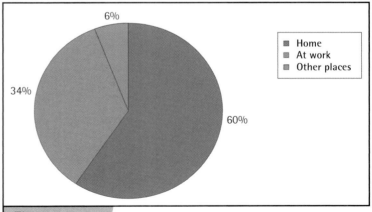

Figure 4.3

Share of Online Time, U.S. Net Users

Source: Norman H. Nie, Alberto Simpser, Irena Stepanikova, and Lu Zheng, "Ten Years After the Birth of the Internet, How Do Americans use the Internet in Their Daily Lives?," paper, Stanford Center for the Quantitative Study of Society, December 2004, 6.

> Time Allocation

Figure 4.2 highlights the pattern of Internet usage time. The highest usage countries, such as Korea and Singapore, average more than two hours per day online. With the many competing demands on time, this high level of online activity testifies to the power of the Net to complete tasks more efficiently while also providing amusement and connection.

Table 4.1

The Wide Range of Internet Usage				
The tasks of everyday life and the Internet				
Of those Internet users who ever do a given activity in their lives, the percentages who do them online; and of those who do that activity at any point in their lives, the percentages who do them online exclusively, offline exclusively, or both online and offline.				
Activity or task	Percent of Internet users who have done this online	Percent of those who do the activity who do it online only	Percent who do it offline only	Percent who do it offline and online (Broken down further into the percent of this group who do the task mostly online or mostly offline)
Commonplace information searches				
Look for a map or driving directions	87%	56%	14%	31% (48% of them do it mostly online and 40% do it mostly offline)
Check weather reports	69	31	31	39% (26% of them do it mostly online and 69% do it mostly offline)
Get news	63	17	38	45% (22% of them get it mostly online and 71% get it mostly offline)
Look up telephone numbers, addresses	50	19	50	31% (34% of them get it mostly online and 61% get it mostly offline)
Check sports scores	55	26	45	30% (32% of them get it mostly online and 61% get it mostly offline)
Commonplace transactions				
Buy tickets for concerts movies	55	28	45	27% (38% of them do it mostly online and 57% do it mostly offline)
Pay bills, do banking	44	20	56	26% (34% of them do it mostly online and 54% do it mostly offline)
Purchase everyday items like books, groceries, CDs	33	9	68	19% (5% of them do it mostly online and 93% do it mostly offline
Schedule appointments or meetings	22	9	78	13% (39% of them do it mostly online and 55% do it mostly offline)

Table 4.1

The Wide Range of Internet Usage (continued)			
Everyday kinds of communications			
Communicate with friends and family	79	21	20	59% (17% of them do it mostly online and 72% do it mostly offline)
Send greeting cards, invitations	52	17	47	36% (26% of them do it mostly online and 66% do it mostly offline)
Plan get-togethers for clubs or groups	46	20	53	26% (24% of them do it mostly online and 66% do it mostly offline)
Look for new people to meet or date	26	12	76	16% (18% of them do it mostly online and 60% do it mostly offline)
Everyday entertainment activities			
Play games	46	20	54	27% (33% of them do it mostly online and 60% do it mostly offline)
Pursue hobbies	34	10	66	25% (16% of them do it mostly online and 68% do it mostly offline)
Listen to music or radio	23	6	77	17% (10% of them do it mostly online and 84% do it mostly offline)
Read for pleasure	18	5	82	13% (24% of them do it mostly online and 68% do it mostly offline)
Watch videos, previews, cartoons	16	4	84	11% (9% of them do it mostly online and 87% do it mostly offline)

Source: Pew Internet Project.

Further analysis of this data, as well as other studies, demonstrates the power of access quality in promoting time spent online. Those countries with the most time devoted to online activities tend to have widespread broadband access. This is especially important in promoting media consumption and online gaming, important time-using applications.

Online usage spreads throughout the day and week over many different tasks. Table 4.1 highlights the many commonplace activities for which the Internet improves daily life. Weather checks and travel mapping in the morning help prepare for the upcoming day's events. Access from work or school leads to communication with colleagues, efficient distribution of work tasks, and up to the minute synchronization of data. At the same time, workers may use their Net access for personal matters and hobbies, complicating measures of productivity. While leisure and entertainment dominate at home usage, the resources, communications, and information used at work are often available by secure connection and can lead to late-night completion of work activities.

A useful category breakdown of online user activity is

> *commerce*[11] (sites and applications designed primarily for shopping online),
> *communications* (sites and applications designed primarily to facilitate the exchange of thoughts, messages, or information directly between individuals or groups),
> *content* (sites and applications designed primarily to provide news, information, and entertainment), and
> *search* (sites and applications designed primarily to provide prioritized results based on user requests).

Despite month-to-month variation, several trends are apparent in how U.S. users spend their time online. The leading usage of time online is the combined activities of communication and content, accounting for roughly 80% throughout the sample period shown in Table 4.2. This 80% has been shifting somewhat more toward content and away from communications. Communications clearly dominated at the beginning of the sample, while content rose in share to approximately equal communications by the end. The share devoted to commerce shows seasonality, rising during the holiday season, but staying roughly constant overall. Search, while strategically very important, occurs quickly and leads to these other categories of use.

Especially among younger users, multi-tasking is common and important. As early as the late 1990s, careful surveys of media time usage by teens found what seemed to be a paradox and a serious data problem.[12] When asked to list the amount of time at home spent consuming different media (such as television, radio, music, Internet, and video games), teens responded with estimates exceeding the number of hours available (Figure 4.4). Follow-up analysis showed the data to

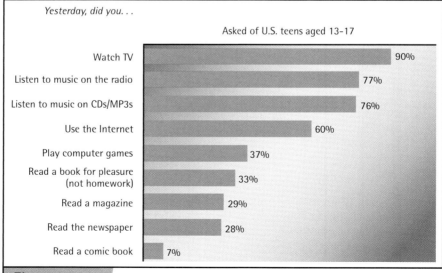

Yesterday, did you. . .

Asked of U.S. teens aged 13-17

Watch TV	90%
Listen to music on the radio	77%
Listen to music on CDs/MP3s	76%
Use the Internet	60%
Play computer games	37%
Read a book for pleasure (not homework)	33%
Read a magazine	29%
Read the newspaper	28%
Read a comic book	7%

Figure 4.4

How Is this Possible—by Multi-Tasking

Source: October 2004, Gallup Survey.

Table 4.2

Allocation of Usage Time by Category

Share of Time Spent Online (%)												
	Jan04	Feb04	Mar04	Apr04	May04	Jun04	Jul04	Aug04	Sep04	Oct04	Nov04	Dec04	Jan05
Commerce	17.0	17.7	17.6	16.4	16.4	15.7	15.2	16.1	15.2	15.8	17.0	18.6	17.8
Communications	44.2	43.4	43.4	43.1	42.9	43.3	41.6	41.4	39.8	39.8	40.1	39.2	40.0
Content	34.9	35.0	35.6	35.9	36.1	36.5	38.9	38.3	41.0	40.2	38.7	38.1	37.7
Search	3.8	3.9	3.5	4.6	4.6	4.4	4.2	4.1	4.0	4.3	4.3	4.2	4.5

% Change in Share of Time, Month-Over-Month												
	Jan04	Feb04	Mar04	Apr04	May04	Jun04	Jul04	Aug04	Sep04	Oct04	Nov04	Dec04	Jan05
Commerce	↓6.6	↑4.1	↓0.6	↓6.8	0.0	↓4.3	↓3.2	↑5.9	↓5.6	↑3.9	↑7.6	↑9.4	↓4.3
Communications	↑0.2	↓1.8	0.0	↓0.7	↓0.5	↑0.9	↓3.9	↓0.5	↓3.9	0.0	↑0.8	↑2.2	↑2.0
Content	↑2.6	↑0.3	↑1.7	↑0.8	↑0.6	↑1.1	↑6.6	↑1.5	↑7.0	↓2.0	↓3.7	↓1.6	↓1.0
Search	↑2.7	↑2.6	↓10.3	↑31.4	0.0	↓4.3	↓4.5	↓2.4	↑2.4	↑7.5	0.0	↓2.3	↑7.1

Notes: Excludes .gov and .edu web sites, as well as pornographic domains. *Percentage change* indicates the percentage increase or decrease from the previous month's value (December 2003 values not shown). Share of Time data based on Total Time values.

Source: Based on data from Online Publishers Association (OPA) and Nielsen/Net Ratings.

be correct, but an implicit assumption of dedicated media consumption wrong. Teens media multi-task, having chat rooms available while gaming, talking on the cell phone while surfing, and listening to music while doing all of the above. Attention was shifting back and forth between all of these simultaneous activities, complicating both the design and measurement of media. Marketers cannot assume that users are currently watching every media connection, as attention may have shifted to a different window or activity.

Multi-tasking is a shift toward hybrid Internet usage. As Net usage matures, it integrates into a wider media consumption pattern. While the Internet has always existed in a sea of other media, younger users are fluidly combining and relying on different media forms for different purposes. The Net has replaced earlier media types, but only partially. Communication experts observe that a new medium typically steals from, but does not completely replace, an existing medium. This pattern holds for the Internet.

> *Internet User Demographics*

Table 1.1 demonstrated that approximately 60% of the population is online in many advanced economies.[13] The remaining 40% or so of the population that are nonusers is explained by a combination of factors, such as age, education, income, and disabilities. Age and education, in particular, play a large role in limiting these late potential adopters.

The proper methodology for forecasting a specific individual's likelihood to be an Internet user simultaneously considers the impacts of location, income, age, education, and other important factors. This is challenging. We typically do not have enough high-quality detailed data to do this. Even when the data is available, it requires a statistical model to determine the joint impacts of these factors.

Because of these limitations, the typical first step in an analysis of Net usage is to look at each of these Internet usage factors in isolation. While potentially misleading, it is a useful beginning point. The problem with treating each factor separately arises when Net factors are correlated. For example, seniors have the lowest likelihood to be online. Without care it is difficult to know whether this is an age issue, or because they are retired and have lower income. The correct method to address the question of relative importance is to consider the variables simultaneously. In the case of disabilities, research shows this can lead to surprising conclusions.

> Age

Figure 4.5 shows the consistent strength and high market penetration of the Internet among younger users regardless of the country considered. In high-usage countries, such as the United States and South Korea, more than 90% of the youngest cohort uses the Internet. Older cohorts have much lower usage rates, strikingly so in the case of Korea. As the younger cohorts age, the market penetration of the Net will slowly rise, even in advanced countries.[14]

The peak of Net usage among younger users is not a new phenomenon. In the United States, the relative importance of the college segment was even larger in the early days of the commercial Net. Over time, the distribution curve has flattened as both younger and older cohorts converged toward the college cohort usage. A flattening of the adoption curve, as seen in Figure 4.6, highlights how the Internet population in the United States is becoming more similar to the general population.[15] Despite this trend, the average Net user is still much younger than the average for the population as a whole.

The most challenging age cohort to move online continues to be seniors. Despite the many benefits of the Internet for managing chronic health conditions, communicating with friends and family, and offsetting diminished mobility, the Net remains a mystery for many older citizens. Lack of familiarity, fear of computers and online content, poor eyesight, lack of training,

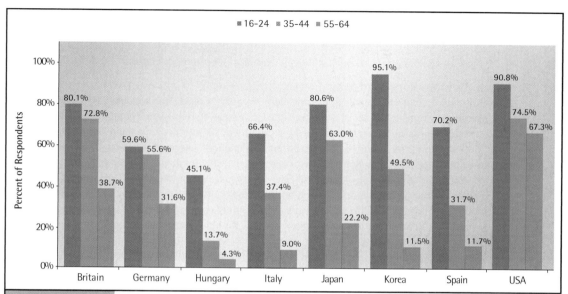

Figure 4.5

Age Distribution of Net Users by Country

Source: The World Internet Report - "Surveying the Digital Future," Center for the Digital Future, USC Annenberg School.

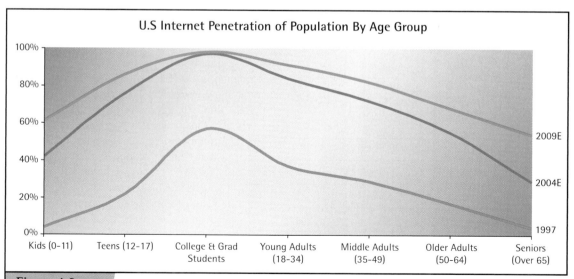

Figure 4.6

Bringing the Missing Cohorts Online in the United States

Source: Jupiter Research

and lack of control over living space are all factors hindering seniors from going online. Over the longer term, as the current working population ages into retirement, a number of these factors will lessen in importance. Better and more accessible visual displays, plus the incorporation of voice control and voice output, will assist this late-adopting population.

> ## Gender, Race, and Employment Status

Early adopters of the Net have historically been heavily male. This bias has disappeared in most advanced countries. The latest data from the U.S. Census Bureau, which conducts in-depth surveys about online usage every two years, finds Net usage slightly higher among females than males. While there are still important gender differences in online usage, especially with regard to aspects of ecommerce and gaming, gender has ceased to be influential with respect to Net access.

Race and employment status are hard to evaluate separately from income and education. Studies on the digital divide by race find that controlling for income and education makes race much less of a predictor. In other words, once a study corrects for the tendency of minorities to have lower income and fewer advanced degrees than average, there ceases to be much impact of race on online access. While less studied, the impact of unemployment is probably similar. Viewed in isolation, the unemployed have a much lower likelihood of being online. As the unemployed are also much more likely to have lower income and education, the independent effect of employment status falls in importance when these other factors are included.

> ## Education

Education is important in determining Net usage, either separately or in combination with other variables. Higher education is strongly correlated with higher Net access rates. Table 4.3 compares the Census results in the United States for 2001 and 2003. While there was small growth in the adoption rates of each cohort, the highest educated group was nearly five times more likely to be online than the lowest educational group.

One of the reasons for education's importance is the cognitive challenge involved in Internet use. The Net requires linguistic and cognitive skills for a number of activities, such as search or online self-service. Education is both a signal of these skills and a method of improving them.

> ## Income

Household income remains influential in determining Internet access and access quality, even within wealthier countries. Figure 4.7a illustrates how more than 80% of U.S. individuals in households with income greater than $75,000 have Internet access, while the number is less than 40% for individuals in households making less than $25,000.

The income–broadband diffusion curve is even steeper than simple access. Figure 4.7b shows that poorer households are much less likely to have broadband than wealthier groups. The current pattern for broadband adoption by income is similar to that of simple Net access in the 1990s.

> ## Disabilities

Disabilities reduce both the value of the Internet and the time spent using it.[16]

Table 4.3

U.S. Net Usage by Educational Attainment		
Educational Attainment	**September 2001**	**October 2003**
Less than high school	13.7	15.5
High school diploma/ GED	41.1	44.5
Some college	63.5	68.6
Bachelor's degree	82.2	84.9
Beyond bachelor's degree	85.0	88.0

Source: U.S. Census Bureau

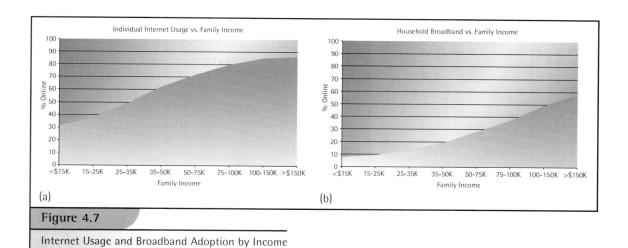

Figure 4.7

Internet Usage and Broadband Adoption by Income

Source: U.S. Census Bureau

Overall, users with disabilities have lower levels of computer ownership and Net usage. This shows up especially strongly with visual or multiple disabilities.

A simultaneous treatment of disabilities with income, age, and education is highly useful in clarifying the role disabilities play in online access and online usage. When controlled appropriately, users with disabilities tend to have computers and Net access at approximately the same rates as other groups. They do, however, spend significantly less time online. The challenges of online usage reduce its benefits, but this shows up in time online and not the presence or absence of the Net in the home.

Many web sites fail to provide adequately for access by those with visual or other physical limitations. This is increasingly unnecessary. A variety of organizations exist providing suggestions, alternatives, and improvements to sites that make them much more accessible while having minimal design impacts. Parallel sites provide another alternative when design conflicts force difficult tradeoffs.

> Access Quality

Part of the explanation for high Internet usage by the young and the working cohorts in the United States is a higher quality online experience. High-speed access at school or work creates a more positive rating of the online experience, and eliminates the "world wide wait" so common among dial-up users. Having experienced this form of the Net, these users are much more likely to spend the additional money for broadband access. Figure 4.8 shows the steady improvement in home broadband adoption.

High-quality access creates a platform for a variety of additional online services that further drive usage. These include voice-over-IP telephony, on-demand media streaming, support of interactive television services, home media sharing, and an increasingly wide array of interactive content in education and other areas.

U.S. broadband penetration lags behind that of several other advanced economies. Both Japan and Korea are especially notable for much higher penetration and much faster online access. Applications such as video-on-demand and video collaboration are much easier when

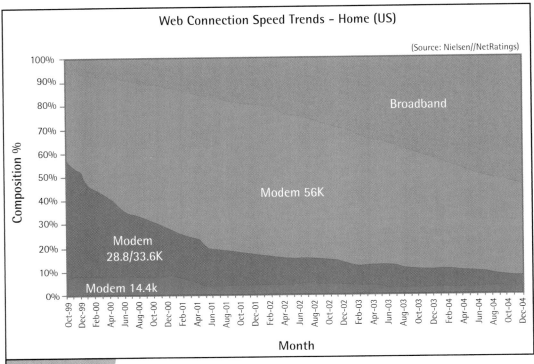

Figure 4.8

Internet Home Access Methods in the United States

Source: Based on data from Nielsen/NetRatings.

broadband dominates dial-up. Internet observers need a global perspective to track market leaders.

In summary, the Internet user in an advanced country is becoming much more representative of the average citizen. The Net is mainstream. The biggest differences are age (the average Net user is younger), income (the average Net user is somewhat more affluent), and education (the average Net user is more educated). Net usage grows much more slowly once 60% of the population is online, but the quality of access continues to grow with a transition to faster speeds.

The Behavioral Internet

Throughout its history, many have proclaimed that the Internet "changes everything." Fortunately, this is not the case. Far more of the fundamentals of marketing carry over to the online world than need to be changed. A core reason is that users relate to virtual information with many of the same human traits and tendencies as they do in the physical world. This is extremely useful, as it indicates that traditional experience and guidelines will retain much of their validity in the online world. Marketers do not have to relearn their entire vocabulary.

Why Korea?

South Korea is a world leader in broadband and Internet adoption. This is surprising, as South Korea ranks only 50th in world per capita income, military expenditures consume important resources, and Korea faces the challenge of a unique language and script. Despite this, at the end of 2004 more than 76% of Korean households were online, nearly all of them with broadband service. Three reasons provide much of the explanation, and demonstrate how market competition, appropriate governmental policies, and entrepreneurial spirit can transform a country's Internet landscape.

Apartments in Seoul, Korea
Source: © Photodisc Green/Getty Images

Reason 1: Low Prices

Just as MCI challenged AT&T following long-distance deregulation in the United States, the entrant Hanaro Telecommunications challenged the broadband incumbent Korea Telecom (KT) in the late 1990s. From the start, Hanaro offered extremely fast Internet service at a price just above US$20. This price was especially attractive compared to dial-up service, with relatively high per minute connect charges and slow connect speeds. While Hanaro offered high-quality service at a low price, the many small cable television companies in Korea offered lower quality broadband at prices below US$10. Forced to respond, the incumbent KT matched Hanaro's broadband pricing.

Reason 2: High Population Density

High population density favors broadband. Most Koreans live in high-rise apartments or condominiums. High-rise living, especially if the buildings are new enough to contain modern outlets and conduit, makes wiring for broadband much cheaper than wiring single family homes. Almost all of the thousands of high-rise buildings came after the Korean War, with ready accommodation for modern phone and electrical systems.

Reason 3: The "PC Bang" Phenomena

Another factor with a unique Korean flavor is the influence of computer gaming and Internet cafes (known as PC Bangs). For historical reasons, the South Korean government prohibited the import of many forms of Japanese culture from 1945 until 2000. Along with movies and television, this included Japanese video game systems such as Nintendo or PlayStation. Instead, young Koreans played computer games from the United States and elsewhere. Computer gaming requires powerful computers, and PC bangs started as computer gaming parlors. With the Internet, they added high-speed access and multi-person games. Experience with these high-speed PC bang connections, and a desire to compete on an equal basis, created a demand among gamers for high-speed access at their homes.

Korean firms face the challenge of creating applications that use this excellent Internet system. Industry observers the world over are watching the South Korean market for best practices and emerging opportunities.

There are differences, however, between offline and online. One difference, especially with technologies such as email, is a lack of social cues and a sparseness of communication. Print messages are just not the same as a phone call or face-to-face meeting. This leads to important differences in the types of communication and interaction that occur with this limited communication method. The result can be inappropriate behavior.

There is also a sparseness of quality cues. One of the oldest cartoons about the Internet shows two dogs online, with one commenting to the other that on the Net no one knows you are a dog. That may be a virtue for a dog, but it is a problem for a high-quality site trying to build reputation and trust. If it is hard to recognize quality, it can be hard to justify creating it.

Online information can be difficult to find. While the past five years have created many new and effective search tools, this is still an active area of research. Making information accessible and retrievable continues to be a challenging problem. Many users have a hard time tracking down the information they want.

The combinations of rewards and difficulties make the online experience range from highly enjoyable to deeply frustrating. When there is a balance between challenge and skills, users experience satisfaction and entertainment. Too little challenge leads to boredom; too much, to frustration. This leads to the concept of flow, where the right online balance can be instrumental in consumers' enjoyment of the medium.

> *The Media Equation*

One of the most surprising results concerning consumers' reactions to online content is how similar it can be to behavior in the physical world. Technology users relate to the virtual world in many of the basic social ways they interact with people in their normal conduct of life. Reeves and Nass call this the media equation.

> Media = Real Life

This strong finding is the result of a lengthy research project conducted by psychologists Byron Reeves and Clifford Nass.[17] They find many examples in which users treat machines and software as they treat people. Among their examples are similarities with regard to politeness, personality, gender, and media fidelity. Each has important consequences as marketers attempt to create connections between themselves and their customers.

The media equation is a highly useful intuitive starting point for evaluating online content and design. It means we do not have to understand an entirely new set of rules, behaviors, and etiquette online. As we make web sites, and increasingly as we create digital environments, marketers can bring to these sites the judgments, experiences, and intuition that govern their daily life. More often than not, these judgments will be as valid online as they are in person.

A good example is politeness. Users prefer polite computers, react positively to flattery by a computer, and act politely toward action on the screen. Rude behavior in real life is considered rude onscreen. This can conflict with common design procedures. For example, computer users are uncomfortable "clicking" on the picture of a person, feeling it an aggressive action. Often participants deny these social behaviors. They consciously find it silly to be polite toward a machine. Yet, in controlled studies, users behave civilly and politely to their machines and software. Computers are sufficiently convincing as social entities to which good manners are expected.

The media equation also applies to personality. One of the most common results in sales force effectiveness studies is the importance of personality. In short, buyers react favorably toward salespeople matching their own personalities. The same result holds online. In particular, users react online as they would in real life to online character's attributes of dominance and friendliness. Dominant personalities tend to like computers that exhibit "dominant" characteristics such as bold design, strong opinions, and even dominant-sounding machine names. Consumers with submissive personalities prefer computer designs similar to themselves.

Moon (2002) documents the power of personality matching for online advice and content.[18] During an initial phase, she had participants answer a survey designed to identify an individual's basic personality traits. These included standard measures such as dominance versus submissiveness, agreeableness, dependability, emotional stability, and openness to experience. The participants then engaged in computer-mediated tasks. Participants received online messages matching or conflicting with their personality type. In all cases, individuals preferred messages matching their personality. Matching messages were more persuasive, the source had more expertise, and information quality was higher than when message tone clashed. Content ranking of music and humor also shifted with the same bias when messages matched or clashed.

Stereotypes are one unfortunate aspect of the media equation. They persist online as they do in the real world. An example is gender. Different groups rated information very differently depending on which computer-generated voice they heard. If the information was about a topic viewed as stereotypically male, users rated the male voice as more authoritative. If the information concerned traditionally female interest areas, the female voice got a higher score. In all cases, the voices were purely synthetic, and the information was identical. Users assign genders to artificial personalities and react to them with many of their normal biases.

Interesting tradeoffs occur in system performance and social perception. It may be better to use deliberately stylized images rather than photo-realistic images when system performance is limited. Figure 4.9 shows three conditions from a study with the goal of creating a feeling of "co-presence," the idea that another social actor was available to provide assistance. In condition (a), a highly anthropomorphic figure is used. In (b) a cartoonlike face represents the agent. In condition (3), the system provides advice without a visual agent. Automated advice occurred in all cases, advice was the same, and performance was somewhat limited.

The simple eyes and mouth cartoon figure (b) performed the highest in generating a feeling of social co-presence. Realistic images raise expectations of similarly realistic advice performance. As the automated system could not achieve that, users were disappointed. The cartoon image better matched expectations. Visuals did help, as both (a) and (b) were preferred to condition (c).

A.   B.   C.

Figure 4.9

Matching Expectations to Performance Is Important

Source: Courtesy of Dr. Frank Biocca

Figure 4.10

Meeting Oneself Online

Source: © Terri Miller/E-Visual Communications Inc.

Expectations and social interaction matter when tradeoffs occur due to limitations of bandwidth. Designers find that online users prefer high-fidelity sound and a static picture to low-resolution video. Jerky video is more disturbing and threatening, while high-quality audio provides much more immersion. Reeves and Nass recommend devoting scarce bandwidth to audio rather than video when a tradeoff is necessary.

Researchers at the University of California, Santa Barbara conducted a variant of the media equation studies[19] that creates amusing possibilities. They asked what would happen if an individual entered virtual reality and encountered an agent with their own face compared to the situation where the agent had a different face (Figure 4.10). Specifically, they measured whether the virtual personal space, the perceived closeness with which people approach the virtual agent, changed between the two conditions. First, they found that the personal space accorded a "virtual other" was very similar to the space accorded in the real world. Second, they found that the virtual space given to an agent with their own face was much smaller. People felt more comfortable getting closer to an agent that had their own face, even though an external computer program controlled the actions of both agents. In addition, individuals were more willing to commit an embarrassing act in front of their "own face" agent than with a different face.

Many of these results seem puzzling. Why should humans treat machines and media the way they do? Reeves and Nass argue fundamental perceptual abilities drive many of these results. Human perceptual abilities evolved in an era without media. Much of perception is "hard-wired" into the nervous system. Humans process media that looks like the real world as the real world. We are fundamentally social beings. Our perceptions of social actions and actors predate our machines.[20]

> *Flow*

Internet users respond enthusiastically when there is an effective balance between the difficulty of using the Net and its rewards. An experience many new users report with amazement is getting lost in their online activity and suddenly discovering that an hour or two has passed. Of course, some view this as lost work and productivity. From the user's point of view, it has been an enjoyable and stimulating activity.

Exploratory web search declines with experience. However, with experience an online user expands their repertoire of online tools, is more willing to reveal information, and more likely to make a purchase. The hundreds of millions of Net users that have moved online over the past decade typically follow a pattern that evolves in sophistication.

This dynamic pattern of web usage presents a challenge for online site designers. If the goal is to provide an intriguing and pleasant experience, the experience must evolve along with the expertise of the user. The goal is to create what Csikszentmihalyi calls the state of flow. Hoffman and Novak[21] define flow as a state characterized by a seamless sequence of responses, intrinsically enjoyable, accompanied by a loss of self-consciousness, and self-reinforcing.

To achieve flow over time, a user faces a tension between flow, anxiety, and boredom. Figure 4.11 shows a stylized version of this process. Initially, a user is in flow (A1) with the proper balance of challenge and reward. If there is no evolution of the experience while the user's skill develops, it eventually becomes boring (A2). In order to recapture flow, the user seeks a new challenge, moving back into balance (A4). Alternatively, if a user moves toward more challenge without new skills, the result is difficulty and anxiety (A3). Adding new skills and training moves the user back toward a proper balance (again, A4). Thus, we get a spiral upward in user skills and complexity.

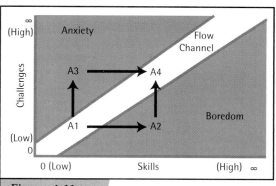

Figure 4.11

Escalating Skills to Maintain Flow

Source: Mihaly Csikszentmihalyi, *Flow: The Psychology of Optimal Experience* (New York: Harper Perennial, 1990), 74. Copyright © 1990 by Mihaly Csikzentmihalyi. Reprinted by permission of HarperCollins Publishers.

Marketing researchers have applied the flow concept to the online experience. One of the most useful distinctions is between goal-directed and experiential online behavior. Goal-directed online behavior attempts to achieve such purposes as answering a question, comparing products and prices, or solving a work-related problem. Experiential online behavior focuses on entertainment and the consumption of time. This includes such online activities as chatting with friends, game playing, media consumption, and participating in an online hobby. Flow is possible for both activities, and the stylized escalation of skills shown in Figure 4.11 applies to both. Somewhat surprisingly, initial research findings suggest online flow may be easier to achieve and maintain for goal-directed behavior.[22] It may be that the Internet is currently better able to escalate challenges and skills for goal-directed activities, and that experiential activities are still limited by performance (such as bandwidth, video capabilities) and techniques (difficulty of creating personalized media, narratives). Online video games seem to be an exception, with the capability of generating flow and even addiction for some.[23]

Flow is a useful concept for designers attempting to build the proper online navigation system for a site. Without individualization, conventional wisdom in software design suggests targeting a site to the "perpetual intermediate." This is a compromise between difficulty and efficiency. With proper authentication and tracking, web site navigation can evolve along with user experience.

Measuring and maintaining flow may be especially important when the goal of the site is education, learning, and training. Chen and McGrath applied the concept of flow to the classroom learning, and found that participatory multimedia projects were highly motivating and successful in self-teaching science.[24] For tasks such as collaborative design, market research, and self-support an attention to flow can raise participation, successful completion, and user satisfaction.

> *Content Accessibility*

Providers of online information face the challenge of making their web sites and other Net communication accessible to a wide range of users, with widely ranging skills and experience. Consumers become frustrated and angry when they are unable to connect to the right page and document, especially if they are convinced it exists and they just cannot locate it. They are also frustrated by difficult navigation, unfamiliar language, and intimidating content. Each of these problems can undermine the goals of the online content, such as customer support, relationship building, and online commerce.

Literacy is fundamental for effective use of the Internet. Accessing online resources is much more challenging and less rewarding for users with reading difficulties. This limits the value of the Net for many of the poor in the world. While only 3% of the U.S. population is illiterate, UNESCO estimates the worldwide illiterate population at nearly 1 billion people. Illiteracy is especially problematic for women in a number of countries, as cultural practices have limited access to schooling for girls. Efforts by the U.N. and others to both raise literacy and to develop access methods more appropriate to illiterate users are underway. This is, however, a challenging and difficult long-term problem requiring substantial resources and time.

Visual and physical handicaps may dramatically limit the accessibility of poorly designed online content. Users may have one or more cognitive challenges. Low-income users may not have the most recent versions of hardware and software, while leading-edge users may have dramatically higher performing systems. The W3C, one of the most influential organizations for Internet operation and design, stress four fundamental principles governing the accessibility of web content:[25]

> Principle 1: Content must be *perceivable.*
> Principle 2: Interface elements in the content must be *operable.*
> Principle 3: Content and controls must be *understandable.*
> Principle 4: Content must be *robust* enough to work with current and future technologies.

As the Internet moves from experimental to fundamental, online marketers must accommodate many users with physical limitations. Fortunately, the W3C and other groups are developing techniques and solutions for many of these physical limitations. Perception can come in many forms. A computer can read aloud a text alternative for visual information. Audio files can have a link to a transcript for those with hearing difficulties. Variable sized fonts help accommodate visual difficulties among seniors. These and many other design approaches expand the groups that can perceive the information presented online.

Operability ensures that visitors can properly operate input devices such as keyboard and mouse or be able to substitute an alternative such as voice recognition. Users with difficulties may be unable to react in time to content timed to make a visual impression, such as scrolling text. In some cases redesign of the site for all may make sense, in other situations a parallel site may be called for.

Principle 3, content must be understandable, is one of the most challenging. This is much more than just the difficulty of the language used. Simply finding information on a comprehensive site presents a major hurdle for many users. The Library of Congress' Thomas site (http://thomas.loc.gov/) provides a good example of many of these challenges (Figure 4.12). The Thomas site is a gateway to the detailed legislative history of Congress, and every American should be able to use it.

The Library must present complicated information, such as the many activities of Congress and the many stages of a potential law, so that individuals can find and understand the content.

First is finding the right information. The Library must decide the best organization of the information for many different levels of user sophistication, ranging from professional legislative researchers down to elementary school children.

The design of the Thomas site reflects lessons learned from decades of study of presenting electronic information. One of the most important is the value of providing both search and browse. Different users use different methods to find information. Experts tend to prefer and rely on search, while beginners tend to prefer and use browse.[26] Successful search is difficult for many users and requires substantial language and cognitive abilities.[27] Browse works best for many novices, as the structure provided by the browsing function helps beginners figure out where to go and provides a mental organization of the content.

Complicating this simple picture is the fact that the same user may switch between browse and search depending on the content sought. For information areas that the user is committed to, and wants to fully understand, browse is often preferred. Browsing leads to the accidental discovery of information and new areas more effectively than does search. It is also appropriate for poorly posed questions, such as when the user does not really understand what appropriate keywords and titles might be. For

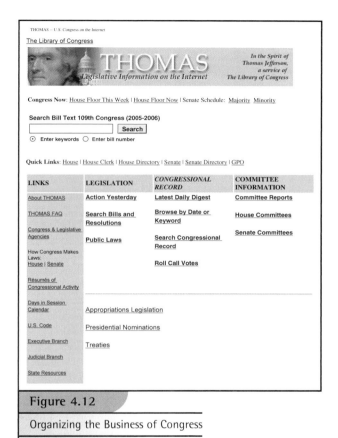

Figure 4.12

Organizing the Business of Congress

Source: Courtesy of www.loc.gov

example, the "Action Yesterday" or the "Latest Daily Digest" buttons let a Congress watcher browse through many of the most recent actions in hearings or on the floor.

Browsing the Thomas site reflects the major divisions of Congress. There is browsing based on which house of Congress is involved as well as by bill topic, title, number, and completion status. There is browsing by committee and browsing by testimony on the floor of Congress. Browsing by Congressional Record index terms provides detailed links and narrow topics.

Search can be highly effective for sophisticated users, with effective and focused keywords. In these cases, a trained user can quickly find the exact documents desired. On the other hand, it is very easy to get extraneous information or to use inappropriate keywords.

Each approach, browse and search, contains valuable lessons. One of the most effective ways of developing a useful browse structure is to capture and use the most commonly searched terms. There is often a high concentration of activity among the top few terms. Making these into separate browse categories, or even subdividing them into several categories capturing important additional terms, can make the browse structure more valuable. Likewise, lessons from the most valuable documents found in the browse mode provide valuable hints to what terms are search synonyms.

The Library of Congress has an easier task than those trying to make information accessible to users with severe limitations. An example is the automated caregiver, in which research groups are attempting to match digital devices and online activities to seniors suffering from Alzheimer's disease or other chronic mental conditions. PDAs (portable digital assistant) and net connections can serve as memory aid, advice giver, and diagnostic tool for early-stage sufferers.

The fundamental lesson that researchers have discovered is the importance of reflecting knowledge about users in the method of finding information. Even simple web issues such as providing a search function require knowledge about the customer base to be effective. This will be most difficult in the early life of a web site but should be easier to refine and become more effective over time. The challenge of Principle 3 is ongoing.

Principle 4, robust content, can be improved but is impossible to guarantee. Testing is crucial. Low-income users may have old hardware and software, and there is substantial upgrade inertia among many users able to afford new technology. Leading-edge users with high-performance systems that do not result in improved performance because of design choices of web sites become frustrated. Robustness is a compromise between innovation and standardization, and requires managing to achieve.

> *Social Cues*

Not all aspects of online interaction mirror the real world, as some means of online communication suffer from limited social cues and limited feedback. Group dynamics and personal communication systematically differ online when the tools of communication lack the subtlety and richness of face-to-face meetings. Decisions reached online can be different from decisions reached through a personal meeting. Differences include both the process and the result.

Social and professional standing heavily influence most meetings between individuals, especially in business and formal situations. As Sproull and Kiesler (1994) put it:

> Most meetings follow a predictable course. Participation is unequal; one person or a minority clique dominates the floor. Member status predicts who will dominate. Managers speak more than subordinates; men speak more than women; the person at the front of the room speaks more than those at the back.[28]

Sproull and Kiesler argue that many of these static cues of hierarchy make meetings predictable, efficient, and cohesive. On the other hand, these patterns breed conformity and elitism and block unpopular views.

Online media, and especially email, alter this pattern. Participation rates, decision quality, and time-to-decision all change when using online methods rather than traditional methods. Sometimes this can be advantageous; other times, disastrous. In either case, it is important to understand that these differences are occurring.

Figure 4.13 captures one of the main effects of using online versus physical meetings. The goal of the experiment was to identify whether the setting of a meeting affected the equality of participation. The studies looked at three types of meeting. The first was a traditional face-to-face discussion. The second was a real-time, text-based computer conference, in essence a text-based chat room. The third setting was email.

Meeting structure strongly affects participation. A score of 1 indicates one person doing all the talking, and a score of 0 reflects equal participation. Face-to-face meetings were significantly more unequal in all the experiments. Text-based chat and email both led to higher and more equal levels of participation. Lower status members of the group were much more likely to participate online.

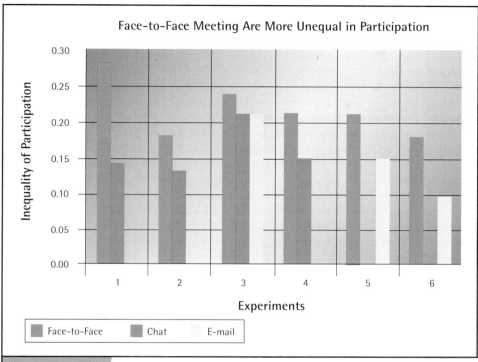

Figure 4.13

Face-to-Face Meetings Are More Unequal in Participation

Source: Lee Sproull and Sara Kiesler. (1994). *Connections: New Ways of Working in the Networked Organization.* MIT Press, 57.

The form of a meeting also affected the conclusions of the group. Going online reduced the influence of the high-status members on the final decision. Online meetings were much more likely to adopt an idea advocated first by a low-status member. Face-to-face meetings stuck with the high-status members' suggestions.

Flaming closely relates to these results. Flaming is to "speak incessantly and/or rabidly on some relatively uninteresting subject or with a patently ridiculous attitude."[29] Three factors contribute to the unfortunate tendency toward flaming. One, the lack of feedback between individuals using email makes it harder to judge disapproval and confusion. Misunderstandings develop without the standard responses that would make individuals stop to explain themselves in face-to-face discussion. There is an absence of dynamic cues, such as gestures, nods, or other expressions. The second is a form of compensation. Because text is not as rich and powerful as personal interaction, writers are tempted to use stronger words and images than otherwise. This can lead to an escalation of feeling and attitudes. Finally, the lack of social cues leads individuals to use these strong words and language to a much wider audience than they ever would in an actual physical discussion. People send email to an entire organization with material they would never discuss in front of the group.

Sending flames to customers is a serious issue. Customers may resort to flames, using highly unpleasant language that is an overstatement of their true feelings. Even worse, employees dealing with customers may fall into the trap of flaming. Because these messages are in writing, they can escalate and lead to tremendously bad press and negative word of mouth. Avoiding customer flaming requires deliberate policies and training.

First impressions suffer due to thin communication channels. First impressions based on video-conferences using lower resolution are less positive than first impressions based on face-to-face meetings.[30] Marwick (2001) found first impressions using high-resolution Internet video were close to those of face-to-face, audio conferences were less effective, and the least effective was text-based chat. Lower bandwidth communication is suited for established relationships, while high bandwidth is much better for initial conversations. In other words, strong ties can use weak communication tools but weak ties need strong communication tools.[31]

The literature on social cues strongly suggests that different online tools are appropriate for different stages of customer interaction. New customer acquisition would seem to benefit the most from high bandwidth and media richness. Less intensive tools are appropriate for more established relationships. For example, an audio channel for tech support might help resolve ambiguity without the higher cost of video. Simple emails and text messages to established customers can announce product releases or upcoming events. The literature also suggests that an occasional high-bandwidth connection, and even fact-to-face meeting, may refresh and renew the strength of social ties and customer relationships.

> Quality Cues

In the classic marketing essay "Making the Intangible Tangible," Theodore Levitt explains why so many of the traditional trappings of business are useful in reinforcing positioning.[32] One example is private banking. This service, provided to wealthy customers, consists of personalized advice, estate planning, and other financial services.

Private bankers' offices are typically posh, elegant, and expensive. Levitt argues that the physical manifestations of business need to reassure customers of the much harder to demonstrate intangible characteristics. A wealthy client wants to be assured that the advice is sound and the banker has a successful track record. One piece of evidence of successful advice is prosperity. Posh surroundings also signal that the company isn't desperate and won't take a risky position just to cover a cash-flow shortage.

The Web is much less able to signal these kinds of messages than traditional "brick and mortar." The smallest startup company can look like a huge global corporation. There are fewer available cues of the quality, durability, and financial position of an online site. There are fewer tangible signals of quality. For example, the web page of JP Morgan private banking is much less impressive than their office in downtown Manhattan.

Hanson and Putler (1996)[33] found that this desire for online quality cues is present and makes consumers vulnerable to manipulation. To demonstrate this point, they conducted a study in which they manipulated a weak signal of online quality. When a user wants to try out some shareware available on AOL, such as a gaming scenario or a graphics utility, he or she would go to the shareware forum.

Figure 4.14 shows the user interface at the time of this study. The only available information was the date of upload, the subject of the file, the title of the file, the cumulative number of downloads since this file appeared, and the date of the last download. From this page, the online user could get more information, download the file immediately, or schedule the file for later download. The authors conjectured that many consumers would use the download count as a signal of quality.

To test this hypothesis, the researchers matched pairs of files with similar descriptions, function, size, and time of original appearance on the shareware system. One of each pair was randomly selected as the treatment file. The other member of the pair was the control. The treatment file was then repeatedly downloaded, artificially inflating the hit count. Treatment levels varied from no impact to 100% of the original baseline number.

The results support the claim that users will flock to the popular items, and artificially inflating the download numbers can cause many more downloads. The more pronounced the lead in the number of files, the more additional downloads were induced. Download counts and other quality cues have an impact (Figure 4.14).

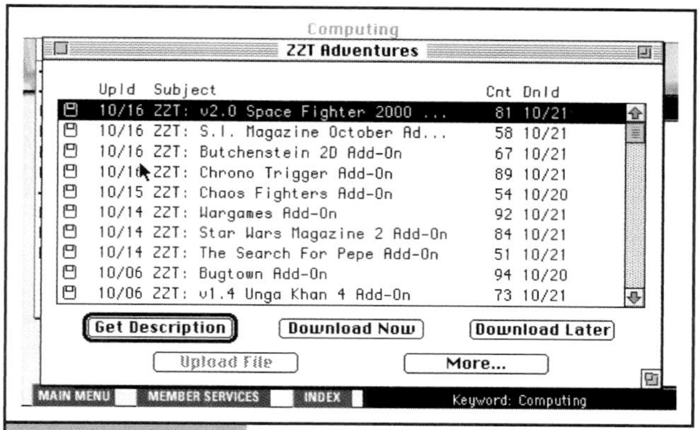

This result suggests that independent verification of web site usage can be important. It was easy and inexpensive for the researchers to manipulate the download counts; it would be even easier for a web site to report incorrect access numbers and steer users toward their preferred files. Online advertisers agree, and independent verification of web site traffic has become an important online service.

Quality cues play a big role in the eBay system. EBay faces the difficult challenge of supporting auctions for thousands of unique items. One important feature is a system for establishing seller reputations. For each auction item, a bidder can investigate the seller based on length of activity, the percentage of positive feedback, comments left by previous buyers, and other items sold by the seller (Figure 4.15). High-quality reputations are valuable. Controlled experiments show that unknown sellers receive significantly less revenue per sale than well-regarded sellers receive for the same item.[34]

Beyond the seller's reputation, eBay provides tools for investigating and verifying auction item features. Pictures and descriptions help. Bidders can ask sellers questions. Extensive bidding information reduces bid manipulation and helps limit bidding rings. The Security and Resolution Center helps resolve problems. Seller assistance tools make it easier for sellers to provide high-quality support. Each of these features provides quality cues, and reduces the risk of bidding and buying online.

Established brands often serve as a guarantor of quality, and play an important role in establishing online quality cues. Chapter 6 discusses this role of brands, and it may be even more important online than in traditional outlets.

> Friendly Technology

Observers comment that technology is technology only if it was invented after you were born. We don't usually think of cars, trains, or airplanes as technology. They seem to have always been around, familiar, and almost natural. The same is true for many electronic

Figure 4.14

Manipulating Weak Quality Cues

Source: Ward Hanson and Daniel Putler, Hits and Misses : Herd Behavior and Online, The Marketing Letters 7, no. 4 (1996): 297–305. Reprinted with kind permission of Springer Science and Business Media.

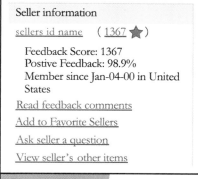

Figure 4.15

Reputation Systems on EBay

Source: "These materials have been reproduced with the permission of eBay Inc." COPYRIGHT © EBAY INC. ALL RIGHTS RESERVED

devices. Televisions, radios, telephones, and some form of VCR have market penetrations in excess of 90% of U.S. households. They have become familiar appliances, expected in almost every home.

Adoption rates fall as products become more complicated, expensive, or specialized. Products need to diffuse and become more general-purpose and less expensive to reach a majority of homes. With this in mind, personal computers have done very well. Despite a relatively high price compared to other consumer electronics, home computers are in over 80% of households in the United States.

The Internet has experienced rapid growth since 1995 largely because the World Wide Web is easy to use and more appliance-like than earlier versions. To reach anything like the 98% of homes with television, the Web must become even easier and friendlier.

The easiest type of online consumer activity is when loyal and experienced users perform simple tasks. Experienced users are familiar with the basic technology and aware of where information is stored and organized. In contrast, naive users will often require training, additional information, phone calls, and other supporting information to make them able to use the site and its features.

Loyal users are easier to handle than the occasional visitor and casual browser, as they are willing to invest time and effort to learn the system. They are much more likely to send information and suggestions to the online site and to tolerate occasional bugs and annoyances. Browsers, on the other hand, will often react quickly and negatively to any delay or problem. Rather than take the time to make suggestions, they will "click and be gone."

Loyal online users will be the consumers who take the time to send emails, take part in beta tests, provide feedback about new products, and otherwise help the company improve its offerings. If these consumers are experienced as well, it makes them able to articulate their concerns and effectively communicate with the company. Casual users lack this incentive and will simply go elsewhere. Naive users may have the personal commitment to the product but lack the basic knowledge and skills to use the online service effectively and provide a helpful "voice."

This type of web interaction also shapes the online difficulty. If all a user wants to do is collect simple company or product information, there is unlikely to be any difficulty. More complicated tasks, such as checking order status or seeking online customer support, require instruction. More risky transactions, such as the exchange of money and personal information, require trust, technical sophistication, and the willingness to pay careful attention to customer needs.

How marketers choose to position a product conditions users' expectations of ease and simplicity. One of the biggest challenges for firms introducing voice-over-IP (VoIP) to the consumer market is the ease and reliability of the traditional phone system. VoIP uses a home's broadband connection to provide phone service, usually at a much cheaper rate than the local phone company. The problem is expectation. People expect dial tone every time they pick up a phone, and they do not expect to have to reboot their phones if a problem arises. Even though VoIP can be very cheap and highly reliable, it looks much riskier if consumers view it as computer related.

INDIVIDUALIZATION AS A GPT

The Individualization GPT

The most innovative aspects of Internet marketing stem from an ability to link specific individuals, allow them to receive individualized information, and permit companies to increasingly refine their direct marketing interactions. Fundamental change happens when a direct connection to specific individuals, specific products, and specific information occurs. This leads to the third general purpose technology (GPT) of Internet marketing.

This GPT is individualization, the ability to (1) recognize individual people, items, and information, (2) remember relevant information and to learn from current activity, and (3) react on an individual basis to the available knowledge and demands. Just as RFIDs allow product tracking with increasingly detailed accuracy, individual usage and information content is increasingly tracked and customized. The semantic web, using technical approaches such as XML, creates detail and meaning for the content of stories and web pages. Companies understand their customers' previous activities better and match them to appropriate products and information.

Individualization is the least developed and most controversial of the three GPTs of Net marketing. It is a combination of technical capabilities and organizational changes. Unlike the performance of a computer or the extent of a network, it is more challenging to measure and compare over time. Earlier major GPTs such as electrification and the factory system, which also combine technical capabilities and organizational changes, provide a closer analogy. These GPTs entered the economy slowly, first in limited ways and in isolated occurrences, and then eventually as a dominant method of operation.

Just as modern networking required earlier breakthroughs in computerization, individualization requires both computing and networking. The pervasiveness of the individualization GPT appears in the databases, web logs, and powerful computing capable of tracking individual usage and handling the complexity of dealing with tens of millions of different users. Networks allow for individuals to share and correct information crucial for improving services and operating at the individual level, and companies to directly communicate at low cost with individuals.

The individualization GPT raises controversy due to fears of privacy invasion and governmental abuses. Part of this is familiarity. At a similar stage of development of computing, science fiction writing and movies were full of robots taking over and dominating humans. While still a popular theme, society has had decades of adapting and benefiting from the many uses of computers and fear of the digital revolution has subsided. Computers seem far more benign now, when they are vastly more powerful, than when some of the most memorable negative images debuted.

Part of the fear and concern is valid and real. It is extremely difficult to forecast the medium- and long-term impacts of any general purpose technology. Society takes time to develop rules to handle abuses and problems. Society eliminates some, and becomes accustomed to others. For example, the general purpose technology of the automobile has had vast repercussions on how we live our daily lives. It changed living patterns, recreation, job locations, family dynamics, and many other aspects of modern life. While few would give up their automobile, its benefits also come with the damages from widespread pollution and over a million traffic fatalities annually around the globe.[35]

One of the defining features of a GPT is the spillover between different industries. The RFID example beginning the chapter demonstrates spillovers between the military, Wal-Mart, and the pharmaceutical industry. Lessons learned in scanning, processing, and reacting to RFID tags in any of these sectors spill over to other industries. Other areas of online use demonstrate individualization spillovers as well. Capabilities for secure access to information learned in online banking spill over to medical or dating services. Techniques used in interactive advertising spill over to online education and tutoring.

Three capabilities underlie individualization as a GPT. These are authentication, association, and interaction. They provide the capabilities to recognize individuals, to remember and learn relevant information, and to react appropriately. This part defines and explains each in turn. Each is part technical and part organizational, and varies somewhat by application. The emphasis here is on online marketing, but as is the case for any GPT, they apply in many industries and business functions.

> *Authentication*

Authentication is the ability to identify an individual user or device. Authentication can be partial or complete. Partial authentication is useful for identifying members of a group, such as a computer located on a specific university campus. Complete authentication identifies a specific user.

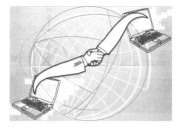

Source: © Photodisc Red/Getty Images

Authentication creates trust in the identity of the person communicating, the information received, and the properties of products and connecting devices. Without authentication, online identity may be counterfeit and unreliable. "Phishing" and "spoofing," where a fraudulent web site or email disguises itself as a credible site, is a serious problem stemming from failed authentication. On the other hand, thousands of secure ecommerce transactions every day are examples of successful authentication.

Authentication is part technical and part social. Technical characteristics establish the possible authentication capabilities, while social factors strongly influence whether actual performance is close to the theoretical ideal. One of the major drivers of identification as a GPT is the establishment of more secure authentication practices, usable in a wide range of settings.

Table 4.4 compares authentication elements using four settings. These are *Ali Baba and the Cave of the 40 Thieves*, a web site with an online password system, an ATM machine for banking,

Table 4.4

Elements of an Authentication System				
Authentication Element	**Cave of the 40 Thieves**	**Password Login**	**ATM Machine**	**Secure Web Server to Client**
1. What is authenticated?	Anyone who knew the password	Authorized user	Owner of a bank account	Web site owner
2. What is the distinguishing characteristic, token, or authenticator?	The password "Open, Sesame"	Secret password	ATM card and PIN	Public key within a certificate
3. Who is the proprietor, system owner, or administrator?	The forty thieves	Enterprise owning the system	Bank	Certificate authority
4. What is the authentication mechanism?	Magical device that responds to the word	Password validation software	Card validation software	Certificate validation software
5. What is the access control mechanism?	Mechanism to roll the stone from in front of the cave	Login process, access controls	Allows banking transactions	Browser marks the page "secure"

Source: Adapted from R. Smith (2002)

and a secure web server's interaction with an online shopper. Successful authentication must address the five questions in the first column.

> Q1: What Is Authenticated?

Authentication begins with the authenticated element. Often it is an individual. In other situations, it something broader such as a household, related family members, or members of a specific club or group. In *Ali Baba*, the band of thieves is the intended authenticated element but knowledge of the password is enough. For an ATM, the specific owner of a bank account is the authentication element. The authentication element connects closely to the concepts of ownership or marketing target.

Services must make decisions when multiple users share an account only authorized for single use. For example, the Rhapsody music service from Real Networks allows anyone knowledgeable of a user name and password combination to log in to the service from any computer. However, if another user logs at the same time with the same user ID and password, the system interrupts the original listener. This both enforces the limit on usage and alerts the original user if unauthorized access has occurred.

> Q2: What Is the Distinguishing Token?

Any authentication system relies on some form of token. These can be passwords, an Internet address, a stored browser cookie, physical smart cards, stored electronic keys and certificates, or user biometric information (Figure 4.16). The choice of token dramatically affects the strength, costs, and reliability of the authentication system. Low value or low threat systems can rely on simple and weaker protection, while high threat or high value systems rely on strong and redundant approaches.

Passwords are the most common authentication token for online use. In principle, passwords for modern online systems are an effective protection against all but the most determined and skilled hacker. Current implementations of Internet Explorer permit 128-bit passwords, difficult for criminals to break if used correctly. The problem, however, is with people and not technology.

A maximally secure password is one that is (1) as long as allowed, (2) uses all allowable letters, numbers, and other characters, and (3) is totally random.[36] Such passwords are very difficult for humans to memorize. Real people resort to simplifications that create security challenges. People choose short passwords, write them down on a slip of paper, use familiar words, family names, phrases, or phone numbers. Special characters, such as # or ~, are almost never used. Password reuse across different systems creates a further risk, as a proprietor of one system could use the shared password to gain access to a different system.

The common authentication approach chosen by Evite.com highlights the tradeoff between password security, password memorability, and customer support cost (Figure 4.17). Evite is a social site, most familiar as a free service for sending party and organizational invitations. Its business model requires very low customer support costs, so it must make customer interaction highly automated. Evite's activities are private, potentially sensitive,

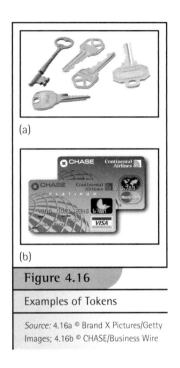

(a)

(b)

Figure 4.16

Examples of Tokens

Source: 4.16a © Brand X Pictures/Getty Images; 4.16b © CHASE/Business Wire

Figure 4.17

Evite Login

Source: Courtesy of Evite

but not financially critical. Their authentication system balances these goals. They use a standard ID + password approach, where the ID is an active email address. This ensures they can contact users automatically. Their password system has no minimum length, is case sensitive, but does not allow for any special symbols or spaces—making it much easier to crack. When a user forgets their password, a request automatically generates an email containing the forgotten password. Thus, anyone with access to an individual's email account could automatically gain access to a target's Evite account. With such an easily discovered ID as an email address, a password cracking system might utilize brute force and a dictionary to gain access.

Authentication with a physical device provides a different approach. Cell phones authenticate based on a pre-established link to the cellular operator. ATM cards combine a physical card with a password, although the password is often very short and easy to crack. Efforts to embed identifiers into each microprocessor, readable by online web sites, have encountered resistance from privacy groups. There has also been resistance to requiring smart cards or biometrics in all but the most security-conscious settings.

> Q3: Who Is the Proprietor?

An authenticated system requires some form of trusted proprietor, the entity responsible for maintaining the security arrangement. One of the reasons that the Internet has struggled with a general form of authentication is no general proprietor exists—no one owns the Net. Attempts to create a universal authentication system so far have proven unsuccessful. An early contender was the Passport system, operated by Microsoft since 1999. Passport relied on a typical login ID + password system, which verified identity to a web site without sharing the user's password.

A well-established and widely adopted system, perhaps based on a combination of physical and logical tokens, would simplify authentication dramatically. It would also raise the stakes for security of the "master token" dramatically, as a hacker who successfully acquires the master token could access multiple accounts and services simultaneously. An individual's financial, social, medical, and personal files would suddenly be unprotected and open to the hacker.

A failure to establish a centralized authentication proprietor for email is a partial cause of the current deluge of email spam. While each Internet service provider has a stake in reducing spam, the currently approved specification for email service does not support or require an effective proprietor. Specifically, the system lacks sender authentication. Anyone wishing to disguise their identity can technically do so without invalidating their outbound email. A proper authentication proprietor could verify the identity of the email sender.

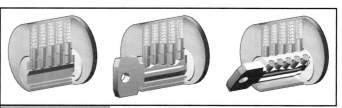

Figure 4.18

Keys (the Token) Embody a "Password" in their Physical Design

> Q4 and Q5: What Is the Authentication and Access Control Mechanism?

An authentication mechanism establishes that the proper token is present, and the access control mechanism grants an approved user entry. Figure 4.18 shows how a familiar key-based lock implements the authentication and control mechanism. When the proper key is inserted the lock-pins line up (the authentication mechanism) allowing the key to turn and the lock to open (the control mechanism). Online systems utilize software that ensures that the proper password or other token is present, and sends the proper messages to other software modules, allowing access.

Authentication is partly a technical choice and partly the result of business strategy. Highly valued assets and secrets can raise the barrier, requiring tokens using a combination of lengthy and temporary passwords, biometric identification, and physical separation. Less secure and valuable information can rely on simpler and cheaper systems. However, as action movies repeatedly show, even the most secure information is crackable by a clever enough adversary willing to devote the resources and skills (as in Figure 4.19). All too often, the weakness in the security is not technical but a human connected with the system proprietor.

Figure 4.19

Cracking the C.I.A.'s Computer

Source: © CORBIS SYGMA

> *Association*

Reliable authentication only sets the stage for individualization. The next step builds on knowledge about the individual. For example, when a web user logs on to a web site, the knowledge might be as simple as calculating the elapsed time since their last visit or as complex as recommending a product based on previous browsing behavior. With authentication comes the potential for a site to remember individual actions and to learn over time. At the heart of association is an ability to connect observable online choices with a customer profile. Key to this step is the precision of the knowledge about the individual.

The extent a marketer can connect actions to individuals is limited by the trust and cooperation that exists between the organization and the user. Figure 4.20 summarizes this into a precision-permission graph. The precision-permission graph connects the accuracy of the authentication mechanism to the implied permission given by a visitor. Low permission methods lead to low precision, while much higher accuracy is possible with higher trust and data access.

At the bottom of the information precision link is the simple web log. While the web log provides some information, it is a one-time snapshot only. No other identifying aspects are contained, and connecting usage to visitors over different sessions is not possible. The web log assists in spotting most popular and least popular pages, isolating trends, and highlighting possible problems. Its main use is diagnostic and historical. Because of its ready access for all sites, we consider it in more detail in Chapter 9.

The next step up in information precision occurs with cookies. From the earliest days of the browser, web sites have had the ability to send and access limited amounts of information to the browser for storage on the user's hard disk. The typical use of a cookie is to keep track of a user within the same session, and to track the user over time by storing a record number in a database maintained by the web site. By connecting a user via a record number, the system can accumulate information across sessions. When a user visits, the web site reads the cookie and looks up the user's information in his or her database. The database modifies the user's history because of the most recent visit, and updates the cookie to point to this new database information.

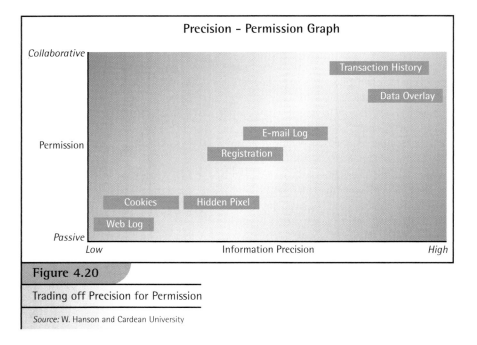

Figure 4.20

Trading off Precision for Permission

Source: W. Hanson and Cardean University

There are limitations to cookies that reduce their precision. One, a cookie is machine specific. If a user has more than one computer, say at home and at work, a cookie-based measure will consider these two different users. Two, cookies don't distinguish alternative individuals sharing a computer, and they count as one person to the web site. Third, cookies may be blocked or periodically deleted. Cookies are only a partial authentication system.

The hidden pixel approach is just a method of creating a multi-site cookie. A variation of the cookie approach occurs when a site uses a hidden file, often called a hidden pixel, to enable cookie writing. These hidden pixels are a small invisible picture, usually made the same color as the page background. The most common reason for hidden pixels is to outsource web site tracking to a firm specializing in online metrics. The hidden pixel allows the metrics firm to write cookies for each page, served from its own web server, and accumulate usage information it reports to the main web site owner.

As seen earlier, registration relies on a user-created identity and password. IDs need not be an actual name, and users may vary their IDs at different sites. Registration works better than cookies across time and machines, and lets the web site track information with fewer missed occasions or double counting. The email log does the same thing for repeated email interactions. The main precision problem with both of these approaches is the self-reported description of the individual. While the same user ID leads to better tracking, individuals may misrepresent their true demographics or other identity characteristics. Multiple individuals may still share the same ID, as long as they coordinate passwords and time of access. Users may create multiple ID names at the same site, so they can pretend to be different personas.

Full authentication occurs when there is a reliable and durable link to actual personal identity. While this may happen with a simple registration system as long as users tell the truth, it becomes much more accurate when personally identifiable identity is verified through a transaction. Using a credit card or a cell phone number reveals much more information than simple registration. Once a web site establishes a user's personal identity, it may choose to augment this information with additional data based on market or financial data service providers.

The evolution of identification technologies pushes many users higher up the permission-precision graph. This sets the stage for a number of benefits and problems. Benefits include a much more personalized web site, access to account information, ease of transactions, and a number of other conveniences. The downside for loss of personal data privacy is also sizable. Companies and governments are struggling with the right balance, and this discussion occurs throughout the coming chapters.

Increased precision is valuable to a marketer. In Chapter 9, we present methods for connecting the precision of the information about an individual with targeting, pricing, and other individualized marketing messages. The challenge is to properly balance the gains from individualization against the costs of making mistakes in inference and association. The higher the precision, the lower the chance of a mistaken action.

> *Interaction*

Diverse and versatile communication modes are a powerful aspect of the Internet. A company can use the Net as a global broadcasting station, a direct marketing vehicle sending targeted specialty messages to niche audiences, or a channel for dialogue with specific individuals. Each of these communications modes has different levels of interaction, uses a different assortment of technologies, and requires different managerial skills. The first step for an online marketer is appreciating these different communications modes. Dell Computer provides valuable lessons on how a company can profitably vary its communication strategy based on characteristics of customers and how it takes advantage of the flexibility of online communication methods.

Dell Computer's online presence reflects this flexibility of communication and the matching of information to customer importance.[37] Different classes of customers receive different amounts of information. Better customers receive information that is more complete, more extensively customized services, and perhaps even better prices. Figure 4.21 shows how this works. The "Dell triangle" reflects the typical inverse relationship between the number of customers in a class and the scope of information they receive. At the top of the triangle is the "all customers" class. This is the broadest category and applies to anyone who visits the Dell site. Successive classes refer to more in-depth relationships. The next step is registration. Contracted customers extend the relationship with formal purchasing agreements. At the peak of the relationship is the platinum class, with extensive quantity and ordering business.

Dell's "all customers" class receives an extensive amount of information and online quality enhancement. This includes product details, ordering information, shipping details, the ability to configure a unique computer and get the list price quote, general technical support, and user forums, as well as general information about Dell as a company. Personalization and additional content begin with registered users. A registered user indicates which pieces of information he or she would like to track. When new information becomes available, it triggers an email message. Online newsletters, customized by account, provide the Web-based information.

Contracted customers have a history of purchasing with Dell, and they can check this history for cumulative sales, custom links, customized offerings, and special discounts. Platinum customers get extensive personalization. Dell translates into 18 different languages and provides web hosting of customer sites in 36 countries. Platinum customers are encouraged to participate in online discussions with product designers to ensure that new products reflect the needs and wishes of the key customers.

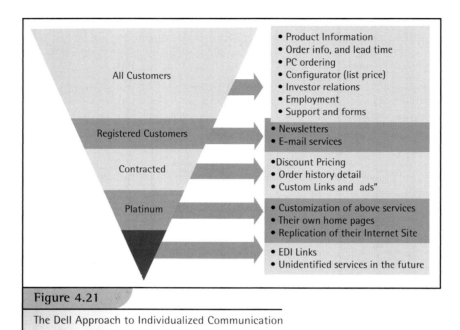

Figure 4.21

The Dell Approach to Individualized Communication

The essential lesson from Dell is as old as marketing. A firm's activities should reflect the specific needs and wishes of individuals. New technologies make it cost-effective to return to an individual-based approach to marketing. Each increase in interactivity lets Dell build and deepen its relationships with customers. To realize this promise, Dell must create effective interactions, and make its system available in ways that reflect customer access, experience, and expectations.

The Dell Triangle indicates that individualization connects naturally to measures of customer profitability and importance. Chapter 5 highlights the many business justifications for online content. Underlying each of these, and more generally, the ability to connect individually, are measures of customer value and lifetime profitability.

ENDNOTES

1. Don Peppers and Martha Rogers. (1997). *Enterprise One to One: Tools for Competing in the Interactive Age.* Currency Doubleday. New York, p. 13.
2. Mihaly Csikszentmihalyi. (1990). *Flow: The Psychology of Optimal Experience.* Harper Perennial. New York.
3. General Accounting Office. (2004). Internet Pharmacies: Some Pose Safety Risks for Consumers. Report to the Chairman. Permanent Subcommittee on Investigations. Committee on governmental Affiars. U.S. Senate. June. p. 2.
4. Special safety conditions applied to Accutane (acne) and Clozaril (schizophrenia) (possible depression and suicide risks). Refrigeration applied to Epogen (anemia) and Humulin (diabetes). Schedule II narcotics included OxyContin (pain), Percocet (pain), and Vicodin (pain). Other leading drugs ordered were Celebrex (arthritis), Combivir (HIV), Crixivan (HIV), Lipitor (cholesterol), Viagra (sexual dysfunction), and Zoloft (depression).
5. Mark Roberti. (2003). "Analysis: RFID—Wal-Mart's Network Effect," *CIO Insight* September 15. Pre-launch estimates have annual savings of $8.35 billion, of which $6.7 billion is due to labor cost savings. Other benefits are $600 million due to lower out-of-stock items; $575 million due to

reduced fraud; $300 million due to better pallet tracking through the supply chain; $180 million due to better visibility of products in supply chain leading to lower required inventory levels. Additional detail of the roll-out of Wal-Mart's plans was presented by Linda Dillman. Chief Information Officer of Wal-Mart, in testimony to the Subcommittee on Commerce. Trade and Consumer Protection. U. S. House of Representatives. July 14. 2004.

6. Bob Brewin. (2003). "Military Orders Suppliers to Use RFID Technology." *ComputerWorld* October 13.

7. Lena Chow. (2003). "The New Challenges of Personalized Medicine," *Medical Marketing and Media*. 38(3), 68–72.

8. Susannah Fox. (2004). "Prescription Drugs Online." *Pew Internet & American Life Project Report*. October.

9. Dan Horsky. (1990). "A Diffusion Model Incorporating Product Benefits. Price. Income and Information," *Marketing Science* 9(4), 342–365. For some interesting complications in the tradeoff of time and money see Erica Mina Okada and Stephen J. Hoch. (2004). "Spending Time versus Spending Money," *Journal of Consumer Research* 31(2) 313–322.

10. Sue Bowden and Avner Offer. (1994). "Household appliances and the use of time: the United States and Britain since the 1920s," *Economic History Review* XLVII, 725–748.

11. Definitions and data from Online Publishers Association.

12. An important early study was D. Roberts. U. Foehr, V. Rideout, and M. Brodie. (1999). *Kids & Media @ the new millennium*. Kaiser Family Foundation. November.

13. Most of the world's population has never been online. This pool of nonusers varies dramatically by country. In poor countries, household income dominates a wide range of telecommunication usage. The single best predictor of online access in these countries is the affluence of a household.

14. While some disadoption may occur for some users as they age, the main impact will be for very high adoption rate cohorts to replace low adoption rate cohorts.

15. Continual growth from the "central cohorts," such as those aged 35–44, may still occur if the actual saturation level continues to rise. If the Internet becomes as basic as television, eventual market penetration rates in the high 90% range may even be possible. Central cohorts are quite large, so any growth in these segments translates to a sizable number of users.

16. H. Stephen Kay. (2003). "Disability and the digital divide: Accounting for lower levels of computer and Internet usage among people with disabilities." presented at APHA, Nov. 17. 2003.

17. Byron Reeves and Clifford Nass. (1996). *The Media Equation: How People Treat Computers, Television, and New Media Like Real People and Places.* Cambridge Press. Also see Clifford Nass and Youngme Moon. (2000). "Machines and Mindlessness: Social Responses to Computers." *Journal of Social Issues* 56(1), 81–103.

18. Youngme Moon. (2002). "Personalization and Personality: Some Effects of Customizing Message Style Based on Consumer Personality." *Journal of Consumer Psychology*. 12(4), 313–326.

19. Bailenson. J.N.. Beall. A.C.. Blascovich. J.. Weisbuch. M.. & Raimmundo. R. (2001). *Intelligent Agents Who Wear Your Face: Users' Reactions to the Virtual Self.* Lecture Notes in Artificial Intelligence. 2190. 86–99.

20. This seems closely connected to what neuroscientists are calling "mirror neurons" in the brain. Brain scans demonstrate striking similarity between an individual doing an action and the same individual watching others do the action.

21. Donna Hoffman and Tom Novak. (1996). "Marketing in Hypermedia Computer-Mediated Environments: Conceptual Foundations," *Journal of Marketing* 60, 50–68.

22. See T. Novak, D. Hoffman, and A. Duhachek. (2003). "The Influence of Goal-Directed and Experiential Activities on Online Flow Experiences." *Journal of Consumer Psychology* 12, 3–16; Charla Mathwick and Edward Rigdon. (2004). "Play, Flow, and the Online Search Experience." *Journal of Consumer Research*. 31, 324–332.

23. See, for example, Ting-Jui Chou and Chih-Chen Ting. (2003). "The Role of Flow Experience in Cyber-Game Addiction." *Cyber Psychology & Addiction* 6(6), 663–675.

24. Pearl Chen and Diane McGrath. (2003). "Moments of Joy: Student Engagement and Conceptual Learning in the Design of Hypermedia Documents." *Journal of Research on Technology in Education* 35(3), 402–421.

25. See the ongoing discussion of accessibility at the w3c.org web site.

26. Annabel Pollock and Andrew Hockley. (1997). "What's Wrong with Internet Searching." *D-Lib Magazine*. March.

27. Thomas K. Landauer. (1996). *The Trouble With Computers: Usefulness. Usability and Productivity*. MIT Press, Cambridge, MA.

28. Lee Sproull and Sara Kiesler. (1994). *Connections: New Ways of Working in the Networked Organization*. MIT Press, Cambridge, MA, 57.

29. *The Hackers Dictionary*. quoted by Sproul and Kiesler (1994), p. 49.

30. See J. Storck and L. Sproul (1995). "Through a glass darkly: what do people learn in videoconferences?" *Human Communication Research*. 22(2), 197–219.

Cited in Gene Rowe and John G. Gammack. (2004). "Promise and perils of electronic public engagement," *Science and Public Policy* February, 39–54.

31. For more on the link with strength of ties see Caroline Haythornthwaite. (2002). "Strong, Weak, and Latent Ties and the Impact of New Media." *The Information Society* 18, 385–401.

32. Theodore Levitt. (1986). *The Marketing Imagination* Free Press, New York.

33. Ward Hanson and Daniel Putler. (1996). "Hits and Misses: Herd Behavior and Online Product Popularity." *Marketing Letters* 7(4), 297–305.

34. For example Patrick Bajari and Ali Hortacsu. (2003). "The winner's curse. reserve prices. and endogenous entry: empirical insights from eBay auctions." *RAND Journal of Economics* 34(2), 329–355.

35. Estimates for worldwide traffic fatalities in 1998 was 1,170,694. *World Health Organization.* "Injury: A Leading Cause of the Global Burden of Disease," 1999.

36. See Jianxin Yan, Alan Blackwell, Ross Anderson, and Alasdair Grant. (2000). "The Memorability and Security of Passwords—Some Empirical Results," working paper. Cambridge University Computer Laboratory.

37. Kenneth Hill. (1997). "Chapter 6: Electronic Marketing: The Dell Computer Experience," in Peterson. *Electronic Marketing and the Consumer.* Sage Publications, Thousand Oaks, CA, 89–99.

part 2:

Essential Skills

Chapter 5: Web Business Models

Chapter 6: Online Branding

Chapter 7: Usability, Credibility, and Persuasion

Chapter 8: Traffic Building

Chapter 9: Personalization

Chapter 10: Creating Commitment

Chapter 11: Innovation and the Net

Chapter 12: Pricing in an Online World

chapter 5:

Web Business Models

" A good business model begins *"* with an insight into human motivations and ends in a rich stream of profits.

Joan Magretta[2]

Even Auctions on Tornados
Source: Photographer: Eric Nguyen

The eBay Ecology

Some call it the Perfect Store.[3] It calls itself the World's Online Marketplace. Hundreds of books provide advice about how best to sell and buy using its services. It has 75.4 million active users, with an active user defined as one who has bid, bought, or listed an item in the previous year.[4] Its first quarter 2006 net revenues, the amount of money it receives for fees and commissions, reached $1.4 billion and split almost evenly between domestic and international sales. It is highly profitable, with GAAP net income after all expenses of $248.3 million.

The firm, of course, is eBay. In less than 10 years, it has become the hub of online commerce and livelihood for millions of individuals around the world. It does this by selling an incredibly wide range of products and services. It has 12 product categories generating more than $1 billion in gross revenue, with the top four being eBay Motors, Consumer Electronics, Computers, and Clothing and Accessories. At the same time, it is the home of many unusual auctions, such as an opportunity to join Midwest tornado specialists chasing storms for two weeks (sale price, $1,495) (Figure 5.1).[5]

EBay wasn't the only, or even the first, site that targeted online auctions. Auction site OnSale.com launched in May of 1995, beating eBay's September launch. However, eBay quickly became the number one site. By August of 1998, it had monthly gross revenues of $70 million with the number 2 and 3 sites at only $5 million.[6]

The Internet provides firms with many profitable opportunities. This chapter highlights the business justifications for online efforts, both direct and indirect. A central concept is customer lifetime value, and the methods for improving lifetime value through online contact.

Topics covered in this chapter include:

> The eBay Ecology

> Customer Lifetime Value

> The Value of Contacts

> Business Justifications

While it launched with an emphasis on collectibles, eBay has grown by constantly solving problems and expanding its geographic coverage and the items and services it provides.

Entering new countries was an early focus. International markets provide balance and diversification, both in terms of economic activity and Internet development. EBay currently has web sites focusing on Australia, Austria, Belgium, Canada, China, France, Germany, Hong Kong, India, Ireland, Italy, Malaysia, the Netherlands, New Zealand, the Philippines, Singapore, South Korea, Spain, Sweden, Switzerland, Taiwan, the United Kingdom, and the United States. It expanded into South America in partnership with MercadoLibre, reaching Argentina, Brazil, Chile, Columbia, Ecuador, Mexico, Peru, Uruguay, and Venezuela. One of its few failures overseas is Japan, dominated by a joint venture between Yahoo! and Softbank. After attempting a late entry, eBay faced the barriers its own competitors face in other markets. It withdrew from Japan, at least temporarily, in 2002.[7]

Auctions work best with a depth of participation. Auction theory and empirical studies demonstrate that the expected revenue from an auction is increasing in the number of participants capable and willing to bid. The 60 million eBay participants are a sizable barrier to any other auction site seeking to compete. Even with its high number of members many auctions at eBay go with 0 or 1 bid only.[8] (See Table 5.1.) It is the unusual auction that leads to a burst of activity. Unless a competitive site can focus on specialty areas, it has a challenging task winning away potential listings for its site.

Investors have rewarded eBay's expansion and high profits despite the ups and downs of the economy and Internet. A comparison between eBay and Amazon.com, shown in Figure 5.2, shows the strong relative showing of eBay. Since 1998, Amazon.com has grown modestly in stock value, while eBay has risen dramatically. EBay's market capitalization, its financial value, is more than three times that of Amazon.[9] While both eBay and Amazon have built a healthy ecosystem of sellers and affiliates, eBay has a more profitable business

Table 5.1

Number of Bids for eBay Listings	
Number of Bids	**% of Total Items**
No bids	54%
1	23%
2	5%
3	4%
4	3%
5	2%
6+	8%

Source: From Auction Software Review sample auctionsoftwarereview.com.

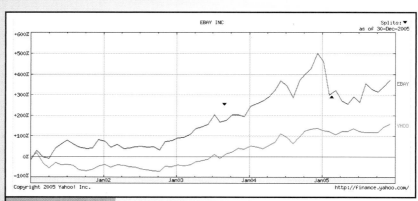

Figure 5.2

The Strong Financial Performance of eBay versus Amazon

Source: Yahoo!, Inc.

model and faces fewer logistics, inventory, and competitive challenges than Amazon. Amazon competes more in the low margin retailing business. EBay has created a system where it plays the role of digital hub of both business-to-consumer and consumer-to-consumer transactions.

Handling consumer-to-consumer payments was an early challenge to growth for online auctions, and remains so in many countries. Buyers are afraid of sending a check prior to receipt of the good, and sellers are afraid to send the good without payment. Sharing credit card information with unknown individuals is risky, requiring some other method. The innovativeness of startups building businesses around eBay, creating eBay support services and an assistance ecology, helped to partially solve the problem. Started in 1998, PayPal emerged as a successful system that provided fraud protection and a method for direct consumer payment. Unlike many other attempts at the time, it grew rapidly with most of its business in support of eBay auctions. In 2002 eBay acquired PayPal, and it now is an important source of revenue as well. PayPal creates yet another stream of commissions when bidders use it to pay for their purchases (Table 5.2). More recently, eBay acquired leading voice-over-IP phone service provider Skype, providing yet another new line of support, fees, and members.

A provider as dominant as eBay becomes a focal point for innovation by others. Examples abound. Time Warner, without any direct involvement of eBay, has added eBay auction tracking to some of its cable systems. This allows television viewers to see the progress of auctions they are tracking over their cable system, without turning on their computer.[10] UPS and AuctionDrop provide a drop-off listing and shipping

Table 5.2

PayPal's Rapid Growth (in millions, except percentages)					
	3Q 2004	4Q 2004	1Q 2005	2Q 2005	3Q 2005
Total Accounts	56.7	63.8	71.6	78.9	86.6
Current quarter vs prior quarter	13%	13%	12%	10%	10%
Current quarter vs prior year quarter	61%	58%	57%	56%	53%
Active Accounts	17.2	20.2	22.1	22.9	24.5
Total Number of Payments	83.4	99.6	110.4	113.2	117.4
Current quarter vs prior quarter	7%	19%	11%	3%	4%
Current quarter vs prior year quarter	45%	46%	39%	46%	41%
Total Payment Volume	$4,637	$5,607	$6,233	$6,471	$6,667
Current quarter vs prior quarter	7%	21%	11%	4%	3%
Current quarter vs prior year quarter	52%	51%	44%	49%	44%
eBay Marketplace as % of total payment vol.	70%	71%	71%	70%	69%
Transaction Rates					
Transaction revenue rate	3.59%	3.57%	3.64%	3.67%	3.60%
Transaction processing expense rate	1.30%	1.27%	1.15%	1.08%	1.11%
Transaction loss rate	0.22%	0.31%	0.30%	0.19%	0.24%

Source: eBay Inc., eBay Announces Q3–05 Earnings, p. 15, http://investor.ebay.com/.

service at the 3,400 UPS outlets throughout the United States. For a fee, they take a photo, run the auction, and handle the shipping and logistics. Current product restrictions require items to weigh less than 25 pounds and sell for more than $75.[11]

To keep this "tornado of growth" going,[12] eBay works to support its sellers and to encourage visits by potential buyers. Among the activities used to bring in bidders is keyword advertising, which bids daily on thousands of keywords related to items currently on auction at eBay. The eBay search team manages one of the most sophisticated keyword advertising efforts as a carefully measured bidder acquisition process. Every auction starts fresh, and the traffic-driving efforts and market strength of eBay combine to funnel interest to as many sellers as possible. These keyword buys are carefully weighed against the fees and commissions received by eBay to maintain their profitability.

VALUING CONTACTS

EBay provides an example of a highly successful online startup, almost perfectly positioned to benefit from DNI (digital-network-individualization) capabilities. EBay relies heavily on digital power to support the millions of users and the thousands of auctions operating simultaneously. Networking, both social and technological, is required to connect the diverse contributions, the flows of product and money, and the shared resources. Commerce at the individual level, from reputation to listings and payments, gives eBay its diverse feel and innovative business practices.

Often throughout this book the phrase "Internet" is used as shorthand for the digital-network-individualization general purpose technologies. The Internet provides opportunities for improved marketing by almost all businesses. These extend from the micro level of valuing electronic contacts to the macro level of new business opportunities it makes possible.

Perhaps the most fundamental level of change is the way businesses interact with customers. The next part discusses how this alters the focus of marketing from the occasional market transaction toward a more careful analysis of continuous and ongoing company and customer contacts, including their impact on customer and brand equity. This includes tools to evaluate and quantify the business value of these near continuous interactions.

At the heart of valuing customer contacts is an appreciation of the interaction between contacts and longer-term relationship benefits. The fundamental metric is customer lifetime value, which highlights the importance of both a long-term perspective for short-term actions and the reality that not all customers have the same economic benefits to a firm. Internet capabilities both reveal differences and create a marketing channel well suited for low-cost individualized interaction.

Technology and Marketing Axioms

In a classic 1972 article, Philip Kotler outlined four axioms of marketing:

1. Marketing involves two or more social units, each consisting of one or more human actors,
2. At least one of the social units is seeking a specific response from one or more other units concerning some social object,
3. The market's response probability is not fixed,
4. Marketing is the attempt to produce the desired response by creating and offering values to the market.

Kotler emphasized the centrality of the transaction, and "the core concern of marketing is that of producing desired responses in free individuals by the judicious creation and offering of values." At the time he wrote his article transactions were the most measurable of consumer responses. Specific customer impacts of television ads, new features, or other aggregate marketing actions are hard to determine. Judging effectiveness requires market surveys, noisy statistical analysis, and a team of researchers for even partial results.

Two decades later, Sheth and Parvatiyar argued that technology and practice shifted marketing toward relationships (with mutual interdependence and cooperation) and away from transactions (with competition and independence). They point out that this is a return to the past, with the industrial era as a temporary dip in attention to relationships.

The authors argue the most important impact of the shift to relationships is a renewed interest in *value creation* and a shift from *value distribution*. It is a move toward what gets created and away from who gets the money.

Sources: Philip Kotler, (1972), A Generic Concept of Marketing, *Journal of Marketing*, Vol. 36, April. Jagdish Sheth and Atul Parvatiyar, (1995), "The Evolution of Relationship Marketing," *International Business Review*, 4, 4: 397–418.

Evaluating customer contacts happens across applications and businesses. It helps to organize these firm opportunities into the indirect benefits of efficiency, effectiveness, and enhancement. There are also the direct benefits of additional revenue sources. These form the building blocks of innovative business approaches.

Marketing Actions and Responses

Online technologies provide the ability to refine marketing actions. When Kotler described the axioms of marketing in the early 1970s he emphasized the eventual transaction (see research box). Two decades later, with the commercialization of the Net and benefits of substantial improvements, marketing could quantify and focus on consumer reactions beyond the purchase. One of the most important business benefits and justifications is at this micro level—where marketers can learn and respond to detailed customer interactions.

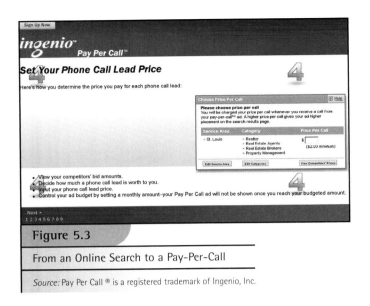

Figure 5.3

From an Online Search to a Pay-Per-Call

Source: Pay Per Call ® is a registered trademark of Ingenio, Inc.

A well-implemented online system can track an online user from a click on a search engine keyword ad, to specific web pages viewed, and on to purchase or exit. Successful online companies such as eBay carefully evaluate their customer acquisition methods, identify the best performing methods, and reallocate spending appropriately.

Better tracking of marketing actions and customer response help create closed-loop marketing, when specific customer responses connect to improved and effective specific marketing actions. For example, if an online ad is run encouraging web site registration, the campaign is closed loop if a firm can track users from ad exposure to registration decision, observe what works and what does not, and change performance and spending accordingly. Closed loop price changes mean tracking the impact of the price change all the way to the purchase decision and profitability analysis, and reacting to these lessons.

Accountability has a tendency to expand. Lessons learned using online tools are helping improve older media. Broadcasters are beginning to incorporate online promotions to better gauge viewer interests. Figure 5.3 shows a company learning from the highly popular pay-per-click search advertising, and applying pay-per-action pricing to situations where the desired customer response is a telephone enquiry.

In addition to accountability, emphasizing closed-loop marketing leads to faster learning. Showing price changes, ad copy, product features, or other marketing variables to a carefully selected sample of consumers leads to low-cost experiments. Marketing becomes more scientific.

Traditional means of communicating within and between businesses used incompatible systems and dedicated approaches. While these worked well enough and could operate globally, they tended to isolate divisions.[13] With the rise of a global Net platform, businesses can much more easily share information, access databases, collaborate on design, and many of the other shared tasks of a global supply chain and customer base.

As marketers learn to track and measure the customer responses to their marketing actions, there is a shift from a focus on customers as a string of isolated transactions to an ongoing process of individualized interaction. This is not automatic, and requires both external and internal capabilities. Figure 5.4 highlights some of the most important features, including:

> a comprehensive customer database that captures the full range of customer interactions,
> a method of classifying and categorizing customers so that interactions can be tailored to specific tastes and requirements,
> a method of forecasting future customer importance, and
> a system of allocating effort and resources to maximize the value of the customer base.

The specifics of the boxes in Figure 5.4 are important. The systems for improving usability of sites covered in Chapter 7 help build the customer database. Traffic-building systems measure the

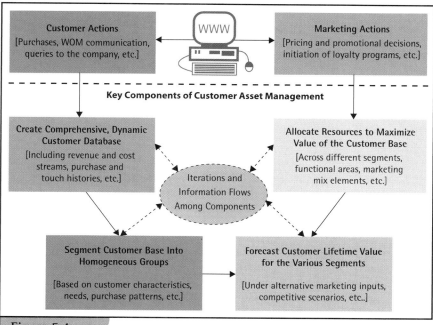

Figure 5.4

Using the Internet to Enhance Customer Value

Source: Adapted from Paul D. Berger and N. Nasr, "Customer Lifetime Value: Marketing Models and Applications," *Journal of Interactive Marketing* 12, no. 1 (1998): 17–30.

connections of marketing actions and response. Systems for personalization covered in Chapter 9 rely heavily on proper customer segmentation and understanding. Indeed, each of the chapters contributes something to make Figure 5.4 less of a goal and more of a reality.

The Value of a Customer Contact

Online customer contacts come in a wide array of forms. Methods are proliferating, especially with always-on broadband and continuously available wireless access. A visitor may type in a web address from memory and arrive at a web site. An animated banner advertisement explains a soon-to-be released product, stimulating a customer to place an early order. A weekly email goes out to previous software purchasers, describing new uses and new options. A web-enabled cell phone user does online price checking while strolling through product displays.

A marketer needs some approach to valuing these customer contacts. Managers of electronic communications need to budget

Figure 5.5

Contact Everywhere

Source: © Terri Miller/E-Visual Communications Inc.

appropriately, which requires understanding how online interactions affect their business. These should include the full impact of electronic connections on customers, suppliers, and channel partners.

Web chain analysis provides a starting point for calculating the benefits of these electronic contacts, whether they are visiting a site, receiving an email, or some other interaction. It does this by creating a list of the possible impacts, quantifying their monetary value, and assigning probabilities that they occur. These probabilities allow the firm to calculate the expected unified value of the contact. The term unified value indicates that the full range of results, good and bad, should be included in the calculation.

Almost any electronic connection can lead to a large number of possible customer actions. Some customers may choose to visit a site but nothing else. Others will finally fill out a registration form after several previous visits. Other customers will move from initial contact to large purchase with the initial contact. A web chain analysis handles these many different possibilities, and weights them according to both their likelihood of happening.

> *The Web Chain Concept*

A web chain of events is the sequence of steps taken as the result of an online contact. It can be as short as a single click, or a hundred different page views. At various steps, different directions and choices are possible. These are event nodes. Eventually the web chain leads to one of the possible end points, labeled as result nodes.

Web chains can start in many different ways. A user may visit Yahoo! or Alta Vista looking for companies selling golf equipment. A search of the keyword "golf" leads to thousands of possible sites, plus keyword ads on the side and top of the return list. An online reader of the *Washington Post* may see a banner ad promoting an online travel agency. A Monday morning email reader finds her email box filled with multiple commercial offers. A visitor to an industry virtual tradeshow sees a link and pursues it.

Figure 5.6 shows several possible sequences for students interested in SAT preparation. Visitor 1 (red arrow) sees the display ad, perhaps subconsciously, but chooses to read some alternative content instead. Visitors 2 and 3 see the ad, become intrigued by the featured book, and click on the banner. Visitor 2 decides a different book is more appropriate, but waits to buy it later. Visitor 3 buys the featured product immediately, using the ecommerce capabilities of the site.

Web chain analysis seeks to put a value on this banner ad by tracking the possible reactions to it, putting values on the results, and systematically comparing them through their expected value. By doing this, a firm can evaluate whether the advertisement is valuable, whether it is the best way to drive traffic to the site, and how valuable online visits are.

As this simple SAT example shows, even a few pages can lead to many alternatives. There are numerous branches different visitors can follow, with each branch leading to another set of possibilities. Even though each of these may be traceable with the help of web logs and customer relationship software, the sheer number of possibilities requires simplification. Choices need clustering into categories, such as read content only, content + registration, and purchase. These grouped alternatives can then be valued. As the web chain calculation requires probabilities, it is important that the list of results account for all possibilities. This ensures that the result probabilities sum to one.

Figure 5.7 presents one clustering easily solvable in a spreadsheet. In this example, each rate corresponds to a yes or no question reflecting steps along the web chain.

> Does the visitor miss the ad? (the no notice rate NNR)
> Does the visitor click through? (the click through rate CTR)

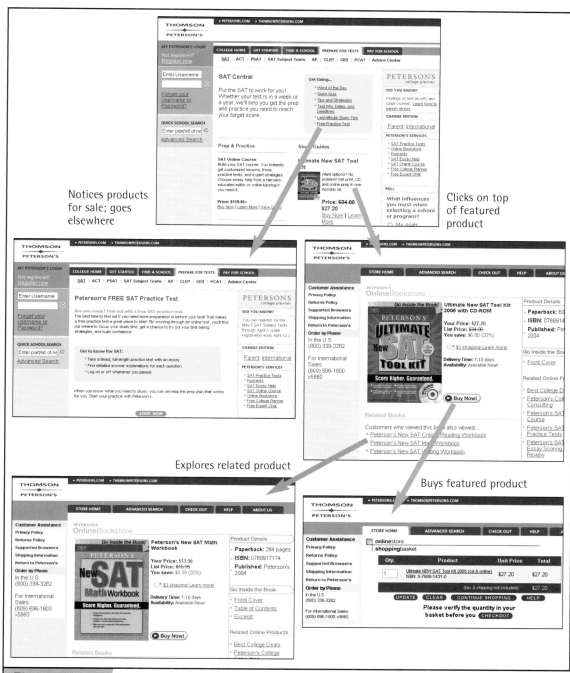

Figure 5.6

Portions of a Web Chain Beginning with a SAT Book Ad

Source: Screen captures reprinted by permission of Peterson's, a division of Thomson Learning: www.thomsonrights.com

> Does the web site convert the visitor? (the prospect conversion rate PCR)
> Did the visit induce an additional offline purchase? (the offline induced buy rate OIB)
> Is the converted visitor a repeat customer? (the repeat buyer rate RR)
> Does this online purchase replace an offline purchase? (the offline buying rate OBR)

Other groupings may be more appropriate in different settings. For example, there may be situations where the goal of initial contact is collecting an email. Events around that result should then be included, probably in detail. Simplifications of the web chain can be useful as well. Traffic-building activities (the focus of Chapter 8) often look only at cost-per-click or cost-per-customer acquisition. These form a two-cluster web chain, the desired action and everything else.

Even though clustering may change from Figure 5.7, going through the steps clarifies the decision making and the method of combining results. Adjustments in the number and precise nature of events and results are then easy to implement.

> Visitors That Don't Click

The chain begins at E1, the first event node. The first result, likely in many cases, is that the ad goes unnoticed. The probability of this is the no notice rate. This leads to the first possible endpoint, result node R1. There is no benefit to the company from these Web impressions.

The no notice rate, sometimes called "banner blindness,"[14] can be both psychological and technological. Familiarity with banner ad locations may lead readers to skip over the content and automatically focus elsewhere. Some laboratory studies find a no notice rate in the range of 60%.[15] An even more permanent blocking occurs through browser or firewall software. Within the Mozilla FireFox browser, for example, it is possible to selectively block images from ad-serving networks without blocking images from the main content page. The page simply appears with blank space where the advertisement would be, eliminating any possibility of noticing the message. This same function is an option for some firewall software.[16]

A second possibility is a visitor who notices the ad but does not click on it. This leads to the ad banner impact result node R2. Advertising professionals have been skeptical about the branding impact of banners, especially early-generation small format static banners. Others argue that as little as a single exposure can have measurable branding results.[17] The web chain approach is agnostic on this issue, and permits any value of branding impact per exposure.

The ad-brand impact is potentially quite important. In almost all banner ad campaigns, the percentage of ads clicked on is small. A click-through rate of .5% is typical for static ads, 1.2% for rich media ads,[18] implying that 99 % of the ad impressions get no click. Web viewers do see a sizable number of impressions. A small but positive ad-brand impact results in a large cumulative impact.

Not all parts of a web chain may be traceable and closed loop. In most actual campaigns, it will be impossible to distinguish between R1 and R2. Both result from "no click," without any immediate feedback. A marketer must resort to samples, surveys, and other indirect methods to tell how many ad viewers actually noticed the ad and chose not to click. The marketer is able to tell how many belong to the combined result R1 and R2 but not the split.

> Unconverted Prospects

Results R3 and R4 reflect a user that clicks on the banner, visits the web site, but is not considered converted, although it may encourage an existing customer to continue or even accelerate

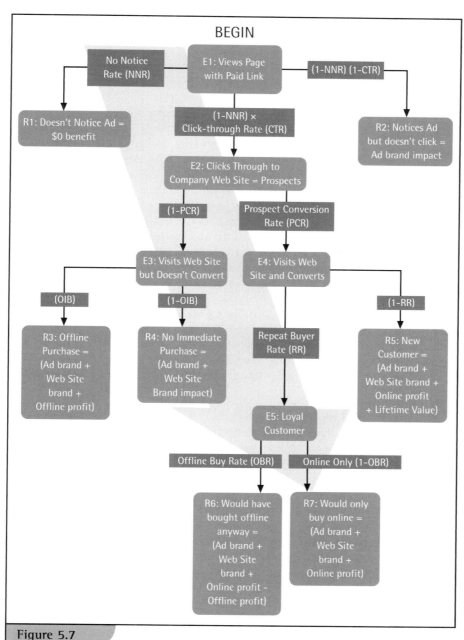

Figure 5.7

A Web Chain of Events

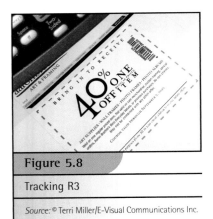

Figure 5.8

Tracking R3

Source: © Terri Miller/E-Visual Communications Inc.

a purchase. Prospects may still obtain the product through traditional channels. If the ad or the visit to the web site stimulates the purchase, it is a positive impact of the ad and the web site visit. This is the link to R3, which shares the traditional problem of linking media advertising with eventual sales (Figure 5.8). Unless active programs are in place to encourage customers to reveal that they used the online site, it will be hard for the company to document this link accurately.

Encoding online discounts with unique identifiers improves the feedback between ad, visit, and purchase. When redeemed, it is possible to match the revenue to the online channel. Proper coding can encode a unique identifier on the coupon allowing a match to the specific visit-generating ad.

Chapter 6 documents how a well-designed site can improve branding. It can build trust and confidence in the company. It can reinforce an image of competence, functionality, and usefulness. It can alert the visitor to the company's range of products and services. It can point out local dealers, upcoming special events, and reasons to come back again.

A web chain analysis requires a translation from these qualitative impacts to monetary terms. This will necessarily be an approximation. The quality of the visit is important. Chapter 7 highlights a number of visit aspects that indicate whether persuasion and credibility are likely to result from a visit. Different routes through a site may influence how big of a web site brand impact results. When this is true, the analyst should define multiple site brand impacts. For this example, we limit it to one impact. At result R4, only the ad and web site brand impact occur.

> Converted Prospects

Prospect conversion occurs if the prospect reaches E4. If the converted prospect is a new customer, he or she is especially valuable. Future profits from this new customer are a valid part of the benefits. This is R5, which for convenience separates out first purchases from remaining customer lifetime value.

Figure 5.7 simplifies the web chain by assuming the same ad and web site brand impact for nonbuyers, first time buyers, and loyal users. This will be fine for some cases, incorrect for others. Each result node could have its own branding impacts, reflecting the different types of customers ending up there.

For many purposes, it is enough to record a purchase and the profit it creates. However, this overstates the benefit if the buyer would have bought through traditional channels. This may still be profitable due to lower costs and higher margins online. The value in R6 acknowledges this cannibalization. In this example, a loyal customer can come from either traditional or online channels. The result is R7. Stimulating additional online sales, with the convenience of immediate action, are especially profitable and boost the value of the entire visit and contact.

> *Evaluating Web Chains*

> Goals of the Evaluation

One of the virtues of web chain analysis is that a marketer can look at any part of the chain and calculate its value.[19] This makes web chains a powerful tool for evaluating a wide range of web strategies and tactics.

The four calculations that matter most are:

> The expected value of a contact: the unified contact value,
> The expected value of a prospect: the unified visit value,
> The expected value of a new customer, and
> The expected value of a repeat buyer.

Each has an understandable and useful meaning. Second, expressing different types of campaigns and customer contacts in a standard format makes efficiency and budgeting comparisons much easier.

> Web Chain Benefits and Probabilities

In order to evaluate a chain we need data for the costs, benefits, and probabilities. This varies widely across different situations. Automatic data feeds and evaluators speed up calculations and reporting, putting real-time data and alerts on the desktop or cell phone of the manager. Figure 5.9 shows one set of web chain data within an evaluator. Chapter 8 uses web chains to evaluate keyword search marketing.

In this case, there are five key monetary inputs into the calculation. The online contribution is the incremental profit received from the online sale. This deducts incremental but not fixed costs. For this example, price minus the incremental costs of the product equals $23.00.

Offline contribution has the same definition as above, but for the sale of products through the standard channel. In this example, offline sales are somewhat less profitable, with a contribution of $15.00.

Ad-brand impact is the value to a visitor that sees the ad but doesn't click. This is an important value, as all but the "no-notice" segment receives this benefit.

Web site brand impact is the monetary benefit of the site impact over and above any sale. It is the monetary value of the impacts discussed in Chapter 6.

New customers are worth their lifetime customer value (defined in the following part). For this application, it does not include acquisition cost or the contribution from the initial sale. Either previous campaigns or test markets provide rate information. In this example the no notice and click through rates appear, and moving the dials provide sensitivity analysis. For this example the other rates are (PCR = 3%, OBR = 30%, and OIB = 5%).

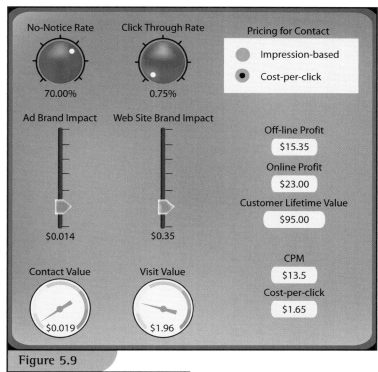

Figure 5.9

A Web Chain Evaluator for the Data

> Calculating Values

The two gauges in Figure 5.9 show the contact value and the visit value using this data. The gauges in the evaluator connect to the campaign pricing. In this case, the firm pays by the click, and the visit value has alert levels if it falls below this price.

Regardless of the pricing mechanism, when there is an ad-brand impact and some viewers notice the ad, the proper comparison is at the top of the web chain. In Table 5.3, this is the sum of all the possible results weighted by their likelihood (shown in green). The visit value is calculated assuming click, and the probabilities in Table 5.3 reflect this assumption.[20]

One of the best uses of web chain analysis is to compare alternative customer acquisition methods and contact methods. A campaign based on simple banners may be cheap but relatively unnoticed and unproductive, while a more comprehensive and highly produced ad may generate more branding and click-throughs. The best campaign will be determined by the full benefits and costs of the campaigns, and the web chain highlights the form of data necessary to balance the quantitative transactional results with the more qualitative, possibly important branding impacts.

> From Web Chains to Closed Loops

Transforming a simple web chain analysis to closed-loop marketing requires tracking that extends from the marketing offer to consumer responses, feedback of results into the campaign management, and improvement based on lessons learned. Web chain analysis attempts to measure the full range of results of a single contact method. Systematic comparisons and a procedure for learning utilize the available data and transform the process.

Commerce platform providers such as eBay, Yahoo!, and Amazon all provide in-depth reporting and tracking capabilities to support their partners. A major movement for large commerce sites during the last few years is to provide web services, permitting programmers access to many of the capabilities and data contained within the commerce platform. EBay has opened up the details of how its system works in detail, allowing third-party vendors to augment alternative reporting and consulting analysis.[21] EBay even publishes user ratings about the reporting systems, even when it shows third parties with a better reporting capability than eBay itself.

Reporting capabilities go far beyond the simple web chain example. Figure 5.10 illustrates transaction tracking. Careful measurement lets a seller observe the characteristics of successful listing, judge their impact, and improve over time. There are many other details and reporting features possible. What to track depends on the goals of the marketing activity, with each requiring their own metrics and benefiting from reporting capabilities.

Sites can use eBay commerce solutions without sending visitors off their site to eBay. Ebay makes many of its tools available through "APIs," the programming software specifications that allow remote sites to display and exchange information.[22] Customers do not need to go to the sites; the

Table 5.3

Unified Value Is the Sum of Expected Results	
Result	Probability of this result
Unified value of the contact	
R1 *	NNR +
R2 *	(1-NNR)* (1-CTR) +
R3 *	(1-NNR)*CTR*(1-PCR)*OIB +
R4 *	(1-NNR)*CTR*(1-PCR)*(1-OIB) +
R5 *	(1-NNR)*CTR*PCR*(1-RR) +
R6 *	(1-NNR)*CTR*PCR*RR*OBR +
R7 *	(1-NNR)*CTR*PCR*RR*(1-OBR)
Value of a visit, assuming a click	
R3 *	(1-PCR)*OIB +
R4 *	(1-PCR)*(1-OIB) +
R5 *	PCR*(1-RR) +
R6 *	PCR*RR*OBR +
R7 *	PCR*RR*(1-OBR)

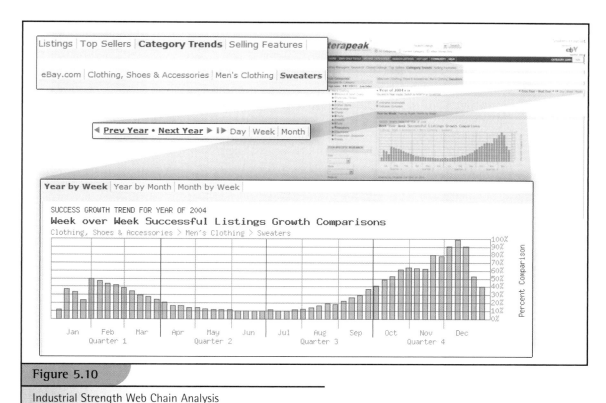

Figure 5.10

Industrial Strength Web Chain Analysis

Source: Terapeak Marketplace Research. © Advanced Economic Research Systems.

software sends the relevant data back and forth to maintain a catalog, run an auction, make the sale, determine shipping costs and logistics, and collect the money. The seller gains by using a high-capacity ecommerce solution, the third-party software vendor profits through software licensing, and eBay benefits through commissions it receives.

Web services such as these allow rapid adoption of commerce and tracking capabilities without extensive software purchases. It makes sophisticated monitoring feasible for a wide array of sites, enabling a much more closed loop marketing approach.

Customer Lifetime Value

Firms increasingly manage their marketing based on customer lifetime value.[23] Customer lifetime value (LTV) is the "present value of the future cash flows attributed to the customer relationship."[24] It depends on a customer's activity level, duration, the firm's retention spending, and other related costs and benefits attachable to that specific customer or customer segment.

The use of LTV models reflects firms' increasing ability to track, store, and analyze individuals and their behavior. Individual data reveals that customers vary widely in retention rates and profitability, both offline and online. Actual market data demonstrates that simple rules can be misleading generalizations. There are customers that are highly profitable, customers whose lifetime value matches the average, and those that actually are "below zero" and suppress cumulative profit.

These differences are clear in a skew diagram, which graphs customer-specific value. Figure 5.11 dramatically shows this dispersion. Customers are first sorted by profitability, with highest value first. The cumulative profit appears on the vertical axis, scaled by the eventual total profits of the full customer base. The curve rises rapidly at first, reflecting the highly profitable customer segments. In this case, the highest 23% of customers are as profitable as the full customer base. Profits continue to rise to their peak at 120% of the eventual total. Beyond this point, roughly the last 45% of customers, contribution is negative. These "BZs" drive cumulative profit down.

Variations in cost to sell create part of the customer skew. Some customers enter their rebuy orders online, even large volumes, without consuming any sales effort. Other customers engage in lengthy discussion, consuming valuable sales calls and resources.

High support costs may drive some customer relationships below zero. Intuit monitors and manages support costs for their Quicken and TurboTax software packages very closely. The software is relatively low priced, and even one phone call for customer support puts a strain on profits for that customer for that year. The ability of customers to find and solve their own problems online, without placing a call to tech support, may be the difference between profit and loss for Intuit.

Customer lifetime value adds a time dimension to customer profitability analysis. The relationship must be maintained (customer retention). It is also the case that future dollars are less

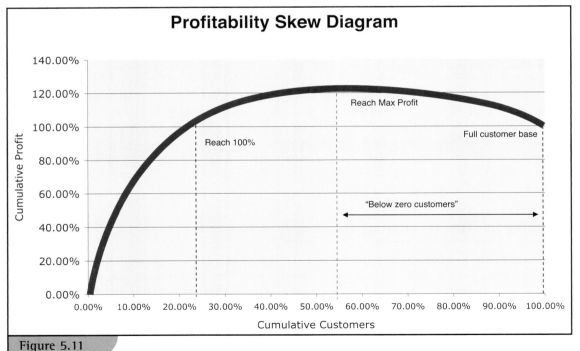

Figure 5.11

A Profitability Skew Diagram

valuable than current dollars. Table 5.4 highlights how the present value of a dollar per period from a retained customer changes with varying retention rates and discount rates. As retention rates fall, or discount rates rise, the present value falls.

Spreadsheet analysis is the standard solution method for customer lifetime value, with the specific assumptions of contribution rates, spending on customer retention, and other factors. For consistency it is important to keep clear whether acquisition costs and first purchases are included in lifetime value. In Figure 5.7 the relevant definitions are:

$$\text{Customer lifetime value customer type } k = \left[\sum_{(t=0, \text{ after first purchase})}^{T} \frac{(r_{kt} - c_{kt})\delta_{kt}}{(1 + i_{kt})^t} \right]$$

$$\text{Customer equity customer type } k = \text{LTV}_k + \text{First purchase contribution}_k - \text{acquisition cost}_k$$

Each period there can be sales and costs. The per-period, per-customer revenue and costs are r_{kt} and c_{kt}. Individual retention rates are δ_{kt}. This particular definition uses the "lost for good" model, where a lost customer disappears forever and must be re-acquired. In other settings a former customer may be much easier or more difficult to reacquire, and should be treated separately. In many settings the first purchase is included in customer lifetime value, and is separated out here only for ease of exposition of the web chain.

Measuring and using customer lifetime value is a very active area of research and plays a vital role in determining many online activities. Attracting and retaining high lifetime value customers provides the motivation for many personalization and customization efforts. It is central to evaluating the profitability of campaigns.

WEB BENEFITS TO FIRMS

The multi-faceted nature of the Internet complicates its business justification. This part looks at the many profitable innovations and benefits that well-conceived and executed online marketing activities provide to firms. These can be both in direct improvements in efficiency and effectiveness, or they can be additional revenue and pricing possibilities. A proper evaluation needs

Table 5.4

Sensitivity of Present Value to Retention and Interest Rates

Value of a Dollar Forever at Different Discount Rates and Retention								
	10.00%	12.50%	15.00%	17.50%	20.00%	22.50%	25.00%	27.50%	30.00%
Retention = 100%	$11.00	$9.00	$7.67	$6.71	$6.00	$5.44	$5.00	$4.64	$4.33
Retention = 95%	$7.33	$6.43	$5.75	$5.22	$4.80	$4.45	$4.17	$3.92	$3.71
Retention = 90%	$5.50	$5.00	$4.60	$4.27	$4.00	$3.77	$3.57	$3.40	$3.25
Retention = 85%	$4.40	$4.09	$3.83	$3.62	$3.43	$3.27	$3.13	$3.00	$2.89

to appreciate these multiple possible benefits. On the other hand, not all online activities are profitable, and getting the right scale of activities matters.

This chapter stops short of the design of new online businesses At the most aggregate level of business model and strategy, the Internet alters many business formats and even creates new ways of competing. Again eBay provides an example. The idea of an auction is ancient. The Internet allows a virtual auction house with a wide assortment of online buyer and seller support tools. Using the perspective that business models are a subset of the full competitive strategy of a firm,[25] the online auction business model provides important sources of customer value and higher profit potential. The fact that eBay and not OnSale emerged as the dominant force involves business model design, proper competitive strategy, and some amount of luck. Entrepreneurial activities and marketing's role in business model design relies on the full range of online skills and opportunities covered in the book. No simple formula exists for constructing an online business model immune from competition and guaranteed to succeed.

Part of this uncertainty is due to the inherently dynamic competition that exists online. Empirical studies find examples where a customer acquisition technique works better early in a firm's online experience, but declines in effectiveness later.[26] Even more challenging, other firms attempting to copy this success may find the approach less suited to later entrants or in their particular sector. Even the proper business format and online business model requires managerial skills and discipline to achieve success. Just getting the idea right is not enough; execution matters as well. The business justification themes raised here appear in detail throughout the book. This discussion highlights the much more in-depth coverage in the chapters that follow.

The challenging environment that faced many online marketers following the shakeout in 2000–2002 instilled a healthy respect for careful business analysis and attention to profitability that should have been there from the beginning. As growth and venture funding returns,[27] business justifications, and attention to profits matter.

Improved Processes

Improvement-based benefits from the Web are the impacts that lead to internal savings, increased marketing effectiveness, and changes in consumers' attitudes. Important examples are lower costs, improved image, higher customer loyalty, and enhanced use of the products offered by companies. They are indirect benefits because they do not immediately lead to a sale and do not immediately generate revenue from customers. Improvement-based benefits are available to almost any firm. A company need not be in an industry centered on technology or information. See Table 5.5.

Table 5.5

Process Improvement Justifications	
Improved Processes	**Examples**
Efficiency & Effectiveness	
Reduced sales & support costs	UPS
Supply chain coordination	Dell Computer
Better market research	Harris Interactive
Enhancement	
Brand support	Burger King
Category building	BP Solar
Online enhancements	NPR

> *Efficiency and Effectiveness*

> Cost Reduction

Cost reduction provides the hard numbers justifying many Web investments by companies. A good example of simple changes saving large sums of money is the posting of manuals and customer-support documents online. Companies like Cisco save hundreds of millions of dollars a year with electronic over traditional publishing of manuals and support documents. Replacing high-cost service encounters is driving many Web activities. Online sites can be the cheapest form of customer interaction. This is especially true for industries like banking, where many customer interactions raise costs rather than lead to additional sales.

An example is transferring money between accounts. Banks have found web-based banking much cheaper than the more traditional "bricks and mortar" or even automated teller machines (ATMs). Studies have found that the incremental cost a bank incurs if a customer comes to a branch and has a teller do the transaction is $1.07. This falls to $.27 if they use an ATM. This four-fold saving caused many banks to push their users toward ATMs in the 1980s and 90s. The Web is much cheaper. The incremental cost of this same transaction over the Web falls to $.01. This is a savings of 99% of the cost of a teller and 95% over an ATM.[28]

Software companies aggressively use the Web for customer service. They were early adopters, with the vast majority of companies using a wide array of online customer support activities. Customer self-service is at the heart of many of these savings. Table 5.6 shows the

Table 5.6

Justifying Capabilities Based on Cost Reduction			
An Efficiency-Improving Web Enhancement			
Before Web Enhancement		*After Web Enhancement*	
YourTaxes software product		*YourTaxes software product*	
Price	49.95	Price	49.95
Incremental cost	12.95	Incremental cost	12.95
Sales level	75,000	Sales level	75,000
Fixed cost	$100,000	Fixed cost	$100,000
Net income before support	$2,675,000	Net income before support	$2,675,000
Standard support costs w/o enhancement		*Standard support costs with enhancement*	
Fixed cost	$500,000	Fixed cost	$500,000
Avg. support contacts per buyer	0.3	Avg. support contacts per buyer	0.1
Labor cost per support contact	$15.00	Labor cost per support contact	$18.00
Standard support costs	$837,500	Standard support costs	$635,000
Web w/o enhancement		*Web with enhancement*	
		One-time Web cost	**$225,000**
Periodic fixed cost	20,000	Periodic fixed cost	35,000
Avg. accesses per buyer	0.3	Avg. accesses per buyer	0.7
Cost per support contact	0.05	Cost per support contact	0.05
Web support costs	$21,125		$37,625
Operating Profits	**$1,816,375**	**Operating Profits**	**$2,002,375**
		First Year Profit	**$1,777,375**
		Change in operating profits	$186,000
		Sales periods until payback	1.21

profit increase that comes by shifting high cost contact points to low cost Web support. Chapter 7 continues this discussion.

A well-designed system may see support costs per phone call actually rise after introducing effective online support. Unique and hard-to-solve problems remain, requiring more skilled and more extensive help. It is also important for the technical support staff to document and write-up findings, solving additional problems online. This appears as higher staff costs, but saves support costs over time.

Reducing the cost of routine sales, as well as building loyalty, provide business benefits throughout ecommerce applications. Online ordering of routine business supplies, package delivery, or consumer pharmaceuticals lowers personnel costs and error rates. At the same time, organizing a customer's system around this ordering capability builds loyalty above that of product or service alone.

Lowering the sales costs of online businesses is a main benefit touted by UPS in its partnership with Yahoo! (Figure 5.12). Tools automatically fulfill many of the shipping and tracking steps, saving money and preventing errors. UPS builds this into the Yahoo! Merchant software, making it easy to implement the capabilities. This benefits UPS by creating a loyal customer base, with a strong incentive to use UPS for its shipping needs.[29]

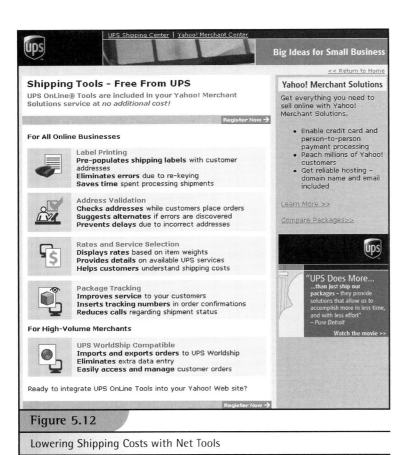

Figure 5.12

Lowering Shipping Costs with Net Tools

Source: Reproduced with permission of Yahoo! Inc. © 2005 by Yahoo! Inc. YAHOO! and the YAHOO! logo are trademarks of Yahoo! Inc.

> Supply Chain Coordination

Effectiveness improvements are another important category of indirect Web benefits. This includes the supply chain of vendors, dealers, and distribution partners. Supply chain effectiveness is a crucial skill in a global economy, affecting both company performance and customer satisfaction.

Dell computer continues to be the leader of supply chain coordination, and it uses the Net to connect directly with both vendors and customers. Ten years ago it carried over 20 days of inventory on hand. Dell has now reduced it to four. Dell is able to manufacture a built-to-order computer in five hours. These reductions in inventory allow it to lower costs, rapidly respond to any changes in the marketplace, and still price aggressively. Supply chain coordination is vital for global sourcing. Chapter 15 looks at these issues in detail, and ways that businesses are using supply chain coordination as a foundation of the high growth in B2B online sales.

> Better Customer Knowledge

Internet-enabled market research and learning through online interactions provide hard-to-measure yet important business justification for online investments. These lessons appear throughout the book, and include:

> Early warning of market changes, both in taste and order size,
> Insight into latent customer tastes and opportunities for new product features,
> Opportunities for collaborative product design through active survey techniques or qualitative feedback,
> Shared market research findings throughout the organization,
> Quantification of relative competitive position, in terms of both satisfaction and online interest, and
> Insight into new offerings and new geographical opportunities by monitoring competitors' and potential partners' web sites.

Improvements such as these are individually small but can be cumulatively important. They may require deliberate training programs and reorganization to generate the proper information flow.

Better access to customer knowledge relies on systems that support easy information exchange through a common platform. Systems developed under earlier technological conditions tended to be specialized. Their design focused on different tradeoffs, when computing and communication was much more expensive. Figure 5.13 shows a more modern design that naturally encourages more information exchange, as different divisions and industries share a common platform.

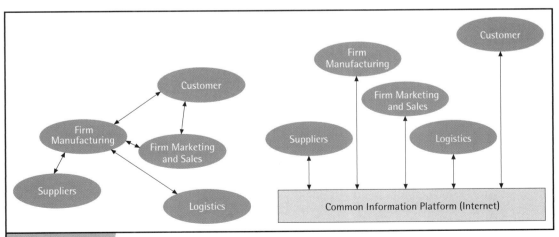

Figure 5.13

Moving from Traditional, but Segmented Business to Business Communication, to a Common Net Platform

Source: Arun Sharma, "Trends in Internet-based business-to-business marketing," *Industrial Marketing Management* 31, no. 2 (2002): 77–84. Copyright 2002. Reprinted with permission from Elsevier.

Better tools for market research benefit both the users and the producers of market information. A company such as Harris augments its standard polling capabilities with an assortment of online tools and survey methods. Clients receive information almost instantly, providing useful feedback and market studies.

> *Brand Enhancement*

Brand building is one of the most important and complex jobs facing marketers. Brands are powerful. They are a method of communicating what a product or service is all about. They are "the flags of marketing. They stake out a certain territory and inform the world that what lies within sight of the flag belongs to those who fly it."[30]

The online world creates new brands and can contribute to existing brand equity for established brands. Chapter 6 discusses both, looking at how online material can contribute to brand equity efforts.

Most branding discussions consider the impact of Procter and Gamble, a dominating force in many consumer categories. With the world's largest advertising budget, P&G is a major shaper of traditional advertising media and marketing practice. P&G has had mixed success online. Its efforts to create the new brand Reflect in cosmetics were unsuccessful, as many new brand efforts often are (Figure 5.14b). Its use of the Net to promote existing brands or brand extensions has been more successful. P&G faces the difficult challenge of augmenting brands that are relatively poorly suited to online sales and may not naturally lead to relationship marketing. Better opportunities, as seen in Tide-to-Go, revolve around new product launch and special price promotions (Figure 5.14a).

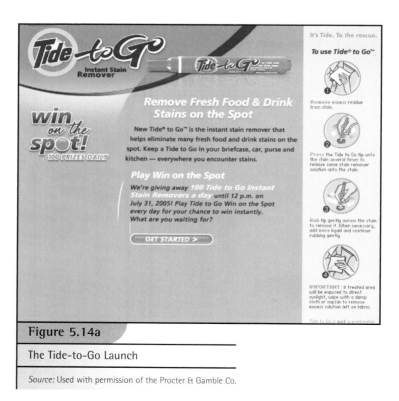

Figure 5.14a

The Tide-to-Go Launch

Source: Used with permission of the Procter & Gamble Co.

One consumer company pioneering edgy and popular brand sites is Burger King, with its "subservient chicken" and "Darth Vader 20 questions" sites. Both provide an unusual interactive experience, geared to generating word-of-mouth among young Web visitors. Like humor in commercials, such efforts are hard to design and can be risky branding. When they work, however, they generate enormous free publicity.

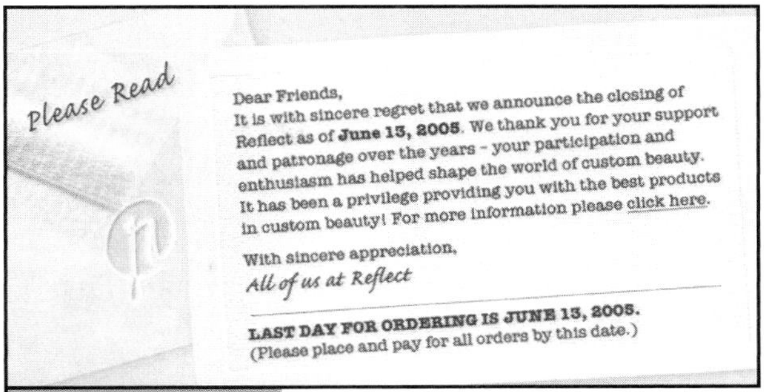

> ### *Category Building*

Another enhancement goal of many sites, especially market leaders, is category development. Rather than focus on specific products, companies use their site to educate visitors about an entire category or capability. Of

please Read

Dear Friends,
It is with sincere regret that we announce the closing of Reflect as of **June 13, 2005**. We thank you for your support and patronage over the years – your participation and enthusiasm has helped shape the world of custom beauty. It has been a privilege providing you with the best products in custom beauty! For more information please click here.

With sincere appreciation,
All of us at Reflect

LAST DAY FOR ORDERING IS JUNE 13, 2005.
(Please place and pay for all orders by this date.)

Figure 5.14b

Closing Reflect.com

Source: Used with Permission of the Procter & Gamble Co.

course, as market leader they can count on getting a large chunk of any additional sales that result from their efforts. Examples include Palm promoting PDAs, BP promoting solar energy, or Intel explaining different computing applications and showcasing them online.

Category-building sites can serve as an early introduction of a concept or technology into the marketplace. Adobe created a web site promoting e-books. Once the market takes off, a firm may phase out the site.[31] This avoids conflict with online retailers, who may wish to use the free books themselves as a traffic-building benefit to their customers.

BP has a web site promoting the use of residential solar energy. A number of pages work to educate the visitor about the economics of solar, the science of photovoltaics, available tax credits, and other information valid for all buyers of solar. As a solar leader, it naturally stands to benefit from some share of additional sales in the category. The same is true for Toyota (see Figure 5.15) and its promotion of energy efficient hybrid cars. Its online hybrid newsletter explains the science, the history of hybrid development, and environmental news.

> ### *Quality Improvement*

Quality improvement is a vital aspect of using the Internet in marketing. Digital material keeps getting cheaper and cheaper. To the extent possible, companies seek to augment and enhance products with online material.

Creativity is the order of the day. Radio historically was at a loss to augment stories with images. This is not necessarily the case anymore. Figure 5.16 is a picture taken by W. Gottlieb showing New York City in 1948. Featured in a story on NPR's All Things Considered, listeners near a computer could now go online to see it. Suddenly the limitations of radio are partially relaxed for those able to go online.[32]

| Revenue Benefits

Internet capabilities and online commerce creates new revenue opportunities. In some situations these services could only operate effectively online. In other cases they are well-known types of businesses, but online commerce creates new opportunities and entrepreneurial openings.

Figure 5.15

Toyota Explaining Hybrid Car Technology and Impacts

Source: Courtesy of Toyota Motor North America, Inc.

Table 5.7 summarizes just some of these new revenue sources. In some cases the additional monies come from other portions of the distribution channel, seeking new customer leads or splitting the revenue these leads bring in. In other cases the final purchaser pays. They are incremental fees when the service would not be possible except online, or the additional products and services that supplement and existing product are heavily influenced by online capabilities.

> *Channel Pays*

Channel-based revenue models have fees paid to an online service by other companies wanting to reach their users. Examples include content sponsorship, banner advertising, prospect fees, and sales commissions. One of the most interesting challenges for Net marketers is to decide on the mix of these revenue sources.

> Permission Sponsorship

The idea of sponsored content goes back to the beginning days of radio. Early radio had three problems. First, performers needed to be paid. Second, there was no way to charge listeners. Third, the running of spot advertising was untested and potentially illegal.[33] The answer was sponsors. National Carbon Company sponsored the Eveready Hour. Clicquot Club Ginger Ale had the Clicquot Club Eskimos singing group. The Happiness Candy Company had the Happiness Boys. Each of these efforts was successful.[34] Eventually sponsorship and exclusivity declined in importance, as radio stations went to networks and spot advertising.

Figure 5.16

NPR's Radio with Pictures: The 52nd Street NY Jazz Scene in 1948

Source: © Copyright 1979 William P. Gottlieb www.jazzphotos.com

Sponsored content also shows up online, as sites attempt to find the best way to pay for high quality and popular content. Figure 5.17 shows an interesting twist, hard to accomplish except online. One either can pay to join Salon Premium, or can choose to watch the sponsor's ad. In this case, a short, 10-second animated commercial lets the viewer arrive at Salon and view content. Absolut Vodka gets an audience that at least nominally asked to see the ad. Although television offers the same choices to viewers for different content (pay for commercial-free HBO or watch a movie on NBC), this is an offer for the same content.

Those following the ad enter an environment very different from a normal ad. First there is a page asking for birth date, ostensibly to verify the user is at least of drinking age. As a side benefit, Absolut Vodka now knows whether the visitor is in his or her twenties or forties. There are additional content choices possible, with animation that reacts to the visitor's choices. At the end, another form of permission enters the picture, as the site gives the user a chance to save the "art work" by supplying an email address.

Table 5.7

New Revenue Opportunities	
New Revenue Sources	**Examples**
Channel pays	
Permission sponsorship	Salon.com
Online advertising	Facebook
Customer leads	Google AdSense
Revenue sharing	Amazon Associates
Purchaser pays	
Product sales	iTunes
Subscriptions	Rhapsody
Versioning	San Jose Mercury News
Bundled sales	Science

Figure 5.17

Pay or Watch? Permission Sponsorship and Information Request

Source: Under permission by V&tS Vin & Sprit AB (publ). ABSOLUT®VODKA. ABSOLUT COUNTRY OF SWEDEN VODKA & LOGO, ABSOLUT, ABSOLUT BOTTLE DESIGN AND ABSOLUT CALLIGRAPHY ARE TRADEMARKS OWNED BY V&tS VIN & SPRIT AB (PUBl). © 2005 V&tS VIN & SPRIT AB (publ).

> ### Banner Advertising

One of the first sources of additional revenue online was the banner ad. As in other media advertising, advertisers go where their target customers spend time and attention. New opportunities exist when the online world provides new highly segmented advertising venues. The on-campus social networking site Facebook has been highly successful in building a big user base among a desirable target market. Advertisers put their banners on the site, knowing exactly the demographics and geographical location of the audience (Figure 5.18).

Performance-based payment systems for ads provide new opportunities. During the early phase of the Net, almost all banners were sold on standard impression pricing. Banner ads establish a point of origin, however, creating the possibility of payment based on impression,

Figure 5.18

Highly Targeted Advertising

Source: Courtesy of Thefacebook

on clicks, on purchases, or on a mixture of all three. To date, no other media has the combination of simultaneity and performance-based flexibility.

> ## Prospect Fees

Click-through ads based on keyword search are a billion-dollar business, and have propelled the rebirth of online advertising. Keyword ads create a tight connection between user search behavior and the ads that appear to the right and the top of the page. What sets them apart from standard advertising is the primary focus on traffic building and generating visitors to the advertiser's web site. Chapter 8 focuses on performance based traffic building, and the implications for customer acquisition.

Keyword-based ads now appear on many publishing sites, driven not by search but by the content of the stories on the page. The logic is the same as search. Someone interested in a particular story may very well be interested in an advertiser related to that topic. Web surfer interest, as expressed by a visit to the content page, is a signal of an underlying characteristic valuable to the advertiser.

An intriguing possibility is a flourishing of content sites related to valuable keywords (such as Figure 5.19). There is substantial variation in keyword prices. Keyword value reflects both high customer lifetime value and a likelihood of converting visitors to customers. Recall Magretta's comment at the beginning of the chapter. For an online business model to be successful, it should start with an insight into behavior and base the technology on that foundation.

Specialty sites do a more general form of content matching. Sites like Edmunds in autos, HomeGain in realty, and WebMD in medicine all partner with sites that use visitor interest as a trigger event. These sites deliver "hot leads," individuals with a much higher probability of being active in the marketplace for these high-value products.

> ## Sales Commissions

Affiliates programs look much the same to consumers as sponsorship, but differ in their payment structure. Like sponsorship, programs involve logos on web sites that link back to the retail partner. Affiliates programs base their payment on the actual revenue from sales.

Figure 5.19

Content Matching Network: Google AdSense with Pet Content

Source: Courtesy of PetPlace.com

Amazon.com has pioneered the online affiliates program. Amazon has over 900,000 sites scattered throughout the world signed up as Amazon affiliates.[35] Each of these affiliates receives a commission for sales that result from a customer originating on their site. Commission rates range from 5–7.5%, down from the rates Amazon used earlier in its existence. Joining is quick and low cost. Amazon's web site makes it possible to join the affiliates program entirely online. This includes creating the special links, displaying product images and content, and setting up royalty arrangements.

The fall in commission rates for affiliates reflects their declining importance to Amazon in generating new traffic and the need for Amazon to focus on profitability. An interesting study comparing Amazon.com, Barnesandnoble.com, CDNOW, and N2K from each of these company's initial public offerings through 2001 found that only Amazon's program had a statistically significant and positive benefit on market value.[36] The other firms seemed to be over-promoting to the point of negative contribution, and for Amazon the benefits were substantially bigger early in its history.

> ## Choosing a Payment Structure

Moving from sponsorship through to commissions is an increase in both accountability and risk for the advertising network, and a reduction in risk for the advertising firm. Sponsorship leads to the same payment regardless of actions by viewers, whereas sales commissions may generate no revenue at all if there are no conversions.

Each of the steps in Figure 5.20 uses different payment and performance criteria. Sponsorships and co-branding arrangements negotiate exclusivity for a fixed length of time. Banner ads price ads based on the total number of impressions. Prospect fees base pricing on actions such as click through or registrations. Finally, commissions are a fraction of sales.[37]

At least four factors determine where on this continuum of risk sharing a specific advertising deal ends up. These are attitude toward risk, the ability to monitor performance, current market emphasis, and negotiating power. In a setting where advertising firms are risk averse but the publisher is neutral toward risk, there will be a movement toward performance-based pricing at a higher cost per click. Pay-per-click is a form of insurance, and the "premium" for this insurance is a higher price.[38] Difficulty in monitoring activities will tend to shift the pricing rule toward the interface between the advertiser and the publisher and away from commissions on sales. There may be a natural market sharing between the impression-based and performance-based, so that as one becomes dominant new advertisers opt for the less popular

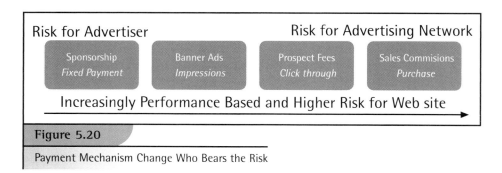

Figure 5.20

Payment Mechanism Change Who Bears the Risk

format.[39] Finally, negotiating power can push a deal toward the preferred solution of the bargainer with the most leverage.

The same site may combine multiple revenue models. *USA Today* Online uses a mixture of sponsorship, banner ads, and performance pricing. Portals such as Yahoo! began with a heavy tilt toward sponsorship and impressions, but over time moved strategically toward performance based click-through ads and revenue sharing.

> *Purchaser Pays*

Numerous pricing innovations are possible online, encouraging businesses to find new sources of revenue and alter their previous pricing approaches. Chapter 12 looks at pricing online in detail, emphasizing the digital nature of price and the changed pricing environment for online products. In some cases the opportunities are beneficial but incremental, such as a golf course adding last minute tee times for a reduced price. In other cases, such as in Apple's iTunes and Real's Rhapsody music service, the innovations are sufficiently major as to rise to a new business format.

The media industry provides examples of the power of the Internet to create new opportunities and challenge existing businesses. The ease of access, sorting, and delivering music leads to innovative online opportunities such as iTunes or Rhapsody. At the same time, music labels and Hollywood live in fear of the impact of music and video piracy. In publishing, the virtual value activities lead to obsolescence for some while creating entirely new opportunities for others. Publishing legends with centuries of experience, such as the Encyclopedia Britannica, face competitive extinction at the same time that open-source offerings such as Wikipedia take off.

New revenue sources may be possible that were impractical prior to the Internet. Figure 5.21 shows four examples, two with music and two with publishing, of media revenue opportunities owing their existence to online commerce. For iTunes, lower transaction costs permit the unbundling of music sales from CDs to single songs. Matched with the iPod digital player, music listening begins to shift from the composite CD to the individual tune. Adelphia Cable provides opportunities to its high speed Internet subscribers to stream music from a large catalog or to purchase songs online.

Some businesses are finding they can expand both their product lines and customer base by using versioning. Versioning targets different product forms at different market segments.[40] One example is the free version of software with reduced capabilities and the premium version with additional features. Newspaper archives are another example, where current stories are free but stories from the archive cost several dollars. At first this seems paradoxical, as current news would seem most useful. The solution is to think of the customer base interested in old news. This is more likely to be an active researcher, possibly willing to pay for that specific story. Charging for archive access or some other form of premium content segments the market.

Finally, bundled digital enhancements are justified through the additional sales they induce of the main product they combine with. Even though the online content has no independent price, it is only available as a bundle with another product. The magazine *Science* uses this approach, encouraging subscriptions to its flagship magazine with access to online material.

Just as an online contact can lead to multiple results with varying profit impacts, different business justifications support online investments. Specific online features and software enhancements may have a close connection to just one business rationale. More comprehensive evaluations and major upgrades should consider multiple impacts, both direct and indirect.

(a) Single songs, free software

(b) Monthly subscriptions and sales

Science (http://www.sciencemag.org)

	Free	Free upon Registration	Free with AAAS Membership*	Available with Paid Institutional Subscription to SCIENCE Online
Science Express: full text articles posted before print publication*			●	Available for an additional fee
Content alert via e-mail	●	●	●	
Enhanced Perspectives*			●	●
Full text of Science Online content from 1996 to the current issue*			●	●
Full text access to historical Science archives back to 1880			●	
Full text of research articles one year after publication		●	●	●
Staff-written summaries of research papers and news stories		●	●	●
Abstracts of current and upcoming research papers		●	●	●
Editorial		●	●	●
Netwatch		●	●	●
Supplementary Material	●	●	●	●
Table of Contents: current and back issues	●	●	●	●
Search Science Online by keyword and author name	●	●	●	●
Browse the tables of contents of back issues	●	●	●	●
Cite Track Research Alerts	●	●	●	●

(c) Flexible online bundling

(d) Versioning newspaper stories: current free but archived cost $2.95 each

Figure 5.21

Online Media Allows New Business Formats

Source: 5.21a © AP / Wide World Photos; 5.21b © PRNewsFoto/Adelphia Communications Corporation; 5.21c Reprinted with permission from AAAS; 5.21d Courtesy of Knight Ridder Digital

ENDNOTES

1. National Research Council. (2001). *The Internet's Coming of Age*. National Academy Press. Washington. D.C., p. 53.

2. Joan Magretta. (2002). "Why Business Models Matter." *Harvard Business Review* May, 86–92.

3. Adam Cohen. (2002). *The Perfect Store: Inside EBay*. Little. Brown.

4. Company press release. "eBay Inc. Announces First Quarter 2006 Financial Results." April 19, 2006.

5. EBay online auction results, category 1468, item 5574436102.

6. David Lucking-Reiley. (2000). "Auctions on the Internet: What's Being Auctioned. and How?" The *Journal of Industrial Economics* XLVIII(3, September), 227–253.

7. Ina Steiner. (2002). "eBay Regroups in Asia: Goodbye Japan. Hello China." *Auction Bytes* February 27.

8. Data from http://www.auctionsoftwarereview.com/article-ebay-statistics.asp.

9. June 9. 2005 intra-day. eBay $50.54 billion. Amazon $14.44 billion.

10. Anthony Crupi. (2005). "TW Dabbles with 'eBay on TV'," *MediaWeek* May 23.

11. Kelly Spors. (2004). "Personal Business: Do I Hear High Fees for Auctions Services?" *Wall Street Journal: Eastern Edition* June 27, 4.

12. See Geoffrey Moore. (1995). *Inside the Tornado*. HarperCollins, New York.

13. Arun Sharma. (2002). "Trends in Internet-based business-to-business marketing," *Industrial Marketing Management* 31, 77–84.

14. J.P. Benway. (1998). "Banner blindness: the irony of attention grabbing on the World Wide Web." *Proceedings of the Human Factors and Ergonomics Society 42nd Annual Meeting*. USA. 1. pp. 463–467.

15. M. E. Bayles and B. Chaparro. (2001). "Recall and recognition of static vs. animated banner advertisements." *Proceedings of the Human Factors and Ergonomics Society 45nd Annual Meeting*. USA. and Michelle Bayles. (2002). "Designing Online Banner Advertisements: Should We Animate?" *CHI 2002*. April.

16. A consequence of this image blocking is to tilt ad serving toward more animated formats, which are not currently blocked by these techniques.

17. Rex Briggs and Nigel Hollis (1997). "Advertising on the Web: Is There Response before Click-Through." *Journal of Advertising Research*. March-April. pp. 33–45. see also Laura Rich. (1997). "A Brand New Game: Does New Research Prove the Branding Value of Banners." *Brandweek*. September 22, 55–56. *Intelliquest* April 10. 2001.

18. In 2005, from DoubleClick data. See Chapter 8.

19. Those familiar with Markov chains will understand the lack of memory being assumed. More complicated web chains, with loops and possible steady states, can be built upon this basic approach.

20. Click-through rate does not matter, as there is assumed to be both a notice of the ad and a click.

21. In addition to developer details provided by eBay, books help programmers and marketers better understand the eBay platform. For example, Ray Rischpater. (2004). *eBay Application Development*. APress. New York outlines the details of the eBay APIs and SDKs and code to access much of the information.

22. See, for example, Ray Rischpater. (2004). *eBay Application Development*, New York, APress.

23. The literature on customer lifetime value, especially estimation and measurement issues, is expanding rapidly. Some notable contributions are Robert Blattberg and John Deighton. (1996). "Manage Marketing by the Customer Equity Test." *Harvard Business Review* (July–August), 136–144. Paul D. Berger and N. Nasr. (1998). "Customer Lifetime Value: Marketing Models and Applications." *Journal of Interactive Marketing* 12(1), 17–30. Francis J. Mulhern. (1999). "Customer Profitability Analysis: Measurement. Concentration. and Research Directions." *Journal of Interactive Marketing*. Vol. 13. No. 1. Winter. pp. 25–40. Robert C. Blattberg. Gary Getz. and Jacquelyn S. Thomas. (2001). *Customer Equity: Building and Managing Relationships as Valuable Assets*. HBS Press. John E. Hogan. Donald R. Lehmann. Maria Merino. Rajendra K. Srivastava. Jacquelyn S. Thomas. and Peter C. Verhoef. (2002), "Linking Customer Assets to Financial Performance." *Journal of Service Research* 5(1), 31. Dipak Jain and S. Singh. (2002). "Customer Lifetime Value Research in Marketing: A Review and Future Directions." *Journal of Interactive Marketing* 16(2), 34–46. Hans Bauer. M. Hammerschmidt. and M. Braehler. (2003). "The Customer Lifetime Value Concept and its Contribution to Corporate Valuation." *Yearbook of Marketing and Consumer Research* 1, 47–67. Ravi Dhar and Rashi Glazer. (2003). "Hedging Customers." *Harvard Business Review* May, 86–92. Rashi Glazer. (2003). "A Strategic Approach to CRM: The Customer Portfolio." CRM Project Volume 4. http://www.crmproject.com. Roland T. Rust. Katherine N. Lemon. and Valerie Zeithaml. (2003). "Return on Marketing: Using Customer Equity to Focus Marketing Strategy." Working

Paper. Robert H. Smith School of Business. University of Maryland. June 5. Peter S. Fader. Bruce G.S. Hardie. and Ka Lok Lee. (2004). "RFM and CLV: Using Iso-value Curves for Customer Base Analysis." Working Paper. July. Phillip E. Pfeifer and Paul W. Farris. (2004). "The Elasticity of Customer Value to Retention: The Duration of a Customer Relationship." *Journal of Interactive Marketing* 18(2), 20–31.

24. Philip Pfeifer, Mark Haskins, and Robert Conroy. (2005). "Customer Lifetime Value, Customer Profitability, and the Treatment of Acquisition Spending." *Journal of Managerial Issues* XVII(1), 11–25.

25. In the sense of Magretta, op. cit, and Peter Seddon and Geoffrey Lewis. (2003). "Strategy and Business Models: What's the Difference?" *7th Pacific Asia Conference on Information Systems.* 10–13 July. Adelaide.

26. See the Amazon Affiliates discussion later in this chapter.

27. Gary Rivlin. (2005). "Venture Capital Rediscovers the Consumer Internet." *New York Times* June 10.

28. This study was conducted by the Booz-Allen consulting group with the data reported in *The Digital Economy.* U.S. Department of Commerce. available at https://www.esa.doc.gov/reports.cfm.

29. For a discussion of UPS and technology, see Jeanne Ross. (2001). "United Parcel Services: Delivering Packages and E-Commerce Solutions." Center for Information Systems Research. Sloan School of Management. August. Also Richard Watson, George Zinkhan, and Leyland Pitt. (2000). "Integrated Internet Marketing." *Communications of the ACM* 43(6).

30. Lynn Upshaw. (1995). *Building Brand Identity: A Strategy for Success in a Hostile Marketplace.* Wiley, New York, xiii.

31. As Adobe has done, phasing out the site in June 2005.

32. The story can be found by searching http://www.npr.org for Gottlieb. The photo can be seen at http://www.jazzphotos.com/52ndst.htm.

33. There was an extended battle on the legality of broadcast advertising, with the Bell System claiming it had retained all rights to spot advertising. Negotiations settled this point, with advertising being cleared from restrictions in late 1924. See Gleason Archer. (1971). *Big Business and Radio.* Arno Press, New York, especially chapters 6 and 7.

34. Susan Smulyan. (1994*). Selling Radio: The Commercialization of American Broadcasting: 1920–1934.* Smithsonian, especially pp. 98–124.

35. Amazon.com. June 2005.

36. Darren Filson. (2004). "The Impact of E-Commerce Strategies on Firm Value: Lessons from Amazon.com and its Early Competitors." *Journal of Business* 77(2), pt. 2

37. For a review of advertising types just before the rise to prominence of search, see T.P. Novak and D.L. Hoffman. (2000). "Advertising and Pricing Models for the Web," in *Internet Publishing and Beyond: The Economics of Digital Information and Intellectual Property.* Deborah Hurley, Brian Kahin and Hal Varian. eds. Cambridge: MIT Press.

38. See Arun Sundararajan. (2003). "Pricing Digital Marketing: Information, Risk Sharing, and Performance." Working Paper. New York University.

39. Ardrea Mangani. (2004). "Online advertising: Pay-per-view versus pay-per-click." *Journal of Revenue and Pricing Management* 2(4).

40. For an excellent discussion of versioning see Carl Shapiro and Hal Varian. (1999). *Information Rules: A Strategic Guide to the Networked Economy.* Harvard Business School Press, especially Chapter 3.

chapter 6:

Online Branding

Figure 6.1

The Uncertain Recep-
tion of Television
Source: © Terri Miller /
E-Visual Communications Inc.

The Chaos Scenario

Traditional media in the United States runs on advertising, much of it geared to building and maintaining brands. By some measures, things appear rosy. With a Summer Olympics, a presidential election, and a recovering economy, broadcast television advertising reached nearly $50 billion in 2004. The top 10 advertising companies spent $16.6 billion, with P&G leading the list at $3.0 billion per year. The automobile industry (including manufacturers, local dealerships, and dealer associations) led industry advertising spending on broadcast and print media with more than $18 billion.[3]

As suggested by the Procter & Gamble (P&G) marketing chief, there are challenges to traditional advertising. Major networks face a shrinking audience, as cable and pay channels proliferate. Programming costs continue to rise. Digital video recorders, such as Tivo, allow consumers to skip many of the advertisements paying for the programming. Television is losing audience minutes to other media, especially among the young and especially in households with broadband.[4]

Other forms of advertising face challenges as well. For decades, the telemarketing industry expanded in both advertising revenue and consumer annoyance. The situation changed dramatically in 2003. Perhaps the most popular U.S. government program of the past decade has been the Do Not Call list restricting telemarketing firms. With some minor exceptions, no one

All organizations engage in branding. Branding is big business, and the Net is changing how it occurs. A major concern is how brand strategy shapes the brand's online presence.

Topics covered in this chapter include:

> **Challenges to Traditional Branding Media**

> **Brands and Online Brand Building**
>> > The branding business
>> > Customer-based brand equity
>> > Online implications of the brand equity framework

signing up should receive an unsolicited phone call from a company seeking new business. Penalties are quite high. Digital technology allowed the federal government to rapidly and cheaply create a list of millions of citizens opting-out of unsolicited calls.[5] All it takes is a call to an automated voice system or a visit to the donotcall.gov web site shown in Figure 6.2. Within three months of launch, the list contained more than 50 million phone numbers. A little more than 60% of these requests occurred online.

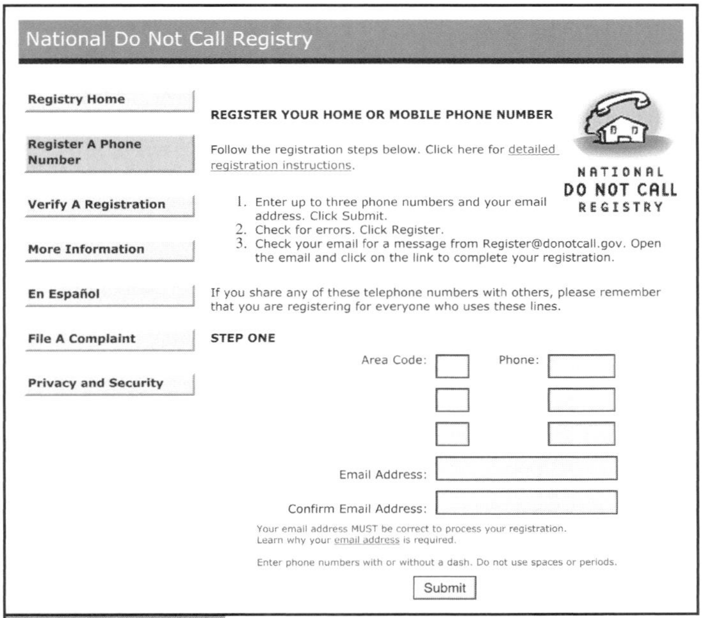

National Do Not Call Registry

Registry Home

Register A Phone Number

Verify A Registration

More Information

En Español

File A Complaint

Privacy and Security

REGISTER YOUR HOME OR MOBILE PHONE NUMBER

Follow the registration steps below. Click here for detailed registration instructions.

NATIONAL DO NOT CALL REGISTRY

1. Enter up to three phone numbers and your email address. Click Submit.
2. Check for errors. Click Register.
3. Check your email for a message from Register@donotcall.gov. Open the email and click on the link to complete your registration.

If you share any of these telephone numbers with others, please remember that you are registering for everyone who uses these lines.

STEP ONE

Area Code: [ ]   Phone: [ ]
[ ]   [ ]
[ ]   [ ]

Email Address: [ ]
Confirm Email Address: [ ]

Your email address MUST be correct to process your registration. Learn why your email address is required.

Enter phone numbers with or without a dash. Do not use spaces or periods.

[Submit]

Figure 6.2

Hanging Up on Telemarketers

Source: Courtesy of www.ftc.gov

These trends are causing media analysts to fear what some call the chaos scenario—a rapid decline in mass media effectiveness prior to the creation of an effective alternative marketing vehicle.[6] Advertisers such as P&G acknowledge the power of the Net to deliver information, inform shoppers of sales and new offerings, and accomplish many other informational tasks. They are less certain about its branding power, and they wonder whether a voluntary and interactive model has the power to brand nearly as well as with traditional television and radio.

Just because new technology and shifting consumer time challenges traditional media does not mean that online media is ready to fill the void. Disappointment with online branding characterized the early years of online marketing. The first online banner appeared in October 2004 on *Hotwired*. While its novelty guaranteed attention, the limitations of banner ads soon became apparent. Web browsers anxious to obtain information easily ignore ads. Space constraints limit the branding message. Indeed, the sponsor of the ad is often hidden or obscure. Even the first ad showed the problem, with there being no mention of the sponsoring advertiser (AT&T) (Figure 6.3).

Banner ads have further limitations. There are limited animation and multimedia opportunities. Browser software can automatically block ads. Sound is typically restricted or absent. Although several industry studies claim these limited banners have measurable branding impacts, enthusiasm for banner ads and their branding impact waned with experience. Banner advertisers focused their branding hopes primarily on the web sites where those willing to click arrive.

Few packaged goods advertisers found the early Web a welcoming branding opportunity, even when they evaluated the impact of their web sites on visitors. The cost of traffic was too high, and Internet capabilities too limited to support many of their familiar image-building tools.

This perception is changing. Companies that dominate the advertising world are spending money to enhance and promote their brands online. Innovative campaigns merge online and offline advertising. Offbeat campaigns get their start online. Companies unable to afford mass media brand building can use their online presence to project a unified branding presence. Marketers able to afford cross-media advertising find each medium capable of different branding impacts, and integrate each into their media buying plans.

Figure 6.3

The First Online Banner Ad

Source: Reproduced with permission, AT&T Corp.

With the expansion of instant messaging, blogs, podcasting, and other new media developments come additional branding opportunities. Some are the rebirth of traditional advertising online, as when a company sponsors a radio podcast over the Net or attempts to influence especially important sources of word of mouth. Some require marketing innovations to match the new technical capabilities. Marketers are working hard to prevent the chaos scenario from occurring.

BRANDS AND ONLINE BRAND BUILDING

The Branding Business

> *The Value of a Strong Brand*

Building strong brands, differentiating them, and maintaining them are critical marketing functions. For centuries, authors and painters identified their work by signing it. Trade guilds in medieval Europe identified their goods with marks to assure the customer of the origin and quality of the merchandise and to provide legal protection to the producer.[7] In modern times, the scope and power of brands have expanded dramatically.

A strong brand provides financial benefits to a firm. Price premiums are one potential benefit. During the mid-1990s, brand research found that IBM was the strongest personal computer brand, able to command $339 more over similarly equipped unbranded "clones." Dell and HP were also fairly strong, receiving $230 and $260, respectively. Apple, partly due to its failing market share at the time, as well as brand equity challenges, could only command $182 over clones. At the bottom, the formerly strong (and soon to be discontinued) Digital brand could only get $10 above the "no names."[8]

A strong brand provides significant advantages for many firms in their distribution channels. A retailer understands that a strong brand name like HP has considerable drawing power, pulling customers into the store and getting them to buy. The availability of the strong brand can enhance the brand image of the retailer. A retailer typically perceives lower risk with a new product from a strong brand name manufacturer. In the case of channel conflict, a strong brand tends to shift power toward the manufacturer. Strong brands enter into consumers' consideration sets, create confidence in purchases, and positively influence product evaluation and choice.[9]

In each of these areas, a firm has created customer-based brand equity. Keller defines this as "the differential effect of brand knowledge on consumer response to the marketing of the brand."[10] He further cites a large body of research documenting these differential benefits—including product evaluation, purchasing rates, market share, quality perceptions, product line extensions, product associations, resistance to negative events, stock market valuation, price sensitivity, advertising recall, and advertising response.[11] In each of these cases, a strong brand improves the efficiency and results of marketing actions. A strong brand complements a firm's marketing activities.

> *Branding and Advertising Services*

> Spending on Branding

Almost all major corporations rely on external ad agencies to manage their branding and advertising creation and spending. In decades past, advertising agencies automatically received a 15% commission of advertising dollars spent by the client. Within the past decade, negotiations and competition based on actual costs have replaced this fee structure for many. DuPont pushed this process even further in 2003 when it used an online reverse auction to allocate its global advertising account. While price was only part of the criteria, an auction dramatically altered the process of awarding business.[12] The 20 competing firms were required to submit proposals showing global capabilities on a list of standardized dimensions. This was highly unusual and was a sharp break from standard practice.

The increased complexity and fragmenting of the media world also drives an increased use of procurement in advertising. In the past, advertising agency creative teams dominated branding decisions and strongly tilted toward radio and television ads. The fragmentation of media, and the rise of the Internet, makes media planning and buying much more complicated. Media buyers now have the upper hand in many decisions, and by nature prefer more cost effective and accountable advertising vehicles.[13] Creative teams are being pushed to offer an integrated, cross-media campaign that skillfully takes advantage of each of the different media strengths and weaknesses.

Any advertising medium can serve different objectives, but each medium has particular capabilities. Advertisers seek to create and maintain brands, to provide information about new products and services, to advertise sales and price promotions, and to direct consumers to the proper retail outlet for their goods. Media differ in their effectiveness at each of these tasks. Sales and promotional spending typically occurs in local and print-oriented media. Brand building and maintenance occurs most frequently in richer and more image-oriented media, such as television, radio, and some national magazines. Customer acquisition, especially by small businesses, works best in directories such as the Yellow Pages, local newspapers, direct mail, or telemarketing. As seen in Figure 6.4, all of these outlets have large amounts of money associated with them.

Diversity exists with online advertising spending as well. While still a small share of total advertising spending, online spending is growing. This is especially true of keyword search, a topic considered in detail in the traffic-building chapter. Keyword search has grown to be the largest share of online advertising, displacing banner ads as the leader.

One of the largest omissions in online spending shown in Figure 6.4 is the amount of money spent on web site content and development. Much of online advertising is to motivate online users to visit a web site, where the branding conversation and conversion actually occurs. These numbers do not reflect the money spent on site development, testing, content creation, and brand-oriented material at company web sites.

Online marketing is becoming an increasingly important part of the brand creation and maintenance process. In part, this reflects the importance of the Internet in consumers' use of time. Any activity, especially one oriented around communication, becomes a potential branding vehicle

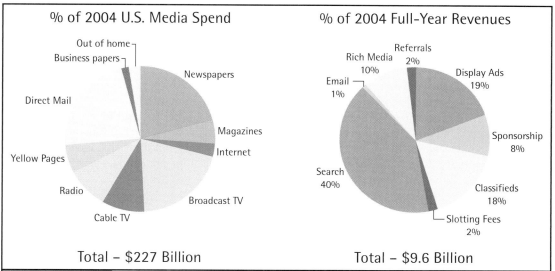

% of 2004 U.S. Media Spend

Out of home
Business papers
Direct Mail
Yellow Pages
Radio
Cable TV
Newspapers
Magazines
Internet
Broadcast TV

Total – $227 Billion

% of 2004 Full-Year Revenues

Referrals 2%
Rich Media 10%
Email 1%
Search 40%
Display Ads 19%
Sponsorship 8%
Classifieds 18%
Slotting Fees 2%

Total – $9.6 Billion

Figure 6.4

Aggregate U.S. Advertising and Online Advertising, by Type

Source: Interactive Advertising Bureau, www.iab.net.

when individuals are spending hours of their time on it each day. Improvements in Net capability are also driving the increased attention to branding. With much more vivid multi-media possibilities, such as podcasting, video streams, and gaming, online marketers have more potential for effectively enhancing brands. Online marketers may indeed fill the gap created by the declining branding effectiveness of traditional media.

A strong brand complements online traffic building. Not only will potential visitors think of the strong brand when considering a category, they will often try the most natural URL, www.thebrandname.com, as a first option. This provides valuable "organic" traffic, but also requires marketers to consider branding when choosing domain names and company URLs. A later section of this chapter develops the domain name–branding connection.

> Innovation, Collaboration and Specialization of Branding Campaigns

As in many other areas of business, the Internet is having an impact on the balance between in-house and outsourced activities. Better communication, improved collaboration tools, and online auction mechanisms are all permitting firms to move more of their activities to remote locations and firms. This creates the potential for tapping of expertise from a much wider range of sources. Best-selling author Thomas Friedman refers to this as "the world has gone flat," with distant service providers able to compete effectively for business. It is dramatically changing the business of advertising.

The application of procurement to marketing services is happening on all levels of the advertising industry. The large amount of advertising spending, in the tens or hundreds of millions of dollars per year for large companies, makes it a tempting target. Procurement managers treat marketing services as another opportunity for achieving cost reductions and improved productivity. They are doing this by establishing specifications and criteria for branding activities.

Branding campaigns require story-telling, technical skills, and media sophistication. With the Internet as a tool, marketers and advertising agencies can reach out to a wide array of professional talent. Skills that needed to be in house at an advertising agency, or with partners located nearby, now are available globally. Figure 6.5 highlights four of these steps, and how the Net is helping this collaborative branding process with global contributions.

A campaign often begins with market research, with focus groups capturing unmet needs or aspirations of potential consumers. Innovative companies commonly collaborate with external research partners. The example shown in (a) is from a youth panel that is surveyed online with *The Take*, an online magazine created as a vehicle for presenting articles, images, and

(a) Youth Panel Newsletter Created Through Online
    Surveys

(b) Searching for Campaign Imagery

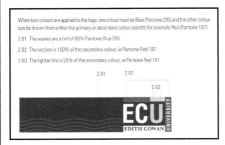

(c) Digitally Archived Style Guides

(d) Podcasting as Permission
    Marketing

Figure 6.5

The Internet Eases Innovation, Collaboration, and Specialization of Branding Process

Source: 6.5a Courtesy of Outlaw Consulting, Inc; 6.5b Courtesy of Storyboards.com; 6.5c Courtesy of Edith Cowan University; 6.5d 360thePitch (360thePitch.com)

new product ideas. Online surveys capture the panel's views, hopefully providing guidance for promising youth-oriented products. Companies share these research results, often including raw data or video feeds when relevant, with the sponsoring company marketing staff and their ad agencies.

Once marketers choose a branding direction, they need to create a campaign. Companies such as Storyboard Online assist in this process. Ad agencies can look through the affiliated artists' portfolios and spot graphic styles and imagery consistent with the emerging campaign. This service makes a rapid, specialized search of artistic styles possible and expands the opportunities for finding the proper look and feel for an ad.

With a storyboard in place, attention turns to creating the advertisements, brochures, print ads, web sites, and other supporting marketing material. Online sharing can lower cost and speed turnaround. Digitally archived style guides, with logos, color schemes, and design criteria, help guarantee both creativity and brand consistency. Panel (c) is from Edith Cowan University in Australia. Any marketing partner can quickly check exactly the color scheme and design features of their logo, without needless phone calls or wasted design iterations. As design and printing is often external as well, standardized elements ease the process whether the printer is across town or on the other side of the globe.

Finally, creative distribution puts the campaign in new and innovative distribution outlets. Video games put branded items into games using product placement. Audio material is podcasted to voluntary subscribers. Archived commercials with email forwarding let friends market to each other and implicitly validate the ad as funny, and possibly persuasive.

Connecting Branding Strategy to Online Presence

Branding is both art and science. The billions of dollars of spending seen in Figure 6.4 lead to many calls for marketers to quantify the impacts of advertising and to provide a scientific basis for brand campaigns. Marketers have developed increasingly sophisticated methods for measuring branding impacts of mass media, direct marketing, and online campaigns.[14] They have been only partially successful. Traditional media's impact is especially hard to track, given its setting, the difficulty of getting accurate responses from consumers about their branding exposure, delays between exposure and measurable actions by consumers, and difficulty in assigning causation between multiple exposures and eventual actions. Even online campaigns are hard to quantify, as branding efforts normally do not have an immediate "call to action." Rather, the goal is to change how consumers view the brand over a longer period.

Even when measurement is possible, and the results of various campaigns are known, it can be very challenging to explain why a particular campaign was more effective than an alternative. Branding campaigns rely on creative elements difficult to explain and even harder to forecast. In some ways, they are like movies. What causes one movie or branding campaign to be a runaway blockbuster, a different campaign to have average results, and another to be a complete bust is a combination of professionalism, story-telling, actor chemistry, and timing that befuddles industry executives. Certain basics must be there, but there is a large element of creative spark as well.

Despite these challenges, marketing researchers have, after devoting much time and study to branding, produced useful frameworks for understanding branding and its constituents. In a series of research papers and brand equity studies, Keller and co-authors present the customer-based brand equity model illustrated in Figure 6.6. It focuses on four key stages composed of six "brand building blocks."[15] The model helps tie together the full range of online branding activities, provides a system for understanding and anticipating online brand enhancement opportunities, and how online brand content can reinforce and create a strong brand.

The four stages of establishing customer-based brand equity, appearing on the left of Figure 6.6 are[16]:

> Establish the proper brand identity.
> Create the appropriate brand meaning.
> Elicit the right brand responses.
> Forge appropriate brand relationships with customers.

Six building blocks implement the four stages. Each building block provides questions for the marketer to ask of its online brand presence. With these in place, the hoped-for results are the benefits shown on the right of Figure 6.6.

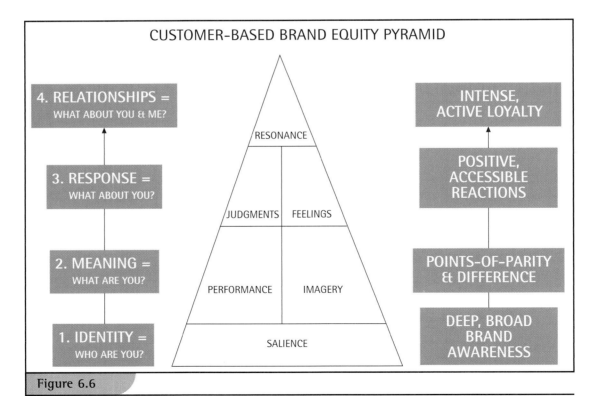

Figure 6.6

Keller's Brand Equity Framework

Source: Kevin Lane Keller, "Conceptualizing, Measuring, and Managing Customer-Based Brand Equity," *Journal of Marketing*, 57 (January 1993): 1–22. Reprinted with the permission of the American Marketing Association.

ONLINE BRAND PRESENCE AND ENHANCEMENT

| Establish Proper Brand Identity

> *Reinforcing Brand Salience*

The first stage in using the Net to enhance a brand is to ensure that the brand has both breadth and depth of brand awareness. The goal is brand salience; when a consumer considers a product category, the brand is automatically included as a possible choice.

Reinforcing brand salience occurs through exposure to web advertising directly or by exposure to the advertiser's web site stimulated by brand advertising.[17] Advertisers are especially interested in the direct web advertising effect. Click-through rates are low, typically under 1%. If the only branding impact of banner advertising occurs through the small fraction of impressions that generate a site visit, the vast majority of online ad dollars contribute little to branding.

The evidence on the direct branding impact of online banners is mixed. While some studies have found immediate branding impacts of ad banners without click-through,[18] industry participants continue to be skeptical. One reason is the design of the studies that found this effect, which have features that tend to overemphasize the branding impact.[19] Even more important for many is the inherent lack of branding tools available for the standard banners and online buttons. Historically, these banners have been small, unanimated images with no sound and little hold on the viewer, making them easy to ignore. This is a very small branding "palette," with few of the tools of television, radio, or full-page magazine ads.

Online banner ads resemble print ads, and they require readers to focus attention away from the main content and to pay attention to the ads. This often does not happen, and it makes online a more challenging brand setting compared to "interruption" marketing. Multimedia capabilities and expanded formats increase the branding capabilities of "banner-like" ads. In a campaign for British Airways, when a visitor lands on a *NY Times* page, the page rotates and the British Airways banner displays on top.[20] After the animated banner completes its message, the content rotates into normal layout and the banner moves to the right side of the page. In comparison with a standard banner ad, the rotating content generated substantially higher brand awareness and recall. Ads based on Flash animation increasingly draw attention through rapid movement and images that cover the page before shrinking back to normal ad banner size.

Brand salience is reinforced when the brand's image and advertising is present at content sites specializing in the category.[21] Geico insurance has maintained an advertising presence on car sites such as Edmunds.com for years, funneling traffic to its call center. This connection between Geico and online car research reinforces the Geico brand for active car shoppers even without immediate transactions. Amazon affiliates, which reach out to thousands of organizations, reinforce the Amazon brand to book buyers. Increasingly, a presence among the results from keyword search serves a similar branding role.

> *Brand Identity and Domain Names*

> Domain Name Goals

The domain name strategy of a company connects closely to an organization's branding and positioning strategy. It serves as a foundation for Web and promotional activity. Once determined, it changes infrequently. While it is always possible to add, delete, or switch domains, it gets increasingly expensive and difficult the more ingrained Net marketing is in the operations and sales efforts of firms.

A domain strategy should accomplish three objectives. It should:

> Reinforce branding
> Build traffic
> Anticipate consumer behavior and mistakes

The ideal domain strategy lets a prospective visitor guess your web site without any help. The visitor simply knows the right address, and types it into the browser. If a name reinforces the basic goals of the firm, so much the better.

A proper domain name strategy requires attention to both the technical and the marketing requirements for domain names. There are technical restrictions, as well as capabilities, that are important to understand. They set the stage for the connection between domain names and brand architecture.

> Defining Domain Names

Hierarchical

Domain names are hierarchical and read from right to left. Primary domain names come in two forms. Form one is a two-letter country code, such as .uk for the United Kingdom or .ru for Russia (typical form 1 domain name: www.bbc.co.uk). Form two is based not on geography but on the type of organization or information involved (typical form 2 domain name: www.stanford.edu). By far the most popular domain category is ".com" for commercial organizations. Other common domain categories are ".edu" for education, ".org" for organization, and ".net" for network.

Additional specialized primary domain names are entering usage. These include .aero, .biz, .coop, .info, .int, .museum, .name, and .pro.[22] While less well known, the hope is that these new extensions will relieve some of the congestion and confusion for individuals or organizations in different categories. They provide additional information and allow for searches that are more sophisticated.

Secondary domain names are the identifying portion of the domain name for most firms. Indeed, the phrase "domain name" typically refers to secondary domain name. Secondary domains are the focus of domain name strategy. They have become the focus of considerable legal battles as well.[23] The owner of the secondary domain name has control of further subdomains. A standard convention is to use "www" as the third-level domain. This is predictable but not required. Some companies use the tertiary domain to refer to organizational structure (referring to the school or division involved, such as gsb), geography (referring to site, such as newyork), or fanciful (mimicking a celebrity or entertainment character, such as gandalf) (see Table 6.1).

One Number, Many Names

Whatever the domain name used by an organization, it must eventually be translated into a proper numerical Internet address. This is the function of domain name servers, a critical piece of Internet architecture. A domain name must uniquely point to a specific Internet address, corresponding to the web server for the site. Although each domain name must uniquely point to an Internet address, more than one domain name can point to the same Internet destination. This technical flexibility is very useful for online marketers. It permits alternative branding possibilities and creates flexibility to reach different audiences.

Figure 6.7 shows four different ways of getting to the Coca-Cola homepage (coca-cola.com, cocacola.com, coke.com, 129.33.95.163).[24] The first three domain names include commonly used

Table 6.1

The Hierarchical Structure of Domain Names				
	Primary Domain	**Secondary Domain**	**Tertiary**	**Full address**
Examples:	.com	discovery (Discovery Network)	tlc (The Learning Channel)	tlc.discovery.com
	.edu	harvard (Harvard University)	library	library.harvard.edu
	.gov	dhs (Dept. of Homeland Security)	www	www.dhs.gov
Goal:	Organization type or location	Branding strategy and identity	Information type or branding	

versions of the brand Coca-Cola, and the fourth is the current IP number used by the server of The Coca-Cola Company. Without domain names a user would have to remember this number, which can change any time a web hosting arrangement changes. Domain names relieve a visitor from the difficult chore of recalling strings of numbers. Alternative domain names pointing to the same site allow traffic to funnel to the site from any of the recalled brand names.

Figure 6.7

Four Different Ways of Getting to the Coca-Cola Home Page

Source: © Bloomberg News /Landov

Alternative naming conventions create new opportunities for potential visitors to find a relevant site. A museum that adopts the museum domain for at least one of its registered domain names gains access to a variety of additional listings and search opportunities. The Art Institute of Chicago is world renowned, with a collection rich in art from the Dutch masters, French impressionists, and ancient art. At the same time, it offers art degrees and programs. It has a short but somewhat confusing domain name — www.artic.edu. For the thousands of tourists searching for information, this is obscure. The Art Institute, among other museums, is registering numerous versions of its name with the museum domain and rerouting this traffic to its site. Less well established is the .aero domain, which targets the aerospace industry. Specialty domains seem especially valuable for medium and small organizations. The additional restriction created by the domain name allows them to stand out in search and browsing.

Memorability

The goal of memorability extends beyond substituting words for numbers. Memorability is limited by length, confusing and unusual strings of letters, artifacts of programming languages, homophones,[25] and names that are difficult to express. Table 6.2 provides some basic guides supporting domain name memorability.

Many consumers simply enter the domain name in a search engine, especially if there is some ambiguity in spelling. In the age of powerful search engines, memorability does not need to be perfect. Potential visitors using one of the major search engines as their starting point only need to get close to the proper domain name (see Table 6.3 for an example from Google). Search

Table 6.2

Basic Guidelines for Domain Name Memorability	
Domain Memorability	**Benefits**
Obtain a Category Domain: Ex: www.jeweler.com	If a small or poorly known firm can secure a category term, it may be able to launch an effective online business.
Avoid Domains Challenging to Encode: Ex: www.dv2u.com	Avoid confusing and difficult to remember domains. Domains should be memorable from both visual and sound cues. Consumers may need to store this in memory from a radio or billboard ad.
Avoid Long and Complicated Domains from Third-Party Hosting Arrangements: Ex: www.viaweb.com/museumcompany/	Third-party hosting should not be an excuse to avoid domain registration. They run into the same problem with user recall.
Avoid Automatic CGI Clutter — Especially for the Homepage Ex: www.companyname.com/ cgi-perscript-sxdil	Some systems store the location of the originating page as a key word in the address. This can confuse users, limit word of mouth, and look strange. Programming scripts can lead to very intimidating addresses as well.
Register Related Items and Common Typos Ex: mcdonalds.com, bigmac.com, goldenarches.com (but they don't have macdonalds.com — a common typo)	The cost of registering domain names is trivial compared to the cost of acquiring traffic. Registering related names, and even common typographical errors, helps build traffic and prevents brand dilution.
Register Domains Matching Company and Consumer Brand Awareness	Structure domain names in a manner reflecting and reinforcing brand name conventions.

Table 6.3

Top Google Brand Searches, Total and Shoe Category, 2004

Popular Brand Names 2004	Popular Shoe Brands 2004
1. louis vuitton	1. ugg boots
2. nikon	2. puma
3. canon	3. adidas
4. treo	4. nike
5. tiffany	5. aerosole
6. rolex	6. manolo blahnik
7. roomba	7. steve madden
8. armani	8. birkenstocks
9. aeron	9. dr martens
10. ray-bans	10. kenneth cole

Source: Courtesy of Google Inc.

expansion is the technique of suggesting closely related search terms. For near misses, either due to memory or typing errors, the search returns a link that is most likely correct as well.

> Choosing the Proper Domain Name

Simple Domain Name Choices

Most top brands reserve a domain name corresponding to their brand. Table 6.4 demonstrates this for the top 10 world brands as ranked by Interbrand for 2004. Typing www.brand.com leads to a web site for all of the top brands, with the minor exception of McDonald's. Apostrophes are not valid in a domain name, so the user must omit it to reach the corporate site. Web sites can redirect visitors, as Disney does when it sends users to its Go properties. Reflecting the tobacco nature of Marlboro, Altria and Phillip Morris redirect traffic to a splash page of the company rather than promoting its specific brand.

Murphy, Raffa, and Mizerski find this form of branding extends far beyond the top 10 brands. They find that by year 2000, 96% of the top 75 brands had web sites corresponding closely to the brand name in the ".com" primary domain. They also provide data on these brands registering under .net (45.3%), .org (49.3%), .au (77.3%), and .fr (80.0%).[26]

Certain mistakes of memory and typing are nearly inevitable. Another simple choice for a brand is to register closely related terms subject to memory or typing errors. For example, it is quite easy to mistype "united.com" as "untied.com." Rather than seamlessly taking the user to the United Airlines site, this alternative spelling site is a criticism site aimed at exposing United's miscues. It would have been far better from a branding point of view, as well as very cheap, for United to have anticipated this and registered the closely related term. For common mistakes, this is a low-cost and prudent precaution.

Top-level domain confusion provides another rationale for registering multiple domains. The BBC emphasizes its home base by using the form 1 version of www.bbc.co.uk. Many users,

Table 6.4

Close Link Between Top World Brands and Domain Names				
Rank	Brand	2004 Brand Value ($billions)	Find using www.brand.com?	Landing URL
1	Coca-Cola	$67.39	yes	www.coca-cola.com
2	Microsoft	61.37	yes	www.microsoft.com
3	IBM	53.79	yes	www.ibm.com
4	GE	44.11	yes	www.ge.com
5	Intel	33.50	yes	www.intel.com
6	Disney	27.11	yes	disney.go.com
7	McDonald's	25.00	yes*	www.mcdonalds.com
8	Nokia	24.04	yes	www.nokia.com
9	Toyota	22.67	yes	www.toyota.com
10	Marlboro	22.13	yes**	www.marlboro.com

Source: Based on data from Interbrand, finfacts.com, authors

*Apostrophes are not valid in a domain name, so the user must omit it to reach the corporate site.

**Reflecting the tobacco nature of Marlboro, Altria and Phillip Morris redirect traffic to a splash page of the company rather than promoting its specific brand.

especially those not in the United Kingdom, would be likely to try www.bbc.com. This alternative address sends the visitor to the preferred page.

The Multi-Brand Problem

Brand Architecture and Domain Names

Few companies face the relatively simple problem of maintaining and enhancing a single brand. Instead, they sell many products and have many potential branding choices. Multi-brand companies face the challenge of branding consistency and brand linkages. Should a company try to keep all of their products together under a common umbrella brand, let each brand stand on its own, or choose some intermediate compromise decision? How does this depend on the type of product or service, the strength of the individual products, or the unique associations of the brands involved? Can the company save branding costs by fitting all of its products into one overall positioning, or does this hopelessly confuse both the brand positioning and the company's consumers? How does a company handle the brands of a company it acquires through a merger? These are the problems of brand architecture. As Aaaker and Joachimsthaler state, the goal is a brand architecture that "will lead to clarity in customer offerings, real synergies in the brands and their communication programs, and an ability to leverage brand assets."[27]

Brand architecture choice is a company-wide, long-term decision. Once chosen, brand architecture is difficult and costly to alter. Because of this, it is important that a company's online presence reflects and reinforces the basics of the preferred brand architecture design.

While the flexibility of online communication allows some branding experimentation and marketing experiments, the first responsibility of the online marketer is to enhance the branding architecture rather than change it. This is especially true for the choice of domain names.

While branding architecture can be complex, the most important choice concerning domain naming is between a branded house and a house of brands. A branded house, chosen by companies such as Virgin, Healthy Choice, and BMW, treats all of its products as an integrated brand. Branding is company wide.[28]

At the other extreme is the house of brands. Branding is product-specific with few, if any, ties to other company brands. The leading example of a house of brands is Procter & Gamble, but it is also a strategy used by many pharmaceutical companies and companies with very separate divisions such as Toyota and Lexus.

Online Implications of Branding Architecture

Brand architecture drives many elements of a company's web presence, such as appropriate domain names, the look and feel of web pages, linking strategies between pages, and proper online traffic-building campaigns. Table 6.5 contrasts the two ends of the brand architecture continuum, the branded house and the house of brands, and summarizes some important online advantages and disadvantages of each method.

A marketer whose company uses a branded house strategy gains a simpler traffic-building challenge and a more complicated set of content and navigation choices. Branded house marketers

Table 6.5

Online Implications of Brand Architecture

	Branded House	**House of Brands**
Important Branding Advantages	Efficient use of branding resources Lowers cost of new product introductions and brand extensions Allows demographic focusing on key user segments, such as targeting the young	Avoids stretching or confusing the brand Can dominate product category associations with a powerful name Helps reduce or minimize channel conflict
Important Online Advantages	Allows traffic-building efforts targeting a single homepage rather than many Reinforces authority status of site by sharing in-bound links Creates multiple reasons for user visits Allows easier tracking of visitors	Allows focused content Permits short click trails from homepage to main interest areas Simplifies the imagery and look-and-feel decisions Allows better measurement of brand-specific campaigns, especially with traditional media
Important Online Challenges	Complicates content choice Creates possible navigation problems for users Creates difficulties for measuring advertising effectiveness by individual brands	Hinders cross-selling opportunities Reduces likelihood of frequent customer visits due to "content fatigue" Relies heavily on customer pull for traffic
URL Choices	Homepage URL is umbrella brand Other brands appear as either brand.umbrellabrand.com or www.umbrellabrand.com/brand Ex: virgin.com/channel/ travel, virgin.com/books, etc.	Separate URLs for each brand Corporate links and other brands downplayed if present at all Ex: www.tide.com, www.pantene.com, etc.

typically funnel traffic to the shared main umbrella brand homepage. Traffic-building efforts (described in detail in Chapter 8) can all link to the main homepage. For example, Virgin's many different enterprises and brands all branch off the main virgin.com page. This creates many opportunities to share traffic-building efforts among the music, travel, and other activities of Virgin.

A branded house strategy makes the content choices of Virgin more complicated. Content appropriate for travel seems out of place for music or books. In Virgin's case, it treats the homepage as a form of mini-portal, with minimal content and a strong emphasis on navigation (Figure 6.8). Channel navigation appears on the left, links to several of the Virgin brands on the bottom. Top tables lead quickly to the most important sites and ease of search is a focus. At each of the main channels or brand content selected, links exist to take the user to other content. A visitor experiences a view of the wide range of offerings from Virgin throughout the web site visit.

A branded house design simplifies customer tracking. Except for sites with password protection, most web sites track visitor sessions using some form of "cookie."[29] With a branded house design, all pages share the same top-level domain name. Because of this, sharing cookies is possible between these pages. This seemingly minor technical point makes tracking much easier. While it is possible to work around this problem, tracking using standard tools and approaches is much easier with a single primary domain name for all of the content.

Advantages and disadvantages tend to be mirror opposites for a house of brands marketer. Figure 6.9 shows the homepages of two P&G brands, Crest and Tide. Having separate pages allows the content to be focused. Category-specific material on laundry need not compete with content appropriate for dentistry. Navigation is also much simpler, with a visitor able to focus quickly on a particular problem or interest.

Building initial and recurring traffic to a house of brands site can be challenging. As each brand stands alone, there is little or no sharing of visitors. This makes it more expensive to attract visitors. It also makes it more difficult to maintain repeat interest in visiting the site. Even a creative brand manager can find it challenging to maintain recurring interest in a focused brand-oriented site. There are only so many questions to ask about a specific shampoo or laundry brand. Content fatigue, whereby repeat visits decline due to boredom or satiation of interest, is hard to avoid.

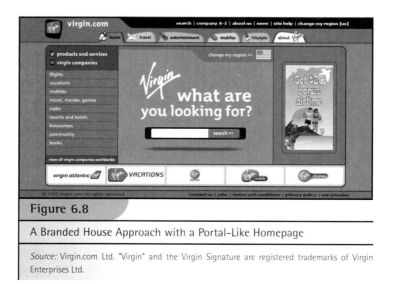

Figure 6.8

A Branded House Approach with a Portal-Like Homepage

Source: Virgin.com Ltd. "Virgin" and the Virgin Signature are registered trademarks of Virgin Enterprises Ltd.

Figure 6.9

No Links Apparent between Two Important P&G Brands

Source: Used with Permission of the Procter & Gamble Co.

A house of brands strategy can assist the tracking of traditional media. For example, traffic to the Virgin site might be due to any of the advertised sub-brands. Traffic arriving to the Crest site links much better to ongoing Crest branding money, with little help from Tide advertising spending.

Intermediate brand architecture choices tend to be compromises between the house of brands and branded house extremes. Endorsed brands, such as Courtyard by Marriott, often have brand-specific domain names (www.courtyard.com) but they also have highly visible endorser brand content and logos. The sub-brand design, being closer to the branded house, more commonly shares the overall corporate domain but also has a sizable content area dedicated to the sub-brand (such as the Deskjet section under hp.com).

An intriguing opportunity for marketers is to use their online presence as a forum for experiments with brand architecture extensions and alterations. This can be very valuable when events force marketers to combine two conflicting brand architecture approaches. Typically this occurs when two companies merge, or a company acquires a new division from another company. Inconsistency between the branding approaches of the two merging companies may be an unavoidable historical fact. The new combined company can experiment with lower risk alternative designs online before committing to a final structure that applies to all branding and all media. Hewlett-Packard faced a difficult version of this problem resulting from its merger with Compaq. HP tried alternative methods of merging the online content, support, and brands of the two companies, finally moving to an HP central approach.

Enhance Brand Meaning

Imagery and functional performance-related information create brand meaning. Brand imagery is more abstract and relates to consumers psychological or social needs. User profiles, purchase and usage situations, personality and values and the history and heritage of the brand all contribute to brand imagery. Functional performance aspects of the product include product features, service, and price.

> *Brand Imagery*

Brand personality refers to the set of human characteristics associated with the brand.[30] For example, IBM's brand personality is button-down corporate America, very secure and low risk. Ragu's personality is Italian grandmother in the kitchen (Figure 6.10). The personality of the brand allows a consumer to express his or her self, an ideal self, or a specific dimension of the self. Brand personality differentiates brands in a product category, drives consumer preference and usage, and is a common denominator for marketing across cultures. A brand's web site can reinforce the brand personality with images and content consistent with the personality of the brand. "Mama," the virtual personality on the Ragu homepage, supports the basic brand characteristics and associations that Ragu aims for (Italian, family, homemade). Positive online experiences consistent with the brand enhance the brand personality.[31]

Online media, with low-cost archives and flexible formats, provides an inexpensive setting to expand brand imagery.[32] For some brands, the goal is a nostalgic connection to simpler times. On the Morton Salt page, the claim is explicit:

> In a world where nothing stays the same, it's reassuring to find the Morton Umbrella girl still standing tall on the famous blue cylinder in your cupboard.

The evolution of brand image shows the tie to the past while maintaining contact with the earliest images (Figure 6.11). At the same time, the most modern version of brand imagery can live side by side. In Figure 6.12 on page 196, a visitor can watch a commercial that ran during the Super Bowl, with three-dimensional animated characters representing some of the best-known grocery store brand figures having dinner together. The commercial is funny, plus it creates a positive association with brands from childhood.

> *Brand Performance*

While television viewers seeing a Ragu or Tide commercial are in a passive entertainment mode ("lean back" media consumption), online users are more commonly in a problem-solving mode

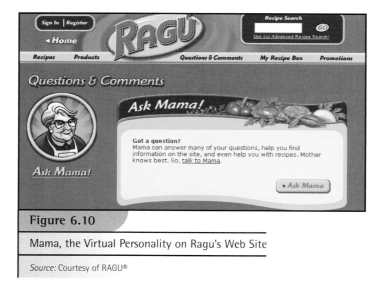

Figure 6.10

Mama, the Virtual Personality on Ragu's Web Site

Source: Courtesy of RAGU®

("lean forward" media consumption). A brand's web site can become an authoritative source for lean forward information—the types of problems for which the brand provides a solution. For example, removing a stain from an item of clothing might drive someone online looking for an answer. The Stain Detective at Tide.com provides relevant content to solve this problem and captures this key association.

Technology companies such as Siebel frequently provide white papers on best practices, case studies, and innovative solutions. Siebel provides white papers on CRM best practices and knowledge gleaned from CRM implementations (Figure 6.13). Digital Impact, a direct email vendor, provides information on email marketing best practices and industry efforts to fight spam. Flextronics, a large provider of outsourced manufacturing services for the electronics industry, provides information on the use of technology in contract manufacturing services as a key association that supports its positioning. In each of these examples, the web site deepens the associations between the brand and important characteristics in the category.

Digital content allows much more frequent modifications compared to traditional media. Performance information can be dynamic and localized. Allegra, a leading allergy brand, uses this approach for its online site. Pollen counts change on a daily basis. A visitor can obtain local weather and ragweed pollen counts by zip code. A map provides pollen counts in adjacent areas. Frequent updates to this information are possible.

Figure 6.11

The Morton Umbrella Girl over the Years

Source: Registered trademarks of Morton International, Inc. Used with permission.

Reinforce Right Brand Responses

When a brand manager's goals escalate to the higher stage of brand response, the interactive and participatory power of the Web becomes increasingly helpful. While earlier brand-building steps may benefit from media specialization, evoking a response online requires coordination across media. The goal is integrated marketing communications,[33] which can be difficult because of tensions between branding vehicles.

Part of this difficulty is the importance of different skills, culture, terminology, and institutions of the main branding tools.[34] Television, direct marketing, sales groups, public relations, and

Figure 6.12

Making the Brand Come Alive, Virtually

Source: Registered trademarks of Morton International, Inc. Used with permission.

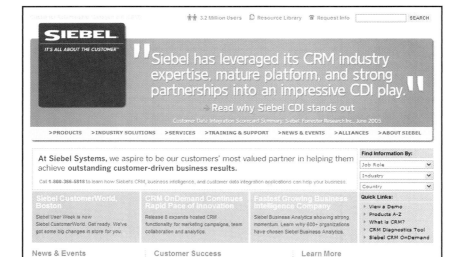

Figure 6.13

Homepage of Siebel Systems

Source: Copyright © 2005 Siebel Systems, Inc. All rights reserved. Siebel and the Siebel Logo are registered trademarks of Siebel Systems, Inc.

online areas have evolved differently. With the ongoing media fragmentation and the move to integrated branding campaigns, online content can provide a unifying role for a brand's message and current campaigns (Figure 6.14). It can also extend a campaign beyond the broadcast phase.

> *Creating a Response*

The strongest proponents of Apple's Macintosh computers are its users. The Apple Switch campaign, launched across multiple media in 2002, uses the emotional connection from current Apple users to reach out to the millions of PC and Linux owners and to encourage a switch to Mac. The campaign uses personal stories and endorsements of a wide range of individuals — some widely known such as Yo-Yo Ma and others just representative Mac users. In other cases the appeal is emotional, with individuals such as the Dalai Lama or Maria Callas representing the spirtual and artistic inclination with no specific claim to ever having used a computer, much less a Mac (Figure 6.15).[35]

Convincing PC users to switch requires telling a reassuring and convincing brand story, with elements including (1) people are switching, (2) switching is beneficial, and (3) all of the core functions that your PC performs are also readily available on the Macintosh. These are complex goals, part rational and part emotional.

Apple's execution of the Switch campaign used the Web as a complementary hub to reinforce its branding appeal. The Switch campaign partitions the campaign into a direct appeal based on testimonials from individuals who have switched, followed by additional content and directions on how to switch. This includes details about steps to follow and software to ease the transition.

Achieving a conversion from PC to Mac user is unlikely based on a single endorser. Using mass broadcasting for multiple messengers is expensive. The Switch campaign built interest with television ads and billboards, each directing consumers to the Apple web site

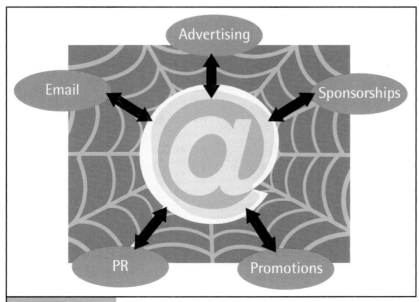

Figure 6.14

The Web as the Natural Glue for Integrated Marketing

(a)   (b)

Figure 6.15

Apple's Campaign Using Endorsements from a Wide Range of Individuals

Source: 6.15a © Michael Newman/PhotoEdit, Inc.; 6.15b © Spencer Grant/PhotoEdit, Inc.

(www.apple.com/switch). Consumers arriving at apple.com for any reason, such as getting iTunes for an iPod or a QuickTime download for a PC, also see a prominent Switch tab on the homepage.

Following this link leads to material attempting to convince the visitor to convert to a Mac. The first subheading titled "Why Switch" lists top 10 reasons to switch to a Mac. A Questions tab provides information that overcomes objections. The tabs titled TV Ads, Real Stories, and Press provide information that reinforces the claims. The Press section is primarily a resource for people who intend to switch and provides reinforcing information from articles written by independent third parties. The last two subheadings aim to close the deal by providing information on How to Switch and How to Buy.

Apple's Switch campaign garnered a tremendous amount of attention. *The Wall Street Journal* designated it as one of the winning ads for 2002.[36] Ellen Feiss, one of the students featured in the ad, has become a minor cult figure, sparking fan sites such as ellenfeiss.net (Figure 6.16a). A number of parodies and spoofs of the campaign have appeared (Figure 6.16b). While such parodies run the risk of confusing target customers, they create free additional exposure to the ad campaign and reflect the irreverent spirit that Apple emphasizes.

Figure 6.16a

The Ellen Feiss Fan Site

Source: Courtesy of flatsoda.com

Figure 6.16b

Foxtrot Cartoon Parody of Apple's Ellen Feiss Ad

Source: FOXTROT © 2002 Bill Amend. Reprinted with permission of UNIVERSAL PRESS SYNDICATE. All rights reserved.

The Apple Switch campaign illustrates a campaign with deep content, elaboration, and reinforcement. In its current form, the Web often lacks the cost-effective reach of traditional media for the initial awareness campaign. Alternatively, billboards and television have limited information because of time constraints and form factor. Pairing mass media with the Web provides opportunities for hybrid media campaigns.[37] Recognizing the strengths and weaknesses of each media type and resulting complementary pairings is a cornerstone of hybrid campaigns.

Figure 6.17 illustrates the handoffs between media in the switch campaign. The campaign progresses from generating interest to convincing, reinforcement, and close. Unless TV ads and billboards funnel traffic to the Web, the switch campaign has limited impact. The versatility of the Web, with its complex mix of information, story-telling ability, and software support, pushes the conversion process along. It demonstrates an increase in the sophistication of integrated marketing communications.

> *Effective Branding Content*

Online marketers are learning from previous campaigns what forms of content work best in a particular brand-building campaign. This requires careful attention to some of the basics of

What Type of Content Has the Largest Impact on Perceived Brand Quality?

A Scandinavian team found that visitors' online expertise predicted the type of content with the largest impact on perceived brand quality. The figure below shows the structure of the experiment. Visitors to a web site viewed online content and performed several tasks. Experimenters split the population into two groups. One group received the basic content and tasks plus personalized content. The other group received the same basic content and tasks plus community-oriented content (such as discussed in the next section). The objective was to measure whether personalization or community building was more influential on brand perception.

The study found that neither type of content worked better for the population as a whole. Rather, personalization content was most effective in raising brand quality perceptions for experienced users, while community content was most effective for novices. At least in this setting, personalization may have been too complicated for beginners while it was welcome by more experienced users. The most important lesson is to test alternative designs on the intended targets, and decide whether brand enhancement features elicit the desired response from the target segments.

Source: Helge Thorbjornsen, Magne Supphellen, Herbjorn Nysveen, Per Egil Pedersen, "Building Brand Relationships Online: A Comparison of Two Interactive Applications," *Journal of Interactive Marketing* 16, no. 3, (summer 2002): 17–34.

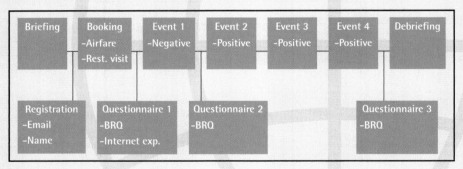

credibility and persuasion. As seen in Chapter 7, these basics include professional-looking design, functioning links, credible sources, and effective navigation. Beyond these basics, research demonstrates that generating the right response may depend on the customer segments targeted by the branding campaign and the nature of the branding process itself.

> *Managing a Brand Crisis*
A crisis can strike a company and its brand image at any time. It can affect consumers' judgments and feelings about the brand. Crises are expensive, lead to lost sales, cause harm to the

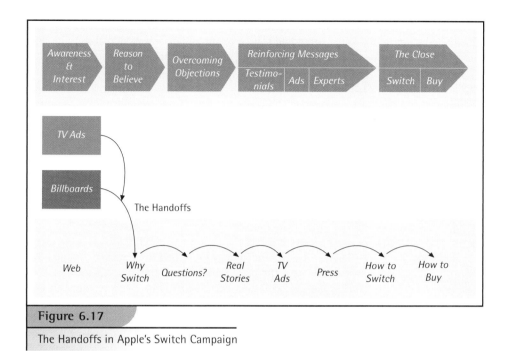

Figure 6.17

The Handoffs in Apple's Switch Campaign

brand image, and potentially result in a failure of the company. The rise of the Internet spreads the crisis story faster than ever before, and it makes it almost impossible to avoid. Just as the Internet makes a brand crisis hard to contain, it also provides some of the best tools for responding quickly and effectively. A quick response is vital, or the brand runs the risk of being permanently associated with the crisis topic.

In a study of corporate crises in Australia, Coleman found multiple crisis sources. These include product defects (36%), operational (24%), financial (8%), organizational (8%), regulatory/legal (4%), and threat/extortion (20%). Consequences are often severe for the company in question. In the Australian case, damages averaged $80 million Australian (US$50 million). Even more troubling, 27% of the Australian firms hit by a crisis during the 1990s did not survive, ending up in liquidation, sale, or merger from the event.[38]

Brand crises strike some of the most well-known products and services. In a number of cases, the cause is a product defect or product tampering. In 1982, six Chicago area residents died because of cyanide-laced Tylenol capsules. Although the FBI failed to find the culprit, maker Johnson & Johnson was able to convince the public not only of its innocence but its integrity as a firm. In other cases, the cause is a company action that strikes consumers as highly inconsistent with a product's positioning. An example of this occurred in 2001, when vegetarians were shocked by the revelation (since changed) that McDonald's added a beef flavoring to their french fries. This was especially problematic in India, where the cow is sacred because of Hindu religious beliefs and beef eating is taboo. In other cases, the crisis arises from error and urban myth. Such a situation faced Ben & Jerry's Ice Cream, when a story emerged erroneously suggesting an unusual presence of the poison dioxin in their products.

In an Internet age, it is critical that companies are prepared to deal with brand crises quickly and effectively. Ben & Jerry's used their web site to inform the public about dioxin and to address the rumor directly. It did this by posting a response on its web site, incorporating a response into its FAQ page, creating a link to the offending source of the rumor and demonstrating its mistakes, and collecting and posting endorsements from such reputable sources as the Physicians for Social Responsibility.[39]

Years later, Ben & Jerry's still maintains online material discussing the issue. This is helpful, as web content tends to survive substantially longer than mass media coverage. Indeed, a Google search on the terms "Ben & Jerry" and "dioxin" produces more than 1000 hits on sites other than benjerry.com. There is very little that Ben & Jerry's can do to affect this content, so the response needs to be durable.

One of the challenges of dealing with a potential brand crisis is determining when a negative story will have "legs" and will develop into a full-fledged threat to the brand. In the case of Tylenol, it was obviously a major story and major crisis. In other situations, such as the Ben & Jerry's case, it is tempting to ignore a story that executives know to be false or misleading.

Three aspects of negative stories seem to affect the need to respond. These are a high level of perceived credibility, dramatic and attention-getting imagery, and the tendency of bad news to travel rapidly.[40] In the Ben & Jerry's case, the mere possibility of contamination of a child's ice cream is enough to call for a rapid and coordinated response. This is where the Web as a media coordination device can play a crucial role.

Forge Brand Relationships

A brand relationship is the commitment and resonance a customer has toward a brand. It goes beyond simple features, functionality, price, or total cost of ownership. It marks the upper point of the brand equity pyramid and represents a goal only some brands are able to obtain. The role of online content is to deepen this brand loyalty, the attachment consumers feel to the brand, the support and sense of community, and to encourage active engagement with the brand.[41]

The higher the commitment to a brand, the more impervious the customer is to the offers of competitors. Higher repurchase probabilities are one measure of this commitment, as are the price premia discussed earlier. Repurchase probabilities raise profits over the long term when more customers repurchase.

Repurchase probability is only one measure of brand loyalty. Another very valuable indicator of brand relationship is a willingness to refer the product to others. For example, a Porsche owner might participate in Porsche clubs and racing events, whereas another owner with a similar level of repurchase probability might not. The former customer is more involved with the brand than the latter. They may differ in their referral activity, with the engaged customer more willing to be a positive source of word of mouth and brand referrals.

Showing the legacy of a brand fosters a brand connection beyond the latest features and capabilities. Understanding the origins of the brand can help enthusiastic loyalists and deepen the brand relationship. For some consumer packaged goods or sporting activities, this brand history stretches back more than a century.

Sporting teams provide an example of brands using their online presence to reinforce a commitment to the game in general and individual brands in particular. Whether it is Manchester United, the Green Bay Packers, or the Tokyo Yomiuri Giants, storied franchises merge their current players with heroes from the past. Organizations promote the sport as a brand by showing past champions (as done by the Tour de France) or great moments in the sport by date. Multimedia brings it alive, with newspaper clippings and radio broadcasts of top moments in the sport. Archives of results and statistics, put into a modern results format, subconsciously connect the accomplishments of the past with the modern teams.

Taking this one step further is the brand connection, which uses brand as a community builder. Sociologists define a community as a network of social relations marked by mutuality and emotional bonds.[42] A brand community is a specialized, non-geographically bound community based on a structured set of social relationships among admirers of the brand.[43] In a brand community, members place a special emphasis on a brand.

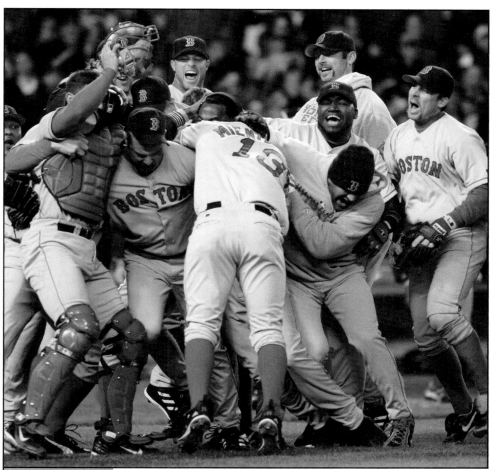

Figure 6.18

Sport Sites Allow Fans to Relive Championship Moments

Source: © MIKE SEGAR/Reuters /Landov

Rather than focus on the brand image from advertising (as seen in panel a of Figure 6.19), the emphasis is much more on the role of brand as the connection point of members (panels b and c). Riding clubs, such as the Harley Hogs or Porsche owners, illustrate how a brand can play a role in constructing this social community and online material help strengthen this connection. Online connection helps these communities overcome limitations of geography and timing.

As in any social network, a brand community has focal individuals that play key roles in establishing and maintaining the community. Muniz and O'Guinn studied these in the context of a small town and its commitment to the brands of Saab automobile, Macintosh computers, and Bronco SUV. Online contributions by community members, in web pages and other online material, helped the authors construct the map shown in Figure 6.20. Important hubs and connectors of the different brand communities emerged. For example, "Bob" is influential in the Saab community while "Bill" and "Steve" play important roles in the Bronco owners' community.

Brand communities tend to be grassroots movements. Many communities, even though they have real and imagined links to each other, begin in specific geographies and have activities that are specific to certain geographies. For example, Harley owners in the San Francisco Bay area would be very interested in rides that are specific to their local area. So the roots and the scope of many brand communities tend to be local in geographic scope. Any particular local brand

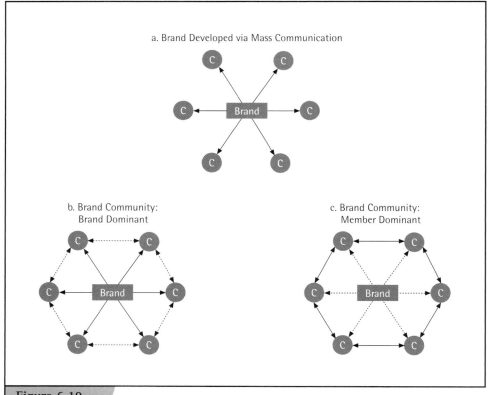

Figure 6.19

Brands as Socially Negotiated Constructs

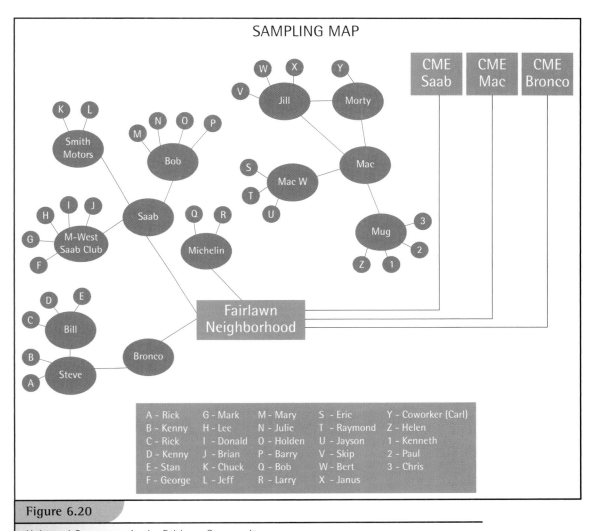

SAMPLING MAP

A – Rick	G – Mark	M – Mary	S – Eric	Y – Coworker (Carl)
B – Kenny	H – Lee	N – Julie	T – Raymond	Z – Helen
C – Rick	I – Donald	O – Holden	U – Jayson	1 – Kenneth
D – Kenny	J – Brian	P – Barry	V – Skip	2 – Paul
E – Stan	K – Chuck	Q – Bob	W – Bert	3 – Chris
F – George	L – Jeff	R – Larry	X – Janus	

Figure 6.20

Hubs and Connectors in the Fairlawn Community

Source: Albert M. Muniz and Thomas C. O'Guinn, "Brand Community," *Journal of Consumer Research* 27 (March 2001): 412–432.

community will not have the scale, resources visibility, or the consensus to take a leadership role in the organization of brand communities on a worldwide basis.

The rise of brand communities poses a dilemma to the brand manager. The transition from building brands mostly by the process outlined in Figure 6.19a to the multiple processes depicted in Figures 6.19b and c requires a shift in the mind set of the brand manger. This requires that a brand manager share some of the ownership and responsibilities of brand building with amorphous geographically diverse entities called brand communities. The brand manager will also need to decide on the right balance between communities dominated by a brand versus one dominated by members.

One useful step is for the brand manager to create and maintain a worldwide coordination page. Over time the homepages of a number of local brand communities will point to or link to the worldwide coordination page, making it a hub in terms of inbound links. This makes it easy for a prospective member to locate the right community member or resource. Porsche is one of the first of the marquee brands that has taken a lead role in setting up a worldwide club coordination page and in setting up a department for this function. Figure 6.21 illustrates the Porsche World Wide Club Coordination page.

This coordination page also supports the interfaces between the company, its dealers, subsidiary companies, and Porsche clubs. Figure 6.22 enumerates the list of services and activities on the coordination page. Figure 6.22 shows that the coordination page provides a worldwide directory of clubs. There are two specific links dedicated to this purpose, one providing a search function and a second link that is available to members only that provides detailed club addresses.

Both these links serve as an easy-to-find central resource for anyone interested in locating Porsche clubs. The Worldmap link provides a summary table that lists the total number of Porsche clubs worldwide and the membership distribution by country. Figure 6.23 on page 208 illustrates this data. This type of information reinforces the notion of an imagined community that is much larger than the local community.

Worldwide Club Coordination

News

Porsche Club Rhein-Main e.V. arranges Porsche Club Marlin Challenge Mauritius from 1st until 6th of March 2003

Exclusive for Clubmembers (password protected):

Services for Clubs   Detailed Club Addresses   Download

The Porsche Club Organization is among the largest and richest in tradition of all marque club organizations. There are currently more than 470 officially recognized Porsche Clubs with around 100,000 members in over 40 countries. The trend is upwards.

Figure 6.21

The Porsche World Wide Club Coordination Page

Source: PORSCHE, the Porsche Crest, BOXSTER®, CARRERA®, and 911® are registered trademarks and the distinctive shapes of Porsche automobiles are trademarks of Dr. Ing. H.c. F. Porsche AG. Used with permission of Porsche Cars North America, Inc. and Dr. Ing. H.c. F. Porsche AG. Copyrighted by Dr. Ing. H.c. F. Porsche AG.

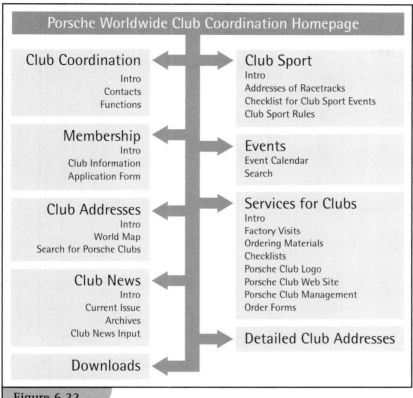

Figure 6.22

Resources on the Porsche World Wide Club Coordination Page

Source: PORSCHE, the Porsche Crest, BOXSTER®, CARRERA®, and 911® are registered trademarks and the distinctive shapes of Porsche automobiles are trademarks of Dr. Ing. H.c. F. Porsche AG. Used with permission of Porsche Cars North America, Inc. and Dr. Ing. H.c. F. Porsche AG. Copyrighted by Dr. Ing. H.c. F. Porsche AG.

Another important marker for communities is traditions and rituals. The brand coordination site can serve as a resource and access point for these brand traditions and rituals. For example, one of the traditions of Porsche owners is a visit to a Porsche factory. Figure 6.22 shows that one of services provided to Porsche clubs worldwide is factory visits. Another tradition for Porsche owners is racing and club sports. The company participates in coordinating these rituals. Downloads that provide access to brand logos, advertising copy, and other materials that are an integral part of the brand rituals and traditions are provided to members.

Brand communities are a special form of online community, where the product or service is the shared defining characteristic of community members. These brand communities can benefit from many of the additional community insights and tools described in Chapter 10. These include innovative tools to provide community content, the proper organization of community content, and methods of ensuring relevance and credibility.

Porshe Clubs	Amount	Members (approx.)
Germany	86	4,200
Europe (except Germany)	108	25,000
USA/Canada	138	50,000
South and Central America/Caribbean	9	850
Asia	26	1,500
Australia/New Zealand	7	2,500
Africa/Middle East	5	1,100
Porshe Classic Clubs		
Germany	33	1,200
Europe (except Germany)	20	3,000
USA/Canada	27	9,000
South and Central America/Caribbean	–	–
Asia	4	150
Australia/New Zealand	3	450
Africa/Middle East	1	150
Other Porshe Clubs		
Tractors/Motorsport/Model Car Clubs	6	650
Total	**473**	**99.750**

Figure 6.23

Summary Statistics on Porsche Clubs Worldwide

Source: PORSCHE, the Porsche Crest, BOXSTER®, CARRERA®, and 911® are registered trademarks and the distinctive shapes of Porsche automobiles are trademarks of Dr. Ing. H.c. F. Porsche AG. Used with permission of Porsche Cars North America, Inc. and Dr. Ing. H.c. F. Porsche AG. Copyrighted by Dr. Ing. H.c. F. Porsche AG.

ENDNOTES

1. David Ogilvy, *Confessions of an Advertising Man* (New York: Ballantine Books, 1971), 87.
2. Quoted in George Raine, "Dot-com ads make a comeback," *SFGate.com,* 10 April 2005.
3. Nielsen News Release, "U.S. Advertising Spending Rose 6.3% in 2004," *Nielsen Monitor-Plus Reports,* 1 March 2005. Available at www.nielsenmonitorplus.com.
4. See, for example, Deborah Fallows, "The Internet and Daily Life," *Pew Internet & American Life Project,* 11 August 2004. Available online at www.pewinternet.org.
5. The FTC reports spending about $3.5 million creating the service, less than ten cents per number evaluated over the first three months.
6. For example, "The Chaos Scenario," On The Media, National Public Radio, April 2005. Transcript and archived broadcast available at www.onthemedia.org.
7. Peter H. Farquhar, "Managing Brand Equity," *Marketing Research* I (1989): 24–34.
8. The Digital brand was eventually phased out after its merger with Compaq. Following the merger of Compaq with HP, a dual-branding strategy was followed, gradually being replaced by HP alone.
9. See, for example, Kevin Lane Keller, "Conceptualizing, Measuring, and Managing Customer-Based Brand Equity," *Journal of Marketing* 57 (1993): 1–22. Steve Hoeffler and Kevin Lane Keller, "The Marketing Advantages of Strong Brands," *Journal of Brand Management* 10, no. 6 (2003): 421–441.
10. Keller (1993), op. cit.
11. Ibid., Tables 1 through 6.

12. Lisa Sanders, "DuPont calls creative auction," *Advertising Age* 74, no. 14 (2003). Sean Callahan, "DuPont consolidates with Ogilvy," *B to B* 88, no. 6 (2003): 3.

13. Devin Leonard, "Nightmare on Madison Avenue," *Fortune* 149, no. 13 (2004).

14. See, for example, Xavier Dreze and Francois-Xavier Hussherr, "Internet Advertising: Is Anybody Watching?" *Journal of Interactive Marketing* 17, no. 4 (2003): 8–23.

15. In addition to references cited earlier, see Kevin Lane Keller, *Strategic Brand Management: Building, Measuring, and Managing Brand Equity* (Upper Saddle River, NJ: Prentice Hall, 1998). K.L. Keller, "Building Customer-Based Brand Equity," *Marketing Management* (July/August 2001). Richard G. Netemeyer, Balaji Krishnan, Chris Pullig, Guangping Wang, Mehmet Yagci, Dwane Dean, Joe Ricks, and Ferdinand Wirth, "Developing and Validating Measures of Facets of Customer-Based Brand Equity," *Journal of Business Research* 57 (2004): 209–224. Niraj Dawar, "What Are Brands Good For?" *MIT Sloan Management Review* (fall 2004).

16. As summarized in Keller (2001), op. cit.

17. Peter J. Danaher and Guy W. Mullarkey, "Factors Affecting Online Advertising Recall: A Study of Students," *Journal of Advertising Research* (September 2003).

18. R. Briggs and N. Hollis, "Advertising on the Web: Is there Response Before ClickThrough?" *Journal of Advertising Research* 37, no. 2 (1997): 33–45. European Interactive Advertising Association, press release, "Online Advertising Builds Brands," 24 September 2004. For a more detailed laboratory study see Dreze and Hussher, op. cit.

19. Early studies tended to intercede shortly after exposure to the online ad for recall and measurement impacts.

20. Internet Advertising Bureau, "British Airways Wimbledon 2002 Sponsorship Online Advertising Case Study." Available at www.iab.net.

21. Lee Sherman and John Deighton, "Banner Advertising: Measuring Effectiveness and Optimizing Placement," *Journal of Interactive Marketing* 15, no. 2 (2001): 60–64.

22. For current information see http://www.icann.org.

23. Domain name cases such as *Jews for Jesus*, *Toeppen vs. Panavision*, and *Planned Parenthood* have established a strong ownership of domain names by firms or organizations with copyrighted or trademarked names. U.S. courts have aggressively defended the rights of trademark owners to their online identity.

24. Note that direct IP addresses can change when an organization switches hosts. This is another major benefit of domain names.

25. For example: to, two, too; mail, male; hour, our.

26. Jamie Murphy, Laura Raffa, and Richard Mizerski, "The Use of Domain Names in e-branding by the World's Top Brands," *Electronic Markets* 13, no. 3 (2003): 222–232.

27. D. Aaker and E. Joachimsthaler, *Brand Leadership: The Next Level of the Brand Revolution* (New York: The Free Press, 2000), 26.

28. For a recent discussion see David A. Aaker, *Brand Portfolio Strategy: Creating Relevance, Differentiation, Energy, Leverage, and Clarity* (New York: Free Press, 2004). A perspective on developing markets is given in Rajagopal and Romulo Sanchez, "Conceptual Analysis of Brand Architecture and Relationships within Product Categories," *Journal of Brand Management* 11, no. 3 (2004): 233–247.

29. Recall the discussion of cookies in Chapter 4.

30. The source for the background information on Brand Personality is Jennifer L. Aaker, "Dimensions of Brand Personality," *Journal of Marketing Research* 34 (1997): 347–356.

31. Brigitte Muller and Jean-Louis Chandon, "The Impact of Visiting a Brand Website on Brand Personality," *Electronic Markets* 13, no. 3 (2003).

32. Jennifer Rowley, "Online Branding," *Online Information Review* 28, no. 2 (2004): 131–138. George Christodoulides and Leslie de Chernatony, "Dimensionalising on- and offline brands' composite equity," *Journal of Product and Brand Management* 13, nos. 2, 3 (2004): 168–179.

33. Don E. Shultz, Stanley I. Tannenbaum, and Robert F. Lauterborn, *Integrated Marketing Communications: Putting it Together and Making it Work* (Lincoln-Wood, IL: NTC Business Books, 1992).

34. Kirthi Kalyanam and Jacques Delacroix, "Customer Loss in the Advertising Industry: Specialization, Agency Size, Age and the Business Environment," Leavey School of Business, Santa Clara University, 2000, working paper.

35. Indeed, Ms. Callas died in 1977 before the Mac was even invented.

36. Suzanne Vranica and Vanessa O'Connell, "2002 Ads: Cheer Up," *The Wall Street Journal* (19 December 2002): B1.

37. For a discussion of hybrid marketing systems in the context of channels of distribution see Rowland T. Moriarty and Ursula Moran, "Managing Hybrid Marketing Systems," *Harvard Business Review* (November/December 1990): 2–11.

38. Les Coleman, "The Frequency and Cost of Corporate Crises," *Journal of Contingencies and Crisis Management* 12, no. 1 (2004): 2–13.

39. Noel Turnbull, "Issues and Crisis Management in a Convergent Environment," *Journal of Public Affairs* 1, no. 1 (2001): 85–92.

40. Beth Hogan Henthorne and Tonyh Henthorne, "The Tarnished Image: Anticipating and Minimizing the Impact of Negative Publicity in Health Services Organizations," *Journal of Consumer Marketing* 11, no. 3 (1994): 44–54.

41. Helge Thorbjornsen and Magne Supphellen, "The Impact of Brand Loyalty on Website Usage," *Journal of Brand Management* 11, no. 3 (2004): 199–207.

42. Thomas Bender, *Community and Social Change in America* (New Brunswick, NJ: Rutgers University Press, 1978).

43. The discussion in this section is drawn from Albert M. Muniz and Thomas C. O'Guinn, "Brand Community," *Journal of Consumer Research* 27 (2001): 412–432. Also see James H. McAlexander, John W. Schouten, and Harold F. Koenig, "Building Brand Community," *Journal of Marketing* 66, no. 1 (2002): 38–54.

chapter 7:

Usability, Credibility, and Persuasion

> " The Web is the ultimate customer-empowering environment. He or she who clicks the mouse gets to decide everything.[1] "
>
> Jakob Nielsen

> " We have entered an era of persuasive technology, of interactive computing systems designed to change people's attitudes and behaviors.[2] "
>
> B. J. Fogg

Helping Hands across the Globe

When a tsunami struck the Indian Ocean on December 26, 2004, news traveled quickly around the world. Within hours, it was clear that a major catastrophe had hit. The full scale of the disaster, with more than 150,000 killed, emerged over the next few days. While the countries of the region, such as Indonesia, Thailand, and Sri Lanka, were the most devastated, countries around the world suffered losses. Concerned families desperately hoped for a phone call or email from loved ones living or vacationing in the region.

Almost as quickly as the spread of the news, the Internet became the focus of a massive amount of individual contributions and fund raising. Established relief agencies created online means for receiving contributions, providing information about relief activities and how to connect with distant relatives, and setting aggressive goals for fund raising. Citizens around the world contributed heavily to relief agencies. One month after the tsunami emergency, the American Red Cross announced it had received sufficient funding commitments to administer its tsunami relief effort and recover program over the next several years. As of July 28, 2005, the American Red Cross has collected $541 million for tsunami relief.

The Red Cross was in a strong position to be a hub of U.S. fund-raising. Established in 1881, the Red Cross has a strong image of humanitarian support and public-oriented services. Whether it is disaster relief, blood bank operations, or health

this chapter

The web site visit is at the heart of online marketing. These visits are often very short, yet an organization faces the challenge of making them useful, believable, and persuasive.

Topics covered in this chapter include:

> Helping Hands Online

> The Elusive Visit

> Creating Useful Information

> Establishing Credibility

> Persuasion Online

education, the Red Cross occupies a trusted position in society. Their web site, redcross.org, reflects these missions and the manner in which volunteers can help (Figure 7.1).

Motivated by the scale of the disaster and powerful images, individuals wanted to help. Many turned online. Each week, Google produces a list of the top search terms gaining or losing popularity (Figure 7.2). Not surprisingly, for the week after the event, tsunami was the top gaining search term. Much of the rest of the list involves seasonal events or celebrities that for some reason were in the news that week. The Red Cross is the only charitable organization making an appearance.

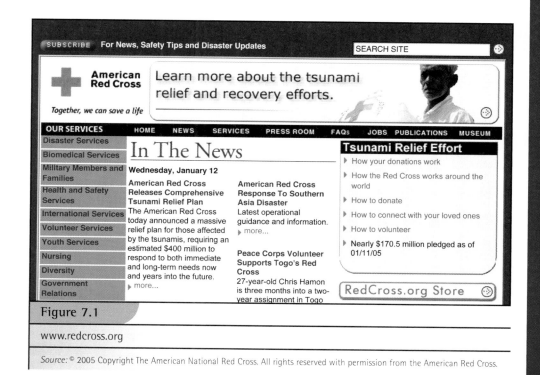

Figure 7.1

www.redcross.org

Source: © 2005 Copyright The American National Red Cross. All rights reserved with permission from the American Red Cross.

Top 10 Gaining Queries
Week Ending Jan. 3, 2005

1. tsunami
2. aishwarya rai
3. petra nemcova
4. red cross
5. new year
6. jerry orbach
7. natalie portman
8. blockbuster
9. delta airlines
10. rose bowl

Figure 7.2

Google.com - Weekly Top Searches

Source: Courtesy of Google Inc.

Potential donors are aware of the Red Cross, and turn to it in times of crisis. Using the Net to do so seems natural to many. Former U.S. president Bill Clinton, asked to assist in motivating donations, said the Internet "democratized the process of charitable giving" similar to how the Internet affected campaign contributions during the 2004 presidential election.[3]

The challenge for the Red Cross is to turn willingness into money. It must persuade visitors to give, and to put their trust into the Red Cross as the vehicle for giving. The Red Cross uses their web site to validate their fund-raising efficiency, reinforce their credibility, and provide specific suggestions for giving.

Establishing online credibility is challenging. Online credibility is a mixture of performance, design, domain name, previous brand image, and previous experience. The Red Cross site works hard to meet these expectations. Despite the heavy load on the site, it performs quickly and efficiently. It has a professional look and feel, and smoothly helps a visitor navigate to key information.

The Red Cross material on the tsunami quickly directs a visitor to appropriate material for contributing. The call-out box on the right of the home page provides a direct link to the most common interests and objectives of a contributor. A visitor does not have to hunt through a wealth of extraneous material. When a visitor lands on the home page, a quick signup form asking name, email, and zip code provides the basis for alerts in the future for other disasters.

Suggestion is also important for persuasion. Figure 7.3 highlights how the site provides concrete examples of how contributions lead to relief supplies, and provides simple measures of what the money buys. For those only able to give a little, $15 suddenly seems like it buys something. Those able to provide more are encouraged to give enough for a family tent.

While straightforward, the choice of domain names reinforces Red Cross credibility and branding. The usage of the organization primary domain ".org" reinforces the nonprofit nature of Red Cross. Each of the main choices off the home page clearly lie within the Red Cross site: redcross.org/news, redcross.org/services, etc. The one exception to

Your Donation at Work

When you give to the American Red Cross International Response Fund, your donation provides tsunami survivors with nutritious food, basic supplies such as tents and hygiene items, basic healthcare and the support that they'll need to cope with the unbelievable trauma they've experienced.

The American Red Cross promises to use each donation dollar in the most efficient and effective manner as possible. Reputable charity "watchdogs" such as www.charitynavigator.org and the American Institute of Philanthropy recognize the commitment of the Red Cross and responded with high marks for the organization in recent ratings.

Thousands of people on the Thai coast have been left homeless by the disaster.
Photo courtesy of the Federation

One hundred percent of every donation made for this disaster goes to tsunami relief and recovery efforts. In order to provide this timely relief, the Red Cross incurs direct support costs, which are less than 6 percent of the total relief costs. These are costs that the American Red Cross would not incur in an everyday working environment and include the coordination of mobilizing relief workers and relief supplies.

Approximate costs of items needed in the tsunamis relief and recovery operation

- $2 – a sleeping mat
- $5 – a mosquito net (essential in areas where malaria is a common disease)
- $15 – a kitchen set for a family of five
- $175 – a waterproof tent for a family of five

Learn how American Red Cross aid will reach tsunami survivors

- Food and safe water
- Immediate family supplies
- Mental health counseling
- Healthcare and disease prevention
- Disaster preparedness and prevention measures

Figure 7.3

Red Cross - Explaining the Usage of Contributions Web Page

Source: © 2005 Copyright The American National Red Cross. All rights reserved with permission from the American Red Cross.

this reinforces the point. The main navigation bar in Figure 7.1 does not have a link to the Red Cross store. This appears to the right with a separate link. Following this link takes you to a site offering first aid kits and vintage Red Cross products (Figure 7.4). These sale items reinforce the brand by offering useful or historical products.

Figure 7.4

Red Cross Store Web Page

Source: © 2005 Copyright The American National Red Cross. All rights reserved with permission from the American Red Cross.

There is a potential problem. Donors may worry that too much effort is going to selling things and commercial operations, and that it taints the core Red Cross mission. The domain strategy partially enforces a separation. The domain name is no longer redcross.org but a separate ".com" domain without the "redcross" name. Red Cross uses a partner to help with its ecommerce activities. While subtle, and perhaps even unintentional, this separation of commercial and charitable activity to different domain names is a good idea. There is clearly co-branding occurring, but the missions are kept at a distance.

Online usability, credibility, and persuasion can help sell philanthropy just as it helps sell soap or computers. While the missions and goals are very different, and cannot operate the same way, nonprofit and for-profit organizations can learn useful lessons from each other in their online techniques. Providing believable information with a call to action is a challenge faced by almost all sites.

THE WEB SITE VISIT

When confronting a natural disaster, the Red Cross seeks to bring potential donors and volunteers to its site and convert them to actual donors and volunteers. In the next chapter, methods for bringing traffic to a site are the focus. This chapter assumes a visitor has already arrived. Now an organization must encourage the visitor to spend time on the site and do something as a result. This chapter covers three fundamentals of the interaction:

> Can visitors find the right information? This raises issues of usability, customer support, and virtual value.
> Do visitors believe the information? This raises issues of credibility, trust, and completeness.
> Do visitors act differently based on the information? This raises the issue of persuasion through online materials.

While Internet marketing increasingly involves multiple communication vehicles (email, instant messaging, podcasts, and more) and multiple platforms (cell phones, PDAs, personal video recorders, and more) the core interaction remains computer access to a web site.[4] While fundamental principles of usability, credibility, and persuasion apply across media, for simplicity most of the discussion in this chapter involves web site interactions.

One of the main roles for an online manager is balancing conflicting objectives and online capabilities. Any sufficiently complicated organization and web site faces conflict in their online approach. Persuasive content may be somewhat harder to use. The most usable format for a beginner is not the same for an expert. Handling these and other conflicts is a management challenge, only partly linked to technology.

Visit Dynamics

> Length of a Visit

The average web site visit is short—less than three page views on many sites.[5] This fundamental reality confronting web site managers is at the heart of the Jakob Nielsen quote that began the chapter. Visitor choices matter a great deal. Unless a site can convince a visitor to remain on the site there is little time available to communicate whatever message the web site hopes to deliver, to establish credibility, build brand, engage in commerce, or to persuade.

Figure 7.5 demonstrates a typical pattern of page views at the Xerox company web site. The horizontal axis is the length of a user's visit to a site measured in the number of page views. The vertical axis is the cumulative percentage of visitors with that number of views or less.[6] Most visits are quite short. There is a heavy bias toward visits of only 1, 2, or 3 pages. Second, there are some very extensive visits lasting 60, 80, or 100 pages. The maximum of the distribution for the site was 110 pages. This skewed distribution implies that the median number of pages visited is a better measure of typical behavior, and is lower than the mean. Third, the fitted curve matches

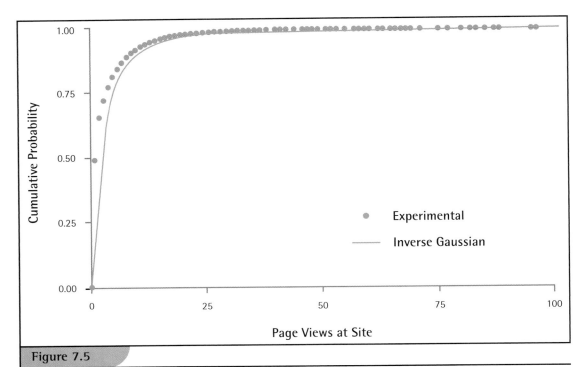

Figure 7.5

The Length of Time Visitors Spend on the Xerox Company Web Site (in page views)

Source: R.M. Lukose and B.A. Huberman, "Surfing as a real option." In Proceedings of the First International Conference on Information and Computation Economies, Charleston, South Carolina, (ACM Press, 1998), 45–51

the data very well. Table 7.1 shows that short visits hold across countries and different web site types.[7] The same study found that on these web sites, more than 90% of page views occurred within five clicks of the entry page.

Two different models explain these very short visits, the random surfer model and the look ahead surfer model. The first is very simple. Researchers using the data summarized in Table 7.1 model web surfing as a simple "flip of the coin." At each page a visitor has a chance to continue the visit or exit. The best empirical fit for the random surfer model has approximately a 50% per page chance of leaving for the first few page views, which then falls to approximately 37% per page chance of exit if the visit continues. This model explains visits of different length, as seen in Figure 7.5, as the result of different runs of luck.

Whereas a simple random model does relatively well in explaining the data, a somewhat better fit and more useful conclusions comes from a different approach. The look ahead model explains the same pattern of many short visits with a very different model of surfing behavior, whereby surfers are not "flipping a coin" about leaving but carefully balancing their time and effort against the chance of finding the information they desire. What is unknown is the ultimate value of continuing their visit. Lukose and Huberman were one of the first to model web surfers as constantly making a judgment about the value of continuing another page view or stopping.[8] Two factors enter this decision. First is the value of the current page. Second is the

Table 7.1

Web Site Visit Length (home page entry)					
Website Code	Type	Country	Recorded Sessions	Average page views	Entry at home page
E1	Educational	Chile	5,500	2.26	84%
E2	Educational	Spain	3,600	2.82	68%
E3	Educational	US	71,300	3.10	42%
C1	Commercial	Chile	12,500	2.85	38%
C2	Commercial	Chile	9,600	2.09	32%
R1	Reference	Chile	36,700	2.08	11%
R2	Reference	Chile	14,000	2.72	22%
O1	Organization	Italy	10,700	2.93	63%
O2	Organization	US	4,500	2.50	1%
OB1	Organization + Blog	Chile	10,000	3.73	31%
OB2	Organization + Blog	Chile	2,000	5.58	84%
B1	Blog	Chile	1,800	9.72	39%
B2	Blog	Chile	3,800	10.39	21%

Source: Ricardo Baeza-Yates and Carlos Castillo: "Crawling the Infinite Web: Five Levels are Enough," Workshop of Algorithms on Web Graphs (WAW), Rome, 2004. In *Springer Lecture Notes in Computer Science* 3243 (2004): 156–167.

value of any pages to come. Any visitor has uncertainty about the value of pages not yet seen. If there is enough of a chance that future pages have high quality, a visit may continue. Surfing continues because of the option value of additional pages.

User expectations and uncertainty lead to the behavior captured in Figure 7.6. If the value of the current page is high, keep going. If the value of a page is below the threshold, then stop and exit the web site. An interesting feature of the model is the upward slope of the curve. Early in a visit to a site, a surfer is willing to keep going even if the value of the current page is low. The uncertainty about future pages creates an incentive to continue sampling the site. Eventually, either the surfer finds the information or decides it does not exist on the site.

Additional research extends the option value surfing model to include page view duration, repeat web site visits, and number of page views. Bucklin and Sismeiro find a very similar pattern for page requests, where the chance of staying falls with the number of pages viewed.[9] They interpret this as the result of both time constraints and involvement with the site. They also find that repeat visits lead to fewer page views, due to learning by the visitor. As seen in Figure 7.7, there is an interesting interaction between page view duration and number of page views. As page views increase, more attention and longer time is devoted to each page. This suggests increasing involvement and better matching of goals with the content.

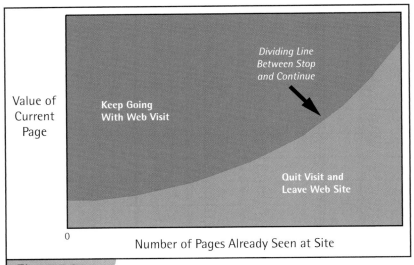

Figure 7.6

The Look Ahead Model of Web Surfing Behavior

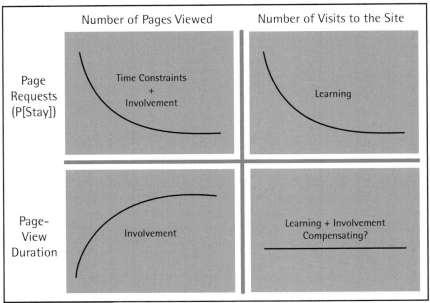

Figure 7.7

Empirical Results and Interpretation of Web Site Browsing Behavior

Source: Randolph E. Bucklin and Catarina Sismeiro, "A Model of Web Site Browsing Behavior Estimated on Clickstream Data," *Journal of Marketing Research* 11 (August 2003): 249–267. Used with permission by the American Marketing Association.

In both the random surfer and the look ahead model, higher average quality content of a site leads to longer expected visits. The models have somewhat different implications about likely exit pages. In a random surfer model, likely exit pages only loosely connect to current page quality. In the surfer option model, the connection is tighter when the page corresponds to accomplishing a task or clarifying that the web site does not match the visitor's goals.

The two different models of web visits may indeed reflect different types of web usage. Novak et al. emphasize[10] the distinction between task-directed and experiential uses. In task-directed web visits the user is attempting to find information to accomplish a task, such as the time of movie, the best route to drive, or the solution to a homework problem. A task-directed surfer is actively engaged in judging the appropriateness and credibility of information, balancing additional information on a page against better alternatives elsewhere.

Experiential surfing is surfing for its own benefit, as a time-using application much like television or a video game. A web site is a form of programming channel, which either offers quality entertainment or does not. Eventually satiation, boredom, or the completion of a task sets in and the visit ends. Many visits end early as the site appears not to match desires (see Table 7.2).

The look ahead model appears the best match for a task-directed visit, while the simple continue or quit model is a more natural model for an experiential surfer not actively engaged in a discovery of specific information. Additional research is needed to further connect the nature of the web site visit to the pattern of visit length it generates.

> *Matching Content to Initial Visit Information*

When web site visits last only one or two page views, limited learning is possible. This makes initial information even more valuable. Each visit starts with three possible pieces of information: the entry page, referral information, and a pre-existing cookie on the visitor's computer. These three sources of information, when available, provide a snapshot of the visitor's identity and possible goals for the particular visit before the visitor makes an additional choice. As most visits are very short, they are especially important sources of understanding users.

The entry page is the start of a visit, and often is the home page. As Table 7.1 demonstrates, there are a number of visits that do not begin on the home page of the site. These specific pages provide useful clues to the goal of the visit. A visitor to redcross.org landing first on the Military Members and Families page probably has very different objectives than someone first appearing on the site at the Blood Donation or Tsunami Relief pages.

Visits that follow a search engine result or from following a web link send this information along with the visitor to the new site. In particular, a search result sends along the search term used. A web link sends its location. Even when the visit starts at the home page, this referral information provides insight into the visitor objectives.

By far the richest source of information on an arriving visitor is contained in the user's "cookie"

Table 7.2	
Contrasts between Online Behavior	
Task-directed Online	**Experiential Online**
Extrinsic motivation	Intrinsic motivation
Situational involvement	Enduring involvement
Utilitarian benefits/value	Hedonic benefits/value
Directed search	Nondirected search, browsing
Goal-directed choice	Navigational choice
Cognitive	Emotional
Work	Fun

Source: Adapted from Thomas P. Novak, Donna L. Hoffman, and Adam Duhachek, "The Influence of Goal-Directed and Experiential Activities on Online Flow Experiences," *Journal of Consumer Psychology* 13, Nos. 1&2 (2003): 3–16.

if it is present. A cookie may be as limited as an indication of the last time the visitor was on the site or as complete as a stored user name and password. Comprehensive snapshots occur when the cookie contains a precise database identifier, a unique user ID, and the web site operator uses it to match the visitor to information stored internally on the web site owner's computers. Once a web site can reliably connect a visitor to a name, some sites fuse extensive outside information with data observed on site. This raises many questions of privacy and privacy policies, discussed in greater detail in Chapters 9 and 17.

While most visits are short, the most important ones are those that tend to last more than a few clicks. As a web site visit evolves, further information accumulates about the motivations and purposes of the particular visit. Sites with dynamic capabilities utilize this growing click-stream data to better match content to users' goals. This occurs when dynamically generated pages contain content based on previous user choices. Dynamic personalization is one of the most powerful online capabilities, combining all three GPTs of digitization, networking, and individualization. Chapter 9 looks at the different types of personalization used by many sites, and the details of information quality, business objectives, and personalization approaches.

Two of the main goals of personalization systems are learning and dialogue, where the interaction between the visitor and the site leads to better understanding and responses that are more appropriate by the system. One view is Figure 7.8, where user choices change the old cartoon about the anonymity of the Internet into personalized interactions. Chapter 10 discusses the methodologies for making such conclusions, and when the chances of mistaking a person for a dog are outweighed by the benefits of providing targeted content.

Even without a completely dynamic and personalized web site, a manager can look at user histories, investigate how good a job the site is doing, and base page content on previous visitor patterns. Content can match weekly, monthly, or annual cycles. Location during a visit provides a signal of the proper time to display content. Two of the standard entries in web log software are the most popular entry and most popular exit pages for visits. Entry pages are the particular web page that a visit begins with; exit pages are the last page viewed during a visit. Tracking software can identify the entry page of a new visit as it occurs by spotting that the visitor has not recently seen any other page on the site. Exit pages, on other hand, are identified only after the fact for any given visit. Augmenting popular entry and exit pages with additional

Figure 7.8

Learning as a Visit Evolves

Source: Cartoon by Nik Scott

information may improve performance. While it might not match a specific visit, reflecting average behavior and typical patterns can still lead to better responses.

Table 7.3 shows several possibilities for matching content with an entry page.[11] Greetings can contain information about special offers, commercial opportunities, and ways to maintain connection over time such as in an electronic magazine or newsletter. Most popular entry pages will naturally be the highest volume pages. This makes advertising a possibility for those entry pages, as advertisers want sufficient volume to avoid duplicating views and reach a large audience.

Days of the week or annual peak demand periods provide a measure of opportune moments for changing content. Seasonal and weekly swings in activity reveal the natural inclination of visitors to come to the site. Lulls in activity provide a window for replacing offers. Launching new offers and promotions makes sense as the most popular days approach. It may also make sense to use external promotional activity, such as search and banner advertising, to reinforce the tendencies of potential visitors and make the advertising more productive.[12]

Table 7.3

Matching Content to Web Site Location For "Static" Sites

Web Analytics Data	Marketers' Potential Responses
Most popular entry pages	*On these pages, do the following:* Place product offers, rotate weekly Promote online store Offer free subscription to an e-zine Sell advertising Include toll-free phone number Remind visitors to bookmark these pages
Visits by day of the week	*Do the following:* Replace offers on the least-visited day Ramp up sales pitch in web page marketing copy daily until most-popular day On days following the most popular one, promote "liquidation" or "last change" sale Increase pay-for-placement positions on search engines during strong-performing days, lower positions on poor-performing days Buy sponsorships in content-related e-zines that email 24–48 hours before best sales days
Most popular exit pages	*On these pages, do the following:* Promote "limited time" offer Offer coupon in exchange for email address Launch exit pop-up survey asking why their needs weren't met (multiple choice)

Source: Adapted from Catherine Seda, *Search Engine Advertising: Buying Your Way to the Top to Increase Sales* (New Riders Press, 2004), 215.

If a site's web log shows a sharp pattern of likely exit pages this information can be used to fix possible problems with the page or augment those pages with additional reasons to stay on the site. These include promotional offers, possible surveys, or other means of either stopping exit or understanding why it is occurring.

CREATING USEFUL INFORMATION

Usability

> *Task-Directed Usability*

The distinction between experiential and task-directed web visits is relevant in more contexts than explaining web session length. It also shapes usability and web site design. In particular, the foundation of many usability approaches matches closely the goals and objectives of a task-directed web surfer. Most usability studies base their analysis on web visitors attempting to solve problems or obtain useful information. A web site that assists users in this process, leads users rapidly to the correct information, and is judged as satisfying and enjoyable by visitors is good design. User goals, not marketer objectives, predominately influence this approach to usability.

The goal for a web site designer seeking a highly usable site is to anticipate problems and create a good design from the start. Ideally, usability tools can catch bad design much like a word processor flags misspelled words and poor grammar. While not perfect, automated writing tools eliminate many of the most common spelling and sentence mistakes and lead to higher quality documents. This is also the goal for usability experts.

The analogy with writing suggests how marketers should approach apparent conflicts between usability and marketing objectives. In order to make a point, sound familiar, or capture dialogue it is occasionally necessary to use nonstandard grammar or spelling. This requires ignoring and overriding automated writing rules. These situations, however, are much less common in professional documents and correspondence than in works of fiction and dramatic settings. There are few cases where task usability and impact must conflict. Conflicts are more likely to be the result of lack of attention to usability concerns rather than necessary tradeoffs.

Tradeoffs that are more fundamental exist between experiential and task-directed usability. While a task-oriented surfer seeks efficiency and time savings, experiential surfing leans toward entertainment and time using. Design rules for a good video game or online experience site are different from design rules for a good customer support site or search engine. The practices of other experiential media, such as television, movies, and music, suggest extreme segmentation is successful and difficulties reaching multiple customer segments with the same experiential content. Not all discussions of usability make this distinction clear, leading to confusion about recommendations. This initial discussion considers task usability, with experiential usability covered second.

Palmer reviews the usability literature and identifies themes that consistently find support as improving usability:[13]

> Fast response time,
> Effective navigation,
> Responsiveness to user goals and desires, and
> Higher interactivity and quality content.

> Response Times and Congestion

Speed of response plays an important part of visitor perceptions of quality of the site.[14] It also affects the capability of the site to achieve its goals of communication and dialogue. A site that takes too long to respond breaks the train of thought of the user. Table 7.4 considers three latencies between user choice and web site response.[15] The first is .1 seconds, which is an upper bound on response perceived as instantaneous. Users perceive delays above one tenth of a second as a lag. Maintaining a flow of thought by a visitor can have delays up to a second. The third latency is 10 seconds, beyond which a user loses the thread of discussion.

Table 7.4

Upper Limit of Delays and Their Impacts	
Delay time	Impact
0.1 second	Upper limit on delay leading to perception of instantaneous response
1.0 second	Upper limit on delay for user's flow of thought to stay uninterrupted
10 seconds	Upper limit on delay to keep user's attention focused on dialogue

Source: Cited in Jakob Nielsen, (2000), Designing Web Usability, New Riders.

Table 7.4 suggests that web site congestion and user broadband connections have subtle but important impacts on the type of communication that feels smooth and persuasive. Even though slower dial-up connections can deliver information, they do not feel instantaneous and require concerted attention by visitors beyond that required by fast connections. Periodic web site congestion can harm site impact relative to uncongested visits, leading to varying user impact.

> Effective Navigation

Effective navigation consistently ranks high among factors explaining web site satisfaction and web site usability.[16] At the same time, screen space devoted to navigation is at the expense of content for that specific page. Balancing content and navigation requires attention to design principles and user goals. Nielsen stresses three questions all users face:[17]

> Where am I?
> Where have I been?
> Where can I go?

Effective navigation helps the user accomplish these three contextual navigation problems quickly and seamlessly.

The tens of millions of web sites existing online have generated thousands of different navigation solutions. One of the most common formats is shown in Figure 7.9, where there are global links horizontally laid out on top (and often bottom), local links laid out vertically, a "breadcrumb" list showing the location of the page in the site, and links within the content spread throughout the page. Users become familiar with the most common layouts and adapt quickly to a site with a similar navigation structure.

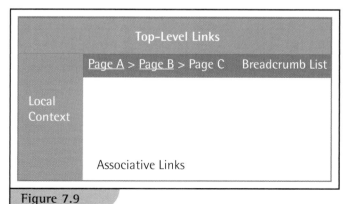

Figure 7.9

A Standard Navigation Layout

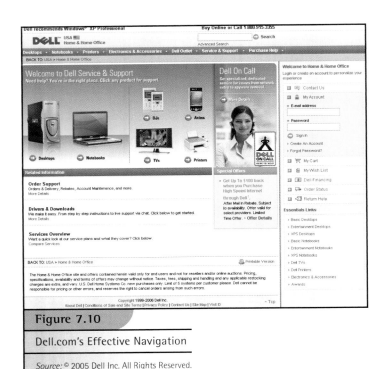

Figure 7.10

Dell.com's Effective Navigation

Source: © 2005 Dell Inc. All Rights Reserved.

Table 7.5

Virtual Value Activities and Customer-Support Solutions

VVAs	Investor Relations	Technical Support
Gathering	Capture SEC filings Record press releases Stock information Analyst reports	Product manuals Product design documents Help desk information Field engineers Warranty information
Organizing	Chronological listing Keyword search News flashes Product group	Product line listing Search Index
Selecting	News flashes SEC reports CEO speeches	FAQs High-hit rate requests Frequent call center requests
Synthesizing	Reporter pages Analyst pages	Getting started pages Solution pages
Distributing	Homepage link Investor channel	Navigation bar links Solution CDs Mass media ads Key customers' intranets

In Figure 7.10, Dell uses this format throughout its award-winning site. The top horizontal bar is global navigation, with the seven main destinations on the site. Each of these provides additional options, as a "mouse-over" of each choice provides three to twelve further detailed navigation choices. The right vertical navigation bar changes with the page visited, providing additional detailed choices of matching the context of the page. A breadcrumb list shows the site map location of the current page.[18] Additional content fills the remainder of the screen space. The goal is quick and efficient navigation requiring a minimum of links and consistency throughout the site.

> Responsiveness to User Goals: Virtual Value Analysis

Nature of Information Sought

Sites that provide information matching user goals receive higher usability ratings. The virtual value activities, briefly discussed in Chapter 3, provide an organizing framework for creating valuable information for visitors to a site. There are nearly unlimited choices for what material, information, and presentations might be on a site. Using the virtual value activities helps identify and limit useful material, as well as spot gaps and opportunities in the current offerings.

Each of the virtual value steps—gathering, organizing, selecting, synthesizing, and distributing—can be customized for different visitor types (Table 7.5). Just as customer-based brand equity adapts brand-building activities to different customer types, adapting the virtual value activities to different visitor segments helps guide managers in designing appropriate online content.

Technical support visitors have different needs than investors checking information about their current or potential investors. Rather than focus on fixing bugs and solving problems, investors want details about revenue forecasts, news flashes, SEC filings, analyst comments, and other information helpful in evaluating investments. A comparison of the virtual value steps for the two types of visitors, investors and customers seeking support, shows very different roles for gathering, organizing, selecting, synthesizing, and distributing information.

Large and small companies share many features on their investor pages, but also have different stories to tell investors. Dell uses their site to emphasize the well-known management team, the strength of the company, and the latest movements of the stock price. Cognizant, ranked as a leading small company, emphasizes less of the personality of managers and more results and commentary by analysts and the financial media (Figure 7.11).

Figure 7.11

Cognizant's Award Winning Investor Support

Source: Courtesy of Cognizant Technology Solutions

User Capabilities

Users arrive at a site with different capabilities. In media where only one design is possible, this creates a problem and a difficult trade off. Targeting beginners allows easy adoption of the service. However, it risks boring both intermediate and advanced users. Targeting advanced users can make the service highly efficient, but possibly obscure and difficult to use. Software designers and user interface specialists suggest targeting the "perpetual intermediate" as the best balance when a fixed approach is required.[19]

Virtual value analysis based on user type allows a different solution. Beginner, intermediate, and advanced users have different abilities and objectives. Maintaining a parallel structure for the web site allows users to self-select their own level of expertise. First-time or advanced users can choose a link that takes them to appropriate content. No choice can remain at the intermediate level.

For beginners, understanding what the site has to offer and how to begin is the correct initial approach. Gathering examples of other beginners, and what they do upon arrival, provides the new visitor an appropriate starting point. Possible organization principles include first visit, how to register, or some other beginning task. Tutorials provide prepackaged solutions. It is probably wise to avoid phrases such as "for beginners," as visitors may resent a forced confession to being a beginner.[20] Getting a beginner to even visit a site may be difficult when they don't understand the site's purpose. Providing demos and examples bundled with new computers or some other natural starting point can be helpful.

Advanced users will typically be frequent users, and do not need as much reminding or as many guidelines on what is available or how to use it. Streamlining frequent requests is more helpful. Even modest improvements in site navigation and operations, such as using shortcuts and remembered information, can save a substantial amount of time and effort for frequent visitors. At the same time, it is more likely that advanced users will be a source of advice to beginners and others. Providing some link, such as to FAQs or customer support comments, may help these advanced users be impromptu volunteer tech support.

User type and information request may interact. An advanced user seeking specific technical information may want to run simulations, test specific solutions, find out the impact of design on costs, and other sophisticated inquiries. Following a user through these tasks, and ensuring an efficient online solution, improves the expert's usability and productivity.

With intermediates, the goal is to provide convenient pathways through the site and to remind and correct key confusion points. Having templates on how best to do occasional tasks helps jog their memory and anticipate mistakes. Reminders, sent out by email and timed appropriately, remind these occasional users of reasons to visit.

A different customer dichotomy is between transactional and relationship customers. Transactional customers are those with a short or nonexistent purchase history, and do not necessarily seek more than a one-time transaction. Relationship customers are repeat customers, with both a history of purchases and an expectation of future purchase opportunities. While research shows both types can be profitable,[21] they have quite different information desires and requirements.

In Chapter 13, the Lands' End site provides an example of catering to the relationship customer. Personal models, stored purchase information, and one-click shopping all reinforce the connection between the shopper and Lands' End. These customers are highly valuable to the retailer, and there is in-depth support for their needs.

Transactional customers can also be profitable online. For example, a family member or friend may wish to buy a gift card for someone who shops at Lands' End even if the purchaser does not. On the gift buying page there are reassurances about privacy and security in a prominent position near the main gift card descriptions. A gift buyer can be a transactional customer, even if the recipient is a relationship buyer. Easing the way to a purchase, and minimizing the need for customer support and interaction with the transactional buyer, can be the difference between a profitable and an unprofitable transaction.

> Interactivity and Content Quality

As broadband reaches the mass market, web designers increasingly turn to multimedia to make a compelling experience. Examples include film clips, pod casts, and flash presentations. Research on multimedia effectiveness suggests that media richness matters, but that implementation makes a great deal of difference as well.

Some visitors to a site are highly motivated to find the proper information. Primary objectives in assisting these users are to make the information usable and understandable. Studies of word-of-mouth reveal that extremes of user reactions to a product or service motivate telling others about the experience. If a goal of a site is information diffusion, then simple comprehension is not enough. Visitors must find the site compelling and enjoyable to motivate positive word-of-mouth.

A study of the best format for presenting medical information regarding cancer looked at five alternative forms and found real differences in multimedia impact on user ratings. The five considered formats were (1) paper presentation, (2) normal web content using standard HTML, (3) audio files, either streamed or downloaded, (4) audio files narrating web pages, and (5) Flash animations combining animation, graphics, and synchronized sound (see Table 7.6). Each focused on the same basic information, "What you need to know about lung cancer."

Results of the study were intriguing. Notably, there was no significant difference in the quality of learning between the five formats. All performed approximately as well when measured with a user quiz covering understanding and retention of the material. Earlier researchers have also found that it is the quality of the implementation rather than any medium choice per se that affects learning.[22]

When it came to rating the content and the method of presentation, there were major differences in enjoyment and satisfaction. Visitors rated the flash animations as more enjoyable and engaging. The results did not follow the level of media richness, as the second rated method was the original paper. The lowest rated methodology was audio narration only, somewhat at odds with the rapid growth in audio podcasting.

The particular ratings given to the different presentation methods may reflect the heavily goal-oriented nature of the setting. Users were attempting to learn about life-and-death issues rather than be entertained. More experiential settings may have quite different ratings.

Table 7.6

Preferred Version of Content for Providing Cancer Communications

Format Choices	Number of Users Selecting Each Ranking				
	1st	2nd	3rd	4th	5th
Flash	32	6	1	1	5
Paper	4	12	9	10	10
Web	4	8	17	13	3
Audio plus Web	5	19	10	5	6
Audio	0	0	8	16	21

Source: Judith L Bader and Nancy Strickman-Stein, "Evaluation of New Multimedia Formats for Cancer Communications," *Journal of Medical Internet Research* 2003 (Aug 29); 5(3):e16. Originally published in the *Journal of Medical Internet Research* and distributed under the terms of the Creative Commons Attribution License.

There are many additional lessons for producing high-quality online content, and the differences between creating content for online presentation and the form of content that works in media such as newspapers or books. These include keeping text short, making it quickly scannable for readers, using plain language, using standard and legible fonts, breaking up material into smaller chunks, effective headlines and titles, using appropriate graphics resolution, making content adaptable to different monitors and displays, and more.[23] Producing high-quality content is a skill requiring training, testing, and talent.

> *Experiential Usability*

Experiential sites are becoming increasingly important online, both as a share of online user time and online revenue. A number of the "stickiest" sites (those with the longest average user duration) are experiential gaming and entertainment sites such as Pokerstars and NeoPets. Some users spend hours, even days, playing online poker.

Experiential online usage is increasingly big business. At more than $30 billion per year in worldwide sales, video games already have larger revenues than box office movie releases. More than 10% of the total revenue is online games, such as multi-person adventure games and simulations.[24] Increasingly, gaming appears as a corporate, military, and college-level educational method.

Experiential online sites are sites with very different objectives and usage patterns from task-oriented sites (recall Table 7.2). Concern shifts from measures of time saved and efficient clicks to measures of joy, beauty, flow, and engagement. As user behavior strongly shapes usability, different factors drive usability for experiential sites.

Experiential usability is a very active research area, with many relevant fields participating, yet lacking the level of consensus of task-directed usability study. It is emerging from a practitioner-dominated field, where game designers and software companies are responsible for results, into research groups in computer science, marketing, psychology, communications, human computer interface, and even economics. Rapid progress is likely in the next few years, as online gaming provides an experimental setting and data to test experiential usability theories.

An example of this active research, and differences in lessons regarding usability, comes from studies of online gaming such as the Xbox Live (Figure 7.13). Increasingly, multi-person games use the Internet to simultaneously play others and communicate with voice to other participants. These can be interactive virtual world settings (adventure games, "God games"), multi-person combat settings ("first person shooter"), or task-oriented simulations. Variations of these include computer-supported cooperative play and computer-supported cooperative work games.

Experiential settings introduce new forms of usability concerns. One example is the challenge of implementing shared social spaces. For example, in the Xbox Live games,

Figure 7.12

On the Internet, Can Anyone Tell if Dogs Are Playing Poker?

Source: © xjlu-00021 John Lund/ Workbook Stock

players use a hands-free microphone to talk to other gamers. Communication can be to teammates, where the goal is coordination, or to opponents, with challenges, taunts, or other discussion. Studies suggest that implementing this feature presents a number of usability challenges. Some players have a difficult time tracking who is talking, reconciling the digital environment they are seeing on their screen with the social setting they are hearing, and handling stray comments and various aspects of social noise.[25] Others find the feature highly motivating. Understanding what causes these widely varying results, and reducing usability problems when they occur, is an active research area.

Bringing new users into a social gaming setting can be a much more difficult transition in experiential settings than for task-oriented sites. As discussed in Chapter 4, maintaining

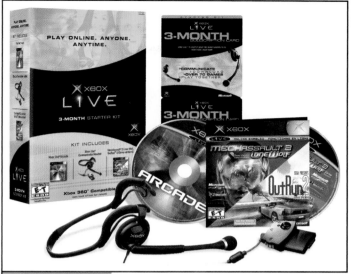

Figure 7.13

New Game Platforms Support Player Interaction

Source: Courtesy of Xbox ® video game system .

flow with rapid learning means escalating the difficulty at the proper pace. Too slow a ramp-up leads to boredom, too fast an escalation to confusion and frustration. Adding a social setting complicates this substantially.[26] Expert gamers do not want to confront newbies all the time, while more experienced players easily exploit beginners. If "training wheels" remain on for beginners until they are ready to face advanced users, the game seems uninspiring and not worth the learning involved.

There are aspects of task-oriented usability that become even more important for experiential sites. An example is latency, the delay between when a user selects an action and when the system actually responds. Net congestion, game server congestion, hardware issues, and even speed-of-light delays cause this for experiential sites. Latency dramatically affects competitive multi-person games, leading to user dissatisfaction and lowered performance. This appears in user feedback and objective results such as lower performance of players. An example is the online version of a game of American football (Figure 7.14).[27] The extraordinary realism of the video game's digital environment may even aggravate the dissatisfaction, which looks very similar to an actual television broadcast.

With the attention of many researchers and the new tools and sources of data, understanding of usability in experiential settings should advance rapidly. This promises to improve the design of games, interactive training, education sites, and the many other forms of experiential content. It may also lead to better understanding of the enjoyment and design of traditional media, such as television, movies, and video advertising.

> *Accessibility*

Not everyone using the Internet and visiting a web site has perfect vision, perfect hearing, full literacy, cognitive skills, or the manual dexterity to handle a keyboard or mouse. Individuals with

User presses pass—nothing happens

After latency delay, throw begins

Defender intercepts, user disgusted

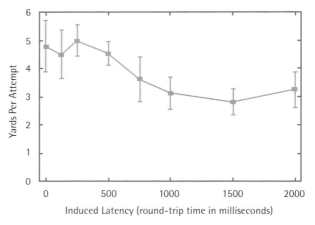

Latency impact on average yards per carry when running

Figure 7.14

Impact of Latency on Performance: Online Multi-person Madden NFL Football

Source: Figures 10, 14, 15, 16 from James Nichols/Mark Claypool, "The Effects of Latency on Online Madden NFL Football," Proceedings of 14th International Workshop on Network and Operating Systems Support in Digital Audio and Video," Cork, ACM Press, 2004, (NOSSDAV'04), pp. 146–151 © 2004 ACM, Inc. Reprinted by permission.

vision restrictions may find small type illegible, those with severe vision challenges may be unable to read it at all. Hearing problems are becoming an increasing problem as web sites add multimedia, animations, and tutorials with spoken instructions. Literacy and cognitive issues make the Web a foreboding challenge. Finally, physical disabilities may limit the fine motor skills necessary to point, click, and type information into a web form or search engine. While many of these ailments become more severe for seniors, there are many possible ailments or physical limitations making the standard Internet less useful than it could and should be for these users.

Digital power, alternative displays of information, and good planning can offset many of these problems. An accessible design works to provide alternative solutions when someone with a disability visits a site. The system can then alter the method of displaying information, say from vision to sound for the vision-impaired or sound to vision for the hearing-impaired. All of these approaches require some amount of good design and advanced thought to work well.

The World Wide Web Consortium (W3C) takes a lead in establishing accessibility guidelines, suggestions, and solutions. The hope is that when a standard page is inaccessible, the technology provides an acceptable alternative. While this secondary solution may lack some of the clarity or impact of the original, it at least allows the visitor to accomplish his or her task. Accessibility tools, like the automated usability methods, attempt to flag problems and suggest solutions.

The core goals of the initiative are simple. They are (1) Content must be perceivable; (2) Interface elements in the content must be operable; (3) Content and controls must be understandable; (4) Content must be robust enough to work with current and future technologies. Site managers should study and adopt as many of the W3C guidelines as possible.

These guidelines seek to provide alternatives for information that would block access or limit usefulness for an impaired user. Unfortunately, even health sites are not immune to accessibility problems. A study in 2004 of the top 30 health sites found many violations of basic accessibility.[28] A typical example is the lack of alternative text when a graphical image or icon is used. A majority of sites failed to provide basic alternative text that would help the visually impaired use the health site or submit a form. Other common mistakes involved frames, icons, and navigation methods.

Rather than rely on extensive testing and post-design problem solving, a better accessibility solution is to prevent problems at the start. Simple training and investment in web design tools can catch many of the accessibility problems. Accessibility checkers exist free online, and their automatic usage can correct many problems before they become difficult to alter.

Customer Support

Each year the Association of Support Professionals bestows honors for the best online customer support sites. Multiple year winners include Cisco, HP, Dell, and Symantec (shown in Figure 7.15) among others. The Symantec site combines functionality, ease-of-use, and comprehensive material. This supports their security software closely, helping customers solve both the recurring problem of keeping their subscriptions up-to-date and the potentially highly stressful problem of dealing with computer viruses and spy ware.

Leading support sites have evolved rapidly from the simple provision of software updates and manuals to a strategic part of a company's business. They can be a direct proof of the commitment of a company to customer service, or evidence pointing the other direction. While each company has unique needs, there are many similarities in the leading sites and the sources of benefits and savings. The Cognos site emphasizes most of these benefits, including (a) inexpensive communications, (b) electronic distribution, (c) online publishing, (d) stored answers and customer self-help, and (e) key notices and events.

> *Inexpensive Communications*
Cognos strongly emphasizes the Web in its customer support. The main navigation encourages using the online Case Management system, stored solutions, and online forums There are many guides to using the service. An important cost-saving goal is to provide a high-quality solution

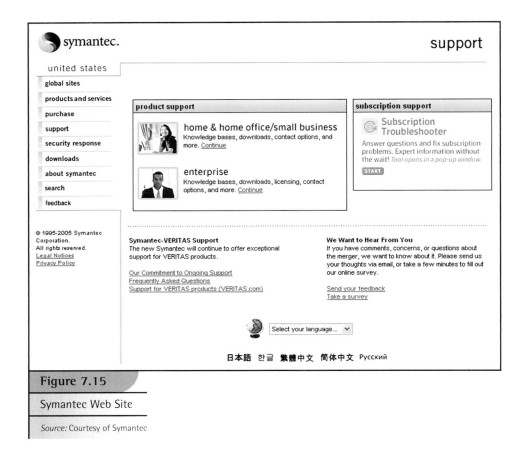

Figure 7.15

Symantec Web Site

Source: Courtesy of Symantec

without the need for human intervention. This reflects the fundamental economics of customer support, which is much cheaper for web interactions than traditional support methods.

Table 7.7 illustrates the opportunities and limitations of traditional and online customer-support methods.[29] Three factors make traditional support mechanisms expensive. These are the agent/customer ratio, the type of interaction, and the type of service. Traditional support is expensive and hard to scale. This is due to the 1:1 ratio and real-time nature of personal contact. Both a sales call and a call center require expensive, assisted, real-time interactions. They are labor intensive and require a large commitment of resources to support prompt and accessible service. Online methods are more flexible. While allowing for 1:1 interaction, online support technology can reach many customers at the same time. Many of the methods break the need for real-time intervention and allow customers to solve their own problems. This permits round-the-clock access to many support resources.

Evidence suggests that web support is especially scalable, while email support for many companies has a cost per incident much closer to traditional call center support (see Table 7.8). Several factors account for this. One, web support is primarily a 1:Many interaction. This allows a much more efficient dissemination of solutions and answers. Once created, there is very little cost for sharing an answer with thousands of users. The higher the usage, the lower the per-interaction cost.

Table 7.7

Traditional and Internet-Based Customer Support

Customer Service Methods	Agent to Customer Ratio	Type of Interaction	Type of Service
Traditional Support			
Sales force	1:1	Real-time	Assisted
Call center	1:1	Real-time	Assisted
Internet Support			
Email	1:1	Messaging	Assisted
Email with A.I.	1:Many	Messaging	Self
Web: FAQ	1:Many	Messaging	Self
Web: self	1:Many	Messaging	Self
Web: chat	1:Many	Real-time	Assisted
Web: phone	1:1	Real-time	Assisted

Source: Adapted from James Wood, (1998), "Five Money-Saving Strategies for Web Customer Service," *Telemarketing and Call Center Solutions*, May pp. 46–55.

Table 7.7 shows two types of email support methods. Regular email is a labor-intensive process requiring personal intervention for each message. At best, techniques such as "smart routing" of email doubles or triples the efficiency of the process by steering email messages to the most appropriate or available support personnel. Electronic outsourcing of support can lower the hourly labor cost. Neither alters the fundamental nature of email as person-to-person communication. Table 7.8 supports this, with email costs similar to phone interactions.[30]

A promising area of development is the merging of email, artificial intelligence, and smart routing. This "mixed mode" email system first tries to automate the response to the customer

Table 7.8

Online Support Provides Much Cheaper Solutions, 2002

Per-transaction costs (median)	Web	Phone	Email	Web/Phone %
By price of best-selling product:				
$10,000+	$16.91	$56.84	$58.34	30%
$1,000–$9,995	$7.94	$36.24	$25.00	22%
Under $1,000	$2.80	$26.67	$39.29	10%
Median	$3.75	$27.78	$28.57	13%

Per-incident costs are calculated by dividing monthly payroll costs for employees who support each delivery method by reported transaction volume.

Source: Association of Support Professionals, (2002), The Economics of Online Support.

Buggy Software, but Great Online Support, the Best for Consumers?

A study by Arora, Caulkins and Telang of Carnegie Mellon University suggests that competition and good customer support leads to companies releasing software earlier and with more bugs. Companies do this knowing that they can fix the problems after release with software patches from online sites.

What is even more surprising about the study is that this is a good thing. A monopolist waits too long to debug their code and under invests in customer support compared to a market with more competitors. Even with some competition, and costly impacts of software problems, society would be better off with even earlier release of software that needs even more patches and fixes.

Behind this surprising result are some of the special features of software: its fixability, a desire by consumers to get new versions, and the fixed cost nature of online support. The model also assumes that software fixes cure the problem immediately. Another intriguing result is the impact of market size—the larger the customer market, the better the customer support system.

Source: Ashish Arora, Jonathan Caulkins, and Rahul Telang, (2003), "Sell First, Fix Later: Impact of Patching on Software Quality," Mimeo, Carnegie Mellon University, August.

email it receives. If the system believes it has a stored response to a customer's email, it automatically retrieves the answer from its database and sends an email with the predicted answer. Auto-respond email becomes a self-service, 1:Many technology.

If an appropriate answer is not forthcoming, the system next tries to predict the best available service agent to handle the request. The system tries to learn from the agent's response by combining this new response into the knowledge database. Over time, the auto-responder is able to handle a larger fraction of the incoming email traffic. Increasingly these interactions are stored, analyzed, and used to improve the entire communications process.

Companies are working to provide internal employees with the tools and capabilities developed for customer support. Employees also benefit from the stored solutions, rapid information retrieval, and understanding to the business necessary to accomplish online customer support. Sharing this information over the company Intranet helps solve internal communication, handle rush orders, and spot opportunities for service improvement and new features.

> *Electronic Distribution*

It is no surprise that all of the "Hall of Fame" customer support sites are high-technology companies. High-technology software and hardware products often suffer from defects, difficult configuration problems, incompatibilities, and security concerns. Electronic distribution of software fixes and corrective information is a costly and vital role for high-tech companies. A strong customer support site is a strategic asset of technology companies.

One of the challenges comes from hacker attacks. A team of Carnegie Mellon researchers analyzed hacker attacks on a group of computers secretly maintained as "honey pots," which are computers that look like normal Internet users but are set up to monitor attacks.[31] One of the results of their study is that software attacks increase sharply after a company announces a software security vulnerability, especially if no solution is immediately available. However, even if the company releases a solution patch the same day, attacks stay high. There are two main reasons for this. First, the announcement alerts hackers to the weakness. Two, users are slow to adopt patches. Hackers increase their attacks knowing many users will not have upgraded. Providing a fix as quickly as possible, and getting users to adopt them, is necessary to maintain security. The Internet aggravates the problem of hacker attacks, while providing an important method of fixing it.

Online software distribution is much faster and much cheaper. By the mid-1990s, Cisco estimated their annual savings from online publishing of software upgrades, patches, and new releases were $130 million. Included in these numbers are packaging, shipping costs, and the difficulty of creating and handling many different version numbers. Using the Internet has dramatically reduced the distribution costs of software. With online distribution, bandwidth charges replace the numerous costs of physical distribution.

Speed increases are even more impressive. Automatic software patch capability, increasingly offered by companies subject to errors and security weaknesses, can respond almost instantaneously to an available patch. With the permission of the user, these automatically download and install.

This capability is very valuable to a company such as Intuit, with its Quicken and TurboTax software. One of the problems of tax software is the short time between when the government finalizes the tax code and the Christmas shopping season—as little as three weeks. It is hard to incorporate the proper tax rules and test the software completely. During one of its release years, Intuit ran into serious bugs in its tax preparation software. Shipping replacement disks to all registered users would have wiped out the profits for Intuit of these sales. It would also have taken months to reach everyone. A much better solution for all was to post the changes and patches online and let customers retrieve the new files. This also meant that Intuit got the changes in the hands of users in days rather than weeks or months.[32] Following this lesson, Intuit made updating the software even easier, and prompts the user to double-check for updates prior to finalizing the tax return.

Business to business fixes can generate huge impacts as well. The National Institute of Standards and Technology issued a major report in 2002 highlighting the costly nature of software bugs and errors, both for the high-technology companies producing the software and the industries using the buggy code. Errors costing billions of dollars occur in industries such as autos, aerospace, and financial services. With losses such as these, rapid response and effective remedies are crucial. Online customer support sites play a central role in limiting the amount of time necessary to find, fix, and distribute software repairs.

> *Online Publishing*

The earliest justification for online customer support came from electronic publishing of product manuals and other material. In the early years of online support, Cisco estimated savings of hundreds of millions of dollars from online publishing. Having established online publishing so well, it is difficult to measure its benefits. Cisco produces far fewer manuals and brochures on paper, making it more of a challenge to even compute the savings from electronic distribution. Cisco is fully aware of its importance however, and promotes it prominently in the main home page navigation bar (Figure 7.16).

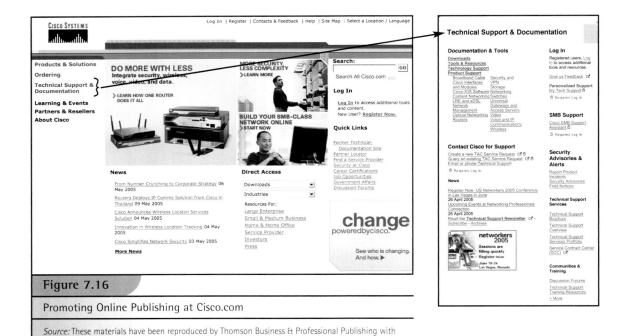

Figure 7.16

Promoting Online Publishing at Cisco.com

> *Stored Answers and Customer Self Help*

Customer problems are rarely isolated occurrences. One of the simplest and most effective methods of customer support is the FAQ—the frequently asked question file. As Cisco emphasizes manuals and publications in the prime navigation bar spot, Cognos emphasizes FAQs. Focusing FAQs by customer and application type, perhaps using a virtual value analysis, helps customers quickly find the right answer. Common alternatives include a product-oriented approach, a search-based method, a customer expertise structure (e.g., newbies, experts), and a problem-based approach. Shared questions and answers emerge naturally in the customer forum site as well, where questions in users' own words may be the easiest links to find.

One of the prime parts of the Cognos support page is devoted to stored answers and getting started guides. These provide valuable step-by-step tutorials for important functions. Some of the least productive calls to consumer support are for questions that are easily resolved once the proper material is located. These "how to" guides eliminate many of these time-consuming customer support calls.

CREDIBILITY AND PERSUASION

| Web Site Credibility

Web site credibility matters to visitors. Web site users realize that anyone can create a site and mere presence online does not certify accuracy. Before information can be valuable or persuasive, it must be believable. Visitors react to basic credibility cues in order to form their judgments. While these cues are not always reliable guides to high-quality information, their common usage makes them important criteria and a checklist for web site managers (Table 7.9).

Organizations investigating online credibility find a cluster of performance cues visitors rely upon.[33] Usability issues play a surprisingly large role shaping user views of site credibility. Credibility limiting usability problems include errors on the page, broken links, confusing site navigation, and sloppy design. While none of these factors necessarily implies low-quality information or an underlying lack of accuracy, they do reflect on the care and professionalism of web site operation. Visitors apparently view these as informative signals of underlying informational quality.[34]

This is not necessarily irrational. Economic models of signaling stress that a signal may have value when it is cheaper and easier for high-quality organizations to provide the signal than for low quality organizations to mimic high quality. Investing in good performance carries with it the signal that the organization may also be delivering credible material. These types of signals have the added advantage of working across information domains. Online visitors develop an appreciation of usability across multiple sites, and use this developed skill to judge unfamiliar sites. Table 7.10 provides a list of credibility guidelines.

Table 7.9

American Views of Credibility Factors	
Evaluating Information *Why some have turned away from a health information site.*	
Health Seekers	%
Site was too commercial	47
You couldn't determine the source of the information	42
You couldn't determine when information was last updated	37
Site lacked endorsement of a trusted independent organization	30
Site appeared sloppy or unprofessional	29
Site contained information you knew to be wrong	26
Information disagreed with own doctor's advice	20

Source: Pew Internet Project.

Table 7.10

Ten Credibility Guidelines	
The Stanford Credibility Guidelines	
1.	Make it easy to verify the accuracy of the information on your site.
2.	Show that there is a real organization behind your site.
3.	Highlight the expertise in your organization and in the content and services you provide.
4.	Show that honest and trustworthy people stand behind your site.
5.	Make it easy to contact you.
6.	Design your site so it looks professional (or is appropriate for your purpose).
7.	Make your site easy to use — and useful.
8.	Update your site's content often (at least show it's been reviewed recently).
9.	If possible, avoid having ads on your site.
10.	Avoid errors of all types, no matter how small they seem.

Source: B.H. Fogg, Stanford Web Credibility Project (2004), Stanford Persuasive Technology Lab, http://captology.stanford.edu.

Visitors also rely upon endorsement signals, such as sponsoring organizations, external reviews from independent organizations, and the identity of individuals associated with the site. Negative cues tend to be signs of commercial interests; visitors seem to view advertisements and paid links as partially undermining the site independence and believability.

Aspects of the actual information do play a role in determining credibility. Obvious errors or inconsistency with the visitor's previous information, such as one's own doctor, lowered credibility in a study of medical sites. Content accuracy and the frequency of updating are additional signals of credibility. Rather than look for information that "has stood the test of time," visitors view a stale site as potentially obsolete and lacking credibility.

The international site of the Red Cross and Red Crescent does a very good job of following credibility guidelines for its web site. The site has an effective and familiar navigation structure.[35] Endorsements and explanations document the organization, its humanitarian purposes, and the immediate charitable needs. Accuracy of information is high, with current news and links to pressing needs. Commercial aspects are absent.

Medical information is one of the most active and important areas for which online trust and credibility matter greatly (see Figure 7.17). Web sites have done reasonably well in acquiring credibility with visitors, with both impressive usage of online medical sites and a growing acceptance of the quality of this source of information. For example, online sites are already the second most trusted source of medical information. While still substantially below doctors, online sites dominate many of the most important other sources of information.[36]

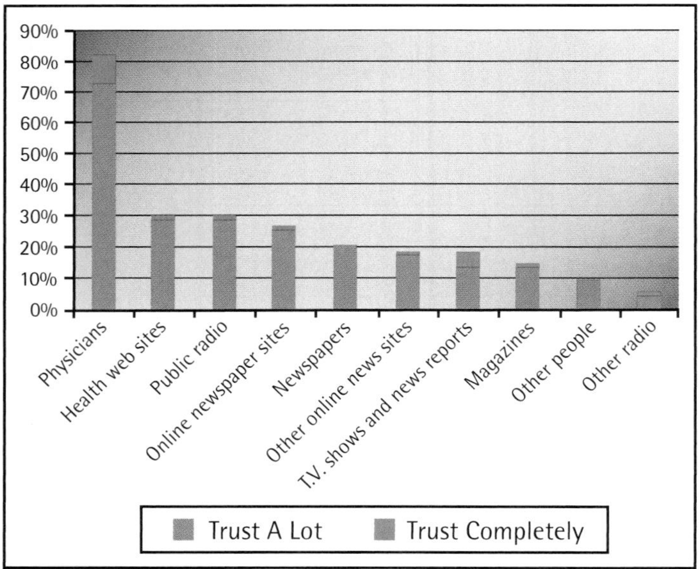

Each disaster has its own need for rapid and credible medical information that the web site can provide. Following Hurricane Katrina and the flooding of New Orleans, the U.S. Red Cross quickly had information about food safety, water treatment, dealing with heat, using generators, providing an evacuation checklist, and more. While those immediately affected by the disaster may have had trouble getting online access, this information helped nearby relief efforts and provided valuable information to those heading to the disaster site.

Information completeness reinforces a visitor's views of site credibility and accuracy,[37] appearing as a top credibility factor in a variety of studies. Completeness augments the other content dimensions of frequent information, professional appearance, and consistency with known information. Missing information seems to be taken as evidence of an inaccurate or slanted viewpoint.

Figure 7.17

Half-full or Half-empty? Trustworthiness of Online Medical Sites

Source: Anne F Kittler, John Hobbs, Lynn A Volk, Gary L Kreps, and David W Bates (2004), "The Internet as a Vehicle to Communicate Health Information During a Public Health Emergency: A Survey Analysis Involving the Anthrax Scare of 2001," *Journal of Medical Internet Research* (Mar 3)6(1):e8. Originally published in the *Journal of Medical Internet Research* and distributed under the terms of the Creative Commons Attribution License.

Completeness and Censorship: The Case of China

One of the most troubling sources of content incompleteness is censorship. This is certainly the case in China, where an elaborate system of humans and software systems review web pages, blogs, discussion boards, and personal email messages. The ONI research organization found that China's filtering system is "the most pervasive, sophisticated, and effective in the world." It occurs throughout the Chinese Internet, especially at the national Internet backbone level. Certain keywords are blocked for both search and discussion forums. Cybercafés, which are an important source of access in China and other Asian countries, must track customers' surfing habits and keep customer records for two months. URLs are blocked based on objectionable content.

Chinese official censorship raises a number of troubling issues for companies operating in China. Censors expect search engines and web directories to conform to the regulations as part of their market participation. Data sharing with the authorities is part of ISPs' and cybercafés'

responsibility. The Chinese government's activities are likely to have a chilling effect on innovations that would make it easier to directly share information between Chinese citizens and circumvent the governmental control.

Religious and political content seems especially controlled. Chinese authorities have heavily restricted the Falun Gong religion, and many of the URLs and keywords relating to the religious group are blocked. Likewise, they block references to Tiananmen Square, human rights, pro-democracy and anti-Communist opposition. The problem is especially severe for content in Chinese, although English sites and content are also restricted.

China is not the only country actively censoring the Net. Saudi Arabia, Cuba, and other totalitarian nations impose serious restrictions, hindering the value of the Net and potentially creating serious ethical issues for Net companies.

Source: ONI, "Internet Filtering in China in 2004–2005: A Country Study," April 2005, working paper. Also Jonathan Zittrain and Benjamin Edelman, "Empirical Analysis of Internet Filtering in China," Berkman Center for Internet & Society, Harvard University.

PHOTO: © Jim Ballard/ Photographer's Choice/ Getty Images

Another useful credibility signal for a site and a page uses the information generated by systems such as Google PageRank, which assigns a rating to sites based on the influence of inbound links to the site. PageRank influences search results and in some settings is independently displayed. Chapter 8 discusses PageRank in some detail, and the steps an organization can use to enhance its rating.

Persuasive Designs

> *Visual Metaphors and Combinations*

While usability experts stress the benefits of online text over imagery and value the simplicity of graphics,[38] marketers have a long tradition of emphasizing imagery for persuasive purposes.[39]

Usability experts stress the negative impacts pictures have on delay and congestion. Marketers, on the other hand, emphasize the power of images to describe brand associations and to communicate a complicated message by combining images that make the brand salient and communicate its appeal. While persuasion and usability are not always in conflict, there can be a tradeoff between straightforward information presentation and other communication goals.

An example of visual metaphor and branding is the use of the Butler as the symbol for Ask Jeeves (Figure 7.18), with the connotation of high-quality searches and personal service. The friendly butler Jeeves is the picture of helpfulness and attention to detail, which is the goal of brand association the site is striving for.

Phillips and McQuarrie make the point that combinations and contrasts of images can have a persuasive impact. Just as advertising using verbal metaphors and puns (e.g., "Why weight for success" in a diet center ad), images communicate brand positioning through their own "language." In order of increasing complexity, images may be juxtaposed (two images seen together), fused (combined into one), or replaced (where an image appears instead of the expected image).

An example of visual metaphor with fusion and replacement is the Pepsi Smash logo in Figure 7.19 used for the music tour and web site pepsismash.com sponsored by Pepsi. Here the Pepsi logo fuses with headphones, symbolizing the music connection to the Pepsi brand. There is also replacement, as the logo replaces the expected image (a person's head) and connects Pepsi to music. The image establishes a connection between Pepsi drinkers and music-lovers.

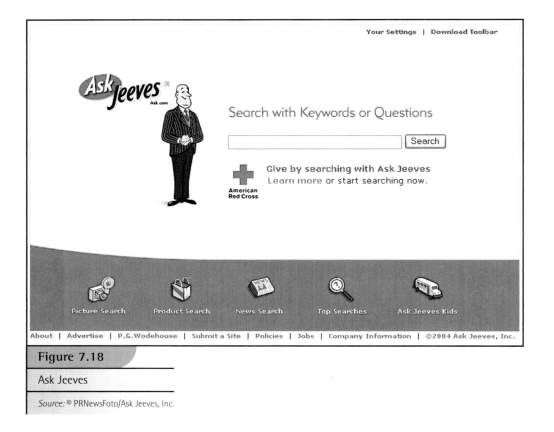

Figure 7.18

Ask Jeeves

Source: © PRNewsFoto/Ask Jeeves, Inc.

The virtual world of avatars and gaming makes the use of commercially oriented visual material an innovative type of product placement. The Sims and other virtual games allow characters, residences, and other community sites to display the logos and brand images of the brand.

Web site operators should be sensitive to these visual techniques for several reasons. With more online branding and persuasion done in-house than through agencies (see Chapter 6) managers need familiarity with visual techniques. Second, there may be combinations and brand associations that are unintended and potentially harmful. Graphic designers may get carried away with digi-

Figure 7.19

Pepsi SMASH

Source: Pepsi-Cola North America

tal imaging tools, creating colorful imagery that is inconsistent with the product's long-term positioning. The speed of online content development and deployment requires more widespread understanding and sensitivity to these issues than might be needed for radio or television, where professional agencies control more of the creative process.

> *Simulations and Tutorials*

Firms are increasingly using simulations and tutorials to educate and persuade employees, customers, and others. These techniques take advantage of increasingly sophisticated methods that combine text, audio, video, and other content into a virtual environment realistic enough to convey a believable scenario. Authoring tools make it possible to create a compelling digital experience, while letting the user choose his or her own route through the material.

Simulations mix realistic scenarios and virtual environments to create didactic and persuasive situations. Users must solve a problem, make decisions, and observe how their choices alter the environment. Scenarios can involve hard skills, such as flying an airplane, or softer skills such as negotiating a contract or dealing with a disgruntled employee.

Simulations often combine learning and persuasion. Research demonstrates the power of digital environments to create a powerful illusion and suspension of disbelief, and call forth responses similar to actual settings.[40] A successful simulation delivers both the knowledge of organization practices with a much more difficult to teach set of company norms and behaviors. By showing real people dealing with realistic problems, and receiving feedback from good and bad choices, a new manager can make mistakes and learn without causing actual consequences. Along the way, there is behavior change and partial assimilation into the company culture.

Tutorials are more task-oriented, and use step-by-step guides to demonstrate how a task is accomplished. Again, the goal is both education and persuasion. Education occurs through the hands-on approach, where the user actually follows the correct procedure to accomplish the task. Along the way, the user may make mistakes, with the guide either pointing them out or allowing for an easy recovery. Combining reading, watching, and doing, a good tutorial allows different modes of learning and memory.

Several persuasive goals are common for tutorials. One goal is to convince an owner of the broad value of a tool or software by demonstrating additional features and applications. In complicated applications, many features are never used. A tutorial provides exposure to these capabilities and a template for adaptation. The more widespread the tool is used, the more loyalty users will have. A good tutorial persuades owners to try the new capability, and lowers the perceived risk of failure.

Business Objects is a software company that develops and markets Xcelsius, an authoring tool for interactive data presentations. Persuading owners to try new capabilities creates more value and wider adoption. To help accomplish this, the company created a learning center demonstrating a wide variety of techniques, solutions, capabilities, and features. Each encourages an owner to try it themselves through the extensive library of examples, some of which are shown in Figure 7.20.

Persuading through simulations and tutorials taps into several psychological processes reinforcing behavior change. As a visitor achieves intermediate successes, the system praises their actions. Often these environments contain periodic reinforcement either randomly awarded or based solely on elapsed time. Despite a lack of direct connection between accomplishment and reward, these forms of operant conditioning can have substantial impact.[41] With growing competence and investment of time, there is a bias toward justifying this investment and the skills acquired.

Xcelsius Examples

Learn how to build these Dashboards (we even give you the files!)

Each of these Xcelsius dashboards contains a demo, a tutorial and even the source files – so you can learn how to build it yourself.

Revenue Forecasting

This forward-looking dashboard simulates a company's revenue structure, and allows the viewer to modify assumptions about future sales and sales targets. The result is an immediate, visual forecast of revenues vs. goals in three categories.

Revenue Forecasting Example

Daily Executive Report

This executive dashboard summarizes the daily status of a hospitality company's key performance measures (KPIs) across 14 locations. It gives the executive an interactive view of the daily and monthly metrics that drive the business.

Daily Executive Report Example

Business Intelligence

This BI dashboard simulates the Return-on-Equity for a bank. It models the six major areas bank executives can influence to improve ROE, allowing them quickly to evaluate the impact of various what-if scenarios on bank profitability.

Business Intelligence Example

Figure 7.20

Persuading through Examples Source: Infommersion

Source: Courtesy of Infommersion, Inc.

> Persuadable Moments

The ancient Greeks distinguished several versions of time. There was chronos, the measure of elapsed time. There was also kairos, the opportune time or favorable moment for an action.[42] Kairos is one of the core strengths of online interaction, the ability to present the right information at the right time. The same information that is ignored or actively disliked when presented at the incorrect time may be valuable and persuasive if it is relevant and appropriate for that moment of the user's online activities. These persuadable moments may arise because of specific location within a visit, predictable swings in user interest and activity, or online activities that reveal new information about the user suggesting an interest.[43]

Figure 7.21 provides an example from real estate. The vertical axis represents different categories of home ownership, such as non-homeowner, satisfied homeowner, selling a home, buying a home, and selling and buying a home simultaneously. The horizontal axis is time. Thus, this particular customer starts as a non-homeowner. There is then a transition to home buyers, satisfied homeowner, and so on. The event graph tracks a specific individual over time, recording all changes in home ownership or their real market activity.

The yellow lines suggest times when an individual is least persuadable, either not being in the market or satisfied with their current state. Green lines represent reasonably active times in the market, anticipating a change in their real estate situation. Circled moments are especially opportune and persuadable moments.

One problem is clear from the event graph. Opportune moments are easier to spot in retrospect than in real time. Observing highly informative online actions, such as researching a car, helps greatly and is at the core of the business models of affiliates, cross-selling on ecommerce sites, and search marketing. Observation of online actions also is an important part of personalization, discussed in Chapter 9.

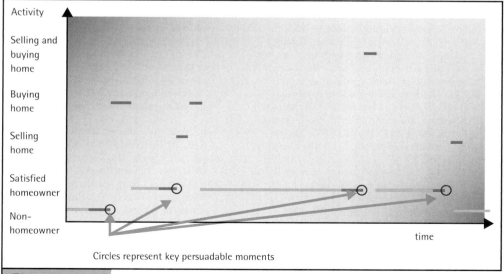

Circles represent key persuadable moments

Figure 7.21

An Event Graph Helps Visualize a Customer's Persuadable Moments

ENDNOTES

1. Jakob Nielsen. (2000). *Designing Web Usability.* New Riders, Indianapolis, IN.

2. B. J. Fogg. (2003). *Persuasive Technology: Using Computers to Change What We Think and Do.* Morgan Kaufmann, San Francisco, 1.

3. Wesley Brown. "Former presidents in town seeking support for tsunami relief." *Arkansas News Bureau.* January 12, 2005.

4. Online managers are beginning to combine online capabilities with serious research on their impact. Multiple perspectives are helpful. Data from web logs, user surveys, and other sources provide methods for testing whether a particular approach has the desired effect. The growing importance of online content stimulates research by companies, nonprofits, and governmental agencies on best practices and effective approaches. Researchers from marketing, communications, sociology, human-computer interactions, and public policy fields are testing different online methods and learning what works.

5. Page views are also called page impressions, and correspond to a page URL. Each file (text, individual pictures, other objects) located on the page is a hit.

6. This particular figure is the distribution of visit lengths that occurred on one day during the summer of 1997 at the Xerox Corporation's web site (http://www.xerox.com). Bernardo A. Huberman, Peter L. T. Pirolli, James E. Pitkow, and Rajan M. Lukose. (1998). "Strong Regularities in World Wide Web Surfing." Science 280(5360), 95–97.

7. Ricardo Baeza-Yates and Carlos Castillo. (2003). "Crawling the Infinite Web: Five Levels are Enough." Working paper. http://www.dcc.uchile.cl/~ccastill/papers/baeza04_crawling_infinite_web.pdf

8. Rajan M. Lukose and Bernardo A. Huberman. (1998). "Surfing as a Real Option." *ICE: 98*: 45–51. Bernardo A. Huberman, Peter L.T. Pirolli, James E. Pitkow, and Rajan M. Lukose. (1998). "Strong Regularities in World Wide Web Surfing." *Science* 280(5360), 95–97.

9. Randolph E. Bucklin and Catarina Sismeiro. (2003). "A Model of Web Site Browsing Behavior Estimated on Clickstream Data." *Journal of Marketing Research* XI (August), 249–267.

10. Thomas P. Novak, Donna L. Hoffman, and Adam Duhachek. (2003). "The Influence of Goal-Directed and Experiential Activities on Online Flow Experiences." *Journal of Consumer Psychology* 13(1,2), 3–16.

11. Catherine Seda. (2004). *Search Engine Advertising: Buying Your Way to the Top to Increase Sales.* New Riders, Indianapolis, IN, 215.

12. Whether advertising is best used to offset natural swings in market activity or reinforce market tendencies is an interesting research question. In a number of settings, it may be more profitable to magnify the underlying demand swings through promotional activity, especially when there are not capacity constraints.

13. Jonathan Palmer. (2002). "Web Site Usability, Design, and Performance Metrics." *Information Systems Research* 13(2), 151–167.

14. For the magnitude of the impact, see Benedict G.C. Dellaert and Barbara Kahn. (1999). "How Tolerable is Delay?: Consumers' Evaluations of Internet Web Sites After Waiting." *Journal of Interactive Marketing* 13(1), 41–54.

15. J. Nielsen. *Usability Engineering.* Chapter 5.

16. See, for example, Mei Xue, Patrick Harker, and Gregory Heim. (2004). "Incorporating the Dual Customer Roles in e-Service Design." Working Paper, Financial Institutions Center. Wharton, March.

17. J. Nielsen. op. cit., p. 188.

18. A breadcrumb listing is often omitted when many visitors link directly to an internal page, as Cognos does for its main support page.

19. Alan Cooper and Robert Reimann. (2003). *About Face 2.0: The Essentials of Interaction Design.* Wiley, Indianapolis, especially pp. 33–38.

20. Ibid., p. 36.

21. Recall transactional and relationship customer discussion of Chapter 5.

22. Mayer, cited in Bader.

23. See, for example, the extensive discussion of usability by the Nielsen/Norman group.

24. Kevin Hew. Martin Gibbs, and Greg Wadley. (2004). "Usability and Sociability of the Xbox Live Voice Channel." Paper presented at Australian Workshop on Interactive Entertainment." Sydney. February.

25. Hew et al., ibid.

26. For example. Steve Cornett. (2004). "The Usability of massively Multiplayer Online Roleplaying Games: Designing for New Users." *CHI 2004* 6(1).

27. James Nichols and Mark Claypool. (2004). "The Effects of Latency on Online Madden NFL Football." *Proceedings of the 14th international workshop on Network and operating systems support for digital audio and video. ACM.* Cork.

28. Michael F. Chiang and Justin Starren. (2004). "Evaluation of Consumer Health Website Accessibility by Users With Sensory and Physical Disabilities." *Medinfo 2004.*

29. James Wood. (1998). "Five Money-Saving Strategies for Web Customer Service." *Telemarketing and Call Center Solutions.* May, 46–55.

30. Association of Support Professionals. (2002). *The Economics of Online Support.*

31. Ashish Arora, Ramayya Krishnan, Anand Nandkumar, Rahul Telang, and Yubao Yang. (2004). "Impact of Vulnerability Disclosure and Patch Availability—An Empirical Analysis." Working paper, Carnegie Mellon University.

32. N. Craig Smith, Robert J. Thomas, and John A. Quelch. (1996). "A Strategic Approach to Managing Product Recalls." *Harvard Business Review.* Boston. September/October.

33. Susannah Fox and Lee Rainie. (2002). *Vital Decisions: How Internet users decide what information to trust when they or their loved ones are sick.* Pew Internet & American Life Project. May 22. Fogg, B.J., Kameda, T., Boyd, J., Marshall, J., Sethi. R., Sockol. M., and Trowbridge, T. (2002). *Stanford-Makovsky Web Credibility Study 2002: Investigating What Makes Web Sites Credible Today.* A Research Report by the Stanford Persuasive Technology Lab & Makovsky & Company. Stanford University. Available at www.webcredibility.org.

34. This is consistent with the economics of signaling. Signals are informative when high-quality providers have an easier time providing the signal than do low-quality and unreliable sites.

35. It is combining global and local navigation in the vertical left bar, another common approach. One nonstandard aspect is the use of Java, which may fail for some browsers and be slow loading on poor connections. However, it also provides a more interactive feel at the expense of a single download.

36. Anne Bates, F. Kittler, John Hobbs, Lynn A. Volk, and Gary L Kreps. (2004). "The Internet as a Vehicle to Communicate Health Information During a Public Health Emergency: A Survey Analysis Involving the Anthrax Scare of 2001." *Journal of Medical Internet Research* 6, no. 1 (March 3): e8.

37. For example, Mohan Dutta-Bergman. (2004). "The Impact of Completeness and Web use Motivation on the Credibility of e-Health Information." *Journal of Communication* June, 253–269.

38. Jakob Nielsen. *Uselt* archives.

39. Barbara Phillips and Edward McQuarrie. (2004). "Beyond visual metaphor: A New typology of visual rhetoric in advertising." *Marketing Theory.* 4, 113–136.

40. Recall the *Media Equation* of Chapter 2.

41. Fogg, *Persuasive Technology.* op. cit., Chapter 3.

42. B.J. Fogg, op. cit.

43. Kirthi Kalyanam and Monte Zweben. (2005). "When is the New What." *Harvard Business Review.* February, "The Perfect Message for the Perfect Moment," *Harvard Business Review,* Vol. 83, no. 11, 112–120.

chapter 8:

Traffic Building

The Price of Words

Mesothelioma is a terrible disease. It is a form of cancer, almost exclusively caused by exposure to asbestos. Each year approximately 3,000 Americans contract mesothelioma. Most are construction workers, shipyard employees, or others who worked with asbestos decades earlier. Once diagnosed, life expectancy is less than two years. Patients suffer increasing pain and disability prior to death.

Mesothelioma is also big business. The tight connection between asbestos exposure and the disease makes mesothelioma a prime candidate for class action lawsuits against businesses that produced or used asbestos. Per patient awards in such a suit, which often end early in a settlement, average around $1 million dollars.[3] Law firms representing clients receive approximately 40% of such awards.

Lucrative awards make attracting the attention of patients a top priority for these law firms. The Internet is a major competitive battleground. The long latency between exposure and disease makes it likely that many of those exposed will have changed jobs and addresses, making it difficult to reach them through phone or mail. A better strategy is to rely on sufferers self-identifying. Online sites are a primary source for a majority of Americans seeking health information.[4] Attracting visits results in some of the highest prices paid for online advertising.

The preferred choice for this advertising is pay-per-click search advertising. Search advertising has grown rapidly in the past few years. While

this chapter

Nothing happens on a web site without visitors. Web content is growing faster than web users. At the same time, much more accountable campaigns result in more rational management of traffic-building campaigns.

Topics covered in this chapter include:

> The Price of Words

> Traffic as Value

> Search Engine marketing

> Traffic by Assocation

it lacks flashy graphics and brand-oriented imagery, the simple text-based ads that appear on Yahoo!, Google, and other sites are accountable and efficient. By connecting advertisers with searchers revealing a specific immediate interest by their search terms, at a price determined by a never-ending auction, search marketing firms are using the power of DNI capabilities.

Table 8.1 illustrates the very high cost of a keyword ad for the phrase "peritoneal mesothelioma" using the Yahoo! search engine. Firms pay as much as $100 per click to generate a visit to their web site. Whenever someone types this phrase in the Yahoo! search page, sees an ad displayed to the right of the normal search terms, and clicks on the ad, the advertiser must pay Yahoo! a fee.

Even though all of the ads generate a link to a web site, the location of the ad matters for attracting attention and generating a visit. On the Yahoo! system, ads appear according to their bid ranking.[5] If you want the highest ranking, you must bid the highest. The second ranking bid gets second position, and so on.

The maximum bid of an advertiser is not the same as the price paid. The actual price an advertiser pays for a click is also determined by the bid of the firm below it in the ranking. Table 8.1 shows both the maximum bids and the resulting costs-per-click of the top five bidders for the phrase. In this case, the top two advertisers are paying much more for their position than positions 3 through 5.

A visit to the top listed web site, costing $99.99 per click, presents something of a puzzle. The majority of the page is dedicated to patient information, without any apparent advertising and few direct links to a sponsor. There is little "call to action," where visitors are asked to do anything commercial.[6]

This approach requires a two-step conversion from visitor to client. First, the sponsoring law firm is boosting source and information credibility by downplaying a commercial connection and emphasizing health concerns. Only then is the visitor likely to find the links to the law firm's specific information. Such a soft-sell approach must be balanced against a failure to convert, especially given the high cost of traffic.

A little math demonstrates how valuable these visitors must be. If 1% of web site visitors

Table 8.1

Bids and Costs of Keyword "Peritoneal Mesothelioma"		
Ad Position	Max Bid	Cost per click
1	$100.00	$99.99
2	$99.99	$99.98
3	$99.98	$30.02
4	$30.01	$25.01
5	$25.00	$20.01

Source: Overture bidding tool, 2/18/05

choose the sponsoring law firm to represent them, a very respectable conversion rate for such an initial stage of interest, the cost of client acquisition is $100/.01 = $10,000. A lower conversion rate boosts the acquisition cost accordingly. Paying $10,000 for a new customer can only be profitable for extremely valuable customers. This is where the tight connection between exposure and disease, and the high value of the lawsuits, enters the picture. A law firm expects to receive hundreds of thousands of dollars in legal fees for each successful client it acquires.

The efficiency of the keyword advertising system relies on competition driving pricing. If law firms find that they cannot convert visitors, or that settlements cease to be as lucrative, keyword prices will fall. Controlling legal fees and class action lawsuits is an ongoing political debate. One consequence of such a legal change would be a fall in the value of these keywords. Alternatively, web site improvements that boost conversion rates from visitor to client would tend to drive up keyword values.

Fortunately for search advertisers, very few words are as expensive as mesothelioma. On Yahoo! and Google bidding starts at a dime or less. The eventual equilibrium price is a combination of keyword focus, alternative methods of customer acquisition, the power of domain names and organic search to stimulate visits, potential customer lifetime value, web site conversion effectiveness, and the intensity of advertising and market competition. The growth of keyword advertising has made a dramatic change in the online world, and has stimulated an emphasis on accountability that is rippling throughout marketing.

This chapter looks at the range of tools capable of generating new visits to a web site. Traffic has value, and an effective traffic-building plan is valuable to any site. Naturally occurring traffic is especially welcome, and should be the centerpiece of any approach. Beyond that, cost-effective and profitable paid advertising injects additional traffic in an accountable and traceable way. In some cases more traditional advertising venues, such as radio or television, may be a valuable addition to the marketing mix.

THE DIFFICULT BATTLE FOR WEB TRAFFIC

| Value and Scarcity

> *Online Content, Attention, and the Diamond–Water Paradox*

The diamond and water paradox is one of the oldest confusions in economics.[7] At first thought, students feel it is obvious that a product's value must determine its price. Something that provides an essential benefit must be valuable, and something without any inherent benefits must be cheap. An immediate difficulty arises when comparing the relative prices of water and diamonds. Deprive someone of water, and an individual dies in days. Diamonds, on the other hand, have no biological benefit and are difficult to work with. Outside of some specialized machine tools, they have few productive uses. They are almost exclusively optional ornaments.

Despite the critical role of water and the inessential nature of diamonds, a diamond is vastly more valuable than water. Of course, scarcity is the key. Water literally falls from the sky, while diamonds are exceedingly rare. Even extraordinary value can be driven down by abundant supply.[8]

The diamond-water paradox lives online in a variety of forms. Email is highly valuable, but users are free to send and receive to their heart's delight. Online mapping sites provide efficient driving to unfamiliar locations, but are supported by online ads without any user fees. Online magazines, travel sites, and global art museums all provide entertaining and educational content to all that arrive.

Although the number of Web users continues to grow, the amount of material on the Web is rising even faster. The battle for attention and traffic is intensifying, and the true scarcity becomes user attention. Every site faces a difficult struggle attracting visitors.

A simple measure of relative scarcity is the number of web pages per user. Figure 8.1 shows the steep increase in content per U.S. Internet user between 1998 and 2004.[9] Even omitting non-English pages from consideration, the readily available online material is much higher than just a few years ago.

Potential visitors to a site use search tools to find valuable content within the billions of alternative web pages. Even though the top search engines index billions of pages, their coverage differs and their ranking of the best matches varies substantially. First-generation search engines were not particularly strong in ranking results effectively, and high value results could be far down the results list. Despite this, a study of Excite users found 58% of users did not look beyond the first page of results. For the search engine Alta Vista, 85.2% of users only looked at the first page of results.[10] Placement on the first page of search results is valuable.

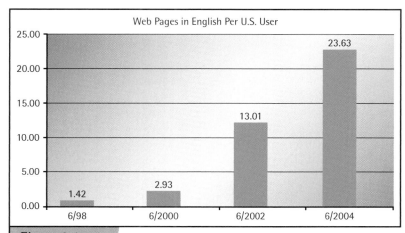

Figure 8.1

The Battle for Attention is Getting More Intense

Figure 8.2 highlights how the Yahoo! and Google top 100 search return items vary dramatically for the same search term, in this case "hybrid car." Only the blue dots appear in the top 100 on both sites, with a line connecting them showing where each appears. For example, the top listing on Yahoo! is the seventh listing on Google. However, the number 4 listing on Google does not appear in the top 100 of Yahoo!, and the same is true for the number 6 listing on Yahoo!. As this tool shows, appearing high on one search engine does not guarantee a high listing on a different engine. Maintaining a top search engine presence is not a simple task as the same approach is not valid for all engines.

> *Novelty No Longer Guarantees Traffic*

In addition to the high volume of online content, online users' growing experience makes attracting new visitors difficult. Exploratory browsing falls with expertise.[11] Faced with busy schedules and seemingly endless new alternatives, many visitors resist adding new destinations and activities (see Figure 8.3). Attracting new visitors requires motivating a visit from locations they visit regularly.

During the early days of the Net, high-quality sites were few and recreational browsing common. The situation was like a small town, where eventually any store gets a view because there isn't much to see. Early sites received large amounts of free publicity. Lead sites in almost every industry were highlighted in books, trade magazines, news-papers, radio, and television. First movers were able to count on traffic boosts due to these reviews. Now, free media is hard to generate, and there are far fewer opportunities to be the first site focusing on a topic.

> *Spending on Traffic Building*

Internet advertising and online traffic-building services help overcome the plentiful supply of content and the challenge of attracting visitors to a site. Online spending has surpassed the boom years, and in its first ten years (1994–2004) has grown faster than the corresponding first ten year growth of either television broadcasting (1949–1958) or cable (1980–1989, all in 2004 dollars). The majority of this is traffic building in nature. For the fourth quarter of 2004, search accounted

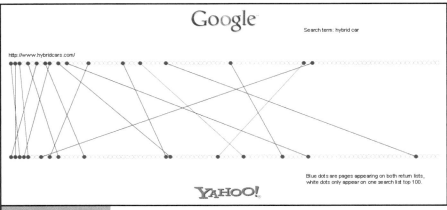

Figure 8.2

Overlap and Differences in Top 100 Returns for Search "Hybrid Car" on Google and Yahoo!

Source: Courtesy of LANGREITER.COM; Yahoo! Logo Courtesy of Yahoo! Inc.; Google Logo Courtesy of Google Inc.

for 40% of the total. These are exclusively devoted to building traffic to a site. Traffic building also drives much of the spending on display ads (18%), classifieds (18%), sponsorship (6%), and referrals (3%) (see Figure 8.4).

There is also a rapidly developing service bureau industry devoted to search engine optimization, search advertising, and other methods of building traffic. While it is possible for small- and medium-size business to do many of the steps themselves, there is a viable outsourcing option for a wide range of traffic-building activities. The major search engines develop networks of advisers, creating advertising "ecosystems" familiar with their tools and approaches.

Search marketing has dominated the recovery in online advertising, primarily the result of highly accountable paid search engine listings, as seen in Table 8.2. This is broken into three categories. The first, organic search engine optimization (SEO), is the spending to ensure that search engines rank a site highly on the relevant search criteria and searchers "organically" find the listing and the site. Search engine marketing (SEM) technology is rather small, and refers to technology spending to

"No, Thursday's out. How about never—is never good for you?"

Figure 8.3

Scarce Time Can Lead to Avoiding Novelty

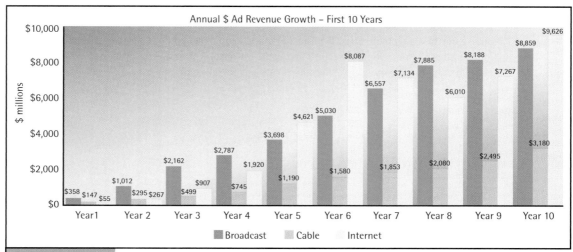

Figure 8.4

Rapid Growth of Internet Advertising, Much of it Traffic Building

Source: Internet Advertising Bureau

Table 8.2

Search Engine Marketing is a Multi-Billion Dollar Industry			
	2004 Advertiser Spending (Million $)	Share of Total	Share of Tactic
Organic SEO	492.1	12.0%	
SEM Agencies	178.8	4.4%	36%
In-house	313.4	5.8%	64%
SEM Technology	71.6	1.8%	
Leasing	30.0	0.7%	42%
SEM Agencies	20.8	0.5%	29%
In-house	20.8	0.5%	29%
Paid Search Advertising	3,523.1	86.2%	
Search Media Firms	3,059.0	74.8%	86.8%
SEM Agencies	181.0	4.4%	5.1%
In-house	283.7	6.9%	8.1%

Source: SEMPO

make onsite search more effective. The dominant share of spending is pay-per-click advertising, on major sites such as Google, Yahoo!, and MSN but also a number of additional more specialized search engines. This growth has led the online advertising rebound.

A WEB TRAFFIC PLAN

Traffic-Building Sources

Without visitors the best web site is a wasted resource. Generating traffic, which can be expensive and difficult, is an essential web marketing skill. Some of the most effective and least cost tools require creativity, imagination, and an attention to qualitative areas of marketing such as branding and publicity. At the same time, quantitative approaches such as keyword advertising and a careful attention to metrics can generate substantial traffic and profits.

A web traffic plan is a combination of strategic and tactical choices that a company makes to build an active user base. It combines one-time actions with choices that can change daily. Traffic sources fall into five main categories. They are (1) branding decisions, (2) search engine marketing, (3) affiliate networks, (4) online banner advertising, and (5) publicity and word of mouth.

> *Branding Choices*

A strong brand creates a ready source of inexpensive online traffic and a natural starting point for many online users seeking information. Figure 8.5 highlights the various sources of traffic to the Club Med web site. One of the most effective sources for Club Med is the power of its well-established brand. The majority of users go to a branded site without first consulting a search engine, external links, or following an ad banner. Rather, they either type the domain name directly into their browser or revisit a site based on a stored bookmark. Both of these are strongly reinforced by the power of the brand.[12]

Chapter 7 discussed how a well-crafted system of domain names naturally builds brand as well as traffic. An appropriate domain name system makes it much easier to include URLs on branded material and to include web addresses into advertisements, billboards, direct mail, and billing statements. A domain system that reflects how consumers view the brand will be memorable and accessible to a web user (and hopefully not like Figure 8.6).

> *Search Engines*

Organic search traffic results from a visitor going to a search engine, typing in a keyword phrase, and following one of the unpaid links to a site. It is free traffic, but it is not easy to achieve. The most important success criterion is an appearance high in the list of search returns. This results from strong content, high visibility, and search engine optimization. While each search engine follows its own approach in constructing its return list, there are commonalities across the leaders and important themes to understand.

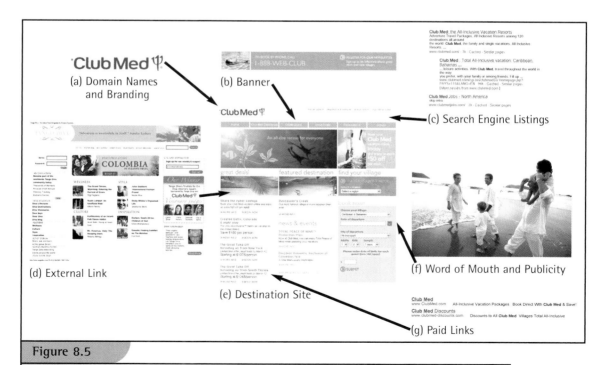

Figure 8.5

Sources of Web Site Traffic

Source: 8.5a, b, e, f Courtesy of Club Med; 8.5d © TangoDiva.com - premier travel magazine for women; 8.5c, g Courtesy of Google Inc.

"It was the only domain name they had left."

Figure 8.6

Domains Need to Match Branding

Paid keyword advertising uses money to move up the search engine return list by purchasing sponsored links and keyword ads. These ads display at the top right, top center, or bottom of the first return page. Keyword advertising has grown very rapidly in the past few years, as Yahoo!, Google, and others discovered the effectiveness of auction allocated keyword ads.

The mesothelioma example demonstrates how keywords can be highly valuable, even without images and branding capabilities. The fundamental benefit is relevance—searchers reveal themselves to be in active information collection mode. The keyword search is a signal of interest.

The rapidly developing industry surrounding paid search engine advertising is based on results. Tools and service bureaus help an advertiser identify the most effective combinations of phrases and bidding strategies. Many of these tools optimize keyword selection around the web chain that follows from this traffic. Visitors from each keyword phrase can be followed throughout their web visit, and in many cases their commercial value tied back to the keyword ad phrase that caught their attention. Promising keywords are kept, disappointing ones discarded.

> Affiliate Networks

Affiliate networks are sites that maintain links in order to receive a potential fee for generating traffic. This charge may be a simple per-click fee, or it may be based on additional actions such as registration or purchase. One of the most interesting aspects of affiliate networks is determining which of these possible actions should be the basis of the fee.

Affiliate networks may be exclusive or non-binding. Online sites such as fatwallet.com are multiple category, multiple vendor sites offering coupons and discounts to shoppers. They have relatively little content and exist around the affiliate fees as a primary business focus. At the other end of the spectrum are sites that have a few affiliate links as an easy extra stream of revenue to go along with their normal content.[13]

> Banner Advertising

Online banner ads are the most visible forms of traffic building. Companies can boost their traffic by placing ad banners on ad-supported web sites. A small but relatively predictable fraction of the viewers of these ads will click through to the web site.

One virtue of online web advertising is scalability. An activity is scaleable when its size can be rapidly expanded without changes in its performance and capability. Online advertising has a wide range of possible advertising exposure levels. A company can buy a few thousand impressions, or with proper care can select millions.

As was the case for keyword advertising, banner ads will vary in productivity by advertising copy and by advertising site. Standard reporting software and ad campaign software creates information tags linking the specific page and ad to an arriving visitor. This permits tracking of acquisition costs and advertising productivity.

> Mass Media Advertising

Under certain circumstances traditional mass media can be an effective online traffic source. Pepsi adopted the Web as an effective medium for reinforcing its branding, partnering with companies such as Yahoo! and Apple that also have very strong appeal with its core market. A co-promotion with Apple is aimed at boosting sales of Pepsi, but also boosting visits to the Apple iTunes site (Figure 8.7). Lucky winners get a free download from Apple on iTunes.

> Word of Mouth and Publicity

An illusive but powerful traffic-building source is publicity, promotion, and word of mouth. Events can make a site famous overnight, with millions of visitors. An amusing example happened during the 2004 Vice-Presidential debates between Dick Cheney and John Edwards. Seeking to make a debating point, Mr. Cheney told viewers that they could go to "factcheck.com" and see for themselves. What he meant to say was "factcheck.org," a nonprofit site run by the Annenberg school. Instead, the factcheck.com site took fifty thousand visitors within the first hour to a site maintained by George Soros, which strongly critiqued the Bush-Cheney team. Only 200 visitors had gone to the site during the previous day.[14]

Consumers consider word-of-mouth recommendations the most persuasive and credible information source. Building natural links into email communications, online visits, and other electronic material helps spread these recommendations. As publicity and word-of-mouth activities have a strong social networking and community connection, a detailed discussion of these efforts is postponed to Chapter 10.

100 million free songs.

Drink Pepsi, 1 in 3 wins. Legally download free music at iTunes.

Figure 8.7

The Pepsi-iTunes Promotion

Source: Courtesy of Pepsi-Cola North America

Traffic Volume and Quality

> *Typical Visit Patterns*

Each step of a web site visit leaves an entry in a web log. Chapter 7 highlighted the information available from web logs about visit duration, common visit entry pages, and common visit exit points and how that shapes content decisions. Chapters 9 and 10 discuss important opportunities for communicating and personalizing messages with visitors based on usage patterns and choices visitors make as they use the site. From a traffic-building perspective, it is important to spot the broad patterns of usage and to determine the cost and productivity of the visits.

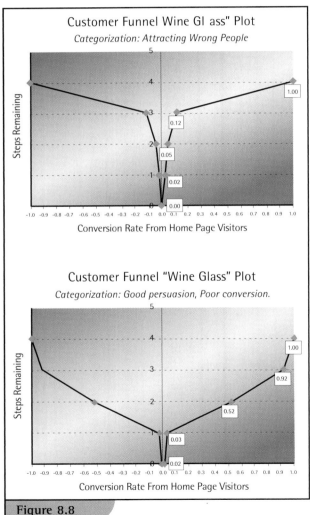

Figure 8.8 shows a "wine glass" plot, a useful web site visualization tool. It presents the average visit pattern of web site visitors, either for all visitors or for a target demographic segment of customers such as women. Starting with arrival, it shows the proportion of visits that exit at each stage. An example would be home page only, additional content pages, completed registration, access a shopping cart, and complete an order. The shape of the "wine glass" helps spot important trends and problems. For example, panel (a) has very steep attrition at the earliest steps. This normally occurs when the traffic building is attracting the wrong type of visitors, who quickly realize this and abandon the site. Panel (b) has a more gradual loss of visitors, but has a very low conversion at the last step. This is much more suggestive of problems with pricing, the costs of shipping, or some other problem with payment and checkout mechanisms.

Building a wine glass plot requires tracking visits from start to exit, selecting the records of users of interest, grouping exit pages into sequential stages, and sending the data to a program for drawing and analyzing the results (such as with a spreadsheet). As seen in Chapter 7, there are many situations where visitors come to a site without sufficient identifying information to categorize them into segments. In those situations, the wine plot must be for the full population. The identity of the sequential changes will change depending on the goals of the traffic-building plan. For commerce-oriented goals, the key steps will focus on shopping and conversion behavior. For branding or persuasion-oriented goals, stages will focus more on the content selection and actions taken with regard to the brand or cause.

Figure 8.8

Summarizing Visit Shapes with a Wine Glass Plot

Source: Concept from Sterne, author data.

Many tools exist to drill down and further analyze web visits. Figure 8.9 demonstrates a "starfield" tool, useful for spotting problems of over and underexposure of individual product items or desirable actions.[15] The size of each box represents its sales importance. In Figure 8.9, showing online sales of IBM laptops, the width of a rectangle is the product price and the height is product margin. For products in the bottom right, many visitors see the product but fail to click through. In the upper left, there is high conversion but relatively low exposure. These forms of visualization help identify outliers, including under- and over-achieving products.

More detailed information can be inferred from statistical analysis of clickstream data. These formal models allow much more careful explanation of the shape and trends of visits. Specific controls can be used for pricing, advertising exposures, the impact of repeat visits, and a variety of other marketing tools.[16] A combination of visualization tools and rigorous quantitative analysis of web log data can explain the patterns of web site usage.

> *Cost-per-Action*

Wine glass plots demonstrate the steady attrition between web visit stages. One of the most useful guides for traffic-building analysis is to compute the cost-per-action, defined as the number of visits that make it to a particular stage (the "action") divided by the campaign costs. Useful measures include the cost per impression, the cost per visit, or the cost per eventual purchase.

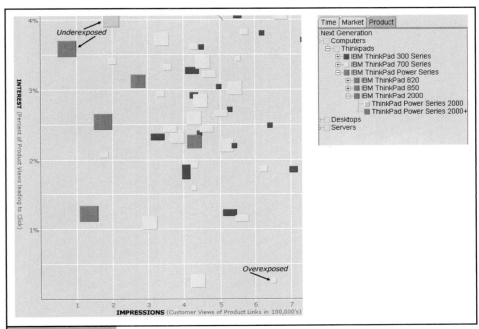

Figure 8.9

Micro-View of Visit Behavior for an Online Retailer

Source: Figure 2 in J. Lee, M. Podlaseck, E. Schonberg, and R. Hoch, "Visualization and Analysis of Clickstream Data of Online Stores for Understanding Web Merchandizing," *Data Mining and Knowledge Discovery* 5, Issue 1–2, (January–April 2001): 59–84. Copyright © 2001 Discovery. Reprinted with kind permission from Springer Science and Business Media.

Figure 8.10 shows results for a relatively productive ad banner campaign. The pricing of the campaign immediately gives the cost per impression. Typically quoted as CPM, or cost per thousand (e.g. mille), the cost per impression in 8.10 is $0.015. While 1.5 cents per impression may seem cheap, banners typically have a low click-through rate. The next stage is a web site visit. If the click-through rate is 2% (a relatively high rate), this gives a cost per visit to the advertiser's web site of $.015/.02 = $0.75. In other words, the average cost of generating a web site visit is 75 cents.

Cost-per-action escalates at each subsequent stage, as the falling success rate appears in the denominator of the cost equation. If the action desired is a purchase, and the conversion rate from web site visit to purchase is 5%, then the cost-per-purchase is $0.015/(.02*.05) = $15.00 per purchase.

Cost-per-action is a simplification of the full web chain analysis presented in Chapter 5. While a web chain analysis tracks all eventual possibilities and evaluates the campaign based on its full range of results, a cost-per-action analysis only focuses on the benefits for one specific desired outcome. When the focus of a campaign is primarily on traffic building for a specific goal, the difference will not be large. When the campaign and the tools used have a considerable branding impact, the difference may be significant. A cost-per-action analysis has the benefit of simplicity, creating a method of quickly comparing alternative traffic-building campaigns. It may

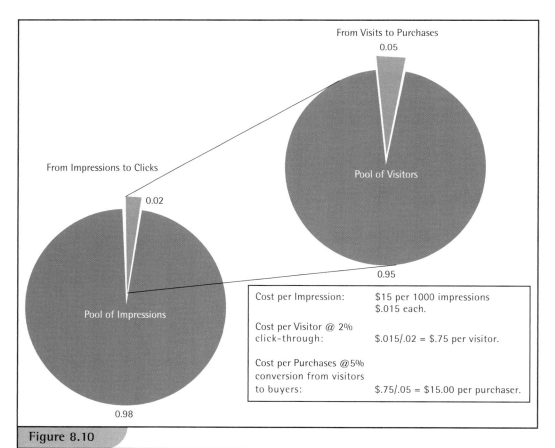

Figure 8.10

Visitors Decline and Costs Rise at Each Stage

understate the full benefits of the campaign when multiple stages and different benefits result from an online ad or web site visit.

The ease of determining campaign costs and campaign results varies greatly between the different traffic approaches illustrated in Figure 8.5. It is difficult to partition the relevant costs for a branding or publicity campaign, and to connect them to the number of visitors arriving at a site. Other sources of traffic, especially search and banners, are much easier to measure and evaluate. Campaigns that permit a cost-per-action calculation lend themselves to much more scientific management, with optimization tools and experimentation leading to substantial lowering of the cost-per-action.

> *Web Visibility and Competitive Analysis*

One of the notable aspects of online marketing is the number of available tools to monitor and improve a web page or web site's visibility and online presence. Many of these are a free and open source, allowing inspection of exactly how they operate and modifications for special situations. These tools provide diagnostics of a site's online presence and help evaluate the impact of advertising, publicity efforts, or some news story.

External links to a site have many benefits. They are crucial ingredients determining how high in the search return list a site appears, as well as a source of web traffic from web surfers following links on other web sites. Tracking the number and location of sites linking to a particular page provides a manager with a highly useful measure of the strength and nature of their online visibility.

The major search engines provide "hooks" into their data, which allow programs to access and report link information. In the sites indexed by Yahoo!, for example, there are 12,200 links to Club Med.[17] A Club Med manager can also capture these links into a spreadsheet, and analyze which sites are heavy linkers and where their coverage is sparse. It is also useful to compare this coverage against other benchmark sites. Some product categories lend themselves to external links much more than others. One method of handling this is to focus less on the absolute number of external links and more on the relative level of visibility within a set of competitors. Benchmarking on competitors can highlight strengths and weaknesses, while ensuring that the comparisons are relevant.

Services such as Alexa allow a web site operator to compare their viewership performance against other web sites. Gathering data from the 10 million users with the Alexa button bar,[18] the system provides daily traffic ranking of site popularity. For example, Figure 8.11 shows that Honda (brown line) and Toyota (red line) rank consistently much higher than the Ford (blue) or GM (green) sites. Both Ford and GM should be concerned

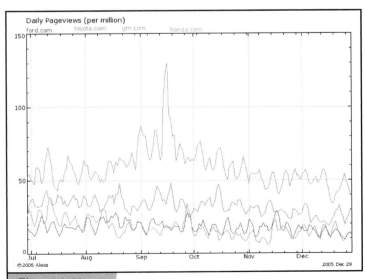

Figure 8.11

Using the Alexa Service to Measure Site Usage

Source: alexa.com

about the low viewership their sites receive compared to Toyota and Honda. This is even more serious if web usage reflects the underlying strength of the brands. A traffic plan might want to focus on both raising site traffic and determining what is causing such low relative performance. Traffic services can also help spot successful promotions and unusual dips that raise concern. Honda's September boost is especially notable and provides important information to both Honda and Honda's competitors.

Club Med gets much less traffic than auto sites, averaging around 30,000th on the Alexa list. The number 1 site is Yahoo!, followed by MSN and Google. The system also allows rankings by browser language used. For example, the top two ranked sites in Arabic are Google and Al Jazeera. In Chinese, the top three are sina.com.cn, baidu.com, and sohu.com. Chapter 16 covers some of the issues in different types of panels and sample issues they raise.

| Traffic-Building Goals

Managers should decide on the goals of a campaign prior to its start. This is good advice for several reasons. One, it helps prevent ex post justifications. There is a natural temptation to focus on the positive results of a campaign when results fall short of the target. A decision to focus on a well-defined objective works against this. Second, it is impossible to effectively test and experiment with different traffic sources or campaign designs without an agreed upon metric of success. Third, it is much easier to contract with outside providers when traffic objectives are well established.

At one level, any traffic-building campaign has the simple goal of attracting the best traffic to the site for the least cost. This is true whether the means are mass media, search engines, external alliances, or some other method. The controversy surrounds the most appropriate and actionable definition of the idea of "best traffic." While maximizing profit is the logical goal for profit-oriented firms, it may be hard to operationalize and may not fit for nonprofit groups. It may be easier to specify and measure alternative goals, such as cost-per-action or the total number of actions accomplished through the traffic campaign.

Setting traffic-building goals is complicated by the relative importance of brand building and offline impacts versus online actions such as registration or first-purchase (Figure 8.12). The web chain analysis of Chapter 5 captures all of these effects into a unified value of an impression and a unified value of a visit. When brand impacts matter, or when a visit to a web site leads some consumers to make beneficial product purchases offline, these should be accounted for

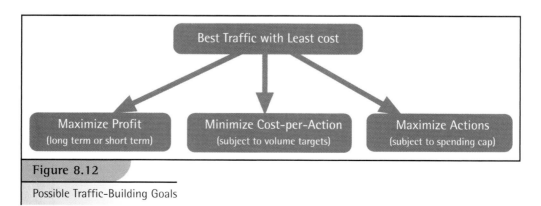

Figure 8.12

Possible Traffic-Building Goals

when setting traffic-building goals. With the push toward online spending accountability, there is a natural tendency to ignore them.

Each of these three approaches has benefits and drawbacks. All three are used by different organizations. For many firms Internet spending has moved beyond experimental money and a lack of accountability, and campaigns are managed for results.

> *Maximize Profit*

A web traffic campaign with profit maximization as its goal has no ex ante spending caps or volume targets. Rather, it is willing to spend on media and traffic as long as the incremental benefits of the traffic exceed the incremental costs. While for many advertising settings, such as television or radio advertising, this guideline can be very challenging to measure and implement, online marketers can often measure the consequences of campaigns they run. This permits traffic building based soundly on profit considerations.

Chapter 5 presented the two essential tools to manage traffic campaigns based on profit maximization. These are customer lifetime value and the unified visit value computed using web chain analysis. Customer lifetime value is the discounted net present value of the expected profits from a new customer. The unified visit value is the full expected benefits arising from a customer's visit to a web site, which includes any branding and purchase impacts. For new and growing firms, the probability of acquiring a new customer multiplied by customer lifetime value is the largest impact of the unified visit value. For more established companies, the largest impact may come through longer term branding.

A traffic-building campaign is not the same thing as an online advertising campaign. Figure 8.13 shows a case where they differ. Far more visitors to the iVillage Health and Beauty page will see the two McDonald's salad ads than ever click through to the McDonald's site. The ad is prominent and well designed, and it is likely to lead to both awareness and recall without a visit to the site. Judging this ad campaign solely on traffic building to the web site would be inappropriate. Its ultimate goal is to drive traffic to McDonald's outlets for lunch or dinner, primarily through longer-term brand impact.

For simplicity, the branding impact of the ads will be ignored in most of what follows. The emphasis is on building traffics to web sites. In cases like Figure 8.13, however, the ad brand impact may be the most important part of the ad campaign.

Focusing only on actions that occur upon arrival at the web site, profit maximization provides the following guideline:

Traffic-building Profit Guideline (web site branding and other impacts included, ad branding impacts ignored)

> Spend on traffic sources that maximize the difference between unified visit value and cost per visit.
> Acquire traffic as long as the cost per visit is less than the unified visit value.

Traffic campaigns that produce a cost per visit lower than the unified visit value are profitable. When the difference is large, the campaign is more profitable.

Some marketers may wish to simplify the web chain analysis and only consider new customers as a valid result. This assumes that the site branding and other impacts do not occur (have zero probability) or have no value (e.g., zero web site brand impact). This can be a useful simplification if there is widespread agreement on customer lifetime value and acquisition cost measures and the other impacts are felt to be minor.

(a)

(b)

Figure 8.13

Online Ads Can Contain Branding and Traffic-Building Impacts

Traffic-building Profit Guideline (branding and other impacts ignored)

> > Spend on traffic sources that maximize the difference between customer lifetime value and online customer acquisition cost.
> > Acquire traffic as long as online customer value exceeds online customer acquisition cost.

The first part of the guideline is another way of saying a traffic campaign should focus on maximizing customer equity, typically defined as the difference between customer lifetime value and customer acquisition cost.[19] The second part states that traffic-building efforts are profitable over the long term as long as customers acquired from the activity bring with them positive customer equity.

It may be easier for some companies to measure customer acquisition cost and manage their traffic building based on that. This is a simplification that assumes brand building is minor and customers produce roughly the same profits after acquisition. Companies and researchers routinely compute customer acquisition cost. For example, a research paper computed customer acquisition costs for Amazon, eBay, Ameritrade, and E*Trade over a five-year period. As seen in Table 8.3, they range from a low of $7.70 to a high of nearly $400.[20] As customer lifetime values for Amazon and eBay were likely to be higher than $10 over this period, these activities look profitable. The threshold for the brokerages is much steeper.

Care needs to be taken when using historical averages. The proper customer acquisition cost and customer lifetime value to use in calculations is forward looking, and historical values may be misleading. Even if E*Trade's acquisition costs were very high during 1997–2002, their acquisition costs going forward could be much lower.

Table 8.3

The Wide Variation in Average Customer Acquisition Costs for Four Net Companies			
Company	Time Period	Acquired Customers	Customer Acq. Cost
Ecommerce companies			
Amazon.com	3/1997->3/2002	33,800,000	$7.70
eBay	12/1996->3/2002	46,100,000	$11.26
Online brokerages			
Ameritrade	9/1997->3/2002	1,877,000	$203.44
E*Trade	12/1997->3/2002	4,117,370	$391.00

Source: Sunil Gupta, Donald R. Lehmann, and Jennifer Ames Stuart, "Valuing Customers," *Journal of Marketing Research* 41, no. 1 (February 2004). Used with permission by the American Marketing Association.

> Minimize Cost-per-Action

Some organizations prefer to manage traffic building with pre-set limits on the total activity rather than the open-ended approach implicit in profit maximization. One popular approach is to set volume targets for some action, and then seek traffic-building approaches that achieve those goals with minimum cost. Possible volume targets are:

> A certain number of unique new visitors,
> A certain number of new registered users providing email addresses,
> A certain number of visitors inquiring about an upcoming new product,
> A certain number of new customers.

One of the virtues of this approach is its ability to handle more than one objective. A campaign may seek the cheapest solution for generating (for instance) 100,000 new visitors and 3,000 new customers. The goal of the campaign planner is to identify the best mixture of traffic-building tools that accomplish these goals. Marketers should be careful, however, that volume goals are not a substitute for thinking carefully about profitability.

> Maximize Actions

Another popular goal is to maximize the number of visitors completing some action subject to a fixed budget. The marketing department may be instructed to generate as many new customers as possible with an online campaign budget of $75,000. Again, it is possible to use this approach for multiple goals or attempt to reach some balance of new visitors, registered users, and new customers.

A goal of maximizing new registrations (for example) requires some form of budget cap to prevent acquisition costs from spiraling out of control. If the goal is simply to bring in as many new registrants as could potentially use the service, more and more advertising will chase ever more difficult to acquire holdouts.

> Tracking Multiple Goals

It is relatively straightforward for a marketer to simultaneously monitor multiple goals and results from traffic-building campaigns. Web hosting and web site tracking firms create management "dashboards" that present results from campaigns on the daily or even hourly basis. Warnings and alerts appear when there is unusual campaign performance, both on the high and low side. Visualization tools increasingly put detailed results in the hands of managers, with intuitive yet real-time connections to live data provided through the Net. These dashboards may also track competitive activity, as online changes may be a leading indicator of changes in competitors' product or pricing plans.

The next section considers search engine marketing, both for organic traffic and paid advertising. Search marketing provides some of the most accountable traffic sources, and has grown rapidly during the past few years.

SEARCH ENGINE MARKETING

Table 8.2 shows how search engine marketing is a vibrant multi-billion-dollar business.[21] The $5.1 billion spent on search in 2005 was 41% of all online advertising.[22] This spending spanned the range from individuals dedicating a few dollars to promoting their personal web sites to major corporations spending millions. Almost any web site can participate, overhead is low, and entry is easy.[23] Regional and local customization is straightforward as well.

Search engine traffic comes in two basic forms. First is organic traffic arising from a search return list, automatically generated by the search engine without any commercial arrangement. Actions taken to boost this traffic are typically referred to as search engine optimization. The other basic form is pay-per-click. The top two keyword search services are Google and Yahoo!, but all major search engines offer some form of the service.[24] Organizations bid on keyword portfolios. Depending on their bid and the bids of others, their ads appear higher or lower on the search returns page. Actions taken to drive this traffic are commonly referred to as keyword management.

Search marketing and keyword analysis provide a highly useful benchmark against which all other traffic-building activities can be judged. The pay-per-click nature of search marketing establishes a hard number for the cost of generating a visit to a web site. Other media can be judged against this cost, and the benefits of an average visit compared as well. Organizationally, the difference between the unified visit value and the cost of acquiring traffic provides a market test of the web site value.

Once an organization decides on its traffic-building goals, it should turn attention toward search engine marketing. The next part considers both search engine optimization and pay-per-click advertising.

Site Optimization

> *The Power of "Above the Fold"*
Newspaper editors have long put their big stories and top news "above the fold." Prominent items naturally attract attention (Figure 8.14). A similar phenomenon holds for search. Searchers' willingness to investigate and respond to the search engine return list falls off steeply as an item falls further down the list. This appears as a

> A much higher click rate on top-rated search items,
> A decay of willingness to look down the list of search returns, and
> A low fraction of searchers going beyond the first page or two of returned items.

This behavior would not be so troublesome if the Web was small, and normal searches didn't return thousands or even millions of hits. Googlefight.com provides an amusing example of how normal searches provide many items. Googlefight uses the number of pages found for each of two searches as the score in a contest, complete with animations of their battle. Celebrity names are one common contest, as are sports teams. For example, a "fight" between the terms Boston Red Sox and New York Yankees leads to a narrow win for the Yankees. What makes for a good game makes for difficult traffic generation for sites beyond the first few hits.

Top placement in search returns is a key to generating organic traffic. Search engine optimizers seek to improve search engine placement by making the main search engines aware of their site, ensuring that content creates the appropriate keywords and details that search engines utilize in their rankings, ensuring that site navigation reinforces search engine algorithms, and cultivating links from other appropriate sites. They provide site guidelines that raise visibility without sacrificing usability and online quality.

Figure 8.14

Top Billing Gets Notice

Source: © FPG/Getty Images

> *Site Guidelines*

> Search Engine Awareness

Any serious site will probably be indexed eventually by the main search engines. Placement services accelerate this process by providing the search engines with addresses and information about the site. Table 8.4 highlights the lags involved in being listed in the main engines. Once part of its listing, each search engine maintains the freshness of its index by occasionally revisiting pages. The importance the search engine gives a page or site partially determines how frequently it is revisited.

> Use Meta-Tags to Flag Important Concepts

Search engines look to the content of the page to determine relevance. Not all content is treated equally. Most of the leading engines weight the page title and keywords listed on the page above words appearing elsewhere in the text. Web designers can assist search engines finding their page with proper emphasis and use of metatags.

Kazanlaw.com demonstrates how good design yields highly valuable traffic through organic search results. Kazanlaw.com ranked in the top three among the organic search results on Google for the high cost phrase "peritoneal mesothelioma" over the course of several months.[25] Rather than pay for high price ads, this top ranking generates very valuable traffic without a fee. Top billing is partially due to the emphasis of the phrase within the title metatag, the keywords metatag, and the description metatag.[26]

Online tools let a marketer check how a search engine indexes a site. These tools simulate how a search "spider," the indexing software used by search engines to read and collate Web

Table 8.4

Search Engine Submission and Costs					
Search Engine	AllTheWeb	AltaVista (Yahoo!)	Google	Inktomi	Teoma
Listing Tied to Submit?	No	Yes	No, but may help	n/a	n/a
Submit Limit	No limit	No limit	No limit	n/a	n/a
Pages Appear	2 to 4 weeks	4 to 6 weeks	About 4 weeks	About 4 weeks	n/a
Overall Freshness	1 day to 4 weeks	1 day to 6 weeks +	1 day to 4 weeks	1 day to 4 weeks	1 day to 4 weeks

Source: SearchEngineWatch.com.

information, reads all the metatags and normal content. Several powerful versions are free and provide a valuable check on programming oversights and missing information. Among the items search engine spiders record are date of last modification, size of page, metatags, image, and textual descriptions.[27]

Web authors must decide which keywords and phrases merit inclusion. This requires an understanding of how consumers view the product or service, and which terms they will use in the search engine. In a health-related site, these keywords will naturally focus on the disease. In other cases the choices are more complex. There can also be legal challenges. In 1998 Playboy Enterprises sued Terri Welles for her use of the keywords "playmate" and "playboy playmate of the year 1981," claiming that these were copyrighted terms owned by Playboy. The Court found that Welles could use the phrases, as they accurately described her past and were a fair use of the terms.[28] Other jurisdictions, such as the European Union, have put stricter limits on the use of brand names within metatags.

While a page can be changed at any time, the lags shown in Table 8.4 imply that keyword choices for search optimization must change relatively infrequently. High placement on multiple keywords is difficult. Firms must focus on the choices which best identify the page and stand out from the competition.

> Structure Web Site Content

The design of a site must satisfy goals of usability, clarity of information, ease of navigation, and entertainment. There are also traffic-building concerns. One of the difficult tradeoffs is between an exciting animation to welcome new viewers and a more informational and search friendly landing page. The site for fans of blues legend John Lee Hooker provides a good example. The first stop for surfers typing in www.johnleehooker.com is an animation providing photos and music, giving a feel for the music prior to landing on a more informational page at www.johnleehooker.com/home.asp.[29] Search engines, however, do not understand this distinction. As the animation does not contain many of the tags and information content that leads to a high ranking, the site's visibility suffers. The same type of concern arises with dynamic pages that change with new content.

There are also influential aspects of site structure that shape the importance of a site or a page in algorithms used to determine site importance. The PageRank algorithm (see next page) of Google uses page links as a form of importance voting. Much of the importance of a site comes from external links, as described in step 5. Within a site, the structure of links also influences rankings. While somewhat technical, there are tools, tutorials, and consulting services that help web site managers structure links and navigation design to better reflect the true importance of pages within a site.

> **Cultivate External Links**

One of the keys to high search engine placement is the number and quality of external links that point at a site. Some search engines use these links as a fundamental feature determining the quality of a page (see description on next page). Even search engines not using links to calculate influence change their indexing behavior based on external links.

A strong network of external links is at least a partial substitute for paid advertising. An example of a site placing high on many search returns for such popular topics as "stem cells" or "health information" is the National Institutes of Health (NIH). Both Alta Vista and Yahoo! show more than 5 million links to the NIH site.

External links provide a snap shot of the connectedness of a web site and the influence it has on the rest of the Web. Each external link is also an opportunity for free traffic. When a site visitor sees a link on a page there is some probability of following it to the web site. Even a small chance on a high volume site can be a valuable source of new visits. External links also provide a variety of clues about fruitful sources of traffic and interest. The search term "link:ford.com" demonstrates that more than 61,000 pages have a link on them pointing toward some page on ford.com. Refining the term to "link: ford.com—site:ford.com" restricts attention to links originating outside of ford.com. Each of these 57,000 pages provides a potential source of traffic to Ford, and insight into companies and organizations that think Ford deserves tracking and monitoring.

"Link farms" are one of the more dubious search engine optimization techniques. These web sites create massive numbers of links, and work out reciprocal links from other sites, in order to concentrate importance weighting through algorithms such as PageRank. Link farms often make their money by charging for establishing a link to a site attempting to move up their ranking. As search engines mature, they are penalizing both link farms and sites that join them for attempting to manipulate rankings with artificial connections.

Keyword Advertising

Site optimization and other sources of naturally occurring web site traffic are valuable sources of visits. Many marketers find it profitable to go beyond these measures and advertise their sites. One of the dramatic online developments since 2000 has been the rapid growth of online keyword pay-per-click advertising.

Small, clickable text-based ads, as shown in Figure 8.15, bring in billions of dollars of advertising revenue. Simple and straightforward, with little or no branding and a basic pitch, their performance is surprisingly effective. These ads steer traffic to an organization's web site, with no money changing hands unless a click occurs.

This section describes the process of keyword advertising, what determines a keyword's value, and how marketers should decide how aggressively to pursue keyword advertising. Many useful online tools make the process easier and more powerful.

PageRank for Marketers

 Google established itself by producing surprisingly effective hits at the top of its search results. At the heart of this success is the PageRank algorithm, and a little knowledge of the Google approach clarifies both its success and the power of external links to a site.

The PageRank algorithm treats links on a web page as a vote of influence. The goal of the PageRank algorithm is to take all the links (the votes) on all the pages of the Web and compute the importance ranking of each page.

The rules of voting are somewhat unusual. The basics are:

> *Ballots aren't secret.* It matters what page is doing the linking.
> *You can't vote for yourself.* Links from Page 1 to Page 1 don't count. Links to other pages within a web site do count.
> *You can vote for as many candidates as you want.* Every page getting a link receives some benefit of the link.
> *No ballot stuffing.* Repeated links only count once.
> *The order of listing on your ballot doesn't matter.*
> *Influence is contagious.* A page receiving many votes is important, and casts important votes.

The most unusual rules are number (3) and number (6). A page with only one link is casting more of its vote to its destination than a page linking to thousands of sites. The

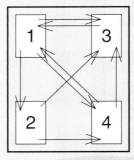

Links are the key to Google's PageRank

PageRank algorithm spreads influence evenly across all outbound links on a page. How much power a page has works through rule (6).

The PageRank algorithm is surprisingly effective. At least partially, it captures the entire influence of all the link information of the entire Web. Second, it does this in a way which is mathematically solvable for billions of web pages. Third, it is relatively immune to manipulation.

Site navigation and link structure concentrates PageRank influence. While an organization can only partly affect external links, it can make design and layout decisions which raise a key page's influence. One of the simplest and most important actions is creating links to the home page on all of the internal pages, reinforcing home page value.

Sources: Sergei Brin and Larry Page, (1998), "The Anatomy of a Large-Scale Hypertextual Web Search Engine," *WWW7/Computer Networks.* Kurt Bryan and Tanya Leise, (2005), "The $20,000,000,000 Eigenvector," working paper, January 26.

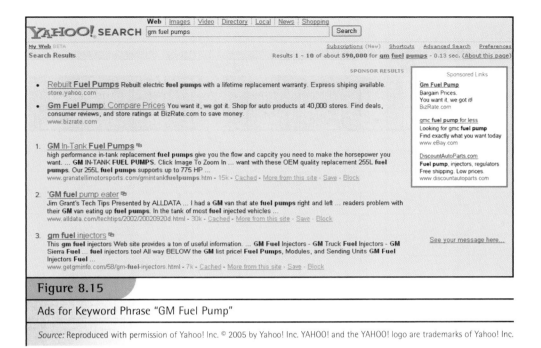

Figure 8.15

Ads for Keyword Phrase "GM Fuel Pump"

Source: Reproduced with permission of Yahoo! Inc. © 2005 by Yahoo! Inc. YAHOO! and the YAHOO! logo are trademarks of Yahoo! Inc.

> Keyword Value

Table 8.5 shows average prices of keywords for major sectors of the economy, compiled by sampling thousands of keywords on a continuous basis.[30] In the automotive sector, the average price per click runs about $1.50, while finance mortgage ads averaged $4.52 a click in May 2005. Wall Street and investors seem to view these prices as important indicators of online activity, and there was a sizable impact on the stock prices of advertising companies following the release of the May dip in keyword prices.[31]

Keyword ads influence billions of web site visits.[32] They also establish a benchmark for the value of traffic from all sources. Traffic is relatively cheap if it can be generated for less than the prevailing keyword price in that sector, and should be refocused if the price is higher than this rate. Traffic cost places a burden on web site managers and usability experts to ensure their sites are sufficiently productive to justify the visit cost.

A few main factors determine keyword value. A keyword only has value if it leads some viewers to click and visit a site and some fraction of those visitors to convert to a desired action. A keyword ad's value to a specific advertiser is driven by its productivity in leading to a desired action and the value of that action. For example, if the desired action is signing up a new customer, then purchase profitability and customer lifetime value strongly influence the value of the keyword.

The connection between keyword ad and action value is possible due to the inherent traceability of keyword advertising. Each arrival to a site is accounted for, and that specific visitor is followed through the "traffic funnel" from visit beginning to visit end. While there are still some uncertainties about what happens offline or on later visits, this level of monitoring is much higher than for almost any other advertising medium.

Table 8.5

Fathom Online's May 2005 Keyword Price Index™ (KPI™)

| | | | | Fathom Online Keyword Price Index™ | | | | | |
Month	Automotive	Consumer-Retail	Consumer-Services	Consumer-Travel Hospitality	Finance-Investing	Finance-Mortgage	Telecom-Broadband	Telecom-Wireless	Avg. of tracked industries
Sep-04	$1.54	$0.32	$0.54	$0.64	$1.76	$3.17	$1.89	$1.09	$1.37
Oct-04	$1.39	$0.48	$0.96	$0.85	$1.60	$4.31	$1.78	$1.06	$1.55
Nov-04	$1.35	$0.60	$1.27	$0.90	$1.70	$4.74	$1.59	$1.09	$1.66
Dec-04	$1.41	$0.58	$1.36	$0.97	$1.76	$4.79	$1.63	$1.09	$1.70
Jan-05	$1.34	$0.52	$1.29	$0.88	$1.73	$4.93	$1.67	$0.79	$1.64
Feb-05	$1.28	$0.46	$1.04	$0.81	$1.65	$5.10	$1.72	$0.77	$1.60
Mar-05	$1.42	$0.51	$1.08	$0.93	$1.86	$5.39	$1.85	$0.95	$1.75
Apr-05	$1.40	$0.52	$1.13	$0.92	$2.03	$6.49	$2.09	$1.01	$1.95
May-05	$1.50	$0.49	$1.09	$0.87	$1.81	$4.52	$2.02	$1.00	$1.67

Source: www.fathomonline.com

Keyword value is driven strongly by competition. Although the specifics differ between major search engines, keyword ads are priced by a continuous auction process. Even if a keyword is extremely valuable to an advertiser, if no other firms bid, its price will be low. However, if there are a number of firms competing for the keyword, the price can be bid up to levels that become unprofitable for some advertisers. Prices can change minute-by-minute, as new bidders enter and current bidders change their offers.

> *Keyword Portfolio Evaluation*

The competitive bidding process creates situations where seemingly close keywords can have very different prices, at least temporarily. Keyword advertisers should monitor activity and follow an iterative process of identification, expansion, testing, trimming, and tracking of campaigns.

Identify main keywords –> Expand the list –> Test –> Bid –> Trim –> Track.

> Identify Possible Keywords

The best place for a company to start building a list of relevant keywords is by reviewing their own web logs. Web log software captures the search terms used by visitors arriving at the site when they click on search engine result items. These are the terms that current visitors generated on their own, and they provide a snapshot of keyword search activity connected to a desire to visit. Some software systems track these natural search terms on to further conversion steps, and high-performing keywords from this list are an especially useful starting point.

Keyword length and alternative phrases are part of keyword list building. Phrases can be of increasing length, and most systems let an advertiser specify near or exact matches. For example, an online battery store selling parts for the Sony Vaio might use any of the following phrases.

> 1-word: battery
> 2-word: laptop battery

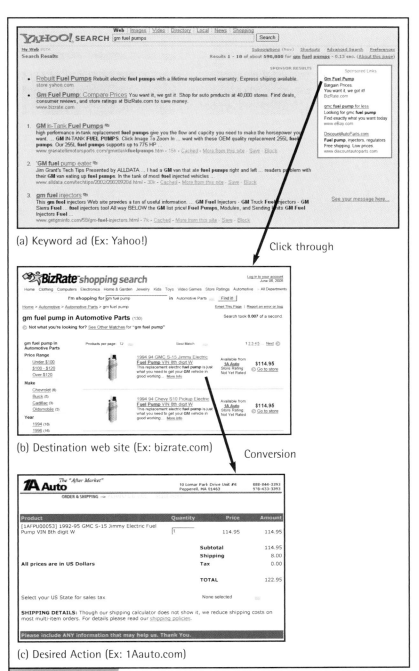

(a) Keyword ad (Ex: Yahoo!)

Click through

(b) Destination web site (Ex: bizrate.com)

Conversion

(c) Desired Action (Ex: 1Aauto.com)

Figure 8.16

Keyword Initiated Traffic

Source: 8.16a Reproduced with permission of Yahoo! Inc. © 2005 by Yahoo! Inc. YAHOO! and the YAHOO! logo are trademarks of Yahoo! Inc.; 8.16b Courtesy of ©2005 Shopzilla, Inc.; 8.16c Courtesy of www.1AAuto.com

> 3-word: Sony laptop battery
> 4-word: Sony Vaio laptop battery
> 5-word: Sony Vaio laptop TR3A battery

Most consumer searches use one or two word phrases, with 39% using one word, 49% using two words, and 9% using three words. Fewer than 5% of searches use four or more words. A marketer may want to augment the keyword list with words or phrases that are especially important to a segment of customers. These can be specific brand names, specific part names, technical phrases, or some other special terms.

> Expand the List

Search providers have tools that help advertisers expand their search term list and find other possible keyword phrases. For example, the Adwords keyword tool suggests more than 100 additional specific keywords for the phrase "fuel pump," such as "mustang fuel pump" or "chevy fuel pump." There is also a long list of additional related topics, such as "gas filter" and "fuel injectors." Depending on the testing strategy, the advertiser can start with a very broad list and trim down or start with a more focused approach and build up from high-performing terms.

> Testing Keywords

Keyword ads vary widely in click-through rates, conversion rates, and cost-per-action productivities. It is very useful to test the keyword list and collect some basic conversion rate and cost-per-action data prior to committing to a keyword plan. Search engines allow advertisers to set daily traffic and budget limits. These permit budgeting for easy and low-risk testing of alternative keyword lists.

Bidding and traffic estimation tools provided by major search providers are a good starting point. For example, the tool lets anyone see the bids placed by advertisers for the phrase "fuel pump." As seen in Figure 8.17, a tester must type the code on the bottom as a protection against software agents constantly checking on prices and overloading the system. Thirty different advertisers bid on this specific phrase, with a range from $.06 to $.47 per click. The system only displays seven ads during an actual search.[33]

There is an extensive literature in statistics on the best strategies for running test markets and how much information to collect. For keyword advertising, the goal is to collect the type of data shown in Table 8.6. This is a list of keyword phrases with their results. Conversion rates, given by conversions/clicks, vary significantly by keyword. The tests should also reveal how

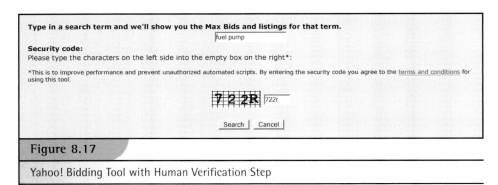

Figure 8.17

Yahoo! Bidding Tool with Human Verification Step

Source: Reproduced with permission of Yahoo! Inc. © 2005 by Yahoo! Inc. YAHOO! and the YAHOO! logo are trademarks of Yahoo! Inc.

Table 8.6

Collecting Keyword Data				
Keyword Phrases	**Clicks**	**Conversions**	**Cost per click to hold position**	**Conversion Rate**
Skylark fuel pump pos. 1	62	6	$0.10	9.68%
GM fuel pump pos. 2	148	18	$0.20	12.16%
Buick parts pos. 2	1246	48	$0.25	3.85%
Used Buick Skylark pos. 1	8678	95	$0.23	1.09%
Buick pos. 3	362	15	$1.37	4.14%
Used car parts pos. 2	17265	98	$0.34	0.57%

productive different keyword positions are, and the prevailing price required to maintain any particular ad position if competitors' prices remain fixed.

> Bid, Trim, and Track

How Search Engines Charge for Ads

The two main keyword-advertising sites, Yahoo! and Google, use two different rules to auction keyword ads. Yahoo! ranks ads according to maximum bid, while Google ranks ads by maximum bid times click-through rate. There are arguments in favor of each approach. Studies suggest that the Google system is somewhat more profitable for the search engine, as better click-through rate ads get "promoted" higher in the list. As the search engine receives money only for click-through, this tends to augment their income by putting low performing ads in less desirable positions. On the other hand, the Yahoo! system is simpler and more transparent. Yahoo! makes public the bids for all keywords, allowing an advertiser to understand what the cost would be to acquire any particular position in the bid list.

A keyword bid sets the maximum price an advertiser is willing to pay for a specific keyword. The actual price paid, and the position on the list, depends on other bids from other advertisers. For an example, assume there are six bidders and a minimum bid of $.10. The system first sorts the bids, from highest to lowest: (.95, .82, .56, .35, .33, .13). The system "works from the bottom." The bottom bidder pays 0.10 and gets the last slot. For an advertiser to show in fifth place instead of sixth it must bid higher than the sixth place maximum bid. Thus, the price of the fifth place is $.14. This continues up to the top. The bids (.95, .82, .56, .35, .33, .13) produce prices paid for six slots of (.83, .57, .36, .34, .14, .10).

The system on Google requires knowledge of estimated click-through rates for each ad. Ranking is no longer based solely on maximum bid, but is also based on the maximum bid time of the estimated click-through rate. Key similarities of the two systems are:

> No payment is required until someone clicks through to the web site,
> Higher bids increase the possibility of a higher keyword position,
> No clicks will cost more than the maximum bid,
> Actual price charged depends on the intensity of competition, and
> The cost-per-click in the marketplace establishes a benchmark for traffic-building activities.

Proper Bidding

A firm placing a keyword ad on Yahoo!, Google, or some other keyword-advertising site must decide which keywords to bid on and how much to bid on each keyword. In order to do this properly, it is necessary to specify the traffic-building goal(s) and to understand keyword specific click-through rates and ultimate conversions to the desired actions.

Several assumptions make the discussion much simpler. When these assumptions do not hold, the proper rules for keyword bidding are more complicated and more of a trial and error approach may be necessary for many firms. Assume that:

> The desired action is new customer acquisition, and all customers have the same dollar value V.
> Competitors' bids are known and they do not change in response to the firm's bids.
> Ads are ranked by maximum bid (the "Yahoo! system").
> We have test market information showing click-through rates and conversion rates for each keyword in each ad position.

These assumptions are obviously very strong,[34] and do not hold in many situations. The real goal is to understand the logic of proper bidding before tackling these complexities. The value V in assumption 1 can be customer lifetime value. It might also be the customer acquisition cost through the next best alternative if this is less than lifetime value.

The solution works in two steps. Step 1 is to calculate the best ad position for each keyword. Once that is determined for each keyword, Step 2 computes which of these keywords to bid for.

Stage 1: Choosing the Proper Position for each Keyword

Stage 1 is a calculation for each keyword separately. It does not imply that the firm will use this keyword, but provides the necessary information to complete stage 2.

If no one else is bidding on a keyword, the firm automatically gets position 1 for the minimum allowed bid. This is currently a dime for Yahoo! in the United States, but in the United Kingdom it is ten pence (or almost twice as high with prevailing exchange rates).

If there are competitors, the firm observes competitor bids (assumption 2). As in Figure 8.18, it can compute from these bids the lowest bid it can make to obtain position 1. Likewise, it can compute the smallest bid that gets position 2, and so on for each of the positions. List these as $(b_k^{(1)}, b_k^{(2)}, ..., b_k^{(n)})$ for the n spots for keyword k. The conversion rate from visit to action for traffic following keyword ad k in position j is $CR_k^{(j)}$. The click-through rate from ad to visit is $CTR_k^{(j)}$.

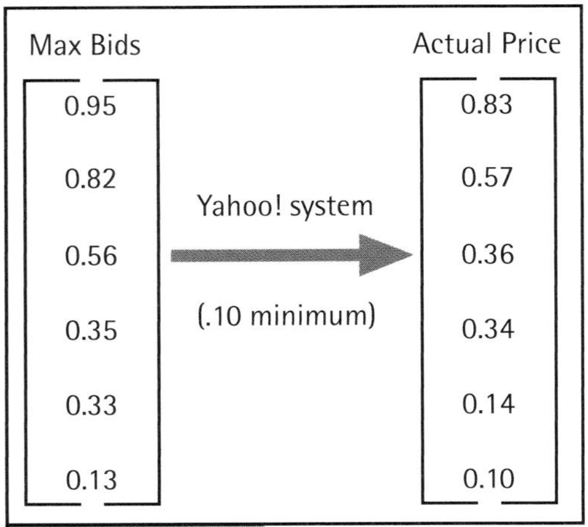

For each of these n spots, compute the expected cost-per-action for that keyword:

$$CPA_k^{(1)} = b_k^{(1)} \div CR_k^{(1)}$$

$$CPA_k^{(2)} = b_k^{(2)} \div CR_k^{(2)}$$

...

$$CPA_k^{(n)} = b_k^{(n)} \div CR_k^{(n)}$$

Only one position is possible per keyword. It is not right to choose the lowest cost-per-action ad position. Both top and lower positions may be profitable, but top positions may generate many more clicks than lower ranking ads.

Max Bids		Actual Price
0.95		0.83
0.82	Yahoo! system	0.57
0.56	→	0.36
0.35	(.10 minimum)	0.34
0.33		0.14
0.13		0.10

Figure 8.18

From Max Bids to Price

What is necessary is to calculate the expected profit per search for the keyword ad in each position:

Expected Profit per Search$_k^{(1)}$ = $(V - CPA_k^{(1)}) \times CTR_k^{(1)} \times CR_k^{(1)}$

Expected Profit per Search$_k^{(2)}$ = $(V - CPA_k^{(2)}) \times CTR_k^{(2)} \times CR_k^{(2)}$

...

Expected Profit per Search$_k^{(n)}$ = $(V - CPA_k^{(n)}) \times CTR_k^{(n)} \times CR_k^{(n)}$

The position that gives the highest expected profit per search is the best position to bid for. This can result from having an especially low cost-per-action, but it can also result from having especially high conversion rates even if the cost-per-action is somewhat higher.

> Stage 1 rule: Choose the ad position with the highest expected profit per search for that keyword. If this is position j, send $CPA_k^{(j)}$ to stage 2.

The solution in Stage 1 almost solves the keyword bidding problem. If the desired position is j for keyword k, then the right bid is either 0 or $b_k^{(j)}$. Stage 2 decides which of these two alternatives is correct for each keyword. In words, either the firm does not bid for keyword k or it bids just enough to win position j.

Stage 2: Choosing which Keywords to Buy
With Stage 1 solved for each keyword, the problem is almost solved. The Stage 2 rule is actually simpler than Stage 1. Rank all of the different keywords by cost-per-action for the chosen position for that keyword. Buy all keywords with cost-per-action lower than V.

> Stage 2 rule: Bid $b_k^{(j)}$ for all keywords with $CPA_k^{(j)} < V$, do not bid on the keyword otherwise.

Tables 8.7 and 8.8 illustrate stages 1 and 2. For the keyword "fuel pump," the data in yellow reflects the test results. For this keyword position 3 is the best location, which is not obvious from either the click-through rate or the cost-per-action. Position 3 wins by combining a low cost-per-action and sufficient volume to generate substantial benefits.

Table 8.8 shows the profitable keywords. The top three have cost-per-action below the Max CPA, the other three are above. Proper keyword bids are just the fee needed to hold that desired position for the profitable keywords, and zero otherwise.

The Stage I and Stage II logic works for both the Yahoo! and Google system, although for the Google system the cost-per-action formula and bid position assignment details change. Online tools help bidders make these adjustments.

> Complications

Competitive Responses
One of the biggest complications to the bidding process is the competitive struggle for desirable keyword positions. The advertiser previously in position 3 for fuel pump will find its ad in position 4. This might be fine. It may also lead to an increased bid high enough to regain position 3. Finding the right solution to the competitive bidding process is an area of active research. Unpublished results suggest there are multiple possible outcomes, and search engines can affect this competitive advertising battle by slightly altering their allocation rules.[35] If competitors can respond, there may be competitive reasons and search engine rules that might make the best bid

Table 8.7

Stage One for Keyword "Fuel Pump"								
V	$15.35							
Keyword Phrases: fuel pump	Clicks	Conversions	Cost per click to hold position	Test impressions	CTR	Conversion Rate	CPA by position	Expected Profit per Search
Position 1	821	29	$0.46	10,000	8.21%	3.53%	$13.02	$0.0067
Position 2	622	19	$0.38	10,000	6.22%	3.05%	$12.44	$0.0055
Position 3	603	22	$0.35	10,000	6.03%	3.65%	$9.59	$0.0127
Position 4	421	12	$0.29	5,000	8.42%	2.85%	$10.17	$0.0124
Position 5	158	4	$0.22	5,000	3.16%	2.53%	$8.69	$0.0053
Position 6	162	6	$0.21	5,000	3.24%	3.70%	$5.67	$0.0116

Table 8.8

Stage Two for Keyword Choice						
Max CPA	15.35					
Keyword Phrases	Clicks	Conversions	Cost per click to hold position	Conversion Rate	CPA	Keyword bid
Skylark fuel pump pos. 1	62	6	$0.10	9.68%	$1.03	$0.10
GM fuel pump pos. 2	148	18	$0.20	12.16%	$1.64	$0.20
Fuel pump pos. 3	603	22	$0.35	3.65%	$9.59	$0.35
Used Buick Skylark pos. 1	8678	95	$0.23	1.09%	$21.01	–
Buick pos. 3	362	15	$1.37	4.14%	$33.06	–
Used car parts pos. 2	17265	98	$0.34	0.57%	$59.90	–

for a keyword higher than just the minimum bid to obtain that position. For example, some search engines break ties between equal bids based on which firm was the first in time to raise the bid to that level. Establishing priority might lead to an "overbid."

Practitioners are used to operating without complete guidance and simple rules. Competitive responses force advertisers to actively manage bidding and keyword position choice in an iterative process. After a period of back and forth caused by a new bidder entering the fray, prices will normally settle down to a new set of values. Equilibrium occurs when all the bidders run the stage one and two procedures and no firm wants to change their keyword bids.[36]

Missing Test Data

The Stage I and II process relies on a firm knowing the click-through and conversion rates of the keywords in question. This data is only partially available, and advertisers must actively choose to collect that information. This can be further complicated if competitors are changing bids during data collection.

The various search engines provide bidding tools to make this estimation easier and less risky. Better data lets an advertiser compete with more assurance. It is likely that the major search firms will continue to improve their assistance to advertisers and make it easier for a firm to understand the productivity of new keywords and different keyword ad positions.

Value per Action Varies by Customer Segment

One of the most important and thorniest complications occurs when customers with different profitability are present in the market and keyword choice partially determines which type of customer responds. This is also an active area of research. It can affect the Stage I and II decisions.

These are not the only complications. Despite these caveats and details, the online keyword ad business provides marketers with a jump in accountability over many other advertising media and is changing the customer acquisition process.

TRAFFIC BY ASSOCIATION

Classic advertising works by association, where marketers put a company's message in front of consumers where they spend their leisure time, where they work, and where they live. Even search advertising works by putting clickable ads near results generated during information collection. Other traffic-building activities shown in Figure 8.5 work by putting the appropriate banner or link in front of individuals where they spend their time, both on and offline.

The full range of traffic-building opportunities and strategies is too wide to cover within one chapter. Chapter 6 focuses on branding, and the strong connection between domain name, brand equity, and getting people to visit a site. Repeat visits and word-of-mouth work by encouraging an existing customer to revisit a site and to spread the word. Chapter 10 covers these, focusing on loyalty-building campaigns online and through email. Chapters 13 and 14 consider retailers and manufacturers use of affiliate networks to drive shoppers to sites. Chapter 16 continues the discussion of online banner advertising, looking at how advertising campaigns find appropriate venues to place banner ads in ways that match desired demographics of online users.

Banner Ads

Banner ads were the initial online advertising format. Introduced in 1994,[37] online revenue from banners grew rapidly during the 1990s, fell sharply in 2000–2002, and is once more experiencing growth.[38] Part of this is a rebound in advertising generally, part is the growth and expansion of households with broadband, and part is the development of new formats.

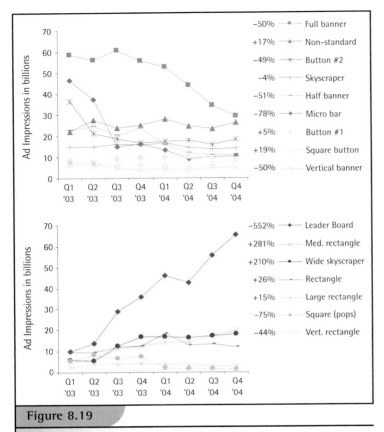

Figure 8.19

Relative Importance of Different Ad Banner Formats

Source: DoubleClick [Rick Bruner], "The Decade in Online Advertising: 1994–2004," DoubleClick (April 2005): 19.

Even after 10 years of online advertising development, there continues to be format innovation and changes in the size and shape of the most popular online ads. Figure 8.19 shows the rapid growth of "Leader Board" ads during 2003–2004.[39] These are a larger format (728 × 90) than the originally more popular full banner (468 × 60) they are displacing. Figure 8.20 illustrates the two. In addition, Leader Board ads often use animation tools such as Flash to make them more eye-catching and interactive.

Advertisers using online banners typically pay by impression, although large advertisers can sometimes negotiate pricing that blends impressions, click-through, and conversions into the pricing formula. Thus, online banner ads have some features of more traditional impression-based advertising as well as performance-based keyword advertising.

In addition to pricing and graphical layout, a major difference between online banners and keyword search ads is the context where they appear. Banner advertising occurs primarily at major portals and publishing sites. Visitors are often engaged in consuming content at the site rather than searching for external information. This leads to low attention paid to banners and low click-through rates (Figure 8.21). There are also software tools that block banner ads from displaying in the browser, making click-through impossible.

Although more sophisticated than search ads, it is still easy and relatively cheap to experiment with a wide range of forms and features within banners. This leads to rapid learning about the important factors causing higher click-through rates. Online advertisers have found higher click-through rates associated with:[40]

> Bold colors
> Top of page placement
> Animation
> Call to action
> Limited frequency of exposure

Figure 8.20

Leader Board Versus Full Banner Format

Source: © Terri Miller/E-Visual Communications Inc.

Despite improvements and innovations, the low banner click-through rates mean that banner ads need to be quite cheap in order to be cost effective. For example, according to data from DoubleClick.com, the average click-through rate for non-rich media ads during the third quarter of 2004 was .2%.[41] For the same time period, Table 8.5 showed the prevailing click-through price for a search ad was approximately $1.50. For a price per impression to result in the same price per click, the CPM rate would have to be $3 (Per impression: X = .2%* $1.50 = .003, per thousand impressions = $3). The richer and more animated the ad, the more likely there is to be a branding impact as well as a traffic generating effect. In that case, evaluating the banner campaign should normally use a web chain analysis and not a simple cost-per-action comparison. The important insight is that comparisons need to be made at the same level of analysis, and this level of analysis should be able to capture all the relevant benefits of the advertising.

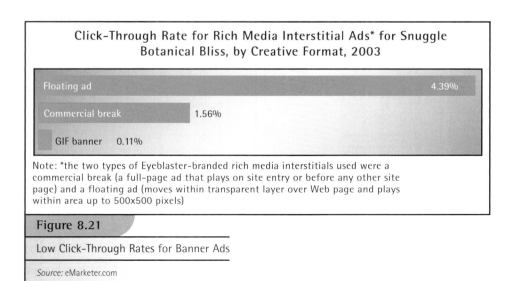

Click-Through Rate for Rich Media Interstitial Ads* for Snuggle Botanical Bliss, by Creative Format, 2003

Floating ad — 4.39%

Commercial break — 1.56%

GIF banner — 0.11%

Note: *the two types of Eyeblaster-branded rich media interstitials used were a commercial break (a full-page ad that plays on site entry or before any other site page) and a floating ad (moves within transparent layer over Web page and plays within area up to 500x500 pixels)

Figure 8.21

Low Click-Through Rates for Banner Ads

Source: eMarketer.com

Co-Branding and Placement

> *URL Placement: Bills, Machines, Bags, and Billboards*

> Software Integration

Some of the most profitable traffic leads to cost reductions rather than new revenue. As shown in Chapter 7, there are many opportunities to save money with online customer and technical support. The primary goal of traffic building in support situations is convenience. If the address is available and online support accessible and easy to use, the online site will replace the more costly phone or sales force methods.

Software companies develop this approach further than most. The proper technical support online addresses are integrated into manuals, warranty cards, and software programs. Microsoft has done this with auto update and help features in their applications and operating system. In fact, the help file in all of the Office applications automatically links into the Microsoft web page (Figure 8.22).

Building the Net into products has numerous benefits. Microsoft's activation policy works against piracy. Updates help control against security problems. Built-in help moves solutions to the cheapest channel to handle the problem. This is much better than requiring the user to find the address and manually type it into the browser.

> Consumer Communications

There are many opportunities for URL placement and inexpensive traffic-building publicity in standard consumer communications. These include shopping bags, billboards, monthly statements, catalogs, television commercials, and store signage. URLs do not have to be prominent to reach some in the audience, as seen in billboard ads used by 21st Century Insurance. With a complicated name, there is not natural parsing into a domain name. The URL on 21st Century Insurance's billboards provide the translation to 21st.com. The company uses a standard placement of

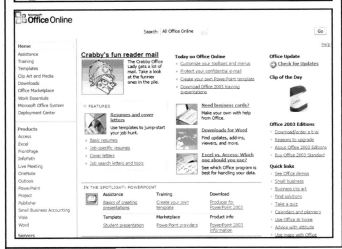

Figure 8.22

Microsoft Office Integrates Links to its Online Support Site

Source: Microsoft product screenshot(s) reprinted with permission from Microsoft Corporation.

seat belt and domain name in the corner of a number of its billboards, whether promoting safe driving or creating an image of driving the Pacific coast. This makes the domain almost part of the logo, further making the domain name and brand connection.

> *Sponsorship and Co-Branding*

Specialized portals are sites acting as a focus of industry news, activities, events, and other content. These have emerged for a wide range of topics, such as health care, real estate, and even marketing. Nonprofit organizations sponsor some, while others are explicitly commercial. Important portals acquire a leadership role within the industry, perhaps through the amount of content, a "must attend" tradeshow, or leading industry publication.

Visible links and sponsorships within these portals may be a cost-effective source of traffic. A regular column within the portal, links appearing to partner sites, or occasional stories with embedded site links all generate a certain number of clicks and visits. Sponsorship arrangements typically lack any volume guarantees. This is similar to corporate sponsorship of sporting and charity events, where the sponsor seeks goodwill and co-branding in a forum frequented by target customers leads to further visits. Online sponsorship has an added advantage of being only a click away from a visit.

Bundled access to a site provides a form of digital sponsorship. *Advertising Age* provides access to the online site and content of its magazine *Point* for subscribers to its main site and publication. It uses its advertising portal site, full of relevant marketing content and news, as a magnet for individuals interested in marketing. Rich media, such as the pop-up film clip they use, is much more noticeable with more impact than a simple banner or link. The co-brand and sponsorship can further drive traffic to additional partner sites.

All the sources of traffic in this chapter have the goal of cost-effectively driving traffic to the advertiser's web site. The ability to track these conversions, to learn what works and what doesn't, creates the opportunity for much more rapid learning than in traditional media. Traffic building is one of the best examples of the move to closed-loop marketing.

ENDNOTES

1. H.A. Simon. (1971). "Designing organizations for an information-rich world," in M. Greenberger (ed.) *Computers, Communications, and the Public Interest*. Baltimore: Johns Hopkins Press. pp. 37–52.
2. David Mamet. *Glengarry Glen Ross*. 1992.
3. Carl Bialik. (2004). "Lawyers Bid Up Value of Web-Search Ads," Wall Street Journal, Eastern Edition. New York, April 8, B.1.
4. Pew Internet Project. (2005). *Health Information Online*. April.
5. Google has a slightly more complicated rule. Bid * click-through rate.
6. As of February 2005. This reinforces the factors discussed in Chapter 7.
7. The Diamond and Water paradox dates at least to Adam Smith's *Wealth of Nations*.
"Nothing is more useful than water: but it will purchase scarce anything; scarce anything can be had in exchange for it. A diamond, on the contrary, has scarce any value in use; but a very great quantity of other goods may frequently be had in exchange for it." Book 1, Chapter IV.
8. In the language of microeconomics, the initial utility of water is much higher than for diamonds but it falls rapidly. The abundant supply makes the price of water nearly free, while the restricted supply of diamonds makes for a steep price.
9. Web pages are calculated as the number of web pages indexed by the largest search engine, as reported by SearchEngineWatch.com. This is known to be an undercount of the total number of pages online, although it is arguably the right measure for a user relying on the particular search engine. During this time interval the fraction of these pages in English appears to have remained roughly constant at about 72% of the

total. It may have fallen with the expansion of the Google index in early 2005. which is not shown in this figure.

10. Amanda Spink, Dietmar Wolfram, B.J. Jansen, and Tefko Saracevic. (2003). "Searching the Web: The Public and their Queries," *Journal of the American Society for Information Science and Technology* 52(3), 226–234.

11. For example, Susannah Fox. (2005). "Internet: The Mainstreaming of Online Life." *Pew Internet Life Project.* January.

12. An internal study by metrics company WebSideStory in 2003 found that 65.5% of users either type the name into the browser address bar or use a book-mark. This is an increase from 58% in the preceding year. The fraction typically rises with the strength of the brand, and falls off for more generic sites or lesser known brands. Brian Morrissey. (2003). "Search Guiding More Web Activity." *Clickz News.* March 12.

13. See additional discussion in Chapter 14.

14. CNN Money. (2004). "Cheney directs surfers to anti-Bush site." October 6.

15. For more discussion, see Juhnyoung Lee and Mark Podlasceck. (2000). "Using a Starfield Visualization for Analyzing Product Performance of Online Stores." *EC'00 ACM,* October. J. Lee, M. Podlascek, Edith Schonberg, Robert Hoch, and Stephen Gomory. (2000). "Analysis and Visualization of Metrics for Online Merchandising," *WEBKDD'99,* in B. Masand and M. Spiliopoulou (ed). Springer-Verlag: Berlin, New York: 126–141. J. Lee, M. Podlaseck, E. Schonberg, and R. Hoch. (2001). "Visualization and Analysis of Clickstream Data of Online Stores for Understanding Web Merchandizing." *Data Mining and Knowledge Discovery* 5, 59–84.

16. For example, Wendy W. Moe and Peter S. Fader. (2004). "Capturing Evolving Visit Behavior in Clickstream Data," *Journal of Interactive Marketing* 18(1), 5–19. Wendy Moe and Peter Fader. "Dynamic Conversion Behavior at E-Commerce Sites." *Management Science* 50(3), 326–335.

17. The Link Harvester tool, hosted at several loca-tions online.

18. Alexa.com. May 30. 2005.

19. Robert Blattberg, Gary Getz, Jacquelyn Thomas. (2001). "Customer Equity: Building and Managing Relationships as Valuable Assets." *Harvard Business School Press*

20. Gupta. Sunil, Donald R. Lehmann, and Jennifer Ames Stuart. (2004). "Valuing Customers," *Journal of Marketing Research* 41(1).

21. SEMPO study.

22. Compared to IAB total for 2005.

23. A simple keyword search campaign can begin in under 10 minutes, with a $5 initialization fee.

24. Discussion of providing services, alliances, out sourcing, etc. from the search engine watch page.

25. Number 1 on 2/5/05, number 2 on 6/2/05.

26. Meta tags are part of the HTML description of a web page, and can viewed with the "View Source" command of a browser.

27. An example is the Spider simulator, provided at se-spider.com.

28. Carl Kaplan. (1999). "Former Playboy Model Wins Right to Use Keywords." *New York Times* December 17.

29. In June 2005.

30. Data from Fathom Online, compiled monthly.

31. "Google, Yahoo! fade on soft ad-spend," *Financial Express.* India. June 8.

32. If we knew the average price per keyword overall all ads clicked, it would be roughly 4 billion/ average price per click. An average of $1 per click. which is probably too high, would mean 4 billion visits generated.

33. June 5, 2005.

34. There are also some additional technical assump-tions necessary given the specific rules of each of the search engines, but the essentials of the argu-ment stay the same.

35. Author personal discussion with Hal Varian and Mark Schwartz, both of the University of California—Berkeley.

36. This is then a Nash equilibrium in multiple key-word prices.

37. Recall the first banner ad, shown in Figure 6.3.

38. Doubleclick cite. IAB cite.

39. Rick Bruner. (2005). *The Decade in Online Advertising: 1994–2004.* DoubleClick. April.

40. Net Results. p. 290.

41. http://www.doubleclick.com/us/knowledge_central

chapter 9

Personalization

> 66 It is the customer who deter- 99
> mines what a business is.
>
> Peter Drucker[1]

> 66 The rediscovery of the customer 99
> is a byproduct—perhaps the most
> important one—of the onset of
> the information revolution.
>
> Robert Blattberg and Rashi Glazer[2]

Personal Procrastination Defense

People procrastinate, especially when it comes to topics like retirement.[3] Young people feel the time is so distant, and current needs so pressing, that they can worry about retirement another day. This procrastination has real impacts. Individuals do not begin to save for retirement until well into their working lives, and they show a tendency to ignore advice about the importance of an early beginning to their savings plan. Relatively modest savings early can lead to very large differences in eventual wealth. Despite the large benefits of starting early, tax advantages that promote savings, and serious issues about the eventual solvency of corporate and public retirement plans, individual retirement savings in the United States is too low.

Individuals that do open retirement savings accounts tend to under-manage them. One problem is status quo bias. Individuals tend to leave things alone, staying with whatever they have set up. One study found that for members of TIAA-CREF, a retirement plan especially geared to university employees, the median number of changes in investment allocations throughout their lifetime of work was zero. That is, whatever choices an individual made when they first began work was the same split of investments they had when they retired. Even very basic financial planning would suggest this is bad, and it creates too much risk for people as they near retirement.

Personalization reflects the fundamental idea in marketing that customers want a product or service that best matches their needs. The Web can serve as the matchmaker that discovers and delivers personal information and individualized products. This chapter discusses how personalization benefits consumers and how companies can best implement personalization.

Topics covered in this chapter include:

> **Personalized Savings**

> **Personalization Benefits**

> **Personalization Approaches**

> > Mass customization

> > Choice assistance

> > Personalized messaging

Different solutions to these problems are possible. One plan showing success is to take advantage of individual inertia and downplaying the future by encouraging workers to create an automatic savings plan out of any future raises. Workers find this easy to do, as a future raise seems about as elusive as getting old. Employees that adopt this plan end up with substantially larger savings than similar groups without the plan's commitment, even though someone in the plan can change their mind at any time and can choose to consume their raise. In this case, inertia results in higher savings.

Online personalization systems provide a different solution to the inertia and status quo problems. Companies are delivering individualized investment advice and automatic investment actions. Rather than rely on the individual to do something they are reluctant and bad at doing, this approach combines modern financial theory with automated online personalized recommendations and actions.

A core reason an individual faces challenges with investment planning is the complexity of the choices involved. Investors face hundreds of possible mutual funds, each with tens or hundreds of

stocks, bonds, or other investments. There are complicated differences in taxes, fees, risk, and reward. Any individual trying to deal with these faces a daunting task. Many just do nothing.

One approach is to rely on endorsement—highly rated investments get five stars, signaling good management. This helps, but is not enough. One of the main retirement goals is diversification. An individual investor has difficulty determining the overlap and differences between different funds. There are different goals depending on someone's income, age, and other goals in life. Somehow, a system must combine an in-depth knowledge of the marketplace with attention to individual personal hopes and limitations.

This is the task of Financial Engines. Its goal is to take the sophistication of big Wall Street investors and use it to help individuals do a better job of handling their retirement accounts. For many of its customers the service is part of an employee's benefits program. A company such as Hewlett-Packard pays the annual fees for Financial Engines to handle employees' retirement accounts. Individuals can also purchase the service themselves.

The system needs two major types of information before making recommendations. First, an individual answers questions about tolerance for risk, goals for retirement, and other future financial needs such as buying a house. Second, the individual provides data on current financial holdings. This lets the system calculate current wealth and allocation into the underlying specific

Source: Courtesy of Financial Engines

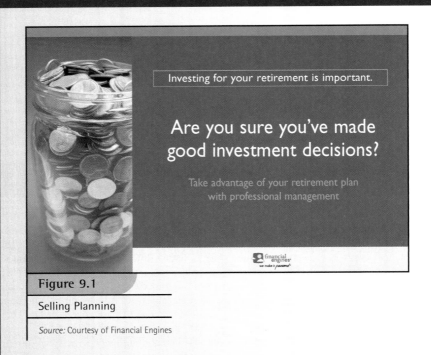

Figure 9.1

Selling Planning

Source: Courtesy of Financial Engines

stocks, bonds, and other investment types. With this detailed knowledge, the system can compute the best adjustments to the current holdings to match the future goals.

This type of information is highly sensitive and requires subscribers to place a great deal of trust in Financial Engines. Endorsement by an employer helps. Other methods of establishing trust and credibility are evident on the web site. A list of current companies hiring Financial Engines to provide advice to their employees include some of the largest and most well-respected entities, including IBM, Kraft, Merck, Nestle USA, the State of Colorado, Visa, Xerox, and numerous financial institutions. This customer list establishes that these highly visible and professionally run corporations that place trust in the service. Endorsement through the credibility of the founders (including a Nobel Prize winner in financial economics), key employees, and advisers further reinforces the competence and sophistication of the system.

Some potential users may be much more distrustful of a purely online system for serious advice, and instead may be more comfortable with routine interactions. Financial Engines addresses this by letting the individual choose to receive information online, by paper, or by phone. They emphasize customer satisfaction statistics. The company's privacy policy is prominent, with simple and clear promises and additional in-depth information.

All that any financial plan can do is improve the chances of reaching some financial goal or objective; it does not guarantee success. One of the most interesting and difficult challenges confronting providers of financial advice is a method of communicating complex messages about risk and likelihood of success. After experimenting with methods of conveying this information, Financial Engines settled on the image of a weather report. Users realize that a weather report is helpful, but is still subject to uncertainty. When Financial Engines concludes that a customer is likely to achieve their goal, the resulting advice shows a high probability of success and a bright sunny day. As the odds of achieving the retirement goals fall, the sunny day turns to partly cloudy or cloudy. When odds are bad due to savings being too low or goals too high, the probability is low and the forecast is rainy.

Personalized and intuitive messages help in recruitment of participation. As part of explaining the service to employees of two major corporations providing Financial Engines as a benefit, personalized snapshots of employee savings rates were provided in the form of stop lights. Green indicated on track, yellow meant insufficient savings, and red showed a serious issue. Participation in the program was more than twice as high in response to this individual message compared to non-personalized appeals.[4]

The Financial Engines system demonstrates many of the features of an online personalization system. It works by combining individualized data with extensive knowledge of the products and services in the marketplace. It combines this with theory and empirical results to create appropriate advice. It presents these in a way that is helpful and understandable. An individual can improve their own choices and results by utilizing a personalization system better at sorting through complicated data to match results to their desires.

PERSONALIZATION BENEFITS

Why Personalization?

Marketing has the responsibility within a firm to reflect customers' goals, needs, and wants. Many tools exist to identify these, including sales calls, surveys, focus groups, test markets, trial samples, and statistical analysis of purchase data. Results from these studies reveal opportunities for new designs and features, as well as show recent failures.

Despite understanding individual differences and the heterogeneity of their customer base, marketers have always had to settle for compromise product and marketing solutions. Companies have thousands, even millions, of customers. They are all somewhat different, with different locations, different purchasing histories, and different preferences. When the costs of product variation are high, as was the case in the mass-market era, these differences are often ignored.

Modern retailing and "big box" stores compete on variety, supporting brand proliferation and variation. This product segmentation creates more choices for individuals, and a dramatically expanded product space can better reflect differences in consumer tastes. The market leader in the United States is Wal-Mart, with its supercenters. These stores average 180,000 square feet and carry an extremely large variety of products ranging from groceries to housewares to pharmacy products. Even a traditional large supermarket carries more than 50,000 unique products on its shelves.[5] In addition to the price savings these large retailers bring to the marketplace,[6] consumers benefit from the increased assortment they offer (as in Figure 9.2). Chapter 13 discusses the benefits the Internet brings in increasing consumer choice and product assortment over even these large supercenters, but supercenters increase choice and consumer benefits over traditional outlets. The market success and rapid growth of this format demonstrates that consumers enjoy both the low prices and the wide range of choices.

Figure 9.2

Product Assortment Has Exploded in the Marketplace

Source: © Lon C. Diehl/Photo Edit

Personalization is a special form of product differentiation. It transforms a standard product or service into a specialized solution for an individual. It changes product design from an inherent compromise to a process of deciding what features would benefit a specific individual. It changes the marketing message from one targeting the average consumer of a broad segment to one reflecting specific individual wants and situation. It can better focus the timing and specificity of the message by triggering communication based on a specific individual's actions. Combined with innovative distribution, it can do a better job of matching consumer tastes without the waste of the current approach.

Personalization is a direct implication of the three general purpose technologies in the DNI framework. Digital technology and computerization makes it possible. Without the power and flexibility of digital technologies, the calculations and data storage underlying personalization could not work. Networking capabilities allow individual data to be used and personal choices communicated to a firm for next to no cost. Individualization technologies create the ability to track, store, verify, and learn an individual's preferences over time. This better matches individual taste while protecting against inappropriate influence and loss of privacy.

The "Democracy of Goods"

Personalized service has always been a sign of luxury and status.[7] Royalty has servants. Personal bankers and private shopping services cater to the wealthy. Movie stars have personal assistants.[8] Well-to-do exercisers hire personal trainers. Top executives in business and government have long used specialized news clipping services to provide focused stories on their areas of interest. They avoid reading irrelevant stories and can read more about what interests them. The pinnacle of this is the president of the United States, who receives a clipping service and briefing book on world issues every morning. Stories are organized and prioritized, with recommendations for action provided by the staff on the most pressing issues.[9]

Personalized goods are also a trademark of the elite. Only the wealthy can afford the cost of personally designed and handmade goods. Original dresses from a top designer cost tens of thousands of dollars. Commissioned art and music has been the province of princes and kings for centuries. Artists approached the courts of Europe and Asia for sponsorship. Musicians such as Mozart and Beethoven were dependent on the courts of Austria and Germany for their patronage.[10]

One of the promises of the Internet is open and low-cost access to personalized service and advice over a much wider range of products, services, and income levels. In the 1920s, this was a commonly advertised benefit of mass production. The factory system had the power to make "Kings in Cottages," who could consume "soap as good as royalty."[11] Technology can now make personalization cheap, as it can be automated, made virtual, and can leverage existing digital assets. Personalization is no longer the sole province of the wealthy.[12]

Turning Experience Goods into Search Goods

Recommendation systems can help a user transform experience goods into search goods.[13] Search goods are products and services that are easy for a consumer to evaluate. A search good is neither good nor bad. A search good is predictable. A consumer can predict benefits and value from a search good with high accuracy. Experience goods, on the other hand, are difficult to judge and evaluate. Products and services can be too complex to judge easily. Different providers may have widely varying skills, capabilities, and expectations. Experience goods may be highly subjective, with personal taste being the most important determinant of usefulness.

Well-known branded products are the most important types of search goods. Gasoline from Texaco, six packs of Coke from different retailers, or a pair of Levi's 501 jeans are closely specified, familiar, and dependable items. When consumers buy a search good, they know what they are getting. Franchised services are an important class of search goods. A visit to McDonald's, Jiffy Lube, or 7-Eleven is highly predictable anywhere in the country. Anyone who has consumed the product or used the service in the past will find another outlet familiar. Unbranded products can be near-search goods if purchasers can test and verify their characteristics with little difficulty. Many agricultural products fit into this category. Simple tests of their composition allow rapid grading and proper classification. Buyers use specifications to create homogeneous commodities.

Services are often experience goods. Health care, dental care, hair stylists, and contractors are just some of the many examples where performance and quality are hard to judge. These services are unstandardized and unique. Even consuming the service may not be enough. A doctor may normally be an excellent diagnostician but lack a critical piece of knowledge to identify a particular disease. A restaurant may look dubious but have wonderful food. A particular dish may sound perfect but end up too spicy or too bland. The first step in providing help is better establishing the quality and understanding of the restaurant such as is accomplished on Zagat.com with rankings and reviews for restaurants around the globe.

Experience goods are especially hard to judge when they are a complex mixture of variety and quality attributes. Everyone wants more quality attributes. In the case of a computer, speed and durability are both quality attributes. Variety attributes stem from different people liking different things. Choosing a health plan is one such complex choice. There are absolute levels of quality that all consumers want more of. There can also be differences in medical philosophy, location, and service schedules. Different consumers can have different desires for these attributes.

The personalization techniques discussed later in the chapter help consumers choose among experience goods. The goal of these approaches is to provide reliable advice about which products to choose and which to avoid. In almost all cases, consumers benefit from reducing their uncertainty about experience goods. An accurate personalization system with an effective way of matching products to tastes can eliminate many unpleasant consumption experiences. Consumers can find movies that they want to rent, books that they enjoy reading, music that they like, and restaurants that match their tastes in food and price.

Turning experience goods into search goods has a complicated impact on firms. It helps high-quality firms build their user base. It also helps low-cost but adequate quality firms find their target customers. At the same time, it can reduce the value of brand and tradition and speed up word of mouth.

| Personalization and the Total Product

> *Levitt and the Source of New Features*

Theodore Levitt and his writings have strongly influenced marketing. One of his classic articles was "Marketing Success through Differentiation—of Anything."[14] In this essay, he gave several insights about differentiating products and services, including:

> There are no commodities. Any product can be customized and made special.
> Products are "problem-solving tools." Think about how different consumers have different problems.
> There is a bias toward emphasizing the measurable. Measurable features may be over-emphasized. Hard to measure parts of a product, such as fun or friendliness, may be ignored.
> Marketers need to make the intangible tangible. Consumers need signals that show them how good and reliable a company is.

Levitt pointed out that all products and services are combinations of features and possibilities. Only the most basic parts of products are commodities. This commodity core is surrounded by increasingly larger rings of differentiation opportunities, the expected and the augmented products.

> *The Total Product in Banking*

While Levitt's arguments point the way toward differentiation opportunities, technological and regulatory change can move an industry away from traditional forms of differentiation and can make product reinvention necessary for survival. This has been the experience of the banking system in the United States during the past 25 years. Deregulation allowed banks to expand and enter new markets. As new technology diffused, involving both consumer interaction and consumer credit-scoring, there has been a wave of consolidation.[15] In just 10 years, the number of banks in the United States declined from roughly 12,000 to 8,000. During the same decade, electronic banking grew rapidly. First, ATMs made consumer visits to a branch less necessary, and then in the late 1990s the rapid growth in banking web sites made a wide range of services available from home or work.

Available individual data makes it possible for large banks to effectively loan money to individuals without the face-to-face knowledge of many small community bankers. Credit-scoring models, using individual credit histories, take much of the judgment and guesswork out of lending for mortgages, autos, or other needs. Measured in importance rather than just number of banks, banking concentration is even more dramatic. From 1980 to 2001, the share of total banking assets controlled by the 10 largest bank holding companies grew from 28% to 76%.[16] Technology allows just a few large banks to serve most of the consumers in the country.

> The Checking Account

With all the electronic and personalized banking capabilities, what constitutes the core, expected, and augmented product is changing rapidly. While direct deposit and ATMs used to be part of the augmented product, for many it is now part of the expected or even core essentials of a checking account. Similarly, the ability to download records electronically has moved from the augmented to the expected.

Levitt argues that the creativity of marketers enters with the augmented product. These new features distinguish different banks from each other. Personalization is a rich area for augmenting the total product. Banking strategists are looking intently at personalized services for online checking. One idea is financial alerts. Rather than waiting for a check to bounce before notification (and penalty), the consumer creates an alert level that triggers a fax or an email message. An alert can signal a missed deposit. While an alert for a payroll check may be unnecessary, a missed alimony payment is all too common. Online expense reporting is another example. Banks are investigating cross-selling possibilities, with personalized offers of loans, insurance, and other financial arrangements triggered by a request or by another customer action.[17]

> Making Online Banking Tangible

Levitt's final point, making intangible benefits tangible, is a difficult challenge for online marketers. Traditionally, a bank illustrated its trustworthiness and stability through architecture, marble, and plush surroundings. This atmosphere combined with conservative business dress provided assurance and comfort that the customer's money was in good hands. In the online world, making features tangible is harder.

Security, reliability, performance, and design can reinforce or jeopardize trust in the bank.[18] Concern is especially high among Web novices. An industry found that with consumers with a year or less online, only 18% viewed Web-based banking as safe.[19]

Personalization can help here as well. One of the most convincing demonstrations of the abilities of FedEx and UPS to handle packages is their package-tracking services. It is a tangible commitment to excellence to be able to track any package in real time throughout the

Does One Electronic Tool Lead to Another?

The figure below shows the rapid rise in ATM usage in the United States during the 1990s, followed by the beginning of a steep rise in transactional banking web sites. Part of this is just the timing of the inventions. A further study suggests that it reflects more important underlying variables.

In a study using detailed individual level data, researchers find that previous exposure to ATMs and other electronic banking techniques made consumers significantly more likely to adopt automatic online bill payment. While the most natural explanation is a sample effect, where early adopters try both technologies first, this study did control for a number of early adopter characteristics (such as age, income, education, and region).

High involvement personalization, such as online bill payment, may require the learning and comfort afforded by previous usage of simpler techniques. While it may be possible to recruit sophisticated users from rival banks, it may be hard to move newly online users all the way to personalized bill payment without a transitional period. Previous experience sets the stage for personalization.

Sources: R. DeYoung, W. Hunter, and G. Udell, "The Past, Present and Probably Future for Community Banks," *Journal of Financial Services Research* 25, no. 2/3 (2004): 85–133; and J. Kolodinsky, J. Hogarth, and M. Hilgert, "The Adoption of electronic banking technologies by US consumers," *International Journal of Bank Marketing* 22, no. 4 (2004): 238–259.

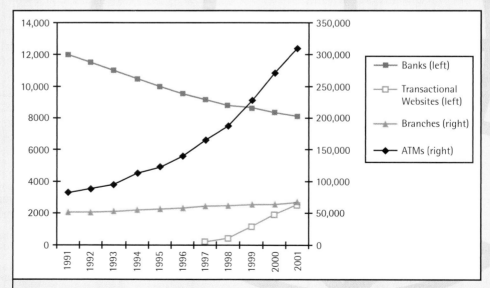

Source: R. DeYoung, W. Hunter, and G. Udell, "The Past, Present and Probably Future for Community Banks," *Journal of Financial Services Research* 25, no. 2/3 (2004): 85–133.

system. This makes the care and information systems seem real. Banks and checking accounts can follow a similar approach by creating methods of demonstrating their care and attention to the money and investments of their customers. Individualized reports that are current and accurate for each customer provide a strong signal to customers of the more intangible levels of the bank's commitments.

> *Adding Switching Costs to Goods*

One source of customer loyalty and competitive advantage arising from personalization is the increasing level of switching costs that an effective personalized system generates. Over time, and with learning and customization, a current service becomes both superior and different from alternatives.[20] This creates a difficult challenge in comparing alternatives, in judging how quickly a new service will adapt, and perhaps a feeling of regret for the amount of time and effort already expended on the current system.[21]

There are many examples of this with online banking. Once a user enters different merchants into the system, complete with user name and account numbers, one-click bill payment is possible. However, a new service requires a different configuration and re-entry of the merchant names and addresses. Increasing the number of accounts and personalized services provided raises switching costs and builds loyalty.

Many of the social networking services, such as Linked In, Face Book, Friendster, and others, increasingly create a barrier to leaving the service. Once friends agree to create a group (Figure 9.3), coordinating a switch to a new service or jumping on one's own becomes a challenge. There is even more inertia when friends belong to multiple and varied groups.

As language recognition becomes an ever more important part of the online interface, personalized training or mobile profiles are necessary for speech-recognition. Unless users train a system on the particular nuances of their voices and equipment, accuracy is very low. Once trained, an alternative approach becomes less attractive. This is especially true if the training is tedious and unproductive, and the system performance is unacceptable without this commitment.

Figure 9.3

Personalized Groups Create Switching Costs

Source: © Colin Hawkins/Stone/Getty Images

| The Personalization Balance

> *Providing Useful Features*

One of the challenges of personalization is determining the proper scale and scope of the activity. The capacity to provide almost unlimited information exists, but consumers do not have unlimited ability or time to process information. One challenge for online marketers is determining what kinds and scope of information consumers will value and use.

Consumer information programs that balance costs and benefits are the most effective. Research has shown that consumers respond better to information programs that properly balance the costs and benefits of using the system. Merely providing new information or just reducing the costs of using information is not enough. The information program should scale consumer difficulties and effort of use against the benefits of the information.

One extensive study of this issue looked at three broad categories of information that could be provided[22]:

> Offer new information to consumers (raise benefits to consumers of using the system)
> Reduce the effort of using existing information (lower costs to consumers)
> Remind consumers to use existing information

Each of these approaches could conceivably help consumers achieve their goals.

None of these three approaches was necessarily successful. The third type, reminding consumers of information they already should know, was notably unsuccessful. In areas such as energy conservation and better nutrition, it was rarely beneficial simply to remind people. This was true even if the programs were extensive and involved a wide range of media.

What mattered most was the particular ratio of costs and benefits to a particular individual. Consumers judged the information programs by their efficiency. Large costs of use are acceptable if the program provides large expected benefits. Even small costs were unacceptable if there were no perceived reasons for using the information.

Personal goals are important predictors of success. Although hard to structure and deliver, researchers found that programs that led consumers to set personal targets and objectives were much more successful. Personalized benefits and goals were much more important than the scale of the information programs. Simple scale and scope of information programs do not lead consumers to take the time to use the information for better decisions.

> *Profitable Personalization*

The best customers of a firm often receive extra care. One of the most common approaches is the use of frequency marketing and continuity programs. Examples include the frequent-flyer programs of airlines, the "gold service" and "premier" plans of hotels and rental cars, and the discount shopping cards of retailers and supermarkets. These continuity programs work to acquire and reward the best customers. By creating a personalized system for tracking usage, customers are encouraged to concentrate their purchases with one firm. This can be very profitable if it attracts the high lifetime profitability customers.

In business-to-business marketing, we see this in the sales force structure. The largest and most important customers are deemed "national accounts" or "key accounts." These key accounts receive dedicated salespeople who pay close attention to their needs. Companies often keep some sales and support staff at the key accounts locations, so they are available when needed.

Personalization, when it works, expands these best customer benefits to a wider range of the customer base. How strongly this boosts profits will vary by application and firm. The success-to-date of personalization as a technology for building competitive advantage and raising profits is somewhat controversial. While most studies find that customer satisfaction and closeness to the customer improves results,[23] there is still debate concerning the role of personalization.[24] Different researchers put a different emphasis on the technical versus the organizational sources of customer-relating capability. Like so many other applications of technology, the best results often require companies to re-organize, train their people, and adapt their business processes to the strengths and weaknesses of the technology. Personalization appears to have the biggest competitive advantage when supported by a widespread dedication by the company to customer-relating capabilities (CRC).

Figure 9.4 shows one representation of how better CRC (including personalization) causes a company to do better than competitors. By improving CRC and matching it with a strategy geared toward customer relationships (motivation and thrust) the firm gains a better position in the marketplace, as well as better performance than its rivals. There are positive influences on both their ability to relate to customers and product features and benefits. These have a positive impact on sales growth, customer retention, and profitability.

One factor not represented in Figure 9.4 is the impact of personalization on improved word of mouth and customer acquisition. As discussed in previous chapters, the most motivated sources of word of mouth are the extremely pleased and the most dissatisfied. When personalization works well, it provides an inducement to share the experience with friends and colleagues. The social connection, as with companies such as Friendster, works well in conjunction with personalization. Personalized service also has something of a "wow factor" when it sorts through millions of possible offerings and suggests something that is highly valuable.

> *Personalization Backlash*

Companies must be careful to be sensitive and realistic about personalization. A natural result of personalization is treating consumers differently. Individuals receive products with different

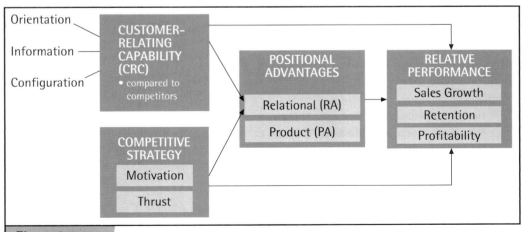

Figure 9.4

Building Competitive Advantage with Customer Capabilities

Source: George Day and Christophe Van den Bulte, "Superiority in Customer Relationship Management: Consequences for Competitive Advantage and Performance," working paper, Wharton School, September 2002.

features. Valuable consumers receive upgrades, special benefits, and preferential treatment. Alliance partners of a firm may also recognize the special status that these highly valued customers have with the company.

A backlash among customers who do not receive this special treatment can happen. Some customers resent that they are not "gold" or "preferred" or "premier" customers. This can cause a sizable chunk of the customer base to feel disadvantaged and underappreciated. Consumers may resent those "more equal" than themselves.

Preferred programs in the physical world are highly visible. Airline passengers see executive premier passengers board the plane first and sit in seats that are more comfortable. Everyone on a rental car shuttle bus sees gold customers dropped off first at their cars, which are already waiting for them. While this distinction may induce some customers to upgrade to preferred status, it can also be a constant and annoying reminder. As one customer commented to researchers, "I spend a lot of money here, too. I should be a valued customer. Instead, the company is making me feel like chopped liver. It made me really mad."[25]

Preventing resentment and backlash may be easier online. Online preferred programs are less visible. With dynamic pages and registration, the level of treatment appropriate to a particular customer is visible only to that customer. Online flexibility can also support smoother upgrades and transitions. Increments in business can cause immediate increments in features and benefits. This may reduce resentment, as the gap in treatment is not as large and some volume benefits are available to all customers.

Companies must be realistic in their expectations of the importance of personalized service. Among many customers and in many product categories, standard products are fine. It is unrealistic to expect consumers to respond to personalization of all of the products and services that they buy. Excessive personalization is cumbersome, confusing, and wastes user time. Personalization must have value to justify the information flow between customer and company. Standardization may be fine for routine and simple products.

PERSONALIZATION APPROACHES

| Overview

This section considers three aspects of personalization and how to implement them. These are mass customization, choice assistance, and personalized messaging. Figure 9.5 highlights these personalization opportunities: (1) the product or service itself, (2) the web site where the customer interacts, and (3) communication and messaging that reaches the customer through a variety of channels and media.[26] After understanding the context for personalization, the rest of the chapter focuses on implementation.

At the heart of all three of these personalization opportunities is the ability of the Net to provide direct communication. Mass customization builds on the ability of the Net to provide low-cost dialogue. Choice assistance and recommendation systems use the full multimedia suite of online interaction to better understand user preferences and provide advice. The communication and messaging choices can be refined to reflect individual nuances of personality, timing, or access device.

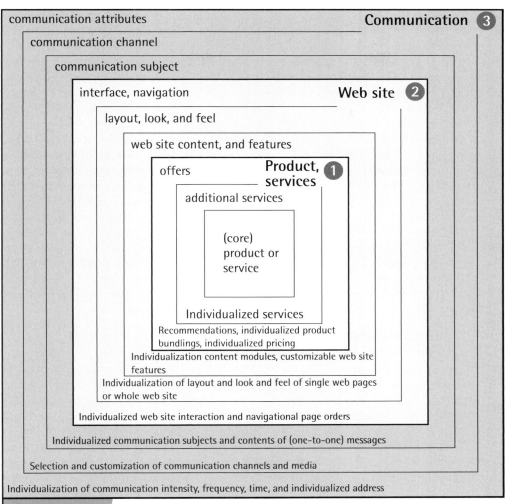

Figure 9.5

The Many Opportunities for Customization and Personalization

Source: Adapted from Kai Riemer and Carsten Totz, "The many faces of personalization—an integrative overview of mass customization and personalization," in M.M. Tseng and F.T. Piller, *The Customer Centric Enterprise: Advances in Mass Customization and Personalization*, S. 35–50 (New York/Berlin: Springer Verlag, 2003).

> *Mass Customization*

Mass customization combines individual-level information and modular production to "the production of goods and services for a relatively large market, which meet exactly the needs of each individual customer with regard to certain product characteristics ... at costs roughly corresponding to those of standard mass-produced goods."[27] Companies in widespread industries such as automobiles, eyeglasses, chemical supplies, and food products delay the final steps of product design and manufacturing until individual choices, tastes, and behavior shape the offering. Through clever design and accurate information, this produces a huge range of potential offerings at competitive costs.

With customization, marketing moves closer to individual consumer satisfaction. By incorporating actual individual preferences and behavior, it more closely reflects the "voice of the customer" into the actual product formulation. Consumers value high variety, where a marketer satisfies both unique needs and tastes that vary over time.[28] Mass customization creates a near infinite number of alternatives.

The Internet is an essential piece of the customization puzzle. The fundamental problem facing many companies trying to customize is accurate, timely, and relevant individual customer information. By providing a direct connection between manufacturers and final customers, companies now have an efficient method of collecting the data they need to power customization. British Airways combines the Web, information collected during the flight, and special software to customize flights for their best travelers. This includes meals, seating, and magazines that match the travelers' tastes.[29]

The connection is even stronger for online services. Online services can implement an advanced version of mass customization. Using specialized software and sophisticated rules, it is possible to deliver truly unique and dynamically personalized web sites in real time. These range from personal windows on information, such as at Yahoo! and Google, to customized software configurations reflecting someone's roles and responsibilities in an organization.

> *Choice Assistance*

The huge array of consumer products and services in the marketplace can be dysfunctional. Providing enough information for consumers to find their preferred product is not easy. The clutter of products leads to a clutter of messages. Broadcast methods work poorly; they are expensive and clumsy. The result is high distribution costs, widespread customer trial, and high levels of customer switching.

Personalization helps consumers deal with this explosion of product variants. An impersonal assortment of products and services can be a headache rather than a resource. Whether it is digital television and 500 possible channels, personal music archives of thousands of songs, grocery shelves with 75,000 choices, online bookstores with millions of titles, or astronomical numbers of configurations of investment portfolios, consumers need help in making intelligent choices. Advice-giving systems combining extensive product category data and a model of the individual's tastes can do better than an individual acting on their limited time and market knowledge.

With online streaming and sales, music is more available than ever. Exposure to new music can result in additional areas of interest, as well as confusion about what choices are best. An example of choice assistance is the Jazz Discovery service at the Barnes & Noble web site (Figure 9.6). Beginners can sample sounds and styles, and can build from what they like to suggestions about artists and albums. The provider of the service, Savage Beast Technologies, is expanding its music recommendations to suggest similar styles and artists based on 400 underlying characteristics of specific songs.[30] Other services base the suggestions on feedback from other users, creating an automated word of mouth. Both approaches are discussed later in the chapter.

One of the challenges and opportunities for recommendation systems is avoiding the best seller and suggesting appropriate back catalog and slow-selling items. Without care, most statistical systems suggest the leading titles and most popular choices. Not only is this

Figure 9.6

Finding Music

Source: Courtesy of Barnes and Noble.com

simplistic, it can lead to a herd mentality and aggressive competition for the top sellers. Systems that tilt toward the appropriate off-topic[31] and cold seller[32] can create choices that are more effective, avoid me-too offerings, and take much better advantage of the wide online assortment.

As seen in Chapters 12 through 14, traditional channels of distribution and retailing still dominate commerce. A desk-based personalization system creates a mismatch between the location of choice (in a store) and access to a personalization system (at a desk). Mobile personalization systems, based on wireless Web access, create a closer connection between advice and decision. Mobile systems, especially with location awareness, can offer reminders about close proximity products, suggestions about available specials, on-demand product reviews and comparisons, price checking against other stores, and personalized and efficient interfaces while on the road.[33]

> *Personalized Interaction*

When a company and a customer have ongoing interactive connections, it makes sense to call it a relationship. Relationship marketing seeks to satisfy a customer's needs over repeated use.[34] It takes choice assistance and customization as a basis for loyal and committed customers. When successful, customers are satisfied and profits are high.

A central ability for appropriate online support of customer relationships is the timing and content of interactions. Too frequent or irrelevant chatter is annoying. Delay in responding is also a problem. Matching the timing of messages requires both an effective model of customer interests and information triggers. These trigger events are normally revealing actions taken by the customer that help a marketer understand immediate needs.

Although increasingly difficult to accomplish, automotive companies hope for ongoing relationships and long-term customer relationships. Within a vehicle's life, profit is much higher when regular maintenance and upkeep using the dealer's facilities follows new car sales. As a consumer matures through different life events, such as parenting and rising income, auto companies hope to offer trade-ups and movement throughout their product line.

General Motors has devoted considerable time and effort in its online presence, including sponsoring research into building trust and loyalty online. Their Owner Center is one example of the results, where a personal connection based on the specific vehicle forms the basis of customized information and interaction (Figure 9.7). Other companies are pursuing these goals as well.[35] The hope is for increased customer loyalty. Proper messaging and proper timing help to achieve this goal.

| Mass Customization

> *Representation and Product Changes*

A framework developed by Gilmore and Pine helps understand mass customization and the role of online interactions. They emphasize two key customer-facing dimensions of mass customization, the representation of the product and the underlying product attributes. Representation is how the company portrays a product or service to the customer. Customization through representation creates a tie between an individual and the packaging, positioning, and imagery used to describe the product. This can be as simple as occasionally using a customer's name, or as complicated as a complete reorganization of information to reflect personal preferences. Product

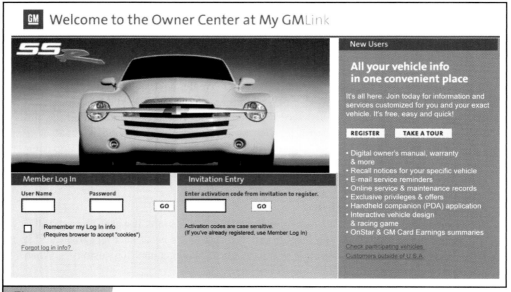

Figure 9.7

Building a Relationship through Personalized Service

Source: General Motors Corp. Used with permission, GM Media Archives

and service attributes are the other customization dimension. Customization can create unique functionality, targeting the specific preferences or behavior of an individual. Product or service specifications change, not just the information linked to the individual.

Figure 9.8 divides these choices into four boxes. Adaptive customization occurs when there is minimal change in either representation or product, yet features of the product naturally customize themselves to the user or can be configured and programmed separately by users to better match needs. In cosmetic mass customization, the emphasis on personalization occurs through the descriptions, packaging, and representation of the product. Transparent customization is the other corner, where no representation changes occur, yet product features do through learning about the consumer. Collaborative customization combines changes in both product and representation to best configure product and information.

Online support for mass customization occurs for physical products configured online, for services ordered online, for digital products created through online interaction, and for the online web site interactions themselves. In all of these situations, there must also be an underlying production and distribution system capable of handling the many possible variations created through mass customization. Chapter 11 discusses the fundamental role of modularity and standards in detail. These are also at the heart of mass customization.

> *Collaborative Customization*

The easiest form of customization to notice online is probably the most direct application of customer and company interaction, collaborative customization. Here potential customers work with an online configuration program, sequentially working through a range of possible

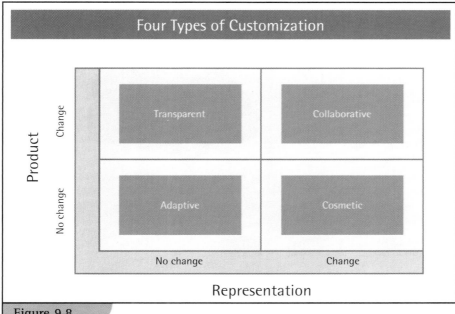

Figure 9.8

Dimensions of Mass Customization

Source: J. H. Gilmore and B.J. Pine, "The four faces of mass customization," *Harvard Business Review* 75, no. 1 (1997): 91–101.

either-or choices, ending up with their own partially designed product. In Figure 9.9, a German interested in a Smart car convertible can pick colors, interior features, and other accessories to arrive at their own personalized automobile.

Collaborative customization combines flexible manufacturing to provide alternatives with little cost over the standard features, and uses the dialogue mechanism of the Net to provide an easy venue for these choices. According to Gilmore and Pine, "Collaborative customizers conduct a dialogue with individual customers to help them articulate their needs, to identify the precise offering that fulfills those needs, and to make customized products for them." This is true one-to-one marketing.

Business-to-business ecommerce is the biggest user of collaborative customization because of the volume of B2B ecommerce and the value of configuration flexibility to businesses. Many companies have extranets to link them with their important suppliers and customers. These extranets are password-protected, and suppliers can offer items and terms not available outside of the established relationship. Technology companies such as Dell and Cisco take extensive advantage of this form of collaborative mass customization. Choices include variations in installed software, the capacity of the systems, and many other technical and packaging alternatives. Configurators can maintain and display the running price total for the choices, so that cost targets and tradeoffs are available to the decision makers.

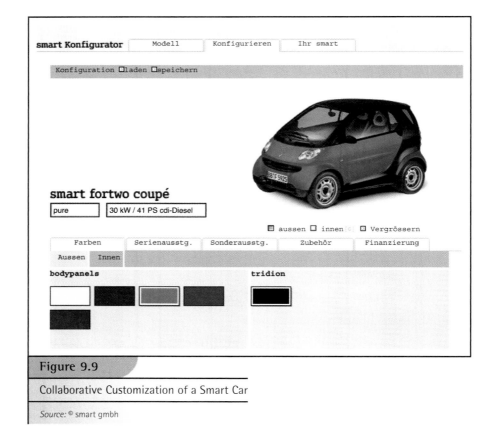

Figure 9.9

Collaborative Customization of a Smart Car

Source: © smart gmbh

> *Cosmetic Customization*

Cosmetic customization postpones the configuration and personalization options until after product assembly, and then permits either the marketer or the customer to alter information or packaging around the essentially standardized product. The emphasis is on packaging, presentation, and small changes that tie it to an individual or group. In the physical world, examples include the private labeling of supermarket goods, a school's name on T-shirts and sweatshirts, and packaging items in different languages for different countries. The exterior of the item changes without alterations to the core product.

One widespread example of online adaptive customization is virtual hosting of web sites. When a user types in the Web address of a firm, it appears that the company has a server that offers the page. More often than not, it does not. Internet standards allow the linking of a company's domain name to any IP address. As long as redirection information gets registered, there can be a split between domain name and actual web site location. It is perfectly acceptable and common for a company's web site to reside entirely on another company's server. It is even acceptable for a foreign company's site, with a domain name referring to a foreign country, to exist on a U.S.-based server. Virtual hosting is a cosmetic customization because many companies' sites can look individual while sharing the same physical Web server location.

The online personalization of the iPod at apple.com provides a way for gift givers and other purchasers to put a customized stamp on the music player (Figure 9.10). It also has a business

Figure 9.10

Cosmetic Customization to an iPod

Source: © Getty Images

implication by creating a product feature easily available online that becomes a hassle, with an extra charge, when done after the purchase. An interesting feature of the approach is that the web site automatically takes you to customization after choosing the model of your choice, and you must opt-out of customization rather than opt-in. This simple difference can have a large impact on the number of purchasers choosing customization.

> *Transparent Customization*

Transparent customization takes the opposite tack from cosmetic customization. In transparent customization, the product itself changes capabilities and performance, matching observed user characteristics or online behavior without representation changes or with minimal attention drawn to the change. Transparent customization works primarily "behind the scenes." The system observes user behavior and adjusts accordingly, making the product or service better match the individual.

Smart ads are one form of transparent customization. Smart ads use observable characteristics and behavior of surfing, reading, or multimedia consumption to show different ads online. Access an advertising-based web site from a university, and you may see an ad targeting visitors from domains ending in ".edu." In some cases, the ad will specifically target the particular university. Listen to a genre of music on a music site and similar music or related styles may appear somewhere on the page without explicitly labeling them as "for you" or "based on your choices." One of the most challenging parts of transparent customization is the recognition of individual needs and preferences without asking.

Google Scholar demonstrates several aspects of transparent customization. This is a service of Google that focuses its indexing on scholarly journals, books, and working papers rather than the full Web. One aspect of transparent customization is the appearance of Google Scholar on the main search page navigation bar when accessing from on a campus, but its relegation to the "more" category when off-campus. This makes sense, as many will be interested in Scholar while on-campus, while users not part of a university will not be. For those who are, a click or two finds the Scholar page.

The transparent customization continues. When a journal article appears in the search results, Google automatically links the result to the proper database and online journal for participating universities. For example, when searching for "mass customization" with Google Scholar on the Stanford campus, the search engine finds a number of articles contained in journals subscribed to by the Stanford library system. A link called "Find it @ Stanford" automatically appears and, if followed, takes the user directly to electronic copy of the relevant journal article. This is a convenience factor made possible by standards for sharing results between the Stanford library system and Google.

> *Adaptive Customization*

A popular approach to online personalization is to offer the same basic products and representation to everyone, but to let users filter out most of the possibilities. This is adaptive customization. In adaptive customization there is a standard offering with many settings. Altering these controls leads to individualized performance. While few physical products have this capability, it is quite common online. An example is the Accuweather site. Entering a Zip code leads to local weather, proper regional maps, and other related geographical material. Adaptive customization allows a few steps of user input to lead to efficiency by sorting through of the many possibilities. It is a form of more durable self-selection in which the user narrows the available selection from a wide range of possibilities.

| Choice Assistance

Choosing the right product or service is easy when needs and product offerings are simple and there are few alternatives. This is not the situation for many product categories.

A trip to the mall finds stores with tens of thousands of items, and online retailers carry even more. Products such as digital cameras vary by size, speed, format, lenses, and tens of other attributes (such as those shown in Figure 9.11). Financial services, such as investing and banking, have complications due to thousands of possible alternatives, taxes, risk, and other financial details. The Yellow Pages in most cities have hundreds of alternatives for auto repair, dentists, or legal help.

Sheer numbers of products are only part of the choice problem. There are many important experience goods and services facing consumers, such as health care or legal advice, where companies and individuals lack the expertise and personal experience necessary to judge quality. New products and services may compete with attributes that are unfamiliar to potential buyers, such as technical formats, and some method of using expert judgment may be necessary.

One of the most important types of web site personalization is choice assistance using recommendation systems. These recommendation systems help consumers sort through the vast array of alternatives in categories such as music, movies, cell phone plans, dating, digital cameras, and many other categories. They provide advice in categories ranging from retirement plans to the type of pet to own.

Choice assistance system operator goals vary. Some work as a consumer's advocate, seeking to provide unbiased advice to help consumers get the best match at the lowest possible price.

Figure 9.11

The Wide Assortment of Choices Available in the Marketplace Can Be Bewildering

Source: ©Bill Freeman/Photo Edit

Others have mixed motives, where commercial selling interests shape results along with customer objectives. Some are advertising-based content sites, some combine advice with market research, and others use choice assistance as an input to a retailing operation.

One of the main challenges to an organization adopting choice assistance on its site is selecting the proper recommendation system. Different product categories require different technical approaches, different types and amounts of data, and different levels of internal and external resources. This section looks at the match between product and category characteristics and the best form of choice assistance.

> *Recommendation Systems*

> Three Questions for Recommendation Systems

In choosing whether to add choice assistance to a site, as well as what type matches the needs of customers, three questions shape the broad outlines of appropriate methodology. These three questions connect customer lifetime value, customer needs, and the nature of the most important product attributes. These three questions are:

> Do customer lifetime values vary significantly?
> Do customer needs vary significantly?
> Are important product attributes qualitative or complex?

Unambiguous answers to these three questions allow a site to pick from among the main choice assistance systems. There may still be implementation problems, especially if the appropriate data or capabilities are not readily available.

Question 1: Do customer lifetime values justify choice assistance?

The first question focuses on the ultimate business justification for the recommendation system. In many of the examples of traditional personalization cited earlier in the chapter, personalization is a benefit awarded to the most valuable customers. There are several reasons for this. One, the economic benefits of high lifetime value support extra customer support. Two, personalization and choice assistance help build switching costs and help create loyalty where it is most valuable. Three, a range of customer lifetime values suggests that uniform policies of customer care might not work. Low value and transactional customers might be hard to cost-effectively personalize for, either because of their low value or because of their transitory interactions with the firm.

Question 2: Do customer needs vary significantly?

One of the major goals of choice assistance is helping potential customers rank the alternatives in the marketplace. The second question looks at the basis for the complexity. If customer needs vary widely, the system's main task is to help sort and comprehend the many alternatives. Widely varying customer needs often translate into a very wide assortment of products in the product category.

Question 3: Are important product attributes qualitative or complex?

Helping customers choose among products is difficult when the underlying attributes are hard to explain or even list. Describing why one piece of music is fun and another unappealing is challenging. The same can be true for many services and products, where customers may know what they like but not exactly why. Recommendation systems are valuable, but they must somehow transcend this difficulty of communication and understanding.

Figure 9.12 highlights four main online recommendation approaches and the situations where they best apply. The right choice of personalization system depends on the customer needs and product attributes. Each system can work well if used in the right setting with the appropriate data.

Rules-based systems use information that a company develops about its customer base as well as an in-depth understanding of product usage to make recommendations without extensive individualized surveys. Because rules-based systems rely on observing behavior and predicting preferences, they work best in situations where the product space is not too complicated, where attributes are quantifiable, and where there exist models and theories about product usage. These models let the system solve the user's problem and find the best matching alternatives.

Endorsement systems work best when the product needs of consumers do not differ greatly, but judging quality and explaining the value of available products are a challenge. In these cases, a simple endorsement can be best. Consumers need to know that a service provider is competent and honest and offers high quality. The endorsement system connects users with local preferred providers.

CASE stands for computer-assisted self-explication. The online system begins by surveying users about their product category preferences (this is the self-explication step). When needs and wants vary widely, such as in music or restaurants, the market normally responds with many alternatives. CASE systems search through their large database of possible choices to help users narrow their choices from thousands of possibilities to a few highly ranked alternatives. Because consumers differ in their tastes and many choices are possible, these systems must have active participation and dialogue with consumers.

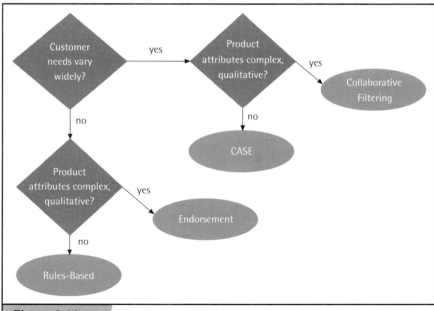

Figure 9.12

A Recommendation System Flowchart

Collaborative filtering is a common approach used when the product space is complicated and preferences are highly subjective, qualitative, and complex. The goal of these systems is educated word of mouth. The system matches different users who seem to share similar tastes. These individuals can then share recommendations and preferences about hard-to-judge products and services.

Figure 9.13 summarizes the choices in the flowchart in a different format. The horizontal axis captures customer need complexity, and the vertical axis captures the nature of product attributes.

> Rules-Based Systems

The heart of an effective rules-based system is a model of user goals and how best to accomplish these goals. This model lets the system use a minimum of customer-supplied responses to draw useful conclusions and make recommendations. Rules-based systems work best when the important product attributes are quantifiable and user needs are not extremely complicated. Both of these support effective modeling of customer choices.

One of the simplest and most common forms of rules-based choice assistance uses geography to help choose what news to pay attention to. Yahoo! and other portals offer information on a vast array of topics. They use a very simple and quantifiable rule: "Show the closest teams" and "Show the local weather." They use Zip code information stored in the customer profile to filter out a huge amount of information based on other locales. Of course, the system allows the user to override these initial options.

A much more powerful model underlies the recommendations provided by the Financial Engines service that began this chapter. When a user joins the Financial Engines service, the user begins by providing a list of his or her current financial assets in his or her retirement account. For example, many universities use TIAA-CREF mutual funds for their plans. A Financial

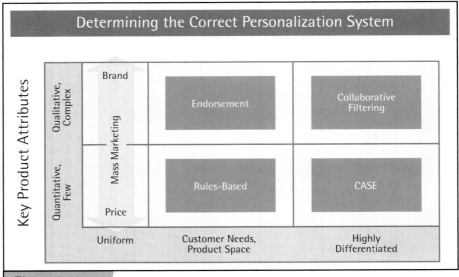

Figure 9.13

Determining the Correct Personalization System

Engines subscriber enters the amounts of each of these funds. Following this the system asks a small number of questions about current age, time until retirement, current income, willingness to accept risk, and other possible major financial requirements (such as child's college fund). With these inputs, the system makes a forecast of the likelihood of achieving these goals and specific suggestions of how to change the portfolio of investments.

In order to make these calculations, the Financial Engines system uses advanced financial theory and a method of handling uncertainty that is the basis for many of the sophisticated Wall Street investment houses. It can apply this cost effectively to an individual user's investments as the system automatically translates a user's current assets and financial goals into specific quantifiable inputs into the model.

Rules-based systems are challenging to develop. Very few areas of daily life and product choice have as well-developed and readily available models as in finance, which condenses the information needed about financial assets into just a limited number of highly quantifiable characteristics. In most cases, users must collaborate more and take a more active role.

> CASE Systems

The basis of a CASE recommendation system is a directed survey of each individual on the importance and acceptability of different product attributes. The process starts with a multi-step questionnaire with several goals:

> Identify unacceptable features or characteristics;
> Identify any "must have" features or characteristics;
> Quantify the user's specific importance weights for the product attributes used to describe products in the category.

One of the core justifications of this approach is that products and services are composed of attributes, and that consumers can do a pretty good job of identifying which attributes are valuable to them. It is this step that benefits from having simpler and more quantifiable attributes.

First-generation online CASE recommenders tended to be standalone systems, handling a wide range of category products, and having a relatively loose connection to online retailers. A good example of these consumer-oriented sites was Personalogic, which was eventually acquired by AOL. The Personalogic system has three main stages. The first stage is education about product features. For each product category, the system wanted to ensure that a consumer understood product features and attribute terminology. A CASE system cannot work well when a respondent does not understand the tradeoff choices. The first step of education can help minimize that problem.

The second step identifies the "must have" and "can't have" features. Price is the most important example of this type of attribute. Consumers typically have a rough idea of the absolute most they would spend for a product. They may also understand the category enough to state minimum price. These two choices can dramatically shrink the number of products. In a choice of bicycles, a price ceiling cut the number of bikes under consideration from more than 4,000 to fewer than 300.

The third stage begins the tradeoff process. Essentially, customers evaluate different attributes and their importance. A surprising result of individual-level marketing research is that a system that directly asks a user's preferences about attributes does a reasonably good job predicting that individual's eventual product choice.[36] Conventional wisdom had held that powerful market research comparison methods were necessary. Current research suggests that good direct user data may be more important than powerful tools. The final step of the system is to present a ranking of the products showing the top choices.

CASE systems can be valuable assistance guides for a consumer. The combination of product category education, a structured elimination of unacceptable features, an efficient tradeoff of product attributes, and an extensive database of product descriptions help simplify a complicated decision process.

For some of these decision guides, it has been a challenge to cover the expenses of building traffic and site operations relying only on advertising or ancillary data services. One alternative is partnering with online retailers. Active Decisions connected with Staples, an office supply retailer. The task for the guide is choosing a laptop. The guide is notably short. Two main factors account for this. First, researchers have found that online surveys need to be brief. Web surfers have become used to quick visits and rapid feedback. As seen in Chapter 7, the average visit tends to be just several clicks. Decision guide makers find that a short initial set of questions works better at maintaining interest than a longer and more comprehensive set of questions. These few questions may not be able to fully cover the product category. Once a user has completed the first set of questions and has seen the initial ranking of products, it is possible to continue the survey and provide more detail. This refines the information, leading to a better match of product ratings and user tastes.

A shorter list of questions is also possible because of a focus on rating and ranking the products carried by the retailer. Even a large store such as Staples carries only a fraction of the product offerings in the category. The goal of the decision guide is to sort through the items carried by Staples and to provide the best match. By limiting attention to the Staples product line, it may be possible to get accurate rankings without as many questions.

> Collaborative Filtering

Choice assistance can be most helpful when it is challenging or impossible for an individual to easily or quickly identify the most promising product to compare in more detail. When products have complex and qualitative attributes, the CASE system starts to break down. Without the ability to trade off and rate attributes, the system cannot calculate and rank products. Some other method of sorting choices is required.

Music is a classic example of this problem. There are more than 3 million CDs to choose from,[37] with a wide range of styles and format. Intense music lovers have different and particular tastes. Further, any two music lovers may agree on choices in one music category but have wide differences in preferences in other categories with different artists. Two friends may both love hip-hop, but one may also love opera, while the other hates opera, but loves jazz. Yet neither may be able to explain what causes their preferences to vary or what aspects of the different music types drive their response.

Collaborative filtering builds on one of the oldest solutions to this problem—ask someone else for a recommendation. The heart of a collaborative filtering approach is a database of user ratings of product variants, with some measure of strength of like or dislike. Once sufficient data exists, the system attempts to find "nearest neighbors," individuals with preferences that are clustered together. These like-minded music lovers can then provide recommendations to each other.

Table 9.1 shows a simplified illustration of how this can work. Through earlier sessions, listeners provide rankings to CDs. Individual A wants to find some new music to listen to. The system searches through the list and finds that Individuals B and C have quite different tastes, but Individual D has tastes on the ranked music that match A's choices fairly closely. Then, the highly ranked choice by D (that A hasn't listened to) is provided as a recommendation for A. Likewise, when D next asks the system for a recommendation, the music highly ranked by A will be a recommendation for D.[38] CD 1 will be recommended to A, while CD 6 will be recommended to D.

Collaborative filtering faces several challenges in generating enough data to make the service useful. One is the "cold start problem." Even the best potential system must generate an initial database somehow. Without previous data, the system must ask users to supply ratings without giving them advice in return. As most services cannot afford to pay users for ratings, and this might even bias their input, the cold start problem presents a serious entry hurdle. This cold start problem reemerges every time a new item enters the database. Until enough users rate the new item to span a range of clusters, the system has a difficult time providing any advice. For example, what does the system advise for music that is about to be released but has not been heard by anyone?

Table 9.1

Collaborative Filtering Based on User Clusters

	Individual A	Individual B	Individual C	Individual D
CD 1	–	4	8	9
CD 2	5	3	7	6
CD 3	9	2	10	8
CD 4	2	8	9	2
CD 5	6	6	1	6
CD 6	10	7	7	–

One solution is to use a form of the CASE system to make recommendations on new releases until enough data is present in order to offer advice based on other users. Visitors answer questions about their favorite music genre, their favorite artists, and perhaps a few additional questions. This generates a list of upcoming releases, perhaps with the ability to listen to a snippet of the new release.

It is also a challenge to get users to continually provide feedback. Without an inflow of new ratings, a collaborative database gets stale and out-of-date. An effective alternative to collecting user ratings is a system based on tracking listening or viewing habits. This is the method used by TIVO, which bases its model of a user's preferences partially on the user's viewing history. TIVO assumes that someone spending an hour a week watching *Survivor* must like it.

Recommendation engines for television shows actually combine several sources of data to deepen their coverage and improve results. Figure 9.14 shows how program information, user preferences, and usage history combine to suggest top shows to watch. Data on the right of the dotted line comes from the user's history, and data on the left comes from program descriptions compiled or licensed by the recommendation system.

Collaborative filtering systems must work to avoid "the Harry Potter" problem, which is a tendency to overemphasize blockbusters. If a system clusters based on book popularity, mega-sellers such as the Harry Potter series will always be near the top. This is not very useful. What users really want is a system clever enough to spot more obscure products that they would enjoy. Collaborative system designers build in special rules in order to emphasize these backlist and specialty items.

Since its earliest days, Amazon.com has been a pioneer in providing online recommendations. Amazon emphasizes what it calls item-to-item collaborative filtering.[39] Partly to alleviate ratings collection problems, and partly to speed up the computation of recommendations for its 30 million customers selecting among several million catalog listings, Amazon clusters based on purchase patterns. Item-by-item systems look for purchase clusters, often doing the time-intensive calculation in "batch mode" and storing the result. That is, the system already has performed many of the calculations necessary to making the recommendation prior to observing a customer putting an item into his or her online shopping cart. This allows Amazon to simultaneously offer suggestions of additional products often paired by other shoppers with the newly chosen item.

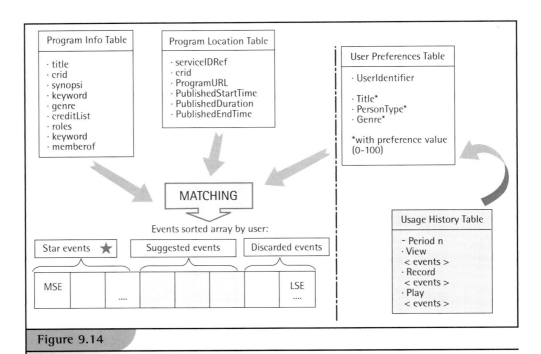

Figure 9.14

Types and Sources of Data for Recommending TV Shows

Figure 9.15

Amazon Explaining Why a Recommendation Was Made

Collaborative filtering, whether based on users or on items, occasionally gives recommendations that seem surprising and curious. One of the most interesting parts of the Amazon.com system is its explanation capability. Most recommendations carry along with them an explanation link. Figure 9.15 illustrates this. Amazon suggested a particular form of HP calculator. The explanation ties this item to a text purchased earlier on corporate finance. As many business students and practitioners do use this calculator in finance, the recommendation is now understandable. If the user already owns the calculator, there is a box to indicate this as well. Amazon's explanation reinforces the credibility of the system, provides the user a chance to correct a mistake, and may even lead to more information provided by the user.

> Endorsement Systems

In complicated settings, with experience goods and qualitative attributes, the best choice assistance may simply be an endorsement by experts in the field. This is especially true when fundamental customer needs and tastes do not vary widely. In this case, the essential problem is often locating a nearby high-quality vendor.

Many local experience goods fit this category. Finding a good dentist, an honest auto repair shop, or a good plumber may have less to do with a complicated list of attributes than just a trustworthy seal of approval. The same is true for online sellers in auction sites. The eBay reputation system provides a form of endorsement where different vendors have different feedback histories. The feedback itself is quite basic, essentially a "thumbs up" or "thumbs down" from each buyer. Nonetheless, buyers value the presence of positive feedback by buyers and it results in a reputation price premium for high-quality sellers.

Many organizations are putting lists of companies on their web sites along with positive and negative endorsements covering topics such as the environment, being family-friendly, having respect for employees, or other social issues. For motivated members of these groups, these guides affect their consumption and investing choices.

> Sources of Data

Figure 9.16 summarizes the different data needs for each of the four choice assistance approaches. Each uses very different inputs. Rules-based and endorsement tend to rely heavily on data supplied primarily by the marketer. Endorsement systems rely on satisfaction databases based on surveys, expert panels, or some other measure of quality. The company needs to collect this data. Rules-based approaches need effective user models. This requires data and modeling expertise by the marketer. User models must tie to observable online triggers. A trigger is some action that a model can use to decide what personalized information to send.

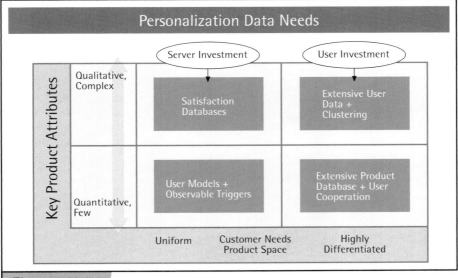

Figure 9.16

Data Needs Change with Methodology

For CASE and collaborative filtering, data from users are the key ingredients. CASE systems typically require less user time than collaborative filtering, but must be augmented by extensive product databases. User data is necessary to effectively match the user and the right product. Collaborative filtering relies on either user ratings or user consumption histories to find proper clusters and recommendation possibilities.

| Personalized Messaging

Personalized messaging uses the tools of personalization to shape the interactions and information presented to a user, often outside of a web site, with email, SMS, or instant messages. As with other forms of the general-purpose individualization technology, personalized messaging combines authenticating the user, associating the individual with some categories or actions, and making appropriate inferences about what messages to send. Each of these has its own difficulties.

> *Authentication for Messaging*

Any form of personalized messaging requires some method of connecting the current situation to previous knowledge. The central piece of information that makes this happen is an address. An address is a method of uniquely identifying an individual that allows cumulative learning to occur. It can be very incomplete, such as an IP address that only reveals some information about a country or organization of origin. In other cases it is nearly total, such as situations where the address reveals a person's real name and a wide range of external data.

Good personalization systems realize and take account of this varying degree of knowledge and certainty (Figure 9.17). Caution is required when making message choices without good information. It may be much better to treat everyone the same than to use a mistaken identity as the basis for the electronic interaction. Marketers using personalized messages need to understand the strengths and weaknesses of their knowledge about customers, and adjust accordingly. As emphasis shifts from providing choice assistance, which involves collaboration with visitors, to marketer-initiated message personalization, this concern grows.

> On the Web

An important feature of the Internet, especially the Web, complicates the use of addresses. The Web is a stateless system. Each mouse click by a user is a separate, standalone transaction. Each request is independent. One of the challenges for an online marketer, especially one interested in personalization, is to merge a collection of stateless requests into an individual history.

Web server information demonstrates the problem:

> *host/ip rfcname authuser* [DD/MMM/YYYY:HH:MM:SS-0000]"METHOD /PATH HTTP/1.0" code bytes

This shows a single entry in a common Web log. For example, this address could have come from the initial request of a company's homepage.[40]

> *host/ip:* The first line is the host/ip name. If the domain name service is working, this will be the name of the computer making the request. More likely, it will be the numerical address of the computer asking for the homepage file.

RFC name: It is technically feasible that the name of the user will be included. This only is true if it is requested, the remote network makes it available, and the user has authorized it. It is typically absent.

authuser: If you are using local authentication and registration, the user's log name will appear. Likewise, if no value is present, a dash (" – ") is substituted. If your site is password protected, the user's login ID will appear here.

datestamp: Current date and time plus an offset from Greenwich Mean Time (for example, Pacific Standard Time is -0800).

retrieval method: The type of request made by the user. Normal types are GET, PUT, POST, or HEAD. Path is the path and file retrieved.

code: HTTP completion code information is shown: 200 is successful, 304 is a reload from cache, 404 is file not found, and so forth. The 404 code shows up when any problem occurs. A 304 means that the file has been reloaded from a previous access.

bytes: The size of the file retrieved, measured in bytes.

Web log analysis software allows a marketer to extract a variety of useful material from a log file. Figure 9.17 shows the increasing amount of knowledge that a Web marketer might possess, depending on choices made by both the online site and the user. The most comprehensive knowledge situation is when a site is password protected and passwords allow retrieval of individual identity. This can occur through a user-supplied ID and password or by a biometric signature built into a keyboard. This is the authentication system.

Many web sites do not use registration or password protection, which makes customization challenging. While the IP address is always available, it is unreliable. Millions of Web browsers use dynamic IP addresses, which are IP addresses assigned by a provider such as AOL that change each time a user dials up the service. A web site tracking only IP addresses will make serious errors if it uses the IP address to represent users over time.

Information stored as browser cookies provides a way of creating a more permanent connection between individuals and information. A line or two of text can be stored on the hard disk of the user's computer. Cookies can be absent because there has been no previous visit, or due to blocking or deletion of cookies written during previous visits. Some users concerned about privacy are adopting software that blocks cookies as well as spyware. Without cookies or authentication, the visitor appears without any previous history available.

Web sites implementing personalized systems of interaction typically blend the use of cookies and login. *The New York Times* uses a common approach. Even though the online paper is free, a visitor must create a user name and password

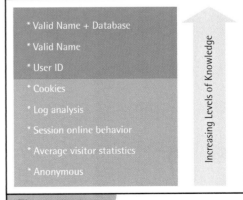

Figure 9.17

Increasing Levels of Knowledge of a Web User

(Figure 9.18). Users deleting a previous cookie must log in to read an article. However, if the user allows the cookie to be rewritten (the "remember me" box is checked) and does not delete it between visits, he or she will be automatically logged in upon returning to the newspaper site.

This system is both flexible and accomplishes the repeat visit-tracking purposes of the *Times*. Logging in every time is tedious for those not worried about the *New York Times'* cookie, while it permits those who "wash" their system of cookies diligently to still enjoy the paper.

> Email and Instant Messaging Addresses

Interaction outside of the web site builds on email and other direct links to the consumer, such as short messages and instant messaging. Each of these also requires a form of address, such as an email address or instant message user ID. Creating and maintaining a valid email list requires ensuring an email address is valid at the start, periodically testing the email connection to make sure it remains valid, and maintaining a process of regular scrubbing of the list to remove invalid email addresses.

Personalized email is at the heart of many retention, loyalty-building, and cross-selling campaigns. One constant finding of electronic direct marketers using these tools is that personalization boosts both the probability of a recipient responding and the response profitability.

> Cell Phone Numbers

Wireless companies that sell devices with online capabilities are in one of the strongest potential market positions for personalized electronic messaging. These companies, such as Vodaphone, NTT DoCoMo, or RIM, have very strong authentication of personal identity because of their billing arrangements. They are fully aware of the name and billing address on a cell phone account, and can match that against extensive external databases. Their geographical awareness of the handset is also increasingly precise, so that they can pinpoint the location of the user in real time.

Whether these wireless providers can or should use this highly authenticated and accurate personal and location information as part of marketing activity is an active debate and public policy controversy. While there are many conceivable benefits from individual geo-coded personalized messages, such as sales and promotions for stores in the vicinity, there are also many concerns about excessive messaging, invasions of privacy, and fair and open competition.

These concerns become more and more important with increasing

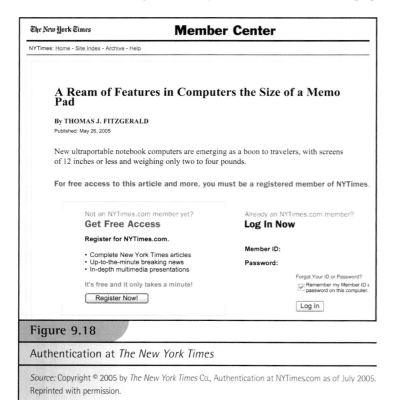

Figure 9.18

Authentication at *The New York Times*

Source: Copyright © 2005 by *The New York Times* Co., Authentication at NYTimes.com as of July 2005. Reprinted with permission.

address accuracy. Discussions of trust, privacy, and permission link closely to all aspects of personalized messaging.

> Association and Personalized Messaging

Once some form of authentication occurs, learning is possible. Over time, and with repeat visits and more observations, the system builds understanding about users. Not all of these will be task- or ecommerce-oriented.

Some of the knowledge helpful for personalization may be style- and taste-oriented. Individuals have different personalities, and adjusting the technology and the messages to better match an individual's preferred method of interaction can make a system seem friendlier and more appropriate. Personalization can begin to make the technology and the messages adapt to the individual, rather than force the individual to make the accommodations.

An example of this is using personalization to create a match between the format used in electronic messages and an individual's own personal style. While it may seem unnecessary, even a bit odd, psychological research suggests that personality matching of messages has a consistent and statistically significant positive impact on user satisfaction.[41] Simply stated, users like a system that talks to them with a style like their own.

Figure 9.19 shows the results from a study demonstrating this phenomenon. The first step of the study, conducted at an earlier time, identified the basic submissive versus dominant personality types of participants. In a subsequent lab setting, participants interacted with a computer demonstrating information on different subjects. The task was similar to a choice-assistance ranking.

Randomly assigned participants received either dominant or submissive style messages. A dominant message would be direct and forceful, such as "You really should put item number 3 high on your list....". A submissive style would have a tone such as "You might want to consider item number 3, as it is very good on a dimension you seem to like."

In all four settings in Figure 9.19, participants ranked the system higher when messages matched their own personality style. Submissive subjects preferred submissive-style messages and dominant subjects preferred dominant-style messages. As the information content and actual rankings of products stayed the same, this highlights how preferred message syntax changes satisfaction.[42]

> Trigger Events and Personalized Messages

Trigger events are important types of user actions that make personalized messaging easier and more accurate. They occur when visitors, current or potential customers, "show their cards" and reveal important new information. A trigger event also means that these users reveal information that creates an opportunity for a valuable interaction. Trigger events combine highly revealing information and an actionable conclusion.[43]

A highly revealing action lets a marketer dramatically improve its estimate of who the user is or what activities the user is trying to accomplish. Recall the dog in the cartoon shown in Figure 7.8. By clicking on a web page that only a dog would be interested in (the bone marrow page), the site updates its estimate from "maybe a dog" to "almost certainly a dog." On a less whimsical note, the site HomeGain uses the action of a visitor checking his or her home value with an online calculator as a revealing action of a home owner potentially interested in selling their property (Figure 9.20).

The second criterion of a trigger event is an actionable conclusion that is justified given the learning that occurred from the revealing action. For HomeGain and the home worth calculator,

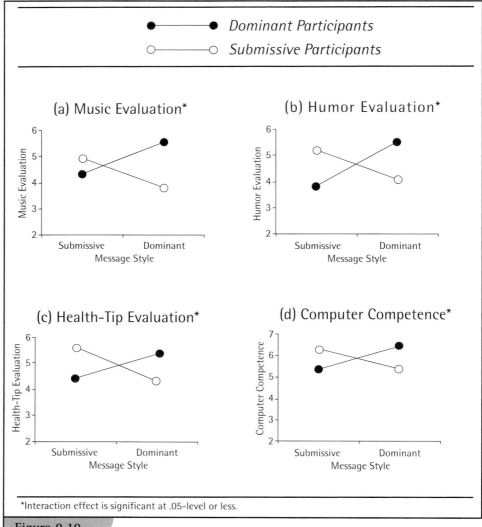

Figure 9.19

Matching Message Language to Personality Type Improves Customer Satisfaction

Source: Youngme Moon, "Personalization and Personality: Some Effects of Customizing Message Style Based on Consumer Personality," *Journal of Consumer Psychology* 12, no. 4 (2002): 313–326.

the action is to promote its real-estate finder service. If the visitor had chosen to look at homes for sale, the action would lead to information customized around potential home buyers.

Chapter 7 already highlighted one of the most useful versions of a trigger event, when the action reveals a persuadable moment. Figure 9.21 illustrates how content selection can be a trigger event. In this case the choice of the house price estimator is a strong, but not perfect, indicator of willingness to sell a home. It could be the visitor merely is curious. On the other

Several Revealing Actions on the HomeGain Site

Source: Courtesy of HomeGain.com, Inc.

hand, it may reveal the very important upcoming transition into selling a home. This content choice, perhaps combined with one or two more actions that separate the curious from the potential home seller, can be a trigger event and can lead to personalized messages around selling a house.

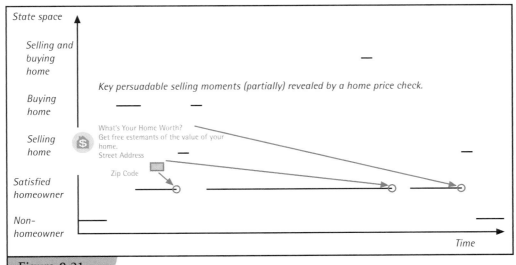

Figure 9.21

Event Graphs Revisited: Content Choices as Trigger Events

Personalized messaging needs to balance the safety and blandness of a generic messaging approach against the effectiveness of customized messaging and risk of mistaken identity. The first may appear to users as a learning failure, the second a rush to judgment or an error-prone firm. Balancing these two problems is tied to the benefits and costs of getting it right or getting it wrong. For example, messaging may vary by the gender of the visitor, with the content and tone of a message for males different from that for females. If the site feels it cannot justify or trust asking the visitor, it must try to reach a conclusion from observing online choices. It must also balance the upside gains and losses from the decision. In some situations the downside is much worse than the improved messaging, and the site should insist on a high degree of confidence. When the downside risk is much less than the upside, the system will be wise to tolerate more mistakes.

There are rigorous statistical procedures to implement these steps, and many of the personalized messaging systems at least partially utilize these decision rules. The technical area is Bayesian decision making, and it forms the basis of both real-time messaging through web sites and sophisticated email systems targeting loyal customers.

ENDNOTES

1. Peter Drucker, *Management: Tasks, Responsibilities, Practices* (New York: HarperCollins Publishers, Inc., 1977), 61.
2. Robert C. Blattberg and Rashi Glazer, "Marketing in the Information Revolution," chap. 1 in *The Marketing Information Revolution* (Boston: Harvard Business School Press, 1994).
3. This discussion of procrastination and status quo bias comes from Richard Thaler and Shlomo Benartzi, "Save More Tomorrow: Using Behavioral Economics to Increase Employee Savings," *Journal of Political Economy* 112, no. 1 (2004): 164–187.
4. Data provided by Financial Engines, June 2005.
5. For a comparison of Wal-Mart Supercenters and their impact on traditional outlets, see Vishal Singh, Karsten Hansen, and Robert Blattberg, "Impact of Wal-Mart Supercenter on a Traditional Supermarket: An Empirical Investigation," working paper. (Carnegie Mellon: 2004), February 11.
6. Ibid. See also Jerry Hausman and Ephraim Leibtag, "CPI Bias from Supercenters: Does the BLS Know that Wal-Mart Exists?" working paper. (MIT, 2004), August 12.
7. Thorstein Veblen, *Theory of the Leisure Class* (New York: Modern Library Random House, 1922), 60–61.
8. "Executives Need Spouse-Equivalent To Manage Chores New-Style Enterprises Create Time–For A Fee," *San Jose Mercury News*, 4 January 1998.
9. The briefing books put together by the White House staff reflect and influence the views of the president. Some presidents have avoided bad news and criticism, while others paid close attention to critiques and covered them in depth. The objectivity and shaping of personal news services is a serious issue in the proper role of personalization.
10. One of Veblen's main arguments was that personalized goods were high status because they were expensive. These types of goods have come to be known as Veblen goods. They are a form of *conspicuous consumption*, valuable because they are wasteful.
11. For these examples and a critical evaluation of the politics of this point of view, see Roland Marchand, "The Parable of the Democracy of Goods," available online.
12. On the other hand, one of the core benefits of personalization is more effective and efficient consumption. The right advice helps someone find the best way to spend and enjoy his or her money. This has the largest absolute impact on those consuming the most. Relative impacts may be another matter. Saving several hundred dollars on life insurance is much more valuable to middle- and lower-income buyers than it is for the rich. Personal advice and choice assistance may be most appreciated by those on the tightest budgets.
13. P. Nelson, "Advertising as Information," *Journal of Political Economy* 81 (1970): 729–754.
14. Theodore Levitt, "Marketing Success Through Differentiation–of Anything," *Harvard Business Review* (January/February 1980). Reprinted in

Theodore Levitt, *The Marketing Imagination* (New York: Free Press, 1986), 72–93.

15. Robert DeYoung, William Hunter, and Gregory Udell, "The Past, Present and Probably Future for Community Banks," *Journal of Financial Services Research* 25, no. 2/3 (2004): 85–133.

16. Ibid, p. 104.

17. Ellen Stark, "Banking from home," *Money*, New York, Summer.

18. Phillip J Britt, "Bankers beware," *Telephony*, 2 June 1997.

19. Bank Marketing Association, "Online banking prospects want a direct connection," *Bank Marketing*, Washington, November.

20. Kai Riemer, and Carsten Totz, "The many faces of personalization—an integrative overview of mass customization and personalization" M. M. Tseng, and F. T. Piller, *The Customer Centric Enterprise: Advances in Mass Customization and Personalization* (New York/Berlin: Springer Verlag, 35–50).

21. Behavioral economics and psychology tend to support the power of sunk costs in motivating choice and satisfaction, even if optimization theory would suggest that sunk costs should be ignored when judging future alternatives.

22. J. Edward Russo and Frace Leclerc, "Characteristics of Successful Product Information Programs," *Journal of Social Issues* 47, no 1 (1991): 73–92. See also J. Edward Russo, "Aiding Purchase Decisions on the Internet," in Veljko Milutinovic (ed.) *Proceedings of the Winter 2002 SSGRR International Conference on Advances in Infrastructure for Electronic Business* (L'Aquila. Italy, 2002).

23. Shivaram Rajgopal, Mohan Venkatachalam, and Suresh Kotha, "Does the Quality of Online Customer Experience Create a Sustainable Competitive Advantage for E-Commerce Firms?" working paper. Stanford University, April 2001.

24. George Day and Christophe Van den Bulte. "Superiority in Customer Relationship Management: Consequences for Competitive Advantage and Performance," working paper. Wharton School, September 2002.

25. Fournier et al., op. cit.

26. See endnote 20.

27. Frank Piller and Melanie Muller, "A New Marketing Approach to Mass Customization," *International Journal of Computer Integrated Manufacturing* 17, no. 7 (2004): 583–593.

28. Barbara Kahn, "Dynamic Relationships with Customers: High-Variety Strategies," *Journal of the Academy of Marketing Science* 26, no. 1 (1998): 45, 53.

29. Bruce Kasanoff, "Are You Ready for Mass Customization," *Training* 35, no 5 (1998): 70–78.

30. National Public Radio interview, *Weekend Edition*, 21 May 2005.

31. Elyon DeKoven, "Off-Topic Recommendations," *Workshop: Beyond Personalization 2005,* working paper. IUI, San Diego, January 9, 2005.

32. Han-Shen Huang, Koung-Lung Lin, Jane Yung-jen Hsu, and Chun-Nan Hsu, "Item-Triggered Recommendation for Identifying Potential Customers of Cold Sellers in Supermarkets," *Workshop: Beyond Personalization 2005*, working paper. IUI, San Diego, January 9, 2005.

33. See Razvan Andonie, J. Edward Russo, and Rishi Dean, "Crossing the Rubicon for an Intelligent Advisor,"*IUI Workshop: Beyond Personalization 2005*," San Diego, January 9, 2005. Bahattin Ozen, Ozgur Kilic, Mehmet Altinel, and Asuman Dogac, "Highly Personalized Information Delivery to Mobile Clients," *Wireless Networks* 10 (2004): 665–683. George Samaras and Christoforos Panayiotou, "A Flexible Personalization Architecture for Wireless Internet Based Mobile Agents," ADBIS 2002, Y Manolopoulos and P. Navrat, eds.

34. M. Jolson, "Broadening the Scope of Relationship Selling," *Journal of Personal Selling and Sales Management* 17, no. 4 (1997): 75–88.

35. Matthew Grimm, "Ford connects: Hatches massive relationship program via Web," *Brandweek,* Jan 4, 1999.

36. V. Srinivasan and Park, "The Surprising Robustness of Self-Explicated," working paper. Stanford University, 1998.

37. Gracenote Music Recognition Services claims more than 3.7 million CDs cataloged in its music service.

38. JC Charlet, "Technology Note: Rules-Based Systems, S-OIT-21. Stanford University Graduate School of Business, March 1998.

39. Greg Linden, Brent Smith, and Jeremy York, "Amazon.com Recommendations: Item-to-Item Collaborative Filtering," *IEEE Internet Computing* (January–February 2003): 76–80.

40. Glen Fleishman, "Web Log Analysis: Who's Doing What, When?" *Web Developer* 2, no. 2 (1996).

41. Youngme Moon, "Personalization and Personality: Some Effects of Customizing Message Style Based on Consumer Personality," *Journal of Consumer Psychology* 12, no. 4 (2002): 313–326.

42. Needless to say, the computer was indifferent between styles.

43. Those familiar with decision modeling will recognize this discussion as Bayesian decision analysis. Initial information is the current prior and a highly revealing action leads to a major change between the prior and posterior distributions. The actionable criterion means there is an action favored with the posterior distribution that was not with the uncertainty prior to the action.

chapter 10:

Creating Commitment

Reach, Serve, and Engage

Every year universities produce a valuable addition to their extended community: a new year's worth of alumni. For seniors completing their undergraduate studies, the university experience is a collection of friendships and transitions and a major part of their identity. For Master's students in professional programs, it is a stepping-stone to a new career. For PhDs, it is the completion of a long journey that for many leads to an academic career. For all, college provides life-changing experiences in which they discover who they are, who they know, and who they will turn to for advice and support.

Most schools work hard to create an ongoing relationship with their new alumni. The Stanford Alumni Association (SAA) sums up its approach with the phrase "Reach, Serve, and Engage," a mission in which the tools of online community building plays an increasingly large role.

The SAA's homepage, Figure 10.1, shows the beginning point of many of these activities. One purpose of the site is to be a virtual window onto campus activities, to temporarily give the alumni a feeling of being back on campus. This takes several forms. One simple but powerful feature is the rotating photo of campus life (a). One image shows students biking on the Quad, while on another day it features a close-up of a campus statue. Headlines for current events are shown, providing insight into what is happening on campus right now.

As a research institution in Silicon Valley, many of the stories emphasize faculty and student innovations. An example is (b), a feature on

this chapter

Customer and member commitment is an elusive holy grail for many organizations. This chapter considers online community development, which can be motivated by commercial or noncommercial motives. More commercial settings lead to a consideration of retention marketing, where continued or additional sales from existing customers provide the incentive.

Topics covered in this chapter include:

> Maintaining Connection

> Reinforcing Community

> Retention Marketing

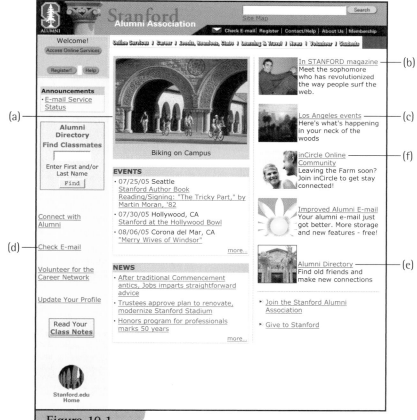

Figure 10.1

The Alumni Association Homepage

Source: Courtesy, Stanford Alumni Association

Stanford undergraduate Blake Ross and his leadership role in creating the Mozilla FireFox browser. Connecting to alumni at home is also important, demonstrated by the featured item (c) showing upcoming Stanford events in Los Angeles and Seattle. These visits provide a physical reinforcement of the virtual connection.

One of the most popular SAA online services is free email (d), available to all Stanford alumni. Free email provides a number of benefits to both alumni and the association. Email continues to be the most frequently used online tool. Each time an alumnus accesses email, it creates a new opportunity to connect to the SAA. Each email is a small endorsement of the Stanford connection.

An email address is a vital part of each alumnus profile. Each month the SAA sends the *@Stanford* email newsletter to all graduates for whom it has email addresses. Satisfaction with the newsletter is very high, with over 115,000 alums receiving the email, an annual unsubscribe rate below .002, and more than a 50% open rate.[3] Providing an email service and online updating of personal information makes it much easier to maintain valid email and physical addresses, despite the many career changes and relocations common in a modern economy.

The SAA strives to provide multiple methods for college friends to remain connected after graduation; finding that peer-to-peer involvement is one of the most powerful inducements to loyalty. There is an online directory, providing news categorized by class year, special events by interest area, and reunion information (e). One of the more innovative tools, which the SAA pioneered with some Stanford graduates, is the InCircle social networking service (f).[4] Launched in January 2003, each member indicates fellow Stanford alumni who are viewed as friends. The service has grown very rapidly, gaining more than 10,000 users in its first month of operation. Unlike open systems such as Friendster and LinkedIn, only those with a Stanford connection may join. A member can send an email to all members with "3 degrees of separation" or less, as well as find the shortest path of people connecting themselves to another member they do not personally know.[5]

One of the most notable items missing from the Alumni Association activities is fund raising. This is deliberate policy. While Figure 10.2 strongly suggests that the SAA online activities build good will and lead to alumni contributions, they do not attempt to collect any money. The goal of the SAA is to build and maintain the Stanford community for those no longer on campus. Online tools help in raising Stanford's visibility, reinforcing personal connections, highlighting future activities, and providing online value through relevant information and useful electronic services.

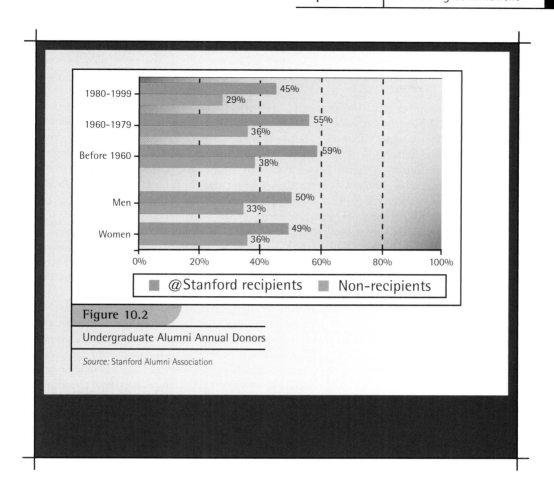

Figure 10.2

Undergraduate Alumni Annual Donors

Source: Stanford Alumni Association

ONLINE COMMUNITY

Community and Loyalty

Online community is a potential source of loyalty, commitment, and increased retention of participants. Just as Stanford University seeks to "reach, serve, and engage," many other organizations seek to build a sense of community among their members as well. This includes consumer sites, business sites, and nonprofit and charitable organizations. Online communities discuss issues as broad as space exploration, as serious as a terminal disease, or as escapist as trivia games.

Online communities seem to magnify commentators' views of the role, impact, and consequence of the Internet. Extreme positions are common – online communities are a social breakthrough or a threat to true civil society. Optimists see online community as one of the true competitive advantages of going online, the gain behind the Net. Pessimists view it as silicon snake oil.[6]

When they work well, online communities are focused social gatherings. Communication is multi-directional, with users responsible for both providing material and consuming information. Repeated interaction reinforces the social features of community, builds trust, and creates loyalty.

Online communities share the important social network features discussed in Chapter 3. As in any network, the community value typically exceeds the individual value. Communities exhibit high local clustering, where connections between close members are much stronger than connections with more distant members. Despite this, most online communities will also be small worlds, where information flows between clusters over weak ties to distant members. Communities have critical hubs and connectors that provide the bulk of interactions. Finally, online communities will normally be robust to the random defection of a typical member but susceptible to the loss of the most important ones.

Community builders face several critical challenges. As always, there is the challenge of gaining attention and building traffic. This is doubly important for communities struggling to reach a critical mass of members. Numerous aspects of online communities benefit from a large user base. These increasing returns provide strong momentum for healthy online communities, but make them more difficult to launch.

There are unique challenges to building and operating an online community. Focus can be lost as communities change and grow. Content generation can break down if members feel unappreciated or apathetic. Incentives that work in smaller groups can fail as the community blossoms. Member attention may wander to other sites, hurting member retention. Community is unfamiliar to many firms that may be more comfortable controlling the messages and information sent to customers. Online marketers should understand how to support communities, how to measure the vitality of their community, and how to moderate content when appropriate.

Table 10.1 provides a straightforward categorization of community types into portal-based, affinity-based, and purpose-built.[7] Portal-based communities, such as Tripod on Lycos or Geocities on Yahoo!, flourish because of services such as free hosting and multiple categorization tools, which link individual content and groups. The convening service benefits from the traffic through online ads and upgraded hosting fees.

Affinity-based communities rely on a closed set of rules defining the community, such as affiliation with a particular university. They can also have open membership for all who share a particular interest, such as the brand-oriented communities discussed in Chapter 6.

Purpose-built communities are organized around a set of tasks and objectives, such as creating open source software or an online encyclopedia. They face a difficult challenge, encouraging the private provision of a public good. Despite the lack of paid compensation or immediate reward, contributors spend large amounts of time and energy providing content and advice freely available to all. One of the main tasks of the community convener is to somehow stimulate and support these contributors without the normal economic means.

Corporations as well as nonprofits can sponsor either affinity or purpose-built virtual communities. The most common is probably the open membership, affinity-based activities in support of the company's product line. In more technical and business to business settings the purpose-built community can provide highly sophisticated alternatives to normal customer and technical support.

Figure 10.3 on page 330 illustrates the diversity of online community efforts. The data comes from a representative sample of U.S. Internet users,[8] showing the percentage of users that have contacted groups of each type. Work and play split the top two categories, with a diverse mix of interests and affinities appearing throughout the rest.

Table 10.1

Types and Functions of Online Community

Community Type		Typical Convener	Main Purpose	Main Sources of Funding	Popular Examples
Portal-based		Large "dot" companies	Provision of information services and resources	Subscription fees, sales, and ads	AOL, Yahoo!, Lycos
Affinity-based	Closed membership	Small groups of like–minded individuals, nonprofits	Interest sharing, etc.	Advertising, sub-scription fees, self–financed by convener	The WELL, Stanford Alumni
	Open membership	Small groups of like–minded individuals, brand managers	Interest sharing, etc.	Advertising, self–financed by convener	USENET, Slashdot, Porsche club
Purpose–built	Vertical assemblages of information	Groups of highly skilled programmers	Production of public goods or clubs (e.g., software)	Governments, Universities, Foundations, self–financed	GNU/Linux, Apache, JBoss
	Horizontal assemblages of information	Groups of highly motivated individuals (not necessarily programmers)	Production of public goods or clubs (e.g., databases and encyclopedias)	Governments, Universities, Foundations, self–financed	Open Directory Project, Wikipedia, Amazon.com reviews

Source: Table 1: Virtual communities: A taxonomy, in Andrea Ciffolilli, "Phantom authority, self–selective recruitment and retention of members in virtual communities: The case of Wikipedia," First Monday, Issue 8 (2003), http://www.firstmonday.org/issues/issue8_12/ciffolilli/.

Positive feedback cycles are important to the growth of online communities.[9] The health of an online community depends on the interplay of its content attractiveness, member loyalty, member profiles, and transaction offerings. Each of these reinforces the value of the community to users and the sponsoring organization, and measuring them provides a snapshot of the state of the online community.

Content attractiveness refers to the depth and relevance of content available for members and produced by members. As more content is available, members find the community even more valuable, and membership increases. Each member has some tendency to produce content, and more members naturally lead to more content.

In some online communities, such as social networking sites MySpace and Friendster, *member profiles* are an important part of the content. These grow as a direct result of new members. In general, membership profiles provide both an opportunity for the sponsor to reach out to individuals with targeted offerings and additional value and connections for other members.

Member loyalty promotes value to members through increased usage and user satisfaction. Peer-to-peer interaction relies on both the number of users and their intensity of use. A

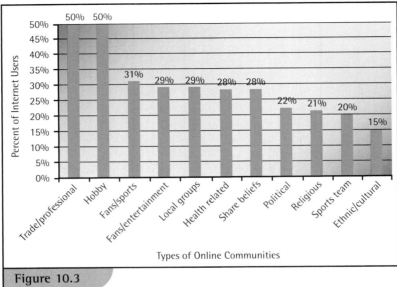

Figure 10.3

The Diversity of Online Communities in the United States

Source: Jenny Preece, Diane Maloney-Krichmar, and Chadia Abras, "History and emergence of online communities," in B. Wellman (Ed.), *Encyclopedia of Community* (Berkshire Publishing Group/Sage, 2003).

commitment to the community leads to volunteering, willingness to help coordinate and manage the community, and an audience for online postings and messages.

As membership grows, the community becomes increasingly attractive to vendors. *Transaction offerings*, selling items related to the interest areas of the community, makes the community even more attractive to members. Other vendors, even in the face of competition, feel compelled to join the community. Advertising and product development work more effectively with increased knowledge.

Each of the four loops in Figure 10.4 presents challenges for the community sponsor. Some organizations, such as the SAA, are dedicated to online community building and find it beneficial. For others, online community experiments have been failures. Some of these disappointments stem from the general difficulty of creating community, both online and offline.[10] Others were a result of poor execution or unrealistic goals.

Increasing returns markets are a double-edged sword. Although they can lead to very rapid growth for successful firms, there will be other failed efforts for sites and communities that fail to achieve a minimum scale. This issue is addressed in more detail in Chapter 11, where the competition between standards has many of the same competitive aspects. This chapter concentrates on the value creating features of online communities rather than competition between communities.

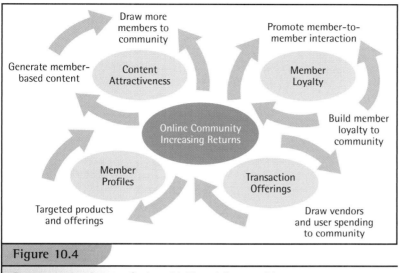

Figure 10.4

Four Increasing Returns Cycles with Virtual Communities

Source: John Hagel, III and Arthur G. Armstrong, *Net gain: expanding markets through virtual communities,* (Boston: Harvard Business School Press, 1997), 51.

Community Content

> *Online Tools*

> Categorizing Online Community Tools

Both communication and content tools reinforce online community. Communication tools support direct, usually simultaneous, exchanges between members. Content tools tend to be indirect, with postings geared less toward specific individuals and time delays between member postings and responses. The terms "communication rings" and "content trees" emphasize these information-flow characteristics in a community context. Communication rings emphasize the social and relational, while content trees tend to be more informational (Table 10.2).[11]

> Communication Rings

Email's simplicity and ubiquity continue to make it the most important of community tools. Email is a highly flexible medium, ranging from one that contains only text messages to one with full graphics and attachments. It easily spans multiple levels of

Table 10.2

Types of Community Tools	
Communication Rings	**Content Trees**
Email and email lists	USENET
SMS	Bulletin boards
Instant messaging	Blogs
Chat rooms	Podcasting
Games and simulation	Web sites

social commitment and hierarchy, with increasingly well-understood and well-developed social etiquette. As mobile access grows in popularity, through cell phone and WiFi, email and short messaging are merging online communities with day-to-day activities.

Community identity can help with current problems plaguing email, including the high rate of spam, identity theft attempts, and unsolicited commercial offerings. Many users and email system operators are turning to spam filters with opt-in rules for permission, allowing only trusted sources of mailings. Such solutions require an address or mailing list be recognized and approved prior to first delivery. After approval, the originating address passes though the filter. As a community address gets added to this trusted list, communication flows easily between members without the burden of spam.

SMS and instant messaging reinforce quick, unstructured communication among close friends and colleagues. Like email, they allow both one-to-one and group communication. Almost by definition they operate within strong ties networks, as a cluster of friends or community participants form a group around an affinity or purpose. Both methods come with a higher expectation of immediate response, imposing a higher cost on the recipient's attention.

While a popular early element of online communities, especially on portals, chat rooms seem to be falling from favor as a community tool. Abuses have caused Yahoo! and MSN, among others, to close their chat rooms. Moderators and community rules that more tightly control access, especially by minors, prevent many of these problems.

Online games and simulations can stimulate communication and serve as a discussion ring. This is the case with the new generation of games, with IP telephony built into the games and communication headsets a standard feature. Competitors and collaborators can comment on the game as it unfolds, bringing a more social connection. As a pioneer of many of the tools of multi-user experience, and the high economic value of top titles, gaming increasingly provides both lessons and a platform for innovative community activities. Countries combining high speed broadband and a tradition of gaming, such as South Korea, are especially interesting.

> Content Trees

Size and growth present scaling problems for communication rings. They do not scale well. Too many messages come from strangers, and many discussions are inappropriate or uninteresting. Organization, focus, and some form of hierarchy are required to handle the flow of information.

Content trees are the other major category of online community-building tools. This includes discussion groups such as USENET, thousands of different dedicated bulletin boards and discussion threads, pod casts delivering audio material, and web sites with member content. Content trees are hierarchies that create manageable discussions. Rather than receive all messages, community members go to topic areas and specialized discussion groups that match their interest. Content trees branch into many subcategories. An example of this structural form is Figure 10.5, a topic oriented hierarchy of the National Science Digital Library. Similar visualization is possible with content sites such as About.com. Each content branch off the homepage reflects a broad interest category. Further divisions occur down the tree. Highly focused topic material and discussion are found on the "leaves" of the tree.

> *Do Online Tools Build Connection?*

Optimists see online communities as a method of rebuilding declining connections between friends and families and restoring social capital. They create new ways of relating. Online communities leverage the new communication tools to empower individuals and organizations. Smart companies harness this power to create loyal customers.

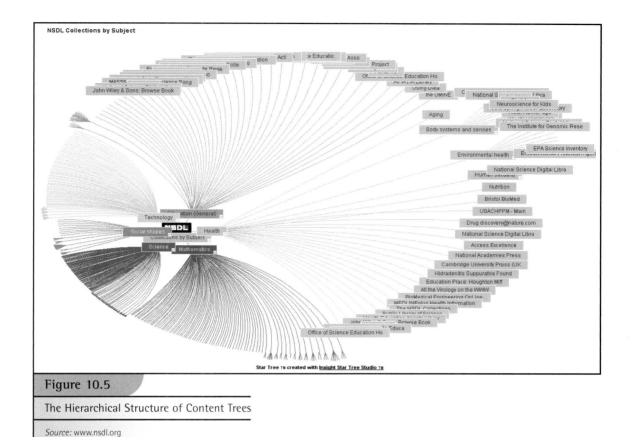

Figure 10.5

The Hierarchical Structure of Content Trees

Source: www.nsdl.org

Pessimists portray these new capabilities as an alienating, and ultimately depressing, time-waster. They see online communities as pale imitations of real, face-to-face interaction. Weak ties between near strangers replace strong ties between friends and neighbors.

> Community Optimists

Proponents of online community highlight the innovative methods of communication. Technologies such as message boards, chat rooms, instant messaging, and virtual worlds are expanding social networks. They allow new forms of communication between close friends, acquaintances, and strangers. These range from simple, single postings of information to in-depth, real-time debates of the most sensitive and personal topics.

A careful individual time diary finds time online allocated across a variety of these social activities. Table 10.3 shows the results of a study capturing detailed time logs of individuals over six sample hours per day.[12] It finds online time dominated by email and browsing, as well as some engagement in a variety of socially oriented activities. The email usage is notable, as the dominant share of email communication is with friends, relatives, and colleagues.

Online communities provide a focus for social interaction. Forums crystallize a wide range of participation. Dedicated members may spend hours per day, while occasional users log in monthly. Groups of friends may be reunited, or new links created among strangers with common interests.

Table 10.3

Online Time for Activities, Minutes per Day from Six Hour Time Slice		
	Male	Female
Email*	23.50	27.53
Internet browsing***	22.10	15.18
Instant messaging	3.31	4.14
Newsgroup/Message boards	3.01	2.20
Chat rooms	2.13	1.65
Creating/Maintaining web sites	2.26	1.47
Social networking	0.53	1.13
Total Internet/Email time	56.84	53.29
*p<.05 **p<.01 ***p<.001 by ANOVA		

Source: Norman Nie, Alberto Simpser, Irena Stepanikova, and Lu Zheng, "Ten Years After the Birth of the Internet, How Do Americans Use the Internet in Their Daily Lives?", report of the Stanford Center for the Quantitative Study of Society, December 2004. p. 17.

The beneficial impact of online interaction on social capital and social networking is felt most strongly by geographically distant friends and family,[13] experienced Internet users,[14] and females.[15] Like Lerma saving individuals worldwide in Figure 10.6, the community tools expand a person's social reach.

> Community Pessimists

Online community pessimists present a very different view. Rather than create value, these observers view the online world as harming individuals and stifling true community: "They (online communities) isolate us from one another and cheapen the meaning of actual experience."[16] Typing at a computer keyboard isn't viewed as true socializing, and social skills online may not be genuine interpersonal skills (Figure 10.7).

Some early studies of Net usage, as the Internet first entered the mainstream, found troubling signs. One study found that novices going online were measurably less well off the more they used the Internet. The more time users spent online, the more negatively they tested on psychological measures of loneliness and depression. This was especially true for teenagers. Paradoxically, users reported themselves pleased with the Internet experience and enjoyed being online.

The authors interpret their results as suggesting time and friendship displacement: "Our hypothesis is there are more cases where you're building shallow relationships (on the Internet),

Figure 10.6

Online Communities Expand Your Social Network and Influence

Source: Cartoon by Nik Scott/Curious Productions

Figure 10.7

Chat Skills Don't Necessarily Carry Over to the Real World

Source: Cartoon by Nik Scott/Curious Productions

leading to an overall decline in feeling of connection to other people".[17] In this sense the Net is having an impact like television, where private time comes at the expense of physical interaction with friends and family.[18] Online time seemed to be coming partially at the expense of traditional community, at least for younger users.

A more recent detailed time survey reinforces this time loss from families. It finds that for an average respondent, the daily three-hour usage of the Internet reduces "face time" with other family members by approximately one hour and ten minutes. It also reduces television watching by about 9 minutes per day and costs about 25 minutes of lost sleep time.[19]

While the 2004 study documents time displacement away from strong face-to-face interaction, it does find a modest overall expansion of time communicating socially when combining online and offline methods. Other research has documented the importance of face-to-face time "cementing" online interaction. Whether the quality of total increased time is equal to the displaced face-to-face time is hard to resolve.

> *Member Produced Content*

> Member Content Has Desirable Features

A well functioning online community has extensive member generated content. Not only is member generated content a sign of a healthy community, it can dominate sponsored content in several ways:

> *Less expensive*—Member material is very cheap to a community sponsor. Sites like Geocities or Tripod provide free web page hosting to their members. This minimal cost results in extensive content areas, many of them rich in material and attractive to advertisers.

> *Current*—Member content reflects their current interests. Active members keep their material current and interesting, updating web sites or blogs hourly. Few topic areas could justify a staff capable of such timely articles.

> *Creative*—Although quality varies widely, thousands of "editors" generate creative energy and unique points of view. Diversity captures emerging trends and provides a barometer of current interest.

> *Credible*—Access-controlled communities, especially those with professional affiliations, lend credibility to online recommendations. For example, doctors trust other doctors more than they trust pharmaceutical salespeople, and fellow alums share a connection to a school.

Not all four of these attributes need hold at the same time. A good example of massive volunteer contributions is the *Wikipedia*, an open source online encyclopedia with more than 1.2 million articles in the English language version.[20] It is somewhat surprising that Wikipedia works at all. All articles are freely editable at any time. While this sounds like a recipe for chaos, a system of after-the-fact reviews and easy restore capabilities leads to improvement over time for many contributions.[21] Two metrics of quality are the number of edits on the contribution and the average length (Figure 10.8). These have risen somewhat over time. Even so, article quality and coverage can be spotty.

> ## Contributions Are Skewed

Community organizers should expect heavily skewed usage and contribution patterns. Accesses to a community discussion area rely on heavy users for most of the page views. Contributions tilt even more toward heavy posters. Most members are passive "lurkers," spending their time reading material posted by others.

The Gnutella peer-to-peer music system, reader reviews at Amazon.com, and the Wikipedia project demonstrate the importance of heavy contributors. In the Gnutella network each member decides the amount of file sharing to the rest of the network. A study conducted in 2000 and again in 2004 found an extreme asymmetry in member file sharing.[22] Approximately 85% of users shared no files at all. The top 1% of file sharers accounted for more than 50% of sharing, and the top 25% accounted for more than 98%.

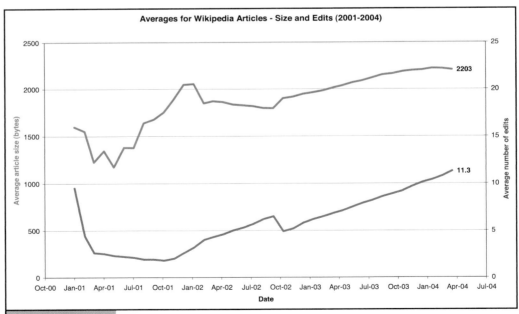

Figure 10.8

Rising Diversity and Length of Contributions to an Online Encyclopedia

Source: Andrew Lih, "Wikipedia as Participatory Journalism: Reliable sources? Metrics for evaluating collaborative media as a news resource," 5th International Symposium on Online Journalism, University of Texas at Austin, April 16–17, 2004, p. 6.

Amazon.com manages a repository of reviews visited by millions of users. Some contributors are highly prolific, with the top reviewers providing almost 10,000 reviews each. The average number of reviews among the top 1,000 reviewers was 150.[23] One reviewer, a former acquisitions librarian, stated that she read two books a day. Amazon wishes to encourage this prosocial behavior, noting heavy contributors for their activity. While monetary rewards are possible, providing status and recognition is often more effective. One common and effective tactic is to promote important contributors into the role of moderator and editor.

Figure 10.9

Amazon Praises its Top Reviewers, but Provides No Monetary Incentives

Wikipedia keeps a running tally of its active members, those who make more than five contributions a month, and its very active members who make more than 100 contributions per month. Figure 10.10 shows the rising participation of very active "wikipedians" in English (red), German (green), and French (blue). Contributors in English alone are responsible for thousands of edits a month.

> Online Tools Expand Discussions

Online tools can encourage users to submit content that would be deemed too personal, sensitive, or difficult to exchange without the tools. This occurs both in personal and professional settings, where online communication ability helps break down both social and geographical distance.

Most individuals have small social networks of people similar to themselves. In a survey conducted prior to the Net, researchers surveyed over 1,500 individuals about their discussion networks.

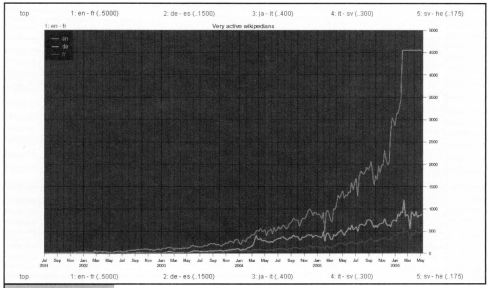

Figure 10.10

The Importance of the Highly Motivated Community Members

Source: Wikipedia.org

Respondents were asked whom they would talk to about important matters. Examples of important matters include family problems, finances, health, and politics.

In 1985 the average American had a discussion group of three people, roughly split between family and nonfamily. As seen in the Table 10.4, many groups had fewer members than this average and few had more than six. Over 58% of individuals had one or no nonkin friends they felt comfortable talking with about important matters. Family networks were also small, over 56% having one or no family members with whom they discuss important matters.

Participation in online communities dramatically expands and changes the nature of discussion networks. Far more individuals participate. These new collaborators span a wider range of personal connection strength. While strong ties may develop online, far more weak ties develop than in traditional discussion networks.

Table 10.4

Pre-Internet Average American Discussion Group Size for "Important Matters"

Network Size	Overall Network	Kin Network	Nonkin Network
0	8.9%	26.4%	36.4%
1	14.9%	29.6%	22.2%
2	15.3%	21.8%	18.9%
3	21.0%	12.6%	13.0%
4	15.2%	6.3%	6.3%
5	19.2%	3.3%	3.1%
6+	5.5%		
Mean	3.01	1.53	1.40

Source: Peter Marsden, "Core Discussion Networks of Americans," *American Sociological Review* 52 (February 1987): 122–131.

The following discussion is a typical example of online personal discussions about issues that are clearly important. This discussion comes from a threaded discussion about attention deficit hyperactivity disorder (ADHD) that is part of a commercial community targeting parents. A new mother raises a very sensitive question about diagnosing ADHD in her baby. Complicating the issue is her husband and in-laws' problems with attention deficit, and their sensitivity and reluctance to talk about it. The online site allows the concerned mom to raise her worries. Reassurance comes from other knowledgeable parents (comments edited slightly for length and privacy).

Original Question: A Quick (Long) Question About ADHD

"Okay, here goes: I have a 4 mo old daughter. Her dad is acute adult ADHD. So are both of his parents... He had horrible experiences in school with both classmates and teachers. He went through endless testing every year with psychologists, etc. He is medicated and doing well – major over achiever – now. However he was reluctant to have children because he was afraid he would pass this along to them. He is still terrified that our children will have to go through even a fraction of what he did. Here's the question: I know girls are less likely to have problems with ADHD but it is possible – his mom is an example – and we also hope one day to have a son. What do I look for and when do I look for it? How early is too early to begin behavior modification techniques, etc? Also, how do I begin to prepare myself to deal with this problem? ... Sorry so long. Just worried about what may lie ahead. Any advice would be appreciated. Thanks "

Reply 1: Re: A Quick (Long) Question)

"I think the stigma that went with add/adhd years ago is not as prevalent today as it was when your husband was in school. (Based on experience with son's school.) It doesn't bother us that other kids know that he has to take med and the kids don't make fun of him."

Reply 2: Re: A Quick (Long) Question)

"Generally speaking, your children would meet a much more progressive attitude in their schooling than your husband did. Sometimes this is not true, and you have to drag the school/teacher kicking and screaming into modern times–but not so often. And there are legal recourses that will force them to comply when necessary. Consistency, structure and good parenting techniques will help a lot. That may be hard for your husband though. On the other hand, he should be able to relate to an ADHD child!"

Original Poster Comments

"Thank you. I am banking on your being right about more advanced techniques in school. And I think you are right about dh doing well if we end up facing this challenge with our kids. ..."

Reply 3: I Can Understand Your Concern

"I have two boys, one with ADHD and one that has a more serious disorder and a daughter from my second marriage. I have always been scared to death that she too will have problems and she has to some extent but only because of what she lives with in our home (a major zoo). I would not spend so much time worrying about it. Enjoy your children now and accept them as they are. If it turns out that they are ADHD, you will know soon enough. In the meantime, educate yourself by reading everything you can about ADHD, skimming the boards here and keep your eyes and ears open. ADHD doesn't have to be a bad thing and in fact has many good aspects about it. Best of luck to you."

Original Poster Comments

"Thanks for your reply. I was hoping someone would just tell me to relax. I know what you mean about good aspects to ADHD. Fell hard for DH because of many of them. Thanks again."

What is striking about the conversation is the amount of personal history and personal concerns revealed to strangers. Anonymity can actually support this level of revelation. While an individual can always reveal his or her true name and identity, discussions start out with privacy protection. The concerned mother doesn't have to worry about close friends and family members viewing her as overly concerned and neurotic.

Communities dedicated to professional collaboration also expand discussion networks. A classic study of physician prescription behavior established the power of word of mouth among doctors. Within each of four Illinois towns, "thought leaders" among the doctors strongly influenced how quickly other doctors prescribed new antibiotics. Positive experiences of the thought leaders showed up in the prescribing behavior of their associates and colleagues.

In this pre-Web setting, physician collaboration was primarily local. No doctor cited word of mouth from a doctor in another town. There was little crossover between cities.[24] Online forums help expand the influence of more distant doctors. Local online dialog is the exception. Online chats with a doctor cross country are more likely than chats across town. An online community allows a doctor's influence to spread nationally, and even internationally.

> *Merge Published and Member Content*

Mixing sponsor and member content creates at least three important risks. The first is the balance between content quality and member freedom. The second risk is the chance that discussions and information posted online may hurt the reputation and brand of the sponsoring organization. Third, member content may involve the sponsor in legal problems.

A lack of control of member content by the sponsoring organization can result in off-topic messages, spam by guerilla marketers, and repetitious discussions of topics previously covered and archived. Too much control stifles member content and creates a perception that material is sponsor sanitized. One of the biggest choices is between real time member posting and built-in delays before the material appears. Real time material, such as immediate postings of discussion threads or chat rooms, makes control difficult. Only highly active moderators are able to intervene quickly enough to intercept inappropriate material. This is both expensive and intrusive.

Authentication deters some of the problems of real time content. Personally identified messages prevent many of the anonymous critical messages. Verification of identity will limit unsolicited messages from nonmembers. The spread of the individualization GPT reinforces the connection between posting and the poster, which can cause problems when sensitive or politically charged discussion is the goal of the online community.

A community sponsor needs to decide its editorial enforcement policy. Once announced, it becomes an expectation and commitment. Table 10.5 highlights examples of control policies and some of the issues raised by each.

Table 10.5

Editorial Control Used by Sponsor			
Example of Online Community	**Control of Member Content**	**Commercial Issues**	**Legal Issues**
Most USENET forums, most general purpose online chat	No control No member has privileged control over postings.	High quality risk Many incomplete postings, off topic spam and mistakes, low quality forums lacking focus.	Low legal risk Community becomes a carrier of information.
Physicians Online[25]	Authentication Member's qualifications for membership are verified, but not content.	Difficult to find a method of authenticating that doesn't create a high barrier to new members.	Depends on authentication quality. Biggest problem areas involve material not suitable for minors.
SeniorNet	Passive Moderator Spamming, profanity, inappropriate content removed as noticed.	Volunteer moderators help create better focus to topics and assist new members.	Creates an expectation of control and possible exposure to liability problems.

Bad word of mouth is a risk for a hybrid commercial community. The high technology industry, and Intel in particular, got a very strong taste of this when online forums documented both a bug in the original Intel Pentium chip and Intel's initial responses. Online forums can magnify and accelerate the spread of bad information.[26]

Forums create the potential for negative comments by members about the community sponsor and its services. In communities closely tied to a product or service, this danger requires careful monitoring by paid staff members of the community sponsor. Some amount of negative commentary is expected. Quick response is vital, not necessarily in terms of pulling the offensive posting, but in responding with the company's point of view.

Legal issues are a concern of many community sponsors. Active control increases the liability of the sponsor. Once a site chooses to control some material, there is an increasing risk that silence on other material constitutes assent. This perspective is one reason why many Internet service providers and forum sponsors view their alternatives as the extremes of exerting no control whatsoever or shutting down the entire forum. Partial editing creates more legal exposure than no editing at all. However, a lack of control makes it more likely that objectionable content appears.

Learning from Online Communities

Online communities provide opportunities for insight into some of the most loyal and profitable customers. With both quantitative and qualitative tools, firms can measure ongoing community efforts, track the success of specific campaigns, map out social networks, and serve as an early warning system for troubling developments and brewing problems. They utilize the customer profiles and online interactions that occur within the community.

> *Community Health*
Table 10.5 highlights some of the metrics for tracking the positive community feedback loops. Together they monitor both the quality of the community content and the quality of the ongoing communication.

> Content Attractiveness
Standard web log reports provide extensive statistics on the attention paid to different content areas, which reflects both content attractiveness and member loyalty. Counts of web page views and most popular paths taken give clear pictures of most popular content. Community organizers and content editors find these to be a valuable source of insights. The information helps reinforce and expand popular areas, fix problem areas, and possibly downplay or eliminate neglected content.

There are statistical measures of the richness of content trees and their diversity. Two simple measures are depth and breadth, as measured by the number of content tree levels and the number of content tree leaves. More complex methods look at the diversity of topics and member usage. Total edits and time since last edit are useful for tracking content freshness.

Emailed articles suggest content eliciting strong emotions. This does not necessarily indicate a satisfactory response, but it at least indicates the story touches a nerve and generates community discussion.

> Member Loyalty
Log analysis provides tools for analyzing member loyalty. Usage and duration patterns can be graphed and compared over time. Usage by members can be compared to see what fraction of

views and content are accounted for by heavy users. Churn and retention measures require additional programming and study, but many support tools are available. Combining the online community activity with activity levels from customer relationship management tools provides insight, as shown in Figure 10.2, linking online tools to monetary rewards.

> Member Profiles

Database marketing methods can be used to evaluate the information collected about community members. We will investigate this issue in some detail in later chapters. In addition to measures of purchasing, community sponsors can use tools of social network analysis to understand the patterns of collaboration in their communities. Interesting insight is sure to emerge, and valuable members will be spotted. This may lead to extra efforts and encouragement for key community leaders to make sure they stay active in the community.

> Transaction Offerings

Transaction offerings are some of the most exciting areas of online marketing.

Table 10.6

Measuring Community Strength

Community Feature	Possible Metrics
Content attractiveness	Access frequency
	Content diversity
	Contributor edits
	Emailed articles
Member loyalty	Access frequency
	Access duration
	Referrals
	Churn, opt-out rates
Member profiles	Database completeness
	User update frequency
	Email bounces
Transaction offerings	Sales revenue
	Active vendors
	Customer LTV
	Items offered

Online commerce is taking off, and the measures listed for online communities can also be used to measure the success of many online commerce activities.

> *Interaction Measures*

Email campaigns provide some of the most direct measures of the underlying community strength. Campaigns can be highly targeted, and each email goes to an identified individual. Metrics from each campaign provide useful feedback on the receptiveness of different segments and the effectiveness of different approaches. For example, the SAA tracks the open rate, the opt-out rate, the click-through rate, the propensity to update an individual's profile, and the willingness of those reading the email to follow additional links. Each of these provides clues to the quality of the dialog.

Different campaigns can reveal the systematic strength of the community and the particulars of individual cohorts or outreach efforts. For a university there will be some classes that consistently outperform other years. Careful tracking and good metrics can separate these factors from the broader trends for multiple cohorts.

More in-depth learning is possible with more information and more powerful approaches. Combining email and web pages, as in Figure 10.11, lets a community sponsor better track social

RTA Code: ___4661___ E-mail Name: ___Class of '94 Reunion announcement: need volunteers (Frosh), March___

Segment Description: ___March Class of '94 email announcement to recruit volunteers(rich text, no graphics)___ Segment ___1___
of ___1___

Please enter your raw data in the yellow boxes below. (where do I find this data?)

Total sent:	1429	Total unique clicks:	80
Total unique views:	937	Total information update clicks:	15
Total unique opt-out (unsubscribe) clicks:	0		

Your e-mail performance results are located in the green boxes below. Type: Promotion (E)

			SAA AVG 2004	Promotion AVG 2004	Your E-mail vs. SAA	vs. E
Open Rate: _How many viewed my e-mail communication?_	(improve it!)	68.30%	52.15%	62.98%	16.15%	5.32%
Opt-Out (Unsubscribe Rate): _How many unsubscribed - ceased further receipt of my e-mail communication?_	(improve it!)	0.00%	0.12%	0.08%	-0.12%	-0.08%
Total Unique Click-Through Rate (CTR): _How many clicked at least one embedded link in my e-mail communication?_	(improve it!)	5.83%	- -	- -	- -	- -
Adjusted Total Unique Click-Through Rate (ACTR): _How many clicked at least one **non-unsubscribe** embedded link in my e-mail communication?_	(improve it!)	5.83%	- -	- -	- -	- -
Information Update Rate: _How many clicked through my e-mail communication to make changes in their online profile?_	(improve it!)	1.09%	0.28%	0.50%	0.81%	0.59%
Click-To-Open Rate (CTOR): _How effective was my e-mail communication in motivating those who opened it to click a link?_	(improve it!)	8.54%	- -	- -	- -	- -
Loss-To-Open Rate (LTOR): _Were a large percentage opening my e-mail communication to unsubscribe?_	(improve it!)	0.00%	0.23%	0.14%	-0.23%	-0.14%

Figure 10.11

Email Tracking by Stanford Alumni Association

Source: Stanford Alumni Association

networks. Figure 10.12 shows an intriguing example of both the social connections present online and a system for learning about them.[27] The email inboxes of members of a professional community were used to identify names of individuals directly communicating. The system then identified as well as possible the relevant homepages of these individuals and the information on the web pages pointing to connected individuals (such as co-authors) and their relevant areas of interest. From this, clustered social networks revealed the underlying linkages between individuals in the group.

What is especially powerful about this type of analysis is the ability to check the clustering against external knowledge of the community. The researchers were able to identify the individuals the software made hubs and authorities, and check the validity against other, more qualitative knowledge.

> Netnography

Research teams are applying *netnography*, the online equivalent of ethnography, in an attempt to capture qualitative insights from commercially relevant online communities.[28] In traditional ethnography an anthropologist or other social scientist spends time living and observing within a social group. The same is true online, although the presence may be overt or in the background.

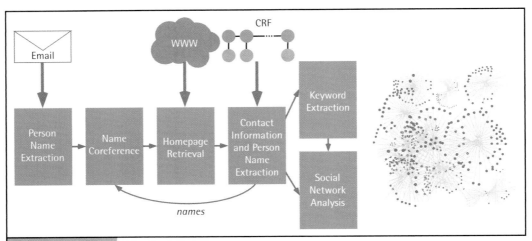

Figure 10.12

Using Email and Homepages to Identify Communities of Interest

Source: Aron Culotta, Ron Bekkerman, and Andrew McCallum, "Extracting Social Networks and Contact Information from Email and the Web," American Association for Artificial Intelligence, 2004, p. 2.

Appropriate sites have more focus, a diverse set of posters, more traffic, detailed messages, and a high volume of between-member interactions.[29]

One study focused on coffee and the various USENET groups devoted to it. The major focus of the study was <alt.coffee>, with a worldwide readership estimated at the time to be around 100,000. This is a top 50 USENET group, with a devoted set of core contributors and far more readers. The study found the online material a useful window into the "coffeephile," and a method for seeing what the highly motivated and intense category fan views as important.

Just as the online sites provide a window on the highly motivated fan, they reveal lessons about the highly motivated critic. Boycott sites can serve as the hubs for complaints and negative word of mouth. They can provide insight into how best to handle a commercial crisis, whether it is a product defect problem or complaints about the ethics of production and employment.[30] Increasingly, companies are contracting with specialists to track online product mentions, both positive and negative.

Online community sites provide a rich setting for determining the motivations for providing online commentary and other contributions. In a study of German online communities, a research team found multiple significant factors driving online word of mouth and four identifiable segments of contributors that had different importance attached to these factors.[31] Motivating factors for community members were a desire to provide platform assistance and vent negative feelings, a concern for other consumers, their extraversion and positive self-enhancement, social benefits, economic incentives, helping the company, and advice seeking. The four clustered segments they labeled "self-interested helpers, "Multiple-motive consumers," "consumer advocates," and "true altruists." They find the first segment the largest at 34%, and heavily driven by economic incentives. The multiple-motive segment assigned high weights to many of the factors, and was the third largest segment with 21% of respondents. The consumer advocates were more narrowly focused, with 17% of respondents fitting into that cluster. The true altruists were the second largest group at 27%, motivated by helping both fellow consumers and the companies involved.

While these factors and segment sizes are community-specific, they indicate both the possibility of using online contributions to reveal the structure of community participation and the different motivations driving online participation. Some community members are in it for their own benefit, while others look to help others. It is a mistake to assume all members of the community share the same motivations in using a community, just as different factors drive the choice of a product or service.

RETENTION MARKETING

Building community is an option for many organizations, both nonprofit and commercial, to reinforce commitment and loyalty among members. Chapter 6 described brand community, which harnesses many of the concepts of the previous part to augment the value provided to current customers. Commercial firms have a number of additional methods to retain customers and to encourage additional purchases.

The previous chapter focused on situations where personalization occurs as a web site visit unfolds. Having an existing relationship makes this personalization work better, as personalization systems take advantage of in-depth profiles to configure products, send appropriate messages, and quote the best terms of sale. One of the weaknesses of approaches relying solely on web site visits is the inertia of the contact. Only if the customer accesses the site is there a possibility of interchange.

With current customers, a firm can initiate contacts through email, messaging, and other marketing activities. These retention activities start with customer profiling, combining personalization tools with outbound communication efforts such as email and marketing programs based on customer classification.

Retention programs go beyond making offers. Maintaining a customer dialogue is a higher level of relationship than personalized advice giving. Creating a dialogue environment requires customer insights, business rules, and software capabilities.

Customer Base Analysis

> *Analyzing Most Profitable Customers*

As seen in Chapter 5, customers vary substantially in lifetime value. This observation leads firms to invest extra resources and online features in their best customers.[32] The first step is identifying the factors driving differences among customer lifetime value.

Figure 5.11 showed the skewed nature of customer profitability. Analysts try to determine what characteristics high value customers on the left of the graph possess. Many direct and online marketers find customer loyalty a prime influence on profitability.[33] Longer duration means lower expenditures on customer acquisition. It creates a longer history of interactions, providing a learning environment and more in-depth profile of interests and preferences. Within business-to-business settings, Chapter 15 shows how longer term contractual relationships encourage investments in automatic buying procedures, electronic connections supporting real-time data, and many other profitable connections. In the B2C setting, consumers purchase services such as Internet access, cell phone service, cable and satellite services, and health club membership on fixed term contracts.

Loyalty receives so much emphasis that it is important to remember that transactional customers can also be quite profitable. Table 10.7 shows the results of a consumer study in a mail-order setting.[34] The study classifies customers into four segments based on the duration of the relationship (long versus short) and lifetime revenue (high versus low). The entry in each cell is the average lifetime profitability of the customer segment.

The upper right hand cell consists of customers with a long duration of relationship and high lifetime revenue. This is the conventional wisdom about the impact of customer duration on profits, and the segment does have the highest lifetime profitability. However, the top left cell and the bottom right cell

Table 10.7

Relationship Duration, Lifetime Revenue, and Lifetime Profitability

	Lifetime Revenue	
Relationship Duration	*Low*	*High*
Long	$50.85	$289.83
Short	$50.49	$257.96

Source: Werner Reinartz and V. Kumar, "The Mismanagement of Customer Loyalty," *Harvard Business Review* 80, no. 7 (July 2002): 86–94.

provide interesting counterpoints. The customers in the bottom right cell are short lived. With an average lifetime profit of $257.96, they are also profitable. There are low profitability customers with both long and short duration.

Profitability depends on much more than just customer loyalty.[35] This has several implications. While loyalty is valuable, loyalty must be balanced against the costs of retention. Second, transactional customers need support and encouragement and cannot be ignored. Value comes from a flexible marketing environment capable of handling both occasional and regular customers.

A sophisticated customer relationship program works to identify profitable customers, reinforce their particular preferences, and match cost-effective marketing programs with features that encourage additional involvement. Online tools can be essential and provide the least expensive methods of direct and personalized interaction. The personalization capabilities of the last chapter often have loyalty and duration as their objectives.

> Loyalty Programs

Loyalty programs are a popular approach to building customer commitment. The most prominent examples are frequent flyer programs pioneered by the airline industry. Firms in industries as diverse as automobile rentals, hotels, retailers, coffee shops and restaurants offer loyalty programs.

Loyalty programs can be simple "buy 10, get 1 free" promotions by a small coffee shop or a global program costing millions to launch and maintain. At Sainsbury, UK, the annual cost of the points in the Nectar program is over 100 million pounds, amounting to one of the largest outsourcing partnerships undertaken.[36] Airlines can spend between 3 and 6% of revenue on frequent flyer programs.[37]

Typical objectives of customer loyalty programs include maintaining sales and profits and improving customer loyalty and incremental sales.[38] Another desired benefit is reduced price competition by inducing switching costs.[39] The benefits and effectiveness of loyalty programs is a subject of keen interest. The types of rewards offered and program effectiveness are inter-related. The fundamental issue is whether a loyalty program encourages consumers to shift from a single-period transaction to a multi-period focus.[40]

Loyalty programs affect different segments in different ways. One study of a reward program found that the best customers redeemed the award more often, but the program had a less beneficial impact on spending than it did with lower profitability customers. In other words, the reward program was generating more incremental spending per customer with less loyal recipients.

Appropriate types of rewards are crucial in motivating buyers.[41] Table 10.8 classifies consumer promotions, emphasizing the timing of rewards. Immediate benefits stimulate new sales and renewal of activity, while delayed benefits help concentrate purchases and build provider loyalty.

Some rewards improve the quality of the underlying service.[42] For example, airlines offer priority check-in and pre-boarding privileges, upgrades to superior seating, and business class flights. Hotels and car rental companies follow similar practices. Some credit card companies such as Discover card offer cash back on purchases. Other credit card companies allow customers to redeem their points on a number of products, sometimes offered in conjunction with a catalog retailer.

Table 10.8		
Loyalty Program Types		
	Timing of Reward	
Type of Reward	*Immediate (acquisition, renewal)*	*Delayed (share of wallet)*
Direct (supports product's value proposition)	Price promotions	Frequent flyers clubs, coupons and tokens
Indirect	Competitions and lotteries	Multi-product frequent-buyer clubs

Large casinos rely on rewards programs in their competition for "heavy rollers" and frequent visitors. The rewards programs offered by Harrah's Casino illustrates a common approach. The entry-level status for the program is Gold. Enrollment in the program provides a member with the Gold status, with just a few immediate benefits (rewards for playing, small discounts at the gift shop, and some bonuses with partners). There is a steep increase in the benefits for the Platinum status, encouraging concentration of purchases to move from Gold to Platinum (birthday gifts, much bigger discounts on tickets and merchandise, and free tournament entry and hotel stays).

Visible differences in service levels can also be an important element, especially for socially consumed products such as casino services. Diamond cardholders use different check in locations and customer service desks, providing higher quality service and status. This type of differentiation appeals to both customer aspirations[43] and exclusivity.[44] In addition to all benefits given Gold and Platinum cardholders, Diamond cardholders receive priority treatment and exclusive dedicated events.

Loyalty programs can span multiple providers. Partnerships and alliances allow customers to pool their spending across different merchants. Ease of participation, ease of use, and ease of management can also help. Trading stamps programs, the precursor of loyalty card programs, did not achieve market penetration because the perceived costs of participating and redemption were too high for many consumers. Digital technologies including magnetic strip cards reduce transaction costs for consumers. These are often alliances of complementary service providers, such as the full range of travel services (flights, car rental, hotels, etc.).

Online documentation of loyalty programs makes them more attractive to customers and less likely to lead to confusion. Interactive explanations and videos of upgrade benefits make distinctions clearer than brochures and tables alone. Online account status can track accumulating miles, help ensure accuracy, lower the need to call customer support, and facilitate low transaction costs when awarding program benefits.

> Switching Costs

Loyalty programs are one example of the more general commitment building that comes from consumer switching costs. Switching costs are the extra expenses, complications, and lost opportunities that arise when a customer switches vendors of a product or service. Switching costs can stem from difficulties of using a vendor, or they can be created deliberately through loyalty programs and strategies of providers.

Switching costs play a fundamental role in cushioning competition between service providers. Without the ability to separate customer types, firms facing segments of loyal and switching customers must decide whether to aggressively pursue switching consumers or to cater to their loyal segments. Loyal customers provide more stability and often higher margins, while switching segments provide additional customer volume. As loyal segments grow in size and commitment, price competition may fall as well. This can be a dynamic additional benefit from loyalty programs.

Competitive effects of switching costs may be more complicated when online tools segment markets effectively. The competition-lessening impact of loyalty might be reduced when personalized offers target each segment without "spilling over" to other segments. It is possible that aggressive online targeting of rival firms' loyal customers can be separated from an immediate price impact on a firm's own loyal customers. Because of this, firms may launch programs to "steal" rivals' loyal customers. Ultimately, this competition could lead to even more aggressive pricing. More research is needed to understand whether the full impact of switching costs is the same with online personalization and targeted pricing approaches.

Even with this competitive uncertainty, in many situations the fundamental impact of switching costs will be to raise existing customer profitability. Figure 10.13 shows three different breakdowns of switching costs.[45] Procedural costs are the time and effort required to make a transition. Financial costs are the lost benefits and out-of-pocket expenses. Relational costs are the lost learning, the lost customization, and the lost emotional connection to a previous vendor.

Some of the most important personalization impacts in financial services work to create switching costs for current customers or mitigate switching costs for a rival's customers. Online banking services create switching costs, especially those with bill paying capabilities. Procedural switching costs are substantial. Experience with the incumbent service is more tangible than any prospective alternative. Set-up and learning costs will be incremental for the new service,

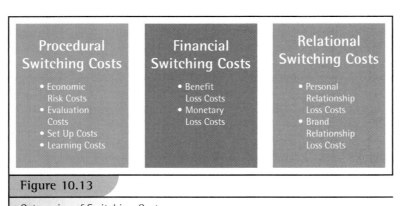

Figure 10.13

Categories of Switching Costs

Source: Adapted from Thomas Burnham, Judy Freis, and Vijay Mahajan, "Consumer Switching Costs: A Typology, Antecedents, and Consequences," *Journal of the Academy of Marketing Science* 31, no. 2 (2003): 109–126.

already incurred for the current provider. Financial costs are potentially very large, if there is a glitch in payments and penalties and ill will accrues. Relational costs exist with preferred rates or capabilities provided to banking customers with multiple services.

On the other hand, a company can invest in reducing consumer switching costs from a rival bank or provider. Software to convert information and transfer from the competitor can reduce the procedural switching costs. Examples, demos, and testimonials can reduce the perceived financial and relational risks. Sign-up bonuses help offset remaining switching costs.

| Dialogue Marketing

The interaction that a good salesperson has with an established customer sets the benchmark for relationship marketing. Effective conversations are "relationship aware" and time sensitive. A good salesperson continues the interaction even after the sale, building the relationship with effective and timely conversations. For example, a salesperson might remember the one-year anniversary of a customer's purchase of an engagement ring and send him a postcard. Effective conversations are also interactive. If a customer does not respond to a message, the salesperson might either follow up with a different message or use a different channel.

The goal of dialogue marketing is to move this capability to the Net. A dialogue is a rich conversation enabled by the three Internet general-purpose technologies, and if possible it is relationship aware, interactive, and closed loop. Just as a good salesperson has an impeccable sense of timing, dialogue targets the most opportune moment. The timing of a dialogue corresponds with the customer's need as opposed to the firm's marketing calendar.

Preventing customer defection is a natural setting for online dialogue marketing. Many firms use exit interviews or other tactics to recover customers as they defect, but by then it might be too late.[46] Consider an example from a catalog retailer. The retailer observes that one of their best customers has suddenly stopped shopping. The retailer wants to know whether the customer is gone, is about to leave, or simply does not need any products at the moment. Each of these states leads to different business issues and possible messaging strategies.

The goal for most models of customer duration is to produce an individual-specific probability that a customer is still active based on the customer's history. One particularly easy to use method computes this probability based on three inputs for each customer:[47]

> the length of time T_j the individual has been a customer,
> the number of purchases n_j within this time interval, and
> the time of the most recent purchase t_j.

Along with certain assumptions, these three specific individual inputs (T_j, n_j, t_j) generate a probability that customer j is active. Probabilities close to one put that specific customer on the right side of Figure 10.14, close to zero on the left.

With the knowledge of an individual's chance of defection, the retailer can immediately launch a dialogue to prevent it. If the customer was high value, the dialogue might be a phone call from an executive. If the customer is low value, an email is more appropriate. If the customer complains of poor service, there might be a follow-up apology that provides them with an incentive to return.

Email is a natural tool for building loyalty online.[48] It reaches out to customers, rather than waiting for them to show up. It can quickly provide information, with a short cycle time from

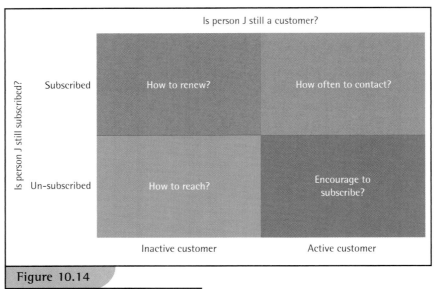

Figure 10.14

Customer State and Contact Questions

the decision to send a message to receipt of that message to the response. Its low cost makes follow-up mailings equally cost effective. As Table 10.9 shows, it is highly measurable. Different responses by customers indicate various stages of involvement. The open rate and click-through rate indicate basic interest and willingness to continue participating. As seen in other contexts, such as search marketing, revenue per message and lifetime value of acquired customer provide the connection between customer behavior and direct profits.

The unsubscribe rate needs to be carefully monitored and is a fundamental variable governing the frequency of contacting customers. The marginal benefit of a mailing needs to exceed the marginal cost, including the value of customers unsubscribing. This is a tight restriction, as any particular mailing that provokes a customer to unsubscribe sacrifices all future contact opportunities, while the marginal benefit is solely from the single mailing's productivity.

Figure 10.15 on page 352 illustrates the design of this type of dialogue using a software platform. The design process begins with a qualification of the status of the customer. A qualification in general assesses the state of the customer. In this case, the qualification is a test of whether the customer is at risk. If the customer qualifies, the next step is to follow a condition. A condition is a rule that specifies what the action should be. For high value customers the action is a follow up phone call. For low value customers the follow up is an email. The follow up actions indicate some aspects of a dialogue can be executed offline with a reminder sent to a salesperson to make a follow up phone call.

The system now monitors for an event defined as a response or lack thereof from the customer. The event examines if the customer does not respond within three weeks. If so, following another condition, high value customers receive a second follow up, whereas the dialogue

Table 10.9

Email Customer Engagement Continuum		
Retention and Loyalty Email Marketing		
Customer Attitude or Goal	*Customer Behavior*	*Metric*
I am reading what you are sending me.	Opens email	Open rate per message delivered
I am interested in the information you provide.	Clicks on links in email	Click-through rate per message delivered
The offers you extend are relevant to me.	Purchases products	Revenue per promotional message delivered
Your program continues to hold my interest.	Maintains subscription; visits web site without prompting; modifies profile; participates in surveys	Rate of subscriber base that has unsubscribed; number of site visits; survey results
I am loyal to your company.	Purchases more products; makes unprompted purchases; refers friends	Lifetime value per customer

Source: Han Peter Brondmo, *The Engaged Customer: The New Rules of Internet Direct Marketing* (New York: Harper Business, 2000), 167 [Table 8.1].

terminates for low value customers. This is the second step in a multi-step dialogue. Since these actions are conditional on the customer's response, they are the follow-through closed-loop aspects of the dialogue.

As this example illustrates, a dialogue specifies a decision tree that executes automatically. Design elements of a dialogue include qualifications, conditions, actions and events. Once specified the dialogue marketing system automatically monitors for a change in a customer state, which can lead to a qualifying event.

Customers go through many transitions in their relationship with a firm. Dialogues can target these transitions and build stronger relationships. A crucial type of customer transition is with respect to the customer's status in the loyalty program. Often customer spending levels might get close enough to tip them into the next loyalty class. Tipping point dialogues remind customers that they are close to a transition point. In the case of an airline, a customer might be ten thousand miles away from the next loyalty level and might have two more months in the year to achieve it. A tipping point dialogue can automatically trigger a message to the customer.

Other tipping points occur around trial and repeat. An online grocery retailer found customers needed to reach a history of at least three purchases before their behavior moved from experimental to loyal customers. Dialogue targeting trial users to encourage further purchases was valuable in stimulating additional activity and reminding them of the service.

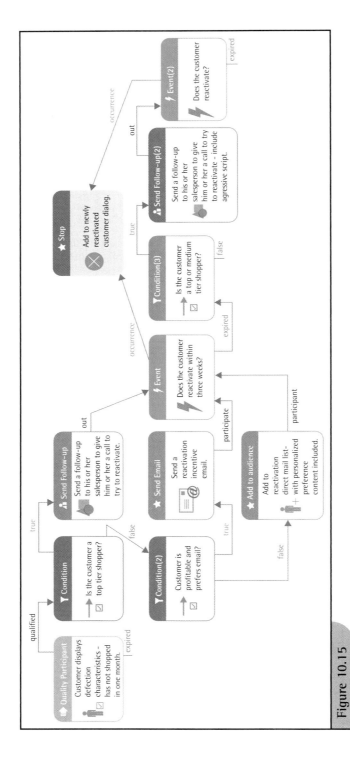

Figure 10.15

A Defection Dialogue that Chooses the Right Channel Based on Customer Value

Source: Kalyanam and Zweben

ENDNOTES

1. Werner Reinartz and V. Kumar. "The Mismanagement of Customer Loyalty." *Harvard Business Review* July 2002.
2. Margaret J. Wheatley and Myron Kellner-Rogers. "The Paradox and Promise of Community." In Hesselbein et.al., Ed, The Community of the Future, The Drucker Foundation, 1998:14.
3. Information provided by the SAA.
4. Now known as Affinity Engines, the InCircle service exists on numerous other campuses. However, at each campus the rule limits connection to that alumni network.
5. Recall from Chapter 3 that someone you know personally is 1 degree, a person that person knows but you do not is 2 degrees, etc. The shortest path is a connection with the fewest number of intermediaries.
6. These terms are taken from two of the influential books about online community, one by Hagel and Armstrong and the other by Stoll.
7. Andrea Ciffolilli. "Phantom Authority: Self-selective recruitment and retention of members in virtual communities: The case of Wikipedia." *First Monday* November 2003. W. Steinmueller. "Virtual communities and the new economy." 2002. In R. Mansell, Ed. *Inside the communication revolution: Evolving patterns of social and technical interaction.* Oxford University Press: Oxford, 2002.
8. Data from Pew Internet Project. Graph appears in Jenny Preece, Diane Maloney-Krichmar, and Chadia Abras. "History and emergence of online communities." In B. Wellman, Ed. Encyclopedia of Community. Berkshire Publishing Group: Sage, 2003.
9. Hagel and Armstrong. Net Gain.
10. For an in-depth discussion of the difficulties of building and maintaining community in the modern world see Robert Putnam. *Bowling Alone: The Collapse and Revival of American Community.* Simon & Schuster: New York, 2000.
11. Miriam Catterall and Pauline Maclaran. "Researching consumers in virtual worlds: A cyberspace odyssey." *Journal of Consumer Behavior* 1(3), 2001: 228–237.
12. Norman Nie, Alberto Simpser, Irena Stepanikova, and Lu Zheng. "Ten Years After the Birth of the Internet, How Do Americans Use the Internet in Their Daily Lives?" Report of the Stanford Center for the Quantitative Study of Society, December 2004.
13. Keith N. Hampton and Barry Wellman. "The Not So Global Village of Netville." In Barry Wellman and Caroline Haythornthwaite, Eds. *The Internet in Everyday Life.* Blackwell Publishing: Oxford, 2002.
14. Andrea Kavanaugh and Scott J. Patterson. 2002, "The Impact of Community Computer Networks on Social Capital and Community Involvement in Blacksburg, in Wellman and Haythornthwaite, ibid.
15. Nie et. al., op. cit.
16. Clifford Stoll. *Silicon Snake Oil,* 1997.
17. "So lonely, I could cry." *Computing Canada.* Willowdale, Sep 14, 1998; Anonymous; citing Carnegie-Mellon Study. Robert Kraut ,Vicki Lundmark, Michael Patterson, Sara Kiesler, Tridas Mukopadhyay, and William Scherlis. *American Psychologist* 53(9), September 1998: 1017–1031.
18. This is the essential argument of Robert Putnam – private time harms community. His main villain is television. Putnam, Robert. "The Strange Disappearance of Civic America." *The American Prospect.* Vol. 24, No. 1, 1996: 34.
19. Nie et. al., op. cit.
20. As of July 2006. For the growth curve, see Figure 11.25 in Chapter 11.
21. See Andrew Lih. "Wikipedia as Participatory Journalism: Reliable source? Metrics for evaluating collaborative media as a news resource." *5th International Symposium on Online Journalism.* University of Texas at Austin, April 16–17, 2004. Also see Andrea Ciffolilli. "Phantom Authority, self-selective recruitment and retention of members in virtual communities: The case of Wikipedia." *First Monday.* No. 8, 12, 2003.
22. E. Adar and B. Huberman. "Free Riding on Gnutella." *First Monday.* October 2000. Daniel Hughes, Geoff Coulson, and James Walkerdine. "Free Riding on Gnutella Revisited: The Bell Tolls? *IEEE DS Online.* 2004.
23. Mani Subramani and Naren Peddibhotla. "Quantity and Quality: Understanding contribution of Knowledge to public document repositories." Working paper: Information and Decision Sciences Department, Carlson School of Management, University of Minnesota, May 3, 2004.
24. Coleman, Katz, Menzel (1966). See also Burt (1987) and Burt and Uchiyama (1989).
25. Now part of WebMD.
26. See Jacob Goldenberg, Barak Libai, Sarit Moldovan, and Eitan Muller. "The Economic Implications of Negative Word of Mouth: A Dynamic Small-World Approach." Working paper: Tel Aviv University, August 2004.

27. Aron Culotta, Ron Bekkerman, and Andrew McCallum. "Extracting Social Networks and Contact Information from Email and the Web." *American Association for Artificial Intelligence* 2004.

28. Robert Kozinets. "The Field Behind the Screen: Using Netnography for Marketing Research in Online Communities." *Journal of Marketing Research* XXXXIX(2), February, 61–72. also Catterall and Maclaran, op.cit. cit.

29. Ibid.

30. R. Kozinets and J. Handelman. "Ensouling Consumption: A Netnographic Exploration of the Meaning of Boycotting Behavior." *Advances in Consumer Research* 25, 1998.

31. Results from Thorsten Hennig-Thurau, Kevin P. Gwinner, Gianfranco Walsh, Dwayne D. Gremler. "Electronic Word-of-Mouth Via Consumer-Driven Platforms: What Motivates Consumers to Articulate Themselves on the Internet?" *Journal of Interactive Marketing* 18(1), Winter 2004. Also see Thorsten Hennig-Thurau and Gianfranco Walsh. "Electronic Word-of-Mouth: Motives for and Consequences of Reading Customer Articulations on the Internet." *International Journal of Electronic Commerce* 8(2), Winter 2003–2004: 51–74.

32. For many demand settings it is better to provide these digital enhancements as a bundled service to the enhanced product, rather than try to price them separately.

33. For example, Frederick Reichheld. *The Loyalty Effect: The Hidden Force Behind Growth, Profits, and Lasting Value.* Harvard Business School Press: Cambridge, 1996.

34. Adapted from Werner J. Reinhartz and V. Kumar. "On the Profitability of Long Life Customers in a Noncontractual Setting: An Empirical Investigation and Implications for Marketing." *Journal of Marketing* 64, October 2000: 17–35.

35. For example Werner Reinartz and V. Kumar. "The Mismanagement of Customer Loyalty." *Harvard Business Review* July 2002: note that managing customers for loyalty is not the same as managing them for profit.

36. John Deighton, ibid. See also Briony Hale. "The Cost of Nectar Loyalty." BBC News February 17, 2003.

37. "Extra Lift for Airlines." Asian Business August 1993: 44–66.

38. Grahame R. Dowling and Mark Uncles. (1997). "Do Customer Loyalty Programs Really Work?" *Sloan Management Review,* 38(4), 1997: 71–82.

39. Paul Klemperer. The Competitiveness of Markets with Switching Costs. *Rand Journal of Economics* 18(1), 1987: 138–150.

40. For an analysis of this longer-term relation perspective as a dynamic optimization problem, see Michael Lewis. The Influence of Loyalty Programs and Short Term Promotions on Customer Retention. *Journal of Marketing Research.* August 2004: 281–292.

41. These five elements are adapted from L. O' Brien and C. Jones. "Do Rewards Really Create Loyalty?" *Harvard Business Review* 73, May–June 1995: 75–82.

42. See Michelle L. Roehm, Ellen Bolman Pullins, and Harper A Roehm Jr. "Designing Loyalty Building Programs for Packaged Goods Brands." *Journal of Marketing Research* 32, May 2002: 202–213 for a discussion of cue compatible incentives and their role in loyalty building programs.

43. Gary Loveman. "Diamonds in the Data Mine." *Harvard Business Review* May 2003.

44. Social consumption can be a powerful motivator – documented by economists and sociologists since the time of Thorstein Veblen.

45. Thomas Burnham, Judy Freis, and Vijay Mahajan. "Consumer Switching Costs: A Typology, Antecedents, and Consequences." *Journal of the Academy of Marketing Science* 31(2), 2003: 109–126.

46. Martin Kon. Stop Customer Churn Before it Starts. *Harvard Management Update* May 2004: argues that customer satisfaction surveys do not capture enough customers who have decided to leave. He cites the example of one European ISP who found that almost 80% of ex customers has described themselves as satisfied or very satisfied in a survey they filled out 12 months before they dropped the service.

47. Peter Fader, Bruce Hardie, Ka Lok Lee. "'Counting Your Customers' the Easy Way: An Alternative to the Pareto/NBD Model." Working paper: Wharton School of the University of Pennsylvania, August 2003.

48. For an excellent discussion of email marketing, see Han Peter Brondmo. *The Engaged Customer: The New Rules of Internet Direct Marketing.* Harper Business: New York, 2000.

chapter 11:

Innovation and the Net

High-Tech Battles and the Browser Wars

Classic rivalries exist throughout sports. Army's football battle against Navy each year gets the attention of veterans everywhere. The Green Bay Packers against the Chicago Bears is a showcase of the National Football League. The Yankees against the Red Sox or the Giants against the Dodgers are rivalries that go back to the 1800s. Every time these teams play, old grudges and decades of history matter as much as the current season and the teams' position in the standings.

Business has its rivals as well. Few are better documented than Coke and its continuing contest with Pepsi. Market shares are tracked carefully. The history of the rivalry is the stuff of books and documentaries.[3] These two companies have battled since they both started in Georgia more than a hundred years ago. New ad campaigns, market promotions, and supermarket deals all are studied with the attention given a war. The battle even entered politics. During the cold war, when trade deals required presidential-level negotiation, the cola wars were there. Pepsi struck first, getting exclusive rights in the Soviet Union (Figure 11.1). Coke retaliated by getting China and negotiating an exclusive deal with its communist leaders.

Rivalries do not seem to last as long in high-technology markets. In the mid-1980s, a fierce battle raged between IBM and Apple over control of the personal-computer market.[4] Now Apple's

A manager responsible for online capabilities should understand how the innovation process occurs online, as well as methods for using the Net to accelerate this process. This chapter covers the need for speed, modularity, and standards in the innovation process.

Topics covered in this chapter include:

> **High-Tech Battles**

> **Speed and Internet Time**

> **Standards Marketing**

> **Improving New Product Development**

Figure 11.1

Vice President Nixon and Soviet Union Premier Khrushchev Having a Pepsi, 1959

Source: © Bettmann/CORBIS

moves regarding music get more notice than on its computers, and IBM exited personal computing by selling its division to a Chinese company. There was a time when the fight between Digital and Data General in minicomputers was inspiring enough to lead to a *New York Times* bestseller chronicling the struggles.[5] Now both companies have faded from the public eye, disappearing in mergers. When Sony led the development of VCRs, it did so with its Betamax format. After a costly battle with VHS, it was forced to drop Beta and switch to making VHS.[6]

Many of the current high-technology wars are being fought on the Internet. One of the most important early battles happened between Netscape and Microsoft. Each attempted to make its browser, its way of "seeing" the Internet, the accepted standard. The stakes were high and strategies differed. The speed of the race was striking. Both companies rapidly developed new versions, which were reviewed widely in the press. Supporters on both sides loudly argued relative merits. Tactics chosen by Microsoft in the browser war became central to antitrust complaints against it.[7]

In less than two years, from 1995 to mid-1997, both Netscape and Microsoft previewed and released generations two, three, and four of their Web browser software. These versions included much more than minor bug fixes and cosmetic improvements. Second-generation browser software included fundamental new features like Java and JavaScript. Third-generation software included document-editing capabilities, much-improved email and newsgroup features, and powerful new security capabilities. The fourth generation brought new ways of computing and sharing information, and even blurred the lines between what was on the Internet and what was on a user's computer.

This was an exhausting pace. It kept employees on 100-hour workweeks. Programmers were as likely to be at their desks at 3 a.m. as 3 p.m. Even more impressively, these new products were clearly better than their predecessors. Many new features were added. Entire new capabilities were created.

The browser battles started with a strong showing by Netscape.[8] For a while it was the fastest-growing software company ever. Pictures of Netscape's leaders were in all the major business and computer magazines, and much of Silicon Valley became its ally. It was not enough. Four generations of browser technology took Microsoft from sideline player to browser king. The battles led to controversy, anti–Microsoft newspaper editorials, and antitrust lawsuits.

Within two years of the opening skirmish, the browser war was a rout, with Microsoft on its way to dominance (see Figure 11.2). Netscape merged with America Online, all but abandoning the browser market. Speed, standards, marketing power, and new features dominated the browser battle. The winner does not get just a few additional market-share points. By mid-2004 Internet Explorer had more than a 95% share of browser usage, even including Mac and Linux operating systems. This is near complete control.[9]

There was, however, a growing guerilla movement. While exiting from browser production, Netscape turned over its code to allow a very different type of software production. The Mozilla Organization accepted the browser code for open source development. In open source, all individuals or organizations are allowed to see, use, and modify the code. The only proviso for using the code is that it inherits a license stipulating that it remains free and accessible to others. Among the projects emerging from this code base is the Firefox browser, with a team of programmers including then

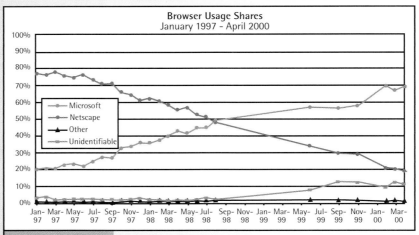

Figure 11.2

The Fall of Netscape's Browser

Source: Rebecca E. Henderson, Government Exhibit 310, Testimony in Microsoft case, February 6, 2000.

Stanford sophomore Blake Ross (shown in Figure 11.3). With a number of innovations, and critical acclaim from reviewers, suddenly competition re-entered the browser world.

By February 2005, Microsoft's shares dipped below 90%. Firefox started to receive significant press attention, both for its features and its innovative approach to software creation. By late April 2005, more than 50 million downloads had occurred worldwide and Firefox's market share grew rapidly. Among lead users, the Firefox market share was much higher than the average market share.[10] After few changes for a number of years, Microsoft announced new features for Internet Explorer version 7, initiating a second round of browser battles.

(a)

(b)

U.S. Browser Usage Share — All OS				
Browser	*4/29/05*	*2/18/05*	*12/3/04*	*6/4/04*
Internet Explorer	88.86%	89.85%	91.80%	95.48%
Firefox	6.75%	5.69%	4.06%	*3.53%
Non-Firefox Netscape and Mozilla Browsers	2.23%	2.47%	2.83%	
Other	2.06%	1.90%	1.25%	0.95%

(c)

Browser Usage Share in Other Countries as of 4/29/05 — All OS		
Browser	*Germany*	*Japan*
Internet Explorer	69.45%	93.92%
Firefox	22.58%	2.79%
Other	4.12%	1.94%
Non-Firefox Netscape and Mozilla Browsers	3.77%	1.26%

Figure 11.3

Source: 11.3a © AP/Wide World Photos; 11.3b, c Courtesy of WebSideStory, Inc.

THE NEED FOR SPEED

Internet Time

"Sleepless in Silicon Valley" is the story that accompanied the 1996 picture shown in Figure 11.4. It wouldn't be so surprising if the sleeper was a new recruit out to prove himself on the job. It's actually Dave Filo, one of the co-founders of Yahoo!, sleeping under his desk.[11] This is well after he was on his way to becoming a thirty-year-old billionaire, with control of one of the strongest brands on the Net. Filo is catching some sleep after pulling an all-night work session on a new Yahoo! feature. Other pictures show impromptu baseball batting practice at two in the morning and other round-the-clock activity. Each of these pictures shows the stress and strain of creating new features and market positions when a new online opportunity emerges, operating on what has come to be known as Internet time.

Internet time has two important aspects. First, it is the rapid change and evolution of Internet tools, marketplace, and business practices. Leading companies and capabilities seem to emerge and change overnight. In the first few years of the commercial Internet it was Yahoo! and Netscape. More recently, it is Google, MySpace, and Skype.

The second part of Internet time reaches far beyond the high-tech centers of Silicon Valley, Boston, or Bangalore. Internet time is the acceleration of new-product development, competitive activity, and business tactics that the Internet has made possible. Internet time seems to be spreading to many other industries, and the lessons learned by companies operating in this environment are lessons most marketers need to understand and anticipate.

Figure 11.4

Living on Internet Time

Source: Photographer Meri Simon/San Jose Mercury News. Copyright 2005 SJMN. All rights reserved.

| Business Implications of Internet Time

Techniques of new product development that use the Net's communication and research capabilities are necessary to stay competitive. An important goal of Net marketers is to facilitate rapid change and new product development. It is marketing's role to make sure that short product cycles and rapid change don't cause consumer tastes and desires to be ignored. It is also marketing's role to make sure the new product development cycle leads to profitable products.

> *Speed and Profits*

The need for speed has become a goal for companies throughout the economy. A major reason is the critical connection between time-to-market and the profitability of new products. Figure 11.5 shows the pattern of profits that Clark and Wheelwright found in consumer electronics.[12] A competitor able to get a new system to market six months earlier than rivals is able to turn this into lifetime profits that are three times larger. Slip to six months late, however, and the profit penalty is severe.

The fraction of revenue and profits accounted for by new products in high technology is even higher. Hewlett-Packard is a typical example. For HP, 77% of revenues derive from products less than two years old.[13]

This profit penalty can make or break companies. High profits from a successful early market entry plowed back into innovative next-generation research lead to new capabilities and further opportunities. Slow entry, and consequent lost profits, leads to erosion of a company's fortunes.

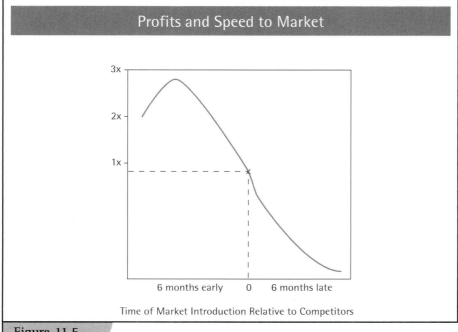

Figure 11.5

Profits and Speed to Market

> *Speed and Innovativeness*

Slowness to market erodes consumers' views of a company. For years, this has frustrated General Motors. It has been especially galling to see rivals get credit for innovations that General Motors created. Speedier rivals have been able to learn from basic research by GM and still beat GM to the marketplace. Consumers form their judgments based on the cars they see, and GM always seemed to be playing catch-up.[14]

Researchers are finding that the best companies, especially in high-technology markets, use a form of time pacing to govern their new product activity. Rather than wait for events such as new technology or changes in consumer tastes to drive new products, time pacing relies on the calendar to guide their efforts.[15] Products are released at fixed time intervals. We have already seen this with Moore's Law. Engineers use the predicted improvement as the benchmark for success. It has also driven the browser wars. Netscape settled on a six-month major product cycle, although some managers argued for a three-month interval.

Rapid product introduction is critical in new product categories. Speed to market leads to learning. By getting products to consumers quickly, companies learn what is desirable and what is just a frill. Early firms in a product category can count on large amounts of consumer interest, feedback, and free advice. Because they are pioneering an important solution, users take the time to provide in-depth information. A company that can use this feedback has an important advantage over later rivals.

Software companies have refined this early release, in-depth customer feedback strategy. They release rough versions, with bugs, mistakes, and flaws, to a set of early users. These beta versions provide extremely valuable sources of feedback. Beta testing has become such an important online process it gets covered in detail later in this chapter.[16]

Proper time pacing shapes customer impressions. If new products are timed for release just as customers are considering their needs, these new products will appear fresh and innovative compared to the competition. Important magazine reviews and trade shows are other external pacing factors.

As companies increase their pace of new product release, they push suppliers to increase their time pace as well. What was a natural pace becomes too slow to accommodate these fast-paced business customers. Faster product cycles are contagious.[17]

> *Speed and Alliances*

Early market entrants, especially in swiftly changing conditions, become a magnet for partners and alliances. Almost without effort, pioneers in a new product or service category are approached with enhancements and improvements. Third-party suppliers can be vital in creating a complete solution for customers. It is far too costly, both in money and in scarce talent, for the market pioneer to provide all of the features on its own. Allies fill in product and marketing gaps in the initial offering.

Distribution creates alliance possibilities. Whenever a company develops a new product or service, it faces many decisions about the best way to bring it to market. Among the most important of these decisions is whether to go it alone or bring in partners. The company must also decide if its particular idea is big enough to build an entire business around. Many companies rely on partnerships to afford to distribute and market their product.

Alliances reduce entry barriers and allow a product to offer many more options by partnering. Internet and software companies benefit greatly from this process. One option for Firefox is to try and build into its browser all of the functionality necessary to support the many online standards, such as Flash, PDFs, and others. This would dramatically slow its ability to release new generations of browsers. It would also dramatically raise the costs of development, with hundreds of programmers and managers required to merge the rapidly changing Firefox capabilities with the fast-changing products of hundreds of other companies.

A better solution is to make the browser modular and to cooperate with these companies' efforts. Cooperation led to the idea of plug-ins. Plug-ins are additional programs that create new browser capabilities without altering the core browser program, often to support proprietary formats and capabilities. Extensions are small programs that extend the browser capabilities, such as viewing standard graphics, storing passwords, or some other function or online utility. Figure 11.6 shows some of the leading plug-ins for Windows operating systems.

Strategic alliances and mergers arise when the product functions being combined are viewed as critical to both companies. While alliances allow companies to retain their independence, product complementarities and a desire for a full product line and joint development can lead to merger. Two of the leading web software companies, Macromedia and Adobe, merged to form a unified software presence.

> *Speed and Standards*

Speed to market can be a critical factor determining what approach becomes the accepted way of accomplishing a task. Early entrants shape the future of the market, even when commercial success escapes the company. Market leaders create standards, either official or de facto, that may last for many years. These standards can be purely technical, or they can be consumer expectations and familiarity with the product category.

Standard setting is one of the most important ways to translate a short-term advantage into a long-term dominant position. The company that defines and defends a standard can be in a strong strategic position for decades. Standards are the main reason why high-technology competition tends to be intense but short-lived. Rivalries between competing standards usually don't last long. It is very expensive for consumers to deal with competing standards. Markets where

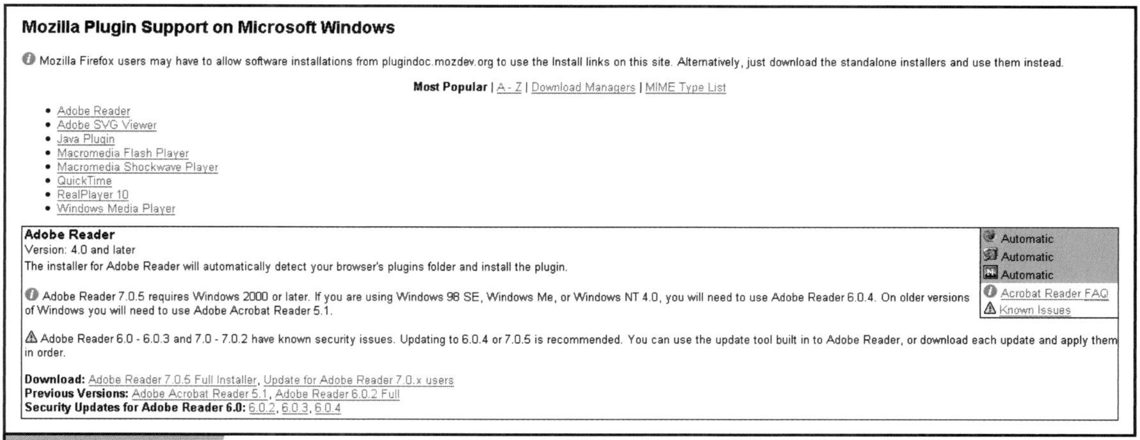

Mozilla Plugin Support on Microsoft Windows

ⓘ Mozilla Firefox users may have to allow software installations from plugindoc.mozdev.org to use the Install links on this site. Alternatively, just download the standalone installers and use them instead.

Most Popular | A - Z | Download Managers | MIME Type List

- Adobe Reader
- Adobe SVG Viewer
- Java Plugin
- Macromedia Flash Player
- Macromedia Shockwave Player
- QuickTime
- RealPlayer 10
- Windows Media Player

Adobe Reader
Version: 4.0 and later
The installer for Adobe Reader will automatically detect your browser's plugins folder and install the plugin.

ⓘ Adobe Reader 7.0.5 requires Windows 2000 or later. If you are using Windows 98 SE, Windows Me, or Windows NT 4.0, you will need to use Adobe Reader 6.0.4. On older versions of Windows you will need to use Adobe Acrobat Reader 5.1.

⚠ Adobe Reader 6.0 - 6.0.3 and 7.0 - 7.0.2 have known security issues. Updating to 6.0.4 or 7.0.5 is recommended. You can use the update tool built in to Adobe Reader, or download each update and apply them in order.

Download: Adobe Reader 7.0.5 Full Installer, Update for Adobe Reader 7.0.x users
Previous Versions: Adobe Acrobat Reader 5.1, Adobe Reader 6.0.2 Full
Security Updates for Adobe Reader 6.0: 6.0.2, 6.0.3, 6.0.4

- Automatic
- Automatic
- Automatic
- Acrobat Reader FAQ
- Known Issues

Figure 11.6

Plug-ins for Enhanced Browser Functionality

Source: Courtesy of Mozilla Corporation

standards are important will normally "tip." That is, once a specific approach becomes established, the marketplace tends to swing dramatically toward it. The losing standards sink quickly. When standards matter, success breeds success. Once established, leads tend to magnify over time.

STANDARDS MARKETING

The Importance of Standards

Standards are a defining feature of high-technology markets. The inside of a computer is dominated by standards determining how hard drives, USB and Firewire devices, screens, keyboards, and memory communicate with each other. Standards determine how computers connect to the Internet. Standards dictate how files and messages are turned into packets. Standards determine how these packets make it to their destination.

Conventions are also important. Conventions are general practices that designers and users have come to expect. Conventions are accepted approaches, but without the formal stamp of approval of a standard's process or controlling organization. Searching and browsing web sites are examples of areas where conventions have developed without the rise of official standards.

In the quick-release, modular style of new product development, standards and conventions play a very useful role. Both make it much easier to share information, with standards the most useful. It is much easier to break a product into modules if a standard is available to specify how the modules communicate. Standards provide a very precise version of the visible design rules of modular design.

Standards are a strong determinant of the success of new products in high-technology markets. An excellent product can be a market failure if it is based on a standard that is losing ground. A mediocre product can be highly profitable if it uses the winning standard. Entire categories of products and services rise and fall because of the evolution and domination of standards.

Competition among standards tends to be intense and brief. Standards are most valuable to users when they are reliable and widespread. On the other hand, standards are most valuable to producers when they create an advantage or at least a level playing field. The worst result for a producer, however, is to be the sponsor of a losing standard.[18]

Figure 11.7

Multiple Wi-Fi Standards

Source: Courtesy of the Wi-Fi Alliance. The term Wi-Fi and the Wi-Fi Alliance logo are registered trademarks of the Wi-Fi Alliance.

One of the most important current standards for online users is wireless Internet access, especially the IEEE 802.11 standard (also known as Wi-Fi). Growth in Wi-Fi adoption has been very rapid. Figure 11.8 charts the certification of compatible products, such as wireless cards and laptops, by the Wi-Fi Alliance. By 2005, nearly 2,000 products form hundreds of vendors, comprising millions of units, could send and receive according to the Wi-Fi standard. Consumers can buy wireless access points, home computers, printers, and many other consumer electronics devices sharing the standard and expect compatibility despite different companies producing the products. Speed increases, such as 802.11g, are also backward-compatible and are able to support earlier slower versions of the standard.

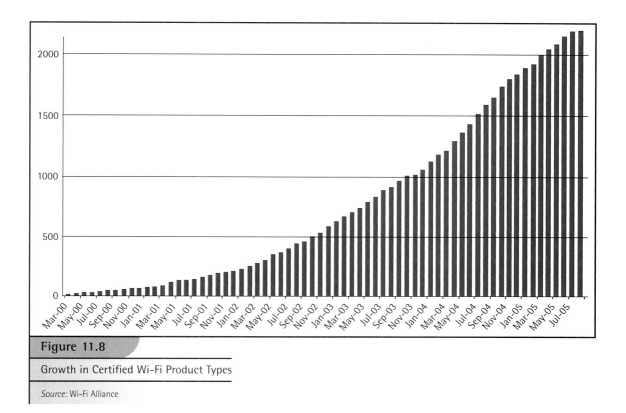

Figure 11.8

Growth in Certified Wi-Fi Product Types

Source: Wi-Fi Alliance

Despite the rapid adoption of Wi-Fi it is unlikely to be the last word in wireless standards. Increasingly, devices use multiple standards to accomplish different tasks. For example, HP builds infrared, Bluetooth, and 802.11b wireless capabilities into some of its PDAs. Figure 11.9 gives one analyst's view of the tradeoffs and capabilities of eight different approaches.[19] These include infrared, used by many remote controllers (IrDA), cellular phone networks, three variants of Wi-Fi (802.11a, b, and g), a European systems for cordless telephony (DECT), Bluetooth used for short-range communication between peripherals and devices, and the ZigBee standard used for wireless sensors.

Introducing standards is often a rocky process, with many battles and delays. Standards battles in technology markets are very common. Understanding these battles, and having a standards strategy, is important for online commerce.

The Two Types of Standards

Two types of standards exist. The first is an open standard, based on an official process of debate, consensus, and voting by an official standards body. The second is a *de facto* standard based entirely on marketplace acceptance. A de facto standard is established when a product or approach is so widely adopted that it becomes expected. In contrast with a convention, a de facto standard is typically controlled by a single company and can be changed at any time.

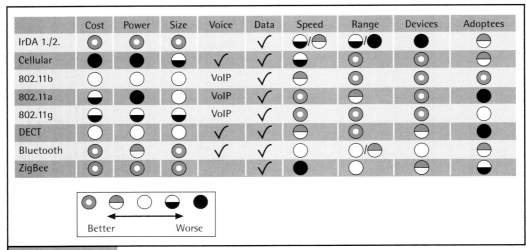

Figure 11.9

Various Wireless Standards and Capabilities

Source: William Saltzstein, "Bluetooth and Beyond: Wireless Options for Medical Devices," Medical Device Link, June 2004. Copyright © 2004 by William Saltzstein, www.codebluecommunications.com

Both kinds of standards are widely used. The choice of a strategy using standards is an important new area of marketing, especially for high-technology markets. Use of an open standard will often lead to widespread adoption and innovation. It will also, however, open the company to competition. De facto standards may be harder to establish and may be resented by consumers and other producers, but they can be more profitable and easier for the company to control.

Standards battles are contentious. During the 1990s, the standards battle surrounding the Java programming language became an important aspect of the antitrust case against Microsoft. In Internet modems, both 3Com and Rockwell battled for control of the 56K modem. Neither 3Com nor Rockwell was able to make its format for 56K modems the standard. Each of these companies aggressively pushed its format for new, higher-speed modems for the home. Each format was incompatible with the other. This forced Internet service providers to either choose, or invest money to support each format. Eventually a compromise was necessary, and a unified standard emerged.

> *Wi-Fi and Open Standards*

IEEE 802.11, better known among the public as Wi-Fi (the name of the corresponding industrial alliance) is an example of an open standard. It is supervised by the 802.11 working group within the IEEE 802 Local Area Networks/Metropolitan Area Networks Standards Committee (LMSC) sponsored by the IEEE.

No one owns an open standard, which emerges by consensus of experts in the area and must be approved by a standards body. In the case of Wi-Fi, when the IEEE endorses a new version of wireless standard, it is further endorsed by the ISO body. The result is a detailed specification of the technical aspects of the wireless protocol. It is publicly available. The standard for 802.11b, for example, is a 96-page document that was approved on September 16, 1999, and was reaffirmed in June 2003.[20]

Regardless of who submits a proposed standard, there are multiple important stages. The steps needed to create an IETF open standard are highlighted in Figure 11.10.[21] The flowchart shows a simplified sequence of events in the creation of an IETF Internet standard. At each step, workability and consensus are the goals. No standard can be just a rough proposal. All must be based on very clear documentation and at least two versions of working code. Not only that, but there must be a consensus regarding the value and best choice for the standard. This puts a high enough difficulty threshold to limit the number of standards that make it all the way through this system.

Figure 11.10 also shows some of the Officers of IEEE 802.11. 802 procedures require a very careful series of formal written ballots in which all voters are allowed to submit written comments and are entitled to written responses. Multiple levels of approval by at least 75% are required.

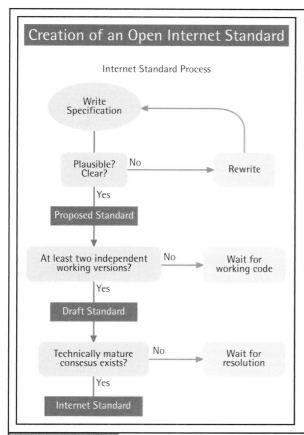

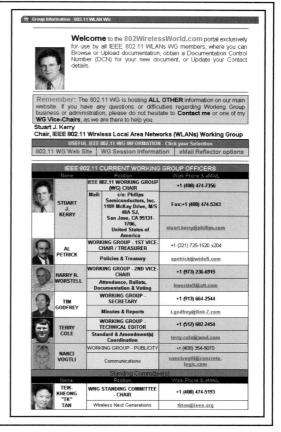

Figure 11.10

Creation of an Open Internet Standard, and the 802.11 Working Group Officers

Source: Courtesy of 802.11 WLAN WG

The form of the procedures is very different in IEEE 802 than in the IETF. 802 is very formal, following Robert's Rules of Order, having defined voting pools and conducting most of its business in face-to-face meetings, while the IETF is very informal, having no defined membership, conducting most of its business by email, and making its working group decisions by humanly judged consensus. Yet both have produced effective standards and require a clear super majority for approval.

Membership on a standards board is a professional honor for members. For some standards it is also a matter of corporate strategy and negotiation. Effective standards bodies attempt to combine technical expertise with a range of company and user participation, so that standards are widely adopted and used. The goal is to serve as a cooperative forum establishing appropriate standards that all can use.

> *Xbox 360 and De Facto Standards*

Proprietary standards are also important in the marketplace. With a proprietary standard, a single company controls and licenses the technical specifications and permission to use the standard. The company may grant these licenses for free or for a very low cost, or it may base its business model on these licensing fees. The success of a de facto standard is determined by the ability of the company to sell the standard and to encourage other companies to license the standard.

Both of the leading video game systems, Playstation from Sony and Xbox from Microsoft, are examples of proprietary de facto standards. Video game makers must get contracts and pay royalties to the companies for using the technical specifications (see Figure 11.11). These licenses are crucial to profitability of the systems, as both Sony and Microsoft essentially subsidize the hardware by keeping machine prices low. Both games and the live network for the Xbox provide Microsoft with the opportunity of recouping its investment.

> *Reaching Compromise*

Standards battles can be costly. This is especially true if the sides are equally matched, if there is no obvious solution, and if confusion slows the entire product category. This was the situation when 56K dial-up modems were introduced. Due to the design of the telephone system, 56K modems are the fastest access speeds available to consumers over standard analog phone lines. Anything faster, such as DSL, requires special digital circuits and more expensive DSL modems. Despite the need for speed, 56K modems were slow to displace earlier generations of modems because of a standards battle that confused and worried both consumers and Internet service providers.

The problem was two incompatible standards: the X2 technology of 3Com and the K56flex technology of Rockwell. These technologies are very similar. But, as one analyst commented, "The technology is basically the same, but they've tweaked it just enough so the two don't talk to each other. Long story short: It's a mess."[22] Potential adopters delayed their modem upgrade, and ISPs were slow to add faster dial-up capacity.[23]

Realizing the standards battle had become stalemated, 3Com and Rockwell agreed to a compromise ratified by the International Telecommunications Union. The resolution of the 56K standard was similar to an earlier battle and solution for 28K modems. This also ended with a compromise. Rather than fight to the finish, a middle ground was found that created a formal, open standard.

Formal standard setting can seem very cumbersome and complicated. While most marketers will not have to directly set a standard, it is useful and important to understand where

Figure 11.11

Proprietary Standards are Established by Market Results and Technology Licensing

Source: Courtesy of Xbox® video game system

the standards come from. These standards bodies directly shape the evolution of the Internet (Table 11.1). Many companies, especially in high tech, have formal staff positions that create their standards strategies. They are responsible for participation in the standards bodies, and for providing educated guesses on which standards seem to be winning.[24]

Table 11.1

International Internet Standards Bodies	
Standards Body	**Description**
The American National Standards Institute (ANSI)	ANSI is "the sole U.S. representative and dues-paying member of the two major non-treaty international standards organizations the (ISO) and the (IEC)." It coordinates a U.S. position to international standards groups.
European Union	Just like ANSI in the United States, the European Union has a standardization body. This report outlines its philosophy and structure.
International Organization for Standardization (ISO)	ISO develops and maintains a very wide range of international standards in almost all areas of the economy.
The International Telecommunications Union (ITU)	The ITU is the dominant world standards organization for telecommunications. This affects much of the Net. Among the Net areas it covers is multimedia and modems.
The Internet Engineering Task Force	IETF is an organization open to anyone interested in the workings of the Net. It develops consensus open standards on a wide range of Net software and services. It is one of the main standards bodies for the Net.
The World Wide Web Consortium	The W3C is an international consortium, with its headquarters at MIT. It concentrates on web interfaces, next-generation Net protocols, and social impact issues. It contributes to other standards organizations.

| Standards Strategy

Managers need to choose which standards strategy they are going to use. Should they immediately pursue an open standard, or should they try to win the battle in the marketplace? When should a standards battle be negotiated?

Standards competition is dynamic. Standards win or lose share over time. A standards "lock-in" happens when a standard becomes so well established that almost all new users choose it. It has come to dominate the marketplace, and other standards in essence go extinct. This type of "winner takes most" market can be very profitable, but it is also competed for very aggressively. In other cases, markets will be shared. No standard emerges that completely dominates, and several competing ways co-exist in the marketplace.[25]

> Market Sharing

Figure 11.12 illustrates standards competition. For this example we will assume there are two competing standards, A and B. Their market shares add to 100%. On the X-axis is the market share of Standard A in period t. The Y-axis shows the *expected market share* of Standard A in the next time period. The 45-degree line is the divide between a standard gaining or losing share. If the expected share is above the 45-degree line, next period's share is expected to be higher than this period. When the curve is below the 45-degree line, it shows the standard is losing ground relative to its current market position. A point on the 45-degree line is a situation where the expected market share next period is the same as the market share this period.

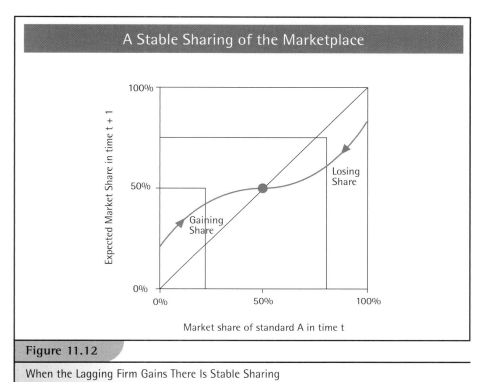

A Stable Sharing of the Marketplace

Expected Market Share in time t + 1

Losing Share

Gaining Share

Market share of standard A in time t

Figure 11.12

When the Lagging Firm Gains There Is Stable Sharing

Source: Ward Hanson, "Bandwagons and Orphans: Dynamic Pricing of Competing Technological Systems Subject to Decreasing Cost" (Ph.D. diss., Stanford University Department of Economics, 1985).

There are a number of reasons why the expected shares can work in this way. It can reflect the reactions of a competitor. When standard A is gaining, standard B is losing. This could result in promotions run by the competitor to catch up. The graph may also reflect the temporary swings in the market caused by large orders. If a large order has temporarily pushed standard A up, it is more likely the next large order will be from the B customers that just happened not to be in the market during period t.

The dynamics in Figure 11.12 leads to market sharing. To the left of 50%, when it is the smaller share standard, A gains share. To the right of 50%, A loses ground. The stable equilibrium point is shown by intersection of the market share curve and the 45-degree line. This competition is stable near the middle because the low share firm tends to gain over time and the high share firm tends to lose. Competition is driving shares toward the middle, and toward a market sharing equilibrium.

> *Bandwagon Markets*

Market sharing is less likely for markets with standards competition and installed base benefits. Many industries experience shakeouts due to both scale and installed base effects. Standards competition occurred in multiple dimensions in the early automobile industry. There was competition between type of engine, such as steam, electric, diesel, and gasoline. There were hundreds of new automobile companies, battling over design and distribution approaches. Leading companies found it easier to grow, attract dealers and repair facilities, build an image in consumers' minds, and receive other benefits from previous success. The early personal computer industry had numerous entrants, such as CompuColor and Radio Shack, with different approaches and alternative operating systems. Video game pioneer Atari has been replaced by Sony and Microsoft.

Online sites subject to standards and installed base effects have gone through a shakeout as well. Auction sites provide a good example of success breeding success. More bidders attract more sellers, and vice versa. At the same time that eBay grew rapidly, other sites such as First Auction had to close down because of lack of scale.

Figure 11.13 illustrates the dynamics where a market lead grows over time. This is a graph of a competition where "success breeds success," leading to a bandwagon effect. In this case, the firm with the higher share is expected to get even more sales in the next period. The smaller share firm is expected to shrink. When a competition like this occurs, we expect to see a de facto standard set by the market winner.

The curve in Figure 11.13 is more common whenever the technology is part of a system requiring investments. In the case of modems, consumers want to know whether their internet service provider supports the format. The ISP wants to know that it is worth investing in that support because the standard will be popular. For Java or Wi-Fi, it's even more obvious. A software developer or computer maker wants to choose a technology with wide appeal and support. This creates a bandwagon effect for the technology with the largest installed base.

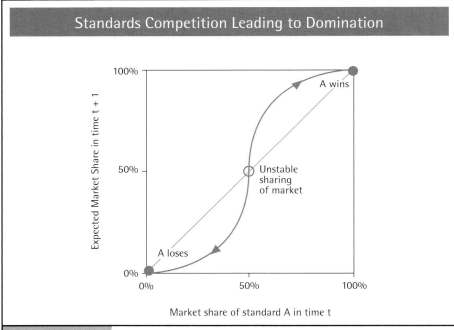

Figure 11.13

A Winner-Take-All Marketplace

Source: Ward Hanson, "Bandwagons and Orphans: Dynamic Pricing of Competing Technological Systems Subject to Decreasing Cost" (Ph.D. diss., Stanford University Department of Economics, 1985).

One interesting feature of standards competition is that it can be much easier to predict that someone will win than who that winner will be. Historical events, often minor, can be crucial if they come at a decisive time.

Standards competitions is aggressive and fast paced because early entrants can often lock up the marketplace. It takes a very strong market competitor to overcome a small share in a bandwagon market. Usually, the only way this can happen is if the small share competitor has a dominant position in a different standard and is able to leverage that power into a new standard. Another possibility is that the leader makes a serious mistake, creating a situation where a trailing firm can catch up.

Alliances can be critical in achieving the critical mass in a standards battle. Some standards battles start with multiple competing approaches, each with a share far below 50%. Users are confused, and there is no clear consensus. In a situation like that, an alliance between several participants to agree on a standard can be decisive. This can propel one of the standards to the status of clear leader and can give it bandwagon momentum.

Endorsements can help establish a standard. For Java, a major early endorsement came from Marc Andreessen. Andreesen was the chief designer of Mosaic, the first popular web browser. He was also the chief designer and co-founder of Netscape. At the time of critical negotiations with Sun, Andreesen proclaimed that "Java has to be the language of the network, it has to be open, so nobody owns it, so all databases speak it. Our job's not done if we don't achieve that." When Andreessen endorsed Java publicly, the chief marketer of Java counted it as "a blessing from the god of the Internet." The endorsement pushed Java to be the clear leader for web enhancement.

NEW PRODUCT DEVELOPMENT ONLINE

Improving Traditional New Product Development

> *The Idea Funnel*

Two main goals shape the traditional new-product development process. The first is to uncover unmet consumer needs. Ideas come from a wide range of sources. Focus groups bring together consumers to talk informally about how they use a product and what features or functions could be improved. Formal research techniques, such as conjoint analysis, try to uncover the importance of these features and put numerical weights on these choices.[26] Companies consult the dealer network and sales force for suggestions and consumer complaints.

The second main concern of traditional new-product methods is to eliminate design mistakes before too much money is spent. For manufactured products, costs escalate swiftly the closer the product is to its actual market introduction. One of the main goals of the process is to create effective "go/no go" decision points that eliminate products that will not sell and do not reach the desired target market.[27]

The combination of these two objectives is often depicted as a funnel. Many different ideas enter the new-product process, and only a few new products emerge. There are two main starting points, perceived customer needs and technological possibilities (Figure 11.14). Perceived needs can emerge from formal market research, analysis of past generations of products, or information flowing back to the company from the distribution channel. The other major source of new possibilities is technology. As new capabilities emerge, such as faster performance or stronger material, these possibilities are investigated for commercial viability.

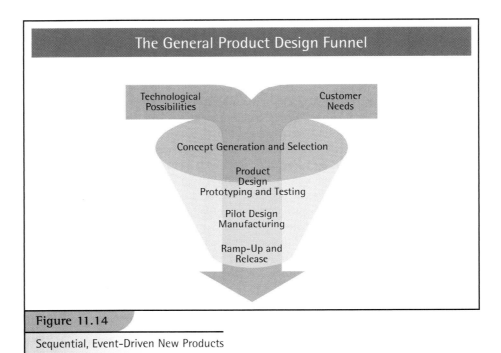

Figure 11.14

Sequential, Event-Driven New Products

After ideas enter the system, they are subject to a series of screens, tests, and refinements. Ideas then are formalized into concepts. Next, the concept is translated into a product design. Testing checks whether the product is feasible to manufacture. Once prototypes are available, they are tested in front of consumers and other partners. Finally, the product is manufactured and released to the marketplace.

It is unlikely that an idea will make it all the way through the funnel. Studies have found that the "batting average" of new products is quite low. A study reviewing the new product literature found an average of less than 1% of the original ideas entering the funnel become commercial successes, although approximately 60% of the commercial launches succeed.[28] Many are rejected early, which is relatively cheap but difficult to do with any certainty. Quite a few make it through some or all of the steps. This is expensive and time consuming.

> *Improving the Product Funnel*

One of the biggest challenges facing new product developers is preventing bad ideas from proceeding through the product design funnel. The further an idea proceeds, the more expense is incurred. Spotting good ideas and killing bad ones not only leads to better products but eliminates considerable research and development waste.

Online market research is helpful in both identifying opportunities and trimming potential losses. An important application is finding the right combination of traditional features, new design elements, and a proper price point for a successful modest innovation. The most likely new product successes are not radical innovations, but are useful improvements on existing approaches.[29] This concept screening can increasingly be done faster and cheaper online.

Dahan and Srinivasan conducted tests of similarity between online and more traditional new concept research, and to predict market share for new product designs. The specific application involved new designs of bicycle pumps.[30] They found Web-based virtual prototyping to work well, matching a physically based market research approach. This is a highly useful result, illustrated in Figure 11.15. The predicted shares of the virtual tasks, using either an animated web site or a static web site, are much closer to the physical prototype than the standard verbal tests used by market researchers. Online testing of new features and new designs is much cheaper than using physical prototypes, is much faster to deploy, and can be shown to a much wider geographic audience.

There is a range of virtual new product approaches. Dahan and Hauser describe a number of these possibilities and their use along the new product development funnel. Some are direct analogues of traditional methods. Others are capabilities difficult to accomplish except online, and they present new research tools and opportunities.

Early steps in the product funnel rely on online versions of conjoint analysis to test and screen ideas. What the researchers call the "information pump" approach is aimed somewhat more at idea generation

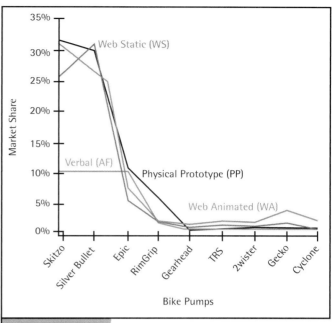

Figure 11.15

When Done Correctly, Virtual Testing Appears to Give Similar Results as Expensive Prototyping for Familiar Products

Source: Ely Dahan and V. Srinivasan, "The Predictive Power of Internet-Based Product Concept Testing Using Visual Depiction and Animation," *Journal of Product Innovation Management* 17 (2000): 99–109.

than testing, and works as a form of online focus group. The goal is to understand how potential consumers think and talk about the product category. See Figure 11.16.

User design and securities trading are methods of consumer-assisted design that would be difficult to do except in a virtual setting. In user design, features and modules can be added or subtracted from products, with immediate visualization and impacts on other features such as price. In securities trading, product features are subject to bidding in a form of auction, letting the revealed price be a measure of product attractiveness. Finally, virtual concept testing attempts to capture elements of choice and likely market share for different final configurations of products.

All of these approaches rely in some degree on the "media equation" discussed in Chapter 2, the tendency of individuals to react to a virtual setting much like they would to a physical environment. At the same time, a virtual setting taps into the power of real-time impact calculations and networked communication.

> *Information Acceleration for Radical Inventions*

The previous methods work on incremental product improvements. Marketers have always struggled with the problem of forecasting the demand for radically new products or services, as well as understanding how consumers will react to different product positioning choices for these major changes.[31] When products such as the Prius hybrid car, the Segway Human Transporter

Method	Description of Respondents' Task	User Interface
WEB-BASED CONJOINT ANALYSIS (WCA)	Sort attribute bundles by clicking on cards. To reduce the number of stimuli per screen, respondent pre-sorts into three piles.	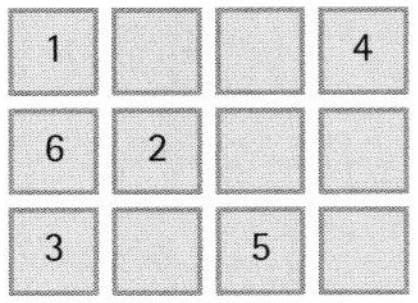
FAST POLYHEDRAL ADAPTIVE CONJOINT ESTIMATION (FP)	Paired comparisons of attribute bundles. Respondent clicks radio buttons to express relative preference between two stimuli.	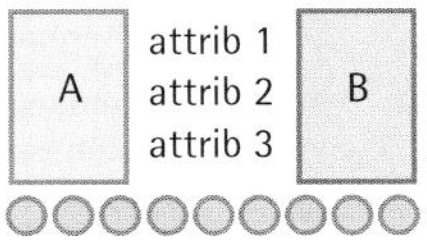
USER DESIGN (UD)	An "ideal" product is configured using visual drag-and-drop. Respondent trades off features against price or performance.	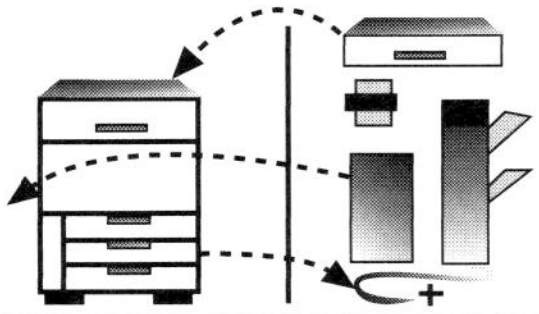
VIRTUAL CONCEPT TESTING (VCT)	"Buy" from among competing concepts based on price and media-rich, integrated concepts. Analyzed as a two-attribute conjoint study.	
SECURITIES TRADING OF CONCEPTS (STOC)	Each product concept is represented by a "security" and is bought and sold by respondents' interacting with one another. Concepts can be richly depicted.	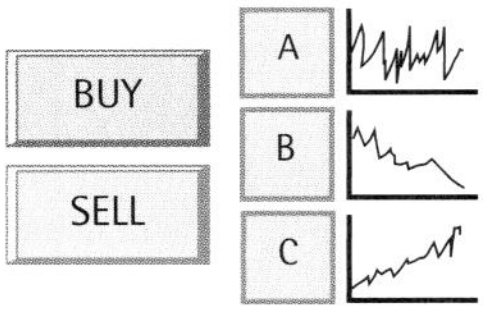
INFORMATION PUMP (IP)	Players formulate questions about products concepts and guess how others will react to their questions. Fine-tuned so respondents think hard and tell the truth.	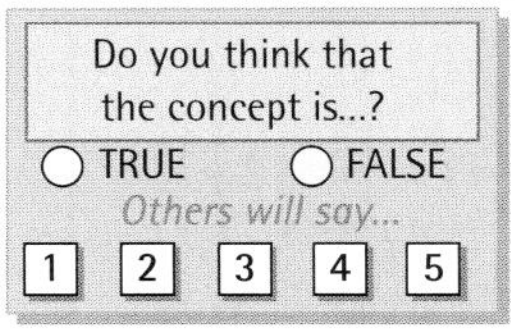

Figure 11.16

Various Online Concept Testing Methods

Source: E. Dahan and J. Hauser, "The Virtual Customer," *Journal of Product Innovation Management* 19 (September 2002): 332–353.

shown in Figure 11.17, or TIVO are introduced they do not fit nicely into preexisting product categories. It is not clear which customer segments will find the product attractive. Consumers have a difficult time understanding what the key attributes are, and whether the product is for them.

Part of the frustration consumers feel is the lack of realistic cues and sources of information when asked their opinion. When faced with a radically new gadget or service, potential buyers

Figure 11.17

How to Explain Very Different Products?

Source: Segway LLC (www.segway.com)

consult other sources of information to learn more. Many people ask a friend or colleague they know to be technologically savvy what it is all about. Others read reviews and newspaper accounts. Some go to a showroom and see the product on display. On their own and without context or experience, individuals may not know their tastes for the product. Forcing them to make a choice without these information sources distorts their responses away from their eventual true response given proper context.

A good example of this type of problem faces companies seeking to develop space tourism. Entrepreneurs such as Richard Branson, Jeff Bezos, and others are working to create private launch capabilities able to take wealthy tourists into space. Branson's *Virgin Galactic* is already taking online reservations for first-year flights, with a refundable $20,000 deposit required to hold a spot for the $200,000 flights. How potential private astronauts really will react to the service is unclear, as is the best positioning for the service (Figure 11.18).

To counteract this difficulty in understanding the demand for truly innovative products, marketers have turned to simulation and digital environments to create more realistic market research settings. One

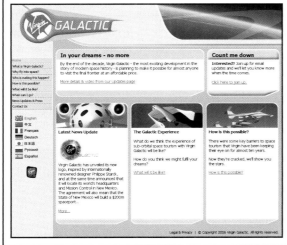

Figure 11.18

No Bucks, No Buck Rogers—Virgin Galactic's Site for Reserving a Space Flight

Source: Courtesy of Virgin Galactic

especially powerful approach, which fits well online, is information acceleration (IA).[32] Urban, Weinberg, and Hauser state that the goal of an IA system is to "place the consumers in a virtual buying environment that simulates the information that is available to the consumer at the time he or she makes a purchase decision."[33] IA systems use digital technologies to create virtual worlds that capture several of the most important aspects of the new product purchase decision. The hope is this increased realism will better represent what an actual consumer would face if the new product is actually produced and marketed.

Early uses of IA concentrated on the information available to consumers at the time of potential purchase. For a study of consumers' future purchases of electric cars, this involved a simulation of:

> Virtual showroom visits
> Advertising (television, magazines, newspapers)
> Review articles and consumer-oriented reports
> Word of mouth

Each of these required the creation of fictitious settings, simulated media, and actors playing different roles.

Any digital environment faces the challenge of being realistic enough to lead to accurate measures of behavior. Creating virtual environments for IA, as opposed to more traditional conjoint analysis, can be expensive. A validation study from the late 1990s estimated the cost of IA as between $100,000 to $750,000 per application. A significant part of this is the upfront cost of creating realistic multimedia content. Another important cost is the difficulty of presenting the information to respondents. At the time of this initial study, respondents needed to either come to a central facility, or a team was needed to carry the equipment to the consumer's location.

Broadband reduces these costs substantially. Using the Net as the delivery vehicle eliminates the very labor-intensive and expensive steps of getting respondents on the IA system. It also speeds up the process, as it eliminates laboratory and staffing capacity constraints. The Wharton FutureView system seen in Figure 11.19 realizes many of these goals. This system combines a wide array of the influences on consumer demand. These include sources of word of mouth, simulated print and broadcast ads, simulated newspaper or magazine articles, a virtual showroom, and more.[34]

Potential consumers are exposed to these different sources, and they often are allowed to dig as deep or as little as they normally would. The goal is to create a much more realistic market research setting. Responses are automatically tracked and analyzed, allowing a rapid evaluation of market research results.

The potential benefits of IA systems are large. If marketers can create realistic systems that measure consumer demands with artificial products and services, it has the potential to dramatically improve the new product process. Virtual simulations can replace expensive prototypes. A much large number of possible product variants can be tried. Valuable new features can be spotted and designed into the next generation of products.

No amount of online material can eliminate the high risks involved in creating and launching a radically different innovation. It can, however, identify many potentially fatal flaws in the concept and improve the chance of success. By exposing would-be consumers to much more realistic information flows of their own choosing, both gaps in the current design and potentially major opportunities can come to light before potentially huge expenses are incurred.

Figure 11.19

The Wharton FutureView System

Source: Courtesy of Alfred R. West Learning Lab, Wharton School, Univ. of Pennsylvania

Modular New Product Development

> *A New Approach*

The traditional methods of new product development lack speed and adaptability, even with online concept screening. In order to serve rapidly changing markets with shrinking product life cycles, technology companies have pioneered new ways of rapidly launching products. These methods maintain flexibility as long as possible and accelerate market feedback. They rely on establishing early release stages, repeatedly receiving market feedback, and quickly fixing any problems with incremental releases.

These methods work especially well for online products. As the products can be delivered using the Net, there is a low cost for multiple releases and small incremental improvements. This allows early sampling and feedback from consumers. Figure 11.20 highlights the process. Each of the blocks represents early versions of the new product. There are multiple points where the product can be changed based on lessons learned from consumers.

Companies able to achieve rapid cycle time rely on a few essential ideas—flexibility, modularity, and rapid feedback. Flexibility allows the new product process to respond effectively to

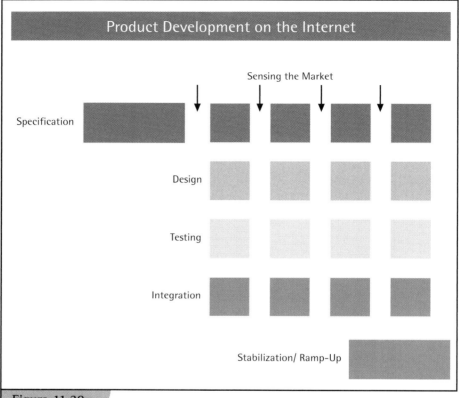

Figure 11.20

Concurrent, Modular Product Development

rapidly changing market conditions. Modularity allows work to proceed in parallel. Teams can work independently and nonsequentially. Finally, improved communication and feedback from early users lead to higher-quality information from customers much earlier than has been possible in the past.[35]

> Modularity in Design

Baldwin and Clark describe how the computer industry is showing the rest of the economy how to handle speed and complexity in new products by using the principle *of modularity in design*.[36] They argue that the computer industry discovered these principles early, many with the development of the IBM 360 system in the 1960s. As the microcomputer, and then the Internet revolution, shortened the product life cycle, this new method grew to even more importance.

Modular design breaks a new product into subsystems, or modules. This allows separate design and testing for each module. Teams can work in parallel, rather than waiting for the preceding group to finish their work. Parallel efforts may take more effort in total, but can dramatically reduce the total time to launch the new product.

Table 11.2 compares the integrated architecture of traditional product development against a modular architecture.[37] Two major points of distinction emerge. First, the integrated architecture

Table 11.2

Comparison of Modular and Integrated Product Architecture	
Integrated Architecture	**Modular Architecture**
A collection of components that implement some functions of a product is called a block.	A collection of components that implement some functions of a product is called a module.
The functional elements of a product are implemented using more than one block.	Same as integrated architecture
A single block implements many functional elements.	A module implements one or a few functional elements in their entirety.
The interactions between blocks are ill-defined and may be incidental to the primary function of the products.	The interactions between modules are well defined and are generally fundamental to the primary function of the product.
Product performance can be enhanced through an integrated architecture.	Product performance may not be enhanced by a modular architecture.
Changing a block in an integrated product may influence many functional elements and may require changes to several related blocks.	Changing a few isolated functional elements of a product may not affect the design of other modules.

Source: Chun-Che Huang, "Overview of Modular Product Development," Proceedings of the National Science Council, Republic of China 24, no. 3 (2000): 149–165.

may yield higher performance if the design is well established and understood. Second, an integrated architecture makes modification difficult because of linkages and dependencies between functional elements. In a proper modular design each module can be altered and improved, without an unknown cascade of effects throughout the product.

Achieving modularity may not be easy. The essential requirement is to sharply divide the product into two types of design features. Information must be partitioned into *visible design rules* and *hidden design parameters*. Baldwin and Clark state that "modularity is beneficial only if this partition is precise, unambiguous, and complete."[38]

Visible design rules are the ways that modules interact with each other. The visible design rules are the critical pieces of information that all teams working on the new product must understand. The visible rules describe exactly how the different modules fit together. They describe what performance each module should have, what each module can expect of other modules, how the modules communicate, and what standards are followed. The visible design rules are the key to successful modular design. The hard part is deciding exactly what is to be expected of each module and making this information available. The visible design rules need to be spelled out very early in the process, during the specification phase. Then each working team can know the constraints they operate under, and what performance is expected of them.

Among the benefits of modularity are future flexibility in the face of uncertainty.[39] Modular design allows substitution of a new solution or avoidance of a fundamental roadblock in any one of the modules. By breaking the design into individual components, the risk of the entire product failing due to one component not being ready is lowered dramatically. In the case of roadblock, a previous solution can be reused. In the case of breakthrough, the new feature and better performance can be rapidly incorporated.

Web alliances take advantage of visible design rules to simplify co-marketing arrangements. One of the big changes in the last few years for sites such as eBay and Amazon is the adoption of modular design and standards for exchanging data between their core databases and independent sellers. Whereas previously this might be done by linking to specific web pages, now there are methods for companies to feed information to eBay and retrieve results from eBay. This is very powerful, and it relies on standards such as XML to describe and exchange the product and sales information.

The APIs, or application program interfaces, are the visible design rules required of a third party. The remainder of the eBay system is hidden, and a third party does not have to understand how it works or worry that changes in the eBay platform beyond the API will cause the third party's application to break. Each team has full flexibility in its choice of the hidden design parameters. As long as the information is exchanged with visible design rules, each has extensive flexibility in producing the site.

The use of Internet standards to let software systems communicate has been dubbed web services, which are growing rapidly (Figure 11.21). These standardized approaches are still mostly internal, but are reaching out to alliance partners.[40]

Dell Computer successfully uses modular hardware design to respond quickly to shifts in the marketplace. One simple example is the decision about the size and speed of the hard disk to include in a family of computers. Dell's visible design rules for each family of computer includes a detailed specification of the standards the computers will use to communicate with the hard disk. This can include SCSI, E-IDE, or any of several other choices. Dell designers will also specify minimum speeds and free space on the disk. With these visible design rules the team working on software knows it has the performance and space available for the operating system and any software bundled with the computer.

An important hidden design rule is the exact capacity of the hard disk. By keeping this a hidden design rule, last-minute shifts in market taste can be reflected. The team responsible for choosing hard disk drives is free to make whatever choice it wants within the visible design rules. This can have a big impact and can save Dell substantial money. In one case, a disk manufacturer approached Dell with a promotion on its current generation of hard drives. However, Dell noticed from its online ordering that many customers had recently shifted to

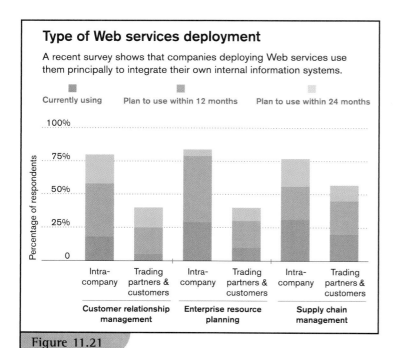

Figure 11.21

Web Services Growing to Support Online Activities

Source: Maryann Jones Thompson, "Web Services Take Hold," *Technology Review* (April 2005): 28. Reproduced with permission of MIT Technology Review in the format Textbook via Copyright Clearance Center.

choosing drives of two or three times the capacity of these promotional drives. Dell declined the offer, and took larger drives. A different computer maker accepted the deal, only to be faced with excess inventory and drives smaller than the market wanted. They ended up having to aggressively discount the systems, costing them more than $100 million in markdowns.

One of the widely noted recent examples of rapid development using modular design is the online open source encyclopedia Wikipedia.[41] Design rules for Wikipedia are extremely simple, containing essentially stripped down HTML commands. Each article is separate. Any information on any topic is fair game, as long as copyright is respected. Any individual can edit almost any article, although other contributors may re-edit the article back to its original state. The result has been remarkable in volume, if occasionally spotty in quality (Figure 11.22). In a little more than five years more than one million articles have been contributed by volunteers in the English language edition. Other languages and content types are under development using the same "wiki" philosophy. This is one of several notable successes of open innovation, where collaborative efforts among large number of volunteers rapidly creates useful and free new products.

Modularity does have its drawbacks.[42] Creating modules may require more redundancy than an integrated design. If modules are used in multiple products there can be excessive capability for some products. Modularity may also lead to a sameness in design between different companies, as companies mix and match the same components. This has been a problem with personal computers, especially among Windows machines.

Early Feedback

Flexible new product development relies on the ability to get meaningful and rapid feedback from customers. This helps spot new opportunities, react to new designs, and to spot declining

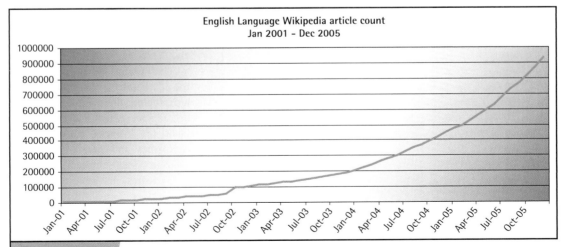

Figure 11.22

Rapid Growth

Source: Wikipedia.org

interest in existing products. All of these methods speed up product cycles and push everyone in the industry to move faster.

Email provides low-cost rapid access to customers and helps gather consumer suggestions for improvements in products. This is especially true for a company with a small or moderate number of customers. In this case, email can be a better solution than extensive customized web pages. The management challenge with email is to make sure it gets handled by the right person in a timely manner.

Raining Data provides multiple addresses for email to the company (Figure 11.23). This strongly hints that the right people will see the message, not just an overworked webmaster.[43] One of the most important findings in new product research over the last 15 years has been the importance of lead users in technical fields in providing important new product ideas.[44] Email can speed this up if there is confidence that a technically sophisticated employee will read the email. This system will give senders much more confidence that the recipient will be able to comprehend the suggestion.

Email also provides a much faster and lower cost method of conducting surveys of existing users. Although not an independent sample of all possible customers, and perhaps inappropriate for new products that are quite different than the current offerings, current users normally provide the core market for a company's new products. An email survey can provide a quick sample of uses and needs.

The prerelease of products to the marketplace has allowed rapid prototyping and testing. This has become an accepted Net strategy. Using the Internet, many software companies and web entrepreneurs utilize a system of alpha-beta product releases. In rapidly changing product categories this has been an especially valuable learning and testing device. As discussed in the usability chapter, this early release of software provides multiple benefits to consumers—even with bugs— as long as feedback and upgrade are also efficient.

Figure 11.23

Extensive Feedback Requires Feedback Systems

Source: Courtesy of Raining Data

The first step in the process is the alpha release stage. Trusted lead users, and often company employees, are asked to participate in alpha testing. These alpha users are typically asked to sign a nondisclosure agreement, where they agree not to share any information about the product with other people and companies. The goal is to shape the product and to understand how functional new ideas and methods are.

At the alpha stage many of the capabilities of products are fluid, and problems are common. Users are asked in-depth questions about the performance of the product and features they might like. Two main reasons account for alpha users' willingness to participate on the "bleeding edge" of technology. First, they feel they can obtain some competitive advantage by early exposure to the technology. Even with its failings, the product lets them accomplish things they couldn't easily do before. The second major reason is to shape and change the features that are part of the product. If the user is committed to the product idea, they have a strong incentive to shape it toward their needs.

Creating the right set of alpha-users is an important strategic choice for successful new product development (Figure 11.24). The goal is to quickly arrive at the right set of features. Research has shown this to be difficult. It is very hard to determine the most important features

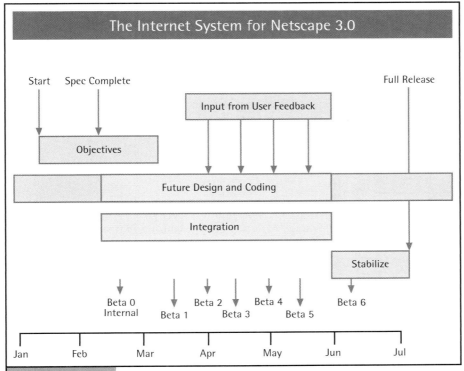

Figure 11.24

The Internet System for Netscape 3.0

Source: Marco Inansiti and Alan MacCormack, "Developing Products on Internet Time," *Harvard Business Review* 75, no. 5 (1997): 108–117.

of new products without talking to a large number of potential users.[45] By encouraging relevant consumers to actually use the product, much more involved and realistic feedback is obtained.

The next step is beta testing, as in Figure 11.24. Now the product or service is made public. The goal is to widely test, and to continue refining the feature set. Key goals now are reliability, compatibility, and fixing user interface problems. Participation is usually obtained by providing the service at a much lower price, typically free. Beta testing also serves as a strong form of advertising and sampling. The ability to temporarily give the product away without establishing a very low reference price allows much more aggressive use of low pricing during development.

Beta testing is a valuable substitute for extensive testing. By relying on customers to find problems, the firm can cut back on its internal testing capabilities. This saves money and dramatically speeds up the process. Widespread testing is critical for a technology that might be accessed by a wide range of computers and differing access capabilities. Traditional methods would slow down the process.

The alpha-beta-version sequence contributes substantially to the pace of competition. "The clock starts ticking" with the release of the alpha product. Now important users know that a product is in the works, and they start hoping for the real version. They may delay purchases of the old version, waiting for the new version. With the beta release the time pressure becomes quite powerful, as users want the problems to disappear in the service they are using. Competitors are alerted much earlier to the full features of the developing product than in the days when testing and development was done internally. This creates the fear of obsolescence and market losses much earlier in their product life cycle. Speed becomes critical, or the competitors' responses to the new entry will follow very closely to the hoped-for competitive breakthrough.

One caution in using the alpha-beta release strategy is a reliance on lead users, which may have unusual demands. The flexible new product process relies heavily on consumer feedback. If beta testers are heavily tilted toward early adopters, as is likely, the suggestions they give may be biased. Even worse, they may be far too forgiving of problems and glitches. A manager needs to be disciplined about getting a wide enough range of feedback, and from different classes of customers.

Rapid Release

Rapid product development simply sets the stage for profitability. The final key to successful and flexible new products is the ability to go to market quickly. Time lost in the distribution cycle is even more damaging than time lost during development. Once the product design is frozen, and manufacturing has taken over, all time lost is a pure cost.

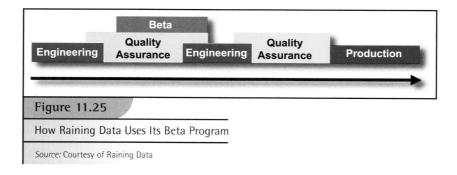

Figure 11.25

How Raining Data Uses Its Beta Program

Source: Courtesy of Raining Data

For products delivered online, the alpha-beta process can be used to accelerate distribution. One effective method is to put a termination date into the beta copies, with an automatic feature leading to a purchase option. Another is to acquire email addresses of beta testers. Once the full version is released, email with embedded links can be sent to the full set of beta users. Upgrades can be quickly and cheaply sent to the appropriate customers, as done with an upgraded version of the Xcelsius software (Figure 11.26).

Explore the all-new Xcelsius!
and get your FREE copy of the release candidate.

(Offer valid only to paid support customers as of May 3, 2005, and expires May 13, 2005 at 12m PT.)

Send me the Xcelsius
Release Candidate

Figure 11.26

Seeding the Customer Base with Beta Versions of a New Product

Source: Courtesy of Infommersion, INC

ENDNOTES

1. From Diogenes Laertius, *Lives of Eminent Philosophers* Cambridge, MA: Harvard University Press, 1938.

2. Jacob Goldenberg, Donald Lehmann, and David Mazursky, "The Idea Itself and the Circumstances of Its Emergence as Predictors of New Product Success," *Management Science* 47, no. 1 (January 2001): 69–84.

3. For example, *The Cola Conquest,* directed by Irene Angelico, Ronin Films, 1998.

4. Timothy F. Bresnahan and Shane Greenstein, "Technological Competition and the Structure of the Computer Industry," *Journal of Industrial Economics* XLVII, no. 1, (March 1999): 1–40.

5. Tracy Kidder, *The Soul of the New Machine* (Boston: Atlantic-Little, Brown, 1981). Note that Digital recently was acquired by Compaq — eventually being swallowed up by one of the personal computer makers whose market they ignored for too long.

6. For a detailed history, see Michael A. Cusamano, Yiorgos Mylonadis, Richard Rosenbloom, "Strategic Maneuvering and Mass-Market Dynamics: The Triumph of VHS over Beta," *The Business History Review* 66, no. 1 (Spring 1992): 55–94.

7. Richard J. Gilbert and Michael Katz, "An Economist's Guide to *U.S. v. Microsoft,*" (May 1, 2001). *Economics Department, University of California, Berkeley,* Working Paper E01-300. http://repositories. cdlib.org/ iber/econ/E01-300

8. Chart comes from Timothy F. Bresnahan and Pai-Ling Yin, "Economic and Technical Drivers of Technology Choice: Browsers," Stanford University, 2003, working paper.

9. From websidestory.com.

10. For some sites, such as W3 Schools, reaching 25% market share in April 2005.

11. "Sleepless in Silicon Valley: Global competition, technology's fast track dictate a lifestyle of working into the wee hours," *San Jose Mercury*, June 21, 1996.

12. Kim Clark and Steven Wheelwright, *Managing New Product and Process Development* (New York: Free Press, 1993).

13. Joel Birnbaum, Senior VP of R&D for Hewlett-Packard, as quoted in: Regis McKenna, *Real Time: Preparing for the Age of the Never Satisfied Customer* (Boston: Harvard Business School Press, 1997).

14. Alex Taylor III, "Is Jack Smith the man to fix GM?" *Fortune* (3 August 1998): 86–92.

15. Kathleen Eisenhardt and Shona Brown, "Time Pacing: Competing in Markets That Won't Stand Still," *Harvard Business Review* (March-April 1998): 59–69.

16. Some researchers have questioned the benefits of being early to market, instead arguing for the benefits of playing a "fast second." An example is Golder and Tellis. They argue that it is better to enter later in the product life cycle when the

market is entering the rapid growth phase. However, for the products in their study this is measured as more than 10 years after the introduction of the first product. This time scale is completely implausible for the Net. While it may be true that a fast second strategy can work for a firm like Microsoft, it still will be measured in months, not years. See Peter Golder and Gerald Tellis, "Pioneer Advantage: Marketing Logic or Marketing Legend," *Journal of Marketing Research* Volume 30, Issue 2. (May 1993): 158–170.

17. Time pacing and Internet time are examples of the Red Queen Effect. The Red Queen Effect owes its name to discussion between Alice and the Red Queen in Alice in Wonderland:

   "Well, in our country," said Alice, still panting a little, "you'd generally get to somewhere else—if you ran very fast for a long time, as we've been doing."

   "A slow sort of country!" said the Queen. "Now, here, you see, it takes all the running you can do, to keep in the same place. If you want to get somewhere else, you must run at least twice as fast as that!"

   Profits may not rise by improving cycle time, but failure to increase the pace may lead to serious profit penalty.

18. For an accessible guide to standards and increasing returns see W. Brian Arthur, "Increasing Returns and the New World of Business," *Harvard Business Review* (July-August 1996): 100–109.

19. William Saltzstein, "Bluetooth and Beyond: Wireless Options for Medical Devices," *Medical Devicelink* (June 2004).

20. IEEE Std. 802.11b-1999 (R2003), "Part 11: Wireless LAN Medium Access Control (MAC) and Physical Layer (PHY) Specifications: Higher-Speed Physical Layer Extension in the 2.4 GHz Band."

21. S. Brander, RFC 2026, 1996: available at http://www.internic.net.

22. Abner Germanow of International Data Quest quoted in Fisher, Lawrence, "Confusion over Modems is Hurting Sales," *New York Times* (24 November 1997).

23. John Rendelman, "56K Rift Deepens Without a Standard," *Internet Week* 685 (13 October 1997).

24. Carl Cargill, *Open Systems Standardization: A Business Approach* (Englewood Cliffs, NJ: Prentice Hall, 1996). Carl Cargill, *Information Technology Standardization: Theory, Process, and Organizations.* (Bedford, MA: Digital Press, 1989).

25. The first analysis in a general multiple period strategic framework that established these curves in the technology system setting can be found in Ward Hanson, "Bandwagons and Orphans: Dynamic Pricing of Competing Technological Systems Subject to Decreasing Cost" (Ph.D. diss., Stanford

University Department of Economics, 1985). The pioneering dynamic analysis in a nonstrategic setting is due to Brian Arthur, *On Competing Technologies and Historical Small Events: The Dynamics of Choice Under Increasing Returns,* International Institute for Applied Systems Analysis, 1983, WP-83-90, working paper. Also see Joseph Farrell and Garth Saloner, "Standardization, Compatibility, and Innovation," *Rand Journal of Economics* 16 (1985): 70–83. Michael Katz and Carl Shapiro, "Technology Adoption in the Presence of Network Externalities," *Journal of Political Economy* 94 (1986): 822–841.

26. As defined by Lilien et al: "Conjoint analysis is a set of methods designed to measure consumer preferences for a multiattribute product. It is the most widely applied and studied method for assessing buyers' multiattribute utility functions." In Gary Lilien, Philip Kotler, Sridhar Moorthy, *Marketing Models* (Englewood Cliffs, NJ: Prentice Hall, 1992), 241.

27. See, for example, Glen Urban and John Hauser, "Ch. 6: An Overview of the Design Process," *Design and Marketing of New Products* (Englewood Cliffs, NJ: Prentice Hall, 1993).

28. Greg Stevens and James Burley, "3000 Raw Ideas = 1 Commercial Success!" *Research Technology Management,* 40. no. 3 (May/June 1997): 16–27.

29. Among many possible sources, see Goldenberg, et al., op. cit.

30. Ely Dahan and V. Srinivasan, "The Predictive Power of Internet-Based Product Concept Testing Using Visual Depiction and Animation," *Journal of Product Innovation Management* 17 (March 2000): 99–109.

31. Gordon Wyner, "Reinventing Research Design," *Marketing Research* (Winter 2003): 6–7. Eric Almquist, Martin Kon, and Wolfgang Bock, "The Science of Demand," *Marketing Management* (March/April 2004): 20–26.

32. Glen Urban, John Hauser, William Qualls, Bruce Weinberg, Jonathan Bohlmann, and Roberta Chicos, "Information Acceleration: Validation and Lessons From the Field," *Journal of Marketing Research* XXXIV (February 1997): 143–153.

33. Glen Urban, Bruce Weinberg, and John Hauser, "Premarket Forecasting of Really-New Products," *Journal of Marketing* 60 (January 1996): 47–60.

34. Timothy Devinney, Jordan Louviere, and Tim Coltman, "A Comprehensive Review of the Theory and Underlying Technology of Information Acceleration Simulators," mimeo, Smart Internet Technology CRC, The Alfred West Jr. Learning Lab, The Wharton School, University of Pennsylvania.

35. Marco Inansiti and Alan MacCormack, "Developing Products on Internet Time," *Harvard Business Review* 75, no. 5 (1997): 108–117.

36. Carliss Baldwin and Kim Clark, "Managing in an Age of Modularity," *Harvard Business Review* (September/October 1997): 84–93.

37. Chun-Che Huang, "Overview of Modular Product Development," *Proceeding National Science Council ROC(A)* 24, no.3 (2000): 149–165.

38. Balwin and Clark, op. cit., p. 86.

39. See, for example, Mark Gaynor and Scott Bradner, "A Real Options Framework to Value Network, Protocol, and Service Architecture," *ACM SIGCOMM Computer Communications Review* 34, no. 5 (October 2004): 31–38.

40. Maryann Jones Thompson, "Web Services Take Hold," *Technology Review* (April 2005): 28.

41. See, for example, Andrew Lih, "The Foundations of Participatory Journalism and the Wikipedia Project,"

presented at *Association for Education in Journalism and Mass Communications,* Toronto, 7 August 2004, and cites within.

42. Huang, op. cit.

43. This use by Pick systems was highlighted by Jim Sterne, *Customer Service on the Internet: Building Relationships, Increasing Loyalty, and Staying Competitive* (New York: Wiley), 59–62.

44. Eric von Hippel has demonstrated this point in his research. For example, Eric von Hippel, "New Product Ideas From 'Lead Users,'" *Research Technology Management* 32, no. 3 (May-June 1989): 24–27.

45. Abbie Griffin and John Hauser, "The Voice of the Customer," *Marketing Science* 12, no. 1 (1993).

chapter 12:

Pricing in an Online World

> **Every price has a life.**
>
> R. Dolan and H. Simon[1]

> **It is only an auctioneer who can equally and impartially admire all schools of art.**
>
> Oscar Wilde[2]

The Price of Vice

Since at least the 1930s, many policy makers view a good tax as one that raises substantial revenue without "distorting" consumer behavior. Typically, this means applying taxes to products with low price sensitivity. When price sensitivity is low, consumers still buy the product even when the price rises due to the tax. In situations where products have harmful effects, such as cigarette smoking, governments around the world put high taxes (often called sin taxes) on the product. In their view, one of two good things will happen.[3] Either consumers look at the high prices and stop buying the product (for cigarettes, stopping smoking and improving health), or they continue buying the product and paying the tax.

The Internet has complicated this policy, especially for high-value and easily shipped products such as cigarettes. In the United States, most of the tax on cigarettes is set by individual state governments. Excise taxes range from very low ($0.03 per pack in tobacco-growing Kentucky) to $2.46 per pack in Rhode Island, plus sales tax.[4] The situation is even more extreme with American Indian sales, many of which sell cigarettes without taxes of any kind from outlets on their tribal lands. Online cigarette sales from low-tax areas are circumventing high state taxes.

Goolsbee and Slemrod looked at how cigarette taxation fared with the rise of the Internet, and the ability of smokers to use the Internet to shop nationally for their smokes. The results are dramatic. Using data on cigarette sales before the

Pricing is the most digital of marketing tactics, and all companies have had their pricing affected the Net. This chapter looks at the most important impacts on pricing sensitivity, using content to reinforce pricing, and taking advantage of the communication abilities of the Net to utilize advanced pricing tactics.

Topics covered in this chapter include:

> **Price Sensitivity and the Net**

> **Advanced Pricing Online**
> > Auction
> > Yield management
> > Rental, trial, and sales
> > Personalized pricing and bundling

Internet became important, they find the measured price elasticity for consumers' purchases of cigarettes to be low (between –.58 and –.68). This is price inelastic, and consistent with the sin tax approach of the states. However, after the Internet becomes important the researchers find a very different situation. Due to shopping across state lines, they find cigarette sales are now elastic (between –1.05 and –1.17). The Internet more than doubled the price elasticity of cigarettes.

Because consumers can get their cigarettes at much lower prices online, many continue to smoke and government tax revenue from cigarettes has fallen sharply (Figure 12.1).[5] The U.S. government estimates lost tax revenue to the states in excess of $1 billion per year due to Internet tobacco sales.[6]

Stopping online cigarette sales, already considered illegal by many states, is a challenge. States or tribal lands where the sales originate have no incentive to prevent them. States where

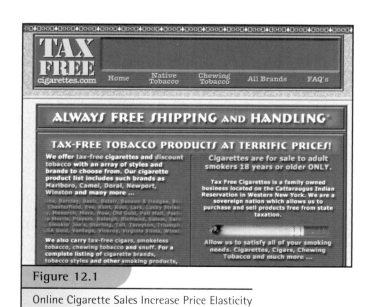

Figure 12.1

Online Cigarette Sales Increase Price Elasticity

Source: Courtesy of www.taxfreecigarettes.com

the sales are shipped have a very difficult time preventing the transaction. Some form of coordination is required.

A path-breaking move involving the Federal Bureau of Tobacco and Firearms, the Attorneys General of a number of taxing states, and the major credit cards and payment systems may be the answer. As of March 2005, all the major credit card companies and online payment systems agreed to no longer support web sites selling cigarettes nationally. Online shoppers will have to use checks, money orders, or some other system to pay for their online cigarette purchases. The states hope this additional barrier will curtail many of the transactions.

Cigarette sales demonstrate a number of the interactions between pricing and the Net. Even price insensitive consumption can become price sensitive when there are different purchase outlets. Smoking is an important cost to heavy users, and smokers are motivated to find low price sources. Using online shopping, this search expands from their neighborhood to the entire country or beyond. Price sensitivity depends on the ability of a shopper to compare alternatives, evaluate deals, and whether the total costs justify the time and effort to find better prices.

The Net has impacts on pricing far beyond simple price reduction. These include many pricing techniques that are difficult to use without online capabilities, such as auctions, yield management, trial pricing, promotions, and peak load pricing. The digital nature of many online products and services makes some pricing tactics much more powerful. Product bundling becomes especially relevant online, as low incremental cost digital products make bundling a profitable pricing approach.

Figure 12.2

Hindering Online Sales of Cigarettes by Banning Credit Card Use

Source: © Terri Miller/E-Visual Communications Inc.

PRICING AND THE NET

The Power of Pricing

Pricing is the most active and dynamic of marketing's fundamental tools. Pricing is an everyday concern of managers. A company, or its competitors, can change price in an instant. A press release, a message to customers, or new sales sheets to the sales force make it a fact.

In many ways, pricing is also the most digital of marketing actions. The price of a product or service is a number, a formula, or an agreement about how much it will cost. These are all information. We have seen how the Internet and information are tightly connected. The informational side of pricing means that every company's pricing actions are affected by the Internet.

The link between pricing and information shows up in many ways. Consumer awareness of prices is critical to proper pricing. Proper pricing also relies on knowledge of different prices from different sources and includes perceptions about fairness. It is crucial that a firm can track changes in costs, customer tastes, and competitive actions.

Studies find a large leverage associated with pricing.[7] In one study of more than 2,400 companies, pricing had the largest impact on profitability (see Figure 12.3) compared with lowering costs or expanding sales.[8] A 1% improvement in price will typically lead to an 11% improvement in profits, a much larger impact than improvements in the other variables.

Pricing's leverage is a two-edged sword. Firms often price incorrectly. Business essayist and observer Peter Drucker has pointed out the power of pricing by making it a central source of

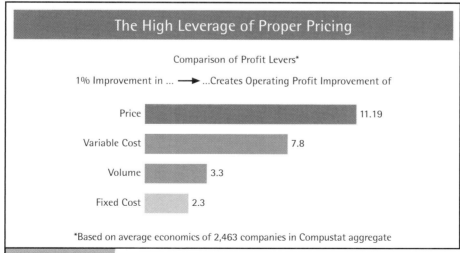

The High Leverage of Proper Pricing

Comparison of Profit Levers*

1% Improvement in ... ⟶ ...Creates Operating Profit Improvement of

Price	11.19
Variable Cost	7.8
Volume	3.3
Fixed Cost	2.3

*Based on average economics of 2,463 companies in Compustat aggregate

Figure 12.3

Pricing is Tightly Linked to Profitability

Source: Michael V. Marn and Robert L. Rosiello, "Managing price, gaining profit," *The McKinsey Quarterly*, Number 4 (1992): pp. 18–37.

business errors. Drucker's *"Five Sins of Business"* are common business mistakes that he observes the world over. Three of the five business sins are directly pricing related:[9]

> *Pricing Sin 1: The Worship of Premium Pricing*—companies try too hard to hold onto high profit margins with small sales.

> *Pricing Sin 2: Skim Pricing of New Products*—companies do not push new products aggressively enough. They serve the most desirable segment first, and forget to adapt to the mainstream.

> *Pricing Sin 3: Cost-Driven Pricing*—cost is internal; value is what customers care about.

The power of pricing also makes it a threat. If a change in the business environment makes it harder to get a good price, profits can drop dramatically. If a 1% pricing improvement can cause an 11% profit increase, a fall in the effective price can drive profits down just as quickly.

The standard pricing solution provides a baseline for understanding the pricing challenges and opportunities arising from the Net. Much of the intuition about pricing builds on the concept of price sensitivity, which summarizes many of the most important features of consumer demand and competition. Much of the impact of the Net on pricing filters through the Net's impact on price sensitivity. Price sensitivity can even help one understand important pricing practices such as auctions and bundling, which go beyond the simple setting of a single price.

Three pricing questions are especially important for Net marketers. They are:

1. How does the presence of the Internet change the price sensitivity of products and services?
2. How can online content be used to influence the price sensitivity of customers?
3. What new pricing tools and methods work better on the Internet than through more traditional methods?

Answering these questions combines an understanding of the capabilities of the DNI framework with an appreciation of how pricing works. It requires coordination of the main pricing functions with online managers. It also sets the stage for a number of the ecommerce activities that follow.

The Standard Pricing Answer

> *The Role of Price Elasticity*

The normal pricing goal for a firm is profit maximization. To do this, a firm must choose price based on three fundamentals: costs, consumer demand, and competition.[10] In some cases, it has enough information about these factors that it can do so precisely. In other situations, it must set price while combining market research, pricing intuition, and experience to get the best return. In an increasing number of situations, it does not even try to set price but relies instead on an auction to determine the best price the product or service can bring.

Even in uncertain and complicated pricing situations, one of the most useful insights comes from the simple textbook setting of a single price when a company knows how its costs and demand change as output changes. In this case, the firm uses the pricing policy of setting marginal revenue equal to marginal cost. Marginal revenue is the revenue it receives from the next unit sold, marginal cost is the incremental cost of the next unit.

When a firm sets price so that marginal revenue equals marginal cost, the firm is making the highest profit possible.[11] If marginal revenue is higher than marginal cost, the company is better off selling more even if it must lower the price to accomplish that. Alternatively, if it is at a point where the marginal cost for new sales is higher than the marginal revenue, cutting back and having fewer sales at a higher price is best. The price that just balances marginal revenue and marginal cost gives the company its maximum profit.

A simple but powerful insight follows from this and guides pricing in a wide range of settings. Even when it does not quite fit, this equation provides the starting point for the correct solution.[12] This is the "inverse elasticity rule." The inverse elasticity rule states that the following must be true when profits are at their highest:[13]

$$\frac{\text{(Best price} - \text{incremental cost)}}{\text{Best price}} = \frac{1}{|\text{Price elasticity of market at best price}|} \quad \text{(12-1)}$$

The left-hand side of the equation is called the contribution margin ratio, which is the fraction of the next sale that is profit. On the right hand side of the equation is the (positive value of) price elasticity of the marketplace. In other words, the optimal contribution margin is the reciprocal of the price elasticity of demand:

$$\text{CMR*} = 1/|\text{price sensitivity of the market at p*}| \quad \text{(12-2)}$$

The major complication of this formula is the price elasticity term, which measures the responsiveness of demand to changes of price.[14] For convenience, we often say that price sensitivity is the negative of price elasticity. The fundamental insight is this: *The more price sensitive a market, the lower the profit-maximizing margin.* When a market becomes more price sensitive, even a monopolist will lower price to maximize profits.

Price sensitivity is so important to pricing that a number of studies have looked at the impact of the Internet on marketplace price sensitivity for a variety of products. If the Internet makes demand more responsive to price, we expect firms to react to this and lower their prices. If the Net does not change price sensitivity, the impact on pricing and the prices consumers pay will be less important.

Equation (12-1) hints at another method by which the Internet might affect pricing. If the incremental cost c falls without affecting price sensitivity, so the right-hand side of (12-1) does not change, a firm will lower its optimal price. We have already discussed this in Chapter 8, where we considered effective ways of substituting the Net for customer support and other costly activities. If firms achieve this without lowering quality, both consumers and the firm benefit.

> ## The Level and Dispersion of Prices
The initial research on the Internet's impact on pricing focused on two questions. One, are goods sold online cheaper than the same goods sold through traditional outlets? Two, are prices online less subject to variation than prices offline? If prices are cheaper online, this creates a strong motivation for consumers to move online. If prices are also less dispersed, this suggests a more efficient marketplace where prices are forced toward the same level.

Judged by these two questions, the initial impact of the Net on the pricing environment was relatively modest. Among the findings on lower prices, these early studies found

> Books, movies, and music were somewhat lower priced online, but more for smaller sellers than market leaders,
> Travel prices were somewhat lower when booked online,

> Automobile prices were lower by a few percent, especially for certain categories of shoppers, than for purchases made face to face. This was partly due to a shift to lower price outlets and partly due to a lower price quoted at the same outlets,

> Except for promotional efforts, prices for many frequently purchased goods such as groceries were higher when shipping and handling costs were included, and

> Price dispersion for books, CDs, electronics, and airline tickets seem larger online than offline. The opposite is found for life insurance and automobiles.[15]

Prices do not converge to a single online offering, and price dispersion remains. This was somewhat surprising, as the power of online search might have forced prices to both go down and be more similar. However, there remain enough search inertia and differentiating features online that prices still vary substantially between sellers.[16]

A major impact of the Net on price sensitivity throughout the economy is the ability of consumers and firms to rapidly compare alternatives for products and services even when they aren't sold online. In industries ranging from life insurance, travel, computers, antiques, and cigarettes the Internet has significantly changed the pricing environment. While raising elasticity typically delivers a lower price to consumers, it can have complicated impacts on sellers and others.

Price Sensitivity and Online Information

Many factors affect customers' price sensitivity. A common perception is that the Net always raises consumer price sensitivity. This isn't true. While the Net tends toward increasing price sensitivity, some companies have skillfully used the Internet to lower their specific marketplace price sensitivity and retain premium prices.

The price sensitivity factors in Table 12.1 provide a useful checklist for combining online strategy and pricing. They are a qualitative first step in helping managers understand when their customers care strongly about price. They can be grouped into three categories corresponding to value uncertainty, purchase importance, and price positioning. They provide an intuitive guide to the factors driving price sensitivity, especially when the data needed for calculating equation (12-2) is missing.

One of the tasks of an online marketer is to understand the implications of the price sensitivity factors for online content. Different companies will have different objectives. A low-price firm will want to use its online presence to enhance price sensitivity and create a focus on price. A premium service-oriented firm, on the other hand, wants online content that reinforces that position and reduces the focus on price. Each of the price sensitivity factors helps the "reverse engineering" from price sensitivity factor to online content.

For example, the shared cost effect applies when there is a separation between purchase decision maker and purchase payer. This occurs regularly in business travel, where a salesperson chooses what airline to fly or hotel to stay at while her company reimburses expenses. The company is much more price sensitive than the traveler. Another example is medicine, where a doctor strongly influences prescription choice, but the patient or health insurance company must pay for the drug. The shared cost effect typically lowers market price sensitivity. The main impact of the shared cost effect on Internet strategy is to create separate content aimed at the decision maker or the payer.

One or more of the price sensitivity factors can operate at the same time for a particular pricing decision. A pricing manager typically must make a decision without the results of controlled

Table 12.1

Price Sensitivity Effects Help Connect Online Strategies and Pricing	
The Price Sensitivity Factors	
Price Sensitivity Factor	*Description*
Value uncertainty	
Reference price effect	Price sensitivity rises when price is perceived as out of line with the alternatives.
Difficult comparison effect	Awareness of more substitutes and lower search costs work to increase price sensitivity.
Switching cost effect	Price sensitivity is reduced when the product is part of a system of complementary products.
Price-quality effect	When price is a signal of quality, price sensitivity is lower.
Purchase importance	
Total expenditures effect	Expensive products, either in absolute or percentage terms, will have higher price sensitivity due to increased search.
End-benefit effect	Important inputs to a production process have higher price sensitivity than less critical items.
Shared cost effect	Separating the decision maker and the payer for a product or service lowers price sensitivity.

Source: Adapted from Thomas T. Nagle and Reed K. Holden, (2002), *The Strategy and Tactics of Pricing*, 3rd Edition, Prentice Hall, New York.

market research and careful statistical studies. Also, online content choices must be regularly made and altered. Having an intuitive understanding of the factors shaping price sensitivity helps pricing managers make good decisions and for online marketers provides a better understanding of how these effects might be altered by online marketing content.[17]

> *Value Uncertainty*

Value uncertainty occurs when customers can not determine the precise quality or applicability of different products to their needs. Another of Wilde's quotes on pricing is to define a cynic as someone "who knows the price of everything and the value of nothing." Cynics are not the only ones troubled by the transformation from product features to ultimate benefits.[18] Consumers may not be able to easily understand the product and make the relevant tradeoffs and comparisons. Value uncertainty affects price sensitivity in several predictable ways. The relevant price sensitivity factors are the reference price effect, the difficult comparison effect, the switching cost effect, and the price-quality effect.

> The Reference Price Effect

The reference price effect connects price sensitivity with the competitive alternatives a potential customer uses to judge the product's price. Price sensitivity increases when a product's price is above those of the perceived alternatives. Perception is important, and the manner in which the product is compared to alternatives can strongly influence price sensitivity.

For sellers of combination mobile devices, the reference price effect suggests very different price reactions if consumers compare a Treo (PDA+ cell phone) to other cell phones or to a PDA

(b) Treo

Is the right comparison for the Treo just another cell phone (which is much cheaper) or another combination phone and PDA (costing about the same) such as a Pocket PC?

(a) Cell Phone

(c) Combination Phone/PDA

Figure 12.4

The Composition of the Reference Set Shapes Price Sensitivity

Source: 12.4a © PRNewsFoto/Nokia; 12.4b © PRNewsFoto/Handspring, Inc.; 12.4c © Market Wire Global Locate

(Figure 12.4). The Treo's price is much higher than Nokia's price, but comparable to an IPAQ. Online material supporting the Treo strongly emphasizes the combination of features, stressing the comparison to the full set of benefits, establishing the more expensive PDA as the reference good.

The reference price effect provides strong motivation for manufacturers to battle for customers' attention and to provide comparison shopping information at their own sites, rather than send consumers to an online shopping site with different comparison sets. Firms competing on low price want to shape the comparisons around basic features and the low prices of their offerings. Sellers of enhanced features need to ensure that the full range of benefits is required for the comparison set. This is a natural tension point between manufacturers and retailers, with retailers less committed to any one aspect of the price and feature spectrum.

Figures 12.5 and 12.6 illustrate this battle. Edmunds.com is an independent comparison site for new and used vehicles. A user can compare by price point or body style, selecting from a wide range of alternatives. For example, a convertible shopper can choose to compare the BMW 6, the Chrysler Sebring, and the Ford Thunderbird. These are very different cars, with a large price gap. This presents a serious problem for both BMW and Ford. Simple tables of attributes do not stress factors such as overall safety, styling, or quality elements that might justify a base price 300% higher than the Chrysler. BMW needs a different comparison set.

The BMW site also contains a comparison tool. However, if a shopper wants to compare the 6 series to other cars, the choices are limited only to those models BMW believes to be most relevant: the Porsche 911, the Cadillac XLR, and the Jaguar XK8. All are close in price to the BMW. The cheapest of these three is the Jaguar, barely 2% lower. With the three alternatives now all being in the mid to high 70K range, the reference price effect is neutral for the BMW rather than harmful. In this case all relevant cars are almost the same price, and the price is appropriate. A somewhat different impact might occur for the BMW 7 Series. BMW officials find that the Lexus LS, which is about $15,000 cheaper than a 750i, is heavily cross-shopped and therefore is included in the comparison set on the web site. In this case the reference effect might work against BMW, as the reference price effect will likely be influenced by this lower price point for the Lexus.

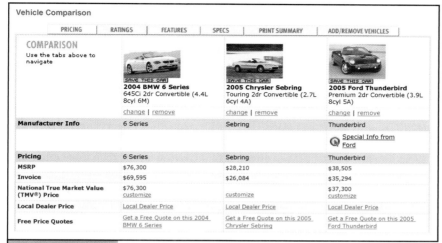

Figure 12.5

Third Party Sites Allow Wide Ranging Comparisons

Source: Courtesy of Edmunds.com, Inc.

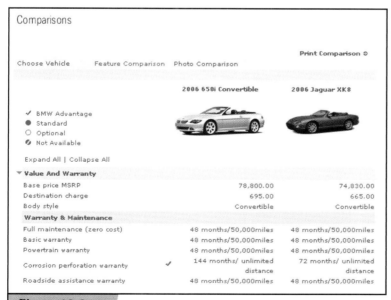

Figure 12.6

Manufacturers Control the Comparison Differently

Source: Courtesy of BMW of North America, LLC. The tradename "BMW," the expression "The Ultimate Driving Machine," the Msport symbol ("///M"), the kidney-shaped grilles, and the BMW Roundel logo are only a few of the federally registered trademarks owned by Bayerische Motoren Werke AG.

Reference prices can be based on expectations of the future as well as current alternatives. One of the dangers of presenting in-depth information about future products online can be the inadvertent creation of a reference price based on a not-yet-released product. The new-generation item, perhaps described online in an attempt to generate buzz and enthusiasm, puts severe pressure on current sales and the evaluation of the incumbent product.

> Difficult Comparison Effect

As seen in the case of online cigarettes, even an addictive product can be price sensitive if there are alternatives available in the market place. The difficult comparison effect connects price sensitivity with the presence and awareness of alternatives. The Internet's biggest impact on price sensitivity may be through the comparison effect, with increasing information leading to lower willingness to pay.[19] A fear of many retailers is that the Internet will create cutthroat competition. Why pay more for a branded item, shipped direct the next day? The concern becomes even more pronounced with the emergence of online services that list the best prices available for products.

Price Watch is an example of a site dedicated at making price comparisons easy for consumers. Price Watch (http://www.pricewatch.com) maintains a database of deals and low price offerings for a wide range of computer systems and peripherals. Users can browse or search, and the system sorts items by price. It gives a limited description of each item, with more details available on request and links to the stores selling the products. Price Watch does not sell the products themselves. Rather, it acts as an information intermediary. Another example is the Quicken Financial Network. Quicken has several different categories of pricing information available any time a consumer wants. One of the most important prices anyone pays is the mortgage loan rate for a house. The Quicken Loans site offers the prospective homebuyer a menu of choices for different loans. If the online information isn't sufficient, or isn't clear, a form is offered leading to a quick callback from a salesperson. The use of a call center is an evolution away from purely online material for Quicken, as it originally relied on online materials and questionnaires to educate prospective borrowers. A mortgage, however, is both a very large and high involvement purchase. Experience has led Quicken to merge online and human interaction in order to educate and comfort customers for their large purchases.

Low cost but high purchase frequency categories also support comparison sites. An example of a comparison service for low price point goods is provided by BestBookDeal.com (Figure 12.7). Searching

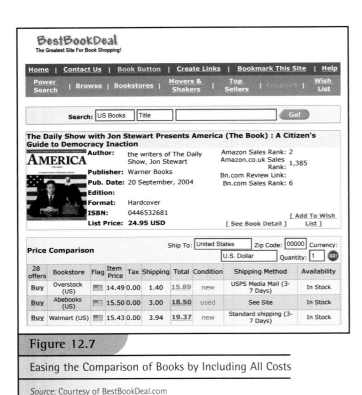

Figure 12.7

Easing the Comparison of Books by Including All Costs

Source: Courtesy of BestBookDeal.com

25 online bookstores in under a minute, the site combines shipping and purchase price to accurately reflect the full total price. Easier price comparison boosts price sensitivity.

The ease of using powerful price comparison sites seems to conflict with research findings stressing the durability of price dispersion and the ability of leading online retailers such as Amazon to maintain a price premium. One answer lies in the motivation of users to visit additional sites, and the trust they place in alternative vendors. Although the prices may be lower, the difficult comparison with respect to on-time delivery and order processing makes it less likely that consumers shop around.

It can be difficult for consumers, even with in-depth online information, to judge the quality of a product or service. One problem is truthfulness and credibility. Is the information online really accurate, or are the company marketers stretching the truth and hiding problems? Another challenge is durability. Even if the product is being honestly described, will it continue to work as advertised? A third issue is commitment. Will the company continue to support the product with service and support? Will the vendor be around in the future? Smith and Brynjolfsson studied consumer behavior at comparison sites and found substantial willingness to pay extra for reliable shipping, both in terms of upgraded shipping and for online retailers with a reputation of shipping on time.[20]

New companies and customers aggravate the problem. As new countries enter the global trading system, due to the Internet or the broader role of globalization, many new consumers find themselves outside their familiar market surroundings. These customers must somehow accurately judge different providers in new countries where they don't have experience or the background purchasing knowledge. Similarly, customers from established markets can now access new sellers, looking for new goods and special deals.

The nature of the product or service involved contributes to the challenge of judging new products or vendors. An important distinction is between search and experience goods.[21] A search good is one in which the goods' features and characteristics, such as quality and price, are easily observable and comparable. An experience good, on the other hand, is one in which it is difficult to judge quality and proper price. For example, many health care providers are difficult to compare, and it is never possible to judge whether a doctor did the proper examination and made the proper diagnosis. Experience goods are naturally more sensitive to the difficult comparison effect and, consequently, less price sensitive.

The evidence from the first few years of online shopping highlights the complexities of the difficult comparison effect. While some firms attempt to use online content to standardize comparison and turn experience goods into search goods, others work toward the opposite objective and seek to make price comparison more challenging. Controlling shopper attention becomes a partial battleground over price sensitivity.

> Switching Cost Effect

Switching costs act to lower price sensitivity, at least in the short run. When a product is part of a system, such as computer plus software or auto plus gasoline, product purchases are less sensitive to changes in the price of one of the components. A rise in the price of gasoline is not responded to aggressively due to the remaining value of the current vehicle. However, when a new car is purchased, the demand for higher efficiency reveals itself and price sensitivity reappears.

Other forms of switching cost occur when a customer must go through an elaborate or confusing set of steps to exit. For example, a brokerage customer may face the challenge of opening a new account elsewhere, transferring money and stocks to the new brokerage, signing new forms, finding new offices, and more. Over time, these switching costs can grow, and consumers may not be able to estimate reliably how this develops.

Chen and Hitt estimated brokerage consumer switching costs using customer flows, online content, site demographics, and other detailed data on the brokerage customer base of a number of brokerages.[22] They found considerable variation in the switching costs, demonstrating both their importance and the challenge they pose for customers. The lowest switching cost was slightly more than half of the high switching cost firms.

Incumbents often strive to raise switching costs.[23] Switching costs based on superior performance, such as superior record keeping and personalized advice, benefit both the incumbent and customer. Artificial switching costs, such as early departure penalties, may sustain profits in the short term while lowering customer satisfaction and breeding resentment. Switching costs that limit customer responses may lead to firm complacency and mistakes. With time and planning, customers can overcome switching costs, and choose better alternatives.

Companies attempting to acquire customers often invest money in lowering customer switching costs. Effective educational material, easy applications, and the ability to transfer data from competitors are all methods one broker can use to steal customers from another provider. Switching costs are a natural battleground between firms. The outcome of this competitive struggle determines how important the switching cost effect will be on price sensitivity.

> Price-Quality Effect

For novel experience goods, consumers try to judge product quality by using whatever information is available, including price. A product's price may act as a cue and signal to consumers of some underlying characteristic of the product that is hard to observe directly. In particular, consumers may believe that a high price signals high quality. If this is true, then price becomes a less responsive tool. The reason is simple. When a firm cuts its price, it makes its product more affordable to a wider customer base. However, this positive benefit of cutting price is partially offset by the negative perception that quality may be lower. Conversely, a price increase makes items more expensive, but for those consumers using price as an informational cue about quality there is a positive perceived quality impact.

When the price-quality effect operates, it may limit the effectiveness of low-cost online outlets. For example, a shopper from Germany may want to buy amber jewelry. If he or she searches online, one of the sites he or she might come across is a Polish jewelry site called Klejnot.pl. The prices may be low, but is the jewelry high quality? This is very difficult to judge remotely. Even with a sophisticated web site, such as Blue Nile, this is difficult. For a simple small business, this is extremely challenging. In such situations, consumers around the world may use price as a cue for quality, and not be willing to order.

Inexperienced consumers tend to rely on the natural correlation between higher price and higher quality. Just as Germans new to the Polish market may associate price with quality, the reverse direction is true as well. Researchers find that Polish consumers, just now being integrated into the European Union marketplace, use price as a partial cue for both product quality and the underlying prestige of the product.[24] Web sites targeting these consumers should address this price-quality effect directly through product education, or indirectly through the prices charged.

The price-quality effect works to the advantage of well-established brands in the face of aggressive price competition by startups and discounters. Some online brokerages, for example, charge much lower prices for stock trades than full-service brokers. If stock trades were all the same, this would seem to be a perfect example of a search good. Established (and higher priced) brokerages have worked to convince investors that all trades are not the same. There can be lags between placing a sell order and the actual trade taking place. Execution matters when prices are changing rapidly. Also, there may be different risks in holding your money at a discount broker relative to a more established firm. These quality risks make a stock account more of an experience good and less susceptible to price competition and high price sensitivity.

The underlying cause of the price quality effect is the lack of appropriate information. This again suggests a potentially strong role for online content when using a low price strategy. Shown below are the two U.S. home pages of E*Trade and Merrill Lynch. There is a striking difference, with the E*Trade site heavily information centric while the Merrill Lynch site is much more brand oriented.

This makes perfect sense for two firms reacting differently to their different position. Merrill Lynch wants to use its well-known bull logo, among other things, to reinforce its decades of investment in branding and to help discourage investors from switching to a low-price vendor. Merrill Lynch uses its page to emphasize brand quality and market size. E*Trade wants to emphasize speed, information, accuracy, and the quality of execution while still delivering a low price per trade. One measure of E*Trade's performance is revealed in a faster loading home page, seen in Figure 12.8. Fast loading may serve as a subtle signal of trade execution speed. Each company is trying to use its online content, at least partially, to reinforce the view of the price-quality effect most advantageous to its own pricing strategy.

> *Purchase Importance*

The monetary and social importance of a purchase increases its price sensitivity. While this may seem obvious, it has interesting implications when pricing is combined with online offerings. The main purchase importance price sensitivity factors are the total expenditures effect, the end benefit effect, and the shared cost effect.

> Total Expenditures Effect

U.S. consumers spend most of their after-tax income on a handful of categories. In 2002, housing dominates at 32.6% of after tax income.[25] Next comes transportation (19.0 %), food (13.6 %),

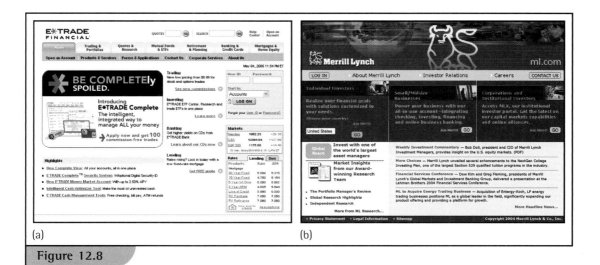

(a) (b)

Figure 12.8

One of the Influences on Content is the Price Quality Effect

Source: 12.8a E*Trade Financial; 12.8b Used with the permission of Merrill Lynch & Co

personal insurance and pensions (9.3%), health care (5.3%), entertainment (5.1%), and apparel and services (4.7%). There are a number of online price shopping services in each of these areas. When customers spend a large fraction of their budget on a product or service, they naturally pay more attention to shopping for the best price. Nagle calls this the total expenditure effect, with consumers most price sensitive for items that are a larger fraction of their budget.

Chronic disease care can be extremely expensive. The American Diabetes Association found that the typical diabetic spends $2,500 a year on supplies alone. Insulin pumps, needed by severe diabetics, can cost $4,000. Diabetics naturally are price sensitive to the price of supplies. Drug prices provide another important example. Many seniors pay a sizable fraction of their retirement income on pharmaceuticals, as do millions of working Americans without health insurance. In order to save money, many are using the Net to purchase cheaper drugs. A major controversy has erupted because of seniors and state governments using the Internet to place orders for their drugs through much cheaper Canadian pharmacies.

Online sites are working to provide seniors and others with guides to the best sources for low price drugs, which is often more complicated than the cartoon in Figure 12.9 would suggest. For example, studies find generic drugs cheaper in the United States while brand name prescriptions are typically cheaper in Canada.[26] Sites such as PharmacyChecker.com find wide ranges of drug prices, with savings in the hundreds of dollars per prescription (Table 12.2).

While health care is 5.1% of consumer expenditures on average, for certain consumer groups it is much higher. These consumers go to extreme measures to save on this category of expenditures, and consequently have higher price sensitivity.

> End Benefit Effect

Price sensitivity tends to work itself up the supply chain. Companies whose customers are price sensitive must be price sensitive themselves when they purchase inputs and design their products. This forms the heart of the end benefit effect. As in the total expenditures effect, the end benefit effect captures the impact of important inputs, justifying additional search and negotiation.

Figure 12.9

The Total Expenditures Effect + the Net Leads Even Consumers Toward Global Purchases

Source: THE SUNSHINE CLUB: © Howie Schneider/Dist. by Newspaper Enterprise Association, Inc.

Additionally, the end benefit effect states that input prices will be more sensitive for the major cost drivers of the final product (Figure 12.10).

Over the last decade, one of the most important generators of price sensitivity among manufacturers has been Wal-Mart. Wal-Mart continually puts pressure on its suppliers to lower their prices. Faced with this pressure, vendors work with their important suppliers to cut costs and lower margins.[27] Part of this occurs in face-to-face negotiations, and part online (Figure 12.11).

The Internet is being used to accomplish many of the important coordination and supply steps allowing manufacturers to roam the world for the lowest possible prices for the inputs they need. While controversial in its impact, with winners and losers in different regions of the world, the supply chains are evolving to provide increasingly better products at lower prices. This is discussed in Chapter 15.

> ## Shared Cost Effect

The shared cost effect connects price sensitivity and the split between decider and payer. Deciders are naturally less price sensitive than payers. Web sites respond to the shared cost effect by customizing their content and approach to these very different objectives. If the target is the decider, sites emphasize amenities while making price appear reasonable. If the target is the payer, cost-effectiveness will be the priority provided there is acceptable quality.

Table 12.2

Large Savings by Any Measure					
Sample Prices and Savings					
Drug	Strength	Qty	LOWEST PRICE	HIGHEST PRICE	POTENTIAL SAVINGS**
Atenolol-Generic	50 mg	100	$8.79	$51.04	83%
Celebrex-Brand	200 mg	100	$129.01	$359.00	64%
Fluoxetine-Generic	20 mg	100	$14.94	$115.50	87%
Lipitor-Brand	20 mg	90	$174.00	$307.99	44%
Lisinopril-Generic	20 mg	100	$17.69	$102.64	83%
Zocor-Brand	20 mg	100	$194.40	$549.75	65%
Zoloft-Brand	50 mg	100	$155.16	$288.63	46%

*Prices do not include shipping or other fees that typically apply to the first drug in an order and are listed in the Compare Prices tables.
**Difference between highest and lowest prices found on PharmacyChecker.com.

Source: PharmacyChecker.com

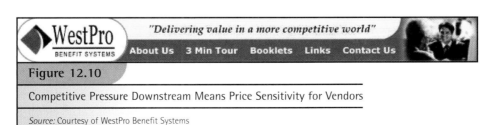

Figure 12.10

Competitive Pressure Downstream Means Price Sensitivity for Vendors

Source: Courtesy of WestPro Benefit Systems

Figure 12.11

Wal-Mart Vendor Support Site

Source: © 2000–2005, Wal-Mart.com USA, LLC and Wal-Mart Stores, Inc.

Hyatt Hotels rewards their frequent visitors with the Gold Passport program (Figure 12.12). You can use the site to enroll in the program, check your award balance, find locations, and make reservations. The site emphasizes all of the different methods business travelers can use to trade their accumulated points for vacations, upgrades, and other awards. Promotions operate by accelerating the granting of additional points and earlier awards.

The emphasis is much different at Howard Johnson, a hotel chain that focuses much more on family travelers and retirees. While still describing amenities, there is much more emphasis on value for the money. Awards are much more immediate, payable in discounts on the stay (Figure 12.13). Further discounts are available to seniors, low price guarantees are given prominence, and sweepstakes based on family-oriented expenses, such as college tuition, have been used for additional sweepstakes promotions.

Many business purchases require a chain of approval, with multiple inputs and veto power from groups without the formal decision authority. For example, the purchase decision for a corporate jet may rest with the board of directors. However, along the way there can be vetoes from the current pilots, maintenance staff, public relations, or other interested parties. This is a different aspect of the shared cost effect. If a firm wishes to compete on price, it may have a much more prepared audience in the directors than it does with the influencers that aren't

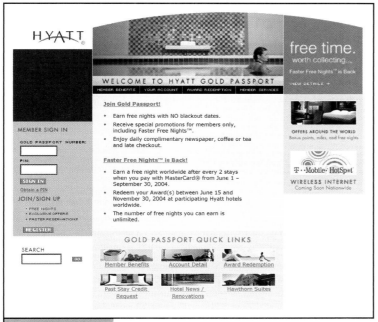

Figure 12.12

A Decider Oriented Site Emphasizing Amenities

Source: Courtesy of Hyatt Corporation

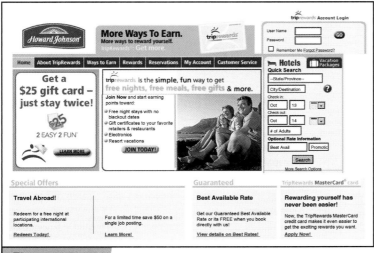

Figure 12.13

A Payer Oriented Site for Howard Johnson

Source: Courtesy of Howard Johnson International, Inc.

responsible for paying. This wider group has lower price sensitivity, due to a lack of financial commitment, than the group required to pay the expense.

The price sensitivity factors help a manager appreciate the power of the Net to affect the everyday pricing situation. Online content has an impact on pricing, and a pricing manager should be aware and included in a firm's web strategies. A prudent pricing manager should also pay close attention to the online content of competitors and the role of pricing intermediaries. Information online makes pricing even more of a managerial full-time commitment than in the past.

ADVANCED PRICING ONLINE

The Net allows pricing strategies that are too complex or too costly to implement without the DNI capabilities. These pricing strategies can be viewed as extensions and refinements of the "inverse price sensitivity" rule. For time-based pricing the Net allows a company to change prices more frequently to reflect dynamic changes in equation (12-1). That is, prices can change over time as demand, costs, or capacity change. Personalized pricing allows pricing to change because equation (12-1) reflects individual-specific demand and cost conditions. In bundle pricing, the Net is used to reduce the complexity of bundled orders and to implement prices that depend on the scope of an order.

1. *Time-based pricing*: Pricing that changes dynamically based on changing demands, costs, or capacity.
2. *Personalized pricing*: Pricing that changes based on the identity of the customer making an enquiry or placing an order.
3. *Bundle pricing*: Pricing that encourages purchasing multiple items.

Dynamic pricing is familiar for stock traders on Wall Street or commodity brokers in Chicago. The only valid price is the price quoted right now "on the Street." The prices of stocks and commodities jump or fall in value in the blink of an eye. Any temporary swing toward a stock bumps its price. Bad news can cause a plunge just as quickly.

Financial markets operate in real time. The number of financial products and commodities sold on exchanges has steadily increased. Information technology has been vital to this growth. Everyone can participate, information flows rapidly, and physical location does not give an inside track. Increasingly, trades happen automatically without human intervention.

The lessons learned in the financial markets are spilling over to the rest of the economy. Companies are using real-time pricing and the power of markets instead of setting price themselves. Partly this stems from efficiency, partly it is caused by necessity. When conditions change so quickly, only real time pricing approaches may be feasible. As in so many other situations, because of the efficiency of the Internet, practices that were once too sophisticated or too costly to be used in everyday marketing are now feasible and profitable.

Personalized pricing can yield much higher prices than a single price for all. Many markets offer coupons to repeat buyers, discounts for senior citizens, or special deals available only to the informed. Pricing in these markets attempts to account for differences among these customer segments, and somehow encourage proper buying by these groups.

Bundling also changes the simple textbook approach. Pricing must be coordinated across a product line, not separately as in the simple pricing approach. Bundle pricing requires a careful calculation of how potential customers evaluate each product individually and in combination.

Products in the same product line partially compete among themselves. Predicting actual consumer choice is difficult.

Time-Based Pricing

> *The Life of a Price*

Dolan and Simon's phrase that opened the chapter summarizes nicely how the underlying conditions making a price the right one change and evolve over time.[28] Sophisticated pricing involves a careful consideration of costs, customers, and competition. When any of these change, the best possible price may also change. Understanding price sensitivity factors can help meet fluctuating conditions. The Internet makes a different answer possible as well. Rather than try to determine a fixed price in changing conditions, many companies are learning techniques of real-time pricing.

This part focuses on how the Net helps with the time customization of price. This includes

> Using auctions for pricing,
> Yield management,
> Renting rather than selling, and
> Running a limited time sale.

Each of these pricing tactics benefits from the power of the Net to rapidly communicate demand and supply information between would be sellers and buyers, making the prices chosen more appropriate for the actual market conditions. At the risk of humanizing a marketing tactic, the Net allows prices to have shorter but more productive lives.

> *Auctions*

> The Growing Importance of Auctions

For many products and services it is hard to know demand before setting price and seeing the market reaction. This creates a serious risk. Set the price too high, and the product does not sell. Set the price too low, and buyers snap up the bargain. The important point is that mistakes do not balance over time. On average, too much is sold when mistakes are made on the low price side and too little is sold when the price is set too high.

Online auctions are a powerful alternative method of price setting. Auctions let the marketplace set the price. A pricing manager moves from setting a price to designing an auction. Once the auction rules are in place, the manager is not required to guess demand and supply conditions. The hope is that the auction finds a solution similar to the profit-maximizing price.

Auctions work well online. In-depth information is available to bidders. Confused bidders can call or email for more information. Participants can join from anywhere on the planet. The Internet is making it possible to auction many more items than were ever practical before. Managers responsible for pricing will increasingly choose not to even set prices, but to schedule auctions instead.

Auctions have always been an important way of selling unique and unusual items, including personal property, real estate, and art. When in fashion, an artist's work can bring millions. Out of fashion, the price of the artist's work declines rapidly. From the days of the ancient Greeks, auction houses thrived in the main urban centers. Auctions are an effective pricing method even when face-to-face selling and negotiation is feasible.

Auctions are also flexible. When the United States government decided to charge for the airwave spectrum for PCS cellular phones, it chose an involved method of electronic multiple-item auctions.[29] These auctions allowed bidders to win compatible frequencies in different cities.

These multi-item auctions were extremely successful, bringing in more than $10 billion. They were vastly better than the lotteries that the government formerly used to distribute licenses, which were subject to favoritism and waste.

Spectrum auctions in Europe demonstrate another important feature of auctions. Auction results may vary substantially due to the auction design. Following the successes of the U.S. spectrum auctions, many governments in Europe decided to auction off spectrum for the new third-generation cellular services, with high-speed data capabilities. Experiences varied widely. Some countries, such as the United Kingdom and Germany, choose auction formats that were highly successful in stimulating bidding, encouraging competition, and raising billions of Euros. Other countries, such as Switzerland and Holland, used auctions that had fundamental flaws.[30] On a per capita basis the Swiss auction earned less than one thirtieth the fee earned in either the United Kingdom or Germany. Clearly, auction design matters.

Economists and marketers have studied auctions extensively over the last few decades. One of the pioneers was William Vickrey, who won the 1995 Nobel Prize in Economics for his work. Researchers have come to understand many of the subtleties of auction form, including lessons on how to set up an auction to get a high price, how to make sure the bidder with the highest true value for the product will bid the most, and how to prevent collusion and bid-rigging.

The biggest problem with auctions has always been the challenge of getting enough bidders together in the same place at the same time. The Internet changes that. Bidders no longer have to be present physically. This factor reduces participants' costs and increases the total number of bidders. This raises the auction price paid and the profitability of the auction to the seller.[31]

Online sites improve the power and efficiency of auctions in two main ways. The first is information. In-depth information improves bidders' understanding of the items being sold. Auction theory has shown that this is profitable to both buyers and sellers.[32] Buyers are more comfortable and feel that they can correctly evaluate the items being sold. Their bids reflect this comfort level. On average, sellers will receive higher winning bids and bidders will more often get items that they truly value. The second benefit of online auction sites is that they expand the number of bidders. This benefits the seller, leading to a higher winning bid. It also works to avoid an auction failure, when no one bids higher than the reserve price, the lowest price that a seller is willing to accept. Increasing the number of bidders makes it more likely that this reserve threshold is reached.

> Lessons from EBay

Any discussion of online auctions must consider eBay, which in ten years has grown to be the largest and most profitable Internet company. Its listings dominate the online auction market. Further, its auction practices set the benchmark and expectations about how auctions work online (Figure 12.14). Both mass market and specialized auction competitors are inevitably contrasted with eBay.

EBay has also contributed to knowledge about auctions, by partnering with academics and providing opportunities to research online practices. This has led to a number of insights, such as:[33]

> *Reputation matters* in online auctions, and bidders respond to reputation rankings. EBay has been innovative in their usage of reputation feedback from participants. High reputation sellers seem to receive a 5–10% benefit in expected revenue, either through higher prices or a lower chance of no one bidding.
> A substantial amount of bidding occurs during the final minutes of an auction. Often called *sniping*, sniping seems to be an attempt by more experienced bidders to avoid prolonged head-to-head bidding with naïve bidders at the risk of losing an opportunity to place a

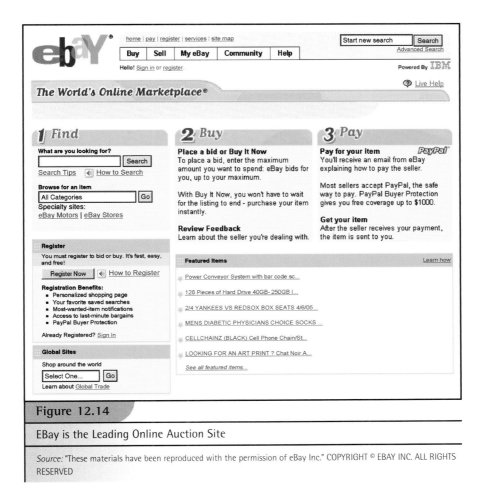

Figure 12.14

EBay is the Leading Online Auction Site

bid.[34] Sniping is significantly less prominent at sites such as Amazon.com, which automatically extend the auction deadline if there is a late bid.

> *Fraud* is an important problem, especially for collectibles. Numerous graded items actually had values lower than declared.

> Bidders are aware of the problem of *winner's curse*, where the winner of an auction finds the value of the item lower than expected, and lowers their bid in response to increased uncertainty or negative information.

> *Minimum bids*, also called *public reserve prices*, are useful and increase the expected revenue from an auction.

> *Secret reserves* are often used on eBay, but evidence is mixed about their profitability. Some studies find lower expected profits and fewer completed sales, but other studies find a modest benefit.

EBay supports its online auctions with a considerable infrastructure, both with internal capabilities and external alliances. Payment is a problem for an auction site, as sellers may not

Figure 12.15

PayPal Eases Online Payments

Source: [PayPal Mark] is a trademark of PayPal, Inc.

process credit cards or want to take the risk of bad checks. EBay acquired PayPal to provide a convenient payment mechanism that is low cost and low risk.

EBay is an ecommerce solution for many small businesses around the world. EBay provides a variety of tools for sellers to use to automate their listings, control inventory, track orders and payment, and monitor the full range of online auction activity. There are discussion groups for sellers to learn from one another, training sessions on how best to sell online, and other support tools to make vendors more successful. Of course, eBay benefits from this as well.

EBay's revenue comes from a combination of insertion fees based on starting or reserve price, the actual item sale price, enhanced graphics and multiple picture listings, and usage for systems such as PayPal or Selling Manager. One of the most attractive features of eBay for the investment community is its high profit margin, as it is able to operate as the intermediary without the difficult logistics of handling the items being sold.

A considerable number of supporting companies surround eBay and complement its activities. One of the challenges for the occasional eBay seller is to provide the level of support expected of more professional sellers. Individuals may not have a reputation established, be a PayPal member, or be available to answer questions of potential bidders. For example, AuctionDrop is a startup company seeking to fill that need, providing thousands of physical locations for drop off and consignment selling. AuctionDrop then attempts to verify the condition of the different items being sold and provide the eBay selling expertise. It charges the seller roughly 40% of the selling price, when fees of both AuctionDrop and eBay are combined.

EBay is able to support this wide range of auction tools due to its high volume of both sellers and buyers. By the end of 2004, eBay had more than 135 million registered users. During 2004, eBay had 1.4 billion listings, $34.2 billion in gross merchandise value, and $3.27 billion in eBay revenue.[35] This is phenomenal worldwide success.

> Specialty Auctions

While eBay dominates online auctions, specialty auctions are also flourishing. The art world online provides examples of the progressive steps a company can use to take advantage of online auction capabilities. The first step for many is consignment selling. The gallery may never take actual possession of the art; instead, it may simply act as a broker. It earns its commission by bringing buyers and sellers together, and adjusting its pricing appropriately.

The Art Brokerage, located in Beverly Hills, is an example of this type of online consignment market.[36] It is a small shop, with only a few employees and a colorful entrepreneurial owner. The online sales and auctions began as an extension of the existing gallery's business. Online dealing started in August 1995. By the summer of 1997 online sales accounted for roughly half of the gallery's sales.[37]

The gallery has several consignment arrangements. Many of its offerings are similar to those found in traditional gallery settings. Pictures have a posted price. A commission is charged to both sellers and buyers if they find art through the system.

A different step toward online auctions is using the web site as an auction enabler. Christie's is one of the largest auction houses in the world for art and expensive collectibles. Christie's represents the next step in the evolution of online auctions. It holds auctions at locations in many of the major art centers of the world. Items sold range from multimillion-dollar paintings by

Van Gogh to old toys and cameras. Each of these auction houses can offset the mass-market volume of eBay with specialty collections, boutique brands, and managerial expertise.

> Designing an Auction

Once a company has decided to use an auction to set price, it needs to choose an auction type and specific auction rules. One of the surprising early results of auction theory was to downplay the impact of auction choice. Under some fairly reasonable assumptions, all of the main auction types are expected to raise the same amount of money. The reason is that smart bidders take into account the specifics of the auction design, and change their bidding strategies accordingly. When these assumptions hold, the firm running the auction can choose whichever auction type is most familiar or convenient.

The most popular auction form, both online and traditional, is the open ascending English auction. This is the familiar kind of auction at which an auctioneer calls out the bids until no one is willing to top the last bid. The high bidder gets the item and pays his or her bid. This is also the format used by eBay. Key benefits of the English auction are the ability to see other bidders' activity, to learn from the intensity of bidding, and the fact that bidding stops close to the highest losing bid (which is a hallmark of auction efficiency). A main weakness of the English auction is a susceptibility to collusion. A bidder trying to break a collusive agreement, and "steal" an auction by bidding higher, can be both observed and punished.

Less common, but still in use, is the Dutch auction. In a Dutch auction the price starts high, and gradually declines. The first bidder gets the item. The Dutch auction (originally named for Dutch flower markets) works in the opposite direction from the English auction. The initial price is set high. It falls at regular time intervals. The first customer willing to bid gets as many of the items as he or she wants at that price. The remaining items continue to have their price cut. Although this sounds strange, we are familiar with it in the discount racks of many clothing retailers. An item starts out at full price. After a certain number of weeks, its price might fall 20%, then 30%, or even 50%.

Dutch auctions have remained common for flower markets and other perishable items. As these flower markets tend to be local, they have not moved online as quickly as auctions where shipping and delivery is simpler. One company using Dutch auctions online is the American Clock, a flower importer based in Miami.[38] Auctions run online several times a week. Bidding occurs while the flowers are in shipment from South America to Miami. Winning bidders are shipped their flowers as soon as they arrive in port.

Figure 12.16 summarizes the evolution toward auctions that companies are undergoing. Consignment selling is one natural path, which emphasizes the brokerage relationship first. This leads to auctions when a company decides to substitute the auction mechanism for its judgment about the proper price. The right-hand path takes existing locally based auctions and starts by enhancing them online. Providing information naturally leads to allowing remote bidders to mix with the bidders that are physically present. Over time the constraints of physical time and place give way to the advantages of purely online auctions.

Assuming a seller wants to use eBay, or a similar auction site, several additional decisions must be made. These include:

> Providing *information* about the product being sold. This includes pictures of the product, a history of its use, perhaps links to a manufacturer's site.
> Setting the *closing time* of the auction. Typically auctions run for several days.
> Selling *single unit* or *multi-units*. If there are multiple units a seller must choose between sequential or simultaneous auctions.

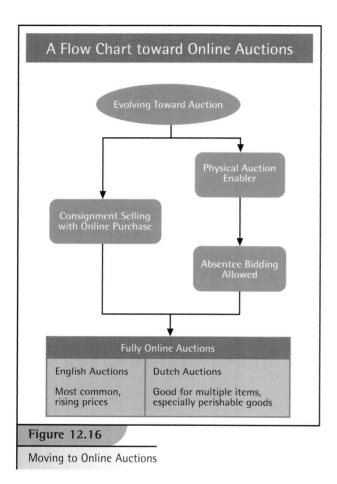

A Flow Chart toward Online Auctions

Figure 12.16

Moving to Online Auctions

> Setting an *initial minimum bid*. Bidding can start at a low price to attract attention, or a much higher price to eliminate this beginning phase.
> Setting a *reserve price*. There can be a price that must be exceeded for the auction to be valid. This can be higher than the initial minimum bid.
> Making this reserve price, if any, *public* or *secret*. If a secret reserve is chosen a bidder may know whether the reserve has been met or not without knowing the exact value.
> Choosing the *shipping terms*. Almost all auctions have some form of shipping or logistics required to get the product to the buyer. Terms and conditions for this need to be specified.
> Choosing the *payment mechanisms*. Most buyers and sellers are not in the same physical location, making some form of credit card, check, or PayPal system necessary.

Sellers can perform all these steps themselves, or use one of the companies such as AuctionDrop as an agent. In the case of AuctionDrop the eventual revenue is split between the company and the seller.

A fundamental insight governing these choices comes from both the theory of auctions and empirical studies of actual auctions. This is the importance of *winner's curse* in shaping an auction's results. Winner's curse is the possibility that the highest bidder is the one with the most over-optimistic information. In other words, the winner of an auction is the bidder making the biggest mistake! Anticipating this, smart bidders react to risk and uncertainty by scaling back their offers. In many cases, a seller actually will make more revenue by sharing information and providing detailed information about the product. As bidders will assume that vague information is a signal of bad quality, good information leads to less fear of winner's curse and more aggressive bidding.

The details of running an auction and establishing a reputation are subjects of active research. Companies such as eBay also conduct extensive training to potential sellers, working with them to improve results and correct seller mistakes. The result is that many companies are turning to auctions as a powerful alternative to the difficulties of setting a fixed price.

> Yield Management

Every traveler is familiar with yield management. Yield management is the sophisticated matching of price and available capacity. Yield management is the system that lets United Airlines and others charge much lower prices to tourists than they get from business travelers. Expensive seats have few restrictions. Low-cost fares are subject to restrictions about use, including advance purchase requirements, required Saturday night stays, off-peak travel times, and other means of separating low willingness-to-pay tourists from high-willingness-to pay business travelers. Other business travel amenities, such as hotels and rental cars, have copied these yield management ideas.

> Conditions for Yield Management

Yield management (sometimes labelled revenue management) has been important for the companies able to implement it. Examining a number of companies using yield management, commentators found that revenue increased approximately 6–8%. Even more importantly, contribution to profits increased between 20–40%. Without yield management, the travel industry would be in even worse financial shape than it currently is.[39]

Several critical characteristics must be present for yield management to be effective. These characteristics are most common in service industries. The first is fixed and perishable capacity. Unsold airplane seats are forever lost as soon as the plane takes off. The same holds true for cargo and freight companies. A ship that sails with spare room has a revenue opportunity that later trips cannot recover. Unsold tee times at a golf course are a pure loss, and can not be stored and saved for another day.

Low incremental cost compared to average cost is also important. The cost of adding an additional guest to a hotel with space is small compared to the total cost of maintaining the hotel. The costs of supplying gas, electricity, or telephone calls are mostly fixed. Additional customers impose minimal costs compared to the upfront costs of creating the capabilities and reaching the customer base.

An important demand characteristic is a customer base with identifiable segments. The core idea of yield management is to give price-sensitive customers a price break to encourage them to fill up the seats without causing a loss of customers willing to pay the regular price. The travel industry has used yield management widely because tourist and business travel are different, in a number of ways. The goal of yield management restrictions is to create problems for business travelers, so that only price-sensitive tourists will use the cheaper tickets.

A final fundamental of yield management is demand uncertainty and enough sophisticated information technology and systems to deal with that uncertainty. Several failed attempts at yield management have occurred in the airline industry because the company was unable to track available

Figure 12.17

Resorts use Yield Management to Attract both Business and Leisure Guests

Source: © PRNewsFoto/The Breakers Palm Beach

seats, reliably quote available capacity to last-minute travelers, and combine historical information into accurate demand forecasts. In response, industrial espionage and corporate raiding of
staff have occurred to acquire these skills.

Cross[40] highlighted seven uncertainties in the marketplace that create or limit the possibilities of yield management. These are (1) perishable products and opportunities, (2) seasonal
and other demand peaks, (3) the product's value in different market segments, (4) product
waste, (5) competition between individual and bulk purchasers, (6) discounting to meet competition, and (7) rapidly changing market circumstances. A revenue management system works
to smooth out these uncertainties, use the system to reach out to different market segments,
and respond appropriately to fast changing conditions.

> Applying Yield Management Online

The Internet is making yield management available to a much wider range of companies. By
combining yield management software with a web site, many more industries are able to use
these capabilities. Small businesses thus may achieve many of the savings and profit boosts that
only the Fortune 500 companies have been able to achieve. Possible industries include tax preparation, auto repair, and medical offices that fit the enabling characteristics.

As an example, consider the possibility of applying yield management to a hair salon. The hair
salon has a web site that potential customers can visit to make reservations. Table 12.3 shows the
major enabling characteristics of revenue management applied to the small owner-operated hair

Table 12.3

Applying Yield Management to an Online Hair Salon Reservation System	
Enabling Characteristics	**Support for Revenue Management**
Fixedness of capacity	High. Stylists can only serve a fixed number of customers per hour, usually one at a time.
Inventory perishability	High. Lost hours are gone.
Demand uncertainty	Medium to high. For high demand stylists there is less uncertainty, as they may be booked days or weeks in advance. For second or third tier stylists, there may be wide swings in use.
Cost fixity	Medium. Most shop costs are fixed; there may be flexibility in the costs faced by the shop, as stylists may be quasi-independent.
Segmentable markets	Medium to high. Basic hair cutting may be similar in valuations, although loyalty programs can be effective. Discretionary services, like coloring and permanents, may be more segmentable.
Ease of preventing arbitrage	High. It is easy to get personalized identification as part of the service.
Advanced reservation requirement	Medium. Discounts can be offered for making reservations at least a week before, especially if combined with loyalty programs.
Historical sales databases	Medium to high. Easy to capture the level of walk in traffic, repeat buying, and swings in requests. Requires data entry and additional work for most shops.
Sales forecast accuracy	Medium. Easier in aggregate, lower for individual.
MIS sophistication	Low. Slow to computerize paper and pencil systems still dominate, unskilled staff.

salon. Yield management seems like a natural fit. There is a high level of fixed cost and perishable capacity. Demand can undergo seasonal and random shifts. There are peak and off-peak times, and discretionary services that can fill the slow times.

The low level of computerization and sophistication of most salon owners is one of the biggest barriers to salons using yield management. This lack may be surmountable by a combined service and software package that is easy to customize to a particular shop. Another concern is cannibalization of regular demand. If it is not possible to keep demand segments separate, the salon may find its regular customers waiting to receive last-minute deals. This potential loss of regular price sales is a serious limit on yield management profitability.

> *Rental Pricing, Trial Pricing, and Sales*

One of the emerging trends for software use is rental versus purchase, which can be tied directly to the power of the Net. The promotional piece by Salesforce.com in Figure 12.18 illustrates the appeal. Rather than acquiring and installing software on a company server, a browser-based approach can outsource many of the total costs of ownership. A hosted application runs on the Salesforce.com site, with links to the subscriber's other data sources.

This linkage requires a highly reliable, highly secure Net. Salesforce.com provides detailed customer and sales information to sales people in the field. For example, a pharmaceutical sales-person might use this software to schedule her day, track information requests, place orders, and monitor her commission check. This is highly sensitive information. Until recently, the Net could not be relied on to have the performance and security to make this feasible. Companies felt it necessary to maintain this data solely in-house. With increased online power comes the flexibility to share data and expertise, and to rent rather than own.

Consumers experience online rental through music subscriptions such as Real Rhapsody and Napster. The Napster system uses the Net to access music streams and download music to MP3 players. Unlike the old Napster, this is perfectly legal. The music comes with digital rights

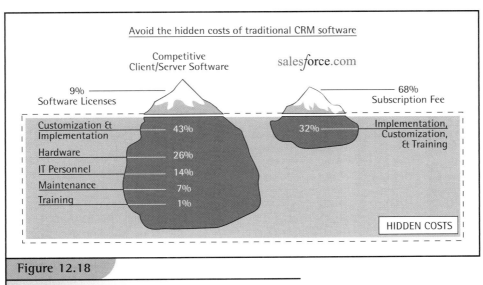

Figure 12.18

A Promotional Piece Extolling Software Rental vs. Purchase

Source: Salesforce.com, Inc.

management, and ceases to work if the monthly rental fee is not paid. Again, the evolution of this capability requires sophisticated security and available broadband support.

We saw in Chapter 10 that the Net is increasingly important in launching new products, sampling opinion on new products, and handling the move from beta to commercial versions. For online products it can be an inexpensive form of limited-time free trial, where new users can experiment with the software or the service and decide whether it meets their needs. This creates a number of opportunities and challenges for pricing. The positives of encouraging trial, generating word of mouth, and benefiting from consumer feedback and testing all must be balanced against the difficulties of moving customers away from a free service toward a pay service. Several steps are required, and they benefit from a coordination of pricing and online marketing steps.

When a free service remains available, marketing material must make clear that the free version is limited in capability and missing key features. Only by establishing the value of the complete solution can a firm convince customers to upgrade. The free trial version is often the most successful competitor against the full pay version, more important than competition from another firm. The move from "free to fee" has challenged many firms.

Real Networks has faced this tradeoff throughout its existence. The promise of a free player is attractive to both users and media sources in Real's struggles against Microsoft, Apple, and others. At the same time, Real includes additional features such as advanced CD burning, accessing certain music online, and support of different MP3 players with its premium player.

The low cost of Net distribution makes it possible for even the smallest organization to take advantage of many of these same capabilities. Software developers are foregoing distribution through traditional channels and selling direct online. One of many examples is *mathStatica*, a small software company located in Australia, which offers students and researchers a powerful statistics program. Bundled with a book explaining the system is a free reduced version that is still powerful enough to be used in coursework and standard statistics classes. For an upgrade price the user can expand the power of the package, adding new features and more customer support.

One of the challenges of trial pricing is the battle over the reference price and the challenges of explaining the new features. MathStatica is trying to position its $89 price against the $159 "regular price" rather than the zero price of the reduced version. At the same time it works to reduce the difficult comparison effect by linking to explanations of important upgrade features (Figure 12.19).

Sellers have relied on promotions and sales to accelerate purchases for millennia. Without the incentive of a limited time offer, customers simply buy items when needed, bypassing the loss of money, flexibility, and inventory costs that go with stockpiling on deal or moving to a new product sooner than they would under a stable pricing regime.

Basic / Student version	Gold (Professional) version
▶ Single user BASIC license	▶ Single user **GOLD** license ...
▶ mathStatica 1.0	▶ mathStatica 1.5 *New!* [See detail]
	✚ **Continuous** Dist. Palette [See pop-up]
	✚ **Discrete** Distribution Palette [See pop-up]
	✚ **Kernels** Palette [See pop-up]
	✚ **HELP System** (detailed) [See pop-up]
	✚ Free **Technical Support** for one year
	✚ Free **Second License** for Home/Notebook[†]
	✚ $30 **Discount** on next major release
Compatible with: *Mathematica* 4 only*	Compatible with: *Mathematica* 4 and 5
Price: Free (for book owners)	**Price:** **$89** special for book owners
	(usual GOLD price is **$159**)

Figure 12.19

Versioning Online

Source: Courtesy of mathStatica.com

The actual mechanics of running a sale with online tools are described in the next chapter on retailing. Whether the goal is to encourage average customers to purchase more and sooner, or to reach out to the most price-sensitive switching segments, this form of time customization is the creation of urgency without any underlying shifts in demand or natural time pressure.

Personalized Pricing

Personalized pricing leads to price differences based on individual differences in willingness to pay, servicing costs, or other individual level distinctions. It takes advantage of the tools and techniques of personalization and individualization. The desire and ability to personalize requires a combination of individual-level data and tools necessary to interact directly with individuals.

Merchants have known for millennia that under the right conditions individual level prices raise profits. When a single price is quoted in the market, such as given by equation (12-1), everyone who buys has a positive *consumer surplus* for the product. That is, essentially every-one who voluntarily purchases an item would have been willing to pay at least a little more. Only the buyer who is indifferent between buying the product in question and doing something else with her money gets zero additional surplus over her next best alternative. There are some buy-ers who would have paid a lot more. If a seller can charge these high value demanders a higher price while still selling at a lower price to others, then profits rise. In some cases, the seller may be able to extract the entire consumer surplus as additional profits.

Of course, there are a number of problems with attempting to target different prices. First, there are a number of circumstances in which charging different prices to different individuals may be illegal, unethical, or lead to a consumer backlash. For example, price differences cannot legally be based on race, religious status, or some other protected status.[41] Despite this, it does happen. There is some evidence that one of the benefits of online car shopping may be as an antidote to discrimination in face-to-face negotiations.[42] Gains from car shopping online were especially large for women and minorities, groups that may face some adverse treatment during traditional automobile negotiations.

A second barrier to personalized pricing is the inability of the seller to identify high-value buyers. Buyers are unlikely to accurately reveal their willingness to pay. High-value demanders are protected by the seller's ignorance, and have an incentive to publicly claim a low value. Low-value demanders have a hard time proving their willingness to pay is actually low and they are not a high-value type in disguise.

A third major obstacle to personalized pricing is consumer resale. If buyer C gets quoted a low price and A is quoted a high price, buyer C can purchase the product and sell it to buyer A and still make a gain. Personalized pricing works best in areas where this resale arbitrage is not possible, such as health care, insurance, or other forms of services.

For personalized pricing to function profitably, individual differences must be identifiable, actionable, and without arbitrage. Consumers should also feel that, at least on average, personal-ized pricing is leading to a benefit. Even with these limitations, there are important applications of personalized pricing. Among the emerging areas in which personalized pricing is being used are:

> Personalized coupons and discounts,
> Loyalty discounts,
> Personalized pricing based on credit scores or other risk measures,
> Personal-level pricing contracts, and
> Personalized bundle offers.

Personalized Coupons and Loyalty Discounts

One of the easiest methods of implementing personalized pricing is through selective discounts based on consumer histories and recent actions. Discounts off the regular price are less objectionable for many consumers. This is especially true when expressed as a reward for loyalty and cumulative purchases. While the pricing is individualized, it strikes many consumers as both a reasonable benefit and ultimately available to any loyal customer.

As we saw with the discussion of loyalty building in earlier chapters, retention email campaigns are often closely tied to personalized pricing. Promotions and specials are targeted to the individual to rekindle interest. The size and category of the promotion is often successfully tied to the specific individual's transaction history. The proper choice balances the lost margin from a sale that would have happened anyway without the discount against the possibility of losing the sale if the discount isn't offered.

Personalized pricing offers may be triggered by a concern that a potential customer is about to leave a web site without buying. Online retail sites are investing in software capable of real-time analysis of click stream data. Certain choices online can suggest that a visitor is about to exit. The site can make one last attempt, perhaps through an offer of free shipping or a coupon such as Figure 12.20, to induce the visitor to become a buyer.

Credit and Risk Scores

One of the most controversial forms of personalized pricing arises when rates and prices for such items as house mortgages, credit cards, and even auto insurance are tied to personal-level data such as credit scores. Loan underwriters and insurance companies have found that a person's credit score is a partial predictor of credit risk and even auto accidents. This leads to rates that vary by individual, based in part on the person's credit rating.

Personal-level Pricing Contracts

Energy conservation and highway congestion provide a different setting for personalized and time-based pricing. Meters in homes and businesses, often connected directly to the Net, can provide real-time electricity pricing to each location based on the contract signed with the power company. This permits smart consumption of electricity. Households received individual-level price quotes, and with further networking can tie appliances and other energy-using systems directly to this changing electricity price.

Personalized Bundling

Personalized bundling is a further sophisticated application of online capabilities with the ability to measure and interact at the individual level. The next part describes bundling and why it is so powerful even without personalization. With personalization, it allows for the use of bundling for exactly those customers where it can benefit the most. In its simplest form, as in the Dell Triangle in Chapter 4, it uses customer importance to determine the range of services provided online.

Figure 12.20

Coupon Clipping Site Coolsavings.com

Source: © CoolSavings, Inc.

Bundle Pricing

Another pricing tactic especially relevant to online content is bundling. Bundling is the combination of products into larger packages. Bundling occurs when products or services that could have been sold separately are instead combined together. While bundling is simple in concept, it can have large effects on competition and consumers.

Eppen, Hanson, and Martin provide a useful categorization of bundling opportunities and situations where bundling is profitable.[43] As part of their study of different industries, including cars, credit cards, health plans, and software, they identified seven different guidelines for using bundling. Bundling is particularly popular online because many of the guidelines for profitable bundling fit the online digital world.

These bundling guidelines can be grouped according to whether they reduce costs, expand markets, or improve product performance (Table 12.4). They provide the strategic goals for bundle pricing. Each can be defended on theoretical grounds, and they also emerge when bundle pricing software is used to calculate the best product line pricing solutions.

> Reduce Costs

The first guideline of bundling is *production efficiency bundling*. In physical production, such as manufacturing automobiles, there are major setup costs when switching between makes and models. One of the incentives for car makers to create option bundles is that it helps smooth production, reduce inventory, and lower distribution costs. In the online world, shipping costs are a common opportunity for production efficiency bundling. As seen in Figure 12.21, Amazon.com offers lower shipping prices for larger orders with a proviso that orders can be grouped into as few shipments as possible. This reduces total freight costs.

Guideline two is *margin spread bundling*. Margin spread bundling reflects the incentive to bundle items together with a high contribution margin ratio, that is, when there is a substantial gap between price and marginal cost. This is the fundamental nature of most digital products, where it is extremely easy and cheap to create additional copies. The idea is to encourage bundles of digital items, while non-digital items tend to be sold separately.

Table 12.4

Many of the Bundling Guidelines Fit Well Online		
Reduce costs	**Expand markets**	**Improve performance**
Production efficiency bundling: Promote bundling when production or shipping has important set-up costs.	*Aggregation bundling:* Target the bundle for an aggregate market and offer higher priced individual items to unusual customer segments.	*Joint performance bundling:* Use pure bundling when components perform better together than separately.
Margin spread bundling: Bundle items with a high contribution margin.	*Trade-up bundling:* In a price insensitive market, create comprehensive bundles when demand is strong and multiple small bundles when demand is weak.	*Product definition bundling:* Consider bundling that helps consumer understand the full range of product and service benefits.
	Loyalty bundling: Use bundling to encourage loyalty and reduce switching.	

Source: Reprinted from "Bundling: New Products, New Markets, Low Risk," by Gary Eppen, Ward Hanson, Kipp Martin, *MIT Sloan Management Review*, Vol. 32, No. 4 (Summer 1991), pp. 7–14, by permission of publisher. Copyright © 1991 by Massachusetts Institute of Technology. All rights reserved.

Super Saver Shipping

FREE on orders over **$25**
Some restrictions apply

How do I take advantage of FREE Super Saver Shipping?

1. Place over $25 of eligible Amazon.com products in your Shopping Cart.*
(Eligible items are indicated as such on their product detail pages.)

2. Proceed to checkout.

3. Ship your items to a single U.S. address.

4. Select Super Saver Shipping as your shipping speed. **Please note that your order will take an additional 3 to 5 days to ship.**

5. Select "Group my items into as few shipments as possible" as your shipping preference.

6. Place your order, and enjoy the free shipping!**

Figure 12.21

Amazon.com's Super Saver Shipping

Source: © 2005 Amazon.com, Inc. All Rights Reserved

One of the most important applications of margin spread bundling is free online support, online technical assistance, and free digital material for a wide range of products and services. Live support and face-to-face consultations, on the other hand, are priced to reflect their higher incremental costs.

> Expand Markets

Some of the most important incentives for online bundling seek to expand total sales volume. This occurs through aggregation bundling, trade-up bundling, and loyalty bundling.

Aggregation bundling is probably the most important type of bundling for online digital products. In aggregation bundling a wide array of products are grouped into a composite sale or monthly subscription. Examples include the music services such as Rhapsody or Napster cited earlier. Rather than offer only individual songs, the services provide the full catalog for listening.

Bakos and Brynjolfsson have developed a useful model of aggregation bundling, which includes why it raises profits.[44] Their model applies when there are hundreds or even thousands of online products that could be offered separately or bundled together. Imagine a song by *Bright Eyes*, another by *Green Day*, and a classical piece by *Bach*. Imagine each consumer views each of these songs independently. For example, some consumers may value all three highly, some may value none highly, and others will be a combination of low, high, and in between. While this is a simplification, which will not work for some situations, it allows us to draw a graph both of consumers' willingness to pay for the bundles and of the market demand curve. For simplicity, assume that the incremental cost to the online music supplier of each consumer using the online service is low enough to ignore.

There is a wide range of consumer valuations and the demand curve for any particular song. In our example, the highest value consumers will pay is a maximum of a penny for each use, but there is a wide range of willingness to pay. This wide spread in customer values gives the linear demand curve shown in Figure 12.22a. If all songs are priced separately, the best price is half a cent, and 50% of the consumers would pay to listen to the song.

Now think of a bundle of *Bright Eyes* and *Green Day*. To some consumers that combination will have a value that's nearly two cents, while to others it will still have a very low value. Most will be concentrated in the middle, with a demand curve that now looks like 12.22b. The best price is a little less than a penny for the two songs, or a little less than .5 cents per song. While it looks like this should lower profits, profits rise because more than half of the market buys the bundle. The lower price, and the fact that more consumers are concentrated near the middle of the valuations distribution, makes the bundle more profitable.

What works a little for the two-song bundle works even better for a bundle of the entire music catalog. If 20 songs are included in a bundle, customer demand now looks like Figure 12.22c. Because so many consumers have a valuation near 10 cents for the bundle, a price just below 10 cents will cause most of the market to purchase the bundle. The small cut in price per song is more than made up for in volume.

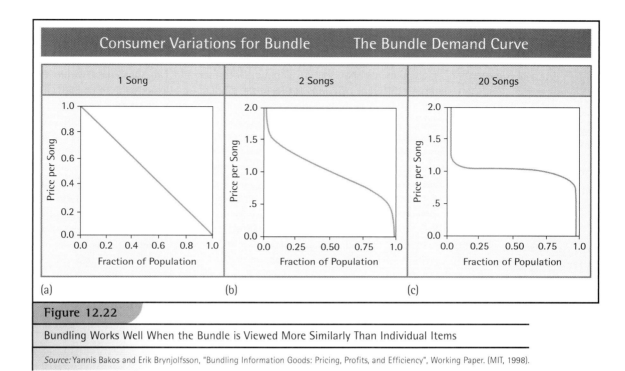

Figure 12.22

Bundling Works Well When the Bundle is Viewed More Similarly Than Individual Items

Source: Yannis Bakos and Erik Brynjolfsson, "Bundling Information Goods: Pricing, Profits, and Efficiency", Working Paper. (MIT, 1998).

Aggregation bundling is effective in stimulating volume. The price per song is still close to half a cent, but now more than 90% of the market is buying the bundle. This expansion from 50% of the market buying rights to listen to each song to 90% buying rights to every song makes this bundling profitable. Even better, make all songs available for a monthly subscription.

There are a number of simplifications used in this model. There are many genres and songs that have different distributions of willingness to pay. Some music may be substitutes, such as alternative recordings of the same music. Other music may reinforce demands. The essential point remains that aggregation bundling works very well for online digital content.

Trade-up bundling is a related form of demand-oriented bundling. Rather than offer many different size bundles, in trade-up bundling there are prefer red bundles encouraging customers to move up to the next bundle size. For example, on the iTunes music service there is a single song price of $0.99 or a per CD price of $9.99 to purchase the music. As many albums have more than 10 songs, this creates an incentive for a purchaser to "move up" to the CD volume. The same form of pricing can be seen for many season ticket offerings.

Loyalty bundling is an important type of bundling, especially for telecommunications and online financial services. The goal of loyalty bundling is to expand the scope of purchases. Banks have found that as customers add additional services, such as combining credit cards, mortgages, and checking accounts, their retention rates for each of the services increases. One of the main motivations for such services as free online bill payment is to cement this relationship, creating switching costs.

> *Improve Performance*

Both *joint performance* and *product definition* bundling use pricing to encourage customers to purchase a complete solution. A standard goal in online joint performance is to encourage joint consumption of components that share a common interface and can share data within the application. Quicken's different offerings for its Intuit product line demonstrate how joint performance bundling can improve both product performance and enhanced revenue per customer. For example, its Bill Pay service automatically funnels information into the Quicken software. Online backup ties together all data files, both the Quicken program and all additional files. The Turbo Tax software can import detailed tax-related information from the tax year in question.

Product definition bundling can be viewed as a form of product versioning, where the enhanced product includes items sold separately for more stripped down versions. As in margin spread bundling, this works extremely well online when the enhancements are digital. A comparison of the Quicken product line demonstrates how these versions include additional functionality with essentially zero incremental cost for Intuit once developed.

The digital, network, and individualized nature of the Internet makes bundling a common and powerful pricing tactic online. While the market expansion incentives are the most influential, each of the seven bundling guidelines suggests useful opportunities for bundling to improve customer satisfaction as well as improve profitability.

ENDNOTES

1. In Robert J. Dolan and Hermann Simon. *Power Pricing*. Free Press, 1996.
2. Oscar Wilde (1854–1900), *The Critic as Artist*, 1891.
3. This "happy tradeoff," as well as the estimates of the impact of the Internet on cigarette elasticity, is contained in Austan Goolsbee and Joel Slemrod. "Playing with Fire: Cigarettes, Taxes and Competition from the Internet." Working paper: University of Chicago, January, 2004.
4. See the Cigarette Tax and Payments table at http://www.brownandwilliamson.com.
5. These results are from data up through 2001, the most recent available to the authors. The researchers control for many of the possible complicating factors, such as differential Internet usage and the demographics of the states. It is likely that the result is even larger now.
6. Michael Gormley. "Public-private deal to prevent Internet cigarette sales." Newsday.com March 17, 2005.
7. Michael V. Marn and Robert L. Rosiello. "Managing price, gaining profit." *The McKinsey Quarterly* 4, 1992: 18–37.
8. The effective price is the price the company actually receives, after accounting for all the discounts, promotions, and deals that it may be involved in.
9. This was pointed out in an article by Stern. "The Pricing Quandary: How to raise 'em when the buyer is boss." *Across the Board*, May 1997: 16–22.
10. Thomas T. Nagle and Reed K. Holden. *The Strategy and Tactics of Pricing*, 3rd Edition. Prentice Hall: New York, 2002.
11. We are assuming throughout this discussion that several conditions must hold. One, everyone pays the same price. If a firm can charge different individuals different prices it can make more money than in the case of a single price. Two, it is pricing a single product and not a product line. When a firm can price across different products in a coordinated way it can also make more money. These newer approaches are talked about in later parts.
12. Bridger Mitchell and Ingo Vogelsang. *Telecommunications Pricing: Theory and Practice*. Cambridge University Press, 1992. They give an excellent example of the general applicability of the "inverse elasticity rule." In it they show it is not only a strong guide for maximizing profits, but a simple change makes it the key guideline to regulators that want to achieve a mix of profits and consumer benefits. It can be adopted to reflect capacity constraints. Robert Wilson. *Nonlinear Pricing*. Oxford University Press: 1993. Further expands its use into a number of nonlinear pricing settings.

13. See Mitchell and Vogelsang. In equation form: $(p^* - c)/p^* = -1/\eta(p^*)$, where $\eta(p^*)$ is $(\Delta Q/\Delta p^*)(p^*/Q)$

14. The price elasticity of demand measures the responsiveness of demand to a change in price. It can be thought of as the percentage change in demand that results from a 1% increase in price. In almost all cases an increase in price will lower sales, so that demand change is negative. To keep things simple we typically define the elasticity as the absolute value of this change. Therefore, if a 1% price increase leads to a 3% fall in demand, the price elasticity is $-(-3\%/+1\%) = 3$. Price elasticities greater than 1 are called elastic, those less than 1 are called price inelastic.

15. Robert J. Kauffman and Dongwon Lee. "Should We Expect Less Price Rigidity in the Digital Economy?," Working paper: Carlson School of Management, University of Minnesota, March 2004.

16. For an estimate of these proportions, see Xing Pan, Brian T. Ratchford, and Venkatesh Shankar. "Can Price Dispersion in Online Markets be Explained by Differences in E-Tailer Service Quality?," *Journal of the Academy of Marketing Science* 30(4), 2002: 433–445. Also see X. Pan, B. Ratchford, and V. Shankar. "Price Dispersion on the Internet: A Review and Directions for Future Research." *Journal of Interactive Marketing* 16(4), Autumn 2004: 116–135 and Michael B. Baye, John Morgan, and Patrick Scholten. "Temporal Price Dispersion: Evidence from an Online Consumer Electronics Market." *Journal of Interactive Marketing* 16(4), Autumn 2004: 101–114.

17. Even in cases where the price sensitivity factors all point in the same direction, making the qualitative impact clear, careful measurement of price sensitivity is ultimately desirable. Earlier chapters, especially Chapters 9 and 10, demonstrate techniques for doing this. In Chapter 16 some of the helpful data systems are discussed.

18. Much of the marketing literature on cognitive biases and choice difficulties emphasize the difficult time consumers have in formulating consistent evaluations in complicated choice circumstances.

19. For example, Lynch and Ariely find that increased information about wine allowed customers to focus more on price. John Lynch and Dan Ariely. "Wine Online: Search Costs Affect Competition on Price, Quality, and Distribution." *Marketing Science* 19(1), 2000: 83–103.

20. Michael D. Smith and Erik Brynjolfsson. "Consumer Decision-Making at an Internet Shopbot: Brand Still Matters." *The Journal of Industrial Economics* XLIX(4), December 2001.

21. Nelson, Phillip. "Information and Consumer Behavior," *Journal of Political Economy*, University of Chicago Press; 78(2), 1970: 311–329.

22. Pei-Yu (Sharon) Chen and Lorin M. Hitt. "Measuring Switching Costs and the Determinants of Customer Retention in Internet-Enabled Businesses: A Study of the Online Brokerage Industry." *Information Systems Research* 13(3), September 2002: 255–274.

23. See, for example, Joachim Buschken. *Higher Profits Through Customer Lock-in.* Thomson, Mason, 2004.

24. Marguerite Moore and Karen McGowan. "The Polish Consumers' Concept of Price as a Marketplace Cue." *Journal of Textile and Apparel Technology and Management* 2(1), Fall 2001.

25. Consumer Expenditure reports available at the BLS web site http://www.bls.gov.

26. Kelly K. Spors. "Online drugs: forget the myths." *Wall Street Journal*, April 18, 2004: 4.

27. For example, Mike Troy. "Ten Things Every Supplier Should Know." *DSN Retailing Today*, December 13, 2004.

28. Robert J. Dolan and Hermann Simon. *Power Pricing: How Managing Price Transforms the Bottom Line.* Free Press, 1996: 248.

29. Federal Communication Commission Auction Page: http://www.fcc.gov/wtb/auctions/. The FCC site documents these auctions, and their results, in detail.

30. For an in-depth discussion see Paul Klemperer. *Auctions: Theory and Practice.* Princeton Paperbacks: Princeton New Jersey, 2004. And Paul Milgrom. *Putting Auction Theory to Work.* Cambridge University Press, Cambridge, 2004. Both of these books are by leading experts in auction theory that assisted the governments in these auction experiments.

31. This is true for almost all forms of auction. This result has been verified theoretically, experimentally, and using actual market auctions. For example see John Riley. "Expected Revenue from Open and Sealed Bid Auctions." *Journal of Economic Perspectives* 3(3), Summer 1989: 41–50; Orley Ashenfelter. "How Auctions Work for Wine and Art," *Journal of Economic Perspectives* 3(3), Summer, 1989: 23–36.

32. Paul Milgrom. "Auctions and Bidding: A Primer." *Journal of Economic Perspectives* 3(3), Summer 1989: 3–22.

33. A very useful summary of these results appears in Patrick Bajari and Ali Hortacsu. "Economic Insights from Internet Auctions." Journal *of Economic Literature* XLII, June 2004,: 457–486.

34. There is a significant amount of controversy regarding the best interpretation of sniping. Other possible explanations include tacit collusion, learning about a common value, a result of simultaneous auctions of other items, or personal uncertainty about the benefits of the good. Roth and Ockenfels find the experienced-naïve bidder

explanation most consistent with the various empirical findings. Alvin E. Roth and Axel Ockenfels, "Last-Minute Bidding and the Rules for Ending Second-Price Auctions: Evidence from eBay and Amazon Auctions on the Internet," *American Economic Review*, 92(4), September 2002: 1093-1103 and Dan Ariely, Axel Ockenfels, and Alvin E. Roth, "Last-Minute and Incremental Bidding: Evidence from the Lab and the Internet," Working paper: Harvard University, 2001.

35. 2005 Analyst Day presentation, 2/10/05. Note that the number of registered eBay users worldwide is equivalent to the population of the ninth largest country. Gross merchandise value is the metric used by eBay to track volume, and corresponds to the market value of all closed auctions. Actual transaction volume will be somewhat less than this, as some auctions that close are never actually consummated in practice due to fraud, logistics, or winning buyers and sellers never shipping product or payment.

36. Site is http://www.artbrokerage.com.

37. "Online auctions: Bid adieu to high prices," HomePC; "Life on the Internet," *Public Broadcasting System*, 1997.

38. http://flowerbuyer.com.

39. Feldman, Joan. "Continental learns to Believe." *Air Transport World*, February 1996, 43–45.

40. Cross, Robert. "Launching the Revenue Rocket: How Revenue Management Can Work for your Business," *Cornell Hotel and Restaurant Administration Quarterly*, April 1997: 32–43.

41. See, for example, John Yinger. "Evidence on Discrimination in Consumer Markets," *Journal of Economic Perspectives* 12(2), 1998: 23–40.

42. See Florian Zettelmeyer, Fiona Scott Morton, and Jorge Silva-Risso. "Cowboys or Cowards: Why are Internet Car Prices Lower," Working paper: University of California-Berkeley, March 2004.

43. Gary Eppen, Ward Hanson, Kipp Martin. "Bundling- New Products, New Markets, Low Risk," *Sloan Management Review* 32(4), Summer 1991. Also see Ward Hanson and Kipp Martin. "Optimal Bundle Pricing", *Management Science* 36(2), February 1990.

44. Yannis Bakos and Erik Brynjolfsson. "Bundling Information Goods: Pricing, Profits, and Efficiency," Working Paper: MIT, 1998.

part 3:

Ecommerce

Chapter 13: Internet Retailing

Chapter 14: Consumer Channels

Chapter 15: B2B Ecommerce

Chapter 16: Online Research

Chapter 17: Organizing for Online Marketing

chapter 13:

Internet Retailing

Best Buy Goes Hybrid

One of the strengths of the U.S. economy, especially when compared to Japan or Europe, is the efficiency of the U.S. retailing sector.[1] A comprehensive study of productivity worldwide found U.S. retailing one of the major sources of U.S. productivity improvement during the previous two decades. While highly beneficial for consumers in providing low prices and wide assortment, this quest for productivity makes the retailing sector highly competitive. U.S. retailers must succeed against sophisticated alternatives or face failure.

The rise of the Internet presents existing retailers with both threat and opportunity. Electronic retailer Best Buy illustrates how some traditional retailers have responded by effectively merging the Net with its standard operations. Ranked as the 20th most visited web site of the 2004 holiday season,[2] Best Buy no longer considers its Net presence as experimental. Best Buy's online retail strategy closely synchronizes with its overall retail strategy and weekly sales promotions. The goal is *cross channel integration*, where consumers shop through whatever channel best matches their goals (Figure 13.1).

Promotional pricing, self-service, and wide assortment are the core of the Best Buy approach.[3] A look at its homepage shows how the Internet site reflects this strategy. The homepage mimics the weekly direct-mail brochure and newspaper insert. Central to this approach are weekly sales. Promotions may involve system bundles, special financing offers, and rebates.

The initial wave of Internet retailing ended in disappointment for many retail startups. Internet retailing is making a strong comeback as established retailers go online and surviving online retailers reach profitability. This chapter examines the growth of Internet retailing, a framework for evaluating online opportunities, successful online tools, and the specific challenges of a hybrid approach.

Topics covered in this chapter include:

> **Internet Retailing Growth and Profitability**

> **The iPace of Internet Shopping**

> **Multi-Channel Shopping Behavior**

Figure 13.1

Best Buy Homepage

Source: Courtesy of Best Buy Enterprise Service, Inc.

Company executives feel that, "The web site has achieved 'promotional parity' with the stores, able to offer financing, the complex product bundling and other deals available in stores. We have eliminated all the barriers that have separated these two channels."[4]

As a *big box* retailer, Best Buy relies on customers to support themselves in terms of information about products and services. The company's web site complements this self-support approach. Figure 13.2 shows a portion of the research center for flat-panel monitors. Best Buy features

similar depth of material for many of the products it carries. Electronic products are typically high involvement, durable good purchases. The online research center cost effectively provides information to consumers and helps them make informed purchases.

Wide assortment and one-stop shopping is the third main element of the Best Buy retailing approach. Once more, the web site seeks to accommodate this. An online site can often feature a broader and deeper assortment, in a more cost effective manner, than a physical outlet. The

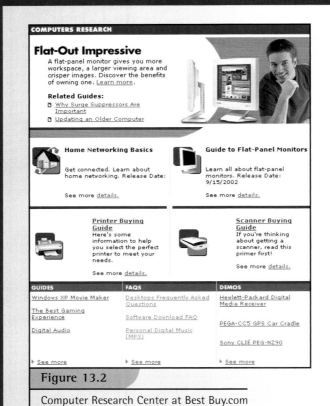

Figure 13.2

Computer Research Center at Best Buy.com

Source: Courtesy of Best Buy Enterprise Service, Inc.

virtual store does not need the inventory and shelf space required of an actual store. In categories such as music and software, the online assortment is much larger than any regular Best Buy outlet. Along with this assortment are comparison guides, allowing a shopper to compare and contrast this expanded offering.

Online retail faces difficulties compared to physical stores. Immediate delivery is a challenge to online retailers, and this is an area where hybrid organizations have an advantage. Many consumers are willing to research and select products online, but would rather not wait for delivery. These consumers find online shopping and in-store pickup attractive. Recognizing this preference, Best Buy invested in technology integration that allows consumers to view the available inventory for a local store of their choice. A consumer can purchase online, arrange for a pickup at a local store, with the assurance of available supply.

Each retail channel has specific strengths and weaknesses. For example, conducting a product test in a set of stores is complex and costly. Such a test requires considerable planning, coordination, and inventory investment. On the other hand, it is relatively easy to conduct a targeted test online. Focused emails can test specific products against specific customer demographics in a quick and unobtrusive manner. Internet retailers are increasingly relying on their online presence to test and determine the most relevant assortment for target customers. As such online testing capabilities mature, it increasingly substitutes for more costly in-store tests.

Startups without a physical location dominated the first wave of online retailing. Later, many traditional retailers adopted an online channel to augment their stores and catalogs. The battle between these forms continues, each with advantages and disadvantages. This chapter discusses the growth and expansion of online retailing, key opportunities for online retailers, the most important tools when competing online, and multi-channel retailing concepts.

ONLINE RETAILING DEVELOPS

Beginning in 1999, the U.S. Census Bureau added ecommerce to its quarterly measurement of U.S. retailing activity. The pattern is one of continual strong growth, with an annual holiday shopping spike in the fourth quarter of each year. Figure 13.3 demonstrates this steady rise, doubling from the beginning amount of under $5 billion in the fourth quarter of 1999 to more than $23 billion in Q4 2005.[5]

Yearly online retail in the United States exceeded $84 billion during 2005. While substantial, it is still only about 2.4% of overall U.S. retail sales. Put differently, total U.S. online retail sales in 2005 were approximately 29% of the U.S. retail sales of the Wal-Mart chain of stores.[6]

There are several reasons why online retail is much more important than its 2.5% share of retailing suggests, including:

> Retail categories where online sales are already a large percentage of total sales
> Continued growth of the online user base stimulates online sales
> Online experience and broadband adoption stimulates online retail
> Properly run online retailers may have superior profitability
> Customer satisfaction with online retailing is high
> Online retailers affect opportunities and expectations of traditional retail

These factors suggest the growing importance and power of online retailing.

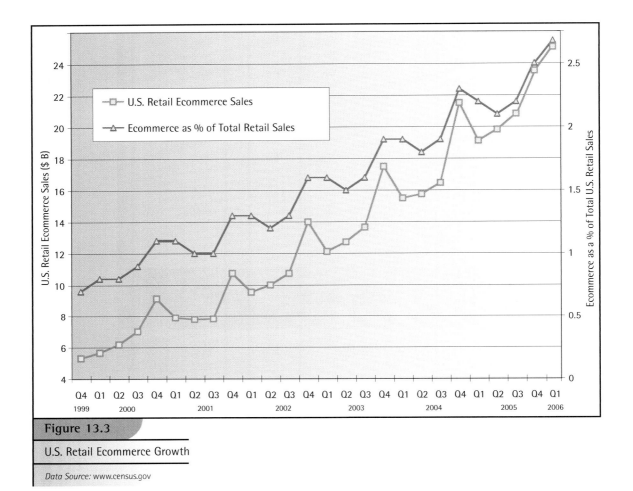

Figure 13.3

U.S. Retail Ecommerce Growth

Data Source: www.census.gov

Online retail percentages vary substantially across product categories, and they are much more important in categories such as computers, tickets, books, and travel. Figure 13.4 highlights this category variation. Computer hardware and software is the highest category with an estimated Internet penetration of 34% by 2003. The second-highest category is tickets, with an estimated Internet penetration of 20%. Books rank third with an estimated penetration of 15%. Jewelry and apparel are right in the middle with penetration of about 5% and 4%, respectively. Product categories like food and auto parts have low penetration rates, ranging around 1%.

Product categories vary significantly in terms of their underlying attributes. The iPACE framework discussed later in this chapter outlines the factors supporting or hindering a category from succeeding online.[7] Some of the top-share categories, such as software and tickets, are essentially digital. Others, such as computers, are information-rich, complex, and high involvement purchases where the online shopping process assists consumers researching their options. Hardware sales also benefit from the strength of direct sellers such as Dell, IBM, and Gateway. Low share products tend to have one or more severe barriers to online retailing. When the Internet excels on the fundamentals driving shoppers, Net retailing can grow to a major share of sales.

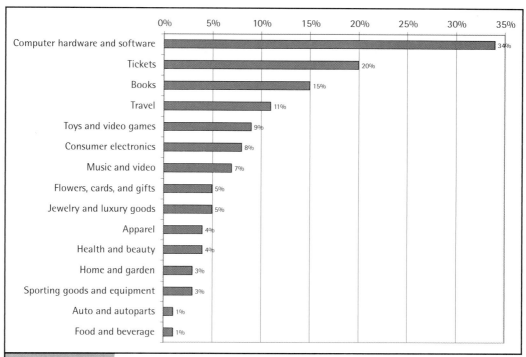

Figure 13.4

Consumer Ecommerce Penetration of Product Categories, 2003

Source: The State of Retail Online, 6.0, a Shop.org Survey conducted by Forrester Research.

Bringing consumers online naturally leads to additional online retail sales. The arrival of new households is fueling growth in online shopping. In 1997, 5 million U.S. households were shopping online. Three years later there were 28.8 million households shopping online, and by 2003 the U.S. online retail population exceeded 43 million. At the same time, average annual online purchases rose from $489 in 1997 to $2,197 in 2003.

Online experience leads to increased trust and comfort with online shopping. Among adults, years online correlates positively with trust and comfort in online shopping. Experience also predicts increasing use of broadband. Growth in online households thus leads to an initial boost because of the increased base, followed by continued growth as these newly minted online shoppers develop expertise and familiarity.

Rich shopping content enhances the online shopping experience. With broadband connections, households can quickly download higher resolution images, three-dimensional views, animations, and short videos. This content helps make retailing web sites more engaging, more informative, and easier to navigate rapidly. Improvements in web site design make it easier for consumers to shop online.

The mainstreaming of online retail has several implications. Mainstream consumers are likely to be less adventuresome and risk taking than early adopters. Familiar brands, simplified ordering and return processes, and local presence all provide additional comfort to new online shoppers.

Usability, simplification, and removing risk are more important to this group of shoppers than cohorts who preceded them.

Online retailer experience, and the elimination of poorly managed companies, is leading to improved profitability of online retailers. Over time, this process of retail evolution helps establish stronger online firms able to fund expansion and growth. This process of adjustment and learning is apparent in the 2002 retailing metrics seen in Table 13.1, when online retailing first made the transition to break-even.

By the end of 2002, online retailers as a group had moved from losing money to break-even. Pure online retailers were still losing money (–16%), but companies mixing online with physical stores (+7%) or online with catalogs (+22%) had achieved online profitability. Several factors drove this improvement. Increasing the scale of operations helps lower the cost of goods. Catalog stores have expertise in shipping and logistics, and this results in lower fulfillment and customer service costs. A physical or catalog presence helps lower the need for high advertising expenditures. Finally, the larger operations of many store and catalog companies lowers the overhead costs captured in the general and administrative category.

Reaching appropriate scale and improving efficiency is an ongoing challenge for all new and growing retailers. During the 1980s and 1990s, Wal-Mart was able to reduce its overhead costs (Selling, General & Administrative) from 23% of revenue to 17%. While only 6%, this improved profitability is very large for a retailer. It created room for Wal-mart to compete aggressively on price. The improved retailing results in Table 13.1, and further improvements after 2002, provide similar improvements in online retailing profitability.

Table 13.1

Financial Metrics for Internet Retailers (2002)					
	2001	2002	2002 by Channel		
Percentage of Revenue	All Companies	All Companies	Web-based Companies	Store-based Companies	Catalog-based Companies
Revenue	100%	100%	100%	100%	100%
Costs of goods sold	66%	50%	59%	40%	51%
Fulfillment	12%	12%	12%	13%	8%
Customer service	3%	4%	5%	4%	2%
Contribution margin	19%	34%	23%	43%	39%
Marketing	11%	11%	14%	8%	8%
Site, technology, content	5%	11%	7%	17%	4%
General and administrative	8%	13%	18%	11%	4%
EBIT	–6%	0%	–16%	7%	22%
Number of retailers in sample	107	130	50	60	20

Source: The State of Retail Online, 6.0, a Shop.org Survey conducted by Forrester Research.

Online retailers do have some advantages. Internet retailers do not invest in brick-and-mortar storefronts or require inventory at multiple locations. Hence, inventory productivity at Internet retailers should be higher. Figure 13.5 provides data on inventory productivity for selected retailers.[8] The data shows that Internet retailers like Amazon.com, Gateway, and Drugstore.com have high inventory productivity. Barnesandnoble.com has more than two times the inventory turnover of Barnes & Noble.

Online retail also favors speed, learning, and customization. Rather than burden the retail channel with multiple versions, or long order delays, an online retailer can quickly respond to changes in the marketplace or a desire for customization. For example, personal computers in inventory rapidly depreciate due to the rapid pace of technological change. Brick-and-mortar computer retailers face difficult challenges of forecasting, planning, building, distributing, and replenishing inventory in the face of demand uncertainty. Online order taking and build-to-order selling systems, such as those used by Dell, eliminate much of this inventory cost.

A further factor driving growth in online retailing is the relatively high levels of customer satisfaction among online shoppers. The American Customer Satisfaction Index (ACSI) measures satisfaction by surveying consumers.[9] Overall, the ecommerce retail sector outperformed traditional retailers in all of the reported measurement periods. With an ACSI score of 87 in 2004, barnesandnoble.com was the top performer not only in the ecommerce sector but also in the retail sector (Figure 13.6).

Surviving online retailers are discovering their best online approach. Sometimes, small and specialty retailers must use a different approach. Rather than try to carve out their own web site, logistics, and online presence, these firms rely on sites such as eBay, Amazon, or Yahoo! as their online "store front" and coordinator.

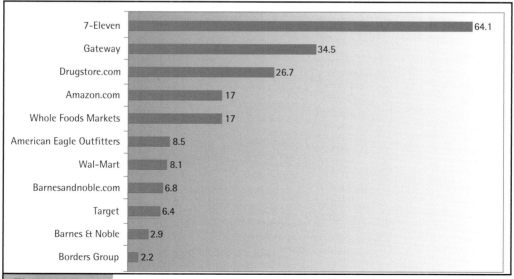

Figure 13.5

Inventory Turnover for Selected Retailers, 2002

Source: Retail Forward.

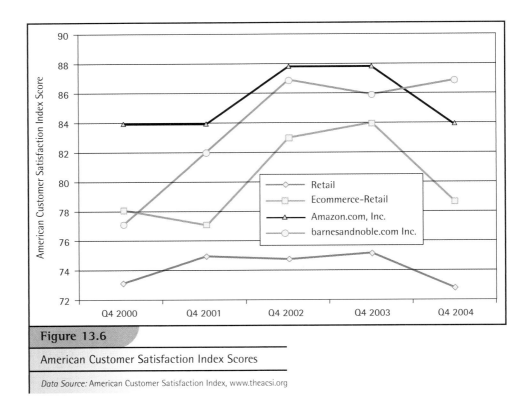

Figure 13.6

American Customer Satisfaction Index Scores

Data Source: American Customer Satisfaction Index, www.theacsi.org

The presence of the online retail channel spills over to traditional outlets. Even in categories with low online purchase rates, many shoppers engage in extensive product research.[10] This online information collection often reveals far more detail than is available in the store, making costs and pricing more transparent.[11] Retailers have less of a monopoly on product information, and find it harder to count on an "ignorance premium" for the majority of shoppers.

INTERNET-ENABLED RETAILING

Consumer shopping needs form the basis of online retailing, as it does for all successful retailing. The most essential of these are information, price, assortment, convenience, and entertainment (iPACE). Internet retailers differentiate themselves around one or more aspects of iPACE. Consumer requirements for iPACE components vary across product categories. The first challenge for an online retailer is understanding the iPACE requirements of potential customers (Figure 13.7).

Implementing iPACE requires matching offerings to target customers. Effective implementation requires a careful understanding of the shopping needs of the target consumer for a particular product category, and providing online features and functionality that support these shopping needs.

Multi-channel retailing includes understanding multi-channel shopping behavior. As in the Best Buy example, a consumer may shop online, select and purchase an item, but pick up the item

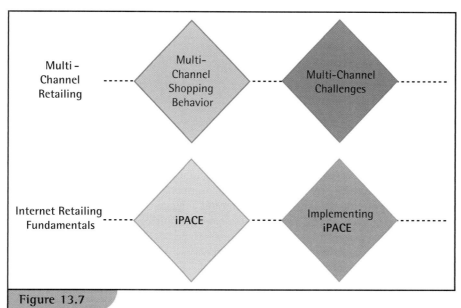

Figure 13.7

Internet-Enabled Retailing Requirements

in the store. As with the basic iPACE approach, retailers have to understand the multi-channel shopping needs in each product category and implement features and functionality that support these needs. For multi-channel retailing, some of these features are on the web site, some in the store, and others link the web site to the store.

Multi-channel retailing involves several challenges that result from conflicts and inconsistencies that arise between the online and physical outlets. Two especially difficult challenges are maintaining consistency of pricing and assortment across channels. It can also be difficult to reward properly activities supporting consumers that result in sales in a different outlet.

iPACE and the Online Shopping Process

Chapter 4 discusses how the dual consumer budget of time and money shapes online activities. In no area are these tradeoffs more important than in shopping. Consumers seek the best value for their money while enjoying the process as much as possible. In some situations the search for the best deal dominates. In others cases the goal is less financial and more amusement, status, or social oriented.

Successful retailers anticipate and react to these consumer goals. The iPACE framework provides a starting point for matching an online retailing environment with consumer shopping needs.[12]

> *Information:* Information about the quality and features of products, how they match consumer needs, use situations, and value comparisons
> *Price:* The price of the product, including the excitement of promotional pricing, the convenience of everyday low pricing and price guarantees

> *Assortment:* The depth of products offered within a category and the breadth of products offered across categories
> *Convenience:* The timing, location, and buying process
> *Entertainment:* The extent to which shopping is fun or playful.[13]

These shopping goals present opportunities for the Internet to better serve customers and deliver higher iPACE value. Failure to provide any of these requirements frustrates shoppers and hinders online retailing.

> *Information*

The most basic requirement of a shopper is information. Figure 13.8 highlights major steps along the consumer shopping cycle, each of which has information requirements. These steps include (1) finding products to consider, (2) collecting general information about these items, (3) evaluating alternatives, (4) placing the order, (5) receiving the product, and (6) dealing with possible disappointments and returns. There is a rich marketing and economics literature on each of these steps, and the following discussion can only touch upon some of the fundamentals.

The first step for a shopper is to find products or services that form his or her initial *consideration set.* A consumer's initial consideration set is the collection of products that comes to mind at the beginning of the shopping process. Forming a consideration set is a complex process tied to previous purchase history, brand perceptions and preferences, and recent marketing exposure.[14]

The flexibility of online shopping makes the consideration set especially important. A consumer may search initially by brand, using a manufacturer's web site as the starting point. Alternatively, shoppers may go to an online retailer as the beginning point and begin the information collection with the products available at that retailer. A third possibility is to begin at an impartial comparison site, with reviews and critiques of the products on the market. Thus, the first step of the information collection process ties closely to both online branding issues and traffic-building steps.

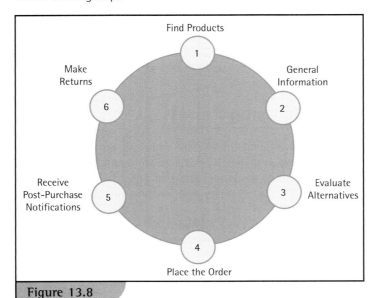

Figure 13.8

The Consumer Shopping Cycle

Does Decomposition of Web Site Activities into User Tasks Improve Prediction of Conversion Rates?

Figure 13.8 decomposes a retail shopping cycle into a number of stages or user tasks. Decomposing web site activities into user tasks is not only logical but can yield valuable information that can improve prediction of conversion rates of visit to transaction.

Sismeiro and Bucklin examine purchasing behavior at an automobile site. They decompose consumer visits into three user tasks:

> Complete Product Configuration

> Input Personal Information
> Complete Order

They find that the task-oriented model improves prediction significantly over a one-step model. As users navigate the site and complete tasks, they provide additional information that is useful in predicting conversion.

Source: Catarina Sismeiro and Randolph Bucklin, "Modeling Purchase Behavior at an E-Commerce Web Site: A Task-Completion Approach," *Journal of Marketing Research* (August 2004): 306–323.

The complexity of the shopping task drives step 2 along the shopping cycle. Products categories such as computers, appliances, and consumer electronics are feature rich. Detailed information describing these features, how to use them, and their benefits help a shopper understand the product better. Online content can include product images, magnification tools, assembly instructions, assembly diagrams, critical reviews, and comparisons.[15]

Step 3 varies dramatically across categories. *Search goods* are those products and services whose important characteristics can be determined with ease.[16] For an experienced traveler, an airplane flight or a rental car is easy to compare, with key features such as price, number of stops, and connection time readily apparent. *Experience goods* are the opposite, where the most important characteristics are challenging to describe and appreciate. A product may be an experience good online because of the importance of hard-to-judge physical properties, as in apparel. It may also be an experience good because of the unstandardized nature of the service, such as for health care or a spa. Most of the high market penetration categories for online retailers shown in Figure 13.4 involve search goods, or digital experience goods that can be downloaded and sampled. One of the biggest challenges for online retailers is to provide information sufficient to at least partially convert experience goods to search goods.

The remaining steps of the shopping cycle also require information. Shoppers may need guidance in choosing the proper outlet and shipping method. Post-purchase information, such as delivery time and return policy, can be influential or intimidating. At each of these stages, the proper information can reinforce or hinder completing a sale.

> Price

The simplest reason to buy online is to save money. In some product categories, online prices are significantly lower than manufacturer's list prices or traditional outlets (recall Table 12.1).

(a) Search goods are easy to specify

(b) Experience goods are challenging

Figure 13.9

Search Goods are Easier to Track; Experience Goods Make Comparison Difficult

Source: 13.9a © Rudi Von Briel/Photo Edit; 13.9b © AP/Wide World Photos

Shoppers use the Internet to find bargains. As seen in the pricing chapter, companies are using the Net to reach customers with last-minute bargains in many travel and other service areas. The first wave of retailers often used price as a customer acquisition method, with online prices significantly cheaper than existing outlets. Innovative online retailers such as eBay create new markets for used and difficult to locate specialty items, often at lower prices than new or local outlets.

Comparison sites help consumers find the best bargain at competing retailers. An electronics shopper can read a digital camera review at CNet, click a link for price comparisons, sort these alternative outlets based on price or other criteria, and choose his or her preferred vendor. The prominence given to product price is often the deciding factor.

Consumer savings can occur with the regular price, taxes, delivery, and shopping/purchasing costs.[17] For a particular product, the full cost of buying online is:

$$\text{Full online price} = [\text{Online price} * (1 + \text{ tax rate})]$$

$$+ \text{ shipping cost}$$

$$+ \text{ expected return costs}$$

Total cost savings promote online sales. Consumers place different weights on reputation, the reliability of shipping, and the difficulties and likelihood of returns. It is also important to know whether shoppers use some form of *price partitioning*. That is, do shoppers consider only the full price, or are some shoppers more price sensitive to some aspects of the full price (such as shipping) than others (such as product price)?

The evidence on price partitioning suggests important situations where consumers do not just sum individual component prices and compare the full online price. One, the difficult comparison effect often makes it harder to observe some of the logistics costs. Conversely, a study by Brynjolfsson and Smith finds online shoppers at comparison sites more price sensitive to shipping costs than product price.[18] At the comparison site used for their study, shipping prices displayed prominently and had a bigger impact on choice than variation in regular prices. Other researchers, using behavioral arguments, find that consumers frame the full online price differently than a sequence of independently presented costs.[19] They argue that repeated charges elicit a more negative reaction, even when summed to the same total, than a composite bundle price. In a series of studies, Simonson and his co-authors document cases where consumers seek out the middle ground in a compromise effect, suggesting the breadth and types of price comparison may affect consumer choices.[20]

> Taxes

In many countries, a national value-added sales tax (VAT) applies uniformly across the country for all retail outlets. In countries such as Germany, France, or England, this VAT raises online and offline prices equally. A national VAT neither favors nor discourages online shopping, applying equally regardless of purchase location.

The United States has a different system, based on state and even local sales taxes. Taxes vary from a low of zero in five states (in Alaska, Delaware, Montana, Nevada, New Hampshire, and Oregon) to a high of 8.25% in California.[21] Further complicating the issue, sales taxes depend on the nature of product delivery and the location of buyer and seller.

Many states exempt purely digital purchases from any taxation. The U.S. Supreme Court further ruled that online sales are taxable only if the seller has a physical presence in the state where the buyer resides. For example, Amazon.com has a physical presence in both Washington and Nevada, but not in California. Thus, someone living in California does not have to pay the 8.25% California sales tax on books purchased from Amazon.

An early study by Goolsbee showed tax rates do stimulate online shopping.[22] Goolsbee used an in-depth survey of online purchasing to see if differences in local taxes changed the amount of online shopping behavior among states. He found that Internet users in high tax states were significantly more likely to shop online than Internet users with less to save because of lower tax rates. Price gaps of a few percent are enough to change behavior. Shoppers do pay attention to the tax savings in the full shopping price equation.

> Shipping Cost

Shipping costs vary from near zero for small file size digital products to prohibitively expensive for bulky items. Shipping costs can negate other price advantages and scare off consumers from making a purchase. This makes shipping costs more than a detail.

Four categories of goods vary considerably in the cost and type of shipping cost.

> *Digital information goods*: Information products delivered electronically
  Examples: airline tickets, research reports
  Shipping cost: Near zero
> *Digital entertainment goods:* Digital audio and video
  Examples: downloaded music, video on demand
  Shipping cost: Key consumer costs are time to transmit and local storage costs. For consumer entertainment products, digital cable systems or very high-speed Internet connections are needed. Key seller costs are bandwidth charges.
> *Hard goods*: Tangible products ordered and paid for online
  Examples: books, compact discs, computers, apparel
  Shipping cost: Depends on weight, bulk, speed of delivery
> *Perishables*: Tangible products subject to rapid spoilage
  Examples: groceries, restaurant meals
  Shipping cost: Potentially high due to waste and inconvenience

Policy Issue: Is the Online Tax Exemption Fair?

Cash-strapped states certainly believe online sales hurt their state tax revenues. As evidence, they cite a study by Forrester Research claiming tens of billions of tax dollars lost to online sales per year. They complain bitterly about both lost revenue and harm to local merchants due to an uneven playing field. Others claim these loss forecasts are too extreme.

As part of their response, many states are proposing simplified national tax rates that are much easier to apply online. As ecommerce grows in importance, and states face tighter and tighter budgets, their complaints will likely increase.

Source: Donald Bruce and William F. Fox, "State and Local Sales Tax Revenue Losses from E-Commerce: Updated Estimates," *State Tax Notes* 22(3) (October 15, 2001): 203–214.

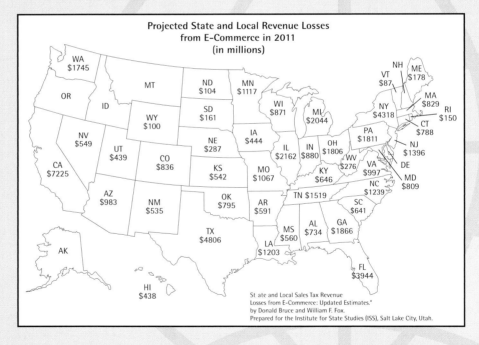

Projected State and Local Revenue Losses from E-Commerce in 2011 (in millions)

WA $1745
OR
MT
ND $104
MN $1117
NH
VT $87
ME $178
ID
WY $100
SD $161
WI $871
MI $2044
NY $4318
MA $829
RI $150
NV $549
UT $439
CO $836
NE $287
IA $444
IL $2162
IN $880
OH $1806
PA $1811
CT $788
NJ $1396
CA $7225
AZ $983
NM $535
KS $542
MO $1067
KY $646
WV $276
VA $997
DE
MD $809
OK $795
AR $591
TN $1519
NC $1239
SC $641
TX $4806
MS $560
AL $734
GA $1866
AK
LA $1203
FL $3944
HI $438

State and Local Sales Tax Revenue Losses from E-Commerce: Updated Estimates."
by Donald Bruce and William F. Fox.
Prepared for the Institute for State Studies (ISS), Salt Lake City, Utah.

Consumer surveys and online shopping behavior demonstrate that consumers notice and react to the cost of shipping. For high-priced and low-weight products, such as a sub-notebook computer, shipping costs are minor compared to the savings in sales taxes. For bulky products like pet food, the high cost of shipping relative to the cost of the product discourages consumers

"Look Inside the Book"

Amazon.com has a feature called "Look inside the Book." Using this feature, a shopper can look inside a book to see the table of contents, the index, and a few chapters. Amazon.com has expanded this capability to allow a shopper to "Search Inside the Book." Here is how this new capability works:

> A shopper types a key word in the search box.
> The search results display relevant titles.

> Underneath each title are excerpts from the pages where the search term appears.
> Clicking each link takes the shopper directly to that page.

Amazon.com announced that sales for the 120,000 titles included in its "Search Inside the Book" program were 9% higher than sales for titles not in the program. While encouraging, the nature of the book titles used in the test would affect the extent to which the results are more generally valid.

Source: Monica Soto Ouchi, "New Amazon Feature Aids Sales," *The Seattle Times*, October 31, 2003.

---

from ordering these products online. Perishable goods are even more trouble. Shipping costs can be very high, with spoilage worries as well.[23]

Not all aspects of electronic commerce and selling online are more efficient than the channels they replace. Shipping to home addresses is such a case. The package delivery system faces higher costs and challenges in order to support the rapid move to online selling (Table 13.2). Jindel points out several factors that make an Internet-based system less efficient than the current retail system:[24]

> Internet retailing shifts deliveries from retail stores to residences, with only a small impact on total retail purchases.
> Package delivery companies are optimized for delivery to commercial addresses.
> Commercial deliveries are more profitable than residential ones.

Companies like DHL, FedEx, and UPS will need to redesign their operations to handle this very different pattern of service. At least in the short term, these demands create pressure for higher delivery fees and shipping charges.[25]

> *Assortment*

> Problems with Traditional Stores

While evidence shows price is important to shoppers, other iPACE factors sometimes dominate. For example, a survey of 1,800 Christmas shoppers' retail dissatisfaction found assortment and convenience the most important factors followed by parking, waiting, and bad selection. Fewer than 2% of the survey mentioned price. Online sites with a huge assortment, helpful advice, and

Table 13.2

Comparison of Normal Retail Delivery System (Commercial) vs. Internet-Driven Delivery System (Residential or Business at Residence)

Characteristics of Commercial and Residential Deliveries			
Service Attributes	*Commercial Delivery*	*Residential Delivery*	*Business at Residence*
Preferred receiving hours	8 a.m. to 12 p.m.	4 p.m. to 8 p.m.	8 a.m. to 8 p.m.
Pickup frequency	Daily	Rarely	Infrequent
Consignee signature upon delivery	Daily	Rarely	Occasionally
Claims exposure with deliveries	Very Low	High	Low
Weekend delivery	Not required	Desirable	Not required
Driver release	Rarely	Frequently	Frequently
Express deliveries	Frequently	Rarely	Occasionally
Tracking and tracing required	Frequently	Frequently	Frequently
Guaranteed delivery commitment	Required	Preferred	Required
Seasonal volume pattern	Low	High	Low
Average weight of parcel	18 lb.	6 lb.	12 lb.
Parcels per delivery stop	2.5	1	1 to 2
Average revenue per parcel	$5.60	$5.20	$5.40
Average revenue per delivery stop	$14.00	$5.20	$8.10
Parcel density	High	Very low	Low

Source: Satish Jindel, "E-commerce's Mixed Blessings Traffic World," February 1, 1999, SJ Consulting Group, Inc., www.jindel.com.

available at all hours from almost all locations provide a powerful alternative to the problems of the mall.

> Advantages of Online Retailers

Shelf space is a critical asset in retailing. Retailers use sophisticated computer programs to choose the best shelf arrangements. They also use algorithms to determine how much inventory of a product should be carried and to determine when a product or category should be dropped. Each product must exceed a minimum profit hurdle to remain on the shelf. These constraints are less binding on Internet retailers. With a good user interface and effective search tools, retailers like Barnes and Noble and Best Buy can "stock" millions of titles.

Online retailing typically has an inventory cost advantage over store-based retailing. Local book and music stores must carry enough inventory to support local demand, plus multiple copies for more popular books. Internet retailers can service demand by maintaining inventory at a centralized location. Internet retailers can also use drop ship capabilities provided by distributors and suppliers. With drop shipping, the retailer accepts the order and a distributor or supplier directly ships the product to the customer. For Internet retailers, these advantages become powerful in product categories that have a large selection, high configurability, rapid price changes, and perishable inventory.

Large Selection

At any point in time, there are millions of book titles in print. A brick-and-mortar retailer can profitably stock only a small fraction of these titles in a store. Researchers find the differences in assortment between Amazon.com and a typical brick-and-mortar physical store striking, as illustrated in Table 13.3.

As a result, consumers shopping at a bookstore often find obscure books out of stock. Out-of-stock titles must be special ordered, a barrier in both time and convenience. Internet shopping from a broad assortment with a known home delivery date is a superior value proposition compared to an out of stock at the store followed by a special order.

Brynjolfsson, Hu, and Smith find the benefits to book shoppers of this increased assortment to be much larger than the impact of lower prices.[26] As the researchers point out, when Amazon makes millions of obscure and backlist books available, this is almost as if millions of new products have entered the market. Economists and marketers have struggled to measure the benefits of new products, and recently have developed some relatively simple and powerful approaches. The study finds that in books alone, this increased assortment created as much as $1 billion worth of extra consumer surplus in the United States during 2000, compared to what would have been consumer book-buying surplus without online book retailers. This large benefit occurs despite the fact that many of these individual titles have limited sales. The consumer benefit from increased assortment is from 7 to 10 times larger than the benefit from lower prices, which they estimate to have been in the range of $100 million in 2000.[27]

The benefits from assortment can be sufficient to overcome shopping difficulty. It would seem unlikely that a retailer can sell shoes to consumers over the Internet without giving them the opportunity to try them on. Zappos.com has succeeded in doing just that. The prices at

Table 13.3

Much Larger Assortment of Products Online		
Product Category	**Amazon.com**	**Typical Large Brick-and-mortar Store**
Books	2,300,000	40,000–100,000
CDs	250,000	5,000–15,000
DVDs	18,000	500–1,500
Digital cameras	213	36
Portable MP3 players	128	16
Flatbed scanners	171	13

Source: Reprinted by permission, Erik Brynjolfsson, Yu Hu, and Michael Smith, "Consumer Surplus in the Digital Economy: Estimating the Value of Increased Product Variety at Online Booksellers," *Management Science* 49, no. 11 (November 2003). Copyright © 2003, the Institute for Operations Research and the Management Sciences (INFORMS), 7240 Parkway Drive, Suite 310, Hanover, MD 21076 USA.

Zappos are comparable to offline stores. The selling point is selection. In a warehouse in Kentucky, Zappos stocks about a half a million pairs of shoes from over 170 brands. In comparison, the typical retail store carries only about a dozen or so brands. Zappos also overcomes consumer hesitancy by waiving delivery fees on all orders and covering return fees.[28]

High Configurability

Products like computers are available in a wide variety of configurations involving different options for processors, memory, storage, and preloaded software. It is very difficult to maintain acceptable stock levels of all possible configurations in a brick-and-mortar retailing environment. The result is that the retailer is frequently out of stock or has excess inventory of product configurations that are not in high demand. Internet retailers can enable the consumer to configure the product of his or her choice and then build the order. The Internet retailer benefits by avoiding the uncertainties of forecasting and stocking multiple configurations.

Rapid Price Changes and Perishable Inventory

Product categories like consumer electronics are subject to rapid price changes. The physical inventory in multiple brick-and-mortar locations can quickly become a liability. The centralized inventory required for Internet retailing operations is better suited for price volatility.

> *Convenience*

Physical shopping and purchasing costs are components of the full online price. These costs include the cost of traveling to the retail store, the cost of parking, the cost of walking through the mall to the store, and the cost of having to rearrange one's schedule to shop during store hours. Shopping costs also include the costs of finding the item in the store and the costs of waiting in line at the checkout. Internet shopping, with in-home access 24 hours a day, seven days a week, enhances convenience by minimizing or eliminating many of these costs.

The holidays are a stressful time for many consumers. They complete their shopping in the short window between Thanksgiving and Christmas. Black Friday, the Friday after Thanksgiving, kicks off the holiday season. Many retailers target special promotions for Black Fridays. This buildup, while exciting to some, is inconvenient to others. Consumers seem to be spreading their shopping over a longer and more convenient window. In a recent study, 53% of respondents said that they started holiday shopping in November, compared to only 43% in the previous year.[29]

The convenience of Internet shopping is an attractive alternative to the pressures of traditional holiday shopping. The data in Figure 13.3 show that the share of Internet as a percentage of total retailing increases during the holiday season. The data in Figure 13.3 also shows that the spike in Internet sales during the holiday season extend into the New Year.

> Repeat Purchase

Like shoes, few would expect perfumes to sell online. If ever a product category seemed to demand in-store sales, fragrances would appear to be it. Despite this, and the fact that online prices match department store prices, Fragrancenet.com has created an online sales site that is attracting national attention and multi-million-dollar sales levels (Figure 13.10).[30] Repeat buying is the key. Over 70% of perfume sales are repeat purchases of a fragrance. The Internet is very convenient for repeat purchase of high-value, low-weight products such as perfume.

Gifts provide an additional opportunity for online perfume sales. Of the 30% of perfume sales that are not a straight rebuy, half are gifts. Fragrancenet.com has a gift adviser system to help select a fragrance based on questions about the relationship between the gift giver and the recipient and personality cues about the recipient.

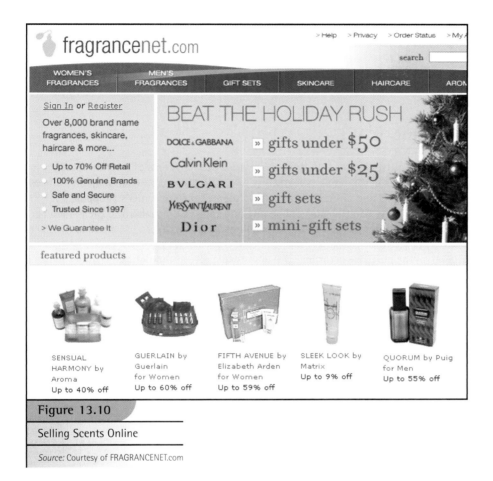

Figure 13.10

Selling Scents Online

Source: Courtesy of FRAGRANCENET.com

> *Entertainment*

For many consumers shopping is about "fun, fantasy, arousal, sensory stimulation and enjoyment."[31] The entertainment component of the Internet is not as developed as many of its functional aspects. Partly this is technical. Consumer access speeds are still too slow for high-quality video and audio. With a broader deployment of broadband connections and full-motion video, the Internet will be capable of a much higher entertainment quotient. Pay-per-view movies, interactive simulations, and video on demand should blur the distinction between the Internet, television, and interactive video games.

There are online sites that combine a heavy dose of entertainment along with commerce, even over slow access lines. Many auction fans on sites like eBay find the competition and thrill of bidding as much a part of the site's benefit as the value of any products purchased. Words like "addictive," "hooked," and "shopping for entertainment" are easy to find among the most devoted bidders.[32] Other sites provide entertainment to users through community-building techniques. Chat rooms, instant messages, and discussion groups have fans that spend hours online.

Limitations on collaborative shopping also limit the entertainment value of current online retail. Many shoppers, especially women, prefer to shop as part of a group. Stores prefer it as well, with studies showing women shopping in a group spend more than they would if shopping alone.[33] It will be intriguing whether younger online users, currently the heaviest users of collaborative tools such as instant messaging and SMS, will merge these tools into their online shopping activities as they age and create a more social shopping experience. Even with these tools, however, the social experience is less than a joint trip to the mall.

Implementing iPACE

The iPACE model identifies factors that drive the relative attractiveness of Internet retailing for shoppers. Implementing iPACE requires marketers understand the consumer shopping process to create matching tools and content. Figure 13.11 merges the consumer's shopping cycle of Figure 13.8 with a variety of important online retailing tools and capabilities. Each stage corresponds to a specific user task, and the capabilities online retailers use to help shoppers accomplish that task.

Depending on the purchase occasion, consumers may proceed through these stages sequentially, or they may jump stages. For example, for a routine item such as a prescription drug refill or the repurchase of a fragrance, the consumer might first find the item and then jump directly to placing the order. If the consumer is shopping across channels, then an extended search might be conducted offline, followed by placing an order on the Internet.

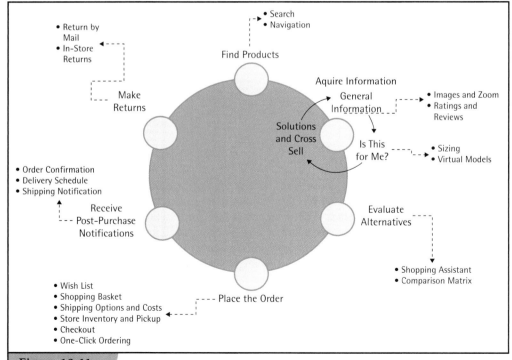

Figure 13.11

The Consumer Shopping Cycle on a Web Site

The stages in the shopping cycle in Figure 13.11 bear similarities to models of consumer decision-making processes,[34] but with several key differences. Models of consumer decision processes typically span multiple retailers. Figure 13.11 focuses on implementation at one retailer. It emphasizes the aspects most relevant to online retailing—for example, the emphasis on placing orders and receiving post-order notifications. Further, it gives priority to actions that a retailer can take to facilitate each stage.

> Find Products

As retail web sites expand, finding the right products quickly becomes difficult. Studies of early online retailing sites report that inability to find a product accounted for more than 40% of failed purchase attempts.[35] Improving on this failure rate provides essential support to the product-finding task.

As seen in Chapter 6, visitors use both search and browsing. As in other settings, experienced shoppers are more likely to search, while novices are more likely to browse. Designing for both types of shoppers involves compromise and understanding of online shopping behavior.

While a general search engine or directory such as Yahoo! needs to handle thousands of different types of visitors per hour, a retailing site normally faces a more limited range of objectives. Indeed, a useful guide to design for both search and browse is the concept of *shopping scenario*. Shopping scenarios take into account a shopper's goals in a particular shopping trip or occasion, creating a "broad context in which a customer does business."[36] The retailer can use shopping scenarios to identify the specific user tasks in each scenario and the key words and navigation associated with each task.

Scenarios help set the proper context for evaluating online tools and capabilities. Example scenarios might be (1) a grandmother buying a book as a gift for her preschool grandson, (2) a business consultant buying a book to read during a vacation; this shopper wants to avoid normal work-related topics and is looking for off-beat novels or stimulating nonfiction, or (3) a dedicated cat owner purchasing supplies for the upcoming month. In each case, important demographic interest and experience help clarify for designers the needs and wants of the buyer.

Shoppers also locate products using the navigation bar to browse a site. Navigation paths that directly support shopping scenarios increase the odds that a customer will find the products that they are looking for. Figure 13.12 provides an example from Wal-Mart.com. The navigation panel provides a number of alternative paths to find products. Which choices to include in the directory can emerge from scenario analysis, study of web logs, and interviews with shoppers. In this case, the emphasis is on product category and age of recipient. This navigation ensures that the site has a "flat" structure and minimizes the number of clicks it takes to find a product. The navigation bar also features frequently used links such as pre-order. The display of the navigation bar is consistent throughout the toy section. Another navigation option is to present products by use occasions. For example, apparel retailers group products based on use occasions such as formal wear, weekend getaway, and night on the town.

As in other areas, retail search effectiveness varies by the specificity of search terms. Figure 13.13 shows the results of a search using "Fancy Feast" (a brand of cat food) as a key word at pet food retailer Petco.com. In this case, search results are accurate—they locate the correct brand. The search also locates the various product types and flavors. The presentation of the search results is easy to read and

Figure 13.12

Navigation on Wal-Mart.com

Source: © 2000-2005, Wal-Mart.com USA, LLC and Wal-Mart Stores, Inc.

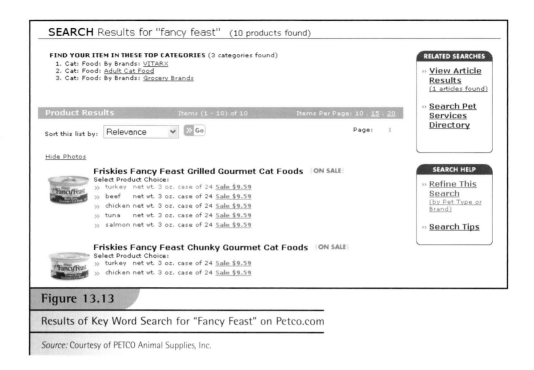

Figure 13.13

Results of Key Word Search for "Fancy Feast" on Petco.com

Source: Courtesy of PETCO Animal Supplies, Inc.

blends with the general look and feel of the site. Thumbnail graphics of the product reconfirm the verbal description in the search results. The results list the price of the item and indicate whether it is on sale. Search results can be sorted using different criteria or refined using other key words. Well-implemented search engines can automatically detect and respond to common spelling errors.

Specific results allow rapid access to information and checkout. Clickable links lead to specific description pages or straight to a shopping cart. This is difficult when a general term leads to unfocused results.

When a shopper uses a broad search term, most online search algorithms return an expansive set of results. Organizing these can be a challenge. For example, a shopper at Macy's might use the key word phrase "wine glasses." This search term and the corresponding results are much broader than the search for a specific brand (see Figure 13.14). Instead of presenting the shopper with multiple pages of search results, Macy's uses a navigation bar to summarize the results by department, brand, design, color, and price, along with a recommendation. This provides multiple ways of looking into the entire selection of wine glasses while still trying to emphasize a preferred result.

> *Acquire Information*

Once a shopper finds the desired products or product category, the next step for a site is to provide product information. In addition to the normal concerns of credibility and relevance, online retailers must take advantage of the capabilities of the Internet and mitigate its retailing limitations (such as the inability to touch and feel merchandise). This includes basic information that answers, "What actually is the product?", personalizing information such as "Is this for me?", and information that connects the product with solutions "Can this be part of an outfit?"

Figure 13.14

Search Results for Key Word "Wine Glasses"

Source: Courtesy of Macy's

> Basic Information

Basic product information includes a detailed attribute-level description, images, and quality indicators. In the case of consumer electronics, the description includes a comprehensive listing of product features and description of their benefits. Annotated images of the product that highlight the features are becoming increasingly common on the web sites of electronics retailers. In categories like apparel, texture is an important attribute. So in addition to product descriptions, high-density images and tools that allow a consumer to magnify or zoom over the product provide additional information.

Images and Zoom

First-generation web technologies struggled with the right balance of imagery and performance for shoppers using slow dial-up access. Consumer broadband and faster Internet infrastructure means fewer tradeoffs between excitement, entertainment, and site performance. Apparel retailers have responded with tools such as zoom. A shopper can drag the tool over any of the images on the page and get a closer look at the fabric texture or patterns. Another feature on apparel retailers' web sites is a color swatch. Color swatches display the image of the product in different colors. Apparel retailers say they consider zoom as a necessary feature and believe that it boosts conversion rates by 7% up to 10%.[37] Other features that complement zoom include high-quality photography, alternate views, and enlarged views.

Online retailers face a difficult choice during the ongoing transition to widespread broadband. One choice is to maintain parallel sites; one site designed to best serve high-speed access and the other to best serve low-speed connections. This is flexible and reaches the full customer base, but may be expensive and difficult to manage. It reflects the lessons of digital environments discussed in Chapter 2. A second choice is compromise, adequate for either speed but not best for either. This is simpler to implement, but vulnerable to competitors that better match customer wants with online capabilities. A third option is to sacrifice the low-end market and design only for high-speed connections. Arguments for this approach are the broadband online shopping bias, the simplicity of managing and promoting a single site, and the clear trend toward high-speed access. While it can be painful for a retailer to exclude any potential customers, an increasing number of online retailers may opt for the third choice.

Making the decision among these approaches requires careful market analysis, cost considerations, and forecasts about the rate of customer adoption of fast access. Different conclusions are possible for different industries. A toy retailer might choose option 1 (entertaining kids, connecting to broadband parents, and still reaching low-speed grandparents), an online bank choosing option 2 (a single secure site with one look and feel), and an online fashion site choosing option 3 (reaching its high-income trendy clientele more likely to have high-speed connections). Again, shopping scenarios can illustrate for online retailers the needs and capabilities of its customers.

Ratings and Reviews

In categories like books, electronics, and entertainment, shoppers use product ratings and reviews. For books and entertainment, editorial reviews are usually available and presented alongside product information. In addition to editorial reviews, some retailers allow consumers to post ratings and reviews. The following excerpt from Circuitcity.com[38] provides insight into the motivation, purpose, and guidelines for these ratings:

> ... [The] Ratings and Reviews feature offers you the opportunity to tell other Circuit City customers about your experience with a product. Are you happy with your purchase? Or do you feel it's not a good value? If you could tell other Circuit City customers something about a product you own, what would it be? We welcome your honest opinions—positive or negative—about any of the products you've used, so our customers can make informed buying decisions.

> Personalized Information

Matching product and individual is one of the most important parts of the shopping process. For experience goods such as apparel, achieving the match is difficult. An outfit that works well for one person can be completely wrong for another. Even more challenging, it may not even be possible to describe exactly why one garment works and another does not.

Online apparel retailers are moving to personalized information to deal with this task. Size and color descriptions only go so far. Shoppers want to know how the outfit specifically looks on them. To partially handle this demand, retailers such as Lands' End offer a virtual model. An individual customizes the digital character to approximate her own characteristics. For women, this involves choices of model's name, body shape, bust size, waist, height, weight, age, eye shape, nose, lips, skin color, hairstyle, and hair color (Figure 13.15).

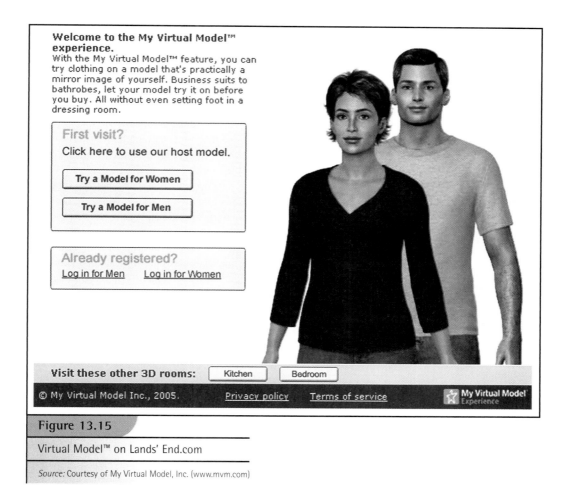

Welcome to the My Virtual Model™ experience.
With the My Virtual Model™ feature, you can try clothing on a model that's practically a mirror image of yourself. Business suits to bathrobes, let your model try it on before you buy. All without even setting foot in a dressing room.

First visit?
Click here to use our host model.

Try a Model for Women

Try a Model for Men

Already registered?
Log in for Men   Log in for Women

Visit these other 3D rooms: Kitchen   Bedroom

© My Virtual Model Inc., 2005.   Privacy policy   Terms of service   My Virtual Model Experience

Figure 13.15

Virtual Model™ on Lands' End.com

Source: Courtesy of My Virtual Model, Inc. (www.mvm.com)

After creating a model, a shopper uses it to visualize the look and fit of outfits. The tool increases shopper confidence in their choices, enabling them to mix and match garments and design outfits. A study conducted by Lands' End concluded that the conversion rate, the percentage of visitors who actually purchased, was 26% higher for shoppers who used the Virtual Model technology compared to the average shopper. The same study also concluded that the average order value was 13% higher for shoppers who used the virtual model technology than shoppers overall.[39]

One of the weaknesses of online shopping, especially for women, is its lack of social interaction. Despite the pressures of work and family, Underhill observes, "The use of shopping as a social activity seems unchanged, however. Women still like to shop with friends, egging each other on and rescuing each other from ill-advised purchases."[40] Once a shopper creates their virtual model and assembles an outfit, she can email the model wearing the outfit to friends. The social feedback can catch a mistake or, as Lands' End hopes, confirms the shopper in her decision. It also provides a social occasion to connect through email, possibly a distant friend with whom local shopping is not possible.

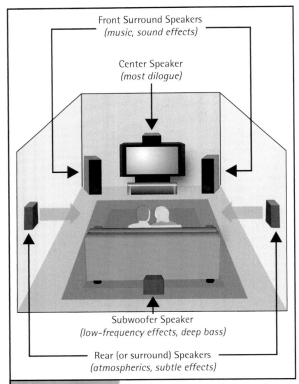

Front Surround Speakers
(music, sound effects)

Center Speaker
(most dilogue)

Subwoofer Speaker
(low-frequency effects, deep bass)

Rear (or surround) Speakers
(atmospherics, subtle effects)

Figure 13.16

Design a Home Theater to Your Own Dimensions

Personalization can help shoppers visualize a product in their own home. A home theater configuration, with television, multiple speakers, and other components may be difficult for many to evaluate (Figure 13.16). Allowing the shopper to use online tools or kiosks in store to mimic their desired layout can illustrate the proper solution. Functional diagrams can highlight the components, while suggesting methods to hide devices and to blend into existing décor.

The essence of this personalized shopping approach is to match a product to its use occasion, thus lowering risk and helping the shopper's imagination. For clothing, the person wearing the clothes is most important. For furniture, it is the room and pre-existing fixtures and furniture. For paint or landscaping, it is the combination of house and lot design. The goal is to augment the reality of existing products and features with the improved look from the new purchase.

> Cross Selling and Solution Selling

Apart from matching products to individuals, virtual model technology allows retailers to go beyond a single product category and present outfits and solutions. Dressing the virtual figure subtly encourages a full assortment of new items, without which the digital mannequin looks incomplete. In consumer electronics, compatibility issues are quite common. Selecting a new device can trigger suggestions of appropriate components and to flag problems with incompatible choices. The home theater design can lead to recommendations regarding speakers, cabling, upgraded video and audio components, and even new furniture.

Another cross selling technique is to provide recommendations based on the consumer's past purchases. As time passes, consumers may want new offerings and be ready to add additional components. Recalling previous purchases and making these suggestions provide cross-selling opportunities.

> Evaluate Alternatives

After identifying several products of interest and collecting information, the next step for the shopper is evaluation. Marketers refer to this comparison, the rules and processes employed by the shopper, as the shopper's *choice model*. Choice models are broadly of two types: *compensatory* and *non-compensatory*. In a compensatory choice model, a consumer compares products and services on all of the product attributes. While attributes vary in their importance, the strength in one attribute can compensate for a shortfall in another attribute. Compensatory models allow for attribute tradeoffs and ranking based on total features.

In non-compensatory models, shoppers first compare products based on certain key attributes. Shoppers eliminate products and services that do not have sufficient levels of these key attributes. Only then do consumers move on to other attributes. They may trade off these further attributes in a compensatory way or rank them individually.

Each of these approaches may challenge the skill and cognitive ability of shoppers.[41] Cramped store environments, hard-to-retrieve information, and the hustle and bustle of foot traffic on the store floor are all factors that make it difficult for consumers to gather information and process it in a physical store. Better alternatives exist online.

While the online world may provide more information, seemingly making the decision problem more difficult, at the same time these online tools may greatly assist the shopper in comparing alternatives. One such interactive tool is a shopping assistant. Shopping assistants help consumers screen choices based on prespecified criteria. Another interactive tool, a comparison matrix, helps compare alternatives by providing detailed information on attributes in a side-by-side manner.[42]

> Shopping Assistants

Shopping assistants screen a large set of alternatives based on preferences expressed by consumers, and from this pool select a relevant high-scoring subset. Consumers can provide preferences in a number of different ways, supporting both compensatory and non-compensatory choice models. Non-compensatory rules, such as no cameras below 3.2 mega pixels or prices above $600, are possible. Compensatory approaches get consumers to provide weights for different attributes. Using the weights, the shopping assistant computes an overall attractiveness score for each product. Fine-tuning of weights is possible through a variety of methods.

> Comparison Matrix

Rather than try to re-create a shopper's preferences, some sites instead focus on presenting the information in a manner that lets the shopper form their judgments in whatever manner they desire. A standard approach for this is the comparison matrix, with side-by-side listing of the different products and their attributes. Best Buy, Circuit City, and Macy's have implemented this feature. Figure 13.17 provides an example of a comparison matrix implemented at Circuit City.com. The comparison feature allows the shopper to compare as many as five products at a time. Each column is a product and each row provides details regarding an attribute. Some implementations allow sorting the products based on the levels of a particular attribute. Comparison matrices can compare products across price and quality tiers or compare products within the same tier. This shopping tool does not require consumers to store detailed attribute information in memory.

Alternative formats to the comparison matrix include a brand-centric presentation, where each page contains detailed information on a brand; and an attribute-oriented presentation, a page for each attribute. Controlled experiments show that the nature of the format has a strong impact on how the information is processed. For example, a brand-oriented presentation leads to a strategy of processing by brands and an attribute-oriented presentation leads to a strategy of processing by attributes.[43]

> The Impact of Shopping Tools

Haubl and Trifts studied the effects of comparison matrices and shopping assistants in a series of controlled experiments. They hypothesized that shopping tools reduce the effort required and increase the accuracy of consumer decisions. In order to measure effort reduction, the researchers examined the number of alternatives considered and the amount of information

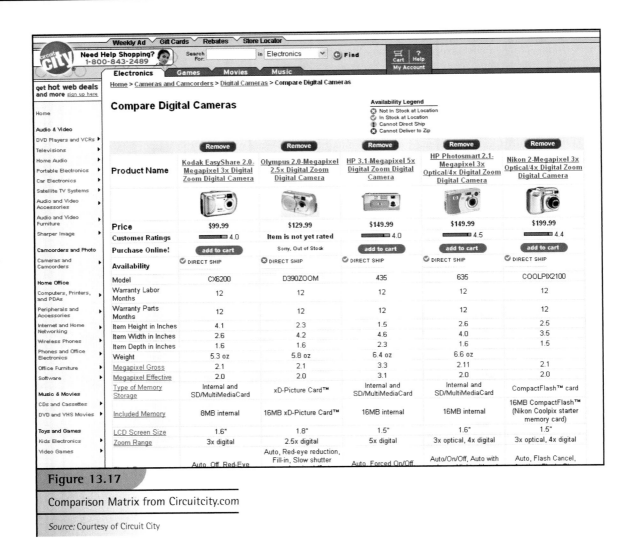

Figure 13.17

Comparison Matrix from Circuitcity.com

Source: Courtesy of Circuit City

used to evaluate alternatives. In order to measure accuracy, the researchers examined consumer confidence in the decision and their willingness to switch to another alternative after the decision.

The researchers found that the shopping tools do indeed have a strong impact, reducing effort and increasing accuracy. While their results indicate that both tools are useful, they find that a shopping assistant that screens products has the strongest impact on consumer accuracy.

> Place the Order

> The Checkout Process

The next step in the shopping cycle, after evaluating products and selecting a particular alternative, is to make the purchase. While this step should be simple, research studies show that a number of Internet shoppers fail to complete an attempted purchase. For example, one study[44]

Research Finding:
The Impact of Shopping Tools

Haubl and Trifts find that while both a shopping assistant and comparison matrix improve the shopping process and choice results, a shopping assistant has a much stronger impact on accuracy.

	Effort Reduction	Improvement in Accuracy
Shoppingnt	✓	✓✓✓
Comparison Matrix	✓	✓

Source: Gerald Haubl and Valerie Trifts, "Consumer Decision Making in Online Environments: The Effects of Decision Aids," *Marketing Science* 19, no. 1 (2000). Copyright © 2000, the Institute for Operations Research and the Management Sciences (INFORMS), 7240 Parkway Drive, Suite 310, Hanover, MD 21076 USA.

put this number as high as 43%. Another newsworthy statistic in Internet retailing is the number of abandoned shopping carts.

However, it is not clear that every abandoned cart means a lost sale. Some consumers use the shopping cart to create a shopping list. In other situations, consumers might just be recording their intent and postpone purchase of the item. Retailers can support this type of postponement behavior with features like wish lists or shopping lists that enable consumers to save their shopping cart for later completion. Providing wish lists can also help the retailer understand the "true" number and value of abandoned shopping baskets. In turn, this can help isolate specific issues due to a lack of functionality or problems in the checkout process.

Information design problems may result in artificially high abandonment rates. Some sites require a shopper to put in their credit card number, register, or submit other types of personal information before they provide shipping costs. Studies suggest these requirements inhibit shoppers.[45] Making shipping costs more transparent is a better solution.

Figure 13.18 provides an example of an enhanced shopping cart at the Watergate Hotel that combines animation software and well-designed information to augment the checkout process. There are three panels on this checkout page. Shoppers use the lefthand panel to select their check-in and check-out dates, to view room availability, and to input the number of guests. Shoppers use the middle panel to select the type of room, and to view a picture and details of the room and the typical average room rate. Once the shopper selects the type of room he or she is interested in, the calendar on the lefthand panel is automatically updated with availability and current pricing information for every day selected, including weekday and weekend rates. The right-most panel acts as a reservation form, providing a summary of the reservation with

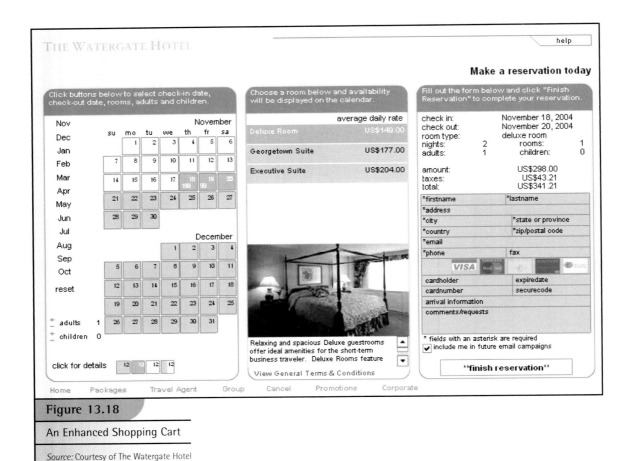

Figure 13.18

An Enhanced Shopping Cart

Source: Courtesy of The Watergate Hotel

automatic updates based on changes made to the other two panels. As this example illustrates, enhanced shopping carts improve the ease of shopping and checkout in situations where the product or service involves multiple options and configurations.[46]

> Efficient Reordering and Routine Purchases

The nature of the shopping task determines the extent of information search. Very little information is necessary for repurchase of routine items or the refilling of a prescription. The ideal shopping process consists of finding the item and placing the order. This same scenario can occur even if it is not a repurchase. The consumer might have shopped in a store, made a choice, and now might want to place the order online.

Recognizing this type of shopping need, Amazon.com created a feature called 1-Click® ordering. One click ordering is available for shoppers who have an account with the retailer. After logging in to their account, shoppers can turn on one click ordering and proceed to shop at the site. A special button appears on every product page (Figure 13.19). Information stored in the shopper's profile automatically determines the preferred payment option and shipping address. Amazon also groups all orders placed within 90 minutes to minimize shipping charges.

Catalog retailers have created a feature on their Internet sites called catalog quick order. A consumer, after shopping the catalog, can order on the web site by typing product codes in the catalog quick order box, then creating a shopping cart and placing the order. This type of feature can reduce the time it takes a consumer to place an order and minimize transaction costs. The retailer can also benefit by not incurring call center costs.

A further benefit of quick ordering comes from the marketing accountability it helps foster. The simplest approach creates a unique match between catalog mailed and the product ordered. For example, a catalog marketer might use 14 different catalogs throughout the year, with different designs and product assortment. A unique code for the catalog can help identify the best and worst performing catalogs. A cycle of improvement based on these measurements can dramatically improve the R.O.I. of the catalog process.

Figure 13.19

1-Click® Ordering on Amazon.com

> *Post-Purchase Notifications and Returns*

> Post-Purchase Notifications

In a physical store, shoppers typically take immediate possession of their merchandise once they pay. With online purchasing there is a time delay between placing the order and receiving the merchandise. This delay creates some additional issues for the shopper. Important details include order confirmation, total price, shipping date, and expected delivery date.

Internet retailers have developed a number of techniques directed at reducing post-purchase uncertainty. Immediately upon receipt of the order, most sites create an individualized invoice, listing these details. Confirmation emails provide a more durable record and can occasionally reveal fraudulent orders. Further emails might provide an update on the actual shipping date, delivery status, and tracking codes. Providing these updates requires coordination of shipping and handling details, linking them to the customer's order.

> Returns

A final aspect of the shopping process is the difficult issue of returns. Returns can be quite expensive, yet without an adequate returns process shoppers may balk from ordering. Given the touch and feel limitations of the Internet for some types of merchandise, shoppers may remain uncertain about what they have bought until they actually receive the merchandise and they get to touch and feel it. Anticipating this concern, some retailers emphasize return information prominently in their shopping baskets to overcome last-minute buyer hesitation.

A common technique facilitating returns by catalogers is to include a prepaid return label with an order. Some retailers even have arrangements with delivery services so that the shopper can call and schedule a merchandise pickup. Multi-channel retailers have the additional opportunity of offering customers the option of returning merchandise at any store location. However, in order to implement store returns, store information systems need to have the capability to recognize the product codes and receipts issued by the web site.

MULTI-CHANNEL RETAILING

| Multi-Channel Shopping Behavior

In their book stressing the impact of consumers using multi-channels for their shopping and information collection, Wind, Mahajan, and Gunther refer to these consumers as "centaurs."[47] Centaurs were the mythic combination of horse and man. The centaur captures the spirit of speed, while still having intelligence and cunning. The centaur is the hybrid consumer willing to shop online and buy in a store, or conversely, trying an item at the mall and going online for a different brand or better price. Jones and Spiegel, in their look at the impact of hybrid shopping, also resort to mythology, this time Mars and Venus, to reflect the differing perspectives of marketing personnel and IT staff necessary to make an integrated online retail approach work well.[48]

The iPACE model provides the dimensions by which online or physical outlets provide these "centaurs" with a better option. Consumers can benefit by mixing channels, using whatever channel best meets their current shopping needs.

> *Cross-Channel Buying and Influence*

Purchase experience provides one measure of the frequency of multi-channel shopping. Table 13.4 presents data from an industry study focused demonstrating the relative tendencies of shoppers to use multiple channels.[49] The study classified shoppers as buying primarily from one of three channels—Online, Store, and Catalog. For example, the first row of the table represent shoppers classified as primarily online. The second row are those shoppers that rely most heavily on physical stores, and the third row are primarily catalog.

Physical store shoppers are the least likely to use multiple channels. While 22% of "primarily store" also use a catalog, only 6% also shop online. This is the least centaur-like consumer group.

Both "primarily online" and "primarily catalog shoppers" are much more likely to rely on other channels for some of their purchases. Online shoppers (78%) reported buying at the retailer's stores. Forty-five percent of online buyers also purchased through the retailer's catalog channel. Catalog buyers also purchased at the retailers online channels (23%) and at the store (36%). Store shoppers were less likely to exhibit multi-channel buying with only 6% reporting buying from the online channel and 22% reporting buying from the retailer's catalog channel.

The situation is more symmetric and more centaur-like when the question is influence rather than purchase. For example, a shopper might see a product featured on the cover of a retailer's catalog and may purchase this product from a nearby store. A second example is that of a shopper who sees a product on the cover of a catalog and then purchases it online. A third example is that of a shopper who sees a product in a store, finds that the store is out of stock in her size, and purchases the product online.

The most significant cross-channel influences are between catalog and online channels. An impressive 68% of

Table 13.4

Percentage of Customers from One Channel Who Purchased in Another Channel			
Shopper Classification	% Purchasing in Channel		
	Online	Store	Catalog
Online	100%	78%	45%
Store	6%	100%	22%
Catalog	23%	36%	100%

Source: The State of Retail Online, 5.0, Shop.org.

Some Cross-Channel Customer Activities

> Browse the store flyer online
> Find store locations online
> Look up store inventory

> Schedule a pickup in the store
> Make a return to the store
> Create and manage gift registries

online buyers reported buying something that they had previously seen in the retailer's catalog. Thirty-nine percent of catalog buyers reported buying something that they had previously seen online. Table 13.5 also shows significant cross-channel influences between the store and catalog and between the store and online channels.

Tables 13.4 and 13.5 highlight the behavior of these multi-channel shoppers. A different view is their preference for a particular channel. Figure 13.20 finds some interesting patterns when these consumers were surveyed about where they prefer to perform their buying or research. A preference for online research is quite strong with both online and store shoppers, with catalog shoppers more neutral. Buying preference, however, follows a much more polarized pattern.

Consumers engage in a number of other cross-channel activities that retailers can support.[50] Consumers look at a retailer's weekly flyers or circulars online. Consumers also use retailers' web sites to find out if a specific item is in stock at a particular location before going to make a purchase. Consumers also look at catalogs online. Since these activities seem simple, it is easy to ignore them or to underestimate their importance and the frequency with which they occur. Recognizing this need, a retailer like Target allows consumers to browse the weekly ad flyer on Target.com. Target gives the online weekly ad flyer a prominent placement at the top of its homepage.

Table 13.5

Percentage of Buyers Who Purchased Something in One Channel Previously Seen in Another Channel

Shopper Classification	% Reporting a Purchase Influenced By		
	Online	Store	Catalog
Online	100%	25%	68%
Store	22%	100%	26%
Catalog	39%	26%	100%

Source: Company reports as compiled by Forward Retailing, Inc.

Multi-Channel Challenges

One of the challenges for multi-channel retailers is determining what products to carry in regular retail stores, what products to carry online, and what products to feature in the catalog. In

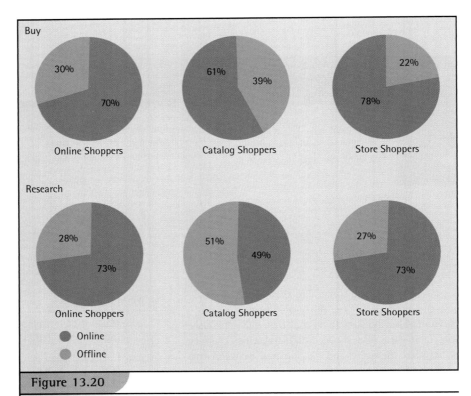

Figure 13.20

Percentage of Shopper Groups Indicating a Channel Preference for Research and Buying

Source: The State of Retail Online, 5.0, Shop.org

some cases, the freedom from space constraints and costly inventory leads to many more choices online. In other situations it is the online outlet with a more limited selection.

Retail space is a key cost driver for store-based retailing, but not for Internet retailing. Store-based retailers can offer an expanded assortment of colors and sizes online. Apparel retailers such as the Gap advertise and rely on their Gap.com outlet for a wider array of sizes, styles, and items than their physical outlets (Figure 13.21). Best Buy puts more limited market appeal products online, so they do not have to support them throughout their physical stores. Discontinued items may find their final sales location online for the same reason.

In some product categories, bulky items, legal restrictions, and contractual arrangements limit the online assortment. Online pharmacies face all three problems. Physical pharmacies often include bulky paper products, alcohol, tobacco, and prescription pharmaceuticals. Online pharmacies carry a more limited assortment. They drop low-value bulky items because of shipping costs. Legal and age restrictions make it challenging to send alcohol and tobacco. Pharmaceuticals may be restricted because of existing contracts, as a number of insurance plans limit online prescription reimbursement to contracted online fulfillment centers. For companies such as CVS or Walgreens, the Internet channel has an edited assortment compared to a typical store.

A substantial difference between online and offline channels can complicate communication and logistics. Online-only products limit the usefulness of in-store pickup. Physical store-only

Figure 13.21

Expanded Assortment at Gap.com

Source: ©David Young-Wolff/Photo Edit

products limit the usefulness of online research, or create online products that allow research but no online ordering.

While assortment creates a challenge of consistency, the pricing problem is even more difficult. Zone pricing, where a retail chain quotes different regional prices for the same product, is a reality in many physical retail outlets. Markets vary in costs, competition, and price sensitivity, leading to price variation. This can create some tension, which becomes much more of a problem with an online channel. If the company adopts a national price, it may be higher than some zone prices. If a company tries to retain zone pricing, it faces the difficulty of listing prices online. Staples requests consumers provide their Zip code prior to quoting prices or displaying advertised specials. Difficulties emerge when a shopper tries different Zip codes and receives a different quote, not just determined by shipping cost or tax rates.

Promotions such as bundle pricing, buy one get one free, free maintenance, and so on are difficult. Implementing these promotions uniformly in all channels can also be complex. Unexpected differences between demand and supply create pricing and promotional opportunities in certain channels. For example, a catalog retailer might face excess inventory in a product category. Catalog production cycles preclude quickly reacting to this type of situation. A quick response on the Internet site or by an email blast are more timely alternatives. Similarly end-of-season markdowns and clearances need a timely pricing response. Some retailers have created a markdown section on their web sites so that clearance merchandise is always available to consumers. Figure 13.22 illustrates the clearance markdown section on the web site of Wehkamp, a catalog- and Internet-retailer based in the Netherlands.

Multiple channels may also be difficult to reward appropriately. As seen in Tables 13.4 and 13.5, many shoppers research in one channel and buy in another. It is difficult to adequately reward the research channel, and the purchasing outlet may receive undue credit for the sale. Using sales as a measure of the value added by a channel can create distortions. Multi-channel retailers need to have measurements and compensation schemes in place that correctly recognize the contribution of a channel so that they can mitigate channel conflict. This form of "free-riding" is even more problematic when management or ownership differs across channels, as discussed in Chapter 14.

Figure 13.22

Using the Internet for Markdowns

Source: Courtesy of Wehkamp

ENDNOTES

1. For an in-depth discussion of retailing productivity worldwide, see William Lewis, *The Power of Productivity*, (Chicago: University of Chicago Press, 2004).

2. Comscore Networks, November 2004.

3. See, for example, Hoover.com's profile of Best Buy. Accessed February 2005.

4. "Best Buy relaunch crowns long-term multi-channel strategy," *Internet Retailer*, Thursday, August 14, 2003.

5. "Quarterly Retail E-Commerce Sales: 4th Quarter 2005," U. S. Department of Commerce News. Available at www.census.gov/estats.

6. Wal-Mart 2005 Annual Report, p. 51. U.S. Wal-Mart sales are $191.8 billion in 2005 (page 17). Sam's Club was $37.1 (page 19), and Wal-Mart International was $56.3 billion (page 21).

7. For a discussion of attributes of product categories that make them more or less suited for Internet retailing, see Thomas Eisenmann and Alastair Brown, Online Retailers, *Harvard Business School* Note, 2000: 9-801-306.

8. James Crawford, *E-Retail Economics: Multi-Channel Rules.* Retail Forward (2002): 10.

9. See www.theacsi.org

10. Jupiter Research, "U.S. Automotive Forecast, 2004 to 2009," February 2005.

11. For example, I. Sinha, "Cost Transparency: The Net's Real Threat to Prices and Brands," *Harvard Business Review,* 2000.

12. The iPace framework extends the traditional retailing approach. For an example, see Michael Levy and Barton Weitz, *Retailing Management,* 5th ed. (Boston: McGraw Hill, 2004). This discusses the retailing mix, which contains many of these retailing basics.

13. For example see Barry Babin, William R. Darden, and Mitch Griffin, "Work and/or Fun: Measuring Hedonic and Utilitarian Shopping Value." *Journal of Consumer Research* 20 (March 1994): 644–656.

14. John R. Hauser and Birger Wernerfelt, "An Evaluation Cost Model of Consideration Sets," *Journal of Consumer Research* 16, no. 4: 393–408.

15. "Bombay's Web Site Takes the Surprise out of Assembly Required," Internet Retailer, Thursday, November 11, 2004.

16. Phillip Nelson, "Information and Consumer Behavior," *Journal of Political Economy* 78: 311–329.

17. For a discussion of a decomposition of shopping costs into fixed and variable components, see David R Bell, Teck-Hua Ho, and Christopher S. Tang, "Determining Where to Shop: Fixed and Variable Costs of Shopping," *Journal of Marketing Research* 35 (August 1998).

18. Erik Brynjolfsson and Michael Smith, "The Great Equalizer? Consumer Choice Behavior at Internet Shopbots." Sloan working paper, 4208-01, October 2001.

19. Dipanker Chakravarti, Rajan Krish, Pallab Paul, and Joydeep Srinvastava, "Partitioned Presentation of Multicomponent Bundle Prices: Evaluation, Choice and Underlying Processing Effects," *Journal of Consumer Psychology* 12, no. 3: 215–229.

20. Ravi Dhar and Itamar Simonson, "The Effect of Forced Choice on Choice," *Journal of Marketing Research* XL (May 2003): 146–160.

21. As of 1/1/2005, Federation of Tax Administrators, www.taxadmin.org.

22. Austan Goolsbee, "In a World Without Borders: The Impact of Taxes on Internet Commerce," University of Chicago: Graduate School of Business and N.B.E.R., November 1998.

23. Shipping cost references here.

24. Satish Jindel, "E-commerce's Mixed Blessings," *TrafficWorld* (February 1, 1999): 47–48.

25. Both UPS and FedEx have publicly expressed concerns about the shift to home delivery. A spokesman for UPS commented, "We're just covering costs on residential delivery. We know we have to be ready for growth in residential deliveries. The answers aren't easy; they may even be painful." A business-to-business division of FedEx commented, "The real difficulty in residential delivery is how to make a buck". See Larry Kahaner, "Is trucking ready for Internet deliveries?" *Fleet Owner* 93, no. 12 (December 1999): 63–65.

26. Erik Brynjolfsson, Yu Hu, and Michael Smith, "Consumer Surplus in the Digital Economy: Estimating the Value of Increased Product Variety at Online Booksellers," *Management Science* 49, no. 11 (November 2003): 1580–1596.

27. Implicit in the specific approach used by Brynjolfsson et. al. is equal shopping cost between online and offline. As discussed in the section on convenience, online shopping may be more convenient. Thus, the authors observe that the estimate of Internet price savings in the study may be somewhat low.

28. Nick Wingfield, "E-tailing comes of age," *Wall Street Journal* (December 8, 2003).

29. "More consumers started holiday shopping earlier this year than last," *Internet Retailer,* December 9, 2003.

30. Thomas Weber, "Making the Sale – Nothing to Sniff At: How Fragrance Counter has managed to overcome the obvious obstacles and become an online success," *Wall Street Journal* (December 7, 1999).

31. Elizabeth C. Hirschmann and Morris B. Holbrook, "Hedonic consumption: Emerging concepts, methods and propositions," *Journal of Marketing* 46, no. 3, (1983): 92–101.

32. Tina Kelley, "Buying Is Only a Click (Oops!) Away," *New York Times* (February 11, 1999).

33. Paco Underhill, *Why We Buy: The Science of Shopping* (New York: Simon & Schuster, 1999), especially Chapter 9.

34. For example see Jagdish Sheth, Banwari Mittal, and Bruce Newman, *Customer Behavior: Consumer Behavior and Beyond.* (Orlando: Dryden Press, 1999), 520.

35. *DMnews.com,* E-tailers missing big sales, December 12, 2000.

36. Patricia Seybold, "Get Inside the Lives of Your Customers," *Harvard Business Review* (May 2001): 80–89.

37. Personal communication with Gene Domecus, V.P. eCommerce, Macys.com, November 2003.

38. www.circuitcity.com

39. New data from Lands' End shows value of Virtual Model™ Technology, My Virtual Model™ Press Release, September 25, 2001. The press release does not provide the details of the sampling scheme used in the study.

40. Underhill, op. cit., p. 115.

41. Steven M. Shugan, "The Cost of Thinking," *Journal of Consumer Research* 7 (September 1980): 99–111.

42. Some of the material in this section is adapted from Gerald Haubl and Valerie Trifts, "Consumer Decision Making in Online Environments: The Effects of Decision Aids," *Marketing Science* 19, no. 1, (2000): 4–21. They investigate two decision aids, a recommendation agent (which we call a shopping assistant), and a comparison matrix.

43. James R. Bettman and Pradeep Kakkar, "Effects of Information Presentation Format on Consumer Information Acquisition Strategies," *Journal of Consumer Research* 3 (March 1977): 233–240.

44. Research by the Boston Consulting Group. Cited in www.thestandard.com. Close encounters with E-Commerce, April 3, 2000.

45. Randy K. Souza, *The Best of Retail Site Design*, Forrester Research, October 2000.

46. Marcelo Prince, "Online Retailers Turn to New Shopping Carts to Drive Sales," *Wall Street Journal* (November 9, 2004).

47. Yoram Wind, Vijay Mahajan, and Robert Gunther, *Convergence Marketing: Strategies for Reaching the New Hybrid Consumer.* (New Jersey: Prentice Hall, 2002).

48. Susan Jones and Ted Spiegel, *Marketing Convergence: How the Leading Companies are Profiting from Integrating Online and Offline Marketing Strategies.* (Mason: Thomson, 2003).

49. The Multi Channel Retail Report Executive Summary, Shop.org, 2001.

50. James Crawford, ibid, 9: 2002.

chapter 14

Consumer Channels

> **❝** New distribution channels change who the customers are. They change not only how customers buy but also what they buy. They change consumer behavior, savings pattern, industry structure—in short, the entire economy. **❞**
>
> Peter Drucker[1]

> **❝** For traditional manufacturers, channel conflict is the thorniest issue of all on the Internet. **❞**
>
> Mary Modahl[2]

Web Sales Click for the Travel Industry

The travel industry is no stranger to electronic commerce.[3] Even before the arrival of the Internet, airlines, hotels, and car rental companies were selling tickets directly to travelers using telephone call centers. Many companies relied on their call center as an important direct sales channel. At the same time, they sold tickets through travel agents.

The arrival of the Internet provided the travel industry with an additional ecommerce boost (Table 14.1). Digital delivery of travel tickets via the Internet eliminates the costs of printing and mailing. Internet direct sales reduce distribution costs by eliminating fees and agent commissions. A direct connection to travelers allows firms to promote their frequent traveler programs more easily and to learn about travel shopping behavior.

From 1998 to 1999, the online travel market grew from $2.6 billion to about $7 billion with over 70% of these online ticket sales going to leisure travelers. A new class of online travel agents, firms such as Expedia and Travelocity, accounted for a significant proportion of these sales. While these sites have many benefits for users, they do not necessarily connect travel providers, such as the airlines, more directly to consumers. The major airlines responded with Orbitz, an online multi-carrier site booking flights, hotels, and rental cars. At the same time, individual airlines were strengthening their own direct booking capabilities.

this chapter

This chapter investigates consumer channels from the perspective of manufacturers and service providers. Opportunities exist for providers to improve the consumer shopping process, to better support retailers, and to use the Net as an entry into direct to consumer sales.

Topics covered in this chapter include:

> Consumer Channels and the Net

> Net-enabled Channel Opportunities

> Selling Direct and Channel Conflict

> Expanding Markets

Table 14.1

Internet Ticket Sales: Key Statistics about the Travel Industry	
% of U.S. adult population using the Internet for travel planning FY 2004	30%
% of U.S. adult population booking at least one travel service FY 2004	21%
% of Internet travel bookings on supplier web sites FY 2004	56%
Reduction in average travel commissions FY 1996 to FY 2001	41%

Source: Adapted and based on data compiled from industry reports.

By the third half of 2000, the airlines' efforts were paying off. A travel industry study reported that online sales increased to 9% of all travel revenue from 2% a year earlier. Further, the airlines' own web sites accounted for 58% of all Internet air-travel bookings. Analysts estimate that travel commissions declined from 8.7% of passenger revenue in 1996 to 5.1% in 2001, saving approximately $6 billion in commissions during this period.

Like the airlines, hotels initially moved onto the Internet with booking services on their own sites. From 2000 to 2003, the percentage of online bookings rose from less than 5% to about 13%. The new online travel agents were at the forefront of this trend. They invested in creating an online presence and obtained the ability to take large blocks of rooms to consumers.

The success of the online travel agents has attracted competition from the hotels themselves. One industry study found that every room sold through an intermediary lowers the margins that a hotel operator earns by 40%. Many hotel chains urged their franchisees not to dump their excess inventories on the online travel agents' web sites. Price matching guarantees and restrictions on frequent purchase points also encourage travelers to book directly. For example, Choice hotels announced that if a traveler finds a lower price on a web site other than the hotel's own, it would undercut the lower price by 10%. Taking a page from Orbitz, some leading hotel chains created the Hotel Distribution Network and Travelweb.com to compete against Expedia and Hotels.com. This web site boasts a direct electronic link to the central reservations systems of participating hotel chains and automated confirmation capabilities. An important difference in the hotel industry is the presence of many small and independent hotels eager to create a method for booking rooms online.

Hotels and online brokers are learning to cooperate with one another for mutual benefit. Some hotel chains such as Starwood and Marriott have signed agreements with online travel agents, giving them direct electronic access to their centralized reservation systems. In return, the hotel chains have asked their franchisees to refrain from dumping their rooms directly onto the web sites of the online travel agents. This allows the hotel chains to retain centralized visibility of inventory and retain the ability to conduct yield management.

The effects of airlines and hotels offering their lowest fares online can be complex. Posting low fares highlights how the travel industry is willing to offer some guests very low prices. This can breed unhappiness for full-fare travelers and can sensitize the market to price. It complicates yield management, a key feature of revenue management.

The travel industry highlights the powerful and disruptive effects of the Internet onto channels of distribution. The Internet is an especially cost-effective distribution channel for digital products such as tickets, music, movies, and software. The Internet can also have a powerful channel impact even for products not suited for digital delivery. The Internet enables direct sales—producers selling directly to end users. Producers can reach existing customers using new intermediaries such as Internet travel agents. For information-intensive and high-involvement products, the Internet can facilitate presales support. Using the Internet, producers can expand markets and more effectively conduct closeout sales.

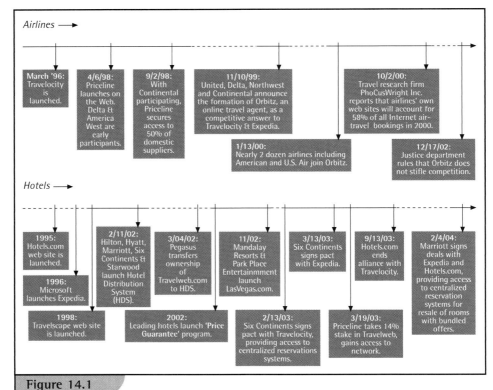

Figure 14.1

A Timeline of the Evolution of Internet Distribution in the Travel Industry

CONSUMER CHANNELS AND THE INTERNET

Overview

A marketing channel is a set of interdependent organizations involved in the process of making a product or service available for use or consumption.[4] Consumer marketing channels include producers of the product, intermediaries specializing in logistics, distribution, and assortment, and consumers. The most basic role of the marketing channel is making products available for purchase. Often, the channel is where a consumer discovers a product, learns about it, compares it with competitive offerings, and understands its relative positioning and value. When problems arise, the channel provides service, maintenance, and returns.

Figure 14.2 shows increasingly indirect channel configurations. The direct channel, with no intermediaries between the producer and the consumer, is the simplest. As a channel adds levels of intermediaries, it becomes longer and more difficult for a producer to influence. After designing the channel, producers orchestrate a number of flows through channels such as information, product, orders, credit, and risk.

A very different picture emerges if the focus is on the number of contacts as opposed to the number of intermediaries. Figure 14.3 captures one of the most important standard arguments for using an indirect channel. Direct distribution requires consumers and providers to deal directly with each other. This means many contacts, with each provider dealing with each customer. If there are 50 providers and 1 million customers, this is 50*1,000,000 = 50,000,000 contacts.

Now introduce a retail intermediary that can reach the entire market. Each of the 50 providers must interact with the retailer, and each of the million customers deals with the retailer. This reduces the number of contacts to 50 + 1,000,000 = 1,000,050 contacts. This is a dramatic reduction of effort, especially for providers but also for customers.

This simple math is true for online channels, but the costs and benefits of contact are very different. Contact costs are high in the physical world but lower online. Companies can afford a wider span of contact with customers.

Simplicity in Figure 14.2 means a direct channel, with few intermediaries and their associated costs. Simplicity in Figure 14.3 means wholesalers and retailers, reducing the total number of contacts dramatically. The tensions between Figures 14.2 and 14.3 are one of the reasons that Modahl finds channel conflict one of the "thorniest issues" for manufacturers. There is no easy solution, yet the opportunities and changes caused by the Internet are too big to ignore.

Channel Design

Deciding to go direct or to use intermediaries is one of the most fundamental issues in the design of marketing channels. A make or buy decision framework is useful in analyzing this

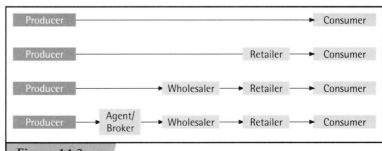

Figure 14.2

Typical Business-to-Consumer Channels

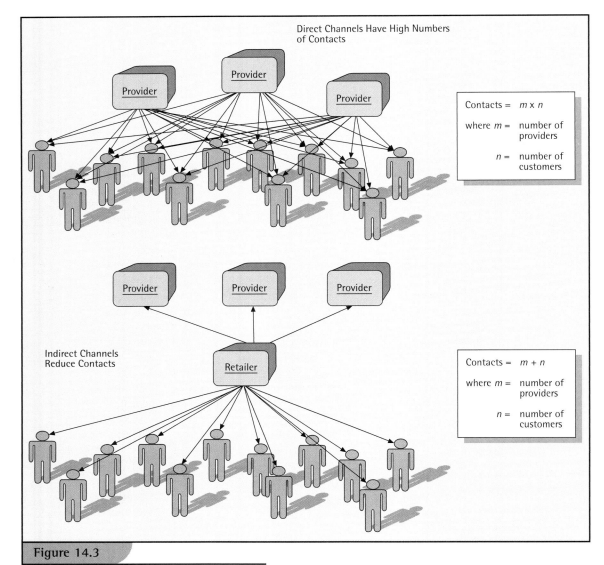

Direct Channels Have High Numbers of Contacts

Contacts = $m \times n$

where m = number of providers

n = number of customers

Indirect Channels Reduce Contacts

Contacts = $m + n$

where m = number of providers

n = number of customers

Figure 14.3

Intermediaries Reduce Total Number of Contacts

decision.[5] The standard answer combines an analysis of consumer requirements for service outputs with a make or buy analysis of the most effective manner of providing those services.

> *iPACE and Channel Services*

The iPACE discussion in the previous chapter captures the basic channel requirements of consumers. Reviewing these in a channel context helps in channel design decisions.[6]

> *Information:* Consumers seek information during the shopping process. This includes information on the product, comparison to other products, and compatibility. Consumers

seek a high level of information particularly for products that are new, are technically complicated, or have a rapidly changing technical component. When information needs are high, transmission of information to consumers via intermediaries can be complicated and error prone.

> *Price Sensitivity:* Channel design can both affect and reflect shopper price sensitivity. For highly price-sensitive categories, efficiency will drive the design. In addition, the presence of aggressive retailers such as Wal-Mart shapes the channel decisions of other market participants.

> *Assortment:* Assortment refers to a broad range of products across categories (breadth) or within a product category (depth). A family with children might have a large shopping basket because of the need to purchase goods for different family members. In this case, breadth of assortment gives consumers the benefits of one-stop shopping. Consumers may require breadth so that they can assemble a complementary bundle all under one roof. Consumers may need depth so that they can compare multiple alternatives and multiple providers.

> *Customization:* Many products require modification to fit the needs of the consumer. Alternations or adjustments are a good example of the type of customization that occurs in retail channels. Personal computers are available in several different configurations of memory, hard drive size, and processor speed. The manufacturing process at a factory might be more effective for this type of customization.

> *Convenience:* Some buying situations require a high degree of convenience and immediate product availability. Last-minute gifts, prescription drugs for acute care, or ingredients for an immediate meal all require rapid distribution. Consumers prefer channels with immediate availability when consumption needs are uncertain.

> *Entertainment:* Style-oriented manufacturers may want a direct channel to provide an experience to consumers. Nike, Sony, and Apple all use a physical outlet to surround their brands with expertise and ambience while also providing other channel services.

Figure 14.4 illustrates the standard channel services reconsidered in light of the Internet. While the Internet is indeed very capable of providing rich information, it is less suited for questions of

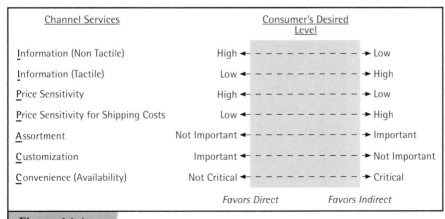

Channel Services	Consumer's Desired Level	
Information (Non Tactile)	High ← – – – – – – – – →	Low
Information (Tactile)	Low ← – – – – – – – – →	High
Price Sensitivity	High ← – – – – – – – – →	Low
Price Sensitivity for Shipping Costs	Low ← – – – – – – – – →	High
Assortment	Not Important ← – – – – – – – →	Important
Customization	Important ← – – – – – – – →	Not Important
Convenience (Availability)	Not Critical ← – – – – – – – →	Critical
	Favors Direct	*Favors Indirect*

Figure 14.4

Internet Impact on Channel Services

touch-and-feel. Price sensitivity can differ for product and shipping. While in some cases a simpler channel helps avoid intermediary costs, it also introduces shipping costs. As seen in the personalization chapter, mass customization favors a direct connection. Each of these services is easier or more difficult to provide depending on channel configuration. Balancing these tradeoffs leads to the make or buy decision.

> *The Make or Buy Decision*

Channel intermediaries subject to competitive forces often provide the best solution for a producer. Channel researchers suggest that a manufacturer should presume that channel outsourcing is more attractive than vertical integration.[7] For example, retailing is a notoriously competitive business and can provide highly efficient channel activities. Going direct must provide sufficient benefits to overcome this hurdle.

Even when serious performance problems exist, a fully direct channel may not be necessary. Cosmetics manufacturers partially integrate forward by providing their own sales associates, but they rent or buy the space from the department store. From a consumer's viewpoint the full assortment and convenience of the department store remains, while the manufacturer can ensure proper information and support.

Implicit in the make or buy decision is an analysis of channel compensation. The most basic form of compensation is to provide a margin on the product sold. However, manufacturers often provide other funds, such as merchandise development funds, and cooperative advertising to channel members to motivate the channel to provide other services.

The Internet alters channel economics and expands the range of channel alternatives. The Internet provides many more producers with a low-cost direct consumer connection. New classes of Internet-based intermediaries are available. In addition, existing intermediaries adapt to the Internet and change how they interact with consumers. Figure 14.5a illustrates these expanded

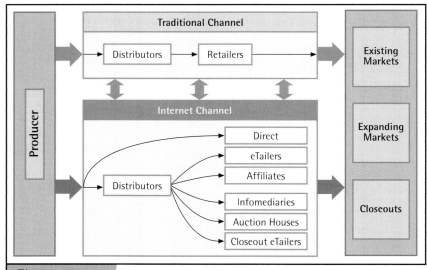

Figure 14.5a

The Internet Channel Complements and Extends the Traditional Channel options.[8] New classes of online intermediaries include online retailers, or eTailers, affiliate networks, infomediaries, online auction houses, and closeout eTailers. These can better reach existing customers, expand markets, and implement closeout sales.

Traditional and Internet channels are interconnected, both in terms of product and information flows. An automobile buyer can visit an infomediary like Edmunds, obtain information, then go to another intermediary such as Auto-by-Tel to locate a dealer who has the model in stock, and end up buying a car from a traditional automobile dealer. The Internet channel complements and extends the traditional channel. Figure 14.5b illustrates some of the new channel capabilities and issues that arise when distributing online.

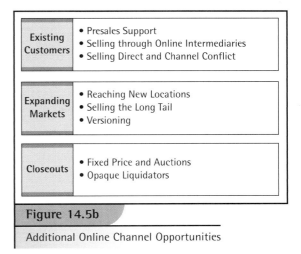

Existing Customers	• Presales Support • Selling through Online Intermediaries • Selling Direct and Channel Conflict
Expanding Markets	• Reaching New Locations • Selling the Long Tail • Versioning
Closeouts	• Fixed Price and Auctions • Opaque Liquidators

Figure 14.5b

Additional Online Channel Opportunities

EXISTING CUSTOMERS

Presales Information

Traditional indirect channels give producers few opportunities to provide in-depth information directly to consumers. Unless already selling direct, information must filter through the distribution channel to consumers. Serious gaps and omissions are common.

Intense retailer competition can aggravate this problem as retailers cut back on customer service, sales associates training, and other forms of presales information to lower retail costs. Online activities by manufacturers or other intermediaries can partially offset these cutbacks and improve customer satisfaction with the entire purchase process. Manufacturers can assist shoppers in the shopping cycle demonstrated in Figure 13.11, either directly at their own web sites or by supporting the information activities of channel members.

The consumer automobile market illustrates many of these trends. Automakers have seen shopping behavior change dramatically. Prior to the Internet, consumers rated buying a car as one of their worst experiences. High-pressure sales tactics at dealerships and a lack of accurate information on product pricing and features contributed to negative customer reactions.

Online information has changed auto buying. J.D. Power reports over 60% of new car buyers used the Internet; with some brands, over 80% of buyers use the Internet (see Table 14.2). There has been a dramatic shift in the balance of power between consumers and automobile dealers. An online automobile shopper can shop at a manufacturer's web site, a third-party web site such as Consumer Reports or Edmunds, a combination sales and information site such as Auto-by-Tel, or a web site of a traditional auto dealer. A much more comprehensive view of the marketplace, available options, and prevailing prices is possible.

Table 14.2

Internet Use by Automobile Buyers	
Brand	**% of Buyers Using the Internet**
Acura	82
Audi	82
Porsche	81
BMW	81
Volkswagen	78
Industry Average	60
Dodge	52
Mercury	51
Lincoln	41
Cadillac	41
Buick	39

Source: Adapted and based on data from J.D. Power and Associates and Autoshoper.com (2002).

.> Manufacturer's Web Site

A manufacturer's web site is a natural place for consumers to learn about products. Consumers can learn about the entire product line. For each product, they can research standard features, product performance information, service, and warranty. Solution guides and configurators help shoppers identify which products best fit their requirements.[9]

In some cases manufacturers even bring competitive products into the mix to provide a more comprehensive research environment. Credibility and completeness are a concern for shoppers visiting manufacturer web sites.

> Third-Party Sites

As seen in Chapter 7, independent sites tend to have higher credibility with consumers. In the automobile market, consumers prefer by a margin of 3 to 1 to go to third-party web sites that provide information on a full range of auto brands.[10] In addition to credibility, third-party sites may have more flexible information presentation, in-depth reviews of latest trends and offerings from all manufacturers, information on products not yet on the marketplace that are worth waiting for, and other material unlikely to exist on any particular manufacturer's site.[11]

In addition to increased satisfaction, online auto information saves consumers valuable shopping time and leads to a better purchase price. Comparing pre- and post-Internet auto shopping results, one study found a benefit of $322 per car. Saved time accounted for $38 of the savings, with the remaining $294 in lower price. Other researchers have found even bigger savings.[12]

In the automobile industry, the quality and multiplicity of sources for obtaining information online have dramatically improved. Consumers can obtain information from manufacturers' web sites, multiple infomediaries, and a number of dealer web sites. According to the National Association of Automobile Dealers, over 90% of automobile dealers are using the Web to interact with their customers.[13] For a majority of new car buyers, the Net is at the heart of their car buying process. For brands that appeal to younger and more educated buyers, the number is even higher. For example, Table 14.2 shows that about 82% of Acura buyers used the Internet for gathering information online.

| Selling Through Online Intermediaries

Producers need not create a direct sales network to receive some of the benefits of online retailing. Instead, they can encourage their current channel to add online retailing to their retailing system. The previous discussion highlighted how presale support helps consumers. There are also

Research Finding:
The Confusing Web of Auto Industry Web Sites

More than 2,000 web sites cover automobile buying, in a wide mix of presale support. Urban and Hoffer find the "virtual dealership" has not arisen, with many diverse sources of information concentrated at one location. Despite benefits of a composite site, business strategies and regulation appear to be blocking its development.

Manufacturer Sites

> Collect information about desired model and options
> Compute suggested retail price of vehicle
> Order a catalog, find a dealer
> Observe concept cars
> Request a dealer quote

Dealers

> Provide dealer description, hours, location, etc.
> Inventory searches
> Email and chat for questions
> Set up test drives
> Provide leasing information
> Arrange vehicle pickup

Informers

> Report model reviews and technical specifications
> List dealer invoice and suggested retail prices
> Report safety data, insurance, and theft statistics
> Provide dealer locations

Advisors

> Offer lessons in vehicle buying
> Suggest most economical purchases: new vs. used, lease vs. purchase, trade-in or sell, size of down payment
> Calculate loan and lease payments
> Calculate appropriate auto expenses for budget
> Recommend accessories

Servers and Ancillary Servicers

> Act as purchasing agent
> Advertise used vehicles
> Bring buyers and sellers together
> Provide service contracts, insurance, additional items.

Sources: "Research Finding: The Confusing Web of Auto Industry Web Sites" – "The Virtual Automotive Dealership Revisited", David J Urban; George E Hoffer – *Journal of Consumer Marketing* (2003, Vol.20, No.6) © MCB UP Limited http://www.emeraldinsight.com/jcm.htm

efficiencies and benefits when manufacturers support channel partners' online activities and encourage innovative online retailer formats.

> *Online Retailer Support*

> Web-Ready Merchandise

Manufacturers can support Internet retailers with "web-ready" merchandise. The roots of web-ready merchandise lie in its physical store counterpart called floor-ready merchandise. Manufacturers add price tags and labels to make merchandise floor ready. Floor-ready merchandise can be unpacked and displayed with little additional work.

Similarly, merchandise is web ready when the producer provides descriptions, suggestions, search terms, promotional messages, and digital images that a retailer can readily load onto its web page. For example, Danskin has set up a section on its web site where retailers can download product logos and images for its women's fitness apparel. Lowering stocking and shipping costs helps online retailers include low sales rate items into their assortment.

Apart from product descriptions, the producer might consider including suggestions regarding special occasion promotions. For example, the Vermont Teddy Bear company might include text or tags that position the Teddy Bear as a Valentine's Day gift. The company could also include a sentence or two that describes why the Teddy Bear is an excellent gift for Valentine's Day and suggest search terms or key words.

> Supply Chain Coordination

Channel support opportunities extend far beyond product images and digital archives of branding material. Channel partners are a form of customers, and channel support is a form of business-to-business marketing discussed extensively in the next chapter. In particular, there are many opportunities for providing useful links and logistics support. Connecting to a provider's supply-chain information provides retailers with up-to-date inventory levels, delivery schedules, and new product availability (Figure 14.6). Access to the provider's corporate intranet directories and messaging system helps speed communication and direct problems to the right managers.

Previous systems for such detailed information exchange, such as EDI, required costly setup and operating expenses. With the Net, these capabilities are within the reach of essentially all providers and retailers.

> Establish Authorization Policies and Minimum Advertised Prices (MAP)

Producers can establish authorization criteria and minimum advertised price policies (MAP) for online retailers. Authorization policies specify what stock-keeping units (SKUs) a particular retailer can carry. By specifying an authorization policy, producers can help match the product to the retailer's target customers. Producers also designate certain SKUs for "open distribution."

MAP policies specify the minimum advertised price level for each item to qualify for an allocation of cooperative advertising funds. In the context of online retailers, producers have to decide whether to extend their MAP policies to the Web and how to interpret these policies. Case

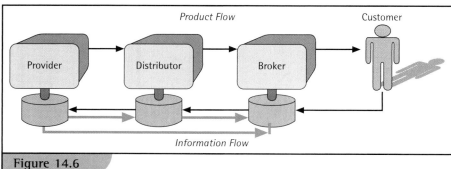

Figure 14.6

Using Online Connections to Inform the Channel

studies suggest that authorization and MAP policies are important ingredients of selling through online intermediaries.

> Encourage Affiliate Networks

Affiliate networks are a new distribution tier available online.[14] As discussed in Chapter 5, affiliates are typically independent third-party sites specializing in certain content types or affinity groups. They funnel traffic and sales leads to online retailers for which they receive a commission. Examples include web directories such as looksmart.com, sites like ebates.com that provide online rebates, and sites that focus on charitable giving such as schoolpop.com.

Affiliate networks are driving a substantial portion of the online sales. For example, Amazon.com reports that it has 900,000 affiliates.[15] In a study by an industry-retailing group, 55% of industry respondents said that they were using affiliate marketing,[16] and it was the third most important tactic. In the same study, 99% of the respondents rated affiliate marketing as effective or very effective, making it one of the highest rated inbound marketing approaches.

Many retailers have built networks consisting of thousands of affiliates. Recruiting and managing such a large number of affiliates is resource intensive. In addition to recruiting affiliates, ecommerce sites have to manage them by providing links to products and descriptions, tracking sales, and making payments. After recruiting affiliates, ecommerce sites also have to communicate with them on an ongoing basis about special promotional offers.

Manufacturers can support these efforts with online support activities for affiliates as well as online retailers. With the small scale of many affiliates, this needs to be especially accessible and simple. Online pages explaining new products and offerings will encourage coverage by affiliates. Software tools such as RSS feeds can automatically alert all interested in new developments. The goal in all of these activities is to encourage the affiliate system to link to and promote the provider's product line through the retail channel.

Affiliates become even more important to providers who use the Net to sell directly to consumers. In this situation affiliates move from a customer lead source for channel partners to a source of direct sales for the provider. In either case, affiliates help intensify distribution for products and services recommended by the affiliate network (Figure 14.7).

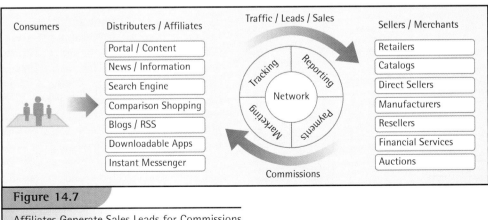

Figure 14.7

Affiliates Generate Sales Leads for Commissions

Source: LinkShare Corp.

| Direct Sales

Direct sales provide some of the most exciting online opportunities for organizations. Producers have always felt the limitations of not having direct contact with end users. Prior to the Internet, going direct was often not feasible. Manufacturers needed to open their own physical stores or set up some form of costly catalog or direct marketing operation. Now, a company can launch online sales much more rapidly and with less financial commitment.

> *Why Sell Direct Online?*

> Meet Consumer Shopping Needs

Intermediaries may not meet consumer shopping needs. Intermediaries might not carry the entire product line of the manufacturer. Some of this selectivity is due to a focus on the top sellers by many retail chains.[17] Some of it is due to a desire by a retailer to differentiate and avoid head-on competition with another retailer.[18] For example, a local bike shop might not want to carry the same models of bicycles that are available at a nearby discount chain. The discount chain might find that not all the models from a particular manufacturer appeal to its target customer. A consumer is unable to view the manufacturer's entire product line at any one retailer.

Retail inventory and availability may be lower at retailers than desired by a manufacturer. This can lead to a frustrating shopping trip, where the consumer is ready to buy but the retailer is out of stock on that item. When this happens, a consumer might substitute a competitive brand that is in stock. Substitution does not affect the manufacturer and the retailer equally. The out of stock manufacturer loses the sale, but the retailer may benefit equally from the sale of either brand.

Some consumers prefer to buy direct from the manufacturer. Consumers might feel that they are getting authentic or new products when they buy directly from the manufacturer. Consumers might also feel that manufacturers are more committed to standing behind their products. Consumers may also find it more convenient to make repeat purchases directly online from well-known manufacturers with extensive product lines.

Consumers may want custom products that are difficult to supply except online. Dell Computer has harnessed this direct sales and build-to-order approach, first with telephone sales and now increasingly with the Web, and has turned it into an engine of growth. Direct selling enables many of the mass customization steps discussed in Chapter 9. It is possible for Dell to receive a unique computer order over the Web, complete with special software and configuration choices, and to ship the newly built computer in four hours. Figure 14.8 shows how Nike offers the option of customizing products as part of its direct sales capability on its web site. This is difficult, if even possible, within a standard retail outlet.

Figure 14.8

Designing a Custom Shoe at Nike.com

Source: David Young-Wolff/Photo Edit

> Expand into a New Profit Pool

A manufacturer may use direct sales to ease entry into complementary products or services that expand the total transaction with the consumer. Major purchases like automobiles, vacation airline tickets, or personal computers are trigger events associated with other complementary purchases. A direct connection to a customer at the time of the trigger event makes it easier to expand into these other markets.

Gadiesh and Gilbert[19] define a profit pool as the total profits earned in an industry at all points along the industry's value chain. A profit pool identifies the different products and services in an industry and calculates their share of revenue and profitability. The structure of the profit pool in an industry can be quite complex. Parts of an industry that account for a large fraction of revenue may have low profits, while modest revenue generators may be very profitable.

Figure 14.9 highlights the profit pool in selling a car. Car manufacturers and dealers account for almost 60% of the sales in the industry, dominating the revenue pool. However, these core

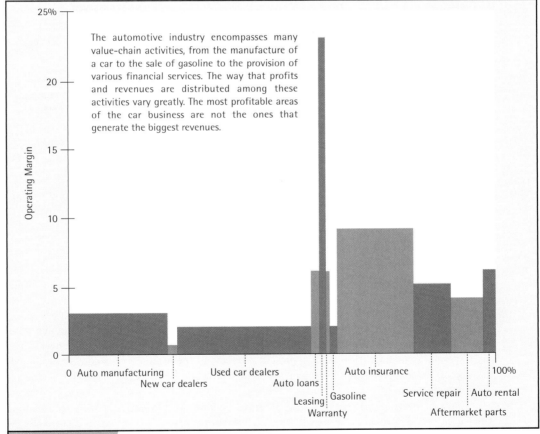

The automotive industry encompasses many value-chain activities, from the manufacture of a car to the sale of gasoline to the provision of various financial services. The way that profits and revenues are distributed among these activities vary greatly. The most profitable areas of the car business are not the ones that generate the biggest revenues.

Figure 14.9

The Distribution of Profits in the Automobile Industry

Source: Orit Gadiesh and James Gilbert, "Profit Pools: A Fresh Look at Strategy," *Harvard Business Review* 76, no. 3 (May–June 1998): pp. 139–147.

activities are low margin. Other segments of the industry, such as financing and leasing, provide much higher profit rates. In the late 1990s, Ford generated as much as 50% of its profits from financing, even though financing accounted for less than one-fifth of the company's revenues.

The trigger event nature of an airline ticket provides an incentive for the airlines to book direct over and above commission savings. A vacation traveler needs hotel rooms and local transportation as part of his or her itinerary. Early purchases in the process provide an opportunity for making complementary sales.

> Getting Closer to End Users by Direct and Regular Interactions

Producers with online sales have constant interaction with end users. When end users visit the web site, web logs capture data on shopping patterns. Purchases provide comprehensive data about end users, including identity and address. Additional data accrues when the customer contacts the web site after the purchase for product registration, additional purchases, service issues, or support.

Learning from direct customer connection has many benefits.[20] It helps providers identify high lifetime value customers and their special needs. It leads to a better understanding of product feature popularity and emerging product trends. It helps refine online offerings and provide a better total experience. It dramatically eases communication with customers, which can be very difficult to achieve with layers of channel intermediaries. Jeff Bezos, the founder and CEO of Amazon.com, emphasizes the benefits for spotting gaps and opportunities:

> We've gotten more feedback in the last four years than most traditional companies have in 40 years. We use it to improve our services. One simple—and very effective—thing we do is to email a question to 3,000 randomly selected customers. We might ask them: Besides the things already in our stores, what else would you like to see us sell? The responses can be incredibly interesting.

> Email in general is a very useful feedback mechanism. That is because email turns off the politeness gene in human beings. People are more willing to be rude and truthful by email than they ever would be in person or over the phone. For a company, that is wonderful.

> Focus groups are great for developing intuitions. However, your total sample size is maybe 20 or 25 people. If you use that to answer questions, you're in great danger of making anecdotal conclusions.

> Hedge against Uncertainty

Intermediaries can face market crises of various forms. A large retail partner or a particular retail channel can enter bankruptcy or drastically shift directions. This can hamper a producer's ability to reach his target customer or to present products to the customer in a consistent manner on a year-round basis. Having a direct sales capability provides a hedge against this type of channel uncertainty.

Another source of uncertainty is the potential magnitude of direct sales itself. It takes time and resources to develop direct capabilities. Manufacturers may not have a clear picture of how direct sales can evolve and the eventual share of the direct sales component. Developing a direct channel provides the possibility of rapid growth should it take off. If the provider fails to experiment and invest in a direct capability, it may not be able to compete effectively with firms that previously invested resources and developed online expertise.

> *Channel Conflict and Channel Performance*

Conflict with pre-existing channel members is one of the main concerns of companies as they add Internet direct sales. Producers going direct threaten existing distribution channels. Channel partners may retaliate, reducing support or even dropping the company's products. Since most of their current sales are from the existing channel, and direct sales might take years to reach comparable scale, serious channel conflict may threaten the majority of current revenue in the hope of some future benefit. It is a serious business risk.

Channel researchers emphasize three main sources of channel conflict:[21]

> Goal divergence
> Responsibility disputes[22]
> Differing perceptions of reality

A successful direct channel is likely to cause some conflict with existing channels from each of these factors. We briefly consider why.

Goal divergence happens when the objectives of a producer and its channel differ. This can be a fight over prices, conflicts over carrying competitors' products, or any number of other disputes between independent firms. A direct sale over the Internet creates an extreme form of goal divergence. The producer and the intermediary may wind up competing directly with each other for the same customers. Customers may make price comparisons on the producer's web site with prices posted on the retailer's web site. While intermediaries are accustomed to competing with one another, they typically resent competing with suppliers.

Responsibility disputes happen over customer handling, territorial assignments, functions performed, or technology used.[23] Responsibility disputes can be severe, especially after a channel redesign.[24] Contentious issues include allocating effort toward customer education and support, placing of orders, awarding commissions, making deliveries, and controlling customer information.

Even if a manufacturer does not want to eliminate the channel, but only wants to support customers, channel conflict may arise because of differing perceptions by the channel. Differences in perception can occur among internal producer constituencies. The direct sales force of a firm may feel very threatened by an online direct approach. Even actions that are actually in support of the sales force, and not designed to supplant or replace them, may be misconstrued and lead to conflict.

Once established, direct sales activities can lead to ongoing channel acrimony and suspicion. The channel fears favoritism toward the direct sales channel. During product shortages, the availability of products for direct sales on the producer's web site might make retailers wonder whether they received their fair share of the product. Retailers worry that the producer will use cost savings to undercut them in terms of price and promotional offers. Retailers may fear a producer will use warranty and registration information obtained from the retailer's customers and launch a direct sales campaign. Whether a producer actually engages in these behaviors or not, the perceptions regarding these types of possibilities lead to channel conflict.

The impact of channel conflict caused by adding a direct online channel depends on the belief in the extent of disintermediation by both parties and the balance of power between the producer and intermediaries. When both parties believe that the extent of disintermediation is small, then channel conflict is likely to be small. When the provider dominates a channel, then channel intermediaries have little choice but to tolerate the move to direct sales. Conversely, when the threat of lost sales is real and power more evenly balanced, channel members will likely retaliate. Possible actions include

> Sending a warning letter to the producer about the wasted resources in direct sales efforts. For example, The Home Depot sent a letter to its suppliers cautioning them about investing money in direct sales to consumers.[25]
> Stopping sale of products from the producer as a retaliatory measure
> Undermining the product by not granting favorable shelf space or adequate sales support
> Not maintaining adequate inventory or demonstration units of the product
> Developing alternate sources of supply in the short or medium term

> *Balancing Direct Sales Benefits and Channel Conflict*

The tradeoff between the expected benefits of direct sales and the expected effects of channel conflict shape the decision to go direct. Figure 14.10 summarizes potential scenarios and alternative approaches from the point of view of manufacturers and services providers. The vertical axis identifies management's belief regarding the magnitude of the direct sales opportunity. The horizontal axis identifies management's belief regarding whether channel conflict is manageable or not.

Channel conflict may be manageable for a variety of reasons. One is precedent, where some form of direct connection existed prior to the rise of an online direct channel. Obvious success by a competing manufacturer may provide a firm with a rationale for experimentation. Dell Computer's success with direct sales highlights how build-to-order combines with direct sales.

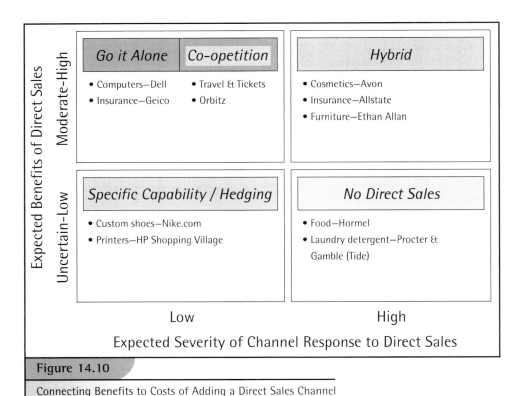

Figure 14.10

Connecting Benefits to Costs of Adding a Direct Sales Channel

This realization can make all players in the industry more accepting of direct sales efforts. Channel conflict can also be manageable when there is a consensus that the direct sales opportunity is small, as in the case of athletic shoes. In this situation, the normal channel views the entry as a specialty line unlikely to threaten their core business.

Channel conflict is less of a concern for powerful brands with strong demand pull. While few producers have such a dominant demand-pull position in a modern global market to completely ignore conflict, it is not credible for individual retailers to attempt to punish such a powerful market force.

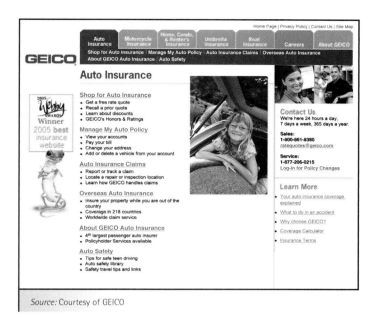

Source: Courtesy of GEICO

> Direct Sales: Go It Alone

Manageable channel conflict and substantial expected benefits lead to direct manufacturer sales as long as this supports a sufficient assortment for consumers or enables efficiencies such as build-to-order. For companies such as Dell and Geico, a direct channel simply reinforced and augmented their previous direct-to-consumer model. Key challenges for these providers are cost-effective customer acquisition and building traffic to the site. Both Geico and Dell combine brand building, direct marketing, online ads, affiliate deals, and investing in the site to reach their customer base.

> Direct Sales: Co-opetition

A manufacturer's direct sales web site might provide an adequately broad assortment for consumers who are brand loyal, or who limit their shopping to the web site of a single producer. However, for consumers who are not very brand loyal, and who want to compare multiple brands, a broader assortment may be necessary.

In this scenario, several producers can collaborate to pool their product lines onto a single web site for Internet sales and meet consumer needs for a broad assortment. The producers can collectively own this Internet sales web site and reduce the need to be dependent on an intermediary that they do not control. Although these producers are competitors, from the perspective of vertical integration into retailing, their offerings are complements. The term co-opetition describes this type of behavior, where competitors collaborate to achieve specific common objectives.[26] Orbitz, Hotels.com, and Fandango each demonstrate joint co-opetition ventures (Table 14-3).

> Specific Capability/Hedging Against Uncertainty

The lower left of Figure 14.10 highlights situations where channel conflict is manageable, but expected gains from an online channel are modest. While many providers in this situation will choose to avoid the complexities of a direct sales channel, others may choose to experiment and create an option for the future. Nike and Hewlett Packard have pursued this approach. The potential for Internet direct sales in the category of athletic shoes is weak. A large and strong brand like Nike sells direct on the Internet and finds the channel conflict manageable. One of

Table 14.3	
Examples of Co-opetition in Internet Direct Sales	
Industry	Co-opetition Venture
Airlines	**ORBITZ** FOR BUSINESS
Hotels	hotels.com BEST PRICES. BEST PLACES. GUARANTEED."®
Movie Tickets	**FANDANGO** You're Good To Go."

Source: Orbitz logo: © PRNewsFoto/Orbitz for Business; Travelport; Hotels.com logo: © PRNewsFoto/Hotels.com; Fandango logo: Courtesy of Fandango, Inc.

the special features of direct sales on Nike.com is the capability to sell custom shoes.

Like Nike, Hewlett Packard has elected to sell printers directly over the Internet to consumers. Hewlett Packard has set up a wholly owned subsidiary called HPShopping.com for Internet direct sales to consumers. Given its strong brand, especially in printers, HP finds channel conflict to be manageable. In the case of HP, direct sales were pursued to satisfy those consumers wanting to buy directly from the company and as a hedge against the possibility that direct sales become the preferred channel for many more customers.[27]

Like Nike and HP, Sony relies on a retail channel for the dominant share of its offerings. At the same time, it is active in a number of media categories, such as music and video content, where the online channel is having a major disruptive effect. Sony's efforts online provide it with a valuable testing ground for online efforts combining its consumer electronics, computing, and media offerings.

The Sony homepage serves as a central location that funnels traffic to the company's various web sites. Sony's direct sales web site is sonystyles.com. With other innovative hardware companies like Apple pioneering online music distribution and hardware sales, Sony's online presence is more strategically important than current online sales would suggest.

> Hybrid

The hybrid approach is appropriate where management expects the direct sales opportunity to be moderate to high, but relies significantly on the existing channel and expects channel conflict. In the hybrid approach, the manufacturer goes direct but in a manner that supports the existing channel members and avoids provoking channel conflict.

As an example, consider Ethan Allan, the furniture manufacturer.[28] Ethan Allan has traditionally sold furniture in over 300 brick-and-mortar stores. Independent licensees own and operate a majority of these stores. One of the company's challenges as it moves into direct sales is maintaining harmony with its storeowners. It does this by sharing the revenue from online sales. Ethan Allan announced that storeowners who provide delivery and service for an item sold over the Internet would get 25% of the sales price. When an item ships directly from the factory, the storeowner in the customer's territory gets 10% of the price. Ethan Allan's approach illustrates the essence of the hybrid model, where compensation is commensurate with sales effort and existing sales territories.

Avon, the world's largest direct seller of beauty products, provides another example of the potentially negative effects of channel conflict with direct selling on the Web.[29] A worldwide network of over 2.8 million representatives sells Avon's products. Over 500,000 representatives operate in the United States market alone. Avon's representatives place orders by putting pencil to paper. The sales representatives receive shipments from Avon and distribute the product to consumers.

Avon estimates that in its U.S. operations, it can save $1 to $3 for every order processed over the Web instead of its traditional paper-and-pencil approach. If Avon processed all of its 650 million orders worldwide over the Internet, it would mean annual savings of between $650 million and $1.95 billion.[30] Avon also experiences a large turnover in its sales force each year. This turnover creates stranded customers, who get cut off from the company.

Avon's sales representatives are not systematically organized.[31] Therefore, the likelihood of organized channel conflict is low. Even so, serious channel conflict is a problem. If sales representatives view online sales as a threat, morale and cooperation will suffer and recruiting will be more difficult.

Avon's Internet direct sales model involves the sales force. When a customer places an order directly over the Web, she can enter the name of her Avon sales representative. The sales representative gets a commission from the sale. If a customer is in need of a representative, Avon assigns her a representative from her area. Figure 14.11 shows the form that Avon has created on its web site so that customers can enter their representative's phone numbers in their orders.

> No Direct Sales

For some industries and product categories, the difficulties of an online channel and the challenges of channel conflict preclude direct sales. Even a global company with top brands such as Tide and Ivory may choose to forego online sales entirely. In these cases the provider can rely instead on presales support and using the Net to provide more effective channel support.

> *Transitioning to Direct Sales*

The transition to direct sales affects not only intermediaries but also employees of the manufacturer that interact with the channel. Reorganization and channel change may threaten existing relationships and job responsibilities. Internal opposition to direct sales sometimes parallels opposition from channel members. Given the continued reliance on traditional channels and the potential sensitivity of traditional channels to direct sales efforts, the transition to direct sales requires careful management.

> Graduated Approach

Many organizations have taken a graduated approach to transitioning to Internet direct sales. Figure 14.12 illustrates the approach used by HP.[32] The transition reflects a series of incremental steps that reduce uncertainty and progress toward the ultimate direct sales approach adopted by the company. The first step toward direct sales was a test of Internet sales of refurbished products. As part of the test, the company developed an online commerce capability and a back-end fulfillment capability in partnership with logistic providers.

The company took the next step after observing traffic on the site, the sales of refurbished products, and the competitive environment. Some high-end models from the current product

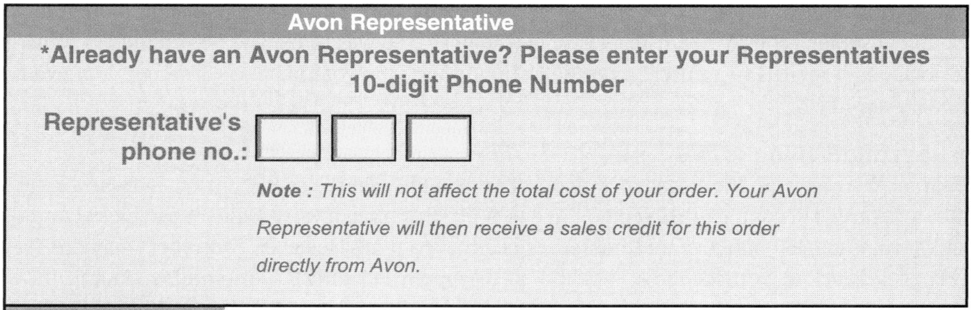

Avon Representative

***Already have an Avon Representative? Please enter your Representatives 10-digit Phone Number**

Representative's phone no.: ☐ ☐ ☐

Note : This will not affect the total cost of your order. Your Avon

Representative will then receive a sales credit for this order

directly from Avon.

Figure 14.11

Option of Entering Avon Rep's Number at Checkout

Source: Courtesy of Avon Products, Inc.

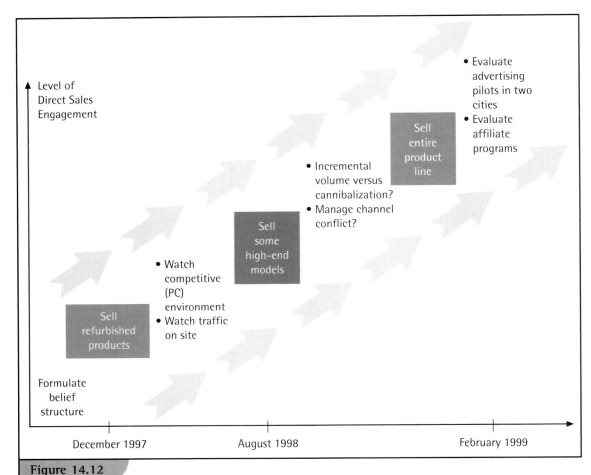

Figure 14.12

How Hewlett Packard Transitioned into Internet Direct Sales to Consumers

line were included in the online assortment. A healthy sales rate of the high-end models indicated consumer's comfort with this channel. The next step was to expand the online assortment to include all models of printers, eventually "morphing" the channel in a graduated and evolutionary approach.[33]

> Setting Online Prices

Product pricing is at the heart of much online channel conflict. One option is to sell at the Manufacturer's Recommended Selling Price (MSRP). This price level, usually at the higher end of the price range, is a safe bet that minimizes channel conflict. However, consumers may not find this price level to be acceptable, leading to disappointing direct sales volume. At the other extreme, the producer could charge prices that are at a lower level than the traditional channel. This is an area of concern. Channel intermediaries understand that the producer has the extra margin to compete with them. This price level would increase channel conflict.

An intermediate price level is the minimum advertised price. Producers usually support the MAP prices with merchandise development funds. The MAP prices are a useful option for

Transitioning to Internet Direct Sales: Lessons from the Hewlett Packard Experience

The experiences of the Hewlett Packard Company highlight the types of issues that arise during the transition to Internet direct sales. Some lessons from this experience:

Follow the Customer

> Learn by participating.
> Take small, discrete, and clear steps.

Manage the Risk

> Be clear and consistent in communications with the channel.
> Stay focused on the customer
> Direct selling prices are crucial.
> Compartmentalize information. Consider a separate physical location, separate IT infrastructure, and email systems for the direct sales group.

Internet direct sales. Hewlett Packard, in its transition to direct sales, used the MAP price level for products sold on HPShopping.com.

In other situations, innovative pricing policies are necessary to encourage customers to use the direct channel rather than intermediaries. The hotel industry uses pricing policies and "frequent stayer" programs to stimulate direct booking.[34] Incentives include bonus miles, free nights, and bonus gifts. Figure 14.13 illustrates the types of price guarantee offered by Choice Hotels. The guarantee promises to match rates and provide an additional 10% discount if the consumer finds a lower price on a comparable room elsewhere. However, there are limits to

---

 Best Choice e-Rate Guarantee

Your rates won't get any better than this!

Looking for the best online rates for Choice Hotels? This is the place. We guarantee the best online rates* for any Choice hotel...and it's easy. Just book your room here. If you find a lower rate for the same hotel and room type on the same date at any other online source, simply let us know. Complete the Best Choice e-Rate Guarantee form and we'll give you the best rate...plus an additional 10% off!

Some limitations apply. Please check Terms and Conditions.

Figure 14.13

Price Guarantee on the Choice Hotels Internet Site

Source: Courtesy of Choice Hotels International

price guarantees. Some hotels honor the prices only if the two rooms are identical. A price found on a liquidation web site like Priceline.com or hotwired.com is not eligible.[35]

Some companies prefer "sticks" to "carrots." One option is to impose penalties on consumers who book through third-party web sites. Hilton Hotels has implemented a rule that stipulates that when a customer books three times at a third-party site, they do not receive benefit points. Wyndham denies membership benefits such as late checkout, frequent flyer airline miles, and free long-distance phone calls on rooms booked through third-party web sites. Some hotel chains report that bookings on their sites have increased after they started enforcing the penalties.

> Direct Access Agreements

Direct access agreements can help coordinate the channel. Under a direct access agreement, an Internet travel agent such as Hotels.com gets direct electronic access into the central reservation systems of the hotel chains. As a result, the travel agent gets access to an expanded inventory with real-time updates. In return, the travel agent agrees not to directly solicit rooms from the franchisees. The chain encourages franchisees to allocate rooms and rates through the centralized system. The centralized systems can automatically raise rates or shut off allotments if a hotel is close to selling out. Both Six Continents and Marriott have signed direct-access pacts with Hotels.com and Expedia.com.

Under these direct access agreements, deeply discounted rooms are bundled with airfares and car rental packages. The tradeoff for the travel site is between the benefits of long-term agreements and access to the entire hotel chain versus the benefits of cutting individual deep discount deals with specific locations. For hotel chains, the access pacts restore the integrity of their yield management systems and restore pricing power.

> Organization and Reporting Structure

The organization and reporting structure of the team that manages direct sales is also an important ongoing issue. Channel members will regard the direct sales team as a competitor. There will be concern that information that they share with the producer might leak to the direct sales team. One approach is partial separation. The producer isolates the direct sales team into a subsidiary, relocating them to a different physical location and even having them operate on a separate IT infrastructure and email system. These precautions build trust with the channel that information shared for mutual advantage will not become a competitive risk with respect to Internet direct sales.

EXPANDING MARKETS

Expanding distribution to reach new markets and new customers is attractive for almost all firms. It can be safer than new product introductions with their high failure rates. It may be easier than intensifying consumption by current customers. It reuses the investments already made in research, development, and commercialization. The Internet provides innovative methods for companies to reach previously unobtainable markets. Opportunities to expand distribution online are particularly attractive for small firms and firms in developing countries.

Market expansion can occur geographically and through enhanced assortment. Geographic expansion can bring customers with demands similar to current customers. Expanding assortment, whether through increased varieties or by expanding the range of qualities offered, can expand the customer base by serving new types of customers with different tastes from existing customers.

New Domestic and International Locations

Throughout history, falling transaction costs have expanded markets. The steamship, the railroad, and the autobahn all expanded the reach of manufacturers and brought distant markets together.[36] This does not happen automatically. Manufacturers must expand into these new markets and develop these new customer bases.

Expanding markets using traditional channels can be costly. Smaller businesses lack the resources to invest in this channel expansion. The Internet provides a cost-effective approach to sell to distant and hard-to-reach customers. These customers may live in markets too small to support a regular store. A study of Internet shopping found that rural U.S. consumers are 16% more likely to shop online compared to urban consumers. The study also concluded that this high propensity of rural Internet users transcends all socioeconomic segments.[37] A high-end retailer such as Neiman Marcus uses online sales to reach customers who fit its customer profile but lack access to a nearby store:[38]

> Internet ... business has been extraordinary, and it is growing like mad. Every village and town has pockets of affluence, but not enough to open a store. Many of these people read the fashion magazines and understand trends but can't in many cases buy it in their towns, so they're coming to us online.

Online sales need not be high-end durable goods. Schwan's Food of Marshall, Minnesota, produces and markets prepared food, both through traditional grocery channels and online. Schwan's traditional distribution channels allow it to reach most of the United States for its package goods. It uses the Internet to reach customers who are hard to reach using traditional channels, including both homebound seniors and those in remote markets. Schwan's uses multiple Internet channels including its own web site, selling its products on eBay.com and on Amazon.com's gourmet site. The company has also launched a new web site called the impromptugourmet.com.[39]

The Internet is making global distribution more efficient, especially for business-to-business commerce (covered in the next chapter). For consumers this most commonly appears in the form of broader selection and lower prices at their regular purchasing locations. The Internet does allow more effective cross-border consumer commerce. Chapter 12 discussed U.S. consumers purchasing pharmaceuticals from Canada and other countries. Internet food sites provide a selection of gourmet foods from many countries. These sites target international travelers who want to continue their consumption of international foods while back at home. These sites, such as the Dutch site Sinterklaasshop.com or the French site zChocolate.com (Figure 14.14), targets citizens living abroad seeking familiar foods or holiday treats.[40]

Figure 14.14

zChocolat.com: A Site That Sells Gourmet French Chocolates

Source: PRNewsFoto/zChocolat

Online distribution allows providers to reach a global market with little investment. This is powerful for services based on digital products such as software, music, tickets, and video content. Sports teams with a global reach can reach fans with video streams provided around the world. While a viewer can theoretically log in from anywhere, congestion problems on international transmission lines lead to higher performance for streams originating closer to the viewer.

There are hidden costs in serving global customers. Round-the-clock customer support may be necessary, possibly in multiple languages. Web site design appropriate for one market may not fit a more distant market with different traditions and culture. Clearly described export and import regulations are necessary to minimize customer confusion and shipment problems. Verification of overseas credit card transactions can be a problem, complicating payment. In some situations, overseas shipping costs can be too high for the price of the product. In spite of these difficulties, some businesses have found the Internet to be a productive channel to expand to overseas markets.[41]

Serious legal issues can confront global service providers. Authorities may block and censor information flow. Services such as gambling are legal in some countries while they are serious legal offences in others. Gambling is causing considerable difficulties within the European Union. While the EU strives to harmonize most commercial laws, gaming regulation is still at the member state level. In some EU countries, such as England, online gambling is legal, and there is an active online casino marketplace. In others, such as Belgium, Sweden, and Italy, it is legal only from the government-sanctioned monopoly provider. Other EU countries ban it entirely. Discussions are under way to harmonize online gaming laws, with a single set of rules for the entire European Union; the patchwork of rules and regulations makes enforcement and compliance complicated.

Selling the Long Tail

Physical distribution has associated fixed and setup costs per item carried. Because of these costs, products have to meet a sales hurdle before they can be profitably distributed using physical channels. Local sales hurdles can be quite steep. For example, a movie theater may not accept a film unless it expects an audience of at least 1,500 over a two-week run. An average record store may require minimum expected sales of two copies of a DVD prior to stocking. National chains may have very high thresholds prior to accepting a title. In the case of broadcast media, technology constraints such as available spectrum also provide hurdles. Products that do not meet the sales hurdle do not receive distribution.[42]

Internet distribution overcomes some of these economic and technological hurdles. In particular, it allows a much wider assortment. A typical Barnes and Noble bookstore stocks about 130,000 titles, whereas Amazon.com launched with 1 million titles. An average Blockbuster video rental store stocks around 3,000 DVD titles. Netflix.com, the online movie rental service, stocks 25,000 DVD titles. This added assortment, which is the right side of the distribution of product sales shown in Figure 14.15, is the "long tail."

The long tail accounts for a substantial fraction of online channel sales. For example, 50% of Amazon.com's sales come from outside its top 30,000 titles. As seen in Figure 14.15, a considerable percentage of Amazon.com, Netflix.com, and Rhapsody sales are from products not stocked in regular stores.

The long tail availability allows obscure titles to enjoy a rebirth of popularity. For readers who previously purchased the book *Into Thin Air* by John Krakhauer, recommendation engines began suggesting a book titled *Touching the Void*, published in 1988 and nearly out of print.

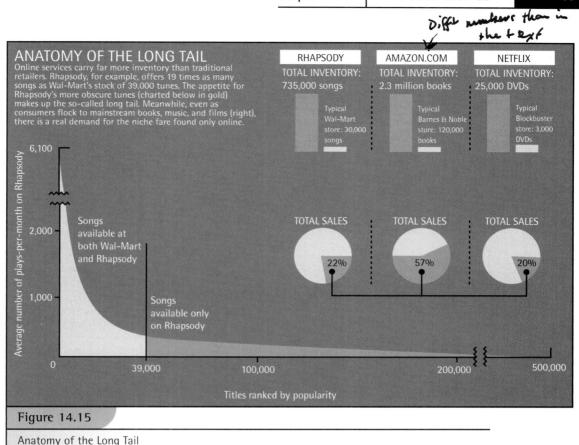

Diff[?] numbers than in the text

Figure 14.15

Anatomy of the Long Tail

Source: Chris Anderson, "The Long Tail," *Wired Magazine* 12, no. 10 (October 2004): 172. Wired © 2004 Conde Nast Publications, Inc.

Touching the Void started selling again. The best–seller provided a point of comparison suggesting a book long gone from normal bookstore shelves.

Versioning

Hollywood has long practiced versioning with its sequential distribution of films. A typical movie appears sequentially in domestic theatrical release, foreign theatrical release, pay per view, and pay television and DVD during its first year. Even later release occurs for foreign TV, network TV, and syndicated networks. Each of these stages contributes to the ultimate profitability of the movie, with some later markets such as DVD dominating the initial box office revenue.[43]

An additional online channel is emerging in markets with sufficiently high bandwidth connection. Speeds such as those in Japan and South Korea eliminate performance compromises. Especially interesting is the combination of an additional online distribution venue with the long tail potential of back catalog movies, television series, and documentaries.[44] Providers of television games are using the Internet to create new versions of their products. These new Internet versions of products are interactive. Game show viewers can play for prizes along with contestants on their favorite shows.[45]

Versioning allows the same core product to effectively reach a much wider range of customers at different price points. High-quality products receive premium prices, while more price-sensitive customers get a reduced feature product or service at a substantial discount. The challenge for the product-line designer is a set of versioned products that effectively target different segments without competing against themselves.[46]

The enhanced assortment capability of online channels makes versioning easier to implement. Shapiro and Varian cite a number of methods for creating versions, with product differences such as delay, user interface, convenience, image resolution, speed of operation, flexibility of use, capability, comprehensiveness, annoyance, and support. An online channel can stock many more of these variations than economically justified in a traditional outlet. Online mass customization using a direct connection can combine versioning with the efficiency of build-to-order.

ONLINE CLOSEOUTS

Excess production and excess inventory are part of the rhythm of many consumer markets. Production and shipping lead times require forecasting consumer tastes several months before the season. Tastes and market conditions can change, leading to excess inventory at the factory, in the warehouse, and in retail stores. Manufacturers need to dispose this excess inventory in a cost-effective manner without disrupting sales in regular channels, pushing down prices of the latest versions, or affecting the image of the brand.

Figure 14.16 illustrates both traditional and Internet channel flows in closeout markets. In the traditional channel, some large manufacturers use factory stores located in outlet malls to

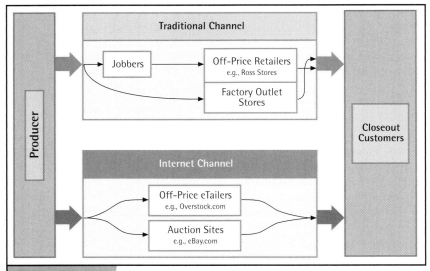

Figure 14.16

Traditional vs. Internet Channel Flows for Closeout Customers dispose of excess inventory. Outlet malls are located at a distance from regular retail markets, minimizing the negative effect on the regular retail channel. Not all manufacturers are big enough to operate factory outlet stores. Another common option is to dispose excess inventory through jobbers. Jobbers are intermediaries who bid on selected lots of merchandise, take title and physical possession, and then dispose of them via closeout retailers.

Traditional closeout methods involve a number of inefficiencies. Using factory stores in outlet malls incurs shipping costs and shipping time to physical locations. Jobbers are often small operations. A manufacturer who wants to dispose of excess inventory in a single transaction might find that no single jobber has the scale required. A second difficulty with jobbers is lack of control and the possibility of regional imbalances. Response times may be slow. When the excess inventory is highly perishable, the time delay in this two-step disposal process of jobber and off-price retailer can be costly.

These inefficiencies create an opportunity for Internet–based approaches. Online auction sites such as eBay are one choice. Many small- and medium–size merchants have been able to use eBay to dispose of closeout merchandise. Online auction sites are less useful for corporations who need to move large volumes of identical items. Listing large volumes of identical items on eBay may suppress price as supply exceeds demand. For example, under these circumstances, one vendor found that they were getting acceptable prices on only 20% of the listed items.[47]

In comparison, online closeout retailers such as Overstock.com have developed a direct connection with consumers interested in purchasing closeout merchandise using fixed prices and auctions (Figure 14.17). An Internet connection to consumers provides Overstock with a much better capability for moving large quantities of identical items. Closeout retailers create scale in a fragmented market. Because of their capitalization and scale, manufacturers can use them as a single outlet for disposing excess inventory. The single contact model provides better control and ability to monitor channel disruptions, and aims to combine the benefits of both channel simplification (Figure 14.2) and lower number of contacts (Figure 14.3).

The Overstock web site reinforces the outlet positioning in many ways, including the page title ("Overstock.com, save up to 80% every day") and the "discount bins" and "shortcuts to savings." There is sufficient urgency to move items rapidly.

Figure 14.17

A Designed Closeout Channel

Source: © Overstock.com, Inc.

Providers can avoid the inefficiencies of physically deploying perishable inventory in geographically dispersed retail outlets.

Online closeouts struggle to control cannibalization of regular channel sales, which eventually would threaten their ability to get products. One method is to combine low prices with a lack of information. This is a method used by travel brokers such as Hotwire. Travel yield management systems, as described in Chapter 12, will inevitably leave some seats unsold. Airlines can offer these at a substantial discount rate through Hotwire.com if these sales can be isolated from the last-minute business traveler. Hotwire.com provides deeply discounted fares for consumers who are flexible about arrival and departure times and the choice of airline. Figure 14.18 shows the results of a search on Hotwire.com. The search results provide a fare and the total cost of the ticket. The site provides flight times and airline names only after the ticket is purchased. Masking the airline name and departure and arrival times keeps the seller anonymous and helps protect against disrupting the regular sales channel. Another approach to this type of anonymous liquidation is the name–your–price approach used by Priceline.com. Table 14.4 lists some of the opaque closeout sites and the details of the approaches implemented on their sites.

Demand cycles complicate the success of closeout channels. When the travel industry is in a slump, travel companies rely heavily on closeout channels for liquidation of excess inventory. However, as the travel market rebounds, closeout channels get less inventory with a lesser discount. The same is true for other product categories, and the size limit of the closeout channel.

Recognizing these limitations, the opaque closeout model is undergoing a significant change. Table 14.4 highlights the types of changes they are making to their business model. The changes include providing more information, such as approximate times and the number of layovers, diversifying into fixed price, non-opaque ticket sales, and diversifying into the sale of hotels and rental cars.

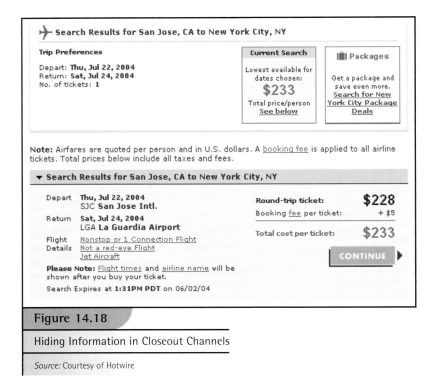

Figure 14.18

Hiding Information in Closeout Channels

Source: Courtesy of Hotwire

Table 14.4

Adjusting Closeout Travel Sites		
Site	How It Works	How They Have Changed
Priceline	Users place a bid on a product, like a hotel room with a specific star rating in a city or an airline ticket from one city to another. Priceline then tries to find a hotel or airline willing to sell at the customer's price and matches up the two. Purchases are non-refundable.	Expanded into retail hotel rooms and rental cars, using a matrix-based interface like the one Orbitz has. It will also launch a research site called MyTravelGuide.
Hotwire	The site lists a hotel room in a city or an airfare between cites at a particular price. Travelers can then choose that price, and click through to purchase. Info revealed after purchase.	Starting in 2005, purchases will be less opaque. For the majority of flights, Hotwire will tell customers roughly what time the flight departs. For all flights, it will also have a link that takes travelers to a page of listed-fare tickets.
SkyAuction	A bid will only be put in at $1 above the highest current bid — so a user with a maximum price of $100 will only pay $75 if the other price in the market is $74. Sometimes, the site can take up to 48 hours to hook a buyer up with a hotel or show.	In 2005, the site started selling some cruises and a few hotels at listed prices.

Source: Avery Johnson, "Travel Web Sites Rethink the Bid and Bargain," *The Wall Street Journal,* (April 7, 2005): D2.

ENDNOTES

1. Peter F. Drucker, "Beyond the Information Revolution," *Atlantic Monthly* 284, no. 6 (October 1999): 47–57.
2. Mary Modahl, *Now or Never: How Companies Must Change Today to Win The Battle for Internet Consumers* (New York: Harper Business, 2000).
3. This discussion on the travel industry is based on the following sources: Travel Industry Association of America press release, "TIA report shows number of online travel bookers continues to grow,; more are also booking all of their travel online," September 2004; Business Wire, "Jupiter Research Forecasts the Online Travel Industry will Reach $91 Billion by 2009, with Supplier Web Sites Increasing Market Share," November 2004; Rob McGann, "U.S. Online Travel Market to Soar," clicks.com, November 2004; Lorraine Sileo and Joshua Friedman, "PhoCusWright's Online Travel Overview: Market Size and Forecasts 2002–2005," *Applied Travel Intelligence,* 2003; Susanna Ray, "Booking Vacations Online Takes Off in Germany," *The Wall Street Journal,* March 11, 2004; Melanie Trottman, "Dropping the Corporate Travel Office," *The Wall Street Journal,* October 28, 2003; Erik Siemers and Edward Harris, "Airline Ticket Sales Begin to Click with Internet-Booking Services," *The Wall Street Journal,* August 2, 1999; Motoko Rich, "Orbitz, Expanding Offerings, Will List Independent Hotels," *The Wall Street Journal,* March 12, 2003; Sonoko Setaishi, "Airlines Go Online to Sang Savvy Fliers Away from Internet Travel Agencies," *The Wall Street Journal,* October 2, 2000; Stephen Power, "'Pre-Internet Age' Rules on Sale Of Airline Tickets to Change," *The Wall Street Journal,* January 2, 2004; Kelly Greene, "Making Your Travel Plans? Consider an Online Rail Sale," *The Wall Street Journal,* March 9, 2003; Christina Binkley, "Harrah's Places a Wager on the Web," *The Wall Street Journal,* November 12, 2003.

4. Coughlan et. al, *Marketing Channels, 6th Edition* (New Jersey: Prentice Hall, 2001), 3.

5. Erin Anderson and Barton Weitz, "Make or Buy Decisions: Vertical Integration and Marketing Productivity," *Sloan Management Review* 27 (Spring 1986): 33–20.

6. Adapted from V. Kasturi Rangan, Melvyn A. J. Menezes and E.P. Maier, "Channel Selection for New Industrial Products: A Framework, Method and Application," *Journal of Marketing* 56 (July 1992): 69–82.

7. Erin Anderson and Barton Weitz, "Make or Buy Decisions: Vertical Integration and Marketing Productivity," *Sloan Management Review* 27 (Spring 1986): 33–20; Coughlan et. al, *Marketing Channels, 6th Edition,* chap. 7 (New Jersey: Prentice Hall, 2001).

8. Figure 14.4 presents traditional channels in a simplified manner. In practice, the traditional channel might be much more complex with additional intermediaries.

9. Mickey Alam Khan, "GM Lets Californians Find their Style Online," *DM News* (April 6, 2004).

10. Gregory L. White, "GM and Auto by Tel Team Up to Test A New Systems for Online Care Shopping," *Wall Street Journal* (February 22, 2001).

11. Adapted from John Hagel and Marc Singer, "Networth: Shaping Markets when Customers Make the Rules," *Harvard Business School Press* (1999).

12. Fiona Scott Morton, Florian Zettelmeyer, and Jorge Silva-Risso, "Internet Car Retailing," *The Journal of Industrial Economics* (December 2001); Brian T. Ratchford, Myung-Soo Lee, and Debabrata Talukdar, "The Impact of the Internet on Information Search for Automobiles," *Journal of Marketing* Research XL (May 2003): 193–209.

13. The discussion on the impact of online learning in the automobile industry is based on Josef Federman, "In the Driver's Seat," *The Wall Street Journal* (May 19, 2003); Shawn Henry, "Consumers Who Think They Know Everything," *Forbes* (April 29, 2002).

14. The discussion in this part draws from the following: Revisiting Affiliate Marketing: A New Sales Tier Emerges in the Digital Commerce Network. An Executive White Paper, Aberdeen Group, September 2003; Charlotte Goddard, "Affiliate Marketing Masterclass: The Revolution Masterclass on Affiliate Marketing," *Revolution: Business and Marketing in the Digital Age* (April 1, 2003); "Interview: Prakesh Bharwani, Senior Manager, Interactive Marketing, 1-800-FLOWERS.com on Affiliates," *Great Minds in Retailing Online* 1, no. 8 (2003); Mark Del Franco and Paul Miller, "Reevaluating Affiliate Marketing," *Catalog Age* (May 3, 2003); Mary Wagner, "The Balancing Act in Affiliate Management," *Internet Retailer* (October, 2003).

15. Data source: Associates section on Amazon.com, June 7, 2004.

16. The State of Retailing Online 2.0. Shop.Org, May 2003.

17. Sarah Ellison, "Retailers Appetite for Top Sellers Has Food Firms Slimming Down," *The Wall Street Journal* (October 28, 2004).

18. See Mark Bergen, Shantanu Dutta, and Steven M. Shugan, "Branded Variants: A Retail Perspective," *Journal of Marketing* 33, no. 1 (1996): 9–19; Steven M. Shugan, "Branded Variants," *Research in Marketing, AMA Educators' Proceedings*, series (Chicago: American Marketing Association, 1989), 33–38.

19. The discussion regarding profit pools is adapted from Orit Gadiesh and James Gilbert, "Profit Pools: A Fresh Look at Strategy," *Harvard Business Review* (May–June 1998): 139–147; Orit Gadiesh and James Gilbert, "Mapping a Profit Pool," *Harvard Business Review* (May–June 1998): 149–162.

20. This has been an important theme of Peppers and Rogers: Don Peppers and Martha Rogers, *The One to One Future* (New York: Currency Doubleday, 1993); Don Peppers and Martha Rogers. *Enterprise One to One* (New York: Currency Doubleday, 1997).

21. Louis Stern, Adel El-Ansary, Anne Coughlan, *Marketing Channels: Fifth Edition* (New Jersey: Prentice Hall, 1996), especially Chapter 7.

22. The authors actually use the phrase "Domain Dissensus," which has been changed due to the likely confusion with the Internet use of the word "domain."

23. Stern et. al., op. cit.

24. Richard Vlosky and David Wilson, "Technology Adoption in Channels: Short-term pain and long-term gain," cited in Stern et. al. (1994) 427.

25. K. Brooker, "E-Rivals Seem to Have Home Depot Awfully Nervous," *Fortune* 140 (August 16, 1999): 28–29.

26. Adam M. Brandenburger and Barry J. Nalebuff, *Co-Opetition: A Revolution Mindset That Combines Competition and Cooperation: The Game Theory Strategy That's Changing the Game of Business* (New York : Doubleday, 1996).

27. Information on HP Shopping comes from Kirthi Kalyanam and Shelby McIntyre "Hewlett Packard Consumer Products Division: Distribution Through E-Commerce Channels," *Journal of Interactive Marketing*, 1999, Vol. 13, No. 4, Autumn. Also see Lee Gomes, "Hewlett Packard is Playing Catch-up in PC's and Printer Sales on the Internet," *The Wall Street Journal* (December 24, 1998). *Internet Retailer,* October 30, 2003, "HPShopping.com Forecasting High Double-digit Holiday Sales Growth," http://www.internetretailer.com.

28. James R. Hagerty, "Ethan Allan Encounters Resistance as it Races Towards Online Sales," *The Wall Street Journal* (July 29, 1999).

29. David Godes, "Avon.com (A)," Harvard Business School Case Study # 9-503-016, 2003.

30. Erin White, "Avon tries to Exploit the Internet without Alienating its Ladies," *The Wall Street Journal* (December 28, 1999).

31. David Godes, "Avon.com (A)," Harvard Business School Case Study # 9-503-016, 2003.

32. Kirthi Kalyanam and Shelby McIntyre, "Teaching Note: The Hewlett Packard Consumer Products Division: Distribution through E*Commerce Channels," Leavey School of Business: Santa Clara University, lsb.scu.edu/kk.

33. Kathleen M. Eisenhardt and Donald N. Sull, "Strategy as Simple Rules," *Harvard Business Review* (January 2001): 107–116.

34. The discussion on the hotel industry is based on the following: Motoko Rich, "Hotels Offer Price Guarantees In Bid to Undercut Travel Sites," *The Wall Street Journal* (March 3, 2003); Julia Angwin and Motoko Rich, "Inn Fighting: Big Hotel Chains Strike Back Against Web Sites," *The Wall Street Journal* (March 3, 2003); Heather Won Tesoriero and Paul Glader, "Book Here—Or Else." *The Wall Street Journal* (March 4, 2004); Christina Binkley, "Marriot Signs Deal With Web Sites," *The Wall Street Journal* (February 4, 2004); Motoko Rich, "Six Continents Tries to Regain Pricing Power in Expedia Pact," *The Wall Street Journal* (March 3, 2003); Julia Angwin and Melanie Trottman, "Hotels.com Ends Travelocity Alliance," *The Wall Street Journal* (September 3, 2003); Greg Sandoval, "Hotels Mimicking Orbitz's Business," *ZD Net News* (February 12, 2002); "Pegasus Transfers Ownership of its Consumer Site TravelWeb.com to HDS," April 5, 2002, http://www.hospitalitynet.org.

35. While not controlling for price differences, Cendant reports that the ratio of people who make a reservation after a search on the Cendant web site increased by 25% since the launch of the price guarantees.

36. Drucker, op. cit.

37. "Rural Consumers 16% more likely than urbanites to shop online study says," *Internet Retailer.* December 8, 2004.

38. Ellen Byron, "Retailing's Velvet Rope," *Wall Street Journal* (December 9, 2004).

39. Janet Moore, "Some Minnesota Food Manufacturers Selling on Amazon.com," *Star Tribune* (November 17, 2003). Also see Katy McLaughlin, "Holiday Dinner, with a Pedigree," *Wall Street Journal* (December 10, 2004); Charles Passy, "Thinking Outside the Lox," *Wall Street Journal* (December 10, 2004).

40. Jeanette Borzo, "Food Fix," *Wall Street Journal* (May 24, 2004).

41. Peter Loftus, "Internet Turns Small Firms into International Businesses," *Wall Street Journal* (December 16, 2003).

42. The discussion in this part is adapted from Chris Anderson, "The Long Tail," *Wired Magazine* (October 2004); Chris Anderson, "The Zen of Jeff Bezos," *Wired Magazine* (January 2005); Lee Gomes, "Web Allows Fans to See Wide Variety of Movies that Were Hard to Get," *The Wall Street Journal* (January 31, 2005). Also see Brynjolfsson, Hu, and Smith, 2003, discussed in Chapter 13.

43. Harold Vogel, *Entertainment Industry Economics: A Guide for Financial Analysis,* 5th ed. (Cambridge: Cambridge University Press, 2001).

44. Michael J. Wolf, "Digitizing MGM's Roar," *Wall Street Journal* (April 27, 2004).

45. Peter Grant, "Place Your Bets," *Wall Street Journal* (May 24, 2004).

46. For an extensive discussion of versioning see Hal Varian and Carl Shapiro, *Information Rules* (Cambridge: HBS Press, 1999).

47. The quote and the material in this paragraph are based on Nick Wingfield, "Overstocked: As eBay Grows, Site Disappoints Some Big Vendors," *Wall Street Journal* (February 26, 2004).

chapter 15:

B2B Ecommerce

❝ In the business world, the rearview mirror is always clearer than the windshield. ❞

Warren Buffett

❝ The world is flat. ❞

Thomas Friedman

Figure 15.1

China Exporting to the World
Source: © Bananastock/Jupiter Images

Selling China to the World

The growth of China's exports has been striking. When it began to open up to foreign trade in 1978, following the disastrous Cultural Revolution, its total exports were approximately $20 billion. By 2004, Chinese worldwide exports exceeded $500 billion and rose above those of Japan.[1] Chinese imports from around the world are also rising rapidly (Figure 15.1). China is heavily investing in Africa and other areas rich in natural resources, seeking to guarantee a supply of materials and energy for its factories.

With the rapid growth in Chinese exports, there was a broadening in the need for buyer's agents. Many suppliers in China are small and regionally based.[2] It is not economically feasible to set up offices in even a regional center. Buyers could travel to find suppliers, but this is costly and fraught with difficulties.

Historically, companies such as Li & Fung Trading filled this market niche with an extensive network of buyer's agents operating through personal contacts and physical presence. Li & Fung would obtain specifications from a buyer, find suppliers matching these specs and receive a commission for this work from the buyer. In addition to matching buyers with sellers, an agent might provide other services such as production monitoring and quality assurance.[3]

While this system works, it introduces costs and delay. The extraordinary growth in China's productive abilities makes it difficult to scale the traditional export support fast enough. Enter new

Business often leads the adoption of new technologies and new methods of operation. This chapter looks at some of the special opportunities and challenges of online commerce between businesses, whether large or small.

Topics covered in this chapter include:

> **What Businesses Buy and How they Buy**

> **B2B Customers and Channels**

> **eProcurement**

> **Supply Chain Integration**

firms such as Alibaba.com, an Internet web site for buyers seeking Chinese suppliers. Based in Hang Zhou in eastern China, Alibaba.com has rapidly grown to be one of the Top 500 global Internet properties.[4] According to the company, its different online properties have more than one million registered users from over 200 countries, and more than 300,000 people visit the site every day.[5]

Alibaba.com currently lists products from 27 industry categories. Basic listing on the web site is free. Buyers and sellers can find each other on the web site (Figure 15.2). However,

Figure 15.2

Alibaba.com: An Online Global Trade Fair

Source: Alibaba.com

they cannot trade online and have to connect offline or via email to close the transaction. The company estimates over $5 billion in trade from buyers and sellers connecting on the web site.

The company gets requests from buyers constantly. It matches a seller's requests to appropriate buyer profiles and provides recommendations. Alibaba.com also participates in trade shows around the world to collect information about buyer needs. The web page of the company features a searchable section called trade leads. Both buyers and sellers can search this section for leads with respect to products of interest.

In order to increase the awareness of business buyers in the United States, the company recently launched an advertising campaign on CNBC. The goal is to attract a small- or medium-sized buyer interested in finding suppliers in China but without prior experience.[6] While it would be prohibitively expensive for a small Chinese seller to advertise in the U.S. market, Alibaba.com can aggregate the power of multiple sellers to provide exposure in a global marketplace.

Alibaba.com takes advantage of some of the most up-to-date and effective online credibility and brand-building techniques. It incorporates its story and examples into case studies and multimedia presentations, such as the Flash overview, seen in Figure 15.3. Its site is professional and fast, with in-depth links to a wide range of material explaining

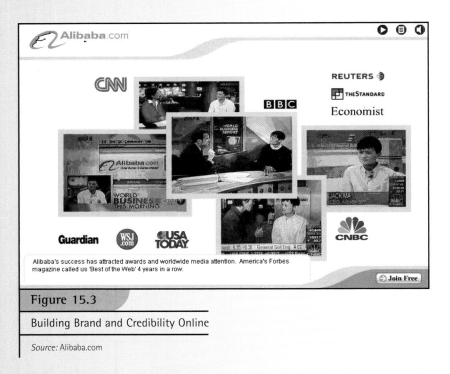

Alibaba's success has attracted awards and worldwide media attention. America's Forbes magazine called us 'Best of the Web' 4 years in a row.

Figure 15.3

Building Brand and Credibility Online

Source: Alibaba.com

the system and the vendor network. Endorsements and stories from many Western media outlets explain and persuade the curious potential buyer.

Matching buyers to sellers is only a small part of the process of actually conducting a transaction. In addition to low price, reliability and quality of the supplier are also crucial. In order to meet this need, Alibaba.com has set up programs to make the quality of suppliers more transparent. For suppliers from China, the company provides a program called Gold Pass®. Third party credit agencies evaluate GoldPass® suppliers. A separate page features these suppliers and provides additional benefits.

According to a survey conducted by the company, one of the top concerns of buyers is authenticity of the supplier. Other concerns include lack of visuals for products, slow feedback, too much information to sort through, and unprofessional suppliers.

In order to address these buyer concerns, the company has established a program called TrustPass® verification, in which a third party confirms the seller's authenticity. The company's survey shows that 85% of buyers are interested in purchasing from sellers who have the TrustPass® qualification. Alibaba also addresses these concerns with extensive supplier information, complete with visuals showing supplier factories and biographies of the companies.

Not everything works perfectly with Alibaba or other companies seeking to provide electronic marketplaces. The Internet infrastructure is still developing in China, especially in the rural areas. There are gaps in payment systems, credit card processing capabilities, an incomplete implementation of electronic signatures, and other factors causing problems online. For users within China there are concerns about governmental censorship and monitoring. Even so, the marketplaces are allowing small and remote suppliers in China to ship their products worldwide. Alibaba helps "flatten" the world.

Ecommerce is shaping business everywhere, with a much larger current impact on business-to-business (B2B) commerce than business to consumers. This chapter looks at ecommerce by considering how businesses buy and sell and how they are buying online. The complications of B2B buying and selling shape how online efficiencies diffuse into the economy.

B2B ECOMMERCE EVOLVES

B2B ecommerce is a much larger fraction of total commerce than it is in either consumer retail or services. B2B ecommerce has already grown to be large in both absolute dollars and percentage of total activity. Figure 15.4 shows that by 2003 ecommerce reached 21.2% of total manufacturing shipments, corresponding to $843 billion. Merchant wholesaling trade was also very large at 16.9% or $730 billion. Ecommerce retailing, on the other hand, was only 1.7% ($56 billion).

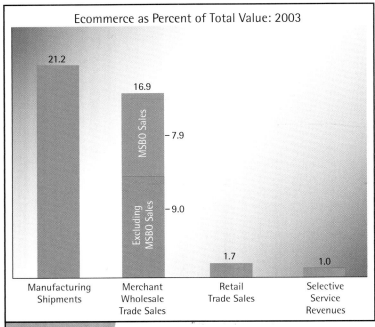

Ecommerce as Percent of Total Value: 2003

Figure 15.4

U.S. Ecommerce Share of Transaction Value

Source: U.S. Census Bureau

As a percent of category shipments, the leading manufacturing sectors included transportation equipment (50.1%), beverage and tobacco product manufacturing (44.0%), and textile product mills (23.5%). Top wholesaling categories were drugs, drug proprietaries, and druggists' sundries (49.1%) and motor vehicles and automotive equipment (25.1%).

Businesses often lead consumers in the adoption of information technology. Online selling builds on a history of computerization, previous use of electronic data interchange, and professional procurement departments in many companies. The use of computers and the Internet caused a rapid increase in productivity throughout the U.S. economy during the late 1990s.[7]

While businesses adopt technology faster than consumers, especially expensive new information systems, it takes time and investment before these tools change business processes.[8] Table 15.1 demonstrates this fact for businesses in the United States. Forman et. al. looked at the adoption of the Internet by businesses at the end of 2000.[9] They split this usage into two types. *Participation* is basic access and usage, having the necessary systems in place to use the Internet. *Enhancement* is deeper; it is the use of the Internet to change business processes. The study finds market size influences the firms in the region, with firms in larger cities more likely to both be online and change business processes.

This chapter concentrates on the usage of the Net in the enhancement of business-to-business commerce. Internet access by businesses reached effective saturation in the United States quickly. Working the Internet into business processes takes more time, more effort, and more training. This diffusion is considerably slower. However, as Figure 15.4 suggests, businesses are going beyond participation. Firms are making the investments and changes necessary to alter their procurement, their supply chains, and their information gathering. Enhancement is beginning to catch up with participation.

Table 15.1

Adoption of Internet by U.S. Businesses, End of 2000		
Firms by Metropolitan Area Size (End of 2000)	Participation	Enhancement
Large MSAs	90.4%	14.7%
Median MSAs	84.9%	11.2%
Small MSAs	75.5%	9.9%

Source: Chris Forman, Avi Goldfarb, and Shane Greenstein. "Digital Dispersion: An Industrial and Geographic Census of Commercial Internet Use," CSIO Working Paper #0031, September 2002.

Figure 15.5 illustrates just some of the complexity of B2B commerce. A manufacturer sells to consumers through distribution centers and retailers. To make this happen, a manufacturer combines indirect materials, research and development, productive capabilities, and services. Many of these flow from a network of suppliers, who have their own suppliers, back to raw materials in the ground. Commerce between a manufacturer and its distributors and retailers consists of the downstream aspects of B2B commerce.[10]

Indirect materials do not go into the production of finished products. Examples of indirect materials include office supplies such as paper, pens and paper clips, janitorial services, and desktop computers and printers. With indirect materials, tight linkages to manufacturing processes are not crucial. Indirect materials do not require specialized services that vary across product categories. For example, the process used to deliver paper clips can be similar to the process used to deliver printer cartridges. A single vendor like Office Depot, Staples, or Grainger can supply many categories. Another feature of many indirect materials is that many industry sectors purchase them using processes that are very similar. These characteristics make indirect materials "horizontal" in nature.

Direct materials are raw materials that go into the production of the finished product. Examples of direct materials include steel for the production of automobiles, or silicon chips used in the production of a personal computer. Tier 1 suppliers provide direct materials. There is tight synchronization between the order and delivery flow of manufacturing inputs and the production process. This tight synchronization is a key aspect that differentiates direct materials from indirect. The supply of direct materials also requires specialized services. For example, the transportation of flat panel displays requires different skills from the transportation of lab chemicals. These specialized services mean that suppliers of direct materials are industry specific: more "vertical" in nature.

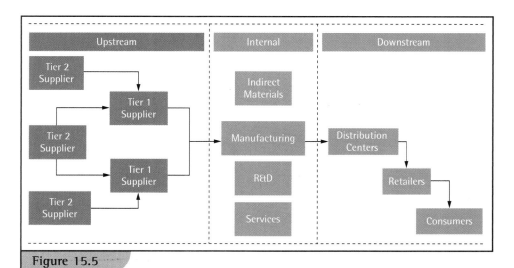

Figure 15.5

Supply Chain for a Manufacturer

Source: Adapted from Robert B Handfield, Ernest L Nichols. *Supply Chain Redesign: Transforming Supply Chains into Integrated Supply Systems* (Upper Saddle River, NJ: Prentice Hall, 1999).

Tier 2 suppliers supply materials to Tier 1 suppliers, and together they constitute the upstream aspects of B2B commerce. When companies outsource manufacturing, Tier 1 suppliers supply raw materials to contract manufacturers. The commerce and coordination activities between the company and the contract manufacturer would also fall into the scope of B2B commerce.

Companies follow systematic processes to compose and run the supply chain. Composing the supply chain involves selecting downstream partners such as distributors and retailers and upstream partners such as Tier 1 suppliers or contract manufacturers. Running the supply chain consists of transacting with the selected partners, booking and placing orders, making and receiving payments, and coordinating the flow of orders and information.

Figure 15.6 shows an example of the steps in the strategic sourcing process. There are process costs and cycle times associated with these steps. Some of these are the costs of hiring professional buyers and supporting their activities. Business buying also involves the costs of placing orders and making payments. Information sharing across entities also adds to costs and cycle time. Other costs are due to lack of timely information exchange; for example, excess inventory levels because buyers and sellers do not share forecasts in a timely manner. Given these inefficiencies in costs and cycle time, companies look to deploy information technology to improve B2B commerce.

Long before the arrival of the public Internet, electronic data interchange (EDI) enabled rudimentary forms of B2B ecommerce. The concept emerged during the 1948 Berlin Airlift, even before commercial computing, as a method of tracking different suppliers.[11] In a typical EDI application, business partners transmit data to each other using a proprietary data network leased from a third party. The third party ensures network security and reliability, and provides software and services that translate data to a standard format—hence the term Value Added Networks (VANs).

EDI communications are now usually computer-to-computer in nature (Figure 15.8). Typical EDI applications are in retail, manufacture, transportation, and government. The most common application in retailing is inventory replenishment. Retail stores might do an inventory count once or twice a day and then upload it to different suppliers. Suppliers confirm the orders and plan deliveries. The operation is sequential and each party transmits data during a specific period in a day. Manufacturing is another common application. A manufacturer can generate weekly or daily demand forecasts, translate them into orders for individual parts and transmit to suppliers.

Security and reliability are two key requirements of EDI. Businesses cannot afford to have important orders lost or duplicated because of glitches in electronic transmissions. An

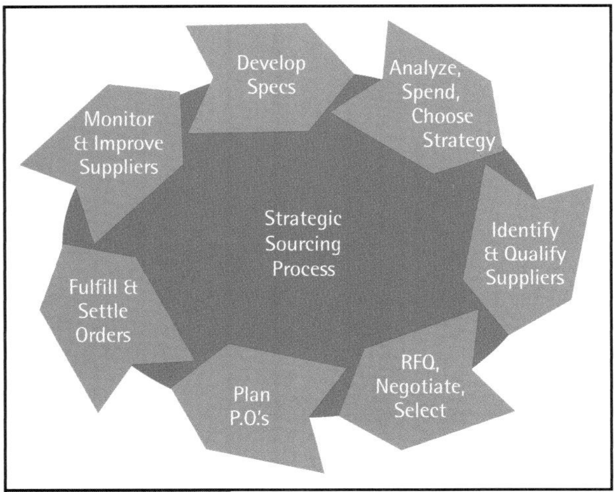

Figure 15.6

Steps in the Strategic Sourcing Process

(a)

(b)

At the height of the Berlin Airlift, two groups of aircraft flew in four-hour blocks around the clock. While one group of aircraft was loaded and serviced, the other group was in the air. On the 264-mile route, 32 aircraft were in the air simultaneously.

Figure 15.7

Co-coordinating Aircraft During the Berlin Airlift

Source: 15.7a © Hulton-Deutsch Collection/CORBIS; 15.7b © Keystone/Getty Images

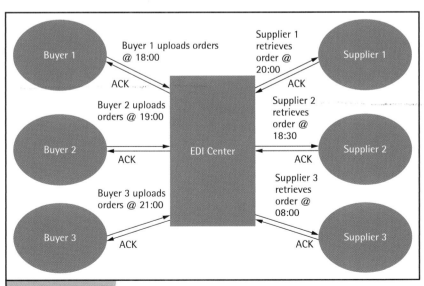

Figure 15.8

Illustration of a Typical EDI Deployment

electronic log of every EDI transmission enables business partners to verify the transmission and receipt of orders. EDI thus provides the electronic equivalent of certified mail. The term used for this capability is non-repudiation. The VAN provider, a third party, facilitates this non-repudiation mechanism.

A key issue in EDI is the format used by the sellers and buyers to transmit the data. In 1968, the U.S. Transportation Data Coordinating Committee formed to coordinate the development of translation rules among existing industry standards. The committee published the first standard, composed of 45 transaction sets, in 1975. Over time, industry-specific standards were developed. Today, X12 and UN/EDIFACT are the most commonly used EDI standards.[12]

The major benefit of EDI is its ability to automate routine order placement and receipt between business partners. It reduces the cycle time of communication between order placement and receipt and eliminates paperwork. Automated transmissions reduce human errors and the strict data formats minimize mistakes.

Unlike the Internet, which is a publicly and ubiquitously available communication medium, EDI uses point-to-point communication. This is an important limitation. It is cumbersome to utilize different point-to-point systems across a multitude of business partners. Connection costs are a barrier for small and medium size businesses. For example, one vendor estimates that customers pay from $10,000 to several hundred thousand dollars to connect to the network. Additionally, companies might have to pay on a per-message basis. Large companies can spend as much as $30,000 per month to send messages. Lack of flexibility is another limiting factor. Unlike the Internet, which uses open public standards, EDI uses proprietary communications that are not flexible to adapt for different applications. This lack of flexibility has also limited the scope of EDI to basic order transmissions. Given these limitations, only 5–10% of businesses currently use EDI, despite its long history.[13]

CUSTOMERS AND CHANNELS

Customer acquisition in B2B markets can be complex. Large order values, multiple decision makers and long selling cycles contribute. Intermediaries are common. Figure 15.9 shows the multiple channels used by Cisco Systems to go to market. As the largest maker of networking products, Cisco sells to large customers using a direct sales force and sells to small- and medium-sized customers using a combination of distributors, resellers, and retailers. Even though Cisco has a direct channel to large customers, a majority of its sales occur through indirect channels. This type of distribution structure is quite common in B2B markets.

The relationship between customers and sellers is often ongoing, with repeat ordering over long periods. Repeat ordering can be either direct or through a sales force. Channel partners such as distributors and retailers also place orders. Order placement in a B2B context involves transaction costs due to order transmission, monitoring receipts, and scheduling payments. The Internet can help improve customer acquisition by providing tailored messages tailored to multiple decision makers. The internet can also reduce transaction costs by automating ordering.

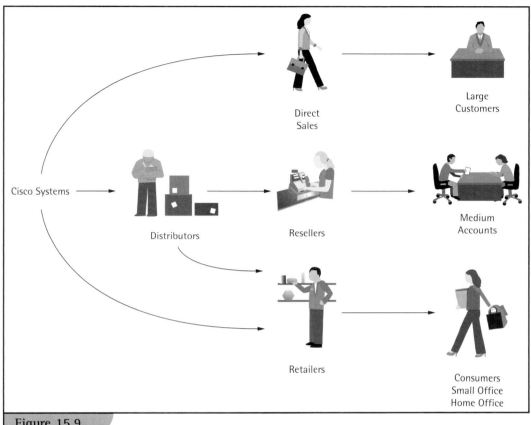

Figure 15.9

Cisco's Distribution Channels

New Sales and Buying Centers

One of the major distinctions between business and consumer purchases is the complexity of the business buying process. B2B buying decisions involve a buying center with multiple decision makers.[14] Buying center participants often have different roles. Some initiate the purchase, some influence it, others decide it, and there are gatekeepers, purchasers, and users. Figure 15.10 uses telecommunications purchases to illustrate six buying center roles encountered in many buying situations. Each individual in the buying center has specific information needs and responds to specific appeals. These needs can be subtle. Selling and marketing efforts that do not tailor messages to these roles can cause confusion and slow down the selling process.

Purchasing a customer relationship management (CRM) software system provides another example. CRM software can be a major capital expenditure for an enterprise. CRM affects the sales force, marketing, production, accounting, and finance divisions. Senior executives, including the

Members of the Buying Center and Their Roles

Initiator   Division general manager proposes to replace the company's telecommunications system

Decider   Vice president of administration selects, with influence from others, the vendor the company will deal with and the system it will buy

Influencers   Corporate telecommunications department and the vice president of data processing have important say about which system and vendor the company will deal with

Purchaser   Corporate purchasing department completes the purchase to specifications by negotiating or bidding

Gatekeepers   Corporate purchasing and corporate telecommunications departments analyze the company's needs and recommend likely matches with potential vendors

Users   All division employees who use the telecommunications equipment

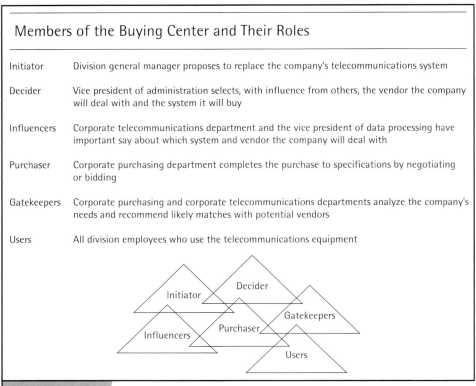

Figure 15.10

The Buying Center

Source: Thomas V. Bonoma, "Major Sales: Who Really Does the Buying?" *Harvard Business Review* 60, no. 3, (May–June 1982), 111–119.

CEO, CFO, CIO, and executives from Sales and Marketing are involved in the buying process. End users such as the sales force and service professionals also participate in the buying. Consultants and system integrators provide input regarding compatibility with legacy systems and cost of integration.

In this buying center, each participant has complex but different information needs. The CEO's concerns might be about how much the system might increase sales and how long it will take. The CFO's concerns might be about total cost of ownership and return on investment. Sales professionals might be more interested in revenue growth and sales effectiveness. Targeting each participant with precisely tailored messages and getting consistent execution in the field is complex.

Online material serves as an archive of continuously available sales presentation and segmentation device. For example, CRM seller Siebel (now part of Oracle) can provide a menu of custom views on the homepage. Each custom view targets a different buying center participant and provides precisely tailored messages. Table 15.2 demonstrates some of the differences between the presentations. Each presentation is a version of the virtual value activities applied to the different functional roles within the buying center. Some presenters seek to promote a decision, while others merely to seek to prevent a veto from that decision maker.

Table 15.2

Siebel Systems Message Hierarchy

Messages on the Web Site of Siebel Systems	Custom Views for Buying Center Participants				
	Executive	Business Manager	Sales Professional	Service Professional	IT Professional
• Siebel Systems Named to Red Herring Top 100	✓	✓	✓	✓	✓
• Industry Analysts Reports	✓	✓	✓	✓	
• The Siebel Difference	✓	✓			✓
• Siebel User Experience	✓			✓	✓
• Build vs. Buy Whitepaper • Total Cost of Ownership Whitepaper • 10 Critical Success Factors for CRM Implementation	✓ ✓ ✓				
• Managing the Demand Chain		✓			
• Grow Revenues More Quickly, Predictably, and Profitably • Enable Strategic Sales Management to Drive Revenue • Better Manage Sales Forecasts, Territories, and Incentives • Mobilize Your Sales Force • Improve Your Sales Effectiveness			✓ ✓ ✓ ✓ ✓		
• Lower Service Costs and Improve Customer Satisfaction • Increase Customer Loyalty and Agent Productivity • Grow Revenues and Improve Service Delivery Processes				✓ ✓ ✓	
• Performance Breakthrough • Siebel Project Implementation Benchmark Whitepaper • Siebel Watch					✓ ✓ ✓

Purchasing a corporate jet is yet another example of decision makers with different information needs. A purchase such as this requires agreement of the top executives that will fly in the plane, the pilots flying and maintaining them, the finance department on whether leasing or owning makes sense, and other parts of the organization. Details of range and speed are of interest to both top management and pilots, while pilots care most about the specifics of the flight controls and required certification. Sites such as Canadian maker Bombardier use their online presence to anticipate and respond to these concerns at any time and around the world. Choice of language and other information customization is easily accomplished.

Facilitating Repeat Purchase

Repeat ordering in B2B settings involves transaction costs. Figure 15.11 contrasts online and traditional ordering flow at Cisco Systems. Customers, sales force, and channel partners faxed orders to customer service representatives. The faxed orders were manually entered into Cisco's order management system. Figure 15.11 also shows some key statistics for this manual process. Only 80% of the orders were entered into the system the same day. Only 60% of the orders were booked or scheduled the same day. This process resulted in a 4–10-day lead-time.

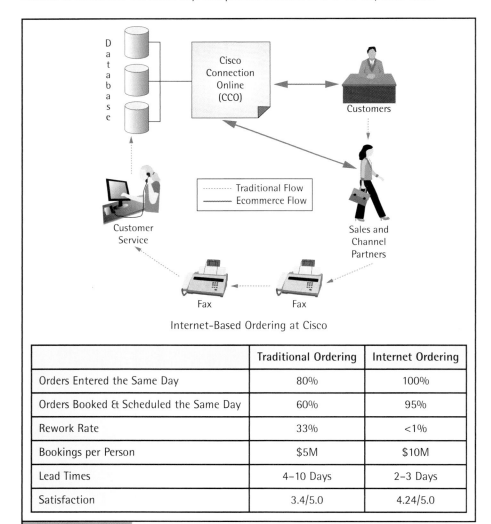

Internet-Based Ordering at Cisco

	Traditional Ordering	Internet Ordering
Orders Entered the Same Day	80%	100%
Orders Booked & Scheduled the Same Day	60%	95%
Rework Rate	33%	<1%
Bookings per Person	$5M	$10M
Lead Times	4–10 Days	2–3 Days
Satisfaction	3.4/5.0	4.24/5.0

Figure 15.11

Metrics for Traditional versus Internet-Based Ordering at Cisco Systems

Source: Cisco Systems

A key aspect of the traditional process was a high order rework rate of 33%. Some of this rework was due to manual errors, and some was due to incorrect product configurations. Some of these errors had to be manually resolved with back and forth phone calls between the customer service representatives, channel partners, and customers. Customer satisfaction with this process was averaging about 3.4 on a 5-point scale.

Cisco introduced Cisco Connection Online (CCO) to help automate the ordering process. CCO is an Internet site that a Cisco customer or channel partner can access to configure products and place orders. CCO has a number of capabilities to support the ordering process including an ordering tool, an invoice generator, a product configuration engine, ability to show pricing, order status, status of contract pricing, and lead times. Customers and channel partners receive email confirmation of orders.

With Internet-based ordering, 100% of orders enter into Cisco's systems on the same day. About 95% of the orders are booked and scheduled on the same day. The order rework rate has decreased to less than 1%. Avoiding configuration errors is one of the key drivers of these reductions. Cisco claims that it is virtually impossible to enter an incorrectly configured order.[15] As a result, the lead-time has been reduced to 2–3 days, a reduction of over 50%. Internet-based ordering has increased satisfaction as well.

The use of Internet-based ordering with customers, direct sales force, and channels is not unique to Cisco. Intel, Pratt, and Dell, are among the companies deploying similar Internet ordering capabilities. Intel has used the Internet to expand its ordering system from its 20 largest computer and electronic customers to thousands of additional customers. Intel has been booking over 95% of its orders over the Internet. The system has reduced errors in the order rate by 75%.[16] Pratt has been in a major push to market refurbished products and services on the web site.[17]

GE Plastics has deployed an Internet-based site for its customers called geplastics.com.[18] The site is the online distribution arm for GE's business. As in the examples of Cisco and Intel, the goal of the site is to help buyers streamline their ordering. Some of the underlying factors that make the site successful include its ability to complement and extend GE's existing sales and distribution structure, its ease of use, and its very high emphasis on online customer service.

Adoption by users is crucial to the success of these Internet ordering systems. Involving customers in the process early on and soliciting their feedback can have powerful results. In the case of GE Plastics an important request from customers was the ability to place and manage orders using the customers' internal part number rather than GE's part number. The site design handles this level of personalization. Each customer has the capability to load their own part numbers and match them to GE's part number. Capabilities such as these can facilitate personalization and deep integration into the customer's internal ordering systems.

Other personalized capabilities include the ability to view orders, check availability, and confirm order and shipment status. Buyers can also create specific templates for frequently ordered products. The site also has research and design tools that provide buyers with technical information. Buyers also receive automated confirmation emails within minutes of placing an order. Without the Internet, this simple process took several manual steps with the buyer having to call a customer service representative to check inventory, getting a call back on delivery dates, and then confirming the deal with a faxed purchase order.

Ease of use is also a crucial factor for adoption. Providing live online support can help usability. GE Plastics uses live online chat to provide customer support. The live support capabilities include the ability for a customer service associate to open windows remotely within the user's browser and guide him or her through the appropriate features or help him or her resolve an issue.

Both GE Plastics and Cisco used a phased approach to site functionality with more complex functionality released later in the cycle. For example, integrating the site with buyers' internal ordering systems or backend enterprise resource planning systems is complex due to the diversity of systems and data formats in existence. GE provided such capabilities, only at a later stage.

These examples show businesses that have moved from simple participation to active enhancement. Even a relatively basic technology deployment such as Internet-based ordering by customers is no exception. In this case, business process change can lead to a more lean and flexible enterprise.

EPROCUREMENT

Direct procurement materials are fundamental to production, while indirect materials support the organization. They differ in a number of dimensions, including their nature, their importance, who can buy, and how bought. Direct materials are strategic, shaping the features and capabilities of the firm's products. Indirect materials are required for operations, but more closely affect costs than output features. See Table 15.3.

Indirect Materials

All companies require supplies in support of operations. These indirect materials, from office supplies to spare parts for machinery, involve procurement. Manual systems, as seen in the top of Figure 15.12, have multiple costs and inefficiencies. This creates opportunities for online savings. Companies are utilizing Internet-based systems to improve their procurement.

Table 15.3

Indirect vs. Direct Materials	
Direct, Production Related Materials	**Indirect, Non-production Materials**
Scheduled	Not scheduled
Production items	Miscellaneous items
Usually no shelf items	Shelf items
Inventory accounts	Expense and asset accounts
Buyers' desktops only	Everybody's desktops
No approvals	Approvals required
Bill of materials	Aggregated catalogs

Source: Udith Gebauer and Arie Segev. "Emerging Technologies to Support Indirect procurement: Two case studies from the petroleum industry," *Information Technology and Management* 1 (2000): 107–128. With kind permission of Springer Science and Business Media.

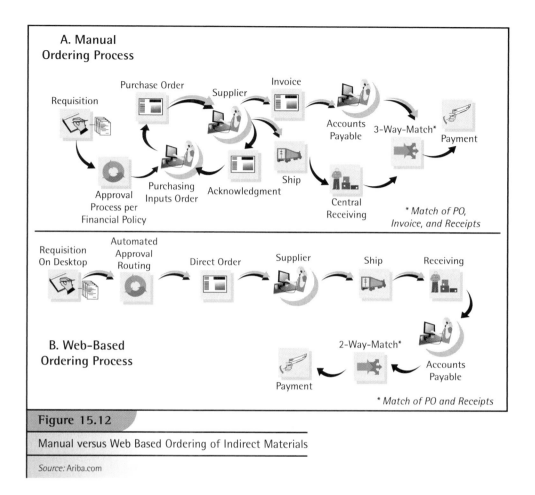

A. Manual Ordering Process

Requisition

Purchase Order

Supplier

Invoice

Accounts Payable

3-Way-Match*

Payment

Approval Process per Financial Policy

Purchasing Inputs Order

Acknowledgment

Ship

Central Receiving

Match of PO, Invoice, and Receipts

Requisition On Desktop

Automated Approval Routing

Direct Order

Supplier

Ship

Receiving

B. Web-Based Ordering Process

2-Way-Match*

Accounts Payable

Payment

Match of PO and Receipts

Figure 15.12

Manual versus Web Based Ordering of Indirect Materials

Source: Ariba.com

Manual procurement is inconvenient and costly for all concerned. Since up-to-date catalogs, specifications, and pricing is typically not readily available, employees engage in costly searches across different vendors. This often leads to "maverick buying"—an industry term for purchases from vendors not on the approved vendor list. For instance, the National Association of Purchasing Managers estimated that 33% of corporate purchases were out of compliance with volume purchasing agreements. With maverick buyers spending approximately 25% more than the approved vendor's price, uncontrolled buying was costly to the enterprise.

Manual procurement often leads to centralization, which creates rigidities and bureaucracy. Employees have trouble tracking the status of orders, fear slow turnaround, and may compensate by over-ordering and stockpiling materials. These inventories prevent shortages, but tie up corporate assets in supplies and inventory of indirect materials.[19] Electronic ordering reduces many of these inefficiencies and decentralizes indirect procurement. Any computer connected to the corporate network, even remotely, can access the web-based ordering system. These usability aspects are crucial in driving adoption of the system, and are much easier to maintain than older "client-server" applications.

Another benefit of the system is a current and updated catalog of indirect materials from the current approved vendors. The web-based catalog has the capability to display images and other multi-media content, providing the look and feel of a retail shopping site. Online catalogs make customization and personalization easier, with items such as personal computers. The availability of a current catalog with updated pricing makes it easy for employees to search for products.

Once an employee places an order, the system sends the order for approval. Organizational rules and hierarchies dictate which individuals have signature authority. A web-based system can capture these rules and hierarchies and route the request for electronic approval. After approval, the system transmits the order to the supplier. Under manual procurement, it can take on average seven to ten days from the time a user places an order until the supplier receives the order. A web-based procurement process can reduce this time to several hours to two or three days at the most. Online ordering eliminates redundant paperwork, minimizes manual errors, and eliminates head count related to order processing and entry in purchasing departments. Receipt of the order triggers a message to accounts payable. The process ends with accounts payable matching the purchase order with the receipt (a two-way match). Web-based procurement automatically captures the orders into an electronic database. Not all suppliers are equipped to receive orders electronically. Many suppliers still receive orders by fax or by phone. Handling dual systems is cumbersome, putting pressure on lagging firms to also adopt and utilize online procurement.

The Institute of Supply Management finds widespread adoption of indirect eprocurement.[20] A survey of 600 organizations, chosen to match the range of U.S. businesses, finds that by the end of 2003 more than 90% of organizations used eprocurement for indirect materials. Non-manufacturing firms utilized the systems the most, buying 15.5% of indirect materials online in 2003, up from 7.1%. Manufacturing firms bought 8.3% of indirect materials electronically in 2003, up from 6.3% in 2001. While exact values are not available about cost savings, a rising number of respondents report both satisfaction and savings.

A different survey of enterprises adopting eprocurement reinforces these results and provides additional detail.[21] Moving to an online system does cause a shift away from off-contract buying, shrinks the requisition-to-order cycle, lowers requisition costs, and moves more spending into the procurement management system (Table 15.4).

Table 15.4

Impact of Adding Eprocurement		
Performance Area	Before Online	After Online
% of spending that is off-contract ("maverick")	38%	14.2%
Price savings on maverick purchases brought into compliance	—	7.3%
Requisition-to-order cycles	20.4 days	3.8 days
Requisition-to-order costs	$56	$23
% of spend under management of the procurement group	56%	69%

Source: Aberdeen Group (2004)

Services

In addition to indirect and direct materials, businesses purchase services from outside vendors. Examples include facilities management, maintenance services, training, information technology consulting, business process consulting, legal services, public relations, marketing, and contingent labor. One study found that 54% of corporate procurement spending is for services.[22] A typical Fortune 500 company could spend as much as $2 billion for services procurement.

Increases in the use of temporary workers are an important driver in the increased procurement of services. Figure 15.13 illustrates the growth in temporary help in the U.S. economy from 1990 to 2004.[23] This is occurring across all skill levels, including IT workers, legal services, and public relations and media staff using temporary or contract positions. An increase in the skill level of temporary workers increases the diversity and complexity of the procurement process. Services are moving toward global sourcing.[24] The Internet provides a powerful, low-cost approach to coordinate global teams.

> *Manual Procurement and Consumption of Services*
The procurement and consumption process varies depending on the type of a service. The terms and conditions of services such as facilities management and maintenance can be part of the

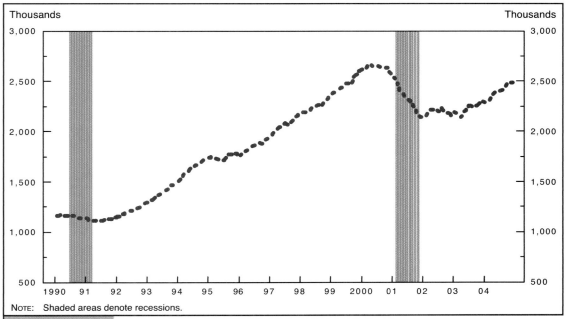

NOTE: Shaded areas denote recessions.

Figure 15.13

Increase in Temporary Workers in the U.S. Economy

Source: Lloyd and Mueller

negotiations of a larger master contract. In addition to pricing, the terms and conditions could include required service level agreements. After negotiation of the master contract, the ordering and consumption of services typically occurs on an incremental basis.

Contingent labor procurement often involves multiple buyers interviewing and scoring candidates. Aggregated scores across multiple buyers inform the final sourcing decisions. Contingent labor procurements also involve service-level agreements.[25] Part of the procurement process for contingent workers includes documenting security clearances. A large business might need to track hundreds or thousands of temporary workers.

Services such as information technology consulting using offshore providers involve additional complexities. Often the buyer and the seller collaborate on developing the specifications. Modification of the specification and change management is also typical. Because of the global nature of the procurement process, expenditures of subcomponents of the contract may occur in different currencies. Despite this, expenditures have to be reconciled against a single master budget.

Similar to the procurement process of indirect materials, a manual approach to procuring services can be slow and error prone. Typical contract procurement can take 3–4 weeks. In addition to procurement, the recording and monitoring of service consumption is an ongoing process. Documenting service consumption with time sheets is cumbersome. Monitoring quality can be difficult. Lack of monitoring capabilities can lead to a low level of vendor compliance. Lack of centralized monitoring data means that a below par employee can leave one department and be rehired in another.[26]

> *Web-Based Procurement and Consumption of Services*

A web-based platform, depending on its features, can automate multiple aspects of the service procurement and consumption process. The buyer and vendor can collaborate on the specifications for the service in a real time manner. They can create specifications for services that are not part of the standard catalog. The use of an internet platform can facilitate collaboration even between a buyer and offshore vendors.

After finalizing specifications, a buyer creates a pool of suppliers for a competitive bidding process (as described in the next part on the procurement of direct materials). The competitive bidding process helps identify the appropriate market price. Companies use additional steps to ensure that suppliers are qualified. In the case of contingent labor, teams can score candidates. The system can also track service consumption using the online time cards.

In a multi-division corporation, it is difficult to control service spending across divisions. As these services proliferate and offshore procurement is common, there can be a loss of control due to lack of timely reporting. Web-based service procurement systems can help. Figure 15.14

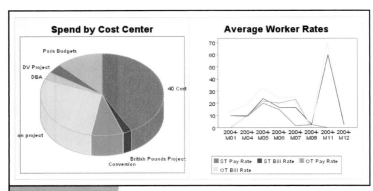

Figure 15.14

Reporting in a Web-Based Services Procurement System

Source: Jai Shekawat, Fieldglass Inc.

demonstrates this type of capability. These management reports help spot trends, catch mistakes, and assist in future contract negotiations.

Direct Materials and Dynamic Bidding

> *Relational versus Transactional Exchanges*

Direct materials are part of the finished goods produced by a manufacturer, listed as cost of goods in the income statements of companies. These direct materials can be undifferentiated commodities (e.g., basic aluminum), specialized and unique items (jet aircraft engine), or somewhere in between (aircraft seats). These costs are highly visible and have an important impact on profitability. Organizations devote considerable time and effort to ensure procurement of direct materials of the right quality at the lowest possible cost.

The nature of the materials shapes the procurement system. A commodity item can utilize an auction among multiple potential suppliers. Competition among the suppliers establishes the market price for the product. Purchase behavior is transactional, with little uncertainty about the input quality and cost reduction a prime objective.

Unique and specialized inputs tend to trade in a more relational and collaborative setting. Firms develop a set of strategic suppliers, working with them to specify products and improve capabilities. Joint development occurs. These partners share information through electronic and face-to-face meetings. With especially important inputs there can be explicit joint ventures.[27]

In the middle of the spectrum lie semi-differentiated products. These products are not commodities nor are they highly specialized. Many of these products involve some customization. An example might be custom metal stampings. A number of suppliers potentially exist. Quality differences across suppliers can be significant. Controlling quality differences and establishing effective bidding requires detailed specifications. Suppliers are motivated to compete for large orders.

Figure 15.15a highlights this process. After identifying suppliers, the buyer prepares a request for a quote. The buyer publicizes the request for quote via different communication channels including its own web site. The procurement group prepares a short list of suppliers from those who responded. The procurement group negotiates on a one-on-one basis with suppliers to finalize terms and conditions and make a final supplier selection.

Buyers face the twin challenges of identifying a qualified slate of suppliers and determining the market price. Identifying a broad slate of qualified suppliers quickly can be challenging. Lack of clear understanding of a supplier's quality is often a problem. Time to market pressures often force buyers to act with limited information and limited competition.

A manual and long drawn out supplier qualification and negotiation process can harm fast growing companies.[28] Supplier qualification and negotiation time increases the cycle time of order transmission into the supply chain. Both buyers and sellers incur selling expenses in the negotiation process. The logistical issues in bringing sellers to one place generally make auctions impractical. Last, many companies rely on sourcing managers to conduct these processes. A short supply of sourcing managers can also be a limiting factor.

Design and process management tools at the industry level help lower costs and improve even the traditional sourcing flow.[29] In the construction industry, a variety of shared specification tools and construction estimation tools exist to lower costs and raise quality of the bidding process. Electronically sharing these specifications helps accelerate and clarify proposals.

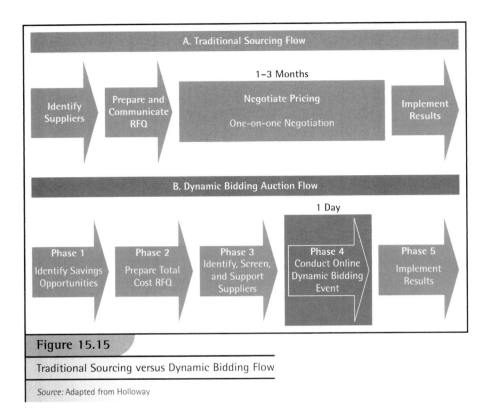

Figure 15.15

Traditional Sourcing versus Dynamic Bidding Flow

Source: Adapted from Holloway

Companies share information through extranets, where select partners receive access to the buyer's internal web sites.[30] These systems help create the modularity and early feedback systems discussed in Chapter 11.

Industry standards reduce the difficulty of creating and using these tools. One of the goals for many trade associations or sponsoring organizations is to create XML definitions for industry practitioners. These libraries of XML definitions create a language for specifying products and services, easing the communication and tracking tasks.

Figure 15.15b illustrates a dynamic bidding process, which can further accelerate the procurement process. The buyer or an agent on behalf of the buyer conducts the process. An auction in the context of enterprise buying usually consists of the following five phases:[31]

Phase 1: Identifying Savings Opportunities: Establishing the product categories in which the buying organization can find savings.

Phase 2: Preparing Total Cost RFQs: The total cost consists of all specifications including drawings, volume forecasts, logistic, and quality requirements. The more precise and detailed the Request for Quote (RFQ), the more informed the supplier. This step also involves dividing the components into several independent lots. These lots are all or nothing in that the suppliers cannot bid on a subdivided part of a lot. The lots must be homogenous from a supplier perspective, involving similar tools, materials, and quality requirements.

Phase 3: Identify Screen and Support Suppliers: Identify a broad slate of suppliers. From this large pool, select a more narrow set of qualified suppliers whose capabilities closely match the requirements of the RFQ. Sometimes suppliers are qualified with a 10–15-page questionnaire.

Phase 4: Conduct Online Competitive Bidding Events: The selected suppliers prepare quotes. Training sessions help them understand the online biding process. The buyer announces the auction rules. Suppliers usually connect over a global network on the day of the actual bidding.

Phase 5: Provide Post Bid Analysis and Award Support: Once the bidding process ends, the buyer analyzes the bids and makes a selection. Depending on the rules of the auction, the supplier with the lowest bid may not be the winner.

> *Buyer Benefits and Supplier Concerns*

Dynamic auctions benefit the buyer by reducing direct materials costs. Industry reports indicate cost savings in the range of 15%.[32] Industry observers attribute this to the dynamic and open bid format that enables suppliers to observe the going market rate for the product and adjust their bidding accordingly. In some cases, the use of Internet auctions enabled the participation of overseas suppliers.

Another benefit to the buyer is the reduction of the cycle time required for determining the final price. A typical one-on-one negotiation process can take up to three months whereas a dynamic bidding process can be completed within a day. This reduction in cycle time can be extremely beneficial to fast-growing companies or to companies subject to time or market pressures.

Dynamic bidding can reduce procurement costs for both buyer and seller, although possibly with some long-term loss in relational connection. Electronic negotiations partially substitute for time-consuming face-to-face interaction. This reduces selling and administrative expenses. The time savings for buying agents can make them more productive by allowing them to handle additional categories. It may, however, lower the personal connection felt between buyers and sellers.

Suppliers worry about auctions leading to an increased importance of price compared to other product or service attributes. Some of these concerns are about the integrity of the auction. For example, suppliers might be concerned that the buyer will use the auction results to award business to an existing preferred supplier. One trade publication reports that suppliers in the automotive industry claim that buyers are abusing auctions and are calling for a formal code of conduct.[33]

Buyers can establish auction rules that can help alleviate supplier concerns. Announcing these auction rules ahead of time helps minimize miscommunication among the participants. Auction rules might cover the following:

> Specifying the exact criteria (lowest price versus others) for the final award.
> Specifying whether the award is subject to a final quality audit or not.
> Restricting suppliers to previous participants.
> Restrictions that eliminate post auction negotiations.
> Restrictions that eliminate "shilling"—buyers placing fictitious bids.

Enhancing the integrity of the auction process is beneficial for both buyers and suppliers, helping to reduce strategic misrepresentations and overly cautious bidding.

Research Finding:
The Relational Impact of Dynamic Bidding

Sandy Jap has studied the impact of the use of dynamic bidding auctions on buyer-seller relationships. In particular she studies whether the use of these auctions increase seller perceptions of opportunistic behavior. Opportunistic behavior is an important construct in the transaction-cost economics framework and is defined as self interest seeking behavior with guile. Oliver Williamson in his book *The Mechanisms of Governance*, describes opportunism as synonymous with misrepresentation, cheating, and deception. The perception of opportunism can undermine trust, hence its importance in Buyer-Seller relationships.

The data were collected in the context of a quasi experiment involving six online auctions of a major industrial buyer. A key finding of the study is that the use of online dynamic bidding auctions increases both new and current suppliers' beliefs that buyers act opportunistically.

Sources: Sandy D Jap. "An Exploratory Study of the Introduction of Online Reverse Auctions," *Journal of Marketing,* July 2003, 96–107. Oliver Williamson. *The Mechanisms of Governance* (New York: Oxford University Press, 1996).

Marketplaces

> *The B2B Marketplace Bubble*

Few areas of the speculative boom of the late 1990s had such dramatic growth and decline as B2B marketplaces. Venture capitalists and existing industry participants sponsored startups to offer electronic marketplaces for all forms of business inputs: indirect materials, services, and direct materials. Marketplaces went public, rising to billions of dollars of market capitalization. Investors hoped that many of the traditional procurement functions would take place through these new online systems.

Marketplace startups argued they could improve procurement efficiency in a number of dimensions, including information exchange, more efficient trading, faster order placement and processing, new forms of auctions, better logistics, collaborative design and learning tools, and better forecasting.[34] Marketplaces would profit from transaction fees, software services, consulting, tradeshows, and other support capabilities.

Part of the lure of these marketplaces was the sheer size of B2B volume, as seen earlier in this chapter. Despite this volume and these possibilities, online marketplaces declined rapidly after reaching their peak in 2001 (Figure 15.16).

Several factors doomed most of these new entrants. Existing firms have been able to add online improvements to their procurement systems. Second, far too many entrants were chasing the same overlapping markets. Like consumer auction sites, marketplaces thrive on

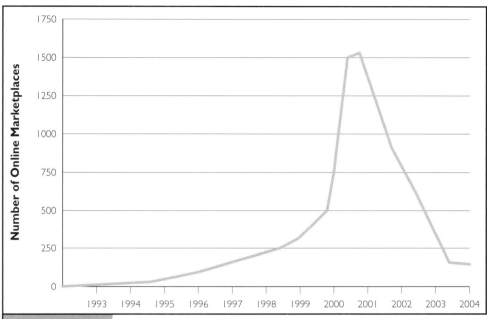

Figure 15.16

The Speculative Boom and Bust in B2B Marketplaces

trading volume. Small specialty sites are difficult to support. Perhaps most importantly, incumbent firms could exploit their existing market position and hinder the rise of these new competitors.

> *Incumbent Backed Marketplaces*

Aspects of these new marketplaces were troubling for both existing buyers and sellers. Disruption of existing procurement arrangements is a concern. New marketplaces require change, which might threaten the security and stability of the supply network. At the least, there would be new procurement processes, systems, and training. While this might promise long-term benefits, there were inevitable short-term costs.

A second concern was the introduction of transaction fees into existing procurement deals. Currently trading buyers and sellers know how to locate each other and the gains through participating in an online marketplace might be marginal.[35] In many markets, there are diminishing returns to discovery of new suppliers. This shifts focus toward managing relationships with existing vendors. New trading marketplaces require fees and possibly a more transactional mentality.

Table 15.5

How Market Structure Favors Different Types of Marketplaces

Market Structure	Impact on Marketplace	Example	Remarks / Challenges
1. Seller Dominated	Favors Seller Driven Marketplace	Transora - Consumer Packaged Goods	• Access to complementary assets is an advantage • Antitrust concerns • Commitment • Goal divergence • Sensitivity to sharing information with competitors • Could face resistance to transaction fees
2. Buyer Dominated	Favors Buyer Driven Marketplace	E2open - Electronics Industry	
3. Fragmented *with* Strong Incumbent Intermediary	Favors Intermediary Driven Marketplace	Avnet - Electronics Distribution	• Business transformation by existing intermediary • Intermediary has access to complementary assets such as product catalogs
4. Fragmented *without* Strong Incumbent Intermediary	Favors Independent Marketplace	Alibaba.com - Procurement from Small and Medium Size Vendors in China	• Content and other complementary assets are barriers

> Supplier Concerns

One of the promised benefits of marketplaces was increased negotiating power for buyers, leading to lower prices. Suppliers were naturally wary of facing further pricing pressure in online environments. Suppliers were also concerned that the marketplaces would reduce the entire transaction to just the one dimension of price. For example, Universal Packaging is a supplier of boxes to Kraft foods. Their production flexibility allows them to supply 126 types of Jell-O boxes.[36] A marketplace emphasizing price might reduce their differentiation advantage and force standardization of their packaging offerings.

Many suppliers worry about independent marketplaces revealing sensitive pricing data or strategic initiatives to the competition. Suppliers are hesitant to expose unique intellectual property or quality benchmark data in a public marketplace. Suppliers' reluctance to join marketplaces meant that digital catalogs were incomplete or sparse. This in turn limited the number of transactions routed through a marketplace.

Ensuring supplier participation was especially problematic for independent exchanges. Buyers would not transact if suppliers were not present and catalogs did not have breadth. Suppliers would not participate if buyers were not transacting, if they could not recoup the costs of creating digital content and participating in a marketplace, and if they faced increased pricing pressure.

> Buyer Concerns

Like suppliers, buyers have concerns about participating in marketplaces. Buyers do not want to reveal their ordering patterns in unprotected environments. They consider their ordering patterns valuable information and want to shield this information from competitors. For example, Dell has always been able to track demand patterns in personal computers extremely well because of its direct to customer model. Participating in public trading environments might partially reveal Dell's market knowledge to competitors.

When existing markets are either supplier-dominated or buyer-dominated, electronic marketplaces tend to be extensions and expansions of their existing procurement systems. Incumbent marketplaces reflect their sponsoring firms, and are sensitive to their concerns. Examples of buyer-backed marketplaces include e2open in the electronics industry, Covisint in the automobile industry and Transora in consumer-packaged goods. Examples of seller-backed marketplaces include Exostar in aerospace and defense.

Compared to independents, incumbent-backed marketplaces have the advantage of having access to complementary assets and better access to buyers or suppliers. This can help the incumbent-backed marketplace obtain content from suppliers for digital catalogs. However, incumbent-based marketplaces face a unique set of challenges. One challenge is regulatory scrutiny. Weeks after the big three automakers formed Covisint, the Federal Trade Commission (FTC)[37] opened an investigation into whether the exchange would spark collusion, illegal price signaling, and other possible sharing of information among competitors. Some exchanges such as the World Wide Retail Exchange restrict themselves to the procurement of goods not available for resale to the public.[38]

Marketplace backers may have diverging goals, leading to conflict and a lack of consensus. The backers may have incompatible software systems and may not be able to agree on a standard. Faced with these issues, incumbent marketplaces may face a lack of commitment as participants hedge their bets between the new online marketplace and their own private efforts.

> *Intermediary Backed and Independent Marketplaces*

> Strong Existing Intermediaries

Strong existing intermediaries were in a natural position to embrace online technologies and marketplaces. In the electronics industry, both Avnet and Arrow demonstrate this type of intermediary. Both companies are electronic parts distributors. They are the primary source of electronic parts distribution for medium and small customers and hence play the role of an intermediary in a segment of the market that is fragmented. These distributors have access to key complementary assets such as existing customer relationships, product catalogs, digital content, pricing, and the ability to provide logistical support. The access to these complementary assets confers an advantage on the incumbent intermediaries who can leverage the Internet and transform themselves into a marketplace.

> Fragmented Markets

Fragmented markets provide a natural setting for marketplaces, with no strong veto role by a dominant buyer or seller. However, the independent marketplace still has the costly customer acquisition problem and the start-up problem of needing to generate sufficient volume of both buyers and sellers. B2B startups like Chemdex initially focused on a market like specialty chemicals, which fit many of these criteria.[39] After promising beginnings, many of these failed to ever achieve profitability and have been forced to scale back, merge, or close their doors.

Surviving marketplaces continue to hone their business models towards long-term viability. Some of them, like Alibaba.com, are finding success by focusing on the rapidly growing trend of global sourcing, particularly from China. They operate as an arms' length sellers' agent, signing up sellers to their site and advertising heavily to attract buyers. Other surviving marketplaces focus on providing a unique functionality such as data synchronization to its members.

SUPPLY CHAIN COORDINATION

Coordinating supply chains can be complicated. Difficulties include tracking demand, managing inventory, introducing new products, and implementing methods of record keeping and data synchronization.

Demand Visibility and Vendor Managed Inventory

Order flows, information flows, and product flows are some of the key functions of a supply chain. Consumers buy products from retailers. Retailers forecast consumer demand and place orders with distributors. The distributors in turn process the orders, forecast demand, and place orders with manufacturers. This process repeats itself through multiple echelons in the supply chain.

Demand variability often increases further "up" the supply chain. For example, the order patterns at a consumer level might be relatively stable. However, orders from the retailer tend to be more variable and the wholesaler even more variable. Figure 15.17 illustrates this effect. This amplification of order variability through the supply chain is the bullwhip (or whiplash) effect.[40]

There are several causes of the bullwhip effect. Demand forecasting contributes to the bullwhip. Order quantities change as forecasts update to reflect data that are more recent. The longer the lead time, the greater is the safety stock and the greater the impact of a change in the order quantity. Batching of orders similarly contributes to variability. Price fluctuations contribute to demand fluctuations and in turn to the amplification of orders. Product shortages lead to inflated orders.[41] Some recent evidence suggests the bullwhip effect is most severe at the wholesale level, less so at manufacturing.[42]

Internet capabilities can partially offset the bullwhip phenomena. Information sharing and integration of the supply chain helps to counteract demand surprises. Information sharing emphasizes creating an information hub, with all parties in the supply chain viewing the same demand information.[43] Another possible remedy is vendor-managed inventory. In a vendor-managed inventory system,[44] a customer provides vendors with access to demand data for the vendors' products. The customer then expects the vendor to manage the supply chain and be more responsive to demand trends. Large customers such as Wal-Mart have aggressively pursued this approach. Wal-Mart expects vendors to manage inventory at its retail stores to deliver to pre-agreed goals of profitability for the product. This is only possible with information sharing. Internet-based information hubs have the potential to allow a broader implementation of vendor-managed inventory systems, beyond just the largest companies.

Low cost Internet information sharing and standardized web-based access is expanding the use of vendor-managed inventory programs between tier 2 and tier 1 suppliers. Autoliv, a manufacturer of auto safety devices, is a tier 1 supplier to automotive companies. Autoliv uses the

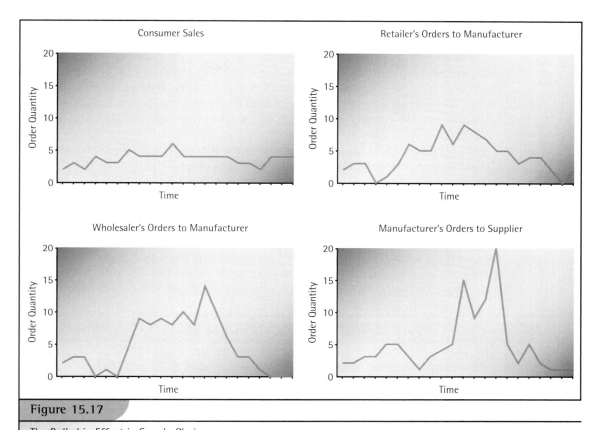

Figure 15.17

The Bullwhip Effect in Supply Chains

Source: Reprinted by permission, Hau L Lee, V Padmanabhan, and Seungjin Whang. "Information Distortion in a Supply Chain: The Bullwhip Effect," *Management Science* 43, no. 4 (April 1997). Copyright © 1997, the Institute for Operations Research and the Management Sciences (INFORMS), 7240 Parkway Drive, Suite 310, Hanover, MD 21076 USA.

Net to coordinate with its suppliers on an hourly basis. Autoliv's vendors can access the data and manage inventory levels of their parts so that Autoliv's production runs in a smooth manner.[45]

The New Product Introduction Process

Handling new product introductions requires coordination of information and new capabilities across the supply chain. Product designs, specifications, and component availability are not static. R&D engineers revise designs based on updated requirements. Procurement managers may recommend a change in components based on availability. Manufacturing engineers might suggest changes based on prototyping. Documenting changes and communicating changes to all parties is an important challenge.

As seen in Chapter 11, new product development increasingly relies on the Net to accelerate the process. Online tools can be used to coordinate new products throughout the supply chain, with the goal of speeding the product to market and making the new product introduction process as parallel and modular as possible.

Outsourcing of manufacturing is a growing trend.[46] Coordination with outsourced manufacturers imposes additional requirements in the new product introduction process. It requires a handoff between the designers and manufacturing. The handoff requires communication and transfer of the design documents and crucial aspects of the design. The communication process is bilateral with the contract manufacturer providing feedback and information back to the design team.

A web-based interface can be used to coordinate new product communications and serve as a repository for related documents. Simultaneous notification of all participants is possible. Tracking capabilities can notify relevant parties of changes in the documents. Since the interface is web based it can allow access to participants both within and outside the organization. A contract manufacturer or a supplier can log in to the system over the web and view documents and observe changes.

Panel C in Figure 15.18 shows the process impact of web-based new product management. For example, a contract manufacturer can get early visibility into a new product design before a design is complete. This can allow the manufacturing engineer to anticipate manufacturing requirements for this product. Similarly, the sourcing group might do some preliminary analysis

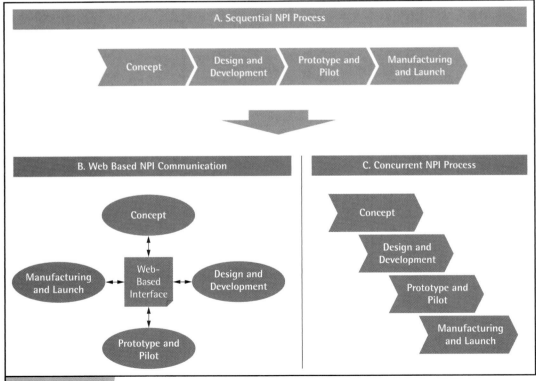

Figure 15.18

Sequential versus Web-Based New Product Introduction (NPI) Process

about the availability of cost-effective substitutes or available in required volumes. There are tradeoffs with respect to what aspects of the work should be concurrent. A web-based process provides visibility to all parties so appropriate tradeoffs can be made.

While large-scale and systematic analysis are not readily available, results from companies that have adopted a web-based platform suggest that there are reductions in cycle time. For example, Johnson and Johnson reports that the use of web-based new product process has resulted in the reduction of cycle time of 52%. Microsoft has reported that its use of a web-based system eliminated several months of cycle time in the introduction of the Xbox.[47]

Global Data Synchronization

Transactions between business partners generate extensive records and documents. Placing an order requires an invoice, payment documents, shipping manifests, and other electronic data and physical documents. Product data are highly dynamic. Introductions of new products, changes in packaging, obsolescence of existing products contribute to the challenge. This is the problem of data synchronization.

The current process for synchronizing data between business partners is often manual, costly, and prone to mistakes. Suppliers send product data in various formats including spreadsheets, faxes, and by express mail. Retailers and contract manufacturers re-enter this data. Since the data arrives in so many forms and formats, errors are inevitable.[48] Virtually identical data creation and updating efforts occur throughout the supply chain, resulting in duplication of effort.

Figure 15.20 hints at the complexity of coordinating a global manufacturing and supply system. Even something as simple as milk comes in hundreds of combinations when all the sources and logistical descriptors are included. Each combination must have codes, tags, and methods of unique identification. Individualization builds on these technological capabilities, such as providing personalized advice and tracking.

Standards simplify data handling dramatically. Both manufacturers and retailers benefit. For manufacturers this provides a single system that they can follow. In the absence of standards, each manufacturer might have to follow the requirements established by multiple retailers, adding costs to the manufacturers operations.

Retailers also benefit from having manufacturers follow a standard. Retailers can make investments in information technology, such as bar code scanning systems, with the assurance that different manufacturers bar codes will work with their scanning system. Additional benefits include

> *Reduction in Out-of-Stocks*—Studies have shown that supply chain delays due to data integrity issues result in approximately 5% of out-of-stocks.[49]
> *Shorter time to Shelf for New Items*—Time to shelf for new items often is a matter of several weeks, and synchronization can reduce this substantially.
> *Reduced Checkout Errors*—Maintaining correct links between checkout systems and inventory reduces "items not being on file" errors and mispricing.

Figure 15.19

UPC Symbol: A Familiar Data Sharing Code

Source: © Tom McCarthy/Photo Edit

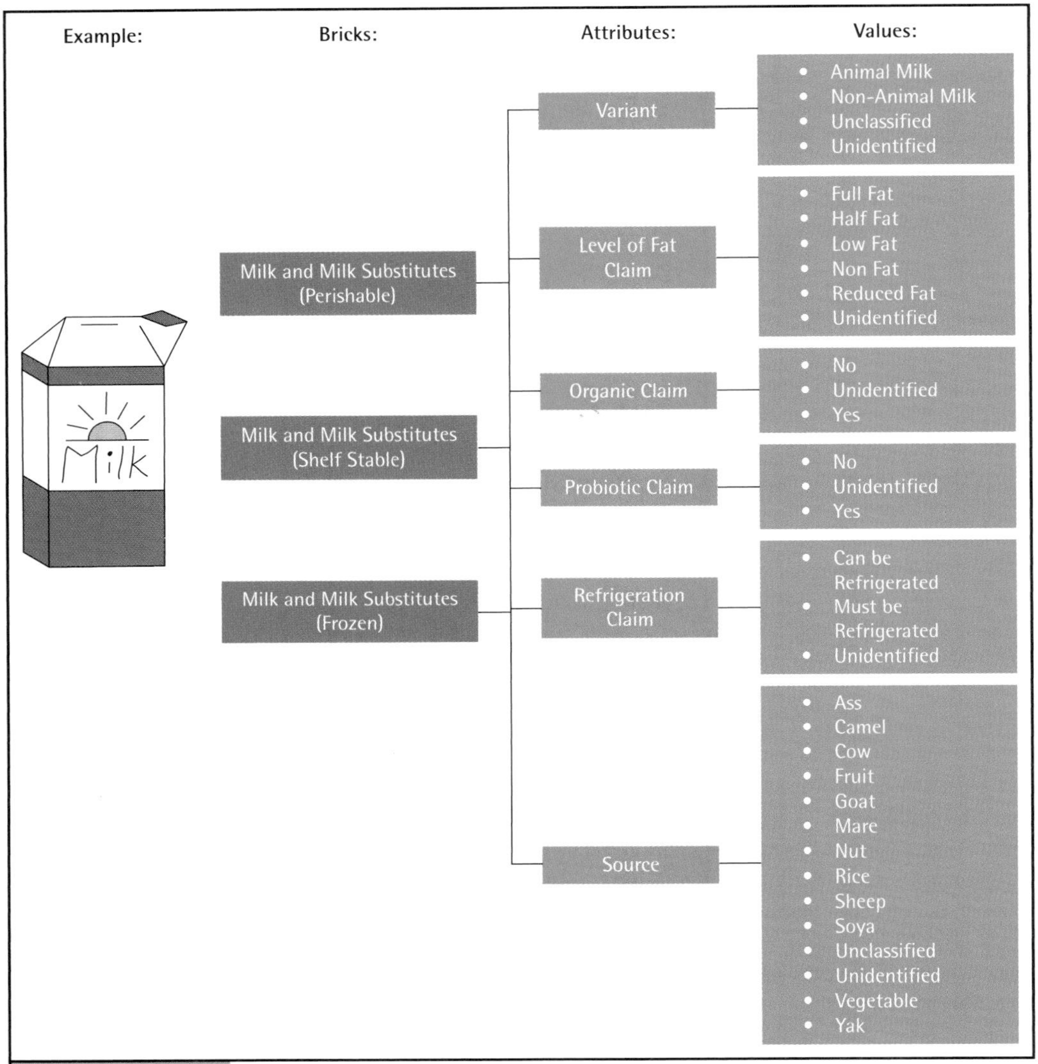

Example:	Bricks:	Attributes:	Values:
		Variant	• Animal Milk • Non-Animal Milk • Unclassified • Unidentified
	Milk and Milk Substitutes (Perishable)	Level of Fat Claim	• Full Fat • Half Fat • Low Fat • Non Fat • Reduced Fat • Unidentified
		Organic Claim	• No • Unidentified • Yes
	Milk and Milk Substitutes (Shelf Stable)	Probiotic Claim	• No • Unidentified • Yes
		Refrigeration Claim	• Can be Refrigerated • Must be Refrigerated • Unidentified
	Milk and Milk Substitutes (Frozen)	Source	• Ass • Camel • Cow • Fruit • Goat • Mare • Nut • Rice • Sheep • Soya • Unclassified • Unidentified • Vegetable • Yak

Figure 15.20

The Complexities of Even Simple Products

Source: EAN.UCC Product Classification Brochure, April 2004. Reprinted by permission from GS1 US.

> *Errors in Purchase Orders*—Eliminating many costly manual checks of purchase orders and deliveries.
> *Reduced Cost for Invoice Reconciliation*—Many invoicing disagreements occur because of data integrity issues. Proper data synchronization reduces "charge backs" and shipping disputes.
> *Reduction in Warehousing Costs*—Synchronized weight and dimension data increases the efficiency of warehousing configuration and logistics.

Creating the proper standards, whether in XML or some other system, requires careful planning and management attention. Benefits are worth it, with companies such as P&G documenting tens of millions of savings from increased supply chain efficiencies. One of the major coordination issues surrounds the global registry (Figure 15.21). Some organization must take the responsibility of maintaining a definitive standard version listing proper codes, details, and new documents. Examples include Transora or World Wide Retail Exchange. The data registry is a potentially valuable resource, with competing groups seeking to be a data hub. An organization such as Alibaba fills much of this role for their vendors and participating buyers. Whether they eventually become part of a larger network, or stay separate, is a strategic decision and an example of the standards battle surrounding supply chain coordination.

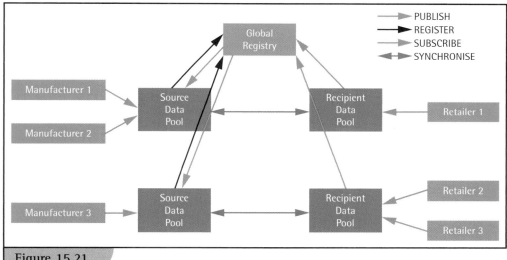

Figure 15.21

The Global Data Synchronization Process

Source: EAN.UCC Global Standard Management Process. Reprinted by permission from GS1 US.

ENDNOTES

1. C.P. Chandrasekhar and Jayati Ghosh. "China's extraordinary export boom." *The Hindu Business Line* May 10, 2005. Ministry of Commerce of the People's Republic of China.
2. "Chinese E-Commerce Site Allows Small Firms to Reach Wider Base." *The Wall Street Journal* February 25, 2004.
3. Jamie O Connell and Gary Loveman, (1995), Li & Fung (Trading) Co., HBS Case # 9-396-075.
4. Alexa.com ranked Alibaba.com as # 38 in its listing of Global 500 sites. Data retrieved on May 13, 2005.
5. Alibaba.com, May 13, 2005.
6. "China's Alibaba.com taking aim at the U.S. Market." Reuters, September 27, 2004.
7. See Erik Brynjolfsson and Lorin Hitt. "Beyond Computation: Information Technology, Organizational Transformation, and Business Practices." *Journal of Economic Perspectives* 14(4), Fall 2000: 23–48. Kevin Stiroh. "Information Technology and the U.S. Productivity Revival: What Do the Industry Data Say?" *The American Economic Review* 92(5), December 2002: 1559–1576.

8. Redesign of business processes can also fail. Scacchi sites a figure as high as 70% of procurement process redesigns failing. Walt Scacchi. "Redesigning Contracted Service Procurement for Internet-based Electronic Commerce: A Case Study." *Information Technology and Management* 2, 2001: 313–334.

9. Chris Forman, Avi Goldfarb and Shane Greenstein. "Digital Dispersion: An Industrial and Geographic Census of Commercial Internet Use." National Bureau of Economic Research, Inc., Working paper WP-02-44, September 2002.

10. An alternative view of the long term structure of B2B channels looks at the functional roles, such as matching, requisitioning and problem solving. See Philip Anderson and Erin Anderson. "The New E-Commerce Intermediaries." *MIT Sloan Management Review* Summer 2002: 53–62.

11. P.M.C. Swatman et al. "The Urgent Case For EDI Standards." 1991. referring to Brawn D. (1989) EDI Developments Abroad and How they Impact on Australia.

12. X12 web site: http://www.x12.org.

13. Nick Wingfield. "In the Beginning there was Electronic Data Interchange and it is Likely to Survive the Internet Quite Well." *Wall Street Journal* May 11, 2001.

14. Thomas V. Bonoma. "Major Sales: Who Really Does all the Buying?" *Harvard Business Review* 1982: 3–11.

15. Retrieved from: Cisco.com, retrieved May 6, 2005.

16. Eric Young. "Web Marketplaces that Really Work." *Business 2.0* November 2001.

17. Andy Pasztor. "Changing Course." *Wall Street Journal* May 21, 2001.

18. The details of the GE Polymerland example are adapted from Alex Frangos. "Just One Word: Plastics." *Wall Street Journal* May 21, 2001.

19. Udith Gebauer and Arie Segev. "Emerging Technologies to Support Indirect procurement: two case studies from the petroleum industry." *Information Technology and Management* 1, 2000: 107–128.

20. David Wyld. "The Weather Report for the Supply Chain: A Longitudinal Analysis of the ISM/Forrester Research Reports on technology in Supply Management 2001–2003." *Management Research News* 27(1), 2004.

21. Aberdeen Group. *The E-Procurement Benchmark Report: Less Hype, More Results.* December 2004.

22. Insert citation for CAPS research study.

23. See Emily Lloyd and Charlotte Mueller. "Payroll Employment Grows in 2004." *Monthly Labor Review* March 2005.

24. For example, Malone and Laubacher (Thomas W. Malone and Robert J. Laubacher. "The Dawn of the E-Lance Economy." *Harvard Business Review* September–October 1998, 145–152) argue that the rise of the Internet as a low-cost coordination mechanism should result in the traditional corporation shrinking and relying more on external parties to get tasks accomplished.

25. The discussion of Information technology consulting, facilities management, and contingent labor is adapted from iSource. Upgrades from eLance and Fieldglass, January 2002.

26. Jai Shekhawat. "Capturing Value from E-Procurement of Services." *Internet World* April 23, 2003.

27. Jan B. Heide. "Inter-organizational Governance in Marketing Channels." *Journal of Marketing* January 1994, 96–107.

28. For example in 1999, the Internet economy was booming and Sun Microsystems was having trouble meeting demand. The cycle time in getting orders into the supply chain had become a gating factor. See Charles A. Holloway, eSourcing Strategy at Sun Microsystems, Stanford Business School, Case Number OIT 34.

29. Thomas Froese and Jeff Rankin. "Representation of Construction Methods in Total Project Systems." *5th Congress on Computing on Civil Engineering* October 1998.

30. See also Goutam Chakraborty, Vishal Lala, David Warren. "An Empirical Investigation of Antecedents of B2B Websites' Effectiveness." *Journal of Interactive Marketing* 16(4), Autumn 2002.

31. These five phases are adapted from Kasturi Rangan. FreeMarkets Online, HBS Case # 9-598-109, 1999.

32. For example, Rangan reports that the weighted average savings from FreeMarkets auctions was 15%, whereas saving in the range of 15–20% are reported by L. Cohn. "B2B: The Hottest Net Bet Yet?" *Business Week* January 17, 2000: 36–37.

33. Ralph Kisiel. "Supplier Group Seeks Code for Auctions." *Automotive News* 67(5974), 2002: 16F.

34. George S. Day, Adam J. Fein and Gregg Ruppersberger. "Shakeouts in Digital Markets: Lessons from B2B Exchanges." *California Management Review* 45(2), Winter 2003, 131–150, identify six core services envisioned by marketplace providers. The six core services that we identify are adapted from their discussion.

35. See Eric Young. "Web Marketplaces that Really Work." *Business 2.0* November 2001.

36. Paul Elias. "Next Generation B2B's Improve Trading." *Red Herring* March 21, 2001.

37. Karen Lundegaard. "Auto Parts Site Next Big Hurdle is Germany's Antitrust Agency." *The Wall Street Journal* September 12, 2000.

38. William M. Bulkeley. "Alliance Led by IBM will Build the World Wide Retail Exchange." *The Wall Street Journal* July 13, 2000.

39. Lynda M. Applegate. Ventro: Builder of B2B Businesses, HBS case # 9-801-274, 2001.

40. Hau L. Lee, V Padmanabhan and Seungjin Whang. "Information Distortion in a Supply Chain: The Bullwhip Effect." *Management Science* 43(4), April 1997: 546–558.

41. See Lee et. al., ibid. Also see David Simchi-Levi, Philip Kaminsky, and Edith Simchi-Levi. *Designing and Managing the Supply Chain.* New York: McGraw Hill, 2003: 103–104.

42. Gerard P. Cachon, Taylor Randall, and Glen M. Schmidt. "In Search of the Bullwhip Effect." Working paper dated April 29, 2005.

43. Hau L. Lee and Seungjin Whang. E-Business and Supply Chain Integration, Stanford Global Supply Chain Forum, SGSCMF-W2-2001, November 2001.

44. Dale D. Achabal, Stephen S. Smith, Shelby S. McIntyre and Kirthi Kalyanam, "A Decision Support System for Vendor Managed Inventory." *Journal of Retailing* 76(4), 2000: 430–454.

45. Karen Lundegaard. "Bumpy Ride." *Wall Street Journal* May 21, 2001.

46. Outsourced manufacturers also called Electronic Manufacturing Service (EMS) providers have enjoyed rapid growth in the 1980's and 1990's. See Ellen Chae and Todd Bailey. "Annual EMS Industry Update." *Prudential Financial* August 7, 2001.

47. Some case studies of improvement in the NPI process are available on the web site of Agile Software. Information retrieved on May 11 2005.

48. See http://www.dcs-is-edi.com/UCCNet.html

49. According to a study by FMI, titled "Retail Out of Stocks: A Worldwide Examination of Extent Causes and Consumers Responses," planning issues including incorrect master data were identified as the causes of out of stock in 18% of the cases.

chapter 16:

Online Research

❝ The first problem of our business is to win an audience, hold an audience, interest an audience. ❞

William Paley[1]

❝ Garbage in, garbage out. ❞

Anonymous

Figure 16.1

Surveys Can Miss the Call
Source: © AP/Wide World Photos

Landon Wins!

Every four years, sample size and margin of error enter the public consciousness. As the presidential campaign heats up, first with the Iowa caucus and then the New Hampshire primary, everyone looks at campaign surveys. This continues up to Election Day, when exit polls and early results start leaking through online campaign blogs. Sometimes results are easy to forecast, with one candidate far in the lead. Often the polls are close to the actual result. Other times, pollsters can end up looking foolish. Market researchers and campaign pollsters have the famous picture in Figure 16.1 burned into their psyche, hoping this is not their year to pull a Dewey.

The problems of 1948 were even worse in 1936. Then a survey by *Literary Digest* magazine, using telephone and auto ownership to recruit a mail survey, predicted victory for Alfred Landon.[2] As the electoral map in Figure 16.2 shows, Franklin Roosevelt actually won re-election in a record-breaking landslide.[3] In 1936, the middle of the Great Depression, owning a telephone or a car was a strong signal of affluence. Many less fortunate leaned toward Roosevelt. There was also a tendency for poorer individuals to decline participation in a telephone survey. People that participated told the truth in the surveys. The huge mistake arose from asking the wrong mix of people in the wrong way for their opinion.[4]

The concerns underlying the polls in 1936 and 1948 have echoes in the Internet world of

Online market research has developed rapidly, for both measuring the online audience and using Net capabilities to improve market research. Not all data is good data. Online data has many advantages of speed and low cost, but care must be taken to use it appropriately.

Topics covered in this chapter include:

> Political Surveys

> Online Surveys

> Finding the Right Audience

> Congestion and Delay

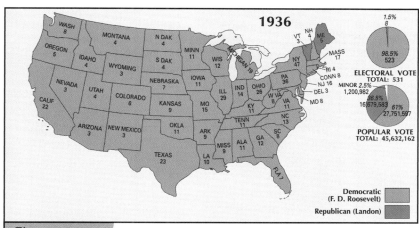

Figure 16.2

Even Worse in 1936

Source: National Atlas of the United States, "Presidential Elections 1978–2000," published 2001, http://nationalatlas.gov.

today. First, the ease of assembling a sample may not be a good guide to the quality of the data. Determining the right sample to ask questions of requires careful attention to any possible sources of bias. This can result from improper recruiting, or differences in the rates of response. Online surveys are extremely easy to create, and often lead to a flood of responses. The quality of this data, however, may be much lower than it could be with attention to sample selection.

Related problems arise when marketers try to recruit an audience to a site. Marketers must decide not just on the volume of traffic, but on the nature of it. While this may show up eventually in conversion rates, efforts to reach out to the wrong groups are frustrating and eat up valuable marketing efforts.

Finding the right audience can sometimes lead to behavior that seems almost paradoxical. The 2004 U.S. presidential campaign provides such an example. The Net was vital to the campaign in many ways. Candidates raised unprecedented amounts of money using online tools. Campaign blogs and online journalists were the new stars in political reporting. Campaign humor and spoofs received millions of hits and head-line coverage. Email lists mobilized campaign workers from the early days of the primaries through the precinct walking and get out the vote efforts. In fact, election 2004 marked the first time that both nominees mentioned their campaign web sites during their convention acceptance speech.[5]

Despite the prominence of the campaign Internet, the online world received very little of the massive amount of campaign advertising. The battle for swing voters in swing states was a television fight. The two campaigns and their supporters spent a total advertising budget of over $900 million dollars. Online advertising received less than $7 million. Both campaigns relied on the traditional approach of using demographic-based gross ratings points (GRPs).[6] This jumps out from the Bush campaign primary spending in the 93 swing markets identified early in the campaign, and shown in Figure 16.3. Each dot represents one of the markets for that target female segment. Campaign planners clearly achieved 10,000 GRPs among older females, half that number for 25–54 year-old females, and half again for the youngest segment. This is classic brand building media scheduling, aimed at selling their candidate prior to the fall campaign.

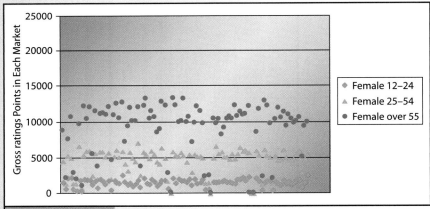

Figure 16.3

Republican Primary Campaign GRPs in 93 Swing Markets

Source: Copyright © 2004 Wisconsin Advertising Project, University of Wisconsin-Madison.

New technologies create new market research opportunities. Each new method has strengths and weaknesses. It takes time to test and learn what works best, and what is unreliable.

There are many fascinating market research questions online. Previous chapters covered some of these, such as new product concept testing in Chapter 11. This chapter looks at the survey and audience selection problem. Like politics, defining and finding the right target segments can mean the difference between success and failure. The chapter concludes with a discussion of congestion and delay, making sure that when the audience arrives, the message actually gets through.

RUNNING A SURVEY

In a survey, a researcher asks a sample of respondents a fixed set of questions.[7] Surveys measure attitudes, perceptions, intentions, and recall. A basic survey is very easy to implement, leading to wide usage. Unfortunately, this also brings with it the potential for confusion and misuse.

Moving surveys online is a natural choice of market researchers. Converting a paper questionnaire to a web page is simple, with results automatically posted to a database or spreadsheet. While this does not necessarily ensure that the online survey is usable or better, it is extremely cost effective. Online surveys can utilize enhanced visuals and video. The network reaches remote respondents. Real-time networking also allows respondents to get instantaneous feedback on how their opinions match the rest of the population. Surveys foster interactivity, resulting in surveys as entertainment.

Reflecting these benefits, the web-based survey industry is growing rapidly. Industry data shows web-based surveys rose from less than 10% of the overall U.S. survey market in 2000 to almost 30% of the market in 2005.[8] This includes investments in the online panels discussed in the next section.[9]

There are inherent speed, reliability, and cost tradeoffs in survey research. Reliability requires carefully constructed random samples. These are costly, and often slow to construct. In other situations, the focus is exploration rather than confirmation, and speed is the key. The early presumption was that web-based survey research techniques would focus on these types of "quick and dirty" research projects.[10] Web-based survey research has rapidly progressed beyond this niche. With innovative approaches to improve quality, web surveys are emerging as a cost-effective and speedier alternative to traditional research techniques. If well constructed, they also achieve comparable reliability.

| Types of Online Surveys

Table 16.1 identifies eight types of web surveys, three of them convenience based and four of them probability based. The distinction between convenience and probability-based surveys is a fundamental one, often ignored in the public press. While a probability-based survey attempts to capture a representative sample of some population, a convenience survey is more opportunistic in who provide answers.

Many sources of bias can contaminate survey accuracy. Table 16.2 illustrates one type of problem, nonparticipation, and the very different results and interpretations it can cause. The survey topic is online privacy. The true population is 50% male and 50% female. Assume that females are much more concerned with privacy (70%) than males (40%). Fifty-five percent of the individuals in the population express concern about online privacy. Of these, 20% of individuals are male *and* concerned about online privacy.

The second part of the table shows the results obtained from a sample subject to nonparticipation. The researcher samples probabilistically from a *sampling frame*—a list of the population. The researcher splits the list into two subgroups, male and female, and randomly samples an equal number of individuals from each subgroup. The researcher encounters a higher rate of non-response among females and as a result has a sample of 70% males.

Table 16.1

Types of Online Surveys	
Convenience Methods	**Probability-Based Methods**
1. Entertainment 2. Unrestricted self-selected surveys 3. Volunteer opt-in panels	4. Intercept surveys 5. List-based surveys 6. Web option in mixed mode surveys 7. Pre-recruited panel of Internet users 8. Pre-recruited panel of full population

Source: Mick C. Couper. "Web Surveys: A Review of Issues and Approaches." *Public Opinion Quarterly* 64, no. 4 (2000): 464–494.

Table 16.2

Projection Error Due to a Non-Representative Sample: An Example						
	Population			**Sample**		
Group	% of Individuals	% Concerned with Online Privacy	% of Individuals Concerned About Online Privacy	% of Individuals	% Concerned with Online Privacy	% of Individuals Concerned About Online Privacy
Male Female	50% 50%	40% 70%	20% 35%	70% 30%	40% 70%	28% 21%
	Actual Proportion →		55%	Sample Estimate →		49%

Consequently, the survey incorrectly finds only 49% of the individuals in the population are concerned about online privacy.

The example illustrates several basic lessons. First, probability sampling requires a sampling frame. Second, the procedure attempts to recruit individuals with a known probability. Third, probability sampling per se does not ensure the results of the survey are not biased. The high rate of non-response among females biases the sample estimate. If researchers notice this differential participation, they can correct for non-response with an appropriate weighting procedure.

When convenience sampling is used a researcher does not know *ex ante* probability of sampling any particular respondent. As a result, it may not be possible to determine the direction or the magnitude of the sample bias. Unknown factors make it difficult to project the sample estimates to the full population. In spite of severe statistical limitations, convenience samples can be useful for certain types of exploratory research as well as entertaining content.

> *Convenience Surveys*

> Entertainment

Opinion polls conducted by news organizations such as CNN or ABC are highly visible. Figure 16.4 shows an opinion poll conducted on CNN's web site. Any visitor to the site can participate. As the caveats beneath the poll results note, the poll is not scientific. These types of polls should be considered as content and as a method for providing interactivity. An individual can express an opinion and get immediate feedback about how the rest of the respondents are thinking. It is not meaningful to discuss margin of error or sample precision.

A second category of entertainment polls enables viewers and fans to exchange opinions about TV shows. Broadcast network web sites host these types of polls, and network executives use them to monitor the sentiments of the fan base and shape the evolution of the storyline.

A third type of entertainment polls simply provides an outlet for people to share opinions and declare brand allegiance. A search on Yahoo! entertainment produced a list of at least 20 sites dedicated to polling on various topics including rating beer, comparing Coke versus Pepsi, and other topics.

> Unrestricted Self-Selected Surveys

Surveys that allow respondents to self-select on a web site or through a banner ad fall into this category. One complication with these types of surveys is repeat responders. Examples of surveys of this type include the WWW user survey conducted by the GVU Center at the University of Georgia, and the National Geographic Society's Survey 2000.[11] These types of surveys yield early insights, but must be used with caution.

A proposed approach to reduce coverage bias is to weight the demographics of the survey respondents to reflect the demographics of a larger universe, such as all Internet users

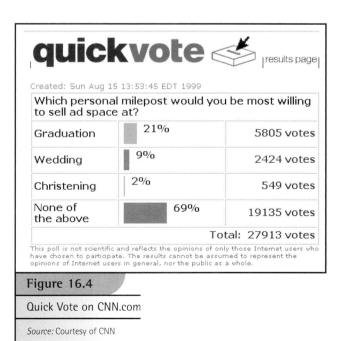

Figure 16.4

Quick Vote on CNN.com

Source: Courtesy of CNN

or the total U.S. population. Such weighting procedures are effective only if responses patterns relate to demographic variables in a simple and systematic manner. For example, in Table 16.2, the type of response varies by the gender of the respondent. This is a relatively simple relationship between the response type and gender, and weighting the respondents by gender can correct sampling bias. However if the relationship between the respondent type and the response is more complex, then simple weighting procedures may not work.

> Volunteer Opt-In Panels

The recruitment process for volunteer opt-in panels is in some ways similar to the process used for unrestricted self-selected surveys. Panelists volunteer to join. Panel operators recruit panelists in many places including their own web site, by placing banners or by purchasing sponsored links or keywords at search engines or recruiting at sites that focus on survey respondents.

In volunteer opt-in panels, the panel operator can control for repeated responses from the same panelists or passing the survey along. Panel operators also use weighting schemes to project the results of the panel to the population. For example, Harris Interactive uses propensity weighting or propensity score adjustment.[12] These types of projection approaches tend to be proprietary in nature.

> *Probability Surveys*

Probability sampling approaches use a sampling frame that provides full coverage of the relevant population. For example if the focus of the research is visitors to a particular site, then sampling every *n*th visitor to the site will provide a random sample. Other applications might require an approach such as random digit dialing (RDD) to generate a random sample. In RDD, a firm places telephone calls randomly to recruit the sample.

> Intercept Surveys

Intercept surveys have a long history in marketing and public opinion research. The purchase intercept technique interviews shoppers before or after they make a purchase in a retail store.[13] Exit polling intercepts voters as they leave poll booths. Intercept techniques are used to study tourists, visitors to events, and mall shoppers.

On the Web, a random process can select visitors before, during, or after a site visit or purchase. In an intercept survey the sampling frame is the set of visitors who visit a web site during a given time period. Cookies can track respondents to control for redundancy.

Third parties can conduct intercept surveys on their own web site or the retailer's web sites. For example, Bizrate.com rates the retail experience of shoppers at online retailers. Bizrate has participating retailers who allow the company to intercept shoppers as soon as they make a purchase. Shoppers receive an email survey that asks them to evaluate the site. The results are available to shoppers in the form of a summary report as illustrated in Figure 16.5.

> List-Based Samples

Sites that have a registered user base, or acquire a relevant list, can use it as a sampling frame. The actual implementation of the survey can use an intercept technique or an email follow up. For example, only registered users can access the online version of the newspaper the *Wall Street Journal*. The *Journal* can intercept these registered users on a random basis and request their participation.

Surveys can also be implemented by email. The email reminds the sample to participate in the survey. Registration data allow further refinements. Researchers may establish a quota for a certain customer type or demographic category. One obvious limitation of the registration list approach is a lack of coverage of prospects or casual visitors.

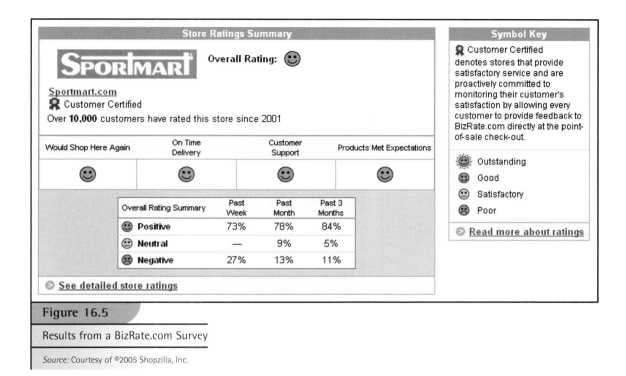

Figure 16.5

Results from a BizRate.com Survey

Source: Courtesy of ©2005 Shopzilla, Inc.

> Mixed Modes, Pre-Recruited Panels, and Full Population Probability Samples

Instead of relying on sampling frames from the Internet, a probability sample based on the full population can be generated using RDD techniques. In this case, the entire sample will not have online access and the researcher has several options regarding implementation of the survey.

One option is a mixed mode design. In a mixed mode design, the Web is one of the many alternative approaches to implement the survey. Initial implementation of mixed mode surveys reported a low response rate for the web-based option. The growth in Internet adoption might change this.

Pre-recruited panels are in many ways similar to opt-in panels discussed in non-probability surveys. A crucial difference is with respect to panelist recruitment, with the pre-recruited panel using probability sampling. Since the panel operator controls the recruitment of the sample there is a known probability of selection. For example, recruitment for panels such as comScore Media Metrix and Nielsen Net Ratings follow a RDD procedure. For hard to reach segments such as educational institutions and business users, recruitment follows an opt-in procedure. A weighting procedure balances the opt-in respondents and the overall panel.[14] After recruitment, respondents complete the survey online.

Survey Quality

The power of lower costs, quick turnaround, and large samples has created a large and growing industry around web-based survey research. Considerations of data quality balance cost and quick turnaround. Sampling, coverage, non-response, and measurement error affect data quality.[15]

> Coverage

Web survey quality depends on coverage, which depends on the penetration of the Internet. One study of tourists found that respondents to web surveys tended to be younger, and have higher income,[16] perhaps reflecting the demographic make up of the Internet at that time. These issues become relevant when researchers project web-based results to a broader population, such as in a poll of presidential candidates. Technology-related issues such as connectivity problems and bounced emails affect coverage as well. Case studies find bounced emails a substantial problem, in some cases exceeding 20% of messages sent.[17] If these errors and bounced messages are regional or due to some bias, sample quality will suffer.

> Self-Selection Bias

Self-selection bias creates another problem area for survey quality. Participants who respond to a survey because they see an item of interest or because of incentives may be different from the rest of the population. For example, one study found men responding more to incentives for computer equipment whereas women respond more for health-oriented topics.[18]

Professional respondents are individuals who participate in multiple panels for compensation and incentives. There appears to be growth in these professional respondents for online studies.[19] An example is the SurveySpy site, focusing on recruiting panelists. Text on the site states that "the more surveys you sign up and complete the more cash and rewards you earn." Such a survey incentive creates the potential for over representation of a special group of respondents.

> Response Rate

Response rates are an area of ongoing concern for online surveys. Some studies report lower response rates in online surveys. Table 16.3 provides a summary of response rates from web surveys reported in a research study. Rates vary from a high of 73% to a low of 6%. Technical issues, coupled with spam and email filters contribute to the non-response rate on an ongoing basis. Non-response contributes to a smaller sample size and the possibility that those who do not respond are different in some unknown way. The virtually zero cost of sending follow up emails can contribute to an over mailing situation that can lower response rates to web surveys across the board.

Response rates can depend on recruitment and implementation modes. If the recruitment mode is offline, it might produce a lower response rate for the online component. Tactics to improve response rates include modifying the language and length of the survey, prior notification, personalization of cover letters,[20] follow-ups, sponsorships, and monetary and non-monetary incentives.

One study reports that a certain type of mixed mode survey received a 72% response rate. In this study there was a mail survey pre-notifying participants followed by a survey mailing. The mail surveys included a link to the web-based survey. An email with a link to the web-based survey followed the postal mail. Finally, about one month after the initial notification there was a postcard mailing. The combination created the high response rate.

> Measurement Errors

The design of survey instruments can change behavior and cause measurement error. Sources of measurement error include confusing wording of questions, incomplete alternatives, order of

Table 16.3

Response Rates in Web Surveys			
Author(s)	Treatments	Response Rate (%)	Response Quality
Sproull 1986	Email Face-to-face	73 87	1.4% item omission rate 0.02% item omission rate
Kiesler & Sproull	Email Mail	67 75	Email had fewer mistakes and a higher item completion rate
Parker 1992	Email Company mail	68 38	Not reported
Schuldt & Totten 1994	Email Mail	19.3 56.5	Not reported
Kittleson 1995	Email Mail	28.1 75.5	Not reported
Mehta & Sivadas 1995	Email Mail	60 58	Similar number of item omissions, email respondents wrote more
Opperman 1995	Email Two mail surveys	49 26/33	Not reported
Tse et al. 1995	Email Mail	6 27	No significant difference in number of item omissions
Bachmann, Elfrink & Vazzana 1996	Email Mail	52.5 65.6	Email respondents were more willing to answer open-ended questions
Weible & Wallace 1998	Email Mail Fax Web Form	30 35.7 31 34.4	Not reported
Schaefer & Dillman 1998	4 mail contacts 4 email contacts mail=>email email=>mail	57.5 58 48 54.4	Email surveys had fewer item omissions and longer answers to open-ended questions
Tse 1998	Email Mail	7 52	No significant difference found
Bachmann, Elfrink & Vazzana 1999	Email Mail	46 19	Email respondents were more expansive, but higher item omission
Dommeyer & Moriarty 2000	Email (attached) Email (embed)	8 37	No significant difference found

Source: Ursula Grandcolas, Ruth Rettie, and Kira Marusenko. "Web Survey Bias: Sample or Mode Effect." *Journal of Marketing Management* 19 (2000): 1–21.

appearance effects and the ineffective use of graphical elements. Graphical elements and color can alter the perception of information. Other design choices include radio buttons, drop-down menus, and ordering of items. Initial research findings suggest that these design choices are not neutral.

Figure 16.6 illustrates the effect of using drop-down boxes compared to radio buttons.[21] The results indicate that drop-down boxes that show a few items have a large order effect. The first five items shown in the drop-down box have a much higher selection propensity compared to other items. These results suggest that the design elements of a web survey are an important choice. Even simple design decisions can alter responses.

Another set of design considerations emerge with narration and multimedia surveys. Some design choices include the use of a male voice versus a female voice for the interviewer. Other voice considerations include tone. For example, a stern versus a cheerful tone of the interviewer's voice might lead to measurement errors. As with voice tone, the expression on the talking face can look stern or pleasant. Research in social interface theory indicates that subjects can be "primed" with subtle cues.[22] The extent to which these effects manifest themselves in web-based surveys is the subject of ongoing research. The challenge for web survey designers is to use the multimedia capabilities of the web to produce high quality survey data without inadvertently causing measurement error.

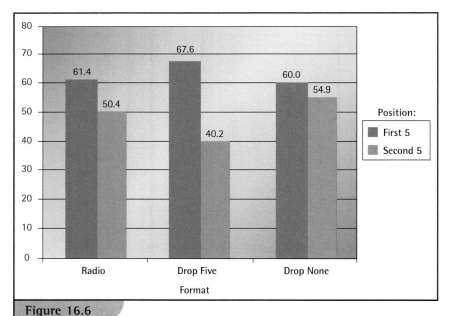

Figure 16.6

Drop Down Boxes Amplify the Ordering Effect

Source: Mick P. Couper, Roger Tourangeau, and Fredrick G. Conrad. "What They See is What We Get: Response Options for Web Surveys." *Social Science Computer Review* 22, no. 1 (2004): 111–127.

FINDING THE RIGHT AUDIENCE

Marketers attempt to find the right audience for their advertising and promotional efforts, whether the medium is television or online sites. Optimizing ad placement through analysis and statistical research can reduce the cost of finding the right audience and raise the effectiveness of activities that follow. One carefully measured study of banner advertising found that proper audience affinities, the tendency of different sites to attract very different readership, boosted visit likelihood by 38% and visit to purchase conversion rates by 24%.[23]

Online sites can extend the traditional media approach of defining a target audience and finding matching media vehicles with the additional capabilities possible with extra information. Online methods, especially those combining tracking with specially recruited and maintained consumer panels, provide data about surfing patterns across web sites. This includes demographics of visitors, time of visit, overall coverage, audience duplication across sites, and coverage of local markets.

The online setting provides additional measurement opportunities and challenges. One difficulty comes from web site domain names. Since many web properties consist of multiple domain names, understanding the hierarchical structure of domains is important to tracking. Traffic variability is another challenge. Online traffic patterns can change rapidly. Monitoring traffic trends is useful (Table 16.4). Internet users tend to visit multiple web sites. Without some measure of audience duplication, visitors may receive multiple versions of promotions and statistics will be inaccurate.

Further measurements help establish the campaign and advertising effectiveness. Digital tracking tools enable tracking sources of traffic to a web site and losses when visitors exit. Online data also provide behavioral measurements, such as identifying if a particular panelist visited a health site or applied for a credit card application online. Online data combined with offline survey data can provide rich behavioral and demographic profiles.

| Panel versus Log File Measurements

Figure 16.7 contrasts two different data sources available for audience analysis. The left side of the figure illustrates the recording of traffic in log files. Large sites have multiple servers that handle requests from the Internet. The servers maintain a log of their requests and the data in these log files provide one basis for measuring site traffic. Auditors analyze the log files and report site traffic. Web sites that sell advertising space provide traffic reports from log files to current and potential advertisers.

Log files need adjustments. They contain traffic from both domestic and international visitors, while the advertiser may only desire exposures for domestic vistors. They do not reflect

Table 16.4								
Online Audience Measurement								
Domains and Tracking	→	Trends and Duplication	→	Source and Loss Analysis	→	Demographic and Behavioral Targeting	→	Reach and Frequency Analysis

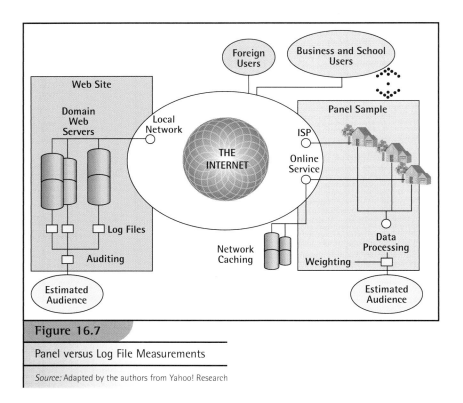

Figure 16.7

Panel versus Log File Measurements

Source: Adapted by the authors from Yahoo! Research

pages served from a local cache or from content delivery networks (discussed later in this chapter). Log files also need adjustments to reflect stopped pages, failed responses, and traffic from search engine indexing programs. In the case of very large sites, traffic reporting is sometimes on sampled logs, not the total files available. Other potential issues with log files include server crashes and corrupted files. Many sites do not require registration or set permanent browser cookies, so estimating unique users requires making some assumptions.

An alternate audience measurement approach uses a panel of households. Household recruitment into a panel typically follows a random digit dialing methodology. In some cases, a panel operator might combine RDD recruitment with other forms of recruitment and balance the sample to the population using a weighting procedure.

Panelists provide demographic information by filling out a survey. A software meter installed on the panelist's PC collects Internet usage data. Some measurement services collect data using a proxy methodology, in which a user's browser unobtrusively routes all page requests through the measurement company's network of dedicated servers.[24]

Panel data provide unique benefits. They capture web site visit patterns for all the sites that a household visits. Using this across-site visit information, panel operators can calculate audience duplication and switching behavior across web sites. Panel data allows the calculation of repeat visit rates. Another unique benefit of panel data is the availability of demographics of the panelists. Merging offline data obtained from third parties with panel data extends the scope of the analysis.[25]

As with other survey methods, an unrepresentative panel can lead to problems. There are many reasons why the households may not reflect the general population. One reason is a biased or unstructured recruiting of the panel. Another reason is non-participation. Certain household types might be less willing to participate. For example, one study showed that panels recruited for tracking consumer-packaged goods tend to have fewer high-income households.[26] Weighting and balancing procedures can reduce some of the issues related to representation.

Domains and Tracking

Online organizations create their site structure with multiple goals in mind. As seen in Chapter 6, branding philosophy influences domain design. Traffic-building considerations may argue for funneling traffic to a main homepage and branching from there. Business model considerations, especially for advertisers seeking to increase their total audience, also bring multiple properties under the same upper-level domain. Usability experts push for flatter site structures, making it easier to navigate quickly to desired information.

The hierarchical structure of a site affects online research, and tracking services have a vocabulary expressing different levels of the hierarchy. Figure 16.8 provides an illustrative example. While one might think of Yahoo! as a single entity, from the perspective of tracking it is a *property*. The term *property* refers to all Yahoo! owned sites and is the top of the media classification hierarchy. Media entities under a property are under common or majority ownership by a single legal entity.[27]

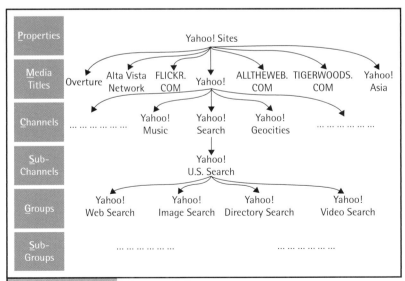

Figure 16.8

Hierarchical Classification Structure Used for Tracking Media Entities

Source: Data Source comScore Media Metrix, Figure Authors

The Yahoo! web site itself is a *media title* and is at the second level of the hierarchy. A media title is an editorially and brand-consistent collection of content. Other media titles at the second level of the hierarchy include Overture, the Alta Vista Network, and Tigerwoods.com. Channels, sub-channels, groups, and subgroups refer to additional classifications of editorially consistent content. For example, Yahoo! Search is a channel. Within Yahoo! Search, U.S. Search is a sub-channel. Web Search, Image Search, Directory Search, and Video Search are groups within the sub-channel search.

The hierarchical classification of media entities affects site metrics. Many crucial site metrics such as number of unique visitors, traffic, demographics, and frequency of repeat visits may vary across the hierarchy. Table 16.5 continues with the example of the Yahoo! properties. Almost all (99%) of the unique visitors at the Yahoo! properties visit the Yahoo! media title. There are considerable differences even within a group such as Yahoo! U.S. Search. Yahoo! Image Search receives only 15% of the unique visitors of Yahoo! Web search, but the data suggest differences in time spent on web search versus image search. For the period, the average minutes spent per usage day by a visitor to image search was 4.0, compared to just 1.5 for Web search.

Trends and Duplication

Traffic patterns at web sites are dynamic. They can change by time of the day, day of the week, and by season. Figure 16.9 illustrates this for professional sports leagues in the United States. With the start of the professional baseball season, there is a sharp increase in traffic at sites such as MLB.com (the official site of Major League Baseball). The effect is even stronger for the NFL. Following the end of the NBA season in June there is a summer dip in fan interest.

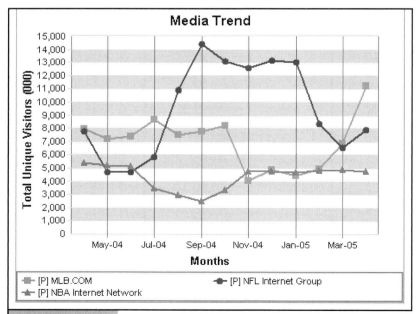

Figure 16.9

Trends in Unique Visitors for Sports Sites

Source: comScore Media Metrix.

Table 16.5

Comparison Metrics for Yahoo! Sites

Classification	Web Entity	Total Unique Visitors (000)	% Reach	Average Daily Visitors (000)	Total Minutes (MM)	Average Minutes per Usage Day	Total Pages Viewed (MM)	Average Pages per Usage Day	Average Minutes per Page	Average Usage Days per Visitor	Average Pages per Visitor	Buying Power Index (BPI)
Property	Yahoo! Sites	116,321	70.5	42,124	33,107	26.2	42,738	33.8	0.8	10.9	367	122
Media Title	Yahoo!	114,803	69.6	41,599	33,047	26.5	42,578	34.1	0.8	10.9	371	123
Media Title	Overture	5,617	3.4	735	15	0.7	55	2.5	0.3	3.9	10	74
Media Title	AltaVista Network	3,956	2.4	336	35	3.5	76	7.5	0.5	2.6	19	192
Media Title	FLICKR.COM	784	0.5	43	3	1.9	9	7.3	0.3	1.6	12	150
Media Title	ALLTHEWEB.COM	515	0.3	51	3	2.3	16	10.6	0.2	3	31	130
Media Title	TIGERWOODS.COM	170	0.1	12	3	8.7	2	6.3	1.4	2.1	13	250
Media Title	Yahoo! Asia	116	0.1	8	0	0.9	0	2.1	0.4	2	4	19
Media Title	YISOU.COM	71	0	4	0	2.4	1	5.2	0.5	1.9	10	55
Group	Yahoo! Web Search	61,395	37.2	11,549	523	1.5	1,612	4.7	0.3	5.6	26	132
Group	Yahoo! Image Search	9,049	5.5	659	78	4	281	14.2	0.3	2.2	31	142
Group	Search	2,219	1.3	96	2	0.7	6	2.2	0.3	1.3	3	103
Group	Yahoo! Video Search	1,859	1.1	91	6	2.1	21	7.8	0.3	1.5	12	47

Source: comScore Media Metrix, April 2005.

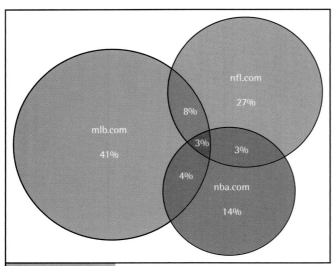

One of the key challenges in audience campaigns is visitor duplication across web sites in a given time period. Depending on the type of campaign and the number of impressions required to convert a customer, some duplication might be desirable. Excessive exposure, however, wastes advertising dollars and consumer attention. Server log files provide detailed information on surfing patterns *within* a web site. Panel data capture information at the household level and hence can provide information on surfing patterns *across* web sites. Combining these two data sources on surfing helps marketers measure and understand audience duplication between a group of sites.

Figure 16.10

Visitor Overlap Across Sports Sites, April 2005

Source: Raw data from comScore Media Metrix, figure by authors.

Figure 16.10 shows duplication across the official baseball (mlb.com), football (nfl.com), and basketball (nba.com) sites. Duplication reflects the unique visitor overlap of these three sports.[28] The total population consists of the panel members that visited at least one site during the month. Only 3% of this group visited all three, while 41% of the unduplicated visitors visited only mlb.com during the month. Another way of viewing this is that 73% of visitors to mlb.com did not visit either the football or basketball sites that month (41/(41+4+3+8)), but 27% did.

In a media campaign analysis, simply adding up the traffic at the three sites would lead to double counting and inflated measures.[29] Even though the overlap between these three sites seems low in an absolute sense, it can add up to a considerable total duplication factor. Overlap statistics may change by month. A month such as September is likely to have more overlap between football and baseball, when both sports are active and fan interest is high.

Source and Loss Analysis

Understanding the context of the shopping trip is very useful in retailing. For example, Wal-Mart's focus on the needs of large basket shoppers and fill-up shopping trips has contributed to its extraordinary success in discount retailing. Other retailers differentiate by focusing on a different type of shopping trip. 7-Eleven finds success by focusing on the specific needs of the convenience shopper.

Understanding the context of the visit helps in the online world as well, with tracking data making it cheaper and easier than traditional settings. Tracking the physical locations that a shopper visited during a shopping trip is cumbersome and costly. Online web logs routinely capture the referring URL, and this enables an understanding of the source of traffic. In addition to the source of traffic, a panel-tracking service can reveal the destinations to which traffic was "lost" and discover where visitors went next.

Source and loss together help create the context of an online session. Source and loss analysis helps improve understanding of visitor motivations and potential sources of traffic. The natural propensity of a source to generate traffic can improve the cost-effectiveness of a media plan. Source loss analysis can guide usability improvements by identifying the reference set of web sites that drive expectations of the online experience. Source loss analysis also helps identify the competition at the level of a site visit. The examples that follow focus on audience building and competitive analysis.

A source loss analysis augments insights from a duplication study. For example, consider the following sequence of site visits for an individual:

$$Logon \rightarrow Site\ A \rightarrow Site\ B \rightarrow Site\ C \rightarrow Site\ D \rightarrow Site\ E \rightarrow Logoff$$

Suppose this sequence is typical of site visit patterns of the population. From a media planning perspective, the audience duplication across any two sites is 100%. However, a source loss analysis conducted for Sites B and D would not show any direct overlap between the two sites. However, a source loss analysis between Sites B and C would show a strong overlap.

Source loss analysis can reveal powerful sites. Table 16.6 presents the #1 source and the #1 loss for the top 10 web properties. Many browsing sessions start and end with Yahoo! or MSN and hence the #1 source and exit for both these portals is a logon and a logoff. This is consistent with many users having the site as their home page.

Figure 16.11 presents the top 20 sources and losses for IRS.GOV for the peak month of April. The largest portals and search sites account for about 38% of all traffic to the site. Slightly over 6% of the traffic came from a logon, which identifies the first site in a browsing session. Sometimes this is because the site was set to be the homepage. As one would expect, a tax software site such as Intuit.com and sites providing support services (HRBlock.com) also provide traffic. Although lower in magnitude compared to the portal, these sites might provide traffic of better quality. A logoff at the end of a browsing session is the number one reason for a loss.

A government agency such as the IRS can use this data to understand the support needs of taxpayers. If a particular software package generates many visitors looking for explanations, the IRS might customize an answer to quickly resolve a common question. Providing forms to other sites might lower congestion. Visits that come from and terminate to the same site, combined with the pages viewed, strongly hint at the context of the visit.

Table 16.6

Source Loss Analysis for Top 10 Web Properties

Property Traffic Rank	Property	Classification	Source		Loss	
			Property	Entries	Property	Exits
1	Yahoo!	Portal	Logon	13.3%	Logoff	11.2%
2	MSN	Portal	Logon	15.0%	Logoff	9.7%
3	Google	Search	Time Warner*	7.5%	Logoff	3.4%
4	eBay	Auctions	Time Warner*	8.7%	Logoff	12.5%
5	Ask Jeeves	Search	Yahoo!	6.9%	Logoff	6.4%
6	Amazon	Retail	Google	7.4%	Logoff	10.5%
7	CNET	News	Time Warner*	8.4%	Time Warner*	8.5%
8	Viacom	Media	Time Warner*	8.2%	Logoff	8.3%
9	Monster	Job Board	Yahoo!	10.7%	Logoff	7.3%
10	NY Times Digital	News	Google	9.0%	Google	6.9%

Reporting Period: April 2005
Source: Raw data from comScore Media Metrix, figure by authors. *Includes AOL.

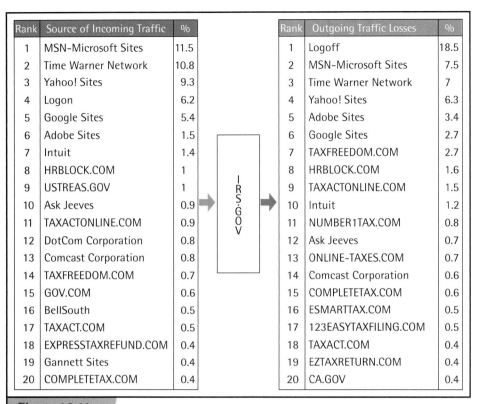

Rank	Source of Incoming Traffic	%
1	MSN-Microsoft Sites	11.5
2	Time Warner Network	10.8
3	Yahoo! Sites	9.3
4	Logon	6.2
5	Google Sites	5.4
6	Adobe Sites	1.5
7	Intuit	1.4
8	HRBLOCK.COM	1
9	USTREAS.GOV	1
10	Ask Jeeves	0.9
11	TAXACTONLINE.COM	0.9
12	DotCom Corporation	0.8
13	Comcast Corporation	0.8
14	TAXFREEDOM.COM	0.7
15	GOV.COM	0.6
16	BellSouth	0.5
17	TAXACT.COM	0.5
18	EXPRESSTAXREFUND.COM	0.4
19	Gannett Sites	0.4
20	COMPLETETAX.COM	0.4

IRS.GOV

Rank	Outgoing Traffic Losses	%
1	Logoff	18.5
2	MSN-Microsoft Sites	7.5
3	Time Warner Network	7
4	Yahoo! Sites	6.3
5	Adobe Sites	3.4
6	Google Sites	2.7
7	TAXFREEDOM.COM	2.7
8	HRBLOCK.COM	1.6
9	TAXACTONLINE.COM	1.5
10	Intuit	1.2
11	NUMBER1TAX.COM	0.8
12	Ask Jeeves	0.7
13	ONLINE-TAXES.COM	0.7
14	Comcast Corporation	0.6
15	COMPLETETAX.COM	0.6
16	ESMARTTAX.COM	0.5
17	123EASYTAXFILING.COM	0.5
18	TAXACT.COM	0.4
19	EZTAXRETURN.COM	0.4
20	CA.GOV	0.4

Figure 16.11

Source Loss Analysis for IRS.Gov, April 2005

Source: Raw data from comScore Media Metrix, figure by authors.

Figure 16.12 provides an example of source loss data used to analyze competitive overlap. The focal site in this case is Bebe.com, the retailer of women's fashion-forward apparel. The top sources of traffic are Portals. The top retailer in terms of source traffic is Nordstrom's, the up-market department store. Federated Department stores is also a source, but at a lower rate due to its mid-market position. Other traffic sources include the Gap and teen-oriented retailers such as Wet Seal. Bebe loses traffic to portals. Bebe also loses traffic to other apparel retailers who appeal to young women such as Abercrombie and Fitch, Guess, Gap, Wet Seal, and Forever 21. The source loss analysis indicates that Bebe is primarily competing with other specialty apparel retailers such as Wet Seal, but there is also some across-format competition with Nordstrom's.[30]

Demographic and Behavioral Composition

There is a long-standing tradition in advertising of matching media vehicles to target audiences using demographics and behavioral variables. This tradition continues in online media selection.

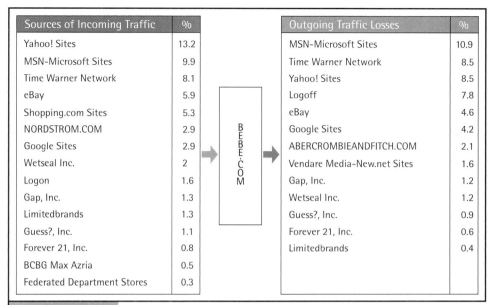

Sources of Incoming Traffic	%
Yahoo! Sites	13.2
MSN-Microsoft Sites	9.9
Time Warner Network	8.1
eBay	5.9
Shopping.com Sites	5.3
NORDSTROM.COM	2.9
Google Sites	2.9
Wetseal Inc.	2
Logon	1.6
Gap, Inc.	1.3
Limitedbrands	1.3
Guess?, Inc.	1.1
Forever 21, Inc.	0.8
BCBG Max Azria	0.5
Federated Department Stores	0.3

Outgoing Traffic Losses	%
MSN-Microsoft Sites	10.9
Time Warner Network	8.5
Yahoo! Sites	8.5
Logoff	7.8
eBay	4.6
Google Sites	4.2
ABERCROMBIEANDFITCH.COM	2.1
Vendare Media-New.net Sites	1.6
Gap, Inc.	1.2
Wetseal Inc.	1.2
Guess?, Inc.	0.9
Forever 21, Inc.	0.6
Limitedbrands	0.4

Figure 16.12

Source Loss Analysis for Bebe.com, April 2005

Source: Raw data from comScore Media Metrix, figure by authors.

Sites that sell advertising space use information from registrations or surveys of visitors to report audience demographics. Panel operators also provide query tools that report on the demographic profile of web sites.

Typical demographics collected from web visitors include race, gender, age, household size, household income, and presence and absence of children in the household. These demographics overlap with the set of variables collected by the population census. Demographic targeting can use a single variable (e.g., gender=female) or combinations of variables (e.g., gender=female, with children in the household).

Demographic profiling of web sites can reveal if visitors with certain demographics tend to visit certain web sites disproportionately. The composition index is the proportion of the traffic at a web site that consists of visitors that match a certain profile. Web sites with a high composition index can be cost effective for advertising. Since more of the visitors fit the target profile, a smaller proportion of the advertising placed on the site is wasted. When sites vary in their ability to attract certain types of traffic, then the composition index is a useful measure to identify sites with profiles that match the target audience.

Panels also report behavioral data. Surveys of panelists regarding their interests or purchase behaviors in specific categories provide the data. Examples of behavioral variables measured include interest or incidence of health issues, financial products, and so on.[31] Behavioral data can be even more actionable than demographic data since it provides information on products and services of recent interest to the consumer. A composition index captures the percent of site visitors with a certain behavioral trait.

Figure 16.13 graphs the site rank for total traffic for the top 400 web sites against the composition index rank for individuals suffering from allergies. The total traffic rank does not correlate to the composition index rank. Individuals who suffer from allergies do not visit all web properties proportionately.

Reach, Frequency, and CPM Analysis

Audience campaigns can have multiple objectives. Many campaigns aim to *reach* a specific number of customers of a given profile over a given period at the lowest cost per thousand impressions (*CPM*). Effectiveness is another consideration. Campaigns can be more effective by improving the creativity used. Campaigns can also be effective by reaching the customer in the right context with the right frequency. Improving reach, frequency, and CPM are important aspects of finding the right audience.

Syndicated audience measurement services provide tools that can help plan and evaluate campaigns against reach and frequency criteria. Figure 16.14 provides an example. The report uses input provided by the media planner to calculate key metrics for the campaign. The media planner provides several important inputs to the tool, including the target audience, a list of web sites, the planned impressions at each site and the CPM. The target audience for this example is

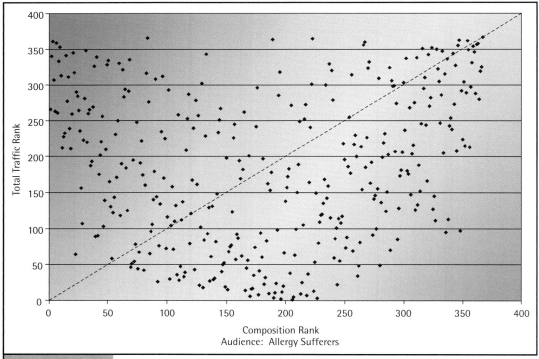

Figure 16.13

Total Traffic Rank versus Composition Rank for Allergy Sufferers, Top 400 Sites

Source: Raw data from comScore Media Metrix, figure by authors.

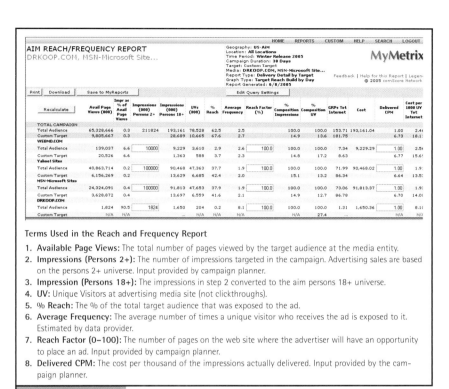

Figure 16.14

Reach and Frequency Report

Source: © comScore Media Metrix

female, allergy sufferers between the ages of 18 and 49. The media planner shortlists two portals, Yahoo! and MSN, for their broad reach. Demographic and targeting analysis indicates that drkoop.com and Webmd.com provide a relevant context for this target audience.

Using these inputs, the reach frequency tool generates a report with several important campaign metrics. The report takes the planned impressions for the audience of 2+ persons and converts them to the 18+ universe used in the planning tool. Based on the impressions of the 18+ universe, the impressions as a percent of total available pages are calculated. For example, the 100 million planned impressions at the MSN site result in 91,813 million impressions for the 18+ universe. This constitutes 0.4% of the 24,324,091 million impressions available on the MSN sites.

In the MSN example, the impressions yield 47,653 unique visitors, a 37.9% reach of the total audience. The impressions also yield 6,559 unique visitors in the target audience, which is a reach of 41%. Assuming a cost per delivered CPM of $1, the MSN sites cost $14 per thousand unique viewers in the target audience.

The first rows of the final columns in the report also provide the cost per 1000 unique visitors for the entire campaign. The report indicates a cost of 1.8 cents per unique visitor in the target audience. For all unique visitors, the cost drops to 0.25 cents per unique visitor. Media planners can evaluate many alternate scenarios including a different mix of sites, ranges of CPMs, and reach factors to identify the most cost effective mix of web sites.

MONITORING CONGESTION AND DELAY

At times, Internet performance itself becomes the object of market research. A number of researchers investigate the importance of congestion and delay in shaping consumer reactions to the online world. These studies provide evidence that delay may become more important with rising expectations, the activity affected, and the perception of control and causation. While studies in gaming show delay to be very influential,[32] studies of the impact of delay in settings similar to dial-up web access have found the connection relatively weak.[33] In other words, rising broadband access may make users significantly less tolerant of delay as they adopt much more congestion-sensitive online activities. Users appear to be more intolerant of delay when they assign the blame to the site rather than the Internet in general. These studies suggest that understanding the source of congestion and the perception of cause is relevant to users.

Retail businesses and service outlets have long realized that consumers respond to fast service. To meet consumer expectations they focus on delivering the right type of service within an acceptable waiting time. Operations managers continuously measure queue times and put in corrective actions to eliminate deviations. In the service businesses, both perception and reality matters. Understanding how customers form perceptions of delay helps managers deal with the adverse effects of actual delay.

The demands of time-starved consumers are evident in online interactions. As the data in Table 16.5 shows, many page views are very short, lasting less than a minute. Consumers react rapidly to congestion and delay, as well as making quick judgments about the value of continuing a visit. Because of this surfing behavior, web sites must track and manage congestion. Delays for a retail site may result in a lost sale; for a content site, a lost viewer. Delays might also have an adverse branding impact. The unified contact value and the visit value models provide a framework to evaluate the monetary impact of a delay.

Despite redundancy and rapid growth in capacity, the Internet is by no means perfect. Breakdowns, outages, congestion, mistakes, accessibility problems, and difficulty of use can create concern and uncertainty among consumers. Internet sites should understand the sources of delay and manage both actual delay and perceptions of it.

Sources of Delays

> *Network Outages*

The Internet uses packet switching, which provides "best effort" but not guaranteed service. Routers attempt to ship each message and its packets as effectively as possible, but the actual time necessary to complete this can vary. When the Net has no problems and plenty of capacity, this works very well.

There are also times, unfortunately, when the Net simply breaks down. The most common cause is a physical break in the communication links connecting key portions of the Net. Even within a redundant system, breakdowns degrade and slow system performance. If a breakdown hits at a point where redundancy is low, a complete loss of service can result.

Exactly this kind of outage struck Stanford University and a number of companies in Silicon Valley.[34] Figure 16.15 shows the culprit. A rat living in the conduits of the university's communication system gnawed through a critical junction cable in the system. This was very bad for the rat's health, as well as the electrical and communication system. A chain reaction ensued, resulting in an electrical blackout that shut down the campus for a number of hours.

Normally, this blackout would not have been a problem for the Internet in general. However, one of the major Internet service providers to many Silicon Valley firms located a principal switching point on the Stanford campus. At the time, this connection did not have sufficient battery backup to keep connections running. It lacked redundancy. As a result, the local Internet went down, and messages from the outside world could not make it through for almost 24 hours.

Network nodes with no redundancy are vulnerable. A failure leaves packets with no alternative routing. A lesson that several companies learned from this incident was to build redundancy into their local network access. A simple method is to use more than one Internet service provider and to locate multiple servers in different locations. Then even freak accidents—and hungry rodents—will not destroy Net access.

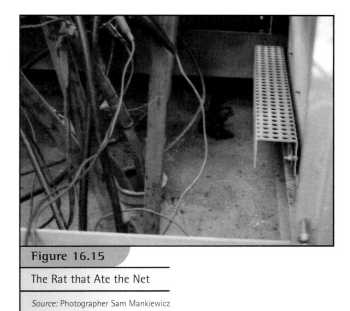

Figure 16.15

The Rat that Ate the Net

Source: Photographer Sam Mankiewicz

> *Delay and Lags*

Complete outages on the Net are quite rare. A much more common result has been congestion and delay. When portions of the Net are overloaded or stop working, bottlenecks develop and performance suffers. Delay also occurs when a site becomes so popular that traffic exceeds even the most generous expectations. Of course, delay is inevitable for users who connect to the Net through slow connections.

Figure 16.16 shows the three categories of lag that can occur when a user makes a request on the Net: access lags, transmission lags, and server lags. Each of these lags can be minimal or severe. Together they generate the total lag experienced by users.

> Server Lags

Server lag is the time that a server takes to recognize and fulfill a user's request. This is itself a combination of several factors. One is the bandwidth capacity of the connection between the server and the ISP. Another is congestion at the firewall or at the security layer. The power and clustering of the hardware employed, the efficiency of the software used, and the size and complexity of the user's request shape congestion at the server. The approach used to implement databases and the number of clusters that are connected impact response.

The typical source of server lag is under capacity relative to sudden shifts in demand. An embarrassing example of this was evident during IBM's coverage of the first Kasparov–Deep Blue chess match. IBM had created a Web site that allowed users to track the chess match (in real time) between the world champion Garry Kasparov and IBM's research project Deep Blue. Unfortunately for IBM's publicity, IBM dramatically underestimated the number of interested chess players who would access the site. Queues, slow performance, and an inability to gain access were the result. A

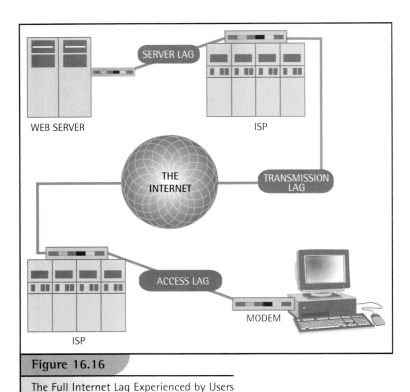

Figure 16.16

The Full Internet Lag Experienced by Users

potentially large publicity boost for IBM turned into a headache. Fortunes for both IBM and Deep Blue were better for the second match. Much larger capacity and parallel sites allowed IBM to handle the demand the second time.

There are multiple ways to reduce server lag. Buying excess capacity for peak loads is only one. Many small sites rely on web hosting and load sharing to handle spikes in demand. A web hosting service spreads the variability in demand of different companies throughout its capacity. The average demand is much more predictable than individual server demand, and flexible operations software makes this transparent to users.

An interesting set of tradeoffs confront online managers in the purchase of content delivery network service (CDN). The market leading firm has a network of 14,000 servers distributed around the world in 65 countries.[35] Clients choose which content to ship directly from their own servers, with more chance of congestion, and which to send via CDN. The most commonly outsourced are large files, such as media or software downloads. Major online publishing companies use CDN services to send many copies of the same pages to millions of users. For a fee, a CDN service reduces the load on a company's server and speeds delivery, by pushing copies of the content much closer to the "edge" of the Internet. A user in Portugal downloading software from a San Jose, California, software company, for example, is likely to receive the content from a geographically close CDN server rather than clog international lines and the company's home server in California. An online manager must decide which content, and possibly which users, deserve this more expensive but faster performing augmented network.

Occasionally server lag is the result of a "denial of service" attack targeting a company. These are coordinated efforts by a hacker or hackers to overload a company's server with bogus requests. These occur from multiple origination points, often as the result of computer viruses programmed to start an attack and take over the communications capabilities of infected computers. Professional criminals launch some of these attacks, while others are the work of a hacker out to have some fun or prove a point.[36]

> Transmission Lags

The next source of Net congestion and delay is transmission lag. This involves the flow of traffic from the user's Internet service provider to the server's Internet service provider. Factors driving transmission lag include distance, the performance of the ISPs involved, the particular path the message packets take, and the level of congestion throughout the Net.

Distance is normally the least important source of transmission lag. Packets traveling over networks travel at the speed of light. An electronic signal can travel around the world seven times in one second. For most applications, other sources of delay swamp this latency. Two important exceptions to this are games and the use of communication satellites for transmission.

As seen in Chapter 7, usability testing measures latencies for gaming in milliseconds. Delay is noticeable if the user and the server are apart by several thousand miles (for example, from New York to Los Angeles). Gaming companies respond to this by putting their servers in multiple locations to get closer to their customers. Even with this, wide geographical separation between players will start to cause lags based on the speed of light.

The speed of light can trigger a problem when satellites provide the long-distance Internet connection. Geosynchronous satellites orbit the Earth at least 25,000 miles above the surface. To make a round trip from user to web site requires at least two "bounces," each with a total length of 50,000 miles. At the speed of light, this round trip of 100,000 miles will take more than a third of a second. This delay can confuse the software that guides how fast to send packets.

When faced with a long delay, some of the standard Internet control software concludes that congestion is slowing packets. The software responds by slowing the rate at which it sends packets. This reduces the effective transmission rate dramatically, even though the congestion is just a function of distance. A response to this problem is to replace satellite links with fiber optic cables whenever possible. This is easiest on land and most expensive when crossing oceans, mountains, and jungles. When this is not possible, low Earth satellites are an option.

Congestion, lack of capacity, and peering arrangements within the ISP network all cause delay. Because the Net is a network of networks, a file may flow over several different private networks. Formal and informal agreements govern how this happens. ISPs might give preferential treatment to their own packets and those of their formal alliance partners. There will be a delay for the other packets, leading to a slowdown.

Combining all these factors leads to fluctuations in Net performance. What is near instantaneous one day can result in delays and wait on another. Sites such as that in Figure 16.17 provide reports on current Net congestion. On this particular day and time, there is a slowdown in Asian performance while Europe and the Americas show few problems.

> Access Lags

Access lags are the delays caused by limited transmission capacity from the user to the Internet. Primarily a bandwidth constraint, they are due to low capacity links from homes, schools, and small businesses. Access lags are much less severe for broadband users, especially for simple surfing and email. While none of the files in Table 16.7 provide much of a challenge for quality broadband, some

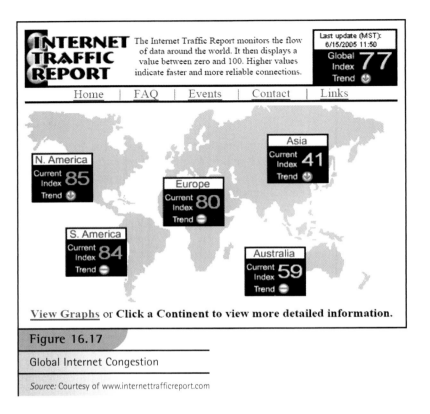

Figure 16.17

Global Internet Congestion

Source: Courtesy of www.internettrafficreport.com

Table 16.7

File Size and Access Times

File Type	File Size	Time to Download at 56K	Comments	Minimal Acceptable Technology
Email	4 Kbyte	0.6 seconds	Standard phone line	14.4 modem, standard phone line
Typical Web page	64 Kbyte	8.8 seconds	10% graphics, rest text	
Complicated interactive Web page	220 Kbyte	31 seconds	75% graphics	28.8 modem, standard phone line
Small PowerPoint slide show	1 MB	2 min., 19 secs.	Or 20 secs AM quality sound file	56K modem, standard phone line
Video clip attached to Web page	3.2 MB	7 min., 24 secs.	Low quality, 2" by 2" window, 60 sec. clip	128 Kbyte ISDN, special phone line and modem
Full-screen video (compressed)	11 MB	38 min.	TV quality, full screen, 256 colors, 60 sec. clip	T1 phone line and modem, or cable modem or ADSL

of the delays may be excessive for dial-up. Some applications, such as video-on-demand and voice-over-IP, can be very sensitive to all forms of lag.

Access lags can be a serious problem with a wide range of user capabilities or high volume files. The same file transmission can take seconds, minutes, or hours depending on connection capacity. The deployment of Wi-Fi adds another layer of complexity beyond the connection to the ISP. A weak wireless signal, physical distance from the access point, interference, and dead spots all contribute to delay.

Monitoring and Managing Delays

> *Monitoring Delays*

The most basic step in researching and managing delays is monitoring. Figure 16.18 shows a typical monitoring console in the network operations center of an ecommerce site. Monitoring tools deployed in servers and other hardware provide real time updates to the network operations center. These tools determine whether all systems are running smoothly.

Data center monitoring tools only provide information on server lags. They do not monitor transmission lags or access lags occurring outside the data center. The total delay faced by the end user is a combination of all three lags. The end user might see delays even when the network monitoring tools indicate that all internal systems are operating properly.

Internet companies do monitor the total user delays. A synthetic monitoring approach uses automated computer requests from different parts of the world to track access, transmission, and server lags. Computers running automated scripts of common user tasks send requests to web sites and monitor page load times—the time it takes a requested page to load on the requesting computer. The network operations center receives analyses of page load times.

Synthetic monitoring uses a sampling approach to monitor web sites. Specific monitors at specific times and locations request pages. Sampling is necessary to avoid clogging the network with these artificial requests. The goal is to detect weaknesses and congestion points without subjecting visitors to the problems.[37]

A different methodology tracks actual user experience of congestion. An independent passive monitoring instrument located in the traffic path recorded the actual page load times. Figure 16.19 compares synthetic monitoring to the response times faced by actual users. In this case, the synthetic services underreport delay.

> *Managing Perceptions of Delay*

Sufficient capacity and CDNs are investments in lower delays. Site design also plays a role in managing actual response. Table 7.4 provided benchmarks for delay time, suggesting perceptual thresholds. Page designs that load within these benchmarks minimize delay. Figure 16.20 shows a non-linear effect between response time and user perceptions. In this study, the user reaction to delay flattens after about four seconds.[38]

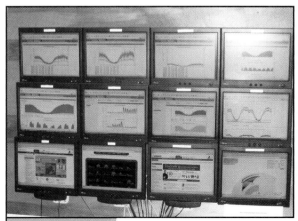

Figure 16.18

Monitoring Console at a Network Operations Center

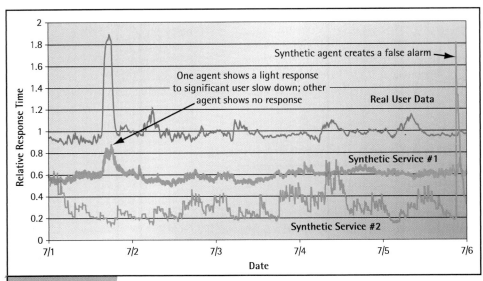

Figure 16.19

Synthetic Measurements Versus Actual User Delays

Source: John Bartlett and Peter Sevcik. "Real vs. Synthetic Web Performance Measurements, a Comparitive Study." Netforecast, Inc. Report 5077 (December 2004): 4.

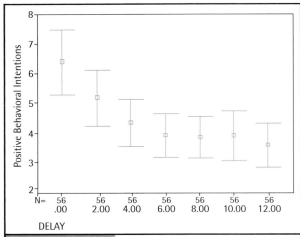

Figure 16.20

Non-Linear Relationship between Actual Delay and Behavioral Intentions

A consistent finding in service quality research is the importance of perceptions.[39] Managing perceived waiting time is part of this process. A common tactic is to provide consumers with duration information or countdown information about the actual waiting times.[40] Sites like Orbitz and Sidestep manage perceptions by showing users a status bar or telling them that the site is processing or searching. A recent research study shows that aesthetic aspects of site design such as color can also influence waiting perceptions.[41]

A study of the sequence of page delays finds[42] an *anchor and adjustment* model can explain user perceptions of delay (Table 16.8). The first few pages of a site influence the user's expectation of site performance. Thus, early experience on the site is the anchor. Future differences move this perception in a gradual way. This implies that a path of (quick, slow, slow) is evaluated differently than (slow, slow, quick).

The specific form of the adjustment is:

$$PWT_p = PWT_{(p-1)} + (1-W) * [AWT_p - R]$$

PWT is the perceived wait time, *p* indexes the page, *AWT* is the actual wait time, and *R* is a reference point. One approach is to set $R = PWT_{(p-1)}$. The strength of the adjustment effect is captured in *W*. When *W*=1 there is no updating of the anchor. When *W*=0 the anchor is averaged with the current delay.

Other things equal, the model suggests it is very important to make the initial pages load quickly. If the total delay of a site is a constant, the pages should be designed so that there is increasing delay.

Table 16.8 illustrates this approach with an example. The pages displayed in increasing order of wait time result in a total perceived wait time of 11.63. The total perceived wait time for pages displayed in decreasing order is 12.38. A large initial delay shifts perceptions, and it takes a number of views to adjust.

Many online tools exist to track the load time and other design issues of individual pages. Figure 16.21 provides an example, analyzing the initial Thomson Learning page for the number of total objects and download times. This particular service then comments on good, bad, and marginal aspects of the page. For example, it suggested that page scripting might be too extensive and the total number of images too high, while the total size of the page and lack of use of multimedia was appropriate.

Table 16.8

Total Perceived Waiting Time for an Anchor and Adjustment Model

	Web Page Order			
	1	*2*	*3*	*Total*
Actual Waiting Time	3	4	5	12
Perceived Waiting Time	3.5	3.75	4.38	11.63
1-W	0.5	0.5	0.5	

Source: Bruce D Weinberg, Paul D. Berger, and Richard C. Hanna. "A Belief Updating Process for Minimizing Waiting Time in Multiple Waiting Time Events: Application to Website Design." *Journal of Interactive Marketing* 17, no. 4 (2003): 24–37.

External Objects		**Download Times**	
External Object	QTY	*Connection Rate*	*Download Time*
Total HTML:	1	14.4K	78.48 seconds
Total HTML Images:	52	28.8K	39.44 seconds
Total CSS Images:	1	33.6K	33.86 seconds
Total Images:	53	56K	20.48 seconds
Total Scripts:	2	ISDN 128K	6.55 seconds
Total CSS Imports:	2	T1 1.44Mbps	0.93 seconds
Total Frames:	0		
Total Iframes:	0		

Thomson Learning Corporate Page   Objects on Page   Download Time

Figure 16.21

Using Page Optimizing Software to Check Individual Pages

ENDNOTES

1. William Paley. *Radio as a Cultural Force.* Testimony before the Federal Communications Commission, (1934).

2. Seymour Sudman and Edward Blair. "Sampling in the Twenty-First Century." *Journal of the Academy of Marketing Science* 27(2) (1999): 269–277.

3. Note that Democrats were the red states in this map.

4. In both elections, there was also a sizable time gap between survey and the election.

5. Michael Cornfield. "Pew Internet Project Data Memo: Presidential Campaign Advertising on the Internet." *Pew Internet & American Life Project.* October, p. 3.

6. Gross ratings points are reach * frequency, where reach is the size of the audience and frequency the number of times the ad is run.

7. This definition is from Edward F McQuarrie. *The Market Research Toolbox: A Concise Guide for Beginners.* Thousand Oaks, CA: Sage Publications, 1996.

8. Jack Honomichl, *Inside Research.*

9. comScore Networks has a panel of over 3 million households, Greenfield claims a global panel of 12 million households, and Harris Interactive a panel of several million households. Data retrieved on June 11 2005.

10. See Mick P. Couper. "Web Surveys: A Review of Issues and Approaches." *Public Opinion Quarterly* 64 (2000): 464–494.

11. Couper, ibid.

12. H. Taylor. "Does Internet Research Work: Comparing Online Survey Result with Telephone Survey." *International Journal of Research in Marketing* 42 (2000): 1, 51–63.

13. Shelby H. McIntyre and Sherry Bender. "The Purchase Intercept Technique (PIT) in Comparison with Telephone and Mail Surveys." *Journal of Retailing* 63 (Winter) (1986): 364–383.

14. However, market researchers have an option to limit their analysis to the RDD sample.

15. R.M. Groves. *Survey Errors and Survey Costs.* New York: Wiley, 1989.

16. Yeong-Hyeon Hwang and Daniel R. Fesenmaier. "Coverage Error Embedded in Self Selected Internet Based Samples: A Case Study of Northern Indiana." *Journal of Travel Research* 42 (2004): 297–304.

17. Stephen J. Sills and Chunyan Song. "Innovations in Survey Research: An Application of Web Based Surveys." *Social Science Computer Review* 20 (2002): 1, 22–30.

18. Gunther Eysenbach and Jeremy Wyatt. "Using the Internet for Surveys and Health Research." *Journal of Medical Internet Research* 4 (2002): 2, e13.

19. *The Professional Respondent Problem in Online Survey Panels Today* Presentation by Gian Fulgoni, Chairman, comScore Networks, to the Marketing Research Association Annual Conference, June, 2005.

20. Dick Heerwegh, Tim Vanhove, Geert Loosveldt, Koen Matthijs. Effects of Personalization on Web Survey Response Rates and Data Quality. Working Paper, Catholic University of Leuven, Belgium.

21. Mick P. Couper, Roger Tourangeau, and Fredrick G. Conrad. "What They See is What We Get: Response Options for Web Surveys." *Social Science Computer Review* 22,1 (2004): 111–127.

22. K.R. Athey, J.E. Coleman, A.P. Reitman and J. Tang. "Two Experiments Showing the Effects of the Interviewers Racial Background on Responses to Questionnaires Concerning Racial Issues." *Journal of Applied Psychology,* 44 (1960): 562–566. Also see B.J. Fogg and C. Nass. "Silicon Sycophants: The Effect of Computers that Flatter." *International Journal of Human Computer Studies* 46 (1997): 551–561.

23. Sherman and Deighton, op. cit.

24. For example see methodology overview of comScore Media Metrix provided by comScore Networks, Reston VA.

25. For a discussion of the unique benefits of panel data in the context of consumer packaged goods see Sachin Gupta, Pradeep Chintagunta, Anil Kaul and Dick Wittink. "Do Household Scanner Data Provide Representative Inferences from Brand Choices: A Comparison with Store Data." *Journal of Marketing Research* Vol. XXXIII November (1996): 383–398.

26. See Makoto Abe and Kirthi Kalyanam. Brand and Category Influences on the Representativeness of Household Panel Data. Working Paper, Santa Clara University.

27. These definitions are adapted from comScore Media Metrix 2.0 documentation. While a particular commercial service may use proprietary terminology, many of the classification issues are generic.

28. Unique visitor overlap collapses repeat visits from the same individual into a visit during the month.

29. In this example, the inflation in reach due to double counting is $2 \times 4\% + 2 \times 3\% + 2 \times 8\% + 3 \times 3\% = 39\%$. Some of the traffic data can be projected and hence may not add up.

30. Hoovers.com accessed on June 06, 2005 lists Donna Karan, Limited Brands, and Wet Seal as top competitors to Bebes.

31. The comScore Media Metrix panel collects data on over 300 behavioral variables and updates it periodically.

32. See Chapter 7 and cites.

33. For example, Diane DiClemente and Donald Hantula. "Optimal foraging Online: Increasing Sensitivity to Delay." *Psychology & Marketing* Vol. 20, No. 9, September (2003). Gregory Rose, Matthew Meuter, and James Curran. "On-line Waiting: The Role of Download Time and Other Important Predictors on Attitude toward E-tailers." *Psychology and Marketing* 22(2) February (2005).

34. Theresa Lee. "Rats May Have Caused Outage." *Stanford Daily Online.* (1996). Accessed October 14.

35. Akamai web site, June 2005.

36. Brian Kladko. "Teen Unleashed Computer Chaos." NewJersey.com. (2005). Accessed June 13.

37. Peter J. Sevcik. "Real vs. Synthetic Measurements of Performance." *BCR* 34 (2004): 11.

38. Dennis F. Galletta, Raymond Henry, Scott McCoy, Peter Polak. "Web Site Delays: How Tolerant are Users?" *Journal of the Association of Information Systems* 5, 1 (2004): 1–28.

39. Dawn Iacobucci. "Services: What We Do Know and Where Shall We Go? A View From Marketing." (1998). In T.E. Swartz, D.E. Bowen, and D Iacobucci (Eds.), Advances in Services Marketing and Management (Vol. 7, pp.1–96), Greenwich, CT: JAI Press, 7.

40. Benedict G.C. Dellaert and Barbara E. Kahn. "How Tolerable is Delay? Consumer's Evaluation of Internet Web Sites After Waiting." *Journal of Interactive Marketing* 13 Winter (1999): 41–54.

41. Gerald J. Gorn, Amitava Chattopadhyay, Jaideep Sengupta and Shashank Tripath. "Waiting for the Web: How Screen Color Affects Time Perception." *Journal of Marketing Research* May (2004): 215–225.

42. Bruce D Weinberg, Paul D. Berger and Richard C. Hanna. "A Belief Updating Process for Minimizing Waiting Time in Multiple Waiting Time Events: Application to Website Design." *Journal of Interactive Marketing* 17, 4 (2003): 24–37.

chapter 17:

Organizing for Online Marketing

Figure 17.1

The Internet Seems to
Accelerate Change
Source: ©Photodisc/Getty Images

The Internet as Appliance

Important parts of the Internet are on their way to becoming utilities and appliances. Ingrained into everyday life, like electricity, the automobile, and the telephone, a utility is available and counted on. Someone puts a compact disc into a computer and, after a brief hesitation, the name of the artist and the music track information appear. This data is not stored on the CD. Without alerting the user, the computer gets the information by matching song number and lengths against an online database. When synchronized, this retrieved information transfers to MP3 players. A similar process works for digital video recorders, where a Net connection gathers program information and suggests shows to watch.

The R.S.S. standard, standing for "really simple syndication," provides yet another example of the emerging utility nature of the Net. Growing rapidly, R.S.S. lets users subscribe anonymously to daily (or even more frequent) feeds of information from media sites, shopping sites, and even classifieds.[3] These feeds automatically provide the latest news, podcasts, product announcements, and then will store them for later viewing on a computer or mobile device. Search advertisers offer services matching ads to R.S.S. content. Interactive agencies are offering longer, more text-oriented ads that seem to work in that environment, and many background services are planned.[4]

For other applications, the utility process works to seamlessly filter out information. Anti-virus and anti-spyware software operate in the

Implementing online marketing and ecommerce raises organizational and legal issues. This new organization needs to reflect changes in online users and their experience, the globalization of the Internet, and future opportunities.

Topics covered in this chapter include:

> The Internet Appliance

> Organizing for Online Tasks

> Looking Forward

background to keep definitions up to date. Part of this data contains lists of suspicious sites and known viruses. When an email arrives from these blacklisted locations the system automatically filters them out, preventing transmission or sending the files to a spam folder for deletion.

Becoming an appliance transforms a product into the well understood and expected (Figure 17.2). A kitchen without a refrigerator, a living room without a television, or a garage without a vehicle is missing an expected good. While 100 years ago these were absent, crude, or extreme luxuries, even in wealthy countries, they are now part of day-to-day life in a modern economy.

Individuals adapt their behavior and expectations to the presence of appliances. Families check medical information from a doctor against web sites, providing an electronic second opinion. Patients arrive with preferences over types of medical treatment because of online and mass media advertising. Advertising and political persuasion move from "closing the deal" during a 30-second spot to motivating a visit to a web site.

In some situations machines use the ubiquitous Internet to call for assistance. From copiers to elevators, expensive infrastructure prone to malfunction increasingly contains enough sensors and communication capabilities to request a service visit. In some cases the machine's call for help happens prior to a malfunction that might actually stop the machine from working. A technical support person appears and makes some adjustments with little or no service interruption. In

other situations the problem is not a malfunction at all, but simply the normal depletion of inventory. Combining digital screening, inventory tracking, point-of-sale monitoring, and network tools, the system automates routine purchasing and shelf replenishment.

There are risks to providing an appliance. Legal and regulatory expectations shift for a product or service used by all. Higher standards of safety and accessibility apply. Graceful accommodation for children and those with cognitive problems is necessary. Discrimination of any kind becomes a legal risk. Adding a new feature or capability to an appliance requires a higher standard of reliability and clarity than adding it to a high-tech product for early adopters.

An Internet appliance is increasingly a reality for the billion users worldwide. For the other 5 billion citizens of the planet the benefits of the Net are indirect or are yet to arrive. As the telegraph and telephone before, the Net provides a more efficient means of connecting a global economy. Increased trade and lower transaction costs should benefit all countries, even those with minimal online resources.

The Net is much more than just a means of faster communication. It is a window into a vast amount of knowledge, culture, and entertainment, creating opportunities for improving education and skills worldwide. It also creates many tensions. Poor nations see these vast stores of content as a public good that should be available at prices they can afford. This leads to tensions over intellectual property control, digital piracy,

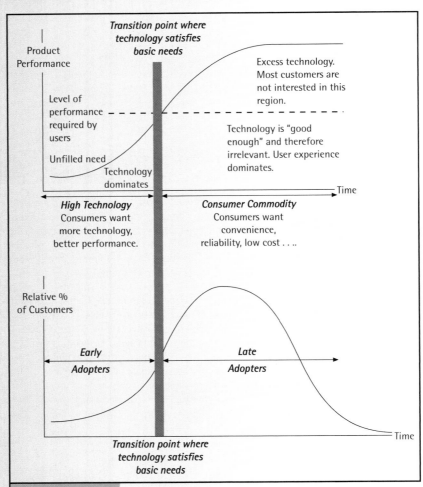

Figure 17.2

Improving Technical Performance Is Less Important as a Technology Becomes an Appliance

Source: Adapted from Donald Norman, *The Invisible Computer* (Cambridge, MA: MIT Press, 1998), 32–33.

and trade battles. Network ownership and control becomes a political concern as the Net becomes a critical facility for business and consumers. Individualization carries with it many opportunities for problems as well as promise.

Complicating all of these issues is the simple fact that the Internet is bigger than any single government or political institution. The Net is a global and local resource. Political and regulatory institutions struggle with issues of jurisdiction, reach, and effective rules when providers of online services can be on the opposite side of the globe almost as easily as they can be next door. The world is spinning faster, with the Net as an integral part and cause of this increasing pace.

ORGANIZING FOR ONLINE TASKS

The online techniques and approaches discussed throughout the book require organizations to share information quickly, often across organizational boundaries. This is disruptive and difficult. Organizational needs escalate with increasing online performance. Simple sites put few strains on a company, while dynamic and personalized sites can challenge long-standing systems. Providing the features and benefits of online marketing and ecommerce selling requires an investment in organizational capability.

Aligning Structure and Strategy

Figure 17.3 highlights how the move from broadcast marketing toward interactivity requires organizational change. While simple techniques require few changes and little investment, crossing the "imitation barrier" requires a commitment of money, training, and time. At some point companies must reorganize to fully benefit from all the online capabilities provided by the three GPTs of digital, network, and individualization.

Much of the difficulty stems from two core challenges. One is real-time interaction, which requires near instantaneous decisions based on appropriate procedures. Traditional marketing approaches tend to isolate real-time capabilities within the sales and distribution channels. Real-time online interactions draw information from multiple departments. The second challenge comes from increasing personalization and customization, which requires careful rules

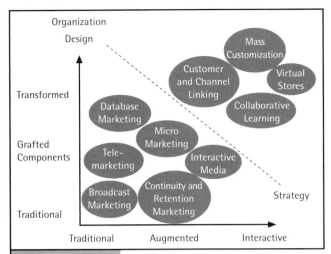

Organization
Design

Transformed

Grafted
Components

Traditional

Traditional   Augmented   Interactive

Mass Customization
Customer and Channel Linking
Virtual Stores
Collaborative Learning
Database Marketing
Micro Marketing
Tele-marketing
Interactive Media
Broadcast Marketing
Continuity and Retention Marketing

Strategy

Figure 17.3

Adopting Internet Technologies Forces Changes in Corporate Organization

Source: George Day, "Organizing for Interactivity," *Journal of Interactive Marketing* 12, no. 1 (Winter 1998): 47–53.

governing the differential treatment of customers. Companies must make sure that all elements of the organization respond appropriately and have an understanding of the appropriate priorities and customer categorization. These challenges escalate when companies move from simple publishing sites to dynamic and personalized information.

> *Organizing for Publishing*

Simple publishing sites are "organizationally easy." Many marketing departments create and maintain their sites by simply converting existing sales documents and product brochures. Technology demands are simple, with little help needed from the rest of the company. This is broadcast marketing in another medium, which fits easily within traditional strategy and organizations.

One of the biggest challenges for static publishing sites is timely information. Even when an organization possesses accurate and timely data, some group must have the responsibility to provide it in the proper format and make sure it is posted. A common solution is decentralized information provision with a centralized "look and feel." The central authority provides templates, leading to a consistent appearance. Individual managers must maintain their information in a timely manner (as in Figure 6.5).

Even these simple publishing sites can create organizational difficulties. Putting information online exposes varying assumptions, duplication of efforts, and gaps in coverage that might not be apparent without the site. Rising consumer expectations are a fact of life for Internet marketers. A company's online presence often shows the current failings and limitations as well as capabilities.

Both business-to-business and consumer expectations of Internet capabilities rise over time. Consumers expect a web site to always be available, with current and accurate information. Sites should be easy to navigate, easy to search, and without long delays or performance glitches. If incomplete information prompts visitors to instant message or to call, support staff response time becomes a factor. Many companies cannot justify continuous access to a human support staff; three-shift customer and technical support is just too expensive. Online material must handle orders and inquiries when human staff is absent.

Diverse consumer access complicates a Net marketer's life. Continual Net access implies a much wider range of Net access devices and locations. While online capabilities of mobile devices are improving, they cannot match desktop screens and keyboards. Even stage I sites must be able to adapt to varying screens, resolutions, and other interface constraints. Many different access devices can slow down the use of new online techniques, especially rich multimedia. It emphasizes simple and widely used technologies such as email. Methods that require downloaded players and plug-ins are a problem, as mobile device versions often lag computer-based versions.

Consumer expectations rise with the demonstration effect of others' usage. Once a web user sees colleagues putting vacation pictures online, it becomes hard for them to understand why a company can't put product repair diagrams there as well. Real-time video by amateurs, even teenagers as in Figure 17.4, makes customers wonder why consulting and training videos are missing. Experience with commercially available encyclopedias, costing less than $50 but containing millions of words of information, show how low digital publishing costs can be.

Access leads to expectations that content should be available.[5] Customers who sign up for insurance online expect to be able to check their policy status material.[6] Librarians find patrons expect to find both online listings and full text material.[7] Government agencies struggle to provide access to all the content describing their programs and functions.[8]

> *Supporting Dynamic Content*

Organizational demands increase with dynamic content. Dynamic retrieval allows users to access databases, track information, and place online orders. At a minimum, dynamic sites require cooperation between marketing and information technology personnel. Other departments soon become involved as more and more customer information becomes accessible online.

Figure 17.4

Widespread Exposure to Real-Time Material Leads to Rising Expectations

Source: Doonesbury© 1998 G.B. Trudeau. Reprinted by permission of UNIVERSAL PRESS SYNDICATE. All rights reserved.

Dynamic sites use different choices by visitors to shape different experiences. Passwords and registration allow information segmentation, with some users having more access than others. One of the most challenging problems at this stage is developing an information access policy. Information must come from multiple sources. Reactions must also be rapid. Decisions increasingly happen in real time in response to individual requests.

Measurement leads to comparison. Dynamic capabilities suffer serious performance problems when capacity planning is poor, sites are ill conceived, or bottlenecks develop. As seen in Chapter 7, lags and performance problems affect both the quality of the experience and consumers' views of the quality of the organization. Marketing managers need to confer with IT staff to ensure sufficient resources to maintain promised performance levels. Figure 17.5 illustrates metrics used by one of the leading performance testing firms to evaluate online brokerages. Differing results shows how performance interacts with design and target customer segments, with some firms concentrating their efforts on performance while others emphasize consistency of user interaction.

Dynamic interaction requires managers to seamlessly coordinate individuals, information, and technology. This includes:

> *Customers* arriving from many sources over the Net
> *Web servers and email servers* that route information to proper applications
> *Application servers* that route information to the right place, include marketing logic, and stitch together online activity
> *Marketing managers* with the ability to change rules, add material, and monitor results
> *Specialty servers* for sales information, transactions, and multimedia
> *Live database* for real-time customer interaction

Managers must assign staff responsibility for keeping information accurate and available to the right groups of individuals. At least two problems arise. First, someone must have ongoing responsibility for tracking and keeping information current. This includes pricing sheets, product descriptions, ongoing offers, current designs, and the full range of customer and technical support.

Management must also set expectations regarding the timing and frequency of changes and notification of other staff members.

A more complicated problem is establishing policies on information access. Many companies, especially if they sell complicated and technical products or services, have in-depth documentation of features, options, and future technical changes. Traditionally, the sales force or product manager made the decision to share information on a case-by-case basis. In an online setting policies are needed. How much access customers should have, and when they should have it, causes problems for many organizations. Errors happen in both directions, with too much kept secret in some cases and too much revealed in others.

Two databases are especially critical. These are the live marketing database and the full customer database. The first shapes reactions by the online marketing system, and the second links past purchases and

Service Level Measures:
- Average high-speed performance (measures below)
- Average dial-up performance (same as high speed)
- Geographic uniformity
- Reliability

Performance Measures:
- Overall transaction response time
- Average page download time
- Homepage download time
- Account list page download
- Account details page download time
- Application process response time
- Average application download time

Figure 17.5

Measuring Dynamic Performance for Online Brokerages

Source: Adapted from Keynote Systems

customer demographics. One of the modeling challenges facing marketers is how to capture much of the customer database into the live marketing database.

The live marketing database sets the limit on real-time marketing actions. Decisions generated in real time rely on this database. Customer information must be stored in a way that allows near-instantaneous access. This requires simplification and a sacrifice of the full amount of information present in the full customer database.

> *Creating a Dialogue*

The demands of real-time personalization affect an entire organization. Pressures mount to reorganize around individual customer information and orders. Personalized and interactive web sites are a window on both the capabilities and the limitations of an entire company. It forces companies to change their logistics and response times. Legal issues are important. Moving to markets of single consumers strains the capabilities of many organizations.

Changes may be required to handle the increased speed, to develop new skills, and to connect with outside resources. It is not an accident that some of the most successful online companies have grown from scratch. Established companies must learn from them while building and maintaining their existing strengths. In particular, they must solve the span-of-control and response problems aggravated by the demands of dialogue marketing.

> The Span-of-Control Problem

The Net is leading companies to question their methods of matching marketplace with marketing staff responsibilities. The requirements of a fully dynamic, fully personalized dialogue with global customers are high. It seems to demand a comprehensive view of all customers, all products, and all markets. This is the underlying logic of managing both brand and customer equity across all possible interactions and geographical operations.

The perfect prescription for handling all customers, all products, and all locations is the complete view and perspective shown in Figure 17.6. This omniscient manager could make the best offers, tradeoffs, and recommendations. It reflects in-depth knowledge of customer needs and purchasing habits, detailed understanding of all the company's products, and a careful feel for the location specific concerns. This is impossible. One person cannot accomplish all of these tasks in a medium or large company.

Reality is always less than this idealized picture. Organizations must realize that the full view is impractical, and smaller pieces of the puzzle should be assigned to individuals. Three different organizing systems are by region, by product, and by customer. Each has strengths and weaknesses. The closest to the complete picture is the *executive view*. Although missing details from the complete view, top executives are responsible for the broad understanding of the full marketplace. Top executives must be able to summarize and respond to problems in any of the three dimensions. However, covering the full range of issues requires delegation and specialization of staff.

The upper-right panel shows a *regional organization*. Managers are responsible for all sales in a certain geographical region, covering all customers living there and products sold to those customers. Regional organization makes the most sense when location-specific knowledge and activities dominate, and shipping and mobility costs are high. It is probably the least appropriate form online. The Net limits the impact and importance of location. Local advertisers, distribution outlets, and shopping environments fall in importance. Global connectivity and activity complicates and pushes companies away from location-based organizational forms.

Product management has been the dominant marketing organization in many industries for decades. Product managers are responsible for understanding the minute details of their product

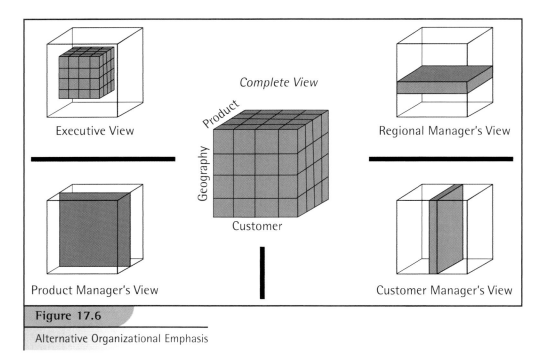

Figure 17.6

Alternative Organizational Emphasis

lines, market shares, and competitive product and service features. A product manager handles the full range of customers and locations. Product management is very good at creating product-specific authority and accountability. It works well with indirect channels of distribution and mass-marketing formats, where managers respond rapidly to falls in share and the impact of competitors' actions.

The product manager view is also less appropriate in the online world. It is challenging in a product management environment to properly evaluate and manage customer acquisition, development, and retention expenses. Likewise, it is a challenge for product managers to understand personalization, cross-selling, and the proper role of online support. These activities repeatedly cross product line boundaries, and are hard to allocate to different product managers. Which product bears the costs of recruiting and retraining customers, and which gets the benefits of increased sales due to personalization and switching costs?

Many Net marketers are finding an organization based on customers makes the most sense. In a *customer management view,* specialization occurs by customer portfolio. Each manager "owns" a group of customers and is responsible for their activity regardless of products or purchase location. A customer management view of the world fits more companies online than it did in traditional settings. It makes it easier to track a particular customer across varying physical locations and product choices. A ubiquitous network lets the customer log in from anywhere in the world. An integrated online shopping system makes it easy to credit a wide range of purchases back to individual accounts. This naturally leads to frequent buyer programs, offers of bundles and specials, new business opportunities, and capturing more of the "customer wallet." It allows the online marketer to offer a consistent user interface, to invest more time and effort in communicating with and training the customer. Customer management simplifies customer value calculations. These better estimates of lifetime value, combined with improvements in closed loop marketing, help make the Net a source of marketing productivity gains.

Customer management requires a wide span of knowledge to serve all of a customer's needs. Effective customer management means answering a much broader range of possible questions and solving many more product issues than in a product management setting. This can only work if individual managers can effectively draw on a wide range of resources and individuals within a company. The effectiveness of online customer managers depends on the internal communication effectiveness of the company. Organizations must effectively move information within internal networks, alliances within the supply chain, and externally with customers.

> The Response Problem

Direct customer dialogue is a new experience for many companies. Traditional marketing relies heavily on intermediaries and one-way communication. While technology creates the capability of two-way communication, Internet marketers must create an organization and system capable of handling communication effectively.

Email is a particular challenge for many organizations. Each email may have individual material that requires unique handling. Its content is unstructured. Compounding the problem, email senders expect rapid response. Email creates an organizational problem requiring technology, financial resources, and a trained staff. It forces managers to create policies about acceptable response rates. Internet marketing departments must decide what turnaround time they will achieve and what resources are necessary to achieve that goal.

Figure 17.7 is a snapshot of the problem many companies have handling email. While email technology permits nearly instantaneous worldwide messaging, firms' actual performance is much slower. Responses are lost and delayed. Only 53% of the retailers in this sample responded to a customer email within the same business day. Fully 26% of the retailers never even responded to an email.[9]

Email performance can be worse than other communication channels. A consumer products company was able to handle 225,000 phone calls out of 264,000 phone calls during a month. This left 15% of the phone calls to its support center unanswered effectively—a problem demanding attention. During this same time the company was only able to handle 2,000 of the 20,000 email inquiries it received—a failure rate of 90%.[10] This is terrible performance.

The 24-hour benchmark is what online users define as acceptable responsiveness from their own friends and colleagues.[11] Delays beyond a day need explanation, either as the recipient being "too busy" or the interpretation as a rejection of the correspondence. With newer technologies, such as Blackberries, expectations are even

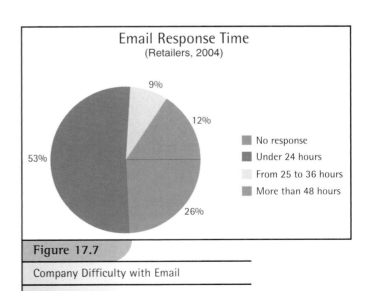

Email Response Time
(Retailers, 2004)

- 9%
- 12%
- 53%
- 26%

■ No response
■ Under 24 hours
□ From 25 to 36 hours
■ More than 48 hours

Figure 17.7

Company Difficulty with Email

Source: Purdue University Benchmark Study, November 2004.

higher. When companies fail to achieve minimal responsiveness, customers may well apply similar rules to their commercial relationship.

Customers know Internet response rates are a business decision. A company can respond faster if it devotes more resources to the job. Marketing managers must determine:

> Resources devoted to rapid response
> Uniqueness of the response
> Appropriateness of the response
> Technology of the interaction

Figure 17.8 shows the problem facing a Net marketer responding to unique incoming requests from customers. Requests could flow from email, web forms, threaded discussions, or other technologies with unique two-directional capabilities. A customer request enters the response system. The first step is an attempt to match the inquiry with a known category of question. If this cannot be done, staff intervention is required. If the category can be matched, the question is compared against previous answers. If special attention is not needed, an answer is automatically sent. Otherwise, the message is routed to the proper staff person to answer.

Resources, previous experience, customer information, and technology affect the matching and attention decisions. An extensive database of answers makes matching easier. Well-structured questions improve matching. New technologies capable of analyzing email content are being developed and introduced to the marketplace.

The special attention step is a classic customer satisfaction choice. It is a tradeoff of response cost and response benefit. Two factors dominate. One is the type of question. Questions indicating serious problems or valuable opportunities should be flagged for special attention. Routine questions easily handled by the system should get an automatic reply. The second factor is customer identity. For a high-value customer almost every question might receive special attention, even if the matching is quite close. The dialogue with lower-value customers will more likely start with an automated response.[12]

The virtue of an automated answer is speed. If a question can be matched without special attention, it can be answered within a minute or two. Once a message is sent for special handling it is delayed. High-value customers get urgent handling, cutting the delay to minutes or hours. Less-valued customers will be answered at a rate depending on the current backlog of questions and the staff capacity. Problems such as Figure 17.7 occur. No human system can respond effectively and accurately with the speed of the Net. Responses measured in seconds must rely on web

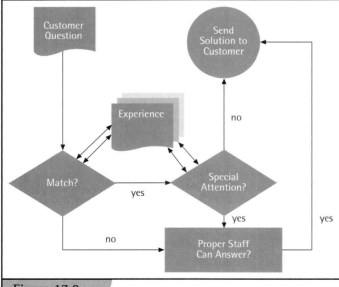

Figure 17.8

Flowchart for Automating Responses

Source: Modified from eGain Corp.

content, fully automatic email systems, or dynamic web pages that generate the correct answers using artificial intelligence.

Automatic response systems are exciting and challenging areas of technology use in marketing. Companies have introduced partial solutions to the speed problem. At its extreme, an automatic response system requires a computer program capable of understanding totally unstructured dialogue and responding appropriately. This is far beyond the scope of currently available software. It is very close to the Turing Test definition of machine intelligence.[13] Even the most optimistic industry observers do not expect this to happen for decades.

In practice, automated answers mean an intelligent matching of frequently asked questions and stock answers. With training and common problems, the system can handle a sizable fraction of incoming email. Urgent and rapid responses to questions require a trained staff augmented by effective systems. One model is purely human responders, with enough training and capacity to achieve high response rates. Increasingly, humans are augmented by technology. Automatic response systems provide the first pass at an answer. Humans check whether the answer is valid, authorize the answer if it fits, and intervene and provide a unique answer if not. New answers are added to the database, and the automatic system is updated.

Less structured systems deliver slower responses. Queuing theory has developed a sophisticated set of tools and theories for deciding how much capacity is needed to handle uncertain customer demands. Support staff needs grow with average demand level, the unpredictability of demand, seasonal peaks, and the desired service rate increase.

The right response to some questions may be no response. Totally inappropriate questions, or questions with inflammatory language, might be best ignored. Any response to the sender may further aggravate the communication problem.

A recent survey found that the most common use of automated email systems (55%) is merely to acknowledge the receipt of the message and to estimate the response time. The next most common (31%) approach has the system select the most appropriate message and forward it to a human agent for review and customization. Only in 14% of the cases does the system automatically choose the appropriate response and send the message without human intervention.[14]

Burger King takes advantage of email-type language parsing to create two amusing online branding sites. At the "subservient chicken" site, a man dressed in a chicken suit responds to typed instructions. Most will be repeats of previous requests (e.g., "flap your wings," "do a dance," etc.). The site automatically plays a short clip showing the action. The system fails gracefully and amusingly when the instruction is not understood or not allowed, with the bird inspecting the camera or doing some other action. At a second site, the user gets to play 20 questions with Darth Vader. Again, the interaction is based on text typed by the user. The game-nature and low stakes of the site reflect the current unreliable quality of the text recognition system. Users are all too familiar with poorly functioning automated voice recognition systems for reservation and customer support systems. Frustrations are lower at an amusement site.

A system such as that shown in Figure 17.8 will go through phases of accuracy and problems. As conditions settle and questions become routine, automation will work well and accuracy will improve. New products, new services, upgrades, and changes by competitors will cause a flurry of new questions and problems that stymie the software and require new learning.

Avoiding Legal Pitfalls

New marketing choices have legal implications.[15] These concerns are partly the newness of the industry. As practices develop, laws are established. Each of the previous chapters raises some

Table 17.1

Matching Technology and Response Rates

Desired Response Rates	Feasible Technologies	Customer–Query pairs
Instantaneous (< 1 minute)	• Web-based search or browse • Automated email • Dynamic web pages	• Standard questions fitting FAQs, content trees • Coded questions, FAQs • Server side AI
Urgent (< 1 hour)	• Email, email initiated voice, custom web links • Highly trained staff	• High-value customers and/or serious problems, premium support
Rapid (< 1 day)	• Email, discussion group moderators • Efficient "call center" structure	• Expertise specific questions, normal priority
Casual (< 1 week)	• Email, web links, Discussion groups • Pooled staff, cross-functional teams	• Baseline support, in-depth technical research
Interruptible (as capacity allows)	• Email, personal visits, or calls	• Highly unusual questions requiring special individuals or special channels
No response	• Content screening	• Inappropriate questions

legal concerns. Examples include online business alliances reconciling and splitting customer lead revenue, the independence and impact of online advice, variations in pricing rules, acceptable performance of ecommerce systems, and numerous others. These legal factors reflect the increasingly important role the Net plays in day-to-day business life.

Fundamental conflicts are also present. Some of the basic features of the Internet create legal complexities. These include the impact of digital environments on intellectual property, the problem the law has dealing with a networked world, and the challenges individual-level marketing creates for honoring individual privacy. Awareness of these conflicts can help avoid unnecessary legal complications.

> *Digital Environments and Intellectual Property*

Digital technology leads to extensive online information. One of the challenges for online management is to ensure that legal rules are not broken as digital environments develop. One area where this is true is site design and implementation. Comprehensive, current, and attractive information can land a company in trouble. Rapidly gathering information from many sources and matching individual needs is a difficult challenge. It forces quick decisions instead of leisurely meetings and reviews. Time pressure and competitive forces can lead to trademark and copyright problems for even the best-intentioned organization.

Tools with legitimate copying functions can violate the law when turned loose on external web material. While imitation may be a high form of flattery, it may also be illegal. Fair use of material can shift into unauthorized copying, timely capture of data may become violations of publishing rights, and marketers' use of online commentary without authorization may violate copyright laws.

The pace of online competition creates serious problems for online marketers and their legal staff. A comfortable publishing pace, where the marketing staff creates documents and a legal team reviews them, does not work well on Internet time. Legal understanding must be decentralized so that staff has a better understanding of the legal rules and constraints. While a little legal knowledge can be a dangerous thing, awareness of the essential rules is useful.[16] These include trademark and copyright, the impact of information accuracy, and rules about unsolicited communication. Staff must make these decisions repeatedly and rapidly.

Online marketers must be careful that providing the highest value to consumers does not shade into copyright violation. Figure 17.9 highlights the steps necessary to determine whether content or material is legal for posting online (under U.S. law—other countries' rules vary). Copyright law balances the desire for free speech and the exchange of knowledge against intellectual property rights. Copying material is legal under several scenarios. If none of these scenarios apply, to avoid legal problems a marketer must decide whether to negotiate for rights or to not use the material.

The first step is to decide if the material is already in the public domain. Copyright[17] applies for a fixed amount of time. Work "created after January 1, 1978 are afforded protection only up to 50 years after the death of the author, or if the works are made for hire, the copyright endures for a term of 75 years from the year of its first publication, or a term of 100 years from the year of its creation, whichever expires first."[18] Once this time expires, the material enters the public domain. Another important source of public domain material is the government. All U.S. government material is automatically part of the public domain.

The next exception to copyright restriction is if the material is an idea or fact, rather than "works of expression." A good example of the difference is the tension in a case between Motorola and the National Basketball Association (NBA). The NBA sued to stop Motorola from collecting and transmitting real-time scores and other details about an ongoing game to hand-held pagers

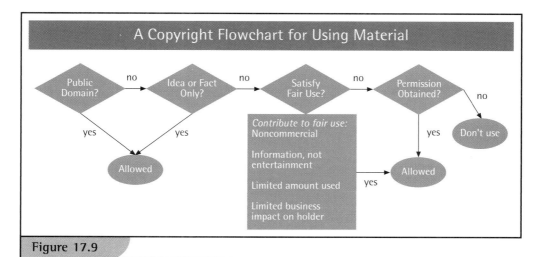

Figure 17.9

When External Material Can Be Used without Copyright Problems of Motorola customers and to a sports section of America Online operated by Motorola. An initial court agreed with the NBA. An appeals court overturned this, ruling the material "strictly factual and therefore without copyright protection." Copyright does protect broadcast of the game, its color commentary, and the full description of the game. The underlying "facts" reported in the broadcast are not protected.[19] There is some point at which the reporting of facts starts to be an illegally competing broadcast, with the facts of the case determining this. The day after the event, the data are clearly just facts. During the event, they might be viewed as a broadcast. Gray areas are often legally risky.

Material that is essentially an idea or formula is also exempt from copyright restrictions. Albert Einstein could copyright his papers on relativity, but not the basic idea and not the formula $E=mc^2$. These are facts of nature and part of the public domain.[20]

Even if material is deemed an "original work...of expression" and copyrightable, it might still fit into the "fair use" provision and its use legal without permission. Fair use is a judgment call, with four major factors:

> Material used for a noncommercial use is more likely to be considered fair use (e.g., use in a public school classroom).
> Material that is primarily informational, as opposed to entertainment, is more likely to be viewed as fair use (e.g., use of Mickey Mouse to demonstrate an animation technique rather than enjoying a cartoon).
> The less material used the more likely it is fair use (e.g., a two-sentence quote rather than an entire page).
> The less negative economic impact it has on the copyright holder the more likely it will be considered fair use (e.g., material from an out-of-date survey material rather than most recent important research results).

Recent laws have strengthened copyright protection and imposed possible criminal penalties. Marketing staff should be trained on the proper use of external material posted online. Training helps avoid both violations and overdue caution.

> *Network Connections and Legal Geography*

The legal system struggles when the connection between activity and location is stretched or broken. Almost all laws apply only within the borders of the government creating the law.[21] The Internet confuses and complicates this. Information and orders flow instantly around the world. A single web transaction can involve multiple states, countries, even different continents, in less than a second. Borders seem almost irrelevant online, yet borders are at the heart of the law.

Marketers are actively debating their online commerce approaches. Important legal questions affect the cost and effectiveness of online business activity. Marketers must also be aware of the commitments they are making when they use a marketing channel with a global, near instantaneous reach.

> Domain Names

It is the responsibility of an individual registering a domain name to verify that no one has a prior claim. U.S. courts have repeatedly ruled that existing businesses and organizations retain their domain name rights even if they have not taken any action to secure the name. This includes the name of the company or organization,[22] the name of trademarked product lines,[23] even trademarked cartoon characters. After registering a domain name, a company is wise to perform an in-depth trademark check before launching a site.[24]

The situation is not as clear if two or more companies have conflicting rights. For example, there are many different companies called AAA Transmission scattered across the country. In Florida alone eight different companies have AAA Transmission in their names. Conflicting claims and unclear ownership makes aaatransmission.com a first-come, first-served domain.

Domains that rely on user mistakes in typing a trademarked domain name may or may not be illegal. These "typosquatters" choose domain names that are very close to some of the most popular web site names, such as "amazom.com," "dismey.com," "wwwamazon.com," or "wwdisney.com." They then place advertising or make referrals to the traffic that arrives. There are conflicting legal rules about whether this violates trademark law.[25] If the resultant site is confusingly similar, it is much more likely to be a violation. If it merely takes advantage of the traffic for a very different reason, it is less of a problem.

International domain names used for commercial reasons present have a murkier legal status. Each country has its own unique two letter country code. For example, Albania has the code ".al," Kuwait has ".kw," and Zimbabwe has ".zw." Several two-letter country codes are attracting attention for their incidental commercial appeal. Tuvalu is a 10-square-mile country made of nine atolls in the Pacific Ocean near Fiji. Its Internet domain code is ".tv." Tuvalu promotes its domain for use by television shows and networks.[26] Thus, in addition to www.cnn.com, Cable News Network might register www.cnn.tv. Likewise, Micronesia sells its ".fm" domain name to fm radio stations (e.g., www.q100.fm), and Turkmenistan its ".tm" code for brand name sites (e.g., pepsi.tm is owned by the Pepsi company). These, and the more than 200 other countries with domain authority, have widely differing legal codes regarding brand name and domain name policy. Only some of these are resolved within the WIPO system of international trade.

> ## Personal Jurisdiction

A general legal rule is that an action may be brought against a person in the state in which that person (a corporation is considered a "legal person") resides, where business is transacted, where a harm occurs, or where a contract was created. The lack of geography on the Internet sometimes makes it hard to apply this definition, and it creates legal uncertainty. The law is not clear on what exactly determines presence in a state or when an online marketer is subject to the jurisdiction of some distant legal system.

Jurisdiction may be created even without a physical presence by the firm. An online marketer has to specifically influence what jurisdiction applies, or multiple jurisdictions may apply. This is especially true for ecommerce. Below is a typical clause establishing jurisdiction, in this case the state of Washington:

> **Choice of Law:**
> This Agreement shall be governed by and construed in accordance with the laws of the State of Washington, without regard to its conflict of laws rules. Any legal action arising of the Agreement shall be litigated and enforced under the laws of the State of Washington. In addition, you agree to submit to the jurisdiction of the courts of the State of Washington, and that any legal action pursued by you shall be within the exclusive jurisdiction of the courts of the State of Washington.[27]

Establishing jurisdiction is more challenging when there is only an Internet presence. New York determined that a Missouri defendant in a trademark case was not subject to New York jurisdiction even though a New York business claimed a trademark infringement. The Missouri web site was visible by New Yorkers, but was solely aimed at its local clientele and lacked any commerce activity. International differences raise more serious concerns.[28] A company may find itself in trouble with distant countries with very different standards of freedom of speech, criticism, or political debate. Jurisdictional issues are complicated by distinctions between civil and criminal, commerce versus presence, and issues of contract. Legal guidance is necessary, especially when adding major functions to a web site.

An increasing number of issues online that used to be settled by individual states are being handled by federal legislation. This reduces the specifics of personal jurisdiction. Similar efforts are underway internationally, attempting to coordinate and rationalize treatment across borders.

> Taxes

The pricing chapter described how state-level cigarette and sales taxes shift purchasing activity. Sales tax on consumer purchases in the United States range from zero in five states to as high as 8.5% in states such as California and New York. Purchases made online avoid sales taxes under two main situations:

> The online firm has no presence in the state of the buyer.
> The sale is for information downloaded over the Net and the state exempts tax on downloaded purchases.

Although some states attempt to collect lost revenue on their income tax forms, without a legal presence in a state (*nexus*) the online transaction does not incur the sales tax during the transaction.

Issues of nexus are strategic for a marketer in a couple of ways. These are:

> Choice of states to locate online activities
> Decisions to have demonstration or customer support stores,
> Sale of products, especially digital products, online or through "shrinkwrap" packages

Taxation rules provide an incentive for an online company to locate in few states, states with no sales tax, and states with small populations. Keeping a company's physical presence limited reduces the number of states where taxes must be charged. Locating in a small population or low sales tax state means few potential customers are affected by the required tax payment. Amazon, for example, uses a distribution center in Reno, Nevada, to service the high sales tax California market.

Tax rules create a difference between hard goods and soft goods bought online. Most states exempt a purely online sale from tax even if there is nexus. Exempting online downloads makes practical sense. Purely digital items can be shipped from anywhere. Taxes could be avoided by creating a different company responsible for downloading software, and then locating them in a low-tax state or overseas.

> *Individualization and Information*

Extensive databases covering consumer choices, tastes, and purchases are fundamental to individual-level marketing. Individual interactions rely on models and data. Of these two, individual data has the most legal implications. The law protects individuals from libel and defamation. It also puts some limits on the types and uses of information. Errors may create damages. Even data transmittal may be restricted if individually identifiable information is involved. Creating a customer-centric organization forces marketers to consider the legal consequences of information accuracy and privacy.

Web site accuracy and performance raise many legal issues. Investors can create simple programs determining when to buy or sell stocks. Companies are adding advice engines that can go further and can trigger stock and retirement portfolio changes based on customer intentions, preferences, and changes in the market. Errors and mistakes in these tools, where millions of dollars are involved, are very serious.

> Inaccurate Information

Some errors and mistakes are inevitable for organizations publishing information and collecting user data. Individualization relies on authentication, association, and inference (see Chapter 4). Errors can happen at each of these steps. Mismatched records can lead to incorrect data in individual user records. The legal system realizes this, and does not hold information providers to an impossible standard. However, several types of information are subject to high standards and legal controls. With the growth of dynamic and individualized communication, marketers run the risk of violating these laws.

Three areas are of special note:

> Information that ends up in credit reports
> Criticism of specific individuals or companies
> Information likely to be used for critical decisions

Errors in this kind of information may result in lawsuits and penalties.

Information and privacy rules are country specific. Countries in the European Union have much stricter protections of privacy and individual information than countries such as the United States and Japan. Reviewing each of the main markets is important for sites active in those countries, but it is beyond the scope of the discussion here. The U.S. situation is used, but other countries may have stricter policies.

Information that Ends Up In Credit Reports

Credit reports are the most widespread example of buying and selling sensitive individual-level data. Applying for a credit card, buying a house or car, applying for life insurance, or applying for a job leads to a credit check. The Fair Credit Reporting Act (FCRA), passed by the U.S. federal government in 1970, established rules on accuracy and liability regarding consumer information. Its goal was to enable the use of credit reports while simultaneously providing consumers with protections against inaccurate information and improper uses of credit reports.

A misconception about credit reports is that they only record information about loans and payment history. Credit reports may legally contain information about drug use, adultery,[29] gambling habits, and arrests.[30] If a plausible connection between a type of information and credit worthiness is possible, a credit report may contain it.

The possibility for abuse is large. The flexibility of the FCRA creates a potentially rich market for personal web site usage data useful for judging credit worthiness. Financial sites might sell information about an individual's access to bankruptcy pages. Sites dealing with marriage issues might report discussions indicating marital problems. Mental health forums might report discussions of depression or other serious disorders capable of disrupting an individual's ability to work. Each of these could be used to score the credit worthiness of a potential borrower, providing a legal justification for the web site to sell the information for credit bureaus.

Selling such information runs the risk of strong consumer backlash. A number of online services offer low-cost or free access to an individual's own credit record. Many consumers will be furious if a firm sells their web data without permission. Companies should think very hard about potential consumer backlash and whether the added revenue justifies the risk and ill will.

Selling information used for credit also has legal implications. Inaccurate information, especially if the firm ignores consumer complaints and corrections, can lead to damages under the

FCRA. The price tag for a FCRA lawsuit can be steep. If a consumer wins they may collect compensatory damages for injury, punitive damages to punish the offending company, and reimbursement of attorneys' fees. Publicity of the lawsuit can lead others to find out about the practice and sue. Class-action suits could result.

Inaccurate Criticism of Individuals or Companies

Community-building tools create a legal risk for their sponsor. One possibility is the defamation and libel of individuals or companies. Private individuals using online forums or chat rooms may post information critical of others. These criticisms may be inaccurate. In some cases, there is serious damage to the business or reputation of an individual.

There are situations where community sponsors may share some of the liability for these criticisms. The more active a role the sponsor plays in editing the forum, the more legal risk the sponsor assumes. Courts have decided that community sponsors that merely host discussions escape most of the legal risk. Exposure to libel grows as a sponsor increases its moderator role. The legal system views an active moderator as a stamp of accuracy for the content. This puts the community sponsor at risk if the criticisms are in error and do harm.

Wise companies are monitoring the Net for both accurate and inappropriate negative comments made about their products or services. Firms get hired to look through USENET, chat rooms, and other online material looking for company commentary. Such comments lead to consumer ill will, a fall in the company stock price, or damage to executives' reputations.[31]

> Privacy Policies

Customers are concerned about their personal information.[32] Consumers are especially concerned about sensitive areas such as health, financial services, and retail transactions. One experiment with European participants clustered responses to privacy policy issues into four clusters. Many of the participants were concerned about revealing any personal information, while others would share some aspects of their profiles.

Privacy statements make clear to customers what types of information are collected and how it is used. These privacy statements lay out the broad guidelines the site follows in handling information collected from individuals through web use, surveys, purchases, or additional data sources merged and matched with online data.

The Federal Trade Commission is responsible for monitoring fair business practices toward consumers. It is the

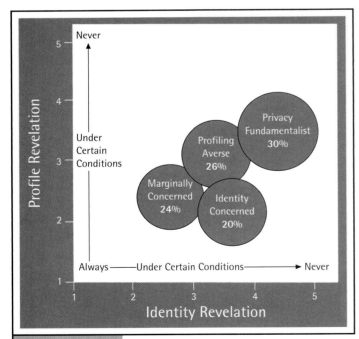

Figure 17.10

Clusters of European Privacy Concerns

Source: Bettina Berendt, Oliver Günther, Sarah Spiekermann, "Privacy in e-commerce: Stated preferences vs. actual behavior." *Communication of the ACM* 48, no. 4 (2005): 101–106.

commission's responsibility, in coordination with individual state attorney generals and governments of other countries, to spot consumer abuses and unfair marketing activities. An important part of that is consumer privacy protection.

The FTC has held a series of detailed hearings on the proper role of consumer information collection online. From these hearings and meetings a consensus has emerged on the important elements of a consumer privacy policy:

> Over the past quarter century, government agencies in the United States, Canada, and Europe have studied the manner in which entities collect and use personal information — their 'information practices' — and the safeguards required to assure those practices are fair and provide adequate privacy protection. .... Common to all of these [fair information practice codes] are five core principles of privacy protection: (1) Notice/Awareness; (2) Choice/Consent; (3) Access/Participation; (4) Integrity/Security; and (5)Enforcement/Redress.[33]

The first step is fundamental. Unless consumers are informed of the information policy of a company they cannot make informed decisions about using the service and disclosing personal data. Several definitions go in to this notice. They are:[34]

1. **Personal Information:** is defined to include any of the following: identifying information, such as name, postal address, email address, telephone number, etc; demographic information (e.g., age, gender, education level, income); and preference information (e.g., hobbies, interests).
2. **A Privacy Policy Notice:** is defined as a comprehensive description of the site's information practices—what the site does with the personal information it collects from visitors to the site. It is located in one place and may be reached by clicking on an icon or hyperlink.
3. **An Information Practice Statement:** is a discrete statement that describes a particular use or practice regarding consumers' personal information and/or a choice offered to consumers about their personal information. Examples include:

> We keep all information confidential.
> We reserve the right to do whatever we want with the information we collect.
> We don't share your information with anyone.
> If you no longer want to be on our mailing list, send us an email at . . ..

Personal information has a wide definition, and it is essentially the information required for any form of personalization and closed-loop marketing. A privacy statement is a comprehensive summary, while parts of a privacy statement that appear in different parts of a site are an information practice statement.

An academic study found limited current acceptance of the fair information practices at the largest companies. Looking at the Fortune 500, they found 383 sites both collect personal identifying information and post a privacy policy. They also found the privacy policy quite incomplete. Only 31% of these 383 sites contain at least one element for each of the first four areas of fair information practices (notice, choice, access, security). They also find only 3% fully comply.[35]

Compliance was not much better for the news media. A different study looked at 405 sites from magazines, weeklies, dailies, and Internet media. While 65% collected personally identifiable data, only 28% had a privacy policy statement. Of those with a policy, 95% covered elements of Notice, 72% Choice, 39% Access, 38% Security, and 71% Redress.[36]

A Template for Creating a Privacy Policy

The following is part of the template suggested by *TrustE* for privacy policy. While firms will differ in their choices, the goal should be to make these choices clear to users.

We store information that we collect through cookies, log files, clear gifs, [and/or] third party sources] to create a "profile" of your preferences. We tie [we do not tie] your personally identifiable information, and [or] your purchasing history, to information in the profile, in order to provide tailored promotions and marketing offers and to improve the content of the site for you.

We share [do not share] your profile with other third parties. [We share your profile in aggregate form only.] [We share your profile together with your personally identifiable information.]

Supplementation of Information

In order to provide certain services [specify] to you, we may on occasion supplement the personal information you submitted to us with information from third-party sources. *[Use all that apply to your business model.]*

Credit Check

To determine if you qualify for one of our credit cards, we use your name and Social Security number to request a credit report. Once we determine your credit-worthiness, we destroy this document.

ID [Address] Verification

We use [THIRD PARTY/THIRD-PARTY SOFTWARE] to verify your [identity] [address] in order to [*state why it is necessary to verify the user's identity or address*].

Enhancement of Profile Information

We purchase marketing data from third parties and add it to our existing user database, to better target our advertising and to provide pertinent offers in which we think you would be interested. To enrich our profiles of individual customers, we tie this information to the personally identifiable information they have provided to us.

Source: TRUSTe Model Privacy Statement

This imbalance creates a number of problems. One, it puts these web sites in violation of a number of governmental standards for appropriate protection, especially the European Community. This makes regulatory action likely. Two, consumers will typically assume the worst. A marketer with a privacy position should have a privacy statement to stand out from the crowd. Otherwise, consumers will be guarded and suspicious of any information gathering. Three, the lack of a privacy statement fosters a lack of trust between consumers and web sites.

The *TrustE* organization has put together a downloadable privacy policy model file that lets an organization choose whatever privacy rules are desired and communicate them to visitors.[37] With a downloadable file, a site can choose alternatives from each of the main provisions of this model. The example above from the language describing consumer profiles shows some of the choices available. The *TrustE* organization is agnostic on the specifics of an individual company's profile. They are committed to explaining the policy clearly and in an understandable way, so that users have informed consent. They stress the need for a company to commit to its policy, to not misrepresent its actions, and to comply fully with its promises.

Privacy choices include the treatment of ordering information, application form information, the limited collection of Social Security numbers, the treatment of survey data, the treatment of referral information such as tell-a-friend, email promotions, email newsletters, emails about service questions, whether a welcoming email is sent, profile information (above), the use of third parties and agents, opt-in versus opt-out, the treatment of log files, the treatment of IP addresses, methods for using cookie data, whether clear gifs are used for tracking, alliances with third-party advertising, links to other sites, exemption of bulletin board and chat, access to personally identifiable data, security understanding, contact method, and methodology for changing privacy policy in the future. *TrustE* also suggests involving a wide range of personnel in the privacy policy. This includes top management, legal, marketing, operations, and engineering. All have important roles to play guaranteeing the commitments of the privacy policy. A number of companies go further, creating the position of Chief Privacy Officer to draft, supervise, and maintain the commitments contained in a company's privacy policy.[38]

LOOKING FORWARD

The Long View

The rapid pace of technical and social change in the world makes it all too easy to focus on very short-term phenomena. Questions revolve around specific technologies of the moment rather than longer-term trends. Specific crises dominate both the front page and the business sections of the press. When dealing with underlying forces, one should also consider the longer view. Looking backward, and at the cautionary insights from history, can help with this dangerous task of looking forward.

The nineteenth century closed like many centuries before it, with people wondering what the next century would bring. A new century breeds hope, instills fear, and demands forecasts. Social thinkers speculate where trends are taking humanity. Technologists extend their own trends and try to guess the shape of future inventions. Business leaders look at these predictions and wonder what it means for their companies, people, and markets. These forecasts share what one author has called "chronocentricity—the egotism that one's own generation is poised on the very cusp of history."[39] Change always seems to be accelerating. We can't imagine it continuing, so some global transformation must occur.

A highly popular nineteenth-century American speculation was the novel *Looking Backward* by Edward Bellamy. It was a bestseller, published in 1887. More than that, it created a vision of the future so compelling that many formed political organizations to invent the predicted future. Its plot, familiar now, has a man from 1887 Boston transported into the future (he falls into a deep hypnotic sleep in a bunker designed to help him deal with insomnia). He survives in stasis undisturbed by a fire that destroys his house until future construction workers finally discover it. The time is now, the beginning of the twenty-first century. As the protagonist learns, the world has changed dramatically. Utopia has arrived.

The novel is as instructive for what it fails to predict as for what it accurately sees. Technology breakthroughs are far too timid. Nowhere in the book are there airplanes, automobiles, movies,

A Year 2000 Boston Shopping Trip *Looking Backward*, Edward Bellamy, 1887

"Where is the clerk?" I asked, for there was no one behind the counter, and no one seemed coming to attend to the customer. "I have no need of the clerk yet," said Edith. "I have not made my selection."

"It was the principal business of clerks to help people to make their selections in my day," I replied.

"What! To tell people what they wanted?" "Yes; and oftener to induce them to buy what they didn't want."

....

"But even a twentieth-century clerk might make himself useful in giving you information about the goods, though he did not tease you to buy them," I suggested. "No," said Edith, "that is not the business of the clerk. These printed cards, for which the government authorities are responsible, give us all the information we can possibly need." I saw then that there was fastened to each sample a card containing in succinct form a complete statement of the make and materials of the goods and all its qualities, as well as price, leaving absolutely no point to hang a question on.

"The clerk has, then, nothing to say about the goods he sells?" I said. "Nothing at all. It is not necessary that he should know or profess to know anything about them. Courtesy and accuracy in taking order are all that are required of him." "What a prodigious amount of lying that simple arrangement saves!"

...

"I have made my selections." With that she touched a button, and in a moment a clerk appeared. He took down her order on a tablet with a pencil which made two copies, of which he gave one to her, and enclosing the counterpart in a small receptacle, dropped it into a transmitting tube. "The duplicate of the order," said Edith as she turned away from the counter, after the clerk had punched the value of her purchases out of the credit card she gave him, "is given to the purchaser, so that any mistakes in filling it can be easily traced and rectified."

"You were very quick about your selections," I said. "May I ask how you knew that you might not have found something to suit you better in some of the other stores? But probably you are required to buy in your own district." "Oh, no," she replied. "We buy where we please, though naturally most often near home. But I should have gained nothing by visiting other stores. The assortment is all exactly the same, representing as it does in each case samples of all the varieties produced or imported by the United States. That is why one can decide quickly, and never need to visit two stores."

The dispatching clerk has a dozen pneumatic transmitters before him answering to the general classes of goods, each communicating with the corresponding department at the warehouse. He drops the box of orders into the tube it calls for, and in a few moments later it drops on the proper desk in the warehouse, together with all the orders of the same sort from other sample stores. The orders are read over, recorded, and sent to be filled, like lightning. ... The packages are then delivered by larger tubes to the city districts, and thence distributed to the houses. You may understand how quickly it is all done when I tell you that my order will probably be at home sooner than I could have carried it from here."

(continued)

"How do you manage in the thinly set-tled rural districts?" I asked.

"The system is the same," Edith explained that the village sample shops are connected by transmitters with the central county ware-house, which may be twenty miles away. The transmission is so swift, though, that the time lost on the way is trifling. But, to save expense, in many counties one set of tubes connect several Villages with the warehouse, and then there is time lost waiting for one another. Sometimes it is two or three hours before goods ordered are received. It was so where I was staying last summer, and I found it quite inconvenient."...

television, atomic power, computers, DNA, or space travel. Technology is an extension and per-fection of late-nineteenth-century tools: the telegraph, pneumatic tubes, electric power, the tele-phone, the railroad, and the factory. These work extremely well and they are fantastically cheap, but they are comprehensible to the visitor from 1887. The major breakthroughs of twentieth-century science and engineering are mostly unanticipated.

Bellamy's social forecasts are far too optimistic. Private markets disappear without unin-tended consequences. Government control of the economy happens without the brutality and inefficiency of communist and fascist regimes. Technical change leads to social progress, but Bellamy ignores technical improvements in war and crime. Population growth and environmen-tal damage are not issues.

Bellamy does get some things right. Elements of the economy held up as wondrous and utopian seem like the modern shopping mall. Some even sound remarkably like ecommerce. The excerpt from *Looking Backward* captures the nineteenth-century man on his first big shopping trip in Boston, the year 2000. It could be Wal-Mart, or even better, Amazon.com.

The essential elements of online shopping are:

> Comprehensive product assortment accessible to all (millions of titles...)
> In-depth information (shopping assistants and buying tutorials)
> Sample stores augmented by the network (Best Buy stores)
> Simple order-taking clerks (easily cast as web forms)
> Credit card transactions
> Accurate and real-time execution (attentive servers rather than invisible warehouses)
> Rapid delivery to the home (FedEx and UPS instead of pneumatic tubes)

Consumer expectations have also risen in the Bellamy world, so a delay of an hour or two becomes annoying as compared to a time when delivery used to take weeks. To a late-nineteenth-century observer, this sounds fantastic and a shopping Utopia. Yet we modern inhabitants of the future already take much of this for granted, and we look for the real change to come in our near future. However, Bellamy would be shocked that material prosperity is so unevenly distributed, and he would be forced to acknowledge that technology is often a two-edged sword.

| If the Net Marketing GPTs Continue to Develop...

Each of the three general-purpose technologies of digitization, networking, and individualization may well continue their rapid pace of development over the next couple of decades. Chapters 2 through 4 provide evidence both of their continuation in the near future and accumulating challenges in the medium to longer term. We have come a far way from the initial observations of Richard Feynman in a 1960 speech, which highlighted how miniaturization of electronics and information had a phenomenal scope for improvement (Figure 17.11). We have seen multiple decades of that already. If each continues for two or three more decades, changes will be profound.

What if the twentieth-century rate continues significantly into the twenty-first century? Some projections are startling, introducing machine intelligence into more and more products and services. Looking three decades hence, one aggressively optimistic forecast leads to a Bellamy-like future. Existing trends continue to a form of perfection, as the problems of artificial intelligence disappear within 30 years of progress.[40]

We may not be able to cost-effectively produce these new designs. Consumer demand for computing power might lag behind engineering capability. Writing software capable of human-like behavior may continue to frustrate researchers, as it has for decades. Digital progress may slow dramatically. Or, mirroring Bellamy, the technology may continue to progress rapidly, but unintended social impacts and consequences cloud the issue.

One area of progress allows computers to better understand the emotional states of users. Work in *affective computing* shows that understanding the emotional context of communication is often necessary to determine what an individual actually means and wants. Especially in areas such as speech recognition, aspects of communication such as tone, speed, and voice pitch provide reliable clues to a user's state of mind.[41] Rather than forcing users to adapt to the limitations of machines, this research seeks to make computers more responsive and adaptive to individuals.

Internet skills are increasingly vital for all companies. Much more than just a convenience, Internet marketing is becoming a primary method of interacting with consumers. The continuing upward spiral of digital technology, network connections, and individual interaction begins to blur the distinction of consumer and tools, between company and software presence. Marketers will have to develop an integrated strategy outlining how:

> Marketing humans interact with human customers
> Marketing digital agents interact with human customers
> Marketing humans interact with customer digital agents
> Marketing digital agents interact with customer digital agents

The lessons of past technology forecasts lead to caution. Our machines are evolving rapidly, humans are not. Software agents and digital tools won't substitute for social needs. Efficiency is not the only driver of consumer wants. Status, equity, and experience will continue to drive purchases in the future as they do now and did 100 years ago.

60nm

As soon as I mention this, people tell me about miniaturization, and how far it has progressed today. They tell me about electric motors that are the size of the nail on your small finger. And there is a device on the market, they tell me, by which you can write the Lord's Prayer on the head of a pin. But that's nothing, that's the most primitive halting step in the direction I intend to discuss. It is a staggeringly small world that is below. In the year 2000, when they look back at this age, they will wonder why it was not until the year 1960 that anybody began seriously to move in this direction.

400nm

Richard P. Feynman 1960

Figure 17.11

Feynman's View Has Proven Correct

The first decade of a commercial Internet has created world-renowned and valuable companies, a boom, a bust, and a recovery, created entirely new forms of publishing and communication, helped raise the productivity of the world's economies, reinforced and accelerated globalization, opened new doors to medicine, education, and many other areas of business and life. This requires no forecast; it has already happened. There is also little forecasting risk in stating the obvious: More progress is coming.

ENDNOTES

1. Quoted in Tom Standage, *The Victorian Internet* (New York: Walker and Company, 1998): 165.
2. Arthur C. Clarke, *Profiles of the Future*, (New York: Harper and Row, 1962).
3. Louise Story, "Marketers See Opportunity as a Web Tool Gains Users," *New York Times* (5 July 2005).
4. Ibid.
5. Leslie Werstein Hann, "E-commerce Can Create Unexpected Challenges," *Best's Review*, P/C (January 1999): 87.
6. Op. cit., quoting Zurich Kemper ecommerce director.
7. Carol Tenopir, "Plagued by Our Own Success," *Library Journal* 123, (1 March 1998): 39–40.
8. Herbert Schorr and Salvatore Stolfo, "A Digital Government for the 21st Century," *Association for Computing Machinery* 41, no. 11 (1998): 15–19.
9. Purdue University/Benchmark study, November 2004.
10. Pamela LiCalzi O'Connell, "We Got Your E-Mail; Just Don't Expect a Reply," *New York Times* (6 July 1998).
11. For example, Yoram Kalman and Sheizaf Rafaeli, "Email Chronemics: Unobtrusive Profiling of Response Times," Proceedings of the 38th Hawaii International Conference on System Sciences, 2005. Also, Joshua Tyler and John C. Tang, "When Can I Expect an Email Response?" 2002, working paper.
12. Lower support quality is typically given to lower-value customers. For example, banks have private bankers for the high-value customers and industrial marketers devote entire teams to their largest customers. An interesting thing about the Net is it forces a finer distinction, perhaps even a continuous adjustment, of service to customer value. Of course, a small customer now might become a large customer in the future; this should be taken into account.
13. Machines can already far surpass humans in some intellectual skills, such as computation and calculus. In the 1940s, Turing proposed a much more difficult and social test. He proposed the test for machine intelligence as the ability to fool a human into thinking they were corresponding with another human when typing messages back and forth.
14. Purdue/Benchmark, op. cit.
15. Russell Beck, "World Wide Web May Mean World Wide Lawsuits," *Direct Marketing* (July 1998): 60–62. Leigh Gregg, "Is Your Web Site Legal," *Executive Journal* (September/October 1998): 18–21. Michael Zugelder, Theresa Flaherty, and James Johnson, "Legal Issues Associated With International Internet Marketing," *International Marketing Review* 17, no. 2 (2000).
16. Each company must find its own balance of review and legal exposure. Competent counsel should review both the training and knowledge of employees making decisions. The information in this section is suggestive, but insufficient for full legal awareness.
17. The official definition is "any original works of authorship fixed in a tangible medium of expression" are afforded federal copyright protection with eight categories receiving specific mention. They include (1) literary works, (2) musical works, (3) dramatic works, (4) pantomimes, (5) pictorial, graphic, and sculptural works, (6) motion pictures and other audiovisual works, (7) sound recordings, and (8) architectural and choreographic works, *17 USC Section 102*.
18. 17 USC Section 30.
19. *National Basketball Association v. Motorola*, 105 F.3rd 841 (2nd Cir. 1997). Also see Lawrence Mifflin, "Court Allows Motorola to Use NBA Scores," *New York Times* (31 January 1997).
20. The hundred years since this publication would also put it in the public domain.
21. Exceptions in the U.S. legal code exist. One of the most important is the Foreign Corrupt Practices Act. This law makes it illegal for a U.S. citizen or corporation to engage in bribery of a foreign official in a foreign country. Another is the Helms-Burton restriction on third-party countries trading with Cuba. Both laws, especially Helms-Burton, are highly controversial. These examples point out

the difficulty of a law reaching beyond a border. The U.S. Constitution restricts a U.S. state efforts to restrict activity outside of its own state border.

22. *Planned Parenthood Federation of America, Inc. v. Bucci*, 65 USLW 2662, 1997 WL 133313 (S.D.N.Y.).

23. *Panavision International v. Toeppen*, (1996), 945 F. Supp. 1296, (C.D. Cal.).

24. There is a delay between reserving a domain name and required payment to Internic. This time period allows for appropriate copyright and trademark search services to investigate any conflicts while the domain is safely reserved.

25. Robert Cumbow, "Day of the Typosquatters," *The Internet Advertising/Marketing Law Report* (11 September 1998). Conflicting cases include *Holiday Inns Inc, v. 800 Reservation Inc,* which suggests that typosquatters are legal, and *Panavision* or *Mobil Oil v. Pegasus Petroleum.*

26. Andrew Raskin, "Buy This Domain: Tuvalu's .tv stands to radically upgrade the country's $10 million GDP," *Wired Magazine*, 6.09 (September 1998).

27. Service Agreement for Qpass, http://www.qpass.com/us/about/terms.asp.

28. *Bensusan Restaurant Corporation v. Richard B. King*, 937 F. Supp. 295 (S.D.N.Y. 1996).

29. *Thorton v. Equifax*, (1980) 619 F.2d 700, woman "living without benefit of matrimony with male companion."

30. *Wiggins v. Equifax*, (1994) 853 Fed. Supp. 500.

31. Matt Richtel, "Trolling for Scuttlebutt on the Internet," *New York Times* (8 March 1999).

32. In addition to the cites below, other examples include Saadi Lahlou, Marc Langheinrich, and Carsten Rocker, "Privacy and Trust Issues with Invisible Computers," *Communications of the ACM* 48, no. 3 (March 2005). Sjaak Nouwt, "Kids

Privacy on the Internet," *Multimedia und Recht* 5, no. 11 (November 2002). Elizabeth Perkins and Mike Markel, "Multinational Data-Privacy Laws: An Introduction for IT Managers," IEEE *Transactions on Professional Communication* 47, no. 2 (June 2004).

33. United States Federal Trade Commission, *Fair Information Practice Principles* (March 1998), available online at http://www.ftc.gov.

34. United States Federal Trade Commission, "Appendix B: Surfer Instructions," *Fair Information Practice Principles* (March 1998), available online at http://www.ftc.gov.

35. Kathy Stewart Schwaig, Gerald C. Kane, Veda C. Storey, "Privacy, Fair Information Practices, and the Fortune 500: The Virtual Reality of Compliance," *The DATA BASE for Advances in Information Systems* 36, no. 1 (2005).

36. Traci Hong, Margaret L. Mclaughlin, Larry Pryor, Christopher Beaudoin, and Paul Grabowicz, "Internet Privacy Practices of News Media and Implications for Online Journalism," *Journalism Studies* 6, no. 2 (2005): 15–28.

37. *TrustE,* Your Online Privacy Policy: An informational paper about drafting your first privacy statement or improving your existing one, 2004. Also, the *TrustE Model Privacy Policy*, available online.

38. Richard Purcell, "Chief Privacy Office," *Harvard Business Review* (December 2000).

39. Sandage, op. cit, 213.

40. Raymond Kurzweil, *The Age of Spiritual Machines: When Computers Exceed Human Intelligence*, (New York: Penguin Books, 1999).

41. Rosalind Picard, *Affective Computing* (Cambridge, MA: MIT Press, 2000).

glossary

access point   A wireless router providing WiFi access to the Internet.

adaptive customization   An offering of the same basic product to everyone, with users having the capability to filter out or alter various attributes of the item.

ad-brand impact   The monetary measure of the brand benefits of an online banner ad, whether or not the visitor takes any immediate action.

affective computing   A computing service capable of recognizing emotional states of users, displaying emotional context to users, or both.

affiliate networks   A system of rewarding remote web sites or other sources of online traffic with commissions for generating visitors or transactions.

affinity-based communities   Affinity-based communities rely on a set of rules defining a community, such as affiliation with a particular university or membership based on a particular interest or hobby.

aggregation bundling   The combining of profitable items targeted toward average consumers.

alpha–beta system   A method of new product development that releases very early versions of a product (the alpha release) to internal users and select trusted external users or closer-to-final release versions (beta releases) to a wider group of external testers.

alpha release stage   The first stage of testing in which lead users, often company employees and loyal customers, test new versions of a product or service.

application program interfaces   Standards for interacting with a software system, which allow a third party to take advantage of many of the software capabilities of the system without complete knowledge of the software. For example, the eBay API allows programmers to externally access some of the data and capabilities of the eBay system.

augmented product   Products formed through addition of features designed to increase differentiation.

authentication mechanism   A method for verifying that someone attempting to use a system is the proper authorized individual.

automatic response system   A software program designed to answer questions without human intervention.

bandwagon effect   The phenomenon by which success breeds success and high market share makes it easier to make additional sales.

banner ads   A form of online advertising. Banner ads are graphic images that can be animated and clicking on the banner takes the user to another web location.

beta testing stage   The testing of preliminary versions of software or products, often with bugs or missing features, by selected customers.

big box retailer   A retailing format featuring corporate stores that are typically large (>50,000 sq. ft.). Examples of big box retailers include Wal-Mart and Target for general merchandise, Best Buy for electronics, and Home Depot for home improvement.

bit   A single, smallest piece of digital information.

blog   A web site containing frequent postings of material, often centered on a specific topic, and typically organized chronologically. Blogs may be the product of a single individual or a collaborative effort among many contributors.

bots   Small software programs capable of simulating some version of online activity, such as search or log in.

brand architecture   For a multi-brand company, brand architecture is the organizing principle linking various brands offered. Common choices are a branded house or a house of brands.

brand awareness   A consumer's familiarity with a brand, either without prompting (unaided brand awareness) or after prompting (aided brand awareness).

brand community   A community organized around ownership and fondness for a branded product or service, such as the Harley Owners' Group.

brand imagery   Associated graphics, images, and logos surrounding a brand.

brand salience   A consumer's strength of association between a brand and its category.

branded house   A brand architecture in which a multi-brand company's offerings are strongly linked together and share the common brand as part of its identity.

breadcrumb list   A technique for displaying the navigation route used to access a page, such as Home Page->Search Page -> Registration.

broadband   High-speed and continually available access to the Internet, such as that provided by fiber, DSL, or cable modem systems.

bullwhip/whiplash effect   The amplification in demand variability as orders move up the supply chain.

bundling   The combining of products into larger packages for sale.

business-to-business (B2B) commerce   Commerce or transactions in which both the seller and the buyer are businesses.

business-to-consumer (B2C) commerce   Commerce or transactions in which the seller is a business and the buyer is a consumer.

CASE system   An online system that asks visitors structured questions about what they like and uses this information to produce rankings and recommendations.

category development   Efforts to build up an entire category of products or services, such as online movie rental, versus specific efforts to promote a particular vendor or brand.

channel   The set of institutions and intermediaries involved in making goods and services available to customers.

channel compensation   Compensation offered to intermediaries in the channel of distribution as remuneration for their effort and services. The most common compensation is a margin on the price of the product. Other forms of compensation include advertising dollars and merchandise development funds.

channel conflict   Problems that arise when a company uses multiple channels to sell a product. Traditional retailers often object to a manufacturer creating a new channel, such as direct ecommerce.

chaos scenario   A phrase referring to a rapid decline in the advertising effectiveness of traditional media, such as the skipping of television ads, without any obvious alternatives for replacing their previous demand-generation capability.

chat rooms   Sites where users can engage in interactive, real-time, text-based discussions.

choice assistance   Advice that helps consumers choose the best products for themselves.

choice model   A mathematical formulation of how a consumer evaluates the attributes and features of a product or service.

closed-loop marketing   The means of tracking customer responses to specific marketing actions and evaluating their productivity and effectiveness.

collaborative customization   The tailoring of a product to meet a customer's unique needs, based on a dialogue between the firm and the customer.

collaborative filtering system   The procedure by which systems match different users with similar tastes for the purpose of sharing recommendations and preferences about hard-to-judge products and services.

communication rings   A shared communication structure. Individuals in a communication ring can send messages to the entire ring, subgroups of the ring, or each other. Examples are email lists and instant messaging buddy lists.

community value   The cumulative value of a network to all of its participants. It is the sum of the individual values of the network over all of its members.

comparison matrix   A matrix provided by Internet retailers to facilitate comparisons of different models in terms of features offered. In a typical implementation, each column of the matrix is devoted to a model and each row describes a feature.

comparison site   A web site that a consumer uses to compare products and services offered by different Internet retail sites.

compensatory model   A mathematical model describing a choice process in which a higher level of one attribute compensates for a lower level of another attribute in a product or service.

consideration set   The set of products that a buyer considers to be potentially acceptable for purchase, from which the ultimate purchase might be made.

consignment selling   A type of sales method in which one party acts as a broker, bringing buyer and seller together, without taking legal ownership of the product.

content delivery network   A service that accelerates online content delivery by pre-loading material, especially large files, onto geographically dispersed web servers.

content tree leaves   Content pages at the bottom of a content tree hierarchy.

content trees   Content hierarchies that organize information. A content tree can break down subjects into topic areas of interest and specialized discussion groups.

continuity programs   Special services and benefits extended to favored customers to encourage volume purchases. Airline frequent flyer programs are an example.

convenience-based sample   A sample that is not generated using a probabilistic sampling process.

conventions   General design practices and traditions that are not official standards.

convergence   The breakdown of technological separations between products or industries, causing them to become more like each other in use and function.

conversion rates   The fraction of successes divided by the total number of successes and failures.

cookie   Special text stored in a file on a user's hard disk by a web site. It serves to maintain information about the current visit, to track site usage over time, and to store information about the user. By convention, a cookie is only readable by the site that originally issues the cookie.

composition index   The proportion of traffic to a web site that consist of visitors that match a certain profile.

co-opetition   A situation when firms both compete and cooperate at the same time. For example, airlines compete with each other in offering air service but cooperate with each other in operating Orbitz.com.

cosmetic customization   The practice of taking a standard product and presenting it differently for different audiences without changing the actual product.

cost-per-action   The conversion rate of a marketing campaign for that action, such as registration or purchase, times the cost of a campaign.

cost–per–visit   The cost-per-action when the desired action is a visit to a web site.

coverage   Extent of the market or audience reached by an advertisement or a more general marketing campaign.

cross channel integration   The extent to which the different channels of a retailer are co-coordinated. Pricing, assortment, and promotions are all facets of cross channel integration.

customer acquisition cost   The marketing expenses incurred to recruit a new customer.

customer–based brand equity   The differential effect of brand knowledge on consumer response to the marketing of the brand.

customer contact   Direct interaction between a firm and its customers.

customer lifetime value (CLV)   The discounted present value of profits that a new customer brings to a firm.

customer management view   Organizing marketing efforts and personnel around portfolios of customers regardless of the products they buy.

customer profitability analysis   Evaluating the profitability over time of specific customer segments, including customer-specific costs and revenue.

customer relationship management (CRM) software   Software designed for maintaining customer contact records, storing transaction information, and identifying profitable direct marketing opportunities.

data synchronization   A process by which manufacturers, distributors, and retailers update product model numbers, taxonomies, and descriptions in their information systems in order to maintain consistency.

de facto standard   A standard established when a product or approach is so widely adopted in the marketplace that it dominates other approaches and standards.

decider   The individual or committee that actually makes a purchase decision, which may not be the same as the person paying for the product or service.

dialogue marketing   A dialogue is a technology-enabled ongoing conversation, intended to target the right customer during opportune moments using the proper method.

diamond–water paradox   The apparent puzzle that critical resources such as water can be very cheap (due to large supply), while unnecessary luxuries such as diamonds can be very expensive (due to limited supply).

difficult comparison effect   A decrease in price sensitivity due to the difficulty of comparing possible substitutes.

diffusion   The adoption over time of a product or service among its potential users.

digital   Any element that has all of its properties and information stored as a string of zeros and ones.

digital convergence   The merging of different industries and technical approaches to a common digital set of technologies capable of sharing and displaying content.

digital environments   A term coined by Janet Murray to capture the procedural, spatial, encyclopedic, and participatory nature of complex digital settings.

digital substitution   Substituting digital content or procedures into business activities.

digitization   The translation of text or other content into digital form.

direct distribution   Direct-to-customer sales in which distribution is not handled by an intermediary.

direct marketing   Targeted marketing activities, often based on specific demographic or individual profiles of recipients.

DNI capabilities   Actions or capabilities that take advantage of the three general purpose technologies: digital, network, and individualization.

domain name   A unique textual web site identifying address.

domain name server   A server responsible for translating web site addresses, such as www.stanford.edu, into a specific numeric address for that web site (171.67.20.37).

domain name strategy The branding and positioning of a firm to allow for ease in finding its web site, especially the domain and subdomains chosen.

downstream partners Channel of distribution partners. From a supply chain perspective, these partners are downstream.

Dutch auction A type of auction in which the price starts high and is periodically reduced. In this case, the first bidder gets the item.

dynamic pricing Pricing that changes over time as demand or supply conditions change.

ecommerce Electronic commerce. The process of shopping, buying, and selling goods and services online. It ranges from purchase influence to ordering and payment settlement.

electronic data exchange (EDI) A process by which buyers and sellers exchange orders and other transaction related information using dedicated and secure electronic communication lines.

end benefit effect Increased price sensitivity due to an input's importance.

entertainment survey An opinion poll allowing respondents to share opinions and obtain immediate feedback on topical issues.

endorsement system A recommendation system that certifies a minimum level of quality or performance.

entry page The beginning page viewed in a web site visit.

eprocurement Procurement transactions and processes conducted over electronic networks. Examples include order placement over EDI networks or the ordering of indirect materials using a web-based software system for transmittal to the supplier.

event nodes Decision points along a web chain.

executive view The broad overall understanding of the full marketplace, which may be lacking detailed specific information.

exit page The last page viewed in a web site visit.

expected product Features and functions of a product or service that are regarded as standard additions to the product's core features. The expected product often expands over time.

experience goods Products and services which are difficult to understand and evaluate in advance.

experiential online behavior Online behavior geared to time-using, leisure activities, such as viewing online video gaming, or browsing content for its enjoyment benefits (as opposed to task-directed online behavior).

FAQs (Frequently Asked Questions) A file of stored answers to the most frequently asked queries.

first level processes The basic value creation that marketing performs.

flaming Overly negative and critical discussion material.

floor-ready merchandise Merchandise that is pre-packed with price tags, hangers, and other labels such that it is ready to be placed on the retail floor with minimum additional processing.

flow The proper balance between the rewards and difficulties of using the Net, which allows the user the optimum experience in terms of entertainment and satisfaction.

free riding Taking advantage of the actions or investments of others without contributing to the service's provision.

frequency marketing Special services and benefits extended to customers making frequent purchases.

friendly technology Methods by which the Net is made easy to use for customers and more appliance-like.

gathering The first of five virtual value activities. Gathering involves collecting information.

general purpose technologies (GPTs) A technology with a pervasive presence that has much room for improvement when introduced and spawns many additional innovations.

goal directed online behavior   Online behavior geared to finding information, solving a task, saving time, or accomplishing a goal (contrast with experiential online behavior).

goal divergence   The conflict that occurs when the objectives of a manufacturer or service provider and its channels differ.

hidden design parameters   The hidden internal workings of modules in a component-based system.

honey pot   A server disguised to look like it contains normal web resources but is actually designed to trap unauthorized users and hackers.

house of brands   A brand architecture that keeps the brands of a multi-brand company separate and uniquely branded, as Proctor & Gamble does with brands such as Tide, Crest, and Ivory (contrast with a branded house).

HTML   Hypertext markup language; the basic page layout system for describing a web page.

hybrid sampling   A procedure in which multiple sampling approaches are used to generate a sample.

incumbent-based marketplace   An electronic marketplace, typically in business-to-business ecommerce, coordinated or operated by a firm that is currently one of the incumbents in the market.

individualization   The emerging general technology base involving identification, the ability to associate identified entities with descriptive information, and the ability to interact appropriately with identified entities.

instant messaging   Direct one-to-one and few-to-few communication; a form of personal chat room.

interactivity   The back and forth flow of information. For a web site, participation plus procedural rules lead to interactivity.

intercept survey   A survey in which the respondents are the randomly selected subset of the visitors to a web site in a given period.

inverse elasticity rule   The equation that states that a profit-maximizing price for a product or service is lower for high elasticity markets.

iPACE   An acronym referring to the importance of information, price, assortment, convenience, and entertainment to consumers' shopping preferences.

joint performance bundling   The combining of products and services due to functionality benefits.

kairos   A Greek word signifying the opportune moment for an action.

keyword advertising   The advertising method relying on the keyword or phrase used in a search at a search engine, with the ranking of displayed ads partially based on an auction for position. Leading keyword advertising sites include Google and Yahoo!.

keyword search ads   Advertising that is typically text based, triggered by a search, and normally displayed either at the top or to the right of the search results.

latency   The delay between the request for an online action and its completion, caused by congestion, distance, or some other factor.

live marketing database   An abbreviated version of a full-customer database. A live marketing database sacrifices some degree of customer information to allow rapid processing.

log file   A database of file requests and transfers maintained by a web server.

long tail   The increased product assortment possible online due to a decrease in transaction costs and centralized inventory. The "long tail" refers to the elongated distribution of products, many with just a few sales, offered by online retailers compared to traditional retailers.

look ahead surfer model   A mathematical model of web surfing behavior in which an individual continually makes judgments about the quality of a site and then leaves the site when the task is completed or the perceived site quality falls below a threshold value.

loyalty bundling Product combinations designed to build customer loyalty and to raise switching costs to other vendors.

loyalty programs Incentive programs and special promotions, such as frequent flyer accounts offered by airlines, used to concentrate purchases.

make or buy decision A channel design choice regarding whether a channel service or activity is performed by the manufacturer (make) or by an intermediary (buy).

margin spread bundling The combination of items that have high contribution margin ratios.

mass customization A system of differentiation achieved through a relatively large number of modular alternatives.

maverick buying Products and services purchased by corporate employees that are not on the list of products and services approved by the purchasing department.

maximally secure password A password using the full length allowed, with a random mixture of all usable characters. Consumers rarely use maximally secure passwords, relying instead on easy-to-remember familiar phrases.

member generated content Content created by members of a community or social networking site rather than created by the site itself.

member profile The accumulated information on an ecommerce or community member.

metadata Descriptive keywords and phrases indicating the content and relevance of information, allowing more refined search and matching.

Metcalfe's Law Generally, the observation that the community value of a network rises much faster than the size of a network. In its original form, the community value of a fully connected network of equal value connections rises at the square of the size of the network.

modularity-in-design principle The separation of a product or information into

well-designed modules allowing easy recombination and alteration of the modules.

Moore's Law The observation, originally noticed by Gordon Moore of Intel, that computing power doubles roughly every 18 months. Commonly used to refer to the ongoing rapid progress of digital technology.

multi-channel retailing A retailing approach that reaches consumers using multiple channels. Typical channels include brick and mortar stores, call centers, and the Internet.

netnography Applying the tools of ethnography to the study of the Internet, especially its social impacts.

newbies Beginning users.

nexus A seller's physical presence, such as a store or warehouse, in a legal jurisdiction, such as a country or state.

no notice rate The probability that an online banner ad will not be noticed by a web page viewer.

online communities Social networks maintained using online tools.

ontology A knowledge hierarchy.

open ascending (or English) auction A standard auction method in which ascending bids are publicly observed with the auction terminating when no higher bid is offered.

open standards Software protocols and operations not controlled by a private company and typically offered for little or no charge to all.

opt-in Active permission given by a customer for use of personalized information or receipt of solicitation. The default is "no permission."

opt-out A customer choice to receive no solicitation or to decline participation. The default is "permission granted."

organic search traffic Unpaid visits arriving from search engines and their results.

origination site Immediately previous web site visited.

packets Small files used to transmit messages over the Internet, containing portions of messages together with routing information.

packet switching   The method used by the Internet to break up communication into multiple information packets, with origin and destination information.

panel data   Data obtained from a set of participating households over a period of time.

pay-per-click   A system of advertising in which an advertiser only pays for an online ad if the web user clicks on the ad.

personal digital assistant (PDA)   A specialized mobile handheld computer.

personalization   A form of product differentiation in which a solution is tailored for a specific individual.

personalized pricing   Pricing based on profile information or individualized transaction history.

phishing   Similar to spoofing, when a fraudulent web site or email mimics a legitimate site in order to trick individuals into providing personal information such as a user ID and password.

plug-ins   Additional programs creating new functions for a web browser without altering the core browser program.

podcast   A digital audio or video program available for download, either manually or by automatic subscription, and playable through a computer or digital player such as an iPod.

point-to-point communication   Communication between a single source and a single receiver.

portal   An initial gateway web site either for specialized information (such as WebMD for medical information) or for more general Internet material (such as Yahoo!).

price elasticity   A mathematical expression representing price sensitivity: the proportionate change in quantity demanded for a proportionate change in price.

price partitioning   Price sensitivities that vary across different components of the full price of a product, such as shipping cost versus product price.

price-quality effect   The observation that customers may use price to judge quality when they lack other reliable cues.

price sensitivity   The impact that price changes have on customers' purchasing habits.

primary domain name   The part of the domain name that indicates the type of organization controlling the web site, such as .com or .edu.

probability sampling   A sampling approach in which the selection of a respondent is specified by an appropriate random process.

procedural costs   The portion of switching costs due to the time and effort involved in changing vendors.

product definition bundling   Combining products to help consumers understand the full range of product and service benefits.

product funnel   The declining fraction of new products surviving from initial concept stage to actual new product release.

production efficiency bundling   Combining multiple products to ensure efficiencies in manufacturing or set-up.

product management view   The limited but detailed perspective of someone responsible for a specific product or service (contrast with executive view).

professional respondents   Individuals repeatedly participating in panels in order to receive monetary compensation or other incentives.

profit pool   The constellation of purchases surrounding a major purchase, and the identification of the dollar value and profitability rates of these related sales.

purpose-built communities   Online communities organized around a task or objectives, such as an open-source software project or some charitable activity.

random digit dialing (RDD)   A telephone survey in which the respondents are randomly recruited from a list, such as a phone book.

random surfer model   A mathematical model of web surfing behavior in which a web site visitor continuously "flips a (weighted) coin" to determine whether to continue a visit or to exit.

radio frequency identification device   A small chip embedded in tags or objects to allow remote sensing and identification.

recommendation system   A system for making personalized purchase suggestions or other types of individual level recommendations.

reference price effect   Changes in price sensitivity caused by the comparison set of alternative products used by a consumer.

relational switching costs   Relational switching costs are the costs of lost learning, lost customization, and lost emotional connection to a previous vendor.

relationship customers   Customers with an ongoing and established repeat buying history; contrast with transactional customers.

representation   The manner in which a product or service is portrayed to a customer.

repurchase probability   The probability that someone who has already purchased a product will repurchase the same product in a particular time period.

request for quote (RFQ)   A request for a quote for a product or a service typically sent out by a purchasing department.

reserve price   The minimum price a seller will accept in an auction. This may be displayed (a posted reserve price) or hidden (private reserve price).

response rate   The fraction of message targets, such as recipients of an email campaign, responding to a marketing effort.

responsibility disputes   Conflicts over customer handling, territorial assignments, functions to be served, or technology to be used.

result node   A termination point of a web chain.

revenue management system   A system combining price incentives, inventory tracking, and demand forecasting to improve the profitability of service providers.

routers   Computers transmitting online packets to their destinations. They form the backbone of the Internet.

R.S.S. standard   An acronym for "really simple syndication;" it is a standard for distributing information through a process of subscribe and publish. Among other applications, it is used in podcasting to alert and deliver new audio or video content.

rules-based system   Software systems using pre-specified criteria to determine the kinds of special offers, promotions, and information provided to a visitor.

sampling frame   A list from which a sample is drawn.

scalability   The ability to accommodate substantial growth.

search engine   A service cataloging online information and providing relevant responses to user queries.

search engine marketing   Efforts to attract web site visitors as a result of search activity.

search goods   Products and services that are easy for a consumer to evaluate.

secondary domain name   The identifying portion of the domain name. For example, Stanford in the domain name stanford.edu.

secret reserve   A private minimum acceptable bid for an auction item.

self-selection bias   Distortions, such as in public opinion sampling, caused by the users of a site or service systematically differing from the general public due to the implicit sorting caused by the service activity. For example, an opinion sample at a college bookstore or at a retirement center will not be representative of the general public due to the special demographics of these users.

semantic web   Extra services and capabilities of the Internet when metatag information is available and utilized.

server lag   Latency in online response caused by congestion and delays at the web site.

shared cost effect   The observation that a market with a division of decider and payer differs from a market in which the same person both chooses and pays.

shilling   Placing bids in an auction to drive up the final price without a desire to actually win the auction.

shopping assistant   A retail site service consumers use to select a subset of products matching their preferences.

shopping scenario   The context, purpose, and specific process of a shopping trip used to evaluate online capabilities.

sniping   Delaying bids until the last moments of an auction, often in an attempt to conceal interest and prevent a response by other bidders.

source loss analysis   An analysis of the origin and eventual destination of web site visitors.

spam   Unsolicited and unwanted email.

span-of-control   The effective managerial reach within an organization.

spatial environment   The virtual space and environments created by web sites or computer games.

sponsorship   Financial support of web content without regard to exact levels of viewership.

spoofing   A fraudulent web site or communication that mimics a real site or message, often for the purpose of tricking the user to provide personal data.

standard   A method or protocol to accomplish a task or technological process.

standards competition   Competition strongly influenced by the standards embedded in the products, which may be incompatible.

standards marketing   Marketing aimed toward creating a proprietary standard.

static web pages   Web pages that are created prior to access and can be indexed by search engines.

"sticky" site   A site with a high visit duration.

strong ties   A close identification and social connection with a group brought about by stringent or extended membership requirements.

switching cost effect   A lowering of short-term price sensitivity for a product when it is used as part of system. For example, consumers may be less price sensitive to gasoline prices when they already own a vehicle than when they are contemplating a vehicle purchase.

switching costs   Transitional expenses which must be paid to switch from one product or service to a competitor. For example, a consumer many need a new cell phone or pay a contractual penalty to switch from one cell phone company to another.

synthesizing   A virtual value activity involving the processing of information gleaned from previous activities.

task-directed online behavior   Online behavior geared to finding specific information, completing a task, or other goal-directed activity (contrast with experiential online behavior).

template   A pre-designed format to speed the creation of content.

tier 1 supplier   Suppliers providing goods or services directly to a company.

tier 2 supplier   Suppliers providing goods and services to tier 1 suppliers.

time-based pricing   Prices partially conditioned on the time of product purchase or rental, such as peak versus off-peak hotel room rates.

time pacing   The practice of producing or introducing new products following a fixed schedule.

total expenditures effect   The tendency of consumers to be more price sensitive to products or services comprising a large portion of their budget.

trade-up bundling   Expanding the scope of a product in a price insensitive market.

traffic building   Efforts devoted to bringing visitors to a web site.

transactional customers   Infrequent or one-time only customers.

transparent customization   Changes in a product brought about as a result of observed user behavior without requiring a user request.

trigger   Some observable action or signal used to initiate a marketing message.

trigger event   An instigating behavior or action, such as getting married or buying a house, which often results in a number of other actions or purchases to occur.

unified visit value   The total expected benefits accruing to a site operator from a visit.

unsubscribe rate   The percentage of subscribers to an email list unsubscribing within a given time period.

upstream partners   Tier 1 suppliers.

URL   A web address (**U**niform **R**esource **L**ocator).

vendor-managed inventory   Retail inventory managed by a vendor or a distributor according to a pre-specified agreement.

venture capital financing   Equity investments made early in a start-up.

versioning   Product alternatives created to serve different price points and market segments. For example, a premium subscription may provide real-time information while a low-cost or free account receives that same information only after a delay.

virtual model   In online retailing, the use of an online figure with similar appearance and body shape to the shopper to display potential purchases.

virtual value activities   The processes firms use to make information more useful.

virtuous cycle   Re-inforcing positive feedback.

visible design rules   Specifications describing how software modules or business processes must perform and interact.

visit duration   The length of time a user spends on a site during a visit or the number of pages viewed at a web site during a visit.

visual metaphor   The use of an image to suggest its online function.

voice-over-IP   Using the Internet to place or receive telephone calls to other computers, land line, or cellular phones.

weak ties   Loose social connections between individuals.

web chain   The potential sequence of actions a visitor to a site can take.

web hosting   A service providing software and bandwidth for a web site's operation.

web log   A database of the transactions and file transfers at a web site.

web site brand impact   The expected branding benefits resulting from a web site visit.

WiFi   A standard for wireless Internet access.

"wine glass" plot   A visual display of the declining fraction of users completing sequential steps at a web site.

winner's curse   The result in which the winner of an auction tends to be the bidder with the most extremely optimistic, and possibly incorrect, view of the value of the item being auctioned.

World Wide Web Consortium (W3C)   A nonprofit organization debating and creating standards for Internet operations and services.

yield management   The matching of price and available capacity.

zone pricing   A pricing practice creating systematic differences in retail price levels depending on the demographics and competitive nature of the retail location.

references

Aaker, David A. *Brand Portfolio Strategy: Creating Relevance, Differentiation, Energy, Leverage, and Clarity.* New York: Free Press, 2004.

Aaker, David A. and **Erich Joachimsthaler.** *Brand Leadership: The Next Level of the Brand Revolution.* New York: Free Press, 2000.

Aaker, Jennifer L. "Dimensions of Brand Personality." *Journal of Marketing Research* 34 (1997): 347–356.

Abe, Makoto and **Kirthi Kalyanam.** "Brand and Category Influences on the Representativeness of Household Panel Data" Working Paper, Santa Clara University, 2004.

Achabal, Dale D., **Stephen S. Smith**, **Shelby S. McIntyre** and **Kirthi Kalyanam.** "A Decision Support System for Vendor Managed Inventory." *Journal of Retailing* 76, No. 4 (2000): 430–454.

Adar, Eytan and **Bernardo A. Huberman.** "Free Riding on Gnutella." Technical Report, Xerox Palo Alto Research Center, 10 August 2000.

Almquist, Eric, **Martin Kon**, and **Wolfgang Bock.** "The Science of Demand." *Marketing Management* (March–April 2004): 20–26.

Anderson, David P. and **John Kubiatowicz.** "The Worldwide Computer." *Scientific America* 286, No. 3 (March 2002).

Anderson, Philip and **Erin Anderson.** "The New E-Commerce Intermediaries." *MIT Sloan Management Review* (Summer 2002): 53–62.

Andonie, Razvan, **J. Edward Russo**, and **Rishi Dean.** "Crossing the Rubicon for an Intelligent Advisor." Working Paper, *IUI Workshop: Beyond Personalization 2005*, San Diego, CA, 9 January 2005.

Archer, Gleason. *Big Business and Radio.* New York: Arno Press, 1971.

Arora, Ashish, **Ramayya Krishnan**, **Anand Nandkumar**, **Rahul Telang**, and **Yubao Yang.** "Impact of Vulnerability Disclosure and Patch Availability - An Empirical Analysis." Working Paper, Carnegie Melon University, 2004.

Arthur, W. Brian. "On Competing Technologies and Historical Small Events: The Dynamics of Choice Under Increasing Returns." Working Paper WP-83-90, International Institute for Applied Systems Analysis, 1983.

_____. "Increasing Returns and the New World of Business." *Harvard Business Review* (July–August 1996): 100–109.

Babin, Barry, **William R. Darden**, and **Mitch Griffin.** "Work and/or Fun: Measuring Hedonic and Utilitarian Shopping Value." *Journal of Consumer Research* 20 (March 1994): 644–656.

Baczewski, Philip. "The Rules of the Internet." *Benchmarks* 13, No. 5 (1992): 12.

Baeza-Yates, Ricardo and **Carlos Castillo.** "Crawling the Infinite Web: Five Levels are Enough." Working Paper, Universidad de Chile, 2003.

Bailenson, J.N., **A.C. Beall**, **J. Blascovich**, **M. Weisbuch**, and **R. Raimmundo.** *Intelligent Agents Who Wear Your Face: Users' Reactions to the Virtual Self.* Lecture Notes in Artificial Intelligence 2190 (2001): 86–99.

Bajari, Patrick and **Ali Horacsu.** "The Winner's Curse, Reserve Prices and Endogenous Entry: Empirical Insights from eBay Auctions." *RAND Journal of Economics* 34, No. 2 (2003): 329–355.

Bajari, Patrick and **Ali Hortacsu.** "Economic Insights from Internet Auctions." *Journal of Economic Literature* XLII (June 2004): 457–486.

Bakos, Yannis and **Erik Brynjolfsson.** "Bundling Information Goods." *Management Science* 45, no. 12 (1999): 1613–1630.

——————. "Bundling and Competition on the Internet." *Marketing Science* 19, no. 1 (Winter 2000): 63–82.

——————. "Aggregating and Disaggregating Information Goods." In Proceedings of Internet Publishing and Beyond: The Economics of Digital Information and Intellectual Property, 1999.

Baldwin, Carliss and **Kim Clark.** "Managing in an Age of Modularity." *Harvard Business Review* (September–October 1997): 84–93.

Barabasi, Albert–Laszlo. *Linked: The New Science of Networks.* New York: Perseus Books Group, 2002.

Barwise, Patrick and **John Farley.** "The State of Interactive Marketing in Seven Countries: Interactive Marketing Comes of Age," *Journal of Interactive Marketing* 19, No. 3 (Summer 2005): 67–80.

Baye, Michael B., **John Morgan**, and **Patrick Scholten.** "Temporal Price Dispersion: Evidence from an Online Consumer Electronics Market." *Journal of Interactive Marketing* 16, No.4 (Autumn 2004): 101–114.

——————. "Price Dispersion in the Small and in the Large: Evidence from an Internet Price Comparison Site, "*The Journal of Industrial Economics* 52", No. 4, (2004): 463–496.

Bayles, M.E. "Designing Online Banner Advertisements: Should We Animate?" *In Proceedings of the SIGCHI conference on Human factors in computing*

systems: Changing our world, changing ourselves, Minneapolis, MN. New York: ACM Press, 2002.

Bayles, M.E. and **B. Chaparro.** "Recall and Recognition of Static vs. Animated Banner Advertisements." *In Proceedings of the Human Factors and Ergonomics Society 45th Annual Meeting,* Minneapolis, MN. Santa Monica, CA: HFES, 2002.

Beck, Russell. "World Wide Web May Mean World Wide Lawsuits." *Direct Marketing* 61, No. 3 (1998): 60–65.

Bellman, Steven, **Eric Johnson**, **Gerald Lohse**, and **Naomi Mandel.** "Designing Marketplaces of the Artificial with Consumers in Mind: Four Approaches to Understanding Consumer Behavior in Electronic Environments," *Journal of Interactive Marketing* 20, No. 1 (Winter 2006): 21–33.

Bender, Thomas. *Community and Social Change in America.* New Brunswick, NJ: Rutgers University Press, 1978.

Benway, J.P. "Banner blindness: The irony of attention grabbing on the World Wide Web." *In Proceedings of the Human Factors and Ergonomics Society 42nd Annual Meeting,* Chicago, IL. Santa Monica, CA: HFES, 1998.

Bergen, Shantanu Dutta, and **Steven M. Shugan.** "Branded Variants: A Retail Perspective." *Journal of Marketing* 33, No. 1 (1996): 9–19.

Berners–Lee, Tim. *Weaving the Web: The Original Design and Ultimate Destiny of the World Wide Web by its Inventor.* New York: Harper-Collins, 1999.

Berners–Lee, Tim, **James Hendler**, and **Ora Lassila.** "The Semantic Web." *Scientific American,* May 2001: 34–43.

Blattberg, Robert C. and **Rashi Glazer.** "Marketing in the Information Revolution." In *The Marketing Information Revolution,* edited by Robert C. Blattberg et al. Cambridge: Harvard Business School Press, 1994.

Blattberg, Robert C., Gary Getz, and Jacquelyn S. Thomas. *Customer Equity: Building and Managing Relationships as Valuable Assets.* Cambridge: Harvard Business School Press, 2001.

Boase, Jeffery, and Barry Wellman. "A Plague of Viruses: Biological, Computer, and Marketing." *Current Sociology* 49, No. 6 (2001): 39–54.

Bowden, Sue and Avner Offer. "Household Appliances and the Use of Time: the United States and Britain since the 1920s." *Economic History Review* XLVII (1994): 725–748.

Bresnahan, Timothy F. and Shane Greenstein. "Technological Competition and the Structure of the Computer Industry." *Journal of Industrial Economics* 47, No. 1 (March 1999): 1–40.

Bresnahan, Timothy F. and Manuel Trajtenberg. "General Purpose Technologies: Engines of Growth?" *Journal of Econometrics* 65 (1995): 83–108.

Bresnahan, Timothy F. and Pai-Ling Yin. "Economic and Technical Drivers of Technology Choice: Browsers." Working Paper, Stanford University, 2003.

Briggs, Rex and Nigel Hollis. "Advertising on the Web: Is There Response before Click-Through." *Journal of Advertising Research* 37, No. 2 (March–April 1997): 33–45.

Broder, A., R. Kumar, F. Maghoul, P. Raghavan, S. Rajagopalan, R. Stata, A. Tomkins, and J. Wiener. "Graph Structure in the Web: Experiments and Models." In *Proceedings of the Ninth Conference on World Wide Web*, Amsterdam, Netherlands. New York: ACM Press, 2000.

Brondmo, Hans Peter. *The Engaged Customer: The New Rules of Internet Direct Marketing.* New York: HarperBusiness, 2000.

Brown, John Seely and Paul Duguid. *The Social Life of Information.* Cambridge: Harvard Business School Press, 2000.

Brown, Jeffrey R. and Austan Goolsbee. "Does the Internet Make Markets More Competitive? Evidence from the Life Insurance Industry," *Journal of Political Economy* 110 (2002): 481–507.

Bruner, Rick E. *The Decade in Online Advertising: 1994–2004.* New York: DoubleClick, 2005.

Brynjolfsson, Erik and Lorin Hitt. "Beyond Computation: Information Technology, Organizational Transformation, and Business Practices." *Journal of Economic Perspectives* 14, No. 4 (Fall 2000): 23–48.

_____. "Computing Productivity: Firm-level Evidence." *Review of Economics and Statistics* 85, No. 4 (2003): 793–808.

Brynjolfsson, Erik, Yu Hu, and Michael Smith. "Consumer Surplus in the Digital Economy: Estimating the Value of Increased Product Variety at Online Booksellers." *Management Science* 49, No. 11 (November 2003): 1580–1596.

Brynjolfsson, Erik and Brian Kahin (Editors). *Understanding the Digital Economy*, Cambridge, MA: MIT Press, 2000.

Bucklin, Randolph E. and Catarina Sismeiro. "A Model of Web Site Browsing Behavior Estimated on Clickstream Data." *Journal of Marketing Research* 37, No. 3 (August 2003): 249–267.

Burnham, Thomas, Judy Freis, and Vijay Mahajan. "Consumer Switching Costs: A Typology, Antecedents, and Consequences." *Journal of the Academy of Marketing Science* 31, No. 2 (2003): 109–126.

Buschken, Joachim. *Higher Profits Through Customer Lock-in.* Mason, OH: Thomson Business and Economics, 2004.

Cargill, Carl. *Information Technology Standardization: Theory, Organizations, and Process.* Burlington, MA: Digital Press, 1989.

_____. *Open Systems Standardization: A Business Approach.* Upper Saddle River, NJ: Prentice Hall, 1996.

Catterall, Miriam and Pauline Maclaran. "Researching Consumers in Virtual Worlds: A Cyberspace Odyssey." *Journal of Consumer Behavior* 1, No. 3 (2001): 228–237.

Chakraborty, Goutam, **Vishal Lala**, and **David Warren.** "An Empirical Investigation of Antecedents of B2B Websites' Effectiveness." *Journal of Interactive Marketing* 16, No. 4 (Autumn 2002): 51–72.

Charlet, J.C. "Technology Note: Rules-Based Systems." Stanford University Graduate School of Business S-OIT-21, March 1998.

Chen, Pearl and **Diane McGrath.** "Moments of Joy: Student Engagement and Conceptual Learning in the Design of Hypermedia Documents." *Journal of Research on Technology in Education* 35, No. 3 (2003): 402–421.

Chen, Pei-Yu and **Lorin M. Hitt.** "Measuring Switching Costs and the Determinants of Customer Retention in Internet-Enabled Businesses: A Study of the Online Brokerage Industry." *Information Systems Research* 13, No. 3 (September 2002): 255–274.

Chen, Yuxin, **Ganesh Iyer**, and **Paddy Padmanabhan.** "Referral Infomediaries and Retail Competition," *Review of Marketing Science Working Papers* 1, No. 2 (2002).

Chevalier, Judith, and **Austan Goolsbee.** "Measuring Prices and Price Competition Online: Amazon.com and BarnesandNoble.com," Quantitative Marketing and Economics 1, No. 2, (June 2003): 1570–1576.

Chiang, Michael F. and **Justin Starren.** "Evaluation of Consumer Health Website Accessibility by Users With Sensory and Physical Disabilities." *Medinfo* 11, Pt. 2 (2004): 1128–32.

Chou, Ting-Jui and **Chih-Chen Teng.** "The Role of Flow Experience in Cyber-Game Addiction." *Cyber Psychology & Addiction* 6, No. 6 (2003): 663–675.

Christodoulides, George and **Leslie de Chernatony.** "Dimensionalising On- and Off-line Brands' Composite Equity." *Journal of Product and Brand Management* 13, No. 3 (2004): 168–179.

Clark, Kim and **Steven Wheelwright.** *Managing New Product and Process Development.* New York: Free Press, 1993.

Clement, Douglas. "Interview with Robert Solow." *Banking and Policy Issues Magazine,* September 2002.

Cohn, Adam. *The Perfect Store: Inside eBay.* New York: Little, Brown and Company, 2002.

Coleman, Les. "The Frequency and Cost of Corporate Crises." *Journal of Contingencies and Crisis Management* 12, No. 1 (2004): 2–13.

Cooper, Alan and **Robert Reimann.** *About Face 2.0: The Essentials of Interaction Design.* New York: John Wiley and Sons, 2003.

Cornett, Steve. "The Usability of Massively Multiplayer Online Roleplaying Games: Designing for New Users." In *Proceedings of the SIGCHI conference on Human factors in Computing Systems,* Vienna, Austria. New York: ACM Press, 2004.

Cotte, June, **Tilottama Chowdhury**, **S. Ratneshwar**, and **Lisa Ricci.** "Pleasure or Utility? Time Planning Style and Web Usage Behaviors," *Journal of Interactive Marketing* 20, No. 1 (Winter 2006): 45–57.

Couper, Mick C. "Web Surveys: A Review of Issues and Approaches." *Public Opinion Quarterly* 64 (2000): 464–494.

Couper, Mick C., **Roger Tourangeau**, and **Fredrick G. Conrad.** "What They See is What We Get: Response Options for Web Surveys." *Social Science Computer Review* 22, No. 1(2004): 111–127.

Cowly, Stacy. "Commerce One Runs out of Cash." *ComputerWorld,* 24 September 2004.

Cox, Brad. *Superdistribution.* Upper Saddle River, NJ: Addison-Wesley, 1996.

Culotta, Aron, **Ron Bekkerman**, and **Andrew McCallum.** "Extracting Social Networks and Contact Information from Email and the Web." In *Proceedings of the First Conference on Email and Anti-Spam (CEAS),* Mountain View, CA, 2004.

Cusamano, Michael A., **Yiorgos Mylonadis**, **Richard Rosenbloom.** "Strategic Maneuvering and Mass-Market Dynamics: The Triumph of VHS over Beta." *The Business History Review* 66, No. 1 (Spring 1992): 55–94.

Csikszentmihalyi, Mihaly. *Flow: The Psychology of Optimal Experience.* New York: Harper & Row, 1990.

Dahan, Ely and **V. Srinivasan.** "The Predictive Power of Internet-Based Product Concept Testing Using Visual Depiction and Animation." *Journal of Product Innovation Management* 17 (2000): 99–109.

Danaher, Peter J. and **Guy W. Mullarkey.** "Factors Affecting Online Advertising Recall: A Study of Students." *Journal of Advertising Research* 43, No. 3 (September 2003): 252–267.

David, Paul A., and **Dominique Foray.** "Economic Fundamentals of the Knowledge Society." Working Paper, Stanford Institute for Economic Policy Research, 13 September 2001.

Dawar, Niraj. "What Are Brands Good For?" *MIT Sloan Management Review* 46, No. 1 (Fall 2004): 31–37.

Day, George and **Christophe Van den Bulte.** "Superiority in Customer Relationship Management: Consequences for Competitive Advantage and Performance." Working Paper, The Wharton School, University of Pennsylvania, September 2002.

Day, George, Adam J. Fein, and **Gregg Ruppersberger.** "Shakeouts in Digital Markets: Lessons from B2B Exchanges." *California Management Review* 45, No. 2 (Winter 2003): 131–150.

DeKoven, Elyon. "Off-Topic Recommendations." Working Paper, *IUI Workshop: Beyond Personalization 2005*, San Diego, CA, 9 January 2005.

Dellaert, Benedict G.C. and **Barbara Kahn.** "How Tolerable is Delay?: Consumers' Evaluations of Internet Web Sites After Waiting." *Journal of Interactive Marketing* 13, No. 1 (1999): 41–54.

Dellarocas, Chrysanthos. "The Digitization of Word of Mouth: Promise and Challenges of Online Feedback Mechanisms." *Management Science* 49, No. 10 (October 2003): 1407–1424.

Devinney, Timothy, Jordan Louviere, and **Tim Coltman.** "A Comprehensive Review of the Theory and Underlying Technology of Information Acceleration Simulators." Working Paper, Smart Internet Technology CRC. The Alfred West Jr. Learning Lab, The Wharton School, University of Pennsylvania, 2003.

DeYoung, Robert, William Hunter, and **Gregory Udell.** "The Past, Present, and Probable Future for Community Banks." *Journal of Financial Services Research* 25, No. 2–3 (April 2004): 85–133.

Dhar, Ravi and **Rashi Glazer.** "Hedging Customers," *Harvard Business Review* (May 2003): 86–92.

DiClemente, Diane and **Donald Hantula.** "Optimal Foraging Online: Increasing Sensitivity to Delay." *Psychology & Marketing* 20, No. 9 (September 2003): 785–809.

Diffie, Whitfield and **Susan Landau.** *Privacy on the Line: The Politics of Wiretapping and Encryption.* Cambridge: MIT Press, 1998.

Dolan, Robert J. and **Hermann.** *Power Pricing.* New York: Free Press, 1996.

Dowling, Grahame R. and **Mark Uncles.** "Do Customer Loyalty Programs Really Work?" *Sloan Management Review* 38, No. 4 (1997): 71–82.

Dreze, Xavier and **Francois-Xavier Hussherr.** "Internet Advertising: Is Anybody Watching?" *Journal of Interactive Marketing* 17, No. 4 (2003): 8–23.

Drucker, Peter. *Management: Tasks, Responsibilities, Practices.* New York: Harper & Row, 1974.

———————. "Beyond the Information Revolution." *Atlantic Monthly* 284, No. 4 (October 1999): 47–57.

Dutta-Bergman, Mohan. "The Impact of Completeness and Web use Motivation on the Credibility of e-Health Information." *Journal of Communication* 5, No. 3 (2003): e21.

Eisenhardt, Kathleen and **Shona Brown.** "Time Pacing: Competing in Markets That

Won't Stand Still." *Harvard Business Review* (March–April 1998): 56–69.

Ellison, Glenn and **Sara Ellison.** "Lessons About Markets from the Internet." *Journal of Economic Perspectives* 19, No. 2 (2005): 139–158.

Eppen, Gary, Ward Hanson, and **Kipp Martin.** "Bundling—New Products, New Markets, Low Risk." *Sloan Management Review* 32, No. 4 (Summer 1991): 7–14.

Fader, Peter, Bruce Hardie, and **Ka Lok Lee.** "'Counting Your Customers' the Easy Way: An Alternative to the Pareto/NBD Model." *Marketing Science* 24, No. 2 (Spring 2005): 275–284.

Farquhar, Peter H. "Managing Brand Equity." *Marketing Research* 1 (September 1989): 24–34.

Farrell, Joseph and **Garth Saloner.** "Standardization, Compatibility, and Innovation." *Rand Journal of Economics* 16 (1985): 70–83.

Filson, Darren. "The Impact of E-Commerce Strategies on Firm Value: Lessons from Amazon.com and its Early Competitors." *Journal of Business* 77, No. 2 (April 2004): S135–S154.

Flake, Gary W., David M. Pennock, and **Daniel C. Fain.** "The Self-Organized Web: The Yin to the Semantic Web's Yang." *IEEE Intelligent Systems,* 2003.

Fogg, B. J. *Persuasive Technology: Using Computers to Change What We Think and Do.* San Francisco: Morgan Kaufmann, 2003.

Fogg, B.J., T. Kameda, J. Boyd, R. Sethi, M. Sockol, and **T. Trowbridge.** *Stanford-Makovsky Web Credibility Study 2002: Investigating What Makes Web Sites Credible Today.* A Research Report by the Stanford Persuasive Technology Lab and Makovsky & Company. Stanford, CA: Stanford University, 2002.

Fox, Susannah and **Lee Rainie.** "Vital Decisions: How Internet Users Decide What Information to Trust When They or Their Loved Ones are Sick." *Pew Internet & American Life Project,* 22 May 2002.

Galletta, Dennis F., Raymond Henry, Scott McCoy, and **Peter Polak.** "Web Site Delays: How Tolerant are Users?" *Journal of the Association of Information Systems* 5, No. 1 (2004): 1–28.

Ganley, Paul and **Ben Allgrove.** "Net Neutrality: A User's Guide," *Computer, Law & Security Report,* 2006.

Garfinkel, Simson. *Database Nation.* Sebastopol: O'Reilly & Associates, 2000.

Gates, Bill. *The Road Ahead.* 2nd ed. New York: Penguin, 1996.

Gaynor, Mark and **Scott Bradner.** "A Real Options Framework to Value Network, Protocol, and Service Architecture." *ACM SIGCOMM Computer Communications Review* 34, No. 5 (October 2004): 31–38.

Goldenberg, Jacob, Donald Lehmann, and **David Mazursky.** "The Idea Itself and the Circumstances of Its Emergence as Predictors of New Product Success." *Management Science* 47, No. 1 (January 2001): 69–84.

Goldenberg, Jacob, Barak Libai, Sarit Moldovan, and **Eitan Muller.** "The Economic Implications of Negative Word of Mouth: A Dynamic Small-World Approach." Working Paper, Tel Aviv University, 1 August 2004.

Golder, Peter and **Gerald Tellis.** "Pioneer Advantage: Marketing Logic or Marketing Legend." *Journal of Marketing Research* 30, No. 2 (May 1993): 158–170.

Goolsbee, Austan. "Competition in the Computer Industry: Online vs. Retail." *Journal of Industrial Economics* 49, no. 4 (2001): 487–499.

_____. "In a World Without Borders: The Impact of Taxes on Internet Commerce." *The Quarterly Journal of Economics 115,* No. 2 (May 2000): 561–576.

Goolsbee, Austan and **Joel Slemrod.** "Playing with Fire: Cigarettes, Taxes and Competition from the Internet." Working paper, University of Chicago, January, 2004

Grannovetter, M. "The Strength of Weak Ties." *American Journal of Sociology* 78 (1973): 1360–1380.

Greenstein, Shane. "The Economic Geography of Internet Infrastructure in the United States." Working Paper 46, Northwestern University, 2004.

Griffin, Abbie and **John R. Hauser.** "The Voice of the Customer." *Marketing Science* 12, No. 1 (Winter 1993): 1–27.

Gupta, Sachin, Pradeep Chintagunta, Anil Kaul and **Dick Wittink.** "Do Household Scanner Data Provide Representative Inferences from Brand Choices: A Comparison with Store Data." *Journal of Marketing Research* XXXIII (November 1996): 383–398.

Gupta, Sunil and **Donald Lehman.** "Customers as Assets." *Journal of Interactive Marketing* 17, No. 1 (Winter 2003): 9–24.

Gupta, Sunil, Donald Lehman, and **Jennifer Ames Stuart.** "Valuing Customers." *Journal of Marketing Research* 41, No. 1 (Feburary 2004): 7–18.

Hafner, K. and **Matthew Long.** *Where Wizards Stay up Late: The Origins of the Internet.* New York: Simon & Schuster, 1996.

Hagel III, John and **Arthur G. Armstrong.** *Net Gain: Expanding Markets Through Virtual Communities.* Cambridge: Harvard Business School Press, 1997.

Hagel III, John and **Marc Singer.** *Networth: Shaping Markets when Customers Make the Rules.* Cambridge: Harvard Business School Press 1999.

Hall, Robert. *Digital Dealing.* New York: W. W. Norton, 2001.

Hampton, Keith N. and **Barry Wellman.** "The Not So Global Village of Netville." In *The Internet in Everyday Life,* edited by Barry Wellman and Caroline Haythornthwaite. Boston: Blackwell Publishing, 2002.

Hanson, Ward. "Bandwagons and Orphans: Dynamic Pricing of Competing Technological Systems Subject to Decreasing Cost." Ph.D. diss., Stanford University, Department of Economics, 1985.

_____. *Principles of Internet Marketing.* Cincinnati, OH: Thomson Learning, 2000.

Hanson, Ward and **Kipp Martin.** "Optimal Bundle Pricing." *Management Science* 36, No. 2 (February): 1990.

Hanson, Ward and **Daniel Putler.** "Hits and Misses: Herd Behavior and Online Product Popularity." *Marketing Letters* 7, No. 4 (1996): 297–305.

Haubl, Gerald and **Valerie Trifts.** "Consumer Decision Making in Online Environments: The Effects of Decision Aids." *Marketing Science* 19, No. 1 (2000): 4–21.

Hausman, Jerry and **Ephraim Leibtag.** "CPI Bias from Supercenters: Does the BLS Know that Wal-Mart Exists?" Working Paper, MIT, August 2004.

Hayes, Brian. "Terabyte Territory." *American Scientist* 90 (May–June 2002): 212–216.

Haythornthwaite, Caroline. "Strong, Weak, and Latent Ties and the Impact of New Media." *The Information Society* 18, No. 5 (2002): 385–401.

Helpman, Elhanan, ed. *General Purpose Technologies and Economic Growth.* Cambridge: MIT Press, 1998.

Hennig-Thurau, Thorsten and **Gianfranco Walsh.** "Electronic Word-of-Mouth: Motives for and Consequences of Reading Customer Articulations on the Internet." *International Journal of Electronic Commerce* 8, No. 2 (Winter 2003/04): 51–74.

Hennig-Thurau, Thorsten, Kevin P. Gwinner, Gianfranco Walsh, and **Dwayne D. Gremler.** "Electronic word-of-mouth via consumer-opinion platforms: What motivates consumers to articulate themselves on the Internet?" Journal of Interactive Marketing 18, No. 1 (Winter 2004): 38–52.

Henthorne, Beth Hogan and **Tony L. Henthorne.** "The Tarnished Image: Anticipating and Minimizing the Impact of Negative Publicity in Health Services Organizations." *Journal of Consumer Marketing* 11, No. 3 (1994): 44–54.

Hew, Kevin, **Martin Gibbs**, and **Greg Wadley.** "Usability and Sociability of the Xbox Live Voice Channel." Paper presented as part of the Australian Workshop on Interactive Entertainment, Sydney, AU, 13 February 2004.

Hicks, Matt. "Google Reveals its Product Formula." *eWeek,* 9 February 2005.

Hiebeler, Robert, **Thomas Kelly**, and **Charles Ketteman.** *Best Practices: Building Your Business with Customer-Focused Solutions.* New York: Simon & Schuster, 1998.

Hill, Kenneth. "Electronic Marketing: The Dell Computer Experience." In *Electronic Marketing and the Consumer,* edited by Robert A. Peterson. Thousand Oaks, CA: SAGE Publications, 1997.

Hillis, Daniel. *The Pattern on the Stone: The Simple Ideas That Make Computers Work.* New York: Basic Books, 1998.

Hitt, Lorin M. and **Pei-Yu Chen.** "Bundling with Customer Self-Selection: A Simple Approach to Bundling Low Marginal Cost Goods." GSIA Working Paper #2003-E33.

Hoeffler, Steve and **Kevin Lane Keller.** "The Marketing Advantages of Strong Brands." *Journal of Brand Management* 10, No. 6 (2003): 421–445.

Hoffman, Donna and **Thomas Novak.** "Marketing in Hypermedia Computer-Mediated Environments: Conceptual Foundations." *Journal of Marketing* 60 (July 1996): 50–68.

_____. "Bridging the Racial Divide on the Internet." *Science* 280, No. 5362 (1998): 390–392.

Hong, Traci, **Margaret L. Mclaughlin**, **Larry Pryor**, **Christopher Beaudoin**, and **Paul Grabowicz.** "Internet Privacy Practices of News Media and Implications for Online Journalism." *Journalism Studies* 6, No. 2 (2005): 15–28.

Horsky, Dan. "A Diffusion Model Incorporating Product Benefits, Price, Income and Information." *Marketing Science* 9, No. 4 (1990): 342–365.

Huang, Chun-Che. "Overview of Modular Product Development." In *Proceeding National Science Council ROC(A)* 24, No. 3 (2000): 149–165.

Huang, Han-Shen, **Koung-Lung Lin**, **Jane Yung-jen Hsu**, and **Chun-Nan Hsu.** "Item-Triggered Recommendation for Identifying Potential Customers of Cold Sellers in Supermarkets." Working Paper, *IUI Workshop: Beyond Personalization 2005*, San Diego, CA, 9 January 2005.

Huberman, Bernardo A., **Peter L. T. Pirolli**, **James E. Pitkow**, and **Rajan M. Lukose.** "Strong Regularities in World Wide Web Surfing." *Science* 280, No. 5360 (1998): 95–97.

Inansiti, Marco and **Alan MacCormack.** "Developing Products on Internet Time." *Harvard Business Review* 75, No. 5 (1997): 108–117.

Jain, Dipak and **S. Singh.** "Customer Lifetime Value Research in Marketing: A Review and Future Directions." *Journal of Interactive Marketing* 16, No. 2 (2002): 34–46.

Johne, Marjo. "Virtual Environments." *CMA Management* 76, No. 10 (Feburary 2003): 12–20.

Johnson, Eric J., **Wendy W. Moe**, **Peter S. Fader**, **Steven Bellman**, and **Gerald L. Lohse.** "On the Depth and Dynamics of Online Search Behavior." *Management Science* 50, No. 3 (March 2004): 306.

Jolson, M.A. "Broadening the Scope of Relationship Selling." *Journal of Personal Selling and Sales Management* 17, No. 4 (1997): 75–88.

Jome, Hiram Leonard. *Economics of the Radio Industry.* Chicago: A.V. Shaw Company, 1925.

Kahn, Barbara. "Dynamic Relationships with Customers: High-Variety Strategies." *Journal of the Academy of Marketing Science* 26, No. 1 (1998): 45–53.

Kalman, Yoram and **Sheizaf Rafaeli.** "Email Chronemics: Unobtrusive Profiling of Response Times." In *Proceedings of the*

38ᵗʰ Hawaii International Conference on System Sciences, 3–6 January 2005.

Kalyanam, Kirthi and **Jacques Delacroix.** "Customer Loss in the Advertising Industry: Specialization, Agency Size, Age, and the Business Environment." Working Paper, Leavey School of Business, Santa Clara University, 2000.

Kalyanam, Kirthi and **Monte Zweben.** "When is the New What." *Harvard Business Review Breakthrough Ideas for 2005* (Feburary 2005): 33–34.

Kasanoff, Bruce. "Are You Ready for Mass Customization." *Training* 35, No. 5 (1998): 70–78.

Katz, Michael and **Carl Shapiro.** "Technology Adoption in the Presence of Network Externalities." *Journal of Political Economy* 94 (1986): 822–841.

Kauffman, Robert J. and **Dongwon Lee.** "Should We Expect Less Price Rigidity in the Digital Economy?" Working paper, Carlson School of Management, University of Minnesota, March 2004.

Kavanaugh, Andrea and **Scott J. Patterson.** "The Impact of Community Computer Networks on Social Capital and Community Involvement in Blacksburg." In *The Internet in Everyday Life*, edited by Barry Wellman and Caroline Haythornthwaite. Boston: Blackwell Publishing, 2002.

Keith, Robert J. "The Marketing Revolution." *Journal of Marketing* 24, No. 3 (January 1960): 35–38.

Keller, Kevin Lane. "Building Customer-Based Brand Equity." *Marketing Management* 28, No. 1 (2001): 35–41.
——————. "Conceptualizing, Measuring, and Managing Customer-Based Brand Equity." *Journal of Marketing* 57, No.1 (January 1993): 1–22.
——————. *Strategic Brand Management: Building. Measuring. and Managing Brand Equity.* Upper Saddle River, NJ: Prentice Hall, 1998.

Kidder, Tracey. *The Soul of the New Machine.* Boston: Little Brown & Co., 1981.

Kinnard, Shannon. *Marketing With E-Mail.* Gulf Breeze: Maximum Press, 2000.

Kittler, Anne F., John Hobbs, Lynn A. Volk, Gary L. Kreps, David W. Bates. "The Internet as a Vehicle to Communicate Health Information During a Public Health Emergency: A Survey Analysis Involving the Anthrax Scare of 2001." *Journal of Medical Internet Research* 6, No. 1 (2004): e8.

Kleijnen, Mirella, Ko de Ruyter, and **Martin Wetzels.** "Consumer Adoption of Wireless Services: Discovering the Rules, While Playing the Game." *Journal of Interactive Marketing* 18, No. 2 (Spring 2004): 51–61.

Klemperer, Paul. "The Competitiveness of Markets with Switching Costs." *Rand Journal of Economics* 18, No. 1 (1987): 138–150.
——————. *Auctions: Theory and Practice.* Princeton: Princeton Paperbacks, 2004.

Kozinets, Robert. "The Field Behind the Screen: Using Netnography for Marketing Research in Online Communities." *Journal of Marketing Research* 39, No. 2 (February 2002): 61–72.

Kozinets, Robert and **Jay M. Handelman.** "Ensouling Consumption: A Netnographic Exploration of Boycotting Behavior." In *Advances in Consumer Research*, ed. J. Alba and W. Hutchinson. Provo, UT: Association for Consumer Research, 1998.

Krauss, Lawrence M. *The Physics of Star Trek.* New York: Harper Collins, 1995.

Kumar, V. and **Rajkumar Venkatesan.** "Who are the multichannel shoppers and how do they perform?: Correlates of multichannel shopping behavior." *Journal of Interactive Marketing* 19, No. 2 (Spring 2005): 44–62.

Kurzweil, Raymond. "When Will HAL Understand What We Are Saying: Computer Speech Recognition and Understanding." In *Hal's Legacy: 2001's Computer as Dream and Reality*, edited by David Stork. Cambridge: MIT Press, 1996.

_____. *The Age of Spiritual Machines: When Computers Exceed Human Intelligence.* New York: Viking Press, 1999.

Lahlou, Saadi, Marc Langheinrich, and **Carsten Rocker.** "Privacy and Trust Issues with Invisible Computers." *Communications of the ACM* 48, No. 3 (March 2005): 59–60.

Landauer, Thomas K. *The Trouble With Computers: Usefulness. Usability and Productivity.* Cambridge: MIT Press, 1996.

Laurel, Brenda. *Computers as Theatre.* Reading: Addison-Wesley, 1991.

Lazarsfeld, Paul, and **Frank Stanton, eds.** *Radio Research.* New York: Duell, Sloan, and Pearce, 1941.

Lee, Hau L., V Padmanabhan, and **Seungjin Whang.** "Information Distortion in a Supply Chain: The Bullwhip Effect." *Management Science* 43, No. 4 (April 1997): 546–558.

Lee, Juhnyoung and **Mark Podlaseck.** "Using a Starfield Visualization for Analyzing Product Performance of Online Stores." In *Proceedings of the 2nd ACM Conference on Electronic Commerce.* New York: ACM Press, 2000.

Lee, Juhnyoung, Mark Podlaseck, Edith Schonberg, and **Robert Hoch.** "Visualization and Analysis of Clickstream Data of Online Stores for Understanding Web Merchandizing." *Data Mining and Knowledge Discovery* 5, Vols. 1–2 (January 2001): 59–84.

Lee, Juhnyoung, Mark Podlaseck, Edith Schonberg, Robert Hoch, and **Stephen Gomory.** "Analysis and Visualization of Metrics for Online Merchandising." In *Web Usage Analysis and User Profiling: International WEBKDD'99 Workshop*, San Diego, CA. New York: Springer, 2000.

Lessig, Lawrence. *The Future of Ideas: The Fate of the Commons in a Connected World.* New York: Random House, 2001.

_____. *Code and Other Laws of Cyberspace.* New York: Basic Books, 1999.

Levitt, Theodore. "Marketing Success Through Differentiation—of Anything." *Harvard Business Review* (January–February 1980): 83–91.

_____. *The Marketing Imagination.* New York: Free Press, 1986.

Lewis, Michael. The Influence of Loyalty Programs and Short-Term Promotions on Customer Retention." *Journal of Marketing Research* 41, No. 3 (August 2004): 281–292.

Lih, Andrew. "Wikipedia as Participatory Journalism: Reliable source? Metrics for evaluating collaborative media as a news resource." Working Paper, *5th International Symposium on Online Journalism.* University of Texas at Austin, 16–17 April 2004.

Linden, Greg, Brent Smith, and **Jeremy York.** "Amazon.com Recommendations: Item-to-Item Collaborative Filtering." *IEEE Internet Computing* 7, No. 1 (January–February 2003): 76–80.

Lucking-Reiley, David. "Auctions on the Internet: What's Being Auctioned. and How?" *The Journal of Industrial Economics* XLVIII, No. 3 (September 2000): 227–253.

Lukose, Rajan M. and **Bernardo A. Huberman.** "Surfing as a Real Option." In *Proceedings of the First International Conference on Information and Computation Economies.* New York: ACM Press, 1998.

Luna, David and **Laura A. Peracchio.** "Advertising to Bilingual Consumers: The Impact of Code-Switching on Persuasion." *Journal of Consumer Research* 31, No. 4 (March 2005): 760–765.

Lyman, Peter and **Hal R. Varian.** "How Much Information? 2003." Retrieved from http://www.sims.berkeley.edu/how-much-info-2003 on 5/15/2006.

Lynch, John and **Dan Ariely.** "Wine Online: Search Costs Affect Competition on Price, Quality, and Distribution." *Marketing Science* 19, No. 1 (2000): 83–103.

Magretta, Joan. "Why Business Models Matter." *Harvard Business Review* 80, No. 5 (May 2002): 86–92.

Malone, Thomas W. and **Robert J. Laubacher.** "The Dawn of the E-Lance Economy." *Harvard Business Review* (September–October 1998): 145–152

Mangani, Andrea. "Online advertising: Pay-per-view versus pay-per-click." *Journal of Revenue and Pricing Management* 2, No. 4 (2004): 295–302.

Mansell, Robin, ed. *Inside the Communication Revolution: Evolving Patterns of Social and Technical Interaction.* Cary, NC: Oxford University Press, 2000.

Marn, Michael V. and **Robert L. Rosiello.** "Managing Price, Gaining Profit." *The McKinsey Quarterly* 4 (1992): 18–37.

Mathwick, Charla and **Edward Rigdon.** "Play, Flow, and the Online Search Experience." *Journal of Consumer Research* 31, No. 2 (2004): 324–332.

McAlexander, James H., John W. Schouten, and **Harold F. Koenig.** "Building Brand Community." *Journal of Marketing* 66, No. 1 (2002): 38–54.

McKenna, Regis. *Relationship Marketing: Successful Strategies for the Age of the Customer.* Reading: Addison-Wesley, 1991.

Milgrom, Paul. "Auctions and Bidding: A Primer." *Journal of Economic Perspectives* 3, No. 3 (Summer 1989): 3–22.

_____. *Putting Auction Theory to Work.* Cambridge: Cambridge University Press, 2004.

Mitchell, Bridger and **Ingo Vogelsang.** *Telecommunications Pricing: Theory and Practice.* Cambridge: Cambridge University Press, 1992

Mitchell, William. *City of Bits: Space, Place, and the Infobahn.* Cambridge: MIT Press, 1995.

Modahl, Mary. *Now or Never: How Companies Must Change Today to Win The Battle for Internet Consumers.* New York: Harper Business, 2000.

Moe, Wendy. "A Field Experiment to Assess the Interruption Effect of Pop-up Promotions." *Journal of Interactive Marketing* 20, No. 1, (Winter 2006): 34–44.

Moe, Wendy W. and **Peter S. Fader.** "Capturing Evolving Visit Behavior in Clickstream Data," *Journal of Interactive Marketing* 18, No. 1 (2004): 5–19.

_____. "Dynamic Conversion Behavior at E-Commerce Sites." *Management Science* 50, No. 3 (2004): 326–335.

Moon, Youngme. "Personalization and Personality: Some Effects of Customizing Message Style Based on Consumer Personality." *Journal of Consumer Psychology* 12, No. 4 (2002): 313–326.

Moore, Geoffrey. *Crossing the Chasm: Marketing and Selling High-Tech Products to Mainstream Customers.* New York: Harper Business, 1991.

_____. *Inside the Tornado: Marketing Strategies from Silicon Valley's Cutting Edge.* New York: HarperCollins, 1995.

Moore, James F. *The Death of Competition: Leadership and Strategy in the Age of Business Ecosystems.* New York: Harperbusiness, 1996.

Morton, Fiona, Florian Zettelmeyer, and **Jorge Silva-Risso.** "Internet Car Retailing." *Journal of Industrial Economics* 49, No. 4 (2001): 501–520.

Mowery, David and **Nathan Rosenberg.** *Paths of Innovation: Technological Change in 20ᵗʰ-Century America.* Cambridge: Cambridge University Press, 1998.

Muller, Brigitte and **Jean-Louis Chandon.** "The Impact of Visiting a Brand Website on Brand Personality." *Electronic Markets* 13, No. 3 (2003): 210–221.

Muniz, Jr., Albert M. and **Thomas C. O'Guinn.** "Brand Community." *Journal of Consumer Research* 27, No. 1 (2001): 412–432.

Muniz, Jr., Albert M. and **Hope Jensen Schau.** "Religiosity in the Abandoned Apple Newton Brand Community." *Journal of Consumer Research* 31, No. 4 (March 2005): 737–747.

Murphy, Jamie, **Laura Raffa**, and **Richard Mizerski**. "The Use of Domain Names in e-branding by the World's Top Brands." *Electronic Markets* 13, No. 3 (2003): 222–232.

Murray, Janet H. *Hamlet on the Holodeck: The Future of Narrative in Cyberspace.* New York: Free Press, 1997.

Nagle, Thomas T. and **Reed K. Holden**. *The Strategy and Tactics of Pricing.* 3rd Edition. New York: Prentice Hall, 2002.

Nass, Clifford and **Youngme Moon**. "Machines and Mindlessness: Social Responses to Computers." *Journal of Social Issues* 56, No. 1 (2000): 81–103.

National Research Council. *The Internet's Coming of Age.* Washington, DC: National Academy Press, 2001.

Negroponte, Nicholas. *Being Digital.* New York: Alfred Knopf, 1995.

Nelson, Phillip. "Advertising as Information." *Journal of Political Economy* 82, No. 4 (July–August 1974): 729–754.

Netemeyer, Richard G., **Balaji Krishnan**, **Chris Pullig**, **Guangping Wang**, **Mehmet Yagci**, **Dwane Dean**, **Joe Ricks**, and **Ferdinand Wirth**. "Developing and Validating Measures of Facets of Customer-based Brand Equity." *Journal of Business Research* 57 (2004): 209–224.

Newell, Frederick. *Loyalty.com.* New York: McGraw-Hill, 2000.

Nichols, James and **Mark Claypool.** "The Effects of Latency on User Performance in Warcraft III." In Proceedings of the 2nd Workshop on Network and System Support for Games, Redwood City, CA. New York: ACM Press, 2003.

——————————. "The Effects of Latency on Online Madden NFL Football." In *Proceedings of the 14th International Workshop on Network and Operating Systems Support for Digital Audio and Video,* Cork, Ireland. New York: ACM Press, 2004.

Nie, Norman, **Alberto Simpser**, **Irena Stepanikova**, and **Lu Zheng**. "Ten Years After the Birth of the Internet, How Do Americans Use the Internet in Their Daily Lives?" *Report of the Stanford Center for the Quantitative Study of Society,* December 2004

Nielsen, Jakob. *Designing Web Usability.* Indianapolis: New Riders Publishing, 2000.

Nordhaus, William. "The Progress of Computing." Working Paper Version 5.2.2., Yale University and National Bureau of Economic Research, 2 March 2002.

Norman, Donald A. *The Invisible Computer: Why Good Products Can Fail, the Personal Computer is so Complex, and Information Appliances are the Solution.* Cambridge: MIT Press, 1999.

——————————. "Why It's Good That Computers Don't Work Like the Brain." In *Beyond Calculation,* edited by Peter Denning and R. Metcalfe. New York: Copernicus, 1997.

Nouwt, Sjaak. "Kids' Privacy on the Internet." *Multimedia und Recht* 5, No. 11 (November 2002): 703–709.

Novak, Thomas and **Donna Hoffman**. "Advertising and Pricing Models for the Web." In *Internet Publishing and Beyond: The Economics of Digital Information and Intellectual Property,* edited by Brian Kahin and Hal R. Varian. Cambridge, MA: MIT Press, 2000.

Novak, Thomas, **Donna Hoffman**, and **A. Duhachek**. "The Influence of Goal-Directed and Experiential Activities on Online Flow Experiences." *Journal of Consumer Psychology* 12, No. 1&2 (2003): 3–16.

Novak, Thomas, **Donna Hoffman**, and **Yiu-Fai Yung**. "Measuring the Customer Experience in Online Environments: A Structural Modeling Approach," *Marketing Science* 19, No. 1, (Winter 2000): 22–42.

Ntoulas, Alexandros, **Junghoo Cho**, and **Christopher Olston**. "What's New on the Web? The Evolution of the Web from a

Search Engine Perspective." In *Proceedings of the 13th International Conference on World Wide Web*, New York, NY. New York: ACM Press, 2004.

O'Brien, L. and C. Jones. "Do Rewards Really Create Loyalty?" *Harvard Business Review* 73 (May/June 1995): 75–82.

O'Keefe, Steve. *Publicity on the Internet.* New York: John Wiley, 1997.

O'Neill, Edward T., Brian Lavoi, and Rick Bennett. "Trends in the evolution of the Public Web: 1998–2002." *D-Lib Magazine*, April 2003.

Okada, Erica Mina and Stephen J. Hoch. "Spending Time versus Spending Money." *Journal of Consumer Research* 31, No. 2 (2004): 313–322.

Ozen, Bahattin, Ozgur Kilic, Mehmet Altinel, and Asuman Dogac. "Highly Personalized Information Delivery to Mobile Clients." *Wireless Networks.* Vol. 10 (2004): 665–683.

Owen, Bruce and Gregory Rosston. "Spectrum Allocation and the Internet." *Stanford Institute for Economic Policy Research Discussion Paper No. 01–09*, December 2001.

Palmer, Jonathan. "Web Site Usability. Design. and Performance Metrics." *Information Systems Research* 13, No. 2 (2002): 151–167.

Pan, Xing, Brian T. Ratchford, and Venkatesh Shankar. "Can Price Dispersion in Online Markets be Explained by Differences in E-Tailer Service Quality?" *Journal of the Academy of Marketing Science* 30, No. 4 (2002): 433–445.

—————————. "Price Dispersion on the Internet: A Review and Directions for Future Research." *Journal of Interactive Marketing* 16, No. 4 (Autumn 2004): 116–135.

Peppers, Don and Martha Rogers. *The One-to-One Future.* New York: Currency Doubleday, 1993.

—————————. *Enterprise One to One: Tools for Competing in the Interactive Age.* New York: Currency Doubleday, 1997.

Perkins, Elizabeth and Mike Markel. "Multinational Data-Privacy Laws: An Introduction for IT Managers." IEEE *Transactions on Professional Communication* 47, No. 2 (June 2004): 85–94.

Peterson, Larry L., and Bruce S. Davie. *Computer Networks: A Systems Approach.* 3rd ed. San Francisco: Morgan Kaufmann, 2003.

Petroski, Henry. *The Evolution of Useful Things: How Everyday Artifacts—From Forks and Pins to Paper Clips and Zippers—Came To Be As They Are.* New York: Alfred A. Knopf, 1992.

Pew/Internet. "How Americans Use Instant Messaging." *Pew Internet & American Life Project,* 1 September 2004.

Pfeifer, Phillip, and Heejung Bang. "Non-parametric Estimation of Mean Customer Lifetime Value." *Journal of Interactive Marketing* 19, No. 4 (Autumn 2005): 48–66.

Pfeifer, Phillip and Paul Farris. "The Elasticity of Customer Value to Retention: The Duration of a Customer Relationship." *Journal of Interactive Marketing* 18, No. 2 (Spring 2004): 20–31.

Pfeifer, Phillip, Mark Haskins, and Robert Conroy. "Customer Lifetime Value, Customer Profitability, and the Treatment of Acquisition Spending." *Journal of Managerial Issues* 17, No. 1 (Spring 2005): 11–25.

Phillips, Barbara and Edward McQuarrie. "Beyond Visual Metaphor: A New Typology of Visual Rhetoric in Advertising." *Marketing Theory* 4, No. 1–2 (2004): 113–136.

Phister, Jr., Montgomery. *Data Processing Technology and Economics.* 2nd ed. Burlington, MA: Digital Press, 1979.

Picard, Rosalind. *Affective Computing.* Cambridge: MIT Press, 1997.

Piller, Frank and **Melanie Muller.** "A New Marketing Approach to Mass Customization." *International Journal of Computer Integrated Manufacturing* 17, No. 7 (2004): 583–593.

Pine, B. Joseph II, and **James Gilmore.** *The Experience Economy: Work is Theatre & Every Business a Stage.* Boston: Harvard Business School Press, 1999.

Pollock, Annabel and **Andrew Hockley.** "What's Wrong with Internet Searching." *D-Lib Magazine,* March 1997.

Preece, Jenny, **Diane Maloney-Krichmar**, and **Chadia Abras.** "History and Emergence of Online Communities." In *Encyclopedia of Community*, edited by B. Wellman. Great Barrington, MA: Berkshire Publishing Group, 2003.

Putnam, Robert D. "The Strange Disappearance of Civic America." *The American Prospect* 7, No. 24 (December 1996): 34–48.

——————————. *Bowling Alone: The Collapse and Revival of American Community.* New York: Simon & Schuster, 2000.

Rajagopal, Priyali and **Romulo Sanchez.** "Conceptual Analysis of Brand Architecture and Relationships within Product Categories." *Journal of Brand Management* 11, No. 3 (2004): 233–247.

Rajagopal, Shivaram, **Mohan Venkatachalam**, and **Suresh Kotha.** "Does the Quality of Online Customer Experience Create a Sustainable Competitive Advantage for E-Commerce Firms?" Working Paper, Stanford University, April 2001.

Raney, Arthur A., **Laura M. Arpan**, **Kartik Pashupati**, and **Dale A. Brill.** At The Movies, On the Web: An Investigation of the Effects of Entertaining and Interactive Web Content on Site and Brand Evaluations." *Journal of Interactive Marketing* 17, No. 4 (Autumn 2003): 38–53.

Rangaswamy, Arvind and **Gerrit Van Bruggen.** "Opportunities and challenges in multichannel marketing: An introduction to the special issue." *Journal of Interactive Marketing* 19, No. 2 (Spring 2005): 5–11.

Ratchford, Brian T., **Myung-Soo Lee** and **Debabrata Talukdar.** "The Impact of the Internet on Information Search for Automobiles." *Journal of Marketing Research* XL (May 2003): 193–209.

Ratliff, John M. "NTT DoCoMo and Its I-mode Success: Origins and Implications." *California Management Review* 44, No. 3 (Spring 2002): 55–71.

Rayport, J.F. and **J. J. Sviokla.** "Exploiting the Virtual Value Chain." *Harvard Business Review* 73, No. 12 (November/December 1995): 75–87.

Reeves, Byron and **Clifford Nass.** *The Media Equation: How People Treat Computers, Television, and New Media Like Real People and Places.* Cambridge: Cambridge University Press, 1996.

Reichheld, Frederick. *The Loyalty Effect: The Hidden Force Behind Growth, Profits, and Lasting Value.* Cambridge: Harvard Business School Press, 1996.

Reinartz, Werner and **V. Kumar.** "On the Profitability of Long-Life Customers in a Noncontractual Setting: An Empirical Investigation and Implications for Marketing." *Journal of Marketing* 64, No. 4 (October 2000): 17–35.

——————————. "The Mismanagement of Customer Loyalty." *Harvard Business Review* (July 2002): 4–12.

Rheingold, Howard. *Smart Mobs: The Next Social Revolution.* New York: Perseus, 2002.

Riemer, Kai and **Carsten Totz.** "The Many Faces of Personalization: An integrative overview of mass customization and personalization." In *The Customer Centric Enterprise: Advances in Mass Customization and Personalization,* edited by M.M. Tseng and F.T. Piller. New York: Springer, 2003.

Rischpater, Ray. *eBay Application Development.* Berkeley, CA: Apress, 2004.

Rivkin, Steve and Fraser Sutherland. *The Making of a Name: The Inside Store of the Brands We Buy.* Oxford: Oxford University Press, 2004.

Roberti, Mark. "Analysis: RFID—Wal-Mart's Network Effect." *CIO Insight,* 15 September 2003.

Roehm, Michelle L., Ellen Bolman Pullins, and Harper A Roehm Jr. "Designing Loyalty Building Programs for Packaged Goods Brands." *Journal of Marketing Research* 32, No. 2 (May 2002): 202–213.

Rosen, Emanuel. *The Anatomy of Buzz: How to Create Word of Mouth Marketing.* New York: Currency Doubleday, 2000.

Rosenberg, Nathan. *Inside the Black Box: Technology and Economics.* Cambridge: Cambridge Press, 1983.

——————. *Exploring the Black Box: Technology, Economics, and History.* Cambridge: Cambridge Press, 1994.

Rowe, Gene and John G. Gammack. "Promise and perils of electronic public engagement." *Science and Public Policy* 31, No. 1 (2004): 39–54.

Rowley, Jennifer. "Online Branding." *Online Information Review* 28, No. 2 (2004): 131–138.

Royce, Walker. *Software Project Management: A Unified Framework.* Upper Saddle River, NJ: Addison-Wesley, 1998.

Russo, J. Edward. "Aiding Purchase Decisions on the Internet." In *Proceedings of the Winter 2002 SSGRR International Conference on Advances in Infrastructure for Electronic Business, Education, and Medicine on the Internet,* edited by Veljko Milutinovic. L'Aquila, Italy, 2002.

Russo, J. Edward and Frace Leclerc. "Characteristics of Successful Product Information Programs." *Journal of Social Issues* 47, No. 1 (1991): 73–92.

Rust, Roland, Katherine Lemon, and Das Narayandas. *Customer Equity Management.* Upper Saddle River, NJ: Prentice Hall, 2005.

Saltzstein, William. "Bluetooth and Beyond: Wireless Options for Medical Devices." *Medical Device and Diagnostic Industry* 26, No. 6 (2004): 78–88.

Samaras, George and Christoforos Panayiotou. "A Flexible Personalization Architecture for Wireless Internet Based Mobile Agents." In *Proceedings of Advances in Databases and Information Systems: 6th East European Conference, ADBIS 2002, Bratislava, Slovakia, September 8–11,* edited by Y. Manolopoulos, P. Návrat. Berlin: Springer, 2002.

Sawhney, Mohanbir, Gianmario Verona, and Emanuela Prandelli. "Collaborating to Create: The Internet as a Platform for Customer Engagement in Product Innovation." *Journal of Interactive Marketing* 19, No. 4 (Autumn 2005): 4–17.

Scacchi, Walt. "Redesigning Contracted Service Procurement for Internet-based Electronic Commerce: A Case Study." *Information Technology and Management* 2 (2001): 313–334.

Schank, Roger. *Tell Me a Story: Narrative and Intelligence.* Evanston: Northwestern University Press, 1998.

Schilling, Melissa A. and Corey Phelps. "Inter-firm Knowledge Networks and Knowledge Creation: The Impact of 'Small-World' Connectivity." Working Paper, New York University, September 2003.

Schlosser, Ann E. "Experiencing Products in the Virtual World: The Role of Goal and Imagery in Influencing Attitudes versus Purchase Intentions." *Journal of Consumer Research* 30, No. 2 (September 2003): 184–198.

Schorr, Herbert and Salvatore Stolfo. "A Digital Government for the 21st Century." *Communications of the ACM* 41, No. 11 (November 1998): 15–19.

Schuler, Douglas. *New Community Networks: Wired for Change.* New York: ACM Press, 1996.

Schwaig, Kathy Stewart, Gerald C. Kane, and Veda C. Storey. "Privacy, Fair

Information Practices, and the Fortune 500: The Virtual Reality of Compliance." *The DATA BASE for Advances in Information Systems* 36, No. 1 (Winter 2005): 49–63.

Seda, Catherine. *Search Engine Advertising: Buying Your Way to the Top to Increase Sales.* Berkeley, CA: New Riders Press, 2004.

Shapiro, B. P., V. K. Rangan, and J. J. Sviokla. "Staple Yourself to an Order." *Harvard Business Review* 70 (July–August 1992): 113–122.

Shapiro, Carl and Hal R. Varian. *Information Rules: A Strategic Guide to the Network Economy.* Cambridge: Harvard Business School Press, 1999.

Sharma, Arun. "Trends in Internet-based Business-to-Business Marketing." *Industrial Marketing Management* 31, No. 2 (2002): 77–84.

Sherman, Lee and John Deighton. "Banner Advertising: Measuring Effectiveness and Optimizing Placement." *Journal of Interactive Marketing* 15, No. 2 (Spring 2001): 60–64.

Shugan, Steven M. "The Impact of Advancing Technology on Marketing and Academic Research." *Marketing Science* 23, No. 4 (Fall 2004): 469–475.

Shultz, Don E., Stanley I. Tannenbaum, and Robert F. Lauterborn. *Integrated Marketing Communications: Putting it Together and Making it Work.* New York: McGraw-Hill, 1993.

Simon, H.A. "Designing Organizations for an Information-Rich World." In *Computers, Communications, and the Public Interest.* Edited by M. Greenberger. Baltimore: Johns Hopkins Press, 1971.

Singh, Vishal, Karsten Hansen, and Robert Blattberg. "Impact of Wal-Mart Supercenter on a Traditional Supermarket: An Empirical Investigation." Working Paper, Carnegie Mellon University, February 2004.

Sinha, Indrajit. "Cost Transparency: The Net's Real Threat to Prices and Brands." *Harvard Business Review*, 2000.

Smith, Richard. *Authentication: From Passwords to Public Keys.* Boston: Addison-Wesley, 2002.

Smulyan, Susan. *Selling Radio: The Commercialization of American Broadcasting, 1920–1934.* Washington, DC: Smithsonian Institution Press, 1994.

Spink, Amanda, Dietmar Wolfram, B.J. Jansen, and Tefko Saracevic. "Searching the Web: The Public and their Queries." *Journal of the American Society for Information Science and Technology* 52, Vol. 3 (2003): 226–234.

Sproull, Lee and Sara Kiesler. *Connections: New Ways of Working in the Networked Organization.* Cambridge: MIT Press, 1994.

Srinivasan, V. and Chan Su Park. "Surprising Robustness of the Self-Explicated Approach to Customer Preference Structure Measurement." Journal of Marketing Research 34, No. 2 (May 1997): 286–291.

Standage, Tom. *The Victorian Internet: The Remarkable Story of the Telegraph and the Nineteenth Century's On-line Pioneers.* New York: Walker, 1998.

Sterne, Jim. *Customer Service on the Internet.* New York: John Wiley and Son, 1996.

Stevens, Greg and James Burley. "3000 Raw Ideas = 1 Commercial Success!" *Research Technology Management* 40, No. 3 (May–June 1997): 16–27.

Stiroh, Kevin. "Information Technology and the U.S. Productivity Revival: What Do the Industry Data Say?" *The American Economic Review* 92, No. 5 (December 2002): 1559–1576.

Storck, J. and L. Sproull. "Through a Glass Darkly: What Do People Learn in Videoconferences?" *Human Communication Research.* 22, No. 2 (1995): 197–219.

Stork, David (Editor). *Hal's Legacy: 2001's Computer as Dream and Reality.* Cambridge: MIT Press, 2000.

Stout, Rick. *Web Site Stats: Tracking Hits and Analyzing Traffic.* Berkeley: Osborne McGraw-Hill, 1997.

Subramani, Mani and **Naren Peddibhotla.** "Quantity and Quality: Understanding Contribution of Knowledge to Public Document Repositories." Working Paper, Information and Decision Sciences Department, Carlson School of Management, University of Minnesota, 3 May 2004.

Sudman, Seymour and **Edward Blair.** "Sampling in the Twenty-First Century." *Journal of the Academy of Marketing Science* 27, No. 2 (1999): 269–277.

Sundararajan, Arun. "Pricing Digital Marketing: Information. Risk Sharing. and Performance." Working Paper, New York University, 2002.

Sunstein, Cass. *Republic.com.* Princeton: Princeton University Press, 2002.

Swire, Peter and **Robert Litan.** *None of Your Business: World Data Flows, Electronic Commerce, and the European Privacy Directive.* Washington DC: Brookings Institution Press, 1998.

Tapscott, Don. *The Digital Economy: Promise and Peril in the Age of Networked Intelligence.* New York: McGraw-Hill, 1996.
————. *Digital Capital: Harnessing the Power of Business Webs.* Boston: Harvard Business School Press, 2000.

Taylor, H. "Does Internet Research Work: Comparing Online Survey Result with Telephone Survey." *International Journal of Research in Marketing* 42, No. 1 (2000): 51–63.

Tedlow, Richard. *New and Improved: The Story of Mass Marketing in America.* Cambridge: Harvard Business School Press, 1996.

Thaler, Richard and **Shlomo Benartzi.** "Save More Tomorrow: Using Behavioral Economics to Increase Employee Savings." *Journal of Political Economy* 112, No. 1 (2004): 164–187.

Thorbjornsen, Helge and **Magne Supphellen.** "The Impact of Brand Loyalty on Website Usage." *Journal of Brand Management* 11, No. 3 (2004): 199–207.

Turnbull, Noel. "Issues and Crisis Management in a Convergent Environment." *Journal of Public Affairs* 1, No. 1 (2001): 85–92.

Underhill, Paco. *Why We Buy: The Science of Shopping.* New York: Simon & Schuster, 1999.
————. *Call of the Mall.* New York: Simon & Schuster, 2004.

Upshaw, Lynn. *Building Brand Identity: A Strategy for Success in a Hostile Marketplace.* New York: John Wiley and Son, 1995.

Urban, Glen, **John Hauser**, **William Qualls**, **Bruce Weinberg**, **Jonathan Bohlmann**, and **Roberta Chicos.** "Information Acceleration: Validation and Lessons From the Field." *Journal of Marketing Research* 34, No. 1 (February 1997): 143–153.

Urban, Glen, **Bruce Weinberg**, and **John Hauser.** "Premarket Forecasting of Really-New Products." *Journal of Marketing* 60, No. 1 (January 1996): 47–60.

Vallee, Jacques. *The Network Revolution: Confessions of a Computer Scientist.* Berkeley: And/Or Press, 1982.

Van Meer, Geoffrey. "Customer Development and Retention on a Web-banking Site." *Journal of Interactive Marketing* 20, No. 1 (Winter 2006): 58–64.

Veblen, Thorstein. *Theory of the Leisure Class: An Economic Study of Institutions.* New York: Modern Library Random House, 1922.

Venkatesan, Rajkumar and **V. Kumar.** "A Customer Lifetime Value Framework for Customer Selection and Resource Allocation Strategy." *Journal of Marketing* 68 (October 2004): 106–125.

Venkatesh, R. and **Rabikar Chatterjee.** "Bundling, Unbundling, and Pricing of Multiform Products: The Case of Magazine Content," *Journal of Interactive Marketing* 20, No. 2 (Spring 2006): 21–40.

Vesanen, Jari and **Mika Raulas.** "Building Bridges for Personalization: A Process Model for Marketing." *Journal of Interactive Marketing* 20, No. 1 (Winter 2006): 5–20.

von Hippel, Eric. "New Product Ideas From 'Lead Users.'" *Research Technology Management* (May–June 1989): 24–27.

Waldrop, M. Mitchell. *The Dream Machine: J.C.R. Licklider and the Revolution That Made Computing Personal.* New York: Penguin Book, 2001.

Watson, Richard T., Leyland Pitt, and **George M. Zinkhan.** "Integrated Internet Marketing." *Communications of the ACM* 43, No. 6 (2000): 97–102.

Watts, Duncan J. *Six Degrees: The Science of a Connected Age.* New York: Norton, 2003.

———. *Small Worlds: The Dynamics of Networks between Order and Randomness.* Princeton: Princeton University Press, 2002.

Weathers, Danny and **Igor Makienko.** "Assessing the Relationships Between E-tail Success and Product and Web Site Factors, *Journal of Interactive Marketing* 20, No. 2 (Spring 2006): 41–54.

Weinberg, Bruce D., Paul D. Berger and **Richard C. Hanna.** "A Belief Updating Process for Minimizing Waiting Time in Multiple Waiting Time Events: Application to Website Design." *Journal of Interactive Marketing* 17, No. 4 (2003): 24–37.

Wheatley, Margaret J. and **Myron Kellner-Rogers.** "The Paradox and Promise of Community." In *The Drucker Foundation: The Community of the Future*, edited by Hesselbein et al. New York: Jossey-Bass, 2000.

Wind, Yoram and **Vijay Mahajan.** "Convergence Marketing." *Journal of Interactive Marketing* 16, No. 2 (Spring 2002): 64–79.

Wind, Yoram, Vijay Mahajan, and **Robert Gunther.** *Convergence Marketing: Strategies for Reaching the New Hybrid Consumer.* Upper Saddle River, NJ: Prentice Hall, 2002.

Wyner, Gordon. "Reinventing Research Design." *Marketing Research* (Winter 2003): 6–7.

Xing, Xiaolin, Zhenlin Yang, and **Fang-Fang Tang.** "A Comparison of Time-Varying Online Price and Price Dispersion Between Multichannel and Dotcom DVD Retailers." *Journal of Interactive Marketing* 20, No. 2 (Spring 2006): 3–20.

Xue, Mei, Patrick Harker, and **Gregory Heim.** "Incorporating the Dual Customer Roles in e-Service Design." Work Paper 03–04, Wharton School Center for Financial Institutions, University of Pennsylvania, 2004.

Yan, Jianxin, Alan Blackwell, Ross Anderson, and **Alasdair Grant.** "The Memorability and Security of Passwords—Some Empirical Results." Working Paper, Cambridge University, 2000.

Yoffie, D. B. "Competing in the Age of Digital Convergence." *California Management Review* 38, No. 4 (Summer 1996): 31–53.

Zugelder, Michael, Theresa Flaherty, and **James Johnson.** "Legal Issues Associated With International Internet Marketing." *International Marketing Review* 17, No. 3 (June 2000): 253–271.

index

Note: Locators followed by f indicate material in figure; locators followed by t indicate material in table.

a

Aaker, D., 209
Aaker, Jennifer L., 209
Abe, Makoto, 564
Abras, Chadia, 353
Access devices, 15–17, 570
Accessibility, 231–233
Access lags, 559–560
Access quality, Internet usage and, 117–118
Access times, files size and, 561t
Accountability, 148
Accuracy, of information, 583–584
Accutane, 138
Achabal, Dale D., 533
ACSI, 435, 436f
Ad agencies, 180
Adaptive customization, 306
Adaptive rules, 51
Adar, Eytan, 103, 353
Ad-brand impact, 155
Adoption rates, of new technology, 130
Advanced users, targeting, 228
Advertising
  See also Banner advertising; Keyword advertising; Search engine marketing
  branding and, 180–183
  challenges facing traditional, 176–178
  mass media, 176, 257
  no notice rate of, 152
  pay-per-click, 170, 248–250, 269–279
  procurement of, 181–182
  spending on, 19–21, 181f, 252–254
  television, 176

Advertising Age, 283
Advertising mediums, 180
AdWords system, 3–4
Affective computing, 590
Affiliate marketing, 169–170, 185, 256, 479, 479f
Affinity-based communities, 328, 329t
Age distribution
  by country, 115t
  Internet usage by, 114, 115t
Aggregation bundling, 422–423
Airline industry, 468–469, 470
Alexa, 261–262, 261f
Alibaba.com, 501–503, 525
Allegra, 195
Alliances, 362–363, 382
Alpha-beta process, 385–387
Alpha release stage, 385–386
Altinel, Mehmet, 323
Alumni communities, 324–327
Amazon.com
  1-Click ordering, 458–459
  affiliate programs, 170, 185, 479
  benefits of feedback to, 482
  choice assistance, 313–314
  vs. eBay, 143–144
  Gold Chest, 52
  "Search Inside the Book" program, 443
  user reviews, 336–337
  web alliances, 382
American Customer Satisfaction Index (ACSI), 435, 436f
American National Standards Institute (ANSI), 370t
Anchor and adjustment model, of user perceptions of delay, 562–563
Anderson, Chris, 499
Anderson, David P., 103
Anderson, Erin, 498, 532
Anderson, Philip, 532
Anderson, Ross, 140
Andonic, Raszvan, 323
Angelico, Irene, 387

Angwin, Julia, 499
AOL-Time Warner, 58
Apparel retailers, 452–454, 462
Apple Computer
  vs. IBM, 356–357
  iPods, 16, 41, 305–306
  Newton, 45, 47
  Switch campaign, 197–199
Applegate, Lynda M., 532
Appliance, Internet as, 566–569
Application program interfaces (APIs), 382
Archer, Gleason, 174
Ariely, Dan, 425
Arora, Ashish, 247
Arpan, Laura M., 66
Art Brokerage, 412
Arthur, Brian, 102, 388
Artificial intelligence (AI), 47
Ashenfelter, Orley, 425
Ask Jeeves, 242f
Association, 135–137, 319
Assortment, product
  channel services and, 473
  defined, 438
  iPACE and, 443–446
  limitations on, 462–463
  long tail and, 492–493
Asynchronous dialogue, 75
Athey, K. R., 564
ATMs (automated teller machines), 52–53, 161, 294
Attention, battle for, 251
  See also Traffic building
Auctions, 409–414
  designing, 413–414
  Dutch, 413
  dynamic bidding, 519–522
  eBay, 410–412
  English, 413
  importance of, 409–410
  specialty, 412–413
Auction sites, 52, 372
  See also eBay
Auction theory, 143

Audience analysis, 545–555
  behavioral composition, 552–554
  CMP analysis, 554–555
  demographics, 552–554
  panel vs. log file measurements
    for, 545–547
  source loss analysis, 550–552
  traffic patterns, 548–550
Augmented reality, 49, 54–55
Austin, Nancy, 102
Authenticated users, 84
Authentication, 132–137
Authentication standards, 84
Authentication systems,
    132–135, 132t
Authorities, 93–94
Authorization policies, 478–479
Autoliv, 526–527
Automated Clearing House
    (ACH), 59
Automatic translation, 45, 47
Automobile industry, 475–476t
  distribution of profits in, 481f
  web sites, 477f
Auto-respond email, 236, 576–577
Avon, 486–487

b

B2B commerce, 500–531
  business buying process, 509–511
  collaborative customization
    and, 304
  complexities of, 505
  customer acquisition, 508
  EDI communications and,
    506–508
  evolution of, 503–508
  facilitating repeat purchases,
    512–514
  marketplaces, 522–526
  procurement, 514–526
  supply chain coordination,
    526–531
Babin, Barry, 465
Bacon, Kevin, 91–93
Baczewski, Phlip, 33
Baeza-Yates, Ricardo, 246
Bailenson, J.N., 139
Bailey, Todd, 533
Bajari, Patrick, 140, 425
Bakos, Yannis, 426
Baldwin, Carliss, 389

Banco Itau, 45, 46f
Bandwagon markets, 371–373
Banking industry, 43–44, 58–59,
    293–295
Banner advertising, 168–169, 178f
  branding impact of, 185
  effectiveness of, 152
  formats, 280f
  vs. keyword advertising, 280
  limitations of, 178
  pricing, 170
  rotating ads, 185
  for traffic building, 256–257,
    279–281
Banner blindness, 152
Barabasi, Albert-Laszlo, 102
Barnes & Noble, 33
Basic product information, 451
Bates, Anne, 247
Bauer, Hans, 173
Baye, Michael, 425
Bayles, M.E., 173
Beall, A.C., 139
Beaudoin, Christopher, 582
Bebe.com, 552, 553f
Beck, Russell, 591
Beginning users, targeting, 228
Bekkerman, Ron, 354
Bell, David R., 465
Bellamy, Edward, 587–589
Bellman, Steven, 101
Ben & Jerry's Ice cream, 201–202
Benartzi, Shlomo, 322
Bender, Sherry, 564
Bender, Thomas, 210
Bennett, Rick, 102
Benway, J.P., 173
Bergen, Mark, 498
Berger, Paul D., 173, 565
Berners-Lee, Tim, 33, 82, 84, 102
BestBookDeal.com, 400–401
Best Buy, 428–430
Betamax, 357
Beta testing, 386
Bettman, James R., 466
Bezos, Jeff, 33
Bid rankings, 249
Big box retailers, 429–430
Binkley, Christina, 497, 499
Birnbaum, Joel, 387
Bits, 38
Blackwell, Alan, 140
Blair, Edward, 564
Blascovich, J., 139
Blattberg, Robert, 173, 284, 322

Blocking software, 178
Blogs, 21, 79–80
BMW, 398–399f
Bohlmann, Jonathan, 388
Bonoma, Thomas V., 532
Borzo, Jeanette, 499
Bowden, Sue, 139
Boyd, J., 247
Bradenburger, Adam M., 498
Brand architecture, domain names
    and, 190–193
Brand communities, 203–208,
    204f, 205f
Brand coordination page, 206–207
Brand crisis, 200–202
Branded house marketing strategy,
    191–192
Brand enhancement, 164–165
Brand equity framework, 184f
Brander, S., 388, 389
Brand identity
  domain names and, 185–193
  establishment of, 185–193
Brand imagery, 193, 194
Branding
  advertising services and,
    180–183
  brand management, 23–24
  business of, 179–183
  campaigns, 181–184
  connecting strategy to online
    presence, 183–184
  content, 199–200
  effective content, 199–200
  enhancing brand meaning,
    193–195
  financial benefits of, 179
  reinforcing right brand responses,
    195–202
  spending on, 180–181
  tracking effectiveness of,
    183–184
  traffic building and, 255
  value of strong, 179–180
  well-designed sites and, 154
Brand loyalty, 202
Brand performance, 193, 194–195
Brand proliferation, 24
Brand relationships, 202–208
Brand salience, 185
Brannan, Shel, 66
Bresnahan, Timothy F., 34, 387
Brewin, Bob, 139
Briggs, R., 173, 209
Brill, Dale A., 66

Britt, Phillip J., 323
Broadband access, 16, 70–72, 109
  ecommerce and, 433, 452
  income levels and, 116, 117f
  Internet usage and, 117–118
  in Japan, 70
  in South Korea, 119
  time usage and, 111
  usability and, 225
Brodie, M., 139
Brondmo, Hans Peter, 102, 354
Brooker, K., 498
Brown, Alastair, 465
Brown, John Seely, 101
Brown, Shona, 387
Brown, Welsey, 246
Browser wars, 356–359
Bruner, Rick, 284
Brynjolfsson, Erik, 66, 425, 426,
  465, 531
Bucklin, Randolph E., 246
Bulkeley, William M., 532
Bullwhip effect, 526–527f
Bundled access, 283
Bundled digital enhancements, 171
Bundle pricing, 408, 421–424, 422t
  market expansion and, 422–423
  performance improvements
    and, 424
  reduce costs from, 422–423
Bundling
  aggregation, 422–423
  consumer demand for, 423f
  joint performance, 424
  loyalty, 423
  product definition, 424
  trade-up, 423
Burger King, 165
Burley, James, 388
Burnham, Thomas, 354
Buschken, Joachim, 425
Business buying process, 509–511
Business justifications
  improved processes,
    160–165, 160t
  revenue benefits, 165–173
Business Objects, 244
Business process point of view,
  63–65
Business-to-business commerce.
  See B2B commerce
Business-to-consumer
  channels, 471f
Buyers
  See also Procurement

buyer-seller relationships, 522
  concerns of, with marketplaces,
    524–525
Buying centers, 509–511, 510f
Byron, Ellen, 499

C

Cargill, Carl, 388
CASE (computer-assisted self-
    explication) systems, 309,
    311–312
Castillo, Carlos, 246
Casual users, 130
Catalog shopping, 460–461
Category building, 165
Catterall, Miriam, 353
Celebrity, 96
Cell phone numbers, 318–319
Cell phones, 68–70
Censorship, 241
Centaurs, 460
Chae, See Ellen, 533
Chakraborty, Goutam, 532
Chakravarti, Dipanker, 465
Chandler, Alfred D., 101
Chandon, Jean-Louis, 209
Chandrasekhar, C.P., 531
Change, rate of web site, 77–78
Channel-based revenue,
    167–171, 474
  banner advertising, 168–169
  payment structures, 170–171
  permission sponsorship,
    167, 168f
  prospect fees, 169
  sales commissions, 169–170
Channel conflict, 483–487
Channels. See Consumer channels;
    Distribution channels
Channel services, 472–474, 473f
Chaos scenario, 178
Chaparro, B., 173
Charlet, J.C., 323
Chat rooms, 21
Chattapadhyay, Amitava, 565
Checking accounts, 293
Checkout process, 456–458
Chen, Pearl, 139
Chen, Pei-Yu, 425
Chernatony, Leslie De, 209
Chiang, Michael F., 246
Chicos, Roberta, 388

Child Online Privacy Protection Act
    (COPPA), 84
China
  censorship in, 241
  growth of Internet in, 14–15
  growth of market in, 500–503
Chintagunta, Pradeep, 564
Cho, Junghoo, 102
Choice assistance, 298, 300–301,
    307–316
  data sources for, 314–315
  recommendation systems for,
    308–316
    CASE, 311–312
    collaborative filtering, 312–314
    endorsement systems, 314
    questions for, 308–310
    rules-based, 310–311
Choice Hotels, 489–490
Choice models, 454–455
Chou, Ting-Jui, 139
Chow, Lena, 139
Christie's, 412–413
Christodoulides, George, 209
Chronos, 245
Ciffolilli, Andrea, 353
Cigarettes, taxes on, 390–392
Cinema, digital, 36–38
Cisco Connection Online (CCO), 513
Cisco Systems, 238f, 508, 509f,
    512f, 513
Clark, Kim, 387, 389
Clark, Philip, 66
Clarke, Arthur C., 591
Claypool, Mark, 246
Clearing House Interbank Payment
    System (CHIPS), 59
Clickstream data, 259
Click-through ads, prospect fees
    and, 169
Click-through rates
  for banner ads, 280–281, 281f
  keyword bidding and, 275
Closed-loop marketing, 148,
    156–157
Closeouts, 494–497
Club Med, 261, 262
Clustering, 69–70, 77, 89–92,
    89f, 91f
Co-branding, 283
Coca-Cola, 186–187
Cognizant, 227f
Cognos, 233–234, 238
Cohen, Adam, 173
Coleman, J. E., 564

Coleman, Les, 209
Collaborative customization,
    303–304
Collaborative filtering, 310, 312–314
Coltman, Tim, 388
Commerce One, 12
Commercial building automation,
    16–17
Commercial Internet
    growth of, 10–13
    impact of, 5–6
Commitment creation, 324–352
    online communities, 327–334
    retention marketing, 345–352
Common information platform, 163f
Communication, online, 75–76
Communication channels,
    information flow across,
    74–75
Communications industry, 58
Communication rings, 331–332
Communication-value pairs, 88
Communication volume, in United
    Kingdom, 74t
Communities. See Online
    communities
Community building
    branding effectiveness and, 200
    through branding, 203
Community network value,
    86–87, 87t
Community optimists, 333–334
Community pessimists, 334–335
Community tools, 331–335,
    337–340
Comparison matrix, 455, 456
Comparison sites, 400–401, 440
Compensatory models, 454
Competitive advantage, 297f
Composition index, 553–554, 554f
Computerized databases, 24
Computer power
    exponential growth of, 41–42
    Moore's Law and, 40
Computer programming, 50–51
Computers, early and modern, 27f
Computing grid, 48
Concept testing methods, 376f
Congestion, 225, 231, 560f
Congestion monitoring, 556–563
Conjoint analysis, 373
Connection devices, 15–17, 570
Connection speed trends, 118f
Connell, Jamie O., 531
Conrad, Frederick G., 564

Conroy, Robert, 174
Consumer behavior, online, 118,
    120–123
Consumer channels, 468–497
    business-to-consumer
        channels, 471f
    channel conflicts, 483–487
    channel design, 471–475
    direct, 471, 472f, 480–490
    existing customers, 475–490
    in expanding markets,
        490–494
    hybrid approach, 486–487
    indirect, 471, 472f
    intermediaries, 471, 472, 474,
        476–480
    iPace and channel services,
        472–474
    long tail and, 492–493, 493f
    make or buy decision,
        474–475
    online closeouts, 494–497
    overview, 471
    versioning, 493–494
Consumer communications,
    282–283
Consumer demand, for computer
    advances, 48–49
Consumer expectations, 96,
    121–122, 570–571
Consumer needs
    shopping, 480
    uncovering, 373
Consumer shopping cycle, 438f,
    439, 448f, 449
Consumer surplus, 419
Content. See Information; Online
    content
Content accessibility, 124–126
Content accuracy, 240
Content attractiveness, 329
Content delivery network (CDN)
    service, 559
Content quality, 229–230
Content sharing systems, 97–98
Content sites, 169
Content trees, 332, 333f
Continuity programs, 296
Convenience, 438
    channel services and, 473
    of online shopping, 446–447
Convenience surveys, 539–540
Conventions, 364, 365
Convergence, 39, 44, 57–65
Conversion rates, prediction of, 439

Cookies, 135–136
    information on, 221–222
    personalization and, 317–318
Cooper, Alan, 246
Coordination page, 206–207
Copyright issues, 578–580, 579f
Cornett, Steve, 246
Cornfield, Michael, 564
Cortada, James W., 101–102
Cosmetic customization, 305–306
Cost-per-action, 259–261, 260f, 265
Cost per impression, 260
Cost per thousand impressions
    (CMP) analysis, 554–555
Cost per visit, 260
Cost reductions
    in computer technology, 40–42
    of online customer support,
        233–236
    web business models and,
        161–162, 161t
Coughlan, Anne, 498
Country codes, 186
Couper, Mick P., 564
Coupons, personalized, 420
Coverage, survey, 542
Cowly, Stacy, 33
Cox, Brad, 65
Crawford, James, 465, 466
Credibility
    establishing online, 214–215
    guidelines, 239t
    views on, 239t
    web site, 238–241
Credit reports, 583–584
Credit scores, 420
Crises, brand, 200–202
Cross, Robert, 426
Cross-channel buying, 460–461
Cross channel integration, 428
Cross selling, 454
Crupi, Anthony, 173
Csikszentmihalyi, Mihaly, 138
Culotta, Aron, 354
Culture, impact of radio on
    mass, 8–9
Cumbow, Robert, 582
Curran, James, 565
Cusamano, Michael A., 387
Customer acquisition
    in B2B commerce, 508
    costs, 265t
    personalization and, 297
Customer activities, cross-channel,
    460–461

Customer base analysis, 345–349
Customer-based brand equity
    model, 179–180, 183, 184f
Customer contacts, valuing,
    146–157
Customer dialogues, 573–577,
    575–577
Customer feedback, 95, 482
Customer interactions, 126–128,
    147–149
Customer knowledge, 163–164
Customer lifetime value (CLV), 25,
    30, 146, 157–159, 263
Customer loyalty, 24
Customer loyalty programs, 346–347
Customer management, 24–25,
    574–575
Customer profiles, association and,
    135–137
Customer-relating capabilities
    (CRC), 297f
Customer relationship management
    (CRM) software, 509–510
Customer responses, 147–149
Customers
    analyzing most profitable,
        345–346
    channels for existing, 475–490
    persuadable moments, 245
    preferred, 296–298
    relationship, 228–229
    tracking, 148
    transactional, 228–229
Customer satisfaction, with online
    retailing, 435, 436f
Customer self-help, 238
Customer support, 233–238
    cost savings from online,
        233–236
    electronic distribution, 236–237
    FAQs, 238
    online publishing, 237, 238f
    personalization of, 301–302
    traffic building and, 282
    Web-based, 161–162
Customer value, using Internet to
    enhance, 149f
Customization
    See also Individualization;
        Personalization
    challenges of, 569–570
    channel services and, 473
    collaborative, 303–304
    mass, 24–25, 298–306
Cyberspace, fictional views of, 53

d

Dahan, Ely, 388
Danaher, Peter J., 209
Darden, William R., 465
Data General, 357
Data synchronization, 529–531, 531f
David, Paul, 102
Davie, Bruce S., 102
Dawar, Niraji, 209
Day, George, 323, 532
Dean, Dwane, 209
Dean, Rishi, 323
Decker, Susan, 101
De facto standards, 365–366, 368
Defamation, 584
Deighton, John, 173, 209, 354
DeKoven, Elyon, 323
Delacroix, Jacques, 209
Delays
    impact of, 556
    lags and, 557–560
    managing perceptions of,
        561–563
    monitoring, 556–563
    sources of, 556–560
Del Franco, Mark, 498
Dellaert, Benedict, G. C., 246, 565
Dell Computer
    modular design and, 382–383
    personalization at, 137–138
    site navigation, 226f
    supply chain coordination,
        162–163
Demand visibility, 526–527
Demographics
    of Internet users, 114–117
    of target audience, 552–554
Denial of service (DOS)
    attacks, 559
Denning, Peter, 66
Design elements, of surveys, 542, 544
Design funnel, 373–375, 374f
Design mistakes, 373, 375–376
Design rules, visible and hidden,
    380, 382
Developing countries, Internet use
    in, 14–15
De Ville, Kenneth, 66
Devinney, Timothy, 388
DeYoung, Robert, 323
Dhar, Ravi, 173, 465
Dialogue creation, 573–577
Dialogue marketing, 349–352, 352f

Diamond-water paradox, 250–252
DiClemente, Diane, 565
Differentiation, 292
Difficult comparison effect, 400–401
Digital applications, 48
Digital cinema, 36–38
Digital computing, 27–28
Digital content, substituting, for
    marketing labor, 43
Digital convergence, 44, 57–65
    converging industries and
        technology, 57–59, 57t
    digitization process and, 59–62
    marketing processes and, 62–65
Digital environments, 39, 49–56
    components of, 50–56
    encyclopedic component, 55–56
    participation, 51–53
    procedural rules, 50–51, 52t
    spatial component, 53–55
Digital marketing. See Internet
    marketing
Digital-network-individualization
    (DNI), 146
Digital revolution, 27–28, 38
Digital sponsorship, 283
Digital substitution, 42–45
    of marketing material, 64
    new capabilities created by,
        45–48
Digital technology, 38, 39
Digital televisions, 37, 49
Digital video recorders (DVRs), 37,
    49, 176
Digital worlds, 53
Digitization
    of marketing processes,
        62–65, 63t
    Moore's Law and, 39–42
    process, 59–62
Dillman, Linda, 139
Direct access agreements, 490
Direct channels, 472f
Direct deposit, 58
Direct marketing, 24–25
Direct materials, 505, 514t, 519–522
Direct payments, 58–59
Direct sales, 480–490
    channel conflicts and, 483–487
    hybrid approach, 486–487
    reasons for, 480–482
    transitioning to, 487–490
Direct sales teams, 490
Disabilities, 116–117, 124,
    231–233

Discussion networks, 337–340
Distributed computing, 48
Distribution, of information, 101
Distribution channels
    See also Consumer channels
    B2B commerce, 509f
    benefits of branding in, 179
    direct sales, 480–490
    marketplaces, 522–526
    procurement process and,
        514–526
Dogac, Asuman, 323
Dolan, Robert J., 424, 425
Domain categories, 186
Domain names
    brand architecture and, 190–193
    brand identity and, 185–193
    choosing, 189–193
    credibility and, 214–216
    defining, 186–189
    goals, 185–186
    hierarchical, 186, 187t, 545,
        547–548
    legal issues, 580–581
    memorability, 188–189, 188t
    registering multiple, 186–188,
        189–190
    of top brands, 190t
    traffic building and, 255
Domain name servers, 186
Do Not Call list, 176–177
Dot-com boom/bust, 11–13
Dowling, Grahame, 354
Download times, 561t, 563f
Dreze, Xavier, 209
Dr. Koop, 33
Drucker, Peter, 322, 497
Duguid, Paul, 101
Duhachek, A., 139, 246
Dutch auctions, 413
Dutta, Shantanu, 498
Dutta-Bergman, Mohan, 247
DVDs, 37
Dynamic bidding, 519–522, 520f
Dynamic content, support for,
    571–573
Dynamic personalization, 222
Dynamic pricing, 408
Dynamic web sites, 18–19

E*Trade, 403
eBay, 129
    business model, 142–146, 160

closeouts and, 495
endorsement system, 315
entertainment component
    of, 447
lessons learned from, 410–412
reporting systems, 156–157
success of, 372
web alliances, 382
Ecommerce. *See* B2B commerce;
    Online retailing
Edmunds.com, 99–101, 398–399f
Education levels, 116, 116t
Effectiveness improvements,
    162–163
Efficiency, 161–162
Eisenhardt, Kathleen, 387, 499
El-Ansary, Adel, 498
Electronic banking, 43–44, 58–59,
    293–295
Electronic data interchange (EDI),
    506–508
Elias, Paul, 532
Ellison, Sarah, 498
Email, 75
    auto-responders, 236, 576–577
    clustering and, 91
    early feedback using, 384
    growth of, 7
    vs. IM, 77t
    incorporating in customer
        dialogue, 76t
    loyalty building through,
        349–351
    personalization and, 318
    response problem, 575–577
    smart routing, 235–236
    surveys, 540
Email addresses, collection of, 89
Email campaigns, 342–343
Email support, 234, 235t
Email viruses, 91
Employment status, 116
End benefit effect, 404–405
Endorsements, 96, 240
Endorsement systems, 309, 314
End users, interaction with, 482
English auctions, 413
Enhancement rates, of U.S.
    business, 504
Entertainment, 438
    channel services and, 473
    online shopping and, 447–448
Entertainment polls, 539
Entry pages, 221, 222–223t
Eppen, Gary, 426
Eprocurement, 514–526

Etickets, 64–65
European Union (EU), 370t, 492
Evaluation, 454–456
Event graphs, 245, 321f
Executive view, 573
Exit pages, 222–223t
Expanding markets, 490–494
Expectations, consumer, 96,
    121–122, 570–571
Experience goods, 291–292,
    439, 440f
Experiential online behavior, 123
Experiential usability, 230–231
Experiential web visits, 221, 224
External links, 261
    cultivation of, 269
    PageRank algorithm and, 270
Eysenbach, Gunther, 564

Facebook, 168
Fader, Peter S., 101, 174, 284, 354
Fain, Daniel C., 102
Fair Credit Reporting Act (FCRA),
    583–584
Fallow, Deborah, 208
FAQs, 238
Farquhar, Peter H., 208
Farrell, Joseph, 102, 388
Farris, Paul W., 174
Fathom Online Keyword Price
    Index, 272t
Federal Trade Commission (FTC),
    582, 584–585
Federman, Josef, 498
FedWire, 59
Feedback
    customer, 95, 482
    on product releases, 383–386
Fein, Adam, 532
Feiss, Ellen, 198, 199f
Feldman, Joan, 426
Fellowship of the Ring (film),
    36–37
Fesenmaier, Daniel R., 564
Feynman, Richard, 48, 65, 590
File compression, 60–61
File size, access times and, 561t
File swapping systems, 97–98
Filo, Dave, 360
Filson, Darren, 174
Financial benefits, of
    branding, 179
Financial booms and busts, 11–13

Financial Engines, 287–289, 311
Financial planning advice, 286–289
Financial sector, 58–59
Firefox browser, 358–359
Firewall software, 152
First-generation Internet, 82
First impressions, 128
Flaherty, Theresa, 591
Flake, Gary W., 102
Flaming, 127–128
Flat-panel televisions, 49
Fleishman, Glen, 323
Flexibility, modular design and, 379–381
Flextronics, 195
Floor-ready merchandise, 477–478
Flow, state of, 122–123
Focus groups, 373
Foehr, U., 139
Fogg, B.J., 247
Folding@Home, 96–97
FOMA (freedom of mobile access), 68, 69
Foray, Dominique, 102
Forman, Chris, 532
Fox, Susannah, 139, 247, 284
Fragmented markets, 525–526
Fragrance.net, 446–447f
Franchised services, 291
Frangos, Alex, 532
Freis, Judy, 354
Frequency marketing, 296
Frequency report, 554, 555f
Frequent flyer programs, 346
Friedman, Thomas, 181
Friendster, 329
Froese, Thomas, 532
Froogle, 3, 5
FTC (Federal Trade Commission), 584–585
Fulgoni, Gian, 564
Functional performance-related information, 193

g

Gadiesh, Orit, 498
Galletta, Dennis F., 565
Gaming sites, 230–231, 232f
Gammack, John G., 140
Gap, 462, 463f
Gaynor, Mark, 389
Gebauer, Udith, 532

Gender, 116, 121
General purpose technologies (GPTs), 25–30
    digital revolution, 27–28
    features of, 71
    future development of, 590–591
    individualization, 29–30, 107–108, 130–138
    of Internet marketing, 26–30
    networking, 28–29
    pervasive presence, 25–26
    room for improvement, 26
    spawn innovations, 26
Genome@Home, 96–97
GE Plastics, 514
Germanow, Abner, 388
Getz, Gary, 173, 284
Gibbs, Martin, 246
Gibson, William, 53
Gigaflops, 42
Gilbert, James, 498
Gilbert, Richard J., 387
Gilman, Laura, 65
Giussani, Bruno, 33
Glader, Paul, 499
Glazer, Rashi, 173, 322
Global data synchronization, 529–531, 531f
Global distribution, 491–492
Global Internet congestion, 560f
Global outsourcing, 517
Global registry, 531
Global service providers, 492
Gnutella, 97–98, 336
Goal-directed online behavior, 123
Goddard, Charlotte, 498
Godes, David, 499
God games, 53
Goldenberg, Jacob, 353, 387
Golder, Peter, 388
Goldfarb, Avi, 532
Gomes, Lee, 498, 499
Gomory, Stephen, 284
Goods
    See also Products
    experience, 291–292, 439, 440f
    search, 291–292, 439, 440f
    switching costs of, 295
Google, 2–5
    Alexa ranking, 262
    keyword bidding on, 275–276
    search marketing and, 266
    top brand searches, 189t
Google AdSense, 169f

Google AdWords, 3–4
Googlefight.com, 267
Google PageRank, 3, 77, 241, 269, 270
Google Scholar, 306
Goolsbee, Austan, 424, 465
Gormley, Michael, 424
Gorn, Gerald, 565
Grabowicz, Paul, 582
Graeber, Catherine, 65
Grannovetter, M., 102
Grant, Alasdair, 140
Grant, Peter, 499
Greene, Kelly, 497
Greenspan, Alan, 65
Greenstein, Shane, 33, 387, 532
Gremler, Dwayne D., 354
Grid computing, 96–98
Griffin, Abbie, 389
Griffin, Mitch, 465
Grimm, Mathew, 323
Gross ratings points (GRPs), 536f
Grove, Andrew, 33, 48
Groves, R. M., 564
Gunther, Robert, 466
Gupta, Sachin, 564
Gupta, Sunil, 34
Gwinner, Kevin P., 354

h

Hacker attacks, 237
Hafner, K., 33
Hagel, John, 498
Hagerty, James R., 499
Hale, Briony, 354
Hammerschmidt, M., 173
Hampton, Keith N., 353
Handelman, J., 354
Handspring Treo Communicator, 44
Hann, Leslie Westein, 591
Hanna, Richard C., 565
Hansen, Karsten, 322
Hanson, Ward, 102, 140, 388, 426
Hantula, 565
Hardie, Bruce, 174, 354
Harker, Patrick, 246
Harris, Edward, 497
Harris, Richard G., 101
Haskins, Mark, 174
Haubl, Gerald, 466
Hauser, John, 388, 389, 465
Hausman, Jerry, 322
Hayes, Brian, 65
Haythornthwaite, Caroline, 140

Health care expenditures, 404
Health information. *See* Medical
    information
Heerwegh, Dick, 564
Heide, Jan B., 532
Heim, Gregory, 246
Helpman, Elhanan, 33, 34, 101
Hendler, James, 102
Hennig-Thurau, Thorsten, 354
Henry, Raymond, 565
Henthorne, Beth Hogan, 210
Henthorne, Tonyh, 210
Herhold, Scott, 33
Heston, Charlton, 102
Hew, Kevin, 246
Hewlett-Packard, 193, 485–486,
    488f, 489
Hicks, Matt, 33
Hidden design parameters, 380, 382
Hidden pixels, 136
Hiebeler, Tobert, 66
Hierarchical domain names, 186,
    187t, 545, 547–548
High-speed access. *See* Broadband
    access
High-tech battles
    browser wars, 356–359
    standards and, 363–364
Hill, Kenneth, 140
Hippel, Eric Von, 389
Hirschmann, Elizabeth C., 465
Hitt, Lorin, 66, 425, 531
Ho, Teck-Hua, 465
Hobbs, John, 247
Hoch, R., 284
Hoch, Stephen, 139
Hockley, Andrew, 139
Hoeffler, Steve, 208
Hoffman, D.L., 139, 174, 246
Hogan, John E., 173
Holbrook, Morris B., 465
Holden, Reed K., 424
Holiday shopping, 446
Hollis, N., 209
Hollis, Nigel, 173
Home pages, 221
Homestore.Com, 33
Hong, Traci, 582
Honomichl, Jack, 564
Hopper, Dennis, 102
Horsky, Dan, 139
Hortacsu, Ali, 140, 425
Hotel industry, 469–470, 489–490
Hotwire, 496
Household appliances, 16
Household income, 116

House of brands marketing strategy,
    191, 192–193
Howard Johnson, 406, 407f
Hsu, Chun-Nan, 323
HTML, 82–84, 83f
Hu, Yu, 465
Huang, Chun-Che, 389
Huang, Han-Shen, 323
Huberman, Bernardo, 103, 246, 353
Hubs, 93–94
Hunter, William, 323
Hurley, Deborah, 174
Hurricane Katrina, 240
Hussherr, Francois-Xavier, 209
Hwang, Yeong-Hyeon, 564
Hyatt Hotels, 406, 407f
Hype, 96

Iacobucci, Dawn, 565
IBM, 194, 356–357
Idea funnel, 373–375, 374f
Identity creation, 104–106
IEEE 802.11, 364–368, 367f
Illiteracy, 124
Image blocking software, 152
Images
    digitizing, 59–61, 60f
    product, 451–452
    visual metaphors, 241–243
Immersion, 49
    See also Digital environments
I-mode, 68
Impression-based pricing, 170
Inaccurate information, 583–584
Inansiti, Marco, 388
Income levels, 116, 117f
Incumbent-backed marketplaces,
    523–525
India, 15
Indirect materials, 505,
    514–516, 514t
Individualization
    See also Customization;
        Personalization
    benefits of, 107
    as general purpose technology,
        29–30, 107–108, 130–138
    association and, 135–137
    authentication and, 132–135
    concerns over, 131
    interaction and, 137–138
    RFIDs and, 105–106
Individual-level interaction, 107–108

Individual marketing concept, 24–25
Industries, convergence of, 57–65
Industry standards, 520
    See also Standards
Information
    See also Online content
    accessibility of, 124–126
    accuracy of, 583–584
    acquisition of, 450–454
    as basic shopper requirement,
        438–439
    channel services and, 472–473
    completeness of, 240–241
    creating useful, 224–238
    in credit reports, 583–584
    distributing, 101
    enhancing value of, 99–101
    flows, 74–75, 74t, 95
    gathering, 99
    initial visit, 221–224
    iPace and, 437
    matching to user goals, 226–229
    online, and price sensitivity,
        396–408
    overload, 73
    personalized, 452–454
    presales, 475–476
    product, 450–454
    production of original, 73–74, 73t
    selecting and organizing, 99–100
    spread of, through clustering,
        89–91
    stored, 73–74
    synthesizing, 100–101
    useful, 296
Information acceleration (IA),
    376–378
Information appliances, 16, 566–569
Information architecture, 99–100
Information gathering, 99
Information requests, permission
    sponsorship and, 167, 168f
Innovative products
    See also Product development
    understanding demand for,
        376–378
Input substitution, 42–45
Instant messaging, 75–76
    vs. email, 77t
    personalization and, 318
Intangible benefits, 292, 293
Integrated marketing
    communications, 195, 197
Integrated media planning, 21
Integrated product
    architecture, 380t

Integrated software solutions, 50–51
Intel Corporation, 39
Intellectual property rights, 578–580
Interaction, 137–138
   of online communities, 342–343
   real-time, 569
Interactive digital storytelling, 53
Interactivity, 51–53, 229–230
Intercept surveys, 540
Intermediaries, 471, 472f, 474f,
   476–480, 525
International locations, 491–492
International Organization for
   Standardization (ISO), 370t
International Telecommunications
   Union (ITU), 370t
Internet
   as appliance, 566–569
   deregulation of, 7
   evolution of, 71–84
     content and communication,
     73–79
     maturation and expansion of,
     71–72
   first-generation, 82
   as global resource, 14–21
   growth explosion, 8–13
   impact of, 5–6
   limits of early, 9–10
   noncommercial beginning
     of, 6–8
   second-generation, 82–84
   technology standards, 81–84
Internet access
   broadband, 70–72, 109, 111,
     116–119, 225, 452
   by country, 14t
   in Japan, 68–70
   standards, 364–365
   via mobile phones, 71
Internet addresses, 186–187
Internet Advertising Bureau
   (IAB), 13f
Internet censorship, 241
Internet companies, stock market
   boom and bust, 11–13
Internet content. See Online content
Internet-enabled retailing. See
   Online retailing
Internet food sites, 491
Internet hosts, 15–16, 15f
Internet marketing
   See also specific types
   challenges faced by, 6
   challenges of, 120
   cost savings from, 43–44

future of, 587–591
GPTs of, 26–30, 107–108,
   130–138
   digital revolution, 27–28
   individualization, 29–30,
     107–108
   networking, 28–29
   organization for, 569–587
Internet Movie Database (IMB),
   55–56, 56t
Internet performance, monitoring,
   556–563
Internet-scale operating system
   (ISCS), 97f
Internet service providers (ISPs), 11f
Internet start-ups, 12–13
Internet time
   business implications of, 361–364
   defined, 360
Internet usage
   access quality and, 117–118
   by activity, 110–111t, 111–114
   by age groups, 115t
   casual, 130
   income levels and, 116, 117t
   individualization and, 107–108
   in Japan, 68–70
   in online communities, 334t, 335
   patterns, 107–130
   in South Korea, 119
   state of flow and, 122–123
   time allocation, 108–114, 109f
Internet users, 14–15
   advanced, 228
   beginner, 228
   casual, 130
   demographics, 114–117
   loyal, 130
   time spent online by, 108–114
   web pages per, 251f
Inventory, vendor managed, 526–527
Inventory turnover, for selected
   retailers, 435f
Investment planning, 286–289
Investor support, 226–227
iPace (information, price,
   assortment, convenience,
   and entertainment), 436–459
   assortment, 438, 443–446, 473
   channel services and, 472–474
   convenience, 438, 446–447, 473
   entertainment, 438,
     447–448, 473
   implementing, 448–459
   information, 437, 438–439,
     472–473

online shopping process and,
   437–448
price, 437, 439–441, 473
iPIX, 61–62
iPodder, 81f
iPods, 16, 41, 41f, 305–306
iTunes, 257f

Jain, Dipak, 173
Jansen, B.J., 284
Jap, Sandy, 522
Japan, 16, 68–70
Jindel, Satish, 465
Joachimsthaler, E., 209
Johnson, Eric J., 101
Johnson, James, 591
Joint performance bundling, 424
Jolson, M., 323
Jome, Hiram, 33
Jones, C., 354
Jones, Susan, 466
Jurisdiction, 581–582

Kahin, Brian, 174
Kahn, Barbara, 246, 323, 565
Kairos, 245
Kakkar, Pradeep, 466
Kalman, Yoram, 591
Kalyanam, Kirthi, 209, 247, 498,
   499, 533, 564
Kameda, T., 247
Kaminski, Philip, 533
Kane, Gerald C., 582
Kaplan, Carl, 284
Kasanoff, Bruce, 323
Katz, Michael, 102, 387
Kaufmann, Robert J., 425
Kaul, Anil, 564
Kavanaugh, Andrea, 353
Kay, H. Stephen, 139
Keitel, Harvey, 102
Keith, Robert J., 34
Keller, Kevin Lane, 208, 209
Kelley, Tina, 465
Kellner-Rogers, Myron, 353
Kelly, Thomas, 66
Ketteman, Charles, 66
Keyword advertising, 19–21,
   248–250, 269–279
   vs. banner advertising, 280

competitive responses and, 277–278
complications in, 277–279
content sites and, 169
Google AdWords, 3–4
growth of, 180
as traffic source, 256
Keyword portfolio evaluation, 272–279
Keywords
  bidding on, 249, 266, 275–277, 278t
  data collection, 275t
  identifying possible, 272–274
  pricing, 169
  testing, 274–275
Key word searches, 449–450
Keyword value, 271–272
Khan, Mickey Alam, 498
Kidder, Tracy, 387
Kiesler, Sara, 140, 353
Kilie, Ozgur, 323
Kisiel, Ralph, 532
Kittler, F., 247
Kladko, Brian, 565
Kleinen, Mirella, 102
Klemperer, Paul, 354, 425
Kodak Photo CD, 60
Koenig, Harold F., 210
Kon, Martin, 354
Kotha, Suresh, 323
Kotler, Philip, 147, 388
Kozinets, Robert, 354
Kraut, Robert, 353
Kreps, Gary L., 247
Krish, Rajan, 465
Krishnan, Balaji, 209
Krishnan, Ramayya, 247
Kumar, V., 34, 353, 354
Kurzweil, Raymond, 47, 66, 582

l

Laertius, Diogenes, 387
Lags, 557–560
  access, 559–560
  server, 557–559
  transmission, 560
Lahlou, Saadi, 582
Lala, Vishal, 532
Landauer, Thomas K., 139
Landon, Alfred, 534
Lands' End, 24, 228–229, 453f
Langheinrich, Marc, 582
Language recognition software, 295

Language translation, 45–47
Lassila, Ora, 102
Latency, 231, 232f
Laubacher, Robert, 532
Lauterborn, Robert F., 209
Lavoi, Brian, 102
Lazarsfeld, Paul, 33
Lean forward information, 194–195
Leclerc, Frace, 323
Lee, Christopher, 102
Lee, Dongwon, 425
Lee, Hau L., 533
Lee, Juhnyoung, 284
Lee, Ka Lok, 174, 354
Lee, Myung-Soo, 498
Lee, Theresa, 565
Legal pitfalls, 577–587
  credit reports and, 583–584
  defamation and libel, 584
  digital environments and
    intellectual property, 578–580
  network connection and legal
    geography, 580–582
  privacy policies and, 584–587
  protection of individual data, 582–587
Lehmann, Donald R., 34, 173, 284, 387
Leibtag, Ephraim, 322
Lemon, Ketherine N., 173
Leonard, Devin, 209
Levitt, Theodore, 128, 140, 292, 293, 322
Levy, Michael, 465
Lewis, Geoffrey, 174
Lewis, William, 464
Libai, Barak, 353
Libel, 584
Library of Congress, 124–126
Lih, Andrew, 353, 389
Lilien, Gary, 388
Lin, Koung-Lung, 323
Linden, Greg, 323
LinkedIn, 92–93
Link farms, 269
List-based samples, 540
Literacy, 124
Lloyd, Emily, 532
Load times, 563, 563f
Loftus, Peter, 499
Log files, 545–547, 550
Lohse, Gerald L., 101
Long, Matthew, 33
Long tail of product sales, 492–493, 493f

Look ahead surfer model, 218–219, 221
Looking Backward (Bellamy), 587–589
Lord of the Rings (film), 36–37, 45
Lossveldt, Geert, 564
Louviere, Jordan, 388
Loveman, Gary, 354, 531
Loyalty bundling, 423
Loyalty discounts, 420
Loyalty programs, 346–347
Loyal users, 130
Lucking-Reiley, David, 173
Lukose, Rajan, 246
Luna, David, 66
Lundegaard, Karen, 532, 533
Lundmark, Vicki, 353
Lynch, John, 425

MacCormack, Alan, 388
Machine intelligence, 47
Maclaran, Pauline, 353
Magnetic media, 73
Magretta, Joan, 173
Mahajan, Vijay, 101, 354, 466
Maier, P., 498
Malone, Thomas W., 532
Maloney-Krichmar, Diane, 353
Mamet, David, 283
Mangani, Ardrea, 174
Mansell, R., 353
Manual procurement, 515, 517–518
Manufacturers
  direct sales by, 480–490
  supply chain, 505–506, 505f
Manufacturer's Recommended
    Selling Price (MRSP), 488
Manufacturer's web sites, 476
Manufacturing, outsourcing of, 528
Marchand, Roland, 322
Marginal costs, 394–395
Marginal revenues, 394–395
Market expansion, 490–494
Marketing
  See also Internet marketing;
    Search engine marketing
  axioms, 147
  brand management, 23–24
  demand building and, 23
  dialogue, 349–353, 352f
  digital benefits for, 39
  direct, 24–25
  frequency, 296

with networks, 94–101
  relationship, 301–302
  retention, 345–352
  standards, 364–373
  technology and, 21–25
Marketing actions, tracking
    responses to, 147–149
Marketing applications, 17–21
Marketing channels. *See* Consumer
    channels
Marketing fundamentals, 118
Marketing material
  digital substitution of, 43, 64
  local storage of, 41
Marketing processes
  digitizing, 62–65, 63t
  redesigning, to use digital
    capabilities, 64–65
Marketing services, procurement
    of, 181–182
Market maturation, 71–72
Marketplaces, B2B, 522–526
  fragmented markets and, 525–526
  incumbent backed, 523–525
  intermediary backed, 525
  market structure and, 524t
  speculative boom in, 522–523f
Market research
  See also Online research
  audience analysis, 545–547,
    545–555
  branding campaigns and,
    182–183
  for innovative products, 376–378
  Internet-enabled, 163–164
  online, 375–376
  online surveys, 535–544
Market segments, shrinking, 25
Market sharing, 370–371, 371f
Market structures, marketplaces
    and, 524f
Marn, Michael V., 424
Marshall, J., 247
Martin, Kipp, 426
Masand, B., 284
Mass customization, 24–25, 298–306
  adaptive, 306
  approaches to, 299–300
  collaborative customization,
    303–304
  cosmetic customization,
    305–306
  dimensions of, 303f
  representation and product
    changes, 302–303
  transparent customization, 306

Mass media
  advertising, 176, 257
  chaos scenario and, 178
Mass production, 22–23, 25
Materials
  direct, 505, 514t, 519–522
  indirect, 505, 514–516, 514t
MathStatica, 418
Mathwick, Charla, 139
Mazursky, David, 387
McAlexander, James H., 210
McCallum, Andrew, 354
McCoy, Scott, 565
McDonald's, 201
McGowan, Karen, 425
McGrath, Diane, 139
McIntyre, Shelby, 498, 499, 533, 564
Mclaughlin, Margaret L., 582
McQuarrie, Edward F., 247, 564
Measurement errors, of online
    surveys, 542, 544
Media equation, 120–122
Media fragmentation, 180
Media impact, tracking, 183
Media industry, opportunities and
    challenges for, 171
Media planning, integrated, 21
Media revenue opportunities, 171
Medical information
  online, 248
  preferred version of content
    for, 229t
  trust and credibility of, 239t,
    240, 240f
Meetings, face-to-face vs. online,
    126–127
Megaflops, 41–42
Member loyalty, 329–330,
    341–342
Member profiles, 329, 342
Memorability, domain name,
    188–189, 188t
Menezes, Melvyn A. J., 498
Mergers, branding issues with, 193
Merino, Maria, 173
Merrill Lynch, 403
Mesothelioma, 248
Metadata, 84
Metatags, 267–268
Metcalfe, R., 66
Metcalfe's Law
  community value and, 86–87
  network value and, 85–86
Meuter, Matthew, 565
Microsoft, 357–359, 368

Milgrom, Paul, 425
Miller, Paul, 498
Milutinovic, Veljko, 323
Miniaturization, 40, 590
Minimum advertised prices (MAP),
    478–479, 488–489
Mitchell, Bridger, 424, 425
Mitchell, William, 66
Mittal, Banwari, 465
Mixed mode email system, 235–236
Mixed-mode surveys, 541
Mizerski, Richard, 209
Mobile devices, 71, 570
Modahl, Mary, 497
Modular product architecture, 380t
Modular product development,
    379–383
Moe, Wendy W., 101, 284
Moldovan, Sarit, 353
Money constraints, 108
Monitoring delays, 560–561
Montgomery Ward, 9
Moon, Youngme, 139, 323
Moore, Geoffrey, 173
Moore, Gordon, 39–40, 65
Moore, J., 102
Moore, Janet, 499
Moore, Marguerite, 425
Moore's Law, 39, 65
  continuation of, 48–49
  digitization and, 39–42
  input substitution, 42–45
  new capabilities, 45–48
  using, 42–48
Moorthy, Sridhar, 388
Moran, Ursula, 209
Morgan, John, 425
Moriarty, Rowland, 209
Morrissey, Brian, 284
Morton, Fiona Scott, 426, 498
Morton Salt, 196f
Movie industry, 36–38
Mozilla, 358
MSN, 262
Mueller, Charlotte, 532
Mukopadhyay, Tridas, 353
Mulhern, Francis J., 173
Mullarkey, Guy W., 209
Muller, Brigitte, 209
Muller, Eitan, 353
Muller, Melanie, 323
Multi-brand problem, 190–191
Multi-channel retailing, 436–437,
    460–464
  challenges of, 461–464
  shopping behavior, 460–461

Multimedia convergence, 58
Multi-person games,
    230–231, 232f
Multi-tasking, 76, 112,
    112f, 114
Muniz, Albert M., 66, 210
Murphy, Jamie, 209
Murray, Janet, 50, 66
Music rentals, 417–418
Music selection, 300–301
Mylonadis, Yiorgos, 387
MySpace, 329

n

Nagle, Thomas, 424
Nalebuff, Barry J., 498
Nandkumar, Anand, 247
Napster, 417–418
Nasr, N., 173
Nass, Clifford, 120, 139
National Research Council, 173
National Science Foundation
    (NSF), 6
Navigation, 54
    effective, 225–226
    flow and, 123
    of online retailers, 449–450
    standard layout, 225f
Negroponte, Nicholas, 38, 65
Nelson, P., 322, 425, 465
Netemeyer, Richard G., 209
Netnography, 343–345
Netscape, 357–359
Network communications, social
    aspects of, 69–70
Network outages, 556–557
Networks, 68–101
    See also Internet
    attacks on, 94
    clustering, 89–91, 91f
    community value of, 86–87
    geometry of social, 85–94
    hubs and authorities, 93–94
    marketing with, 94–101
        expectations, 96
        sharing resources, 96–98
        specialization and, 98
        speed factor and, 95
        ubiquity, 94–95
        virtual value activities, 99–101
    Metcalfe's Law and, 85–87
    small world property, 91–93

specialization and, 97f
    technology standards, 81–84
    WiFi, 72
Network science, 85, 85–94
Network value, 85–88, 86f
Neuromancer (Gibson), 53
Newman, Bruce, 465
New product development. *See*
    Product development
New product introduction (NPI)
    process, 527–529
Newspaper archives, 171, 172f
New York Times, 317–318f
Nichols, James, 246
Nie, Norman, 353
Nielsen, Jakob, 54, 66, 246, 247
Nike, 485–486
Non-compensatory models, 454–455
No notice rate, 152
Nordhaus, William, 40, 48, 65
Norman, Donald A., 33, 51, 66
Novak, Tom, 139, 174, 246
Ntoulas, Alexandros, 102
NTT DoCoMo, 68

o

O'Brien, L., 354
Ockenfels, Axel, 426
O'Connel, Pamela, 591
O'Connell, Vanessa, 209
Odlyzko, Andrew, 101
Offer, Avner, 139
Office automation, 16–17
Ogilvy, David, 208
O'Guinn, Thomas C., 210
Olston, Christopher, 102
    1-Click ordering, 458–459
O'Neill, Edward T., 102
Online activities, time component
    of, 108–109
Online advertising
    See also Advertising
    spending on, 13f,
        180–181, 181f
Online banking, 58–59, 161,
    293–295
Online branding, 176–208
    branding campaigns, 181–183
    business of branding, 179–183
    connecting strategy to online
        presence, 183–184
    disappointment with, 178

enhancing brand meaning,
    193–195
forging brand relationships,
    202–208
identity establishment, 185–193
new opportunities, 179
reinforcing right brand responses,
    195–202
traffic building and, 181
Online channel opportunities,
    474–475f
Online closeouts, 494–497
Online communication, 75–76, 77t,
    126–128
Online communities, 327–334
    challenges to building, 328–331
    content, 331–341
        member-produced, 335–340
        merged published and
            member, 340–341
    diversity of, 330f
    health of, 341–342
    interaction measures, 342–343
    learning from, 341–345
    loyalty and, 327–331
    netnography, 343–345
    types of, 328, 329t
Online companies, advertising
    spending by, 13f
Online content, 76–79
    accessibility of, 124–126
    branding effectiveness and,
        199–200
    creating useful, 224–238
    frequency of update, 240
    matching to initial visit
        information, 221–224
    media equation and, 120–122
    modification of, 195
    of online communities, 331–341
    price sensitivity and, 396–408
    quality of, 229–230
    robust, 126
    structure of, for search engine
        optimization, 268–269
    value and scarcity of, 250–254
Online credibility, 214–215, 239
Online customer service, 43–44,
    161–162
Online gambling sites, 230, 492
Online games, 230–231, 232f
Online intermediaries, 474–475,
    474f, 476–480, 525
Online marketing. *See* Internet
    marketing

Online pharmacies, 104–106, 405t, 462
Online publishing, 237, 238f
Online quality cues, 128–129
Online research, 534–563
  See also Market research
  audience analysis, 545–555
    CMP analysis, 554–555
    demographics and behavioral composition, 552–554
    panel vs. log file measurements for, 545–547
    source loss analysis, 550–552
  on Internet performance, 556–563
  surveys, 535–544
  tracking data, 550–552
  on traffic patterns, 548–550
Online retailers
  financial metrics for, 434t
  profitability of, 434
Online retailer support, 477–478
Online retailing, 19
  advantages of, 429–430, 435, 444–445
  convenience of, 446–447
  development of, 431–436
  difficulties of, 430
  entertainment component of, 447–448
  essential elements of, 589
  evaluation process, 454–456
  hierarchical domains and, 547–548
  importance of, 431
  improved processes, 160–165
  information acquisition and, 450–454
  inventory turnover, 435f
  iPace and, 436–459
  mainstreaming of, 433–434
  order placement process, 456–459
  post-purchase notifications, 459
  product assortment and, 443–446, 462–463
  by product category, 432–433f
  promotions and, 463–464
  reorders, 458–459
  requirements for, 436–437
  returns, 459
  revenue benefits, 165–173
  role of price in, 439–441
  shipping costs and, 441–443
  taxes and, 441, 442
  through intermediaries, 476–479

Online software distribution, 236–237
Online surveys
  advantages of, 537
  convenience surveys, 539–540
  nonrepresentative errors, 538–539, 538t
  probability surveys, 540–541
  problems with, 534–536
  quality of, 541–544
  types of, 538–541
Online ticket sales, 468–470
Online travel agents, 469–470
Online travel industry, 468–470
Online user registration, 88–89
Ontologies, 84
Open standards, 81, 365–368, 367f
Opinion polls, 539
Opportunistic behavior, 522
Opt-in option, 89
Opt-in panels, 540
Opt-out option, 89
Orbitz, 468
Order effect, 544f
Ordering processes, 512–514, 515f
Order placement, 456–459
Organization issues, 569–587
  aligning structure and strategy, 569–577
  alternative organizational emphasis, 574f
  dialogue creation, 573–577
  dynamic content support, 571–573
  publishing sites, 570–571
Organizational approaches, 99–100
Origination sites, 77, 78f
Outlet stores, 495
Outsourcing, 98
  of advertising, 181–182
  of manufacturing, 528
  of services, 517
Overstock.com, 495f
Overture keywords, 5
Ozen, Bahattin, 323

p

Package delivery system, 443, 444t
Padmanabhan, V., 533
PageRank algorithm, 3, 77, 241, 269, 270
Page view duration, 219

Page views, 217–218, 218f, 220f
Paley, William, 564
Palmer, Jonathan, 246
Pan, Xing, 425
Panayiotou, Christoforos, 323
Panel data, 545–547, 550, 553
Parallel sites, 45
Participation rates, of U.S. business, 504
Pashupati, Kartik, 66
Passwords, 133–134
Pasztor, Andy, 532
Patches, software, 237
Pattern of connectedness, 93–94
Patterson, Michael, 353
Patterson, Scott J., 353
Paul, Pallab, 465
Payment structures, choosing, 170–171
PayPal, 144, 145t
Pay-per-click advertising, 170, 248–250, 269–279
  See also Search engine marketing
PC bangs, 119
PDAs, customizing, 37f
Peddibhotla, Naren, 353
Peer-to-peer material, 21
Pennock, David M., 102
Pentaflops, 42
Peppers, Don, 138, 498
Pepsi SMASH logo, 242, 243f
Peracchio, Laura A., 66
Perceived wait time (PWT), 562–563
Perceptual abilities, 121–122
Performance-based payment systems, 168–169, 170
Permission sponsorship, 167, 168f
Personality matching, 120–121, 319, 320f
Personalization, 286–322
  See also Customization; Individualization
  approaches to, 298–322, 299f
    choice assistance, 300–301, 307–316
    mass customization, 302–306
    overview, 298–302
    personalized interaction, 301–302
  backlash, 297–298
  balance, 296–298
  benefits of, 289–298
  challenges of, 569–570

dynamic, 222
experience goods and search
    goods and, 291–292
goals of, 222
of investment advice, 287–289
of marketing, 24–25
personalized messaging,
    316–322
    association and, 319
    authentication for, 316–319
    trigger events and, 319–322
personalized service, 291
profitable, 296–297
real-time, 573
reasons for, 289–291
switching costs and, 295
total product and, 292–295
useful features and, 296
Personalized bundling, 420
Personalized information, 19,
    452–454
    branding effectiveness
        and, 200
    terms on, 89
Personalized interaction, 301–302
Personalized medicine, 106
Personalized messaging, 316–322
    association and, 319
    authentication for, 316–319
    trigger events and, 319–322
Personalized pricing, 408, 419–420
Personal jurisdiction, 581–582
Personal-level pricing contracts, 420
Persuadable moments, 245, 320–321
Persuasion, 241–245
    persuadable moments, 245,
        320–321
    simulation and tutorials,
        243–244
Pervasive presence, 25–26
Peterson, Larry L., 102
Petrosky, Henry, 66
Pew Internet Project, 283, 353
Pfeifer, Philip E., 174
Pharmaceutical companies, 44–45
Phelps, Corey, 102
Phillips, Barbara, 247
Phishing, 132
Phister, Montgomery, 65
Physical limitations, 124
Picard, Rosalind, 582
Piller, Frank, 323
Pirolli, Peter, L. T., 246
Pitkow, James E., 246
Pitt, Leyland, 174

Playstation, 368
Pleasence, Donald, 102
Plug-ins, 363
Podlasceck, Mark, 284
Polak, Peter, 565
Politeness, 120
Pollock, Annabel, 139
Porsche brand community,
    206–208f
Portal-based communities, 328,
    329t
Portal sites, 283
Positive feedback cycles, 329
Post-purchase notifications, 459
Power, Stephen, 497
Preece, Jenny, 353
Preferred customer programs,
    296–298
Preleased products, 384–386
Pre-recruited panels, 541
Presales information, 475–476
    manufacturer's web sites, 476
    third-party sites, 476
Prescription drugs, 104–106,
    404, 405t
Presidential campaigns, 534–536
Price comparison sites, 400–401, 440
Price elasticity
    online cigarette sales and,
        390–392
    role of, 394–396
Price guarantees, 489–490
Price-quality effect, 402–403
Price sensitivity
    channel services and, 473
    online information and, 396–408
    purchase importance and,
        403–408
Price Watch, 400
Pricing, 390–424, 437
    advanced online, 408–424
    bundle, 408, 421–424, 422t
    dynamic, 408
    impact of Internet on, 390–392,
        395–396
    online retailing and, 439–441,
        463
    personalized, 408, 419–420
    power of, 393–394
    price sensitivity and online
        information, 396–408
    product bundling and, 392
    setting online, 488
    standard pricing answer,
        394–396

time-based, 408, 409–419
    auctions, 409–414
    rental pricing, 417–418
    trial, 418
    yield management, 414–417
value uncertainty and, 397–403
    difficult comparison effect,
        400–401
    reference price effect, 397–400
zone, 463
Pricing innovations, 171
Prince, Marcelo, 466
Privacy policies, 584–587
Privacy rules, country specific, 583
Private banking, 128
Probability sampling, 538–539
Probability surveys, 540–541
Procedural rules, for digital
    environments, 50–53
Process improvements,
    160–165, 160t
    brand enhancement, 164–165
    category building, 165
    cost reduction, 161–162, 161t
    customer knowledge, 163–164
    quality improvement, 165
    supply chain coordination,
        162–163
Procrastination, 286
Proctor and Gamble (P&G), 164, 176
Procurement, 514–526
    direct materials, 519–522
    dynamic bidding, 519–522
    indirect materials, 514–516
    marketplaces and, 522–526
    of services, 517–519
Product assortment
    channel services and, 473
    online retailing and, 438,
        443–446, 462–463,
        492–493
Product bundling, 392
Product changes, 302–303
Product convergence, 39
Product cycles, shortened, 95
Product definition bundling, 424
Product development
    concept testing methods,
        376f
    design funnel, 373–375, 374f
    early feedback on, 383–386
    information acceleration,
        376–378
    modular, 379–383
    modular vs. integrated, 380t

online, 373–378, 373–387
radical inventions, 376–378
rapid release, 386–387
speed of, 360–364
standards and, 364–373
supply chain coordination and,
    527–529
Product differentiation, 292
Product evaluations, 454–455
Product images, 451–452
Product information, 450–454
Product introductions, supply
    chain coordination and,
    527–529
Production efficiency bundling,
    422–423
Product management, 573–574
Product manager view, 573–574
Product ratings, 452
Product reviews, 452
Products
    See also Goods
    finding online, 449–450
    prereleasing, 384–386
Product segmentation, 290
Product tests, online, 431
Product tracking, RFIDs, 104–106
Profitability
    analyzing customer, 345–346
    of online retailers, 434
    pricing and, 393–394, 393f
    speed and, 361, 361f
Profitability skew diagram, 158f
Profit maximization
    price elasticity and, 394–396
    through traffic building, 263–264
Profit pools, 481–482
Promotions, 463–464
Property, 547
Proprietors, authentication and, 134
Prospect fees, 169, 170
Prospects
    converted, 154
    unconverted, 152, 154
Prototyping, 375–376
Pryor, Larry, 582
Public domain, 578–580
Publicity, 96, 257
Publishing sites, 570–571
Pullig, Chris, 209
Pullins, Ellen Bolman, 354
Purcell, Richard, 582
Purchase decisions, 405–408
Purchase importance, 403–408
    end benefit effect, 404–405

shared cost effect, 405–408
total expenditures effect,
    403–404
Purchaser-based revenue, 171–172
Purpose-built communities,
    328, 329t
Putler, Daniel, 140
Putnam, Robert, 353

Quality, price-quality effect,
    402–403
Quality cues, 120, 128–129
Quality improvement, 165
Qualls, William, 388
Quelch, John A., 247
Queuing theory, 577
Quicken Financial Network, 400
Quinn, Anthony, 102

Race, 116
Radical inventions, 376–378
Radio, 8–9, 23, 167
Radio frequency identification
    (RFIDs), 104–106, 107, 131
Rafaeli, Sheizaf, 591
Raffa, Laura, 209
Ragu, 194f
Raimmundo, R., 139
Raine, George, 208
Rainie, Lee, 247
Raining Data, 384f, 386f
Rajgopal, Shivaram, 323
Random digit dialing (RDD),
    540, 541
Random surfer model, 218, 221
Raney, Arthur A., 66
Rangan, V. Kasturi, 66, 498
Rangaswamy, Arvind, 34
Rankin, Jeff, 532
Rapid product release, 386–387
Raskin, Andrew, 582
Ratchford, Brian T., 425, 498
Ratings, product, 452
Ray, Susanna, 497
Rayport, Jeffrey, 103
RCA Corporation, 8
Reach, 554

Reach and frequency report,
    554, 555f
Real estate market, 62
Real Networks, 418
Real Rhapsody, 417–418
Real-time interaction, 569
Recommendation systems, 298,
    300–301, 307–316
    CASE, 309, 311–312
    collaborative filtering, 310,
        312–314
    endorsement systems, 309, 314
    flowchart, 309f
    questions for, 308–310
    rules-based, 309, 310–311
Red Cross, 240
Red Queen Effect, 388
Redundant networks, 556–557
Reeves, Byron, 120, 139
Reference price effect, 397–400
Regional organization, 573
Reichheld, Frederick, 354
Reimann, Robert, 246
Reimer, Kai, 323
Reinartz, Werner, 353, 354
Reitman, A. P., 564
Relational exchanges, 519–521
Relationship customers, 228–229
Relationship marketing, 301–302
Rendelman, John, 388
Rental pricing, 417–418
Repeat purchases, 446–447,
    458–459, 508, 512–514
Reporting systems, 156–157
Representation, customization
    through, 302–303
Response rates, 542, 543t,
    575–576, 578t
Response times, 225
Retention marketing, 345–352
    customer base analysis, 345–349
    dialogue marketing, 349–352
    loyalty programs, 346–347
    switching costs and, 347–349
Retirement savings, 286–289
Returns, 459
Revenue benefits, 165–173
    channel-based revenue, 167–171
    new revenue opportunities,
        167t
    purchaser-based revenue,
        171–172
Reviews, product, 452
Rheingold, Howard, 101
Rich, Laura, 173

Rich, Motoko, 499
Ricks, Joe, 209
Rideout, V., 139
Rigdon, Edward, 139
Riley, John, 425
Rischpater, Ray, 173
Risk scores, 420
Riven, 53
Rivlin, Gary, 174
Roberti, Mark, 138
Roberts, D., 139
Rocker, Carsten, 582
Rockwell, 368
Roehm, Harper A., 354
Roehm, Michelle L., 354
Rogers, Martha, 138, 498
Roosevelt, Franklin, 534
Rose, Gregory, 565
Rosen, Emanuel, 102
Rosenber, Nate, 102
Rosenbloom, Richard, 387
Rosiello, Robert L., 424
Ross, Blake, 359
Ross, Jeanne, 174
Roth, Alvin R., 426
Rowe, Gene, 140
Rowley, Jennifer, 209
Royce, Walker, 66
RSS (really simple syndication), 80,
    566–567
Rules-based systems, 309, 310–311
Ruppersberger, Gregg, 532
Russo, J. Edward, 323
Rust, Roland T., 173
Ruyter, Ko De, 102

S

Sales commissions, 169–171
Sales presentations, online, 510–511t
Sales taxes, 441, 582
Saloner, Garth, 102, 388
Saltzstein, William, 388
Samaras, George, 323
Sanchez, Romulo, 209
Sanders, Lisa, 209
Sandoval, Greg, 499
Saracevic, Tefco, 284
Scacchi, Walt, 532
Scalability, 81, 256–257
Scarcity, value and, 250–254
Schau, Hope Jensen, 66
Scherlis, William, 353
Schilling, Melissa A., 102

Schlosser, Ann E., 66
Scholten, Patrick, 425
Schonberg, Edith, 284
Schorr, Herbert, 591
Schouten, John W., 210
Schwaig, Kathy Stewart, 582
Schwan's Food, 491
Schwartz, Mark, 284
Search effectiveness, retail, 449–450
Search engine marketing,
    248–250, 253–254, 266–279
    keyword marketing, 269–279
    site optimization, 266–269
    spending on, 253–254, 254t, 266
    as traffic source, 256
Search engine optimization,
    78–79, 253–254, 266–269
Search engine rankings
    external links and, 261, 269
    optimization of, 78–79,
        253–254, 266–269
    placement in, 266–267
Search engines
    indexing by, 267
    ranking of results by, 251–252
    submission to, 268t
    as traffic source, 255–256
Search engine traffic, 266
Search goods, 291–292, 439, 440f
Second-generation Internet, 82–84
Securities trading, 376
Seda, Catherine, 246
Seddon, Pater, 174
Segev, Arie, 532
Segmentation, 24
Segway, 377f
Self-selected surveys, 539–540
Self-selection bias, 542
Selling concept, 23
Semantic webs, 82, 84
Semiconductors, 39
Semi-differentiated products, 519
Sengupta, Jaideep, 565
Senior citizens, 114, 116
Server lags, 557–559
Server log files, 550
Services, 292, 517–519
Sethi, R., 247
SETI@home, 96
Seybold, Patricia, 466
Shankar, Venkatesh, 425
Shapiro, Benson, 66
Shapiro, Carl, 102, 174
Shared cost effect, 405–408
Sharing resources, 96–98
Sharma, Arun, 173

Shaw, A.W., 33
Sheen, Martin, 102
Shekhawat, Jai, 532
Shelf space, 444
Sherman, Lee, 209
Sheth, Jadish, 465
Shipping costs, 440–443
Shopping assistants, 455
Shopping carts, 456–458f
Shopping scenarios, 449
Shopping tools, impact of,
    455–456, 457f
Short messaging (SMS), 69, 75–76
Shugan, Steven M., 34, 466, 498
Shultz, Don E., 209
Siebel Systems, 195, 196f, 510–511t
Siemers, Erik, 497
Sills, Stephen J., 564
Silva-Risso, Jorge, 426, 498
Sim, 53
Simchi-Levi, David, 533
Simchi-Levi, Edith, 533
Simon, H.A., 283
Simon, Hermann, 424, 425
Simonson, Itamar, 465
Simpser, Alberto, 353
Simulations, 243–244
Singapore, 16
Singer, Marc, 498
Singh, S., 173
Singh, Vishal, 322
Sinha, I., 465
Sin taxes, 390–392
Sismeiro, Catarina, 246
Site metrics, hierarchical structure
    and, 548
Six Degrees of Kevin Bacon,
    91–93
Small world property, 91–93, 95
Smart ads, 306
Smart mobs, 69–70
Smart routing, 235–236
Smart shelves, 105
Smith, Adam, 98, 103
Smith, Brent, 323
Smith, Michael D., 425, 465
Smith, N. Craig, 247
Smith, Robert H., 174
Smith, Stephen S., 533
Smulyan, Susan, 33, 174
Snow, Will, 65
Social cues, 126–128
Social interaction, lack of, with
    online shopping, 453
Social interface theory, 544
Social networking services, 295, 329

Social networks
  See also Online communities
  clustering, 89–91, 89f
  geometry of, 85–94
  hubs and authorities, 93–94
  Metcalfe's Law and, 85–87
  small world property, 91–93
Social perception, 121
Sockol, M., 247
Software
  electronic distribution of,
    236–237
  plug-ins, 363
Software bugs, 236, 237
Software development, 50–51
Software integration, 282
Solution selling, 454
Song, Chunyan, 564
Sony, 368, 486
Source loss analysis, 550–552,
  551t, 552f, 553f
South Korea, 16, 119
Southwest Airlines, 54, 54f
Souza, Randy K., 466
Space tourism, 377f
Spam, 88–89
Spam filters, 88
Span-of-control problem, 573–575
Spatial metaphors, 54
Specialization, 98
Spectrum auctions, 409–410
Speed
  alliances and, 362–363
  innovativeness and, 362
  of networks, 95
  profits and, 361, 361f
  standards and, 363–364
Spegel, Ted, 466
Spiders, 267–268
Spiliopoulou, M., 284
Spink, Amanda, 284
Sponsorship, 283
  vs. commissions, 170
  permission, 167, 168f
Spoofing, 132
Spors, Kelly, 173, 425
Sporting teams, brand relationship
  and, 202–203
Sproull, Lee, 140
Srinivasan, V., 323, 388
Srinvastava, Joydeep, 465
Srivastava, Rajendra K., 173
Standage, Tom, 591
Standards
  battles over, 366
  benefits of, 529–531

competition, 371–373
  compromises over, 368–369
  data synchronization and,
    529–531
  de facto, 365–366, 368
  open, 365–366, 366–368
  speed and, 363–364
  technology, 70, 81–84
  types of, 365–370
  wireless, 364–368, 366f
Standards bodies, 369, 370t
Standards marketing, 364–373
  importance of standards,
    364–365
  strategy, 370–373
    bandwagon markets, 371–373
    market sharing, 370–371, 371f
    types of standards, 365–370
Stanford Alumni Association (SAA),
  324–327
Stanford Research Institute, 6
Stanton, Frank, 33
Starfield tool, 259
Stark, Ellen, 323
Starren, Justin, 246
State sales taxes, 441, 582
Static publishing, 18
Steiger, Rod, 93
Steiner, Ina, 173
Steinmueller, W., 353
Stepanikova, Irena, 353
Stereotypes, 121
Stern, Ouis, 498
Sterne, Jim, 389
Stevens, Greg, 388
Stiroh, Kevin, 531
Stolfo, Salvatore, 591
Stoll, Clifford, 353
Storage technology,
  improvements in, 41
Storck, J., 140
Storey, Veda C., 582
Stork, David, 66
Story, Louise, 591
Storyboard Online, 183
Strategic sourcing process, 506, 506f
Strategy, aligning structure and,
  569–577
Strong ties, 90–91
Structure and strategy alignment,
  569–577
Subramani, Mani, 353
Substitution, digital. *See* Digital
  substitution
Sudman, Seymour, 564
Sull, Donald N., 499

Sundararajan, Arun, 174
Sunil, Gupta, 284
Sun Microsystems, 43
Super Bowl commercials, 194
Supercomputers, 41–42, 42f
Supphellen, Magne, 210
Suppliers
  See also Procurement
  buyer-seller relationships, 522
  concerns of, over dynamic
    bidding, 521
  concerns of, with
    marketplaces, 524
  negotiation with, 519
  qualification of, 519
Supply chain coordination,
  162–163, 478
  B2B commerce and, 526–531
  demand visibility, 526–527
  global data synchronization,
    529–531, 531f
  for manufacturer, 505–506, 505f
  new product introduction
    process, 527–529
  vendor managed inventory,
    526–527
Surveys. *See* Online surveys
Sutherland, Donald, 102
Sviokla, John, 66, 103
Swatman, P.M.C., 532
Switching costs, 295, 347–349
  categories of, 348f
  price sensitivity and, 401–402
Sydow, Max Von, 102
Symantec, 233, 234f
Synthesis, information, 100–101
System performance, 121

Take, The, 182–183
Talukdar, Debabrata, 498
Tang, Christopher S., 465
Tang, J., 564
Tangible benefits, 292, 293
Tannenbaum, Stanley I., 209
Tapscott, Don, 66
Target audience
  demographics and behavioral
    composition, 552–554
  market research on, 545–555
Task-directed usability, 224–230
  effective navigation, 225–226
  interactivity and content quality,
    229–230

response times and congestion, 225
responsiveness to user goals, 226–229
Task-directed web visits, 221
Taxes
    on cigarettes, 390–392
    jurisdiction and, 582
    online retailing and, 442
    state sales, 441, 582
Taylor, Alex, 387
Taylor, H., 564
TCP/IP, 27
Technical support, 226–227
Technology
    becoming an appliance, 566–569
    changes in, 21–25
    convergence of, 57–65
    digital, 38
    friendly, 129–130
    general purpose technologies, 25–30, 107–108, 130–138
    marketing and, 21–25
    marketing axioms and, 147
    matching with response rates, 578t
    pace of change of, 587
Technology forecasting, 49
Technology standards. See Standards
Tedlow, Richard, 34
Telang, Rahul, 247
Telecommunications networks, 28–29
Telegraphs, 28–29
Telemarketing industry, 176–177
Telephone networks, 29
Telephony, 75
Television, 23
    digital, 37, 49
    flat-panel, 49
Television advertising, 176
Tellis, Gerald, 388
Tel-Save, 33
Temporary workers, 517, 517f
Tenopir, Carol, 591
Teraflops, 42
Termination sites, 77, 78f
Thaler, Richard, 322
Third-party sites, 476
Thomas, Jacquelyn, 173, 284
Thomas, Robert J., 247
Thomas site, 124–126
Thompson, Maryann Jones, 389
Thompson, Rory, 34
Thorbjornsen, Helge, 210

3Com, 368
Three-dimensional objects, digitizing, 61–62
Thumb tribes, 69–70
Tide-to-Go launch, 164f
Time-based pricing, 408–419
    auctions, 409–414
    rental pricing, 417–418
    trial pricing, 418
    yield management, 414–417
Time-saving appliances, 108
Time usage, 108–114
Time-using appliances, 108
Time zones, 95
Ting, Chih-Chen, 139
Tivo, 16, 37, 176
Tokens, authentication, 133, 134, 134f
Tolkien, J.R.R., 36
Total expenditures effect, 403–404
Totz, Carsten, 323
Tourangeau, Roger, 564
Toyota, 166f
Tracking, 547–548
Tracking data, 550–552
Tracking systems, 156–157
Trade-up bundling, 423
Traffic building, 248–283
    by association, 279–283
    banner advertising, 279–281
    branding and, 181
    co-branding and placement, 282–283
    competitive analysis, 261–262
    cost-per-action, 259–261
    goals, 262–266, 262f
        action maximization, 265
        cost-per-action minimization, 265
        profit maximization, 263–264
        tacking multiple, 265–266
    novelty and, 252
    outsourcing, 253
    search advertising, 248–250
    search engine marketing, 266–279
    sources, 254–257, 255f
        affiliate networks, 256
        banner advertising, 256–257
        branding choices, 255
        mass media advertising, 257
        search engines, 255–256
        word of mouth, 257
    spending on, 252–254

traffic volume and quality, 258–262
    value and scarcity, 250–254
Traffic patterns, 545, 548–550, 548f
Trajtenberg, Manuel, 33, 34
Transactional customers, 228–229
Transactional exchanges, 519–521
Transaction fees, 523
Transaction offerings, 330, 342
Transactions, 147
Transaction tracking, 156–157f
Translation, 45–47
Transmission lags, 560
Transparent customization, 306
Travel industry, 468–470, 496–497
Treo, 44
Trial pricing, 418
Trifts, Valerie, 466
Trigger events, personalized messaging and, 319–322
Tripath, Shashank, 565
Trottman, Melanie, 497, 499
Trowbridge, T., 247
TrustE organization, 586–587
Tsunami relief, 212–214
Tucker, Bill, 102
Turnbull, Noel, 209
Tutorials, 243–244
24/7 customer support, 95
Tylenol brand crisis, 201

u

Ubiquity, 94–95
Udell, Gregory, 323
Uncles, Mark, 354
Underhill, Paco, 465, 466
Unified value, 156t
Unified visit value, profit maximization and, 263
Unsubscribe rate, 350
UPS, 162
Upshaw, Lynn, 174
Urban, Glen, 388
URL placement, 282–283
Usability, 224–238
    accessibility and, 231–233
    credibility and, 239
    experiential, 230–231
    images and, 241–242
    task-directed, 224–230
        effective navigation, 225–226
        interactivity and content

quality, 229–230
response times and congestion, 225
responsiveness to user goals, 226–229
Usage patterns, traffic building and, 258–259
U.S. businesses, adoption of Internet by, 504t
U.S. ecommerce share of transaction value, 504f
User authentication, 132–135, 316–319
User capabilities, 228–229
User delays. See Delays
User design, 376
User experience, state of flow and, 122–123
User goals, responsiveness to, 226–229
User IDs, 136
Users. See Internet users
U.S. retail ecommerce growth, 432f
U.S. retailing sector, 428

Value
    diamond-water paradox, 250–252
    keyword, 271–272
    network, 85–88
    scarcity and, 250–254
Value-added tax (VAT), 441
Value creation, 147
    with networks, 94–101
    virtual value activities, 99–101
Value distribution, 147
Value uncertainty, 397–403
    difficult comparison effect, 400–401
    price-quality effect, 402–403
    reference price effect, 397–400
    switching cost effect, 401–402
Van Bruggen, Gerrit, 34
Van Den Bulte, Christophe, 323
Vanhove, Tim, 564
Varian, Hal, 174, 284
Veblen, Thorstein, 322
Vendor managed inventory, 526–527
Venkatachalam, Mohan, 323
Venkatesan, Rajkumar, 34
Venture capital, 11
Verhoef, Peter C., 173
Versioning, 171, 172f, 493–494

VHS, vs. Betamax, 357
Vickrey, William, 410
Video games, 53
Virtual environments, for information acceleration, 378
Virtual keyboards, 47f
Virtual model technology, 452–454, 453f
Virtual prototyping, 375–376
Virtual value activities (VVAs), 99–101, 226t
Virtual value analysis, 226–229
Virtual web hosting, 305
Virtuous cycle for Net growth, 10–11, 10f
Visible design rules, 380, 382
Visitor duplication, 550
Visitors, that don't click, 152
Visual metaphors, 241–243
Vlosky, Richard, 498
Vogel, Harold, 499
Vogelsang, Ingo, 424, 425
Voice communication, volume of, 74–75
Voice-over-IP (VoIP), 75, challenges faces by, 130
Voice recognition software, 47
Volk, Lynne A., 247
Volunteer opt-in panels, 540
Vranica, Suzanne, 209

Wadley, Greg, 246
Wagner, Mary, 498
Wal-Mart
    overhead costs, 434
    price sensitivity and, 405, 406f
    vendor-managed inventory and, 526
Walsh, Gianfranco, 354
Wang, Guangping, 209
Warren, David, 532
Watergate Hotel, 458f
Watson, Richard, 174
Watts, Duncan J., 68, 101, 102
Weak ties, 90–91, 91f
Web alliances, 382
Web-based surveys. See Online surveys
Web browser wars, 356–359
Web business models
    benefits of, 159–172
    contact value and, 146–159
    eBay, 142–146

Web chain analysis, 259–261
Web chains, 151f, 153f
    benefits and probabilities, 155
    to closed loops, 156–157
    concept of, 150–154
    evaluating, 154–157
Weber, Thomas, 465
Web log analysis, 135, 272, 316–317
Web pages
    links between, 94
    ranking of, by Google, 3
Web pages per user, 251f
Web-ready merchandise, 477–478
Web services, 156–157
Web site activities, decomposing into user tasks, 439
Web site-brand impact, 155
Web sites
    category building, 165
    consumer shopping cycle on, 448f, 449
    credibility of, 238–241
    customer support, 233–238
    design, for search engine optimization, 268–269
    dynamic, 18–19
    hierarchical structure of, 547–548
    interactive, 51–53
    navigation, 54
    number of public, 80f
    online content, 76–79
    optimization of, 266–269
    page creation, 77–78, 79f
    parallel sites, 45
    persuasive, 241–245
        persuadable moments, 245
        simulation and tutorials, 243–244
        visual metaphors, 241–243
    spending on content and development of, 180
    static publishing, 18
    virtual hosting, 305
Web site visits, 217–224
    dynamics of, 217–224
        length of visit, 217–221, 219t
        matching content to initial visit information, 221–224
    experiential, 221
    task-directed, 221
    typical patterns, 258–259
Web support, 234, 235t
Web surfing models, 218–221, 220f
Web traffic. See Traffic building
Web visibility tools, 261–262
Weinberg, Bruce, 388, 565

Weisbuch, M., 139
Weitz, Barton, 465, 498
Wellman, Barry, 68, 101, 102, 353
Wernerfelt, Birger, 465
Wetzels, Martin, 102
Whang, Seungjin, 533
Wharton FutureView System, 379f
Wheatley, Margaret J., 353
Wheelwright, Steven, 387
White, Erin, 499
White, Gregory L., 498
White, Michael, 65
Wi-Fi, 72, 364–368, 367f
Wikipedia, 336, 336f, 337, 383, 383f
Wilde, Oscar, 424
Wilson, David, 498
Wilson, Robert, 424
Wind, Yoram, 101, 466
Wine glass plot, of usage
    patterns, 258f
Wingfield, Nick, 465, 499, 532
Winner's curse, 414
Wireless networks, 72
Wireless standards, 364–368, 366f
Wirth, Ferdinand, 209
Wittink, Dick, 564
Wolf, Michael J., 499
Wolfram, Dietmar, 284
Won Tesoriero, Heather, 499
Wood, James, 246
Word-of-mouth traffic, 229,
    257, 297

World Cup, 17–19
Worldwide coordination page,
    206–207
World Wide Web
    introduction of, 7–8
    shape of, 76–79, 78f
    virtuous cycle of, 10–11
World Wide Web Consortium
    (W3C), 233, 370t
Wyatt, Jeremy, 564
Wyld, David, 532
Wyner, Gordon, 388

Xbox 360, 368, 369
Xbox Live, 230–231
Xcelsius, 244f
XML definitions, 520
Xue, Mei, 246

Yagci, Mehmet, 209
Yahoo!, 5
    Alexa ranking, 262
    comparison metrics for Yahoo!
        sites, 549t

keyword bidding on, 275–276
    search marketing and, 266
Yahoo! Bidding Tool, 274f
Yahoo! stock prices, 11, 12f
Yan, Jianxin, 140
Yang, Yubao, 247
Yield management, 414–417
    application of, online,
        416–417, 416t
    conditions for, 415–416
Yin, Pai-Ling, 387
Yinger, John, 426
Yotk, Jeremy, 323
Young, Eric, 532
Young users
    multi-tasking by, 112, 114
    percentage of, 114
Yung-jen, Janre, 323

Zappos, 445–446
Zeithaml, Valerie, 173
Zettelmeyer, Florian, 426, 498
Zheng, Lu, 353
Zinkhan, George, 174
Zone pricing, 463
Zoom feature, 452
Zugelder, Michael, 591
Zweben, Monte, 247